British Democracy and Irish Nationalism 1876–1906

A major new study of the impact of Home Rule on liberalism and popular radicalism in Britain and Ireland. Eugenio Biagini argues that between 1876 and 1906 the crisis of public conscience caused by the Home Rule debate acted as the main catalyst in the remaking of popular radicalism. This was not only because of Ireland's intrinsic importance but also because the 'Irish cause' came to be identified with democracy, constitutional freedoms and humanitarianism. The related politics of emotionalism did not aid in finding a solution to either the Home Rule or the Ulster problem but it did create a popular culture of human rights based on the conviction that, ultimately, politics should be guided by non-negotiable moral imperatives. Adopting a comparative perspective, this book explores the common ground between Irish and British democracy and makes a significant contribution to the history of human rights, imperialism and Victorian political culture.

EUGENIO F. BIAGINI is Reader in Modern British and European History at the University of Cambridge and a Fellow of Robinson College, Cambridge. His publications include *Liberty, Retrenchment and Reform: Popular Liberalism in the Age of Gladstone, 1860–1880* (1992), *Gladstone* (2000) and, with Derek Beales, *The Risorgimento and the Unification of Italy* (2002).

For Derek Beales and Peter Clarke

British Democracy and Irish Nationalism 1876–1906

Eugenio F. Biagini

CAMBRIDGE
UNIVERSITY PRESS

CAMBRIDGE UNIVERSITY PRESS
Cambridge, New York, Melbourne, Madrid, Cape Town, Singapore, São Paulo, Delhi

Cambridge University Press
The Edinburgh Building, Cambridge CB2 8RU, UK

Published in the United States of America by Cambridge University Press, New York

www.cambridge.org
Information on this title: www.cambridge.org/9780521841764

First published 2007
Reprinted 2009

Printed in the United Kingdom at the University Press, Cambridge

A catalogue record for this publication is available from the British Library

ISBN 978-0-521-84176-4 hardback

Contents

Acknowledgements

In the preparation of this book I have accumulated many debts of gratitude, in particular to friends and colleagues. Colin Barr, Derek Beales, Paul Bew, Peter Clarke, Vincent Comerford, Almut Hintze, Martin Pugh, Alastair Reid, Deborah Thom and Ian Wilson have read drafts of various chapters and have generously offered their advice and criticism. Phiroza Marker and Danilo Raponi have provided valuable help, working as my research assistants. Moreover, my gratitude goes to my former colleagues in the Department of History of Princeton University, the Master and Fellows of Churchill College Cambridge for electing me to a By-Fellowship in 1995–6, the Pew Charitable Trust for the Evangelical Scholars Fellowship and the Arts and Humanities Research Board (AHRB), each of which helped fund research leave at critical junctures, respectively in 1995–6 and 1999–2000; and especially to the Warden and Fellows of Robinson College Cambridge, whose collegiality, friendship and support I have greatly enjoyed since they elected me one of their number in 1996.

Moreover, I wish to record my thanks to the Library Managers of the Bishopsgate Institute, London, for permission, to quote from the G. Howell Papers; to the Librarian of the Tyne and Wear Archives, Newcastle upon Tyne, for allowing me to quote from the Joseph Cowen Papers; to the Sub-Librarian of the Birmingham University Library for letting me quote from the Joseph Chamberlain Papers; to the Archivist of the Churchill Archives, Cambridge for permission to quote from the C. Dilke and the W. T. Stead Papers; to Mr C. A. Gladstone and the Archivist of the Flintshire Record Office, Hawarden for permission to quote from the Gladstone Papers; to the Librarian of the Sheffield University Library for permission to quote from both the A. J. Mundella Papers and the H. J. Wilson Papers; to the Librarians of the National Library of Scotland and the National Library of Wales and to the Public Archives of Canada. The material reproduced from collections of papers in the National Library of Ireland is the property of the Board of that Library and has been reproduced with their permission. Finally, my thanks are due to DACS on behalf of the Jack B. Yeats Estate, for permission to reproduce the illustration on the book cover.

Note on capitalization

I have used capital initials for nouns and adjectives describing political opinions and movements (e.g. Liberal, Nationalist, Radical, Socialist, Labour, and related nouns) when they refer to membership of, or close association with, political parties or parliamentary groups bearing such name or inspired by related ideologies.

Abbreviations

CW	J. S. Mill, *Collected Works*, ed. by A. P. Robson and A. J. M. Robson, 32 vols. (Toronto and London, 1963–96)
DN	*Daily News*
FJ	*Freeman's Journal*
GD	*The Gladstone Diaries*, ed. by M. R. D. Foot and H. C. G. Matthew, 14 vols. (Oxford, 1968–94)
ILP	Independent Labour Party
INF	Irish National Federation
INL	Irish National League
IRA	Irish Republican Army
JC	Joseph Chamberlain Papers, Birmingham University Library
LCA	Liberal Central Association
LRC	Labour Representation Committee
LW	*Lloyd's Weekly*
NA	National Archives, London
NC	*Newcastle Daily Chronicle*
NDL	National Democratic League
NLF	National Liberal Federation
NLFAR	National Liberal Federation Annual Reports
NLI	National Library of Ireland, Dublin
NLS	National Library of Scotland, Edinburgh
NLW	National Library of Wales, Aberystwyth
NW	*Newcastle Weekly Chronicle*
ODNB	*Oxford Dictionary of National Biography*, ed. by H. C. G. Matthew and B. Harrison (Oxford, 1994)
PRONI	Public Record Office of Northern Ireland, Belfast
RN	*Reynolds's Newspaper*
SDF	Social Democratic Federation
SLA	Scottish Liberal Association
Ti	*The Times*
UIL	United Irish League
WLF	Women's Liberal Federation
WT&E	*Weekly Times & Echo*

1   Home Rule as a 'crisis of public conscience'

Ireland can no longer be governed by the suspension of the safeguards of popular liberty, unless we are prepared to make their suspension the rule rather than the exception.[1]

During the past five years ... [he] has been regarded as the loyal Liberal, and he alone, who followed Mr Gladstone w[h]ithersoever he went ... The great Liberal Party has no creed but Gladstoneism [*sic*]. This is at once its strength and its weakness.[2]

Crisis? What crisis?

'I need scarcely mention that the ministers and religious bodies of all denominations were against us ... Perhaps, after all, the strongest force against me in the fight was that ... it was decided that the Irish vote should go Liberal.'[3] The frustration expressed in these words by a disgruntled candidate reflected a common experience among Independent Labour Party (ILP) parliamentary candidates during the thirty years following the 1886 Home Rule crisis.[4] Yet most historians have argued that the Gladstonian campaign to secure Irish self-government failed to move working-class electors.[5] Indeed, Gladstone's adoption of this cause is

---

[1] L.a., 'The battle of to-day', *NC*, 17 Nov. 1868, 4.
[2] G. Brooks, *Gladstonian liberalism* (1885), ix.
[3] 'Special article by Mr John Robertson on the North East Lanark Election', Lanarkshire Miners' County Union, Reports and Balance Sheets, 1904, 10 (NLS). On the situation in other parts of Scotland see W. M. Walker, 'Irish immigrants in Scotland: their priests, politics and parochial life', *Historical Journal*, 15, 4 (1972), 663–4; I. G. C. Hutchison, 'Glasgow working-class politics', in R. A. Cage (ed.), *The working class in Glasgow, 1750–1914* (1987), 132–3.
[4] For other examples see Ben Tillett, 'The lesson of Attercliffe', *WT&E*, 15 July 1894, 6, and Lawgor, 'South-West Ham', ibid., the latter about Keir Hardie's problems with Michael Davitt and the Irish vote.
[5] G. R. Searle, *The Liberal party: triumph and disintegration, 1886–1929* (1992) discusses the period 1886–1905 under the heading 'The "Problem of Labour"', but does not include a chapter on 'The problem of Ireland', although the latter was much more of a problem for the Liberals at the time.

generally regarded as one of his worst mistakes, brought about by his wish to retain the party leadership and resist the rising tide of social reform[6] – which Joseph Chamberlain and other 'advanced Liberals' felt to be absolutely necessary if the party was to retain its popular following. Consequently, Home Rule has been regarded not as a political strategy which the party adopted rationally, having considered possible alternatives, but as an ageing leader's personal obsession. Allegedly, by imposing Home Rule on his followers, Gladstone first split the party, then lost his working-class supporters – thus indirectly 'causing' the foundation of the Independent Labour Party[7] – and eventually led British Liberalism towards its terminal decline.[8] The Liberals' defeat in the 1886 election and their political impotence over the next twenty years have seemed to bear out this conclusion.

However, there are three main problems with this interpretation, which effectively sidelines the role of the Irish question in British politics. The first is that it takes little note of the fact that until 1921 the United Kingdom included the whole of Ireland and that the total number of Irish MPs accounted for about one-sixth of the House of Commons. Even within England, Scotland and Wales, the Irish, as a result of mass immigration, comprised a sizeable proportion of the working-class voters in many constituencies and knew how to make best use of their electoral muscle.[9] Thus, politically as well as morally, in the 1880s and 1890s the Irish question could not be ignored: indeed, more than social reform or anything else debated in Parliament, Ireland was *the* pressing question of the day and was treated as such by both Liberals and Unionists.

The second problem is that Liberal England did not 'die' in 1886: of course, it was alive and kicking both in 1906, when Gladstone's heirs achieved a memorable election victory, and indeed throughout the 1910s and early 1920s. Moreover, even after its eventual 'decline and fall', liberalism continued to inspire and shape the political outlook of the main parties, and especially Labour, which from 1918 vied with the Liberals for Gladstone's heritage. Thus the question to be answered is not about the demise of liberalism, but about its resilience and

---

[6] J. O'Farrell, *England and Ireland since 1800* (1975), 94; D. A. Hamer, 'The Irish Question and Liberal Politics, 1886–1894', in *Reactions to Irish Nationalism*, intro. by A. O'Day (1987), 253–4.

[7] T. W. Heyck, 'Home Rule, Radicalism and the Liberal party', in *Reactions to Irish Nationalism*, introd. A. O'Day (1987), 259; G. D. H. Cole, *British working class politics* (1941), 82–3.

[8] J. Parry, *The rise and fall of Liberal government in Victorian Britain* (1993), 306–9.

[9] D. A. Hamer, *The politics of electoral pressure: a study in the history of Victorian reform agitations* (1977), 315–17; O'Farrell, *England and Ireland*, 79–80, 91.

pervasiveness, which, rather than undermining, the 1886–94 Home Rule agitation strengthened and further expanded, as Liberal politics went through a period of rapid transformation and redefinition of the very meaning of the 'liberty' to which the party was committed.[10] Indeed, as the Liberal Unionists were electorally squeezed out of the political arena, the Conservative party took on board the rhetoric and some of the policies of old liberalism. The result was that, as John Dunbabin once put it, while before 1914 Britain seemed to have *two* liberal parties, one of which chose to call itself Unionist, after 1918 it had *three*, one of which chose to call itself Labour (significantly, a similar point has been made about politics in 2006).[11]

The third problem is that historians have tended to consider the Home Rule crisis in isolation, when arguably it was part of the broader debate on imperialism, liberty and democracy, which was so important in the United Kingdom during the late Victorian and Edwardian period. Therefore, whether one was in favour of or against Home Rule, the Irish question could not be ignored. Moreover, for those who supported Irish self-government, the latter became a test case of what the French democrats called *fraternité*, which in English could be translated as the politics of humanitarianism. This influenced a range of issues throughout the nineteenth century. It was central to Ernest Jones' Chartist notion of 'the people', those governed by 'their hearts and not their heads': he thought that 'God had created in mankind a natural love for humanity.'[12] It was very influential in the development of late Chartism into popular liberalism and, through pressure groups such as those associated with Exeter Hall, in the mobilization of anti-imperialism against the early manifestations of jingoism.[13] It was often religious in inspiration – as in the anti-slavery campaigns – but always non-sectarian. In fact, as Georgios Varouxakis has argued, a commitment to humanity as a form of enlightened patriotism brought together Positivists like Frederic Harrison, Utilitarians like J. S. Mill, Christian socialists like F. D. Maurice and Idealists like T. H. Green[14] – and we could add, Nonconformists such as the Quaker John Bright and the Baptist John Clifford, campaigners for

---

[10] J. R. Moore, *The transformation of urban liberalism: party politics and urban governance in late nineteenth-century England* (2006), 20, 263.

[11] M. Wolf, ' "Cameronism" is empty at the centre', *Financial Times*, 20 Jan. 2006, 19. Dunbabin's comment was made during the conference 'Popular radicalism and party politics in Britain, 1848–1914', Cambridge, 4–6 April 1989.

[12] M. Taylor, *Ernest Jones, Chartism and the romance of politics, 1819–1869* (2003), 255.

[13] M. Finn, *After Chartism: class and nation in English radical politics, 1848–1874* (1993), 9–11, 177–9, 203–25.

[14] G. Varouxakis, ' "Patriotism", "cosmopolitanism" and "humanity" in Victorian political thought', *European Journal of Political Theory*, 5, 1 (2006), 100–18.

women's rights and moral reform such as Josephine Butler, or indeed leaders of the labour movement including Henry Broadhurst and Robert Knight. In some cases it brought together Evangelicals and Secularists in campaigns against cruel practices.[15] It concerned itself with domestic affairs as much as international crises and, as Gill has argued in one of the most important works on the topic, it targeted the new 'democratic' electorate in an attempt to politicize compassion for electoral gain.[16] As we shall see, it often created a solidarity between Nonconformists and some Irish Nationalists – such as Michael Davitt – and provided much of the energy behind the coalition which supported and inspired the Home Rule 'crusade' from 1886.

Thus the main thrust of the present book is that Irish Home Rule, far from being an ephemeral Liberal aberration and the product of Gladstone's 'obsession', fired the public imagination of the peoples of the United Kingdom and came to dominate their understanding of liberty and citizenship. As politics was transformed both by the rise of the 'caucus' and by an aggressively populist and emotional leadership style, the Gladstonian insistence that policy should reflect moral imperatives made some contemporaries speak of the 'feminization of liberalism'. While this reflected contemporary gender stereotypes rather than any cultural or political reality, the present book argues that the synergy created by the 'Union of Hearts' reshaped popular expectations of liberty and citizenship in both Britain and Ireland, and acted as the single most important catalyst in the remaking of popular radicalism after 1885. Of such a remaking, the present book tries to provide an intellectual history – in other words, it is concerned with popular political ideas and programmes rather than parliamentary manoeuvring and legislative achievements.

In this respect, as well as in its subject matter, *British democracy and Irish nationalism* is the sequel of my *Liberty, retrenchment and reform*.[17] The latter is a study of the post-Chartist generation and their political culture, which I describe as 'popular liberalism'. Like Chartism, the latter was primarily about 'democracy' (as the Victorians understood it). In particular, during the twenty years between the beginning of the agitation for

---

[15] A. J. Reid, 'Old unionism reconsidered: the radicalism of Robert Knight, 1870–1900', in E. F. Biagini and A. J. Reid (eds.), *Currents of Radicalism: liberals, radicals and collective identities in the British Isles, 1865–1931* (1996), 214–43; Chien-Hui Li, 'Mobilizing traditions in the animal defence movement in Britain, 1820–1920', Ph.D. Thesis, University of Cambridge, 2002; M. J. D. Roberts, *Making English morals: voluntary association and moral reform in England, 1787–1886* (2004).

[16] R. Gill, 'Calculating compassion in war: the "New Humanitarian" ethos in Britain 1870–1918', Ph.D. thesis, University of Manchester, 2005, 11.

[17] E. F. Biagini, *Liberty, retrenchment and reform: popular liberalism in the age of Gladstone, 1860–1880* (1992).

the Second Reform Bill in 1864 and the passing of the Third Reform Act in 1884, the extension of the suffrage was regarded as a goal of supreme importance by working-class pressure groups and reform associations, including some large trade unions, such as the coal miners of the North-East of England. These groups were able to establish an alliance with the Liberal party partly because they were prepared to consider compromises (for example, the acceptance of 'household' instead of 'manhood' suffrage), and partly because they were now perceived to be pursuing non-revolutionary social and economic aims, fully compatible with the Gladstonian priorities of 'peace, retrenchment and reform'.

This in turn reflected the emergence of cultural and ideological affinities between middle-class and artisan radicals in the two or three decades after the repeal of the Corn Laws in 1846. The removal of the 'bread tax' and the adoption of free trade were followed by a long period of economic growth, which in due course improved standards of living. The old class-based enmity between Chartists and Liberals – based on the former believing that politics was an aristocratic conspiracy in which the middle classes were willing accomplices – was gradually replaced by a sense of national purpose and the conviction that free-trade economics was in the 'common interest' (and certainly in that of the working-class consumer). Self-help – both individual and collective, through friendly societies, for example – was not a mid-Victorian invention, but acquired a new viability in the climate of optimism and expansion after the 1851 Crystal Palace International Exhibition. 'Freedom' seemed to be all that people were asking for: friendly societies wanted to be 'let alone', trade unions knew the advantages of securing the labour market from the danger of repressive state intervention, while co-operatives and consumer pressure groups expected free trade to give them access to an unprecedented variety of cheap imports from all over the world. Moreover, free trade went together with the demand that all taxes on items of mass consumption be reduced or altogether repealed – in other words, that the working-class family be relieved of most of the fiscal burdens under which they had long been labouring. In turn, this was consistent with the Cobdenite and Gladstonian demand for 'retrenchment', or strict economies, at the Treasury. Slashing state expenditure – which was dominated by the military establishment, the cost of wars and the repayment of the National Debt (itself mainly incurred to pay for past wars) – made sense to working-class radicals. As for social services, such as existed, they were primarily provided by local authorities and funded through the rates, rather than by central government taxation.

A further, important component of the cultural context which made popular liberalism possible was Nonconformity, which had grown rapidly during the first half of the nineteenth century (by 1851 about one-half of churchgoers belonged to one or another of the many Dissenting denominations). Baptists, Congregationalists, Methodists, Free Presbyterians and other groups – including Quakers and Unitarians – were characterized by a non-hierarchical, 'democratic' church polity and by proud self-reliance which made them sympathize with both political radicalism and economic liberalism. They stood for self-help in religion as much as in economics. Their commitment to popular education, temperance, social reform and humanitarian causes overseas was consistent with the traditions of English radicalism. Indeed, the latter had largely been shaped by Dissent especially in the seventeenth century, in the days of Cromwell's republican experiment, the memory of which was rediscovered and celebrated by mid-Victorian radicals from all social backgrounds.

While Dissent, democracy and free trade provided the bulk of the culture, hopes, and ideas behind popular liberalism, the latter was also espoused by a large number of people who were neither religiously nor politically active, but who could, from time to time, be galvanized into activity by the inspiring populism of leaders like Bright and especially Gladstone. Their charismatic leadership helped late nineteenth-century Liberalism to become and remain as much of a mass movement as republicanism in contemporary France or social democracy in Bismarck's Germany.

Liberty had no proper 'Conclusion' and ended, instead, with an analysis of how Gladstone was perceived 'from below'. This was not because of some personal whiggish historical optimism about the rise and progress of liberty personified by Gladstone as a charismatic leader, but because then I was already planning a continuation, a 'volume II' dealing with the question of Home Rule and exploring whether popular liberalism had any counterpart in Ireland. The answer to such questions has now taken the shape of *British democracy and Irish nationalism*. The latter is anything but whiggish in its appraisal of late Victorian radicalism. It ends with radicals demanding a further extension of democracy and formulating a neo-Chartist programme under the banner of the National Democratic League. By 1906 the NDL was bringing together people belonging to various currents of radicalism, including members of socialist societies, who, in context, come across as surprisingly similar to their political forebears of the 1840s. Not much 'progress' here, one might be tempted to conclude. Moreover, the present book starts with a crisis – Home Rule – which proved politically insoluble and dominated the whole period under review. However, *British democracy and Irish nationalism* is not about the failure of a policy, but concerns the popular agitation for its adoption. The book ends in 1906, because I could not discuss the 1910s without opening up a whole series of new problems – including the rise of Labour in Britain and revolutionary nationalism in Ireland – which would require a further book and which, in any case, have already inspired a substantial literature.[18]

As I have already indicated above, this book is mainly an intellectual history not of the Home Rule crisis as such, but of its consequence and impact on the development of popular ideas of liberty and democracy. However, before proceeding, we need briefly to recall the political and electoral events which form the backdrop of our story. The general election of November 1885 was the first to be contested under the new system of uniform household franchise and more equal electoral districts, created throughout the UK by the Reform and Redistribution of Seats Acts of 1884–5. During the electoral campaign the Liberals had appeared to be divided between the moderate wing, headed by the Whig Lord Hartington, heir to the Duke of Devonshire, and the Radicals, led by Joseph Chamberlain. The former stood for continuity with the Palmerstonian tradition; the latter courted the working-class vote and prioritized social reform and church disestablishment. Both were anxious about Gladstone's supposedly imminent retirement and the future leadership of the party. But the Grand Old Man (the GOM, as he was affectionately or derisively called) was not eager to step down. In the past he had used 'big Bills' to renew the unity and purpose of the party at critical junctures, but it was not clear whether he would be able to do so again.

The Liberal party approached the contest with a programme which focused on local government, taxation and the reform of the land laws. Home Rule was not on their agenda but it was clear that something had to be done about Ireland. The latter had been a constant and pressing concern for the Gladstone government in 1880–5, when it had struggled to contain rural unrest, fight terrorism and reform the land laws, which were supposed to be the root cause of all the trouble. Home Rule was the central demand of the powerful National party, led by Charles Stewart Parnell. For months before the election Chamberlain and other radical leaders had been considering various plans to appease Parnell without destroying the parliamentary bond between Britain and Ireland, established by the 1800 Act of Union. On 16 June 1885 Dilke wrote to Grant Duff that although '[t]here is no liking for Ireland or the

---

[18] On these questions see P. F. Clarke, *Lancashire and the New Liberalism* (1971); D. Tanner, *Political change and the Labour party, 1900–1918* (1990); P. Maume, *The long gestation: Irish Nationalist life, 1891–1918* (1999); and P. Bew, *Ideology and the Irish question: Ulster Unionism and Irish Nationalism, 1912–1916* (1994).

Irish', there was 'an almost universal feeling that some form of Home Rule must be tried. My own feeling is that it will be tried too late, as all our remedies are.'[19] Moreover, the issue acquired a new urgency because there was a widespread expectation that – under the new electoral law – the Nationalists would secure a much larger share of the Irish constituencies at the next election. The implications were clear: as Lord Rosebery put it during a speech he delivered (in Gladstone's presence) at a banquet in Edinburgh on 13 November 1885, 'if things turned out in Ireland as they were told they would, that question would absorb the minds of the men of the time and the energy of Parliament to the exclusion of every other'. He continued:

He did not pretend to say how that question would be settled, but he believed it could be settled in only one direction. If they could obtain from the representatives of Ireland a clear and constitutional demand, which would represent the wishes of the people of Ireland, which would not conflict with the union of the two countries, he believed that by satisfying that demand in such a way as not to require readjustment, they would cut off forever the poisonous spring of discontent.[20]

In the speech there was no explicit indication that Home Rule would be considered by the Liberals, although on that very day Gladstone – who was staying at Rosebery's country residence, Dalmeny House – shared with him both 'the idea of constituting a Legislature for Ireland' and a strategy for overcoming the opposition that such a plan was likely to generate within both Parliament and the Liberal party.[21] On the following day, the 14th, Gladstone actually drafted a Home Rule Bill based on the blueprint of a 'Proposed Constitution for Ireland', which Parnell had provided, at his request, on 1 November. Parnell's proposal, which was based on colonial precedents, was indeed 'a clear and constitutional demand' such as the one to which Rosebery had alluded. Moreover, it is important to bear in mind that Gladstone's draft was produced *before* the election itself, when he still hoped that the Liberals would win a majority over the other two parties combined, so that they could deal with Ireland without having to seek the support of the Nationalists.

Even if that had happened, it is highly unlikely that Gladstone would have been able to persuade Hartington to support a Bill such as the one which he had already framed. However, the situation was further complicated by the actual results of the election (the polls were declared from 1 December). Although the Liberals did emerge as the largest party, with

[19] Cited in R. Jenkins, *Dilke: a Victorian tragedy* (1996), 210.
[20] 'Banquet to Lord Rosebery', *Ti*, 14 Nov. 1885, 5.
[21] Gladstone to Lord Rosebery, 13 Nov. 1885, in *GD*, vol. XI, 428.

333 seats to the Conservatives' 251, Parnell secured 86 MPs – more than expected – and the Irish party was now in a position to hold the balance in the new Parliament. Tactical manoeuvring and political bargaining then began. Initially, Parnell decided to keep the Tories in office (Salisbury had formed a caretaker government in April 1885, following Gladstone's defeat over the budget and subsequent resignation). The GOM was obviously in a dilemma, but not over Home Rule – because, as we have seen, he had *already* drafted a Bill before the general election. It was over the feasibility of proceeding with such Bill without an overall Liberal majority and in a situation in which he would be dependent on Nationalist support.

However, on 17 December 1885 Herbert Gladstone leaked to the press the news that his father was planning to adopt Home Rule: this was the so-called 'Hawarden kite', which changed the political landscape completely. As a result the Nationalists were now prepared to oust the Conservative administration, which was defeated on 26 January 1886. On the 30th Gladstone received the Queen's commission to form a government. He intended to explore the viability of Home Rule, but was not, as yet, pledged to any specific proposal. Over the next few months he worked on what he perceived as a comprehensive solution to the Irish problem, consisting of land purchase and devolved government with a Parliament in Dublin.

The reputedly rapacious landowners were perceived as the source of all of Ireland's social problems, but could not be altogether abandoned to the mercy of a Nationalist government. Therefore, in order to restore social stability in rural Ireland, he asked the Treasury to sponsor the purchase and transfer of land from the gentry to the tenant farmers. The farmers would then repay the loan by means of terminable annuities, and the operation would be guaranteed by the newly constituted Irish Parliament. The latter was the subject of the second of Gladstone's 1886 'big Bills'. The Irish assembly would consist of two 'orders': the first would include elected MPs who would be returned – under the UK system of household suffrage – for the existing constituencies. The second would comprise both the Irish hereditary peers and a number of elected senators – men of property and standing who would be returned by a restricted electorate on a £25 franchise. The two orders would sit and deliberate together; however, each would have the power of veto, which could be exercised by voting separately whenever either so desired. The Dublin Parliament would legislate on domestic Irish matters, although the police force remained under imperial control. Moreover, London would retain full control of military defence, foreign affairs and commerce. Trade policy was a sensitive question, because of widespread concern – especially among Ulster industrialists – that a Home Rule Ireland would abandon free trade and introduce tariffs, which Parnell thought necessary to encourage the development of industry in the south. There would be no Irish representation at Westminster.

Unfortunately Gladstone had not prepared the party for such a dramatic development of his Irish policy and the shock was considerable. It soon emerged that the Land Bill had little chance of survival, both because its cost was regarded as prohibitive (amounting, as it did, to some £120 million, which was more than the entire UK budget for 1885), and because it proposed the spending of such a significant amount of money in order to 'bail out' the Irish landowners, a class regarded as particularly undeserving. Gladstone was also in trouble over the Home Rule Bill, particularly because the proposed exclusion of the Irish MPs from the London Parliament was perceived as a step which would inevitably lead both to constitutional clashes and, eventually, to Dublin's full independence. In the end, a majority of the Liberal MPs supported the Prime Minister after he indicated his willingness to reconsider Irish representation at Westminster. However, from the start Hartington refused to join the government, while Chamberlain, having at first accepted, resigned from the Cabinet on 26th March, after realizing the full extent of the Premier's proposals. No doubt, the fact that Gladstone mishandled him so badly contributed to the break between the two statesmen, but, as I shall argue in chapter 5, Chamberlain's opposition to Home Rule sprang from fundamental attitudes, which had been taking shape in 1882–5.

In April the government was defeated by 341 votes to 311. Gladstone immediately decided to take the issue to the country and started a vigorous electoral campaign, which further deepened the party split between the Home Rule majority and the Unionist minority (including both Hartington and Chamberlain).[22] The general election took place on 13 and 14 July 1886. When the results were announced, it emerged that the Home Rule Liberals had secured only 191 seats and the Nationalists 85. The Unionists could count on 316 Conservatives and 78 Liberal dissenters. It was a decisive defeat for Home Rule, but the latter remained a live issue in UK politics: Ireland itself had again overwhelmingly voted for self-government, and Gladstone's proposal had also been endorsed by a majority of Scottish and Welsh electors. The continuing relevance of Home Rule was further highlighted by the Unionist government's

[22] G. D. Goodlad, 'Gladstone and his rivals: popular Liberal perceptions of the party leadership in the political crisis of 1885–1886', in Biagini and Reid, *Currents of Radicalism*, 163–84.

inability to contain unrest among the Irish farmers without introducing new and more stringently repressive measures, which created concern about civil liberty in Britain and outrage and defiance in Ireland. This strengthened the resolve of the Home Rulers, whose campaign resulted in a number of by-election victories for the Liberals. By 1890 the latter had considerably eroded the Unionist majority in the House of Commons.

However, the unity and credibility of the Home Rule coalition was shattered by Parnell's involvement in one of the most celebrated sex scandals of the century. The revelation that he had spent years in an adulterous relationship with Kitty O'Shea, the wife of another Nationalist MP, destroyed his moral prestige. Nevertheless, he refused to step down from the party leadership until forced to do so by a majority of his colleagues after Gladstone indicated that his continuation in power would jeopardize the Liberal alliance. As a consequence, the Irish party split and in 1892 the Home Rulers went to the next general election divided. They managed to win, but secured a majority of only forty, which was too small to force Home Rule – a major constitutional change – on the overwhelmingly Unionist House of Lords. Undeterred, in 1893 Gladstone proceeded to produce a new Home Rule Bill, which tried to address the concerns expressed by his critics in 1886. The new plan retained an Irish representation at Westminster and proposed the creation of a Dublin Parliament consisting of two houses – with 103 MPs elected from the existing constituencies on the system of household franchise, and 48 Council (upper-house) members elected by voters who owned or occupied land with an annual valuation of £200. This Bill was duly passed by the Commons, but rejected by the House of Lords by 419 votes to 41.

Not only did the Lords stop Home Rule, but they also turned down most other Liberal Bills, frustrating the high expectations generated among party supporters by the 1891 Newcastle Programme. The latter included a number of advanced democratic and social reforms to be funded through higher death duties and taxation of land values. Although it was an ambitious programme, Gladstone himself hinted that this was not enough and suggested that the introduction of old age pensions be considered (see below, chapter 4, p. 188). This new radical activism reflected the contemporary shift in British Liberalism towards social concerns and was part of a broader phenomenon within British and European radical culture at the time. By then independent working-class or socialist parties had already been established in most other countries, including Germany, France and Italy. In England a Democratic Federation had been set up in 1881, developing into the Social Democratic Federation (SDF) by 1884. While the SDF adopted a quasi-Marxist revolutionary programme, the Fabian Society, another socialist group also established in 1884, proposed a gradualist approach and the 'permeation' of existing parties.[23] Then in 1893, two years after the Newcastle Programme, a group of democrats and trade unionists established the Independent Labour Party (ILP) in Bradford. All these groups went beyond Liberal radicalism, advocating communal ownership of the means of production, especially the land and the mines. Yet, the socialists failed either to break the mould of British politics or to erode significantly the cultural and political hegemony of the Liberal party on the British left. Their failure was not unrelated to Gladstone's decision to adopt the cause of Irish Home Rule, as it will be further argued below.

The historiography

The two most significant monographs on the Home Rule crisis remain those produced by Hammond in 1938 and Cooke and Vincent in 1974. Each embodies a strong 'thesis' and deserves to be treated with respect even decades after its first appearance. Hammond's *Gladstone and the Irish nation* is a monumental work which failed to attract significant attention when it was first published, in the days of Chamberlain's Munich agreement with Hitler,[24] but has since inspired and provoked generations of scholars. His Gladstonian inclination to interpret the Liberal party schism in terms of the clash of the political forces embodying wealth, social influence and the professions arrayed against 'the Masses' has lost its credibility, although it is quite clear that Liberalism was indeed radicalized by the Irish issue.[25] However, his insistence that the claims of the Irish nation and the Home Rule crisis were turning points in the history of the British Isles cannot be easily rebutted. Methodologically, he was able to combine a focus on 'high' politics with attention to the popular dimension. Whether or not directly influenced by Hammond, Heyck and Barker have continued along similar lines in their important studies. Although they deal primarily with the parliamentary dimension, Barker's work on the National Liberal Federation (NLF) has broken new ground. His suggestion 'that the presence of Gladstone at the head of the Liberal party constituted the

---

[23] H. Pelling, *Origins of the Labour party, 1880–1900* (1983), 18–35.

[24] It first appeared in October 1938. For the contemporary response see S. A. Weaver, *The Hammonds: a marriage in history* (1998), 240–1.

[25] Searle, *Liberal party*, 56; W. C. Lubenow, 'Irish Home Rule and the social basis of the great separation in the Liberal party in 1886', *Historical Journal*, 28, 1 (1885), 125–42; Lubenow, *Parliamentary politics and the Home Rule crisis: the British House of Commons in 1886* (1988).

principal obstacle to the emergence of a coherent and independent labour movement'[26] was one of the starting points for the research embodied in British democracy and Irish nationalism. In fact, the extent to which I am indebted to both Heyck and Barker is considerable, and although I criticize their views on a number of specific issues, on the whole my aim has been to integrate, rather than replace, their perceptive analyses.

Cooke and Vincent have often been cited as shorthand for a whole historiographical tradition. They represent the 'high politics' school which, allegedly, seeks to explain the whole political process in terms of ruthless competition for power between a few individuals at Westminster. This is not entirely fair to their *Governing passion*, let alone to Vincent's later brilliant reappraisal of Gladstone's handling of the Home Rule question. However, their suggestion that Ireland was little more than a pawn in a purely English parliamentary game needs to be challenged, especially because it reflects views widely held among scholars of the period.[27] In particular, Cooke and Vincent's claim that neither the country nor the politicians wanted to know about Ireland in 1885[28] is hardly reconcilable either with the mass of empirical evidence produced at the time by and for Parliament, or with the attention devoted to the Irish question by journalists, political economists and land reformers then, and indeed throughout the period from 1868.

Not only did British politicians and opinion makers 'know' about Ireland, but their awareness of the situation also resulted in radical reforms unprecedented and unparalleled in nineteenth-century Europe. These included the 1881 Land Act, which put an end to absolute property rights in land, and the 1885 Ashbourne Act, which provided Treasury loans for tenants to buy out Irish landlords (farmers would be able to borrow the whole purchase price, to be repaid at 4 per cent annuities over forty-nine years). It was a comparatively small-scale, but highly successful experiment, which, as we have seen, in 1886 Gladstone proposed to develop into a more comprehensive strategy. Although his Bill was defeated, land purchase was gradually implemented by Balfour and Wyndham between 1887 and 1903. By 1891 a British Unionist government had created the Congested District Board – an appointed

---

[26] M. Barker, *Gladstone and radicalism: the reconstruction of Liberal policy in Britain, 1885–1894* (1975), 96; T. W. Heyck, *The dimensions of British radicalism: the case of Ireland, 1874–1895* (1974), 26.

[27] D. A. Hamer, *Liberal politics in the age of Gladstone and Rosebery* (1972); R. Shannon, *Gladstone: Heroic minister, 1865–1898* (1999); P. Stansky, *Ambitions and strategies: the struggle for the leadership of the Liberal party in the 1890s* (1964).

[28] A. B. Cooke and J. R. Vincent, *The governing passion* (1974), 17, 24–5, 163; J. Vincent, 'Gladstone and Ireland', *Proceedings of the British Academy*, (1977), 193–238.

Irish authority, funded by the tax-payer, with wide-ranging powers for the purpose of improving agriculture and developing the road and rail network in the west of the country. By the end of the century its jurisdiction encompassed many counties and included two-thirds of the island. It was a breakthrough in social engineering, in some respects a precursor to F. D. Roosevelt's 1933 Tennessee Valley Authority, which created an infrastructure and sustained employment in a large depressed area cutting across state boundaries. Late Victorian radicals such as George Lansbury and H. W. Massingham had reason to envy the bipartisan consensus which allowed for the mobilization of large economic resources to help the Irish farmer, at a stage when the British working man was being told to look after himself as best as he could.[29] In short, if we considered the amount and extent of reforms carried out in Ireland in 1881–1903, we would be tempted to conclude that in British politics Ireland 'mattered' more than, let us say, Lancashire or Yorkshire. Even Scotland, which produced so many prime ministers during the period, enjoyed no more than a watered-down version of Irish-style land legislation. Moreover, in the specific sphere of self-government, Ireland initiated a debate which continued for generations, as Jackson and Peatling have shown, and affected the subsequent, wider debate on devolution in the United Kingdom.[30]

Irish affairs had been hotly debated at Westminster from 1881 and especially in 1884, when the question was whether to extend the household franchise to Irish tenant farmers and whether proportional representation should be introduced to mitigate the effects of majority rule.[31] Although Home Rule did not feature prominently in the British election in November 1885, behind the scenes not only Gladstone, but also Chamberlain and others worked on various alternative plans for giving Ireland local government and a degree of 'devolution'. Within the Conservative party, Churchill and Carnarvon were equally concerned about the future of Ireland, although they disagreed about the prospects and implications of a Home Rule scheme.[32] As for Salisbury, Cooke and Vincent have stressed that his dismissive, racist and arrogant remarks

---

[29] Barker, *Gladstone and radicalism*, 90.

[30] A. Jackson, *Home Rule: an Irish History, 1820–2000* (2003); G. K. Peatling, *British opinion and Irish self-government, 1865–1925* (2001), J. Kendle, *Ireland and the federal solution: the debate over the United Kingdom constitution, 1870–1921* (1989); G. Boyce, 'Federalism and the Irish question', in A. Bosco (ed.), *The federal idea, vol. I: The history of federalism from the Enlightenment to 1945* (1991).

[31] J. Lubbock and H. O. Arnold-Forster, *Proportional representation: a dialogue* (1884); see J. Hart, *Proportional representation: critics of the British electoral system, 1820–1945* (1992).

[32] P. J. O'Farrell, *Ireland's English question: Anglo-Irish relations, 1534–1970* (1971), 182.

about the Irish being no better than 'the Hottentots' were actually carefully worded provocations to polarize the debate and prevent the formation of a centrist coalition government under Lord Hartington.[33]

In 1977 Vincent published a partial revision of his own analysis, one which has influenced the scholarly debate more than *The governing passion*. In particular, it is now generally accepted that Gladstone's primary aim was to preserve the Union and that he was prepared to introduce all sorts of reforms to secure such an end – including Home Rule.[34] Moreover, Colin Matthew has established that Gladstone was not suddenly 'converted' to Home Rule at the end of 1885, but had privately been considering it from the mid-1870s, while Parry has shown how this was indeed suspected by contemporaries in the parliamentary Liberal party.[35] In fact, from 1881 Gladstone's second government began to experiment with elective self-government also in parts of the empire which had hitherto been run on paternalist and autocratic principles, including India under Lord Ripon and Cyprus under Lord Kimberley.[36]

As a result of Parry's work, the study of high politics has acquired a deeper and richer dimension. His emphasis on the role of ideas, and religion in particular, has transformed the meaning of the 'passion of politics' which his predecessors in this school had too readily interpreted as hunger for power. Moreover, he has corrected Cooke and Vincent's view about the marginality of Ireland in the Liberal party split.[37] He sees Home Rule as a cataclysm which 'turned the Liberal party from a great party of government into a gaggle of outsiders', by giving free rein to sectionalism and populism. However, he also admits that 'Liberal populism neutralised danger from the left by [consigning] Labour to a slow advance through local politics.'[38] In other words, he accepts that, by championing Home Rule, Gladstone tapped into a source of potential support for any independent labour party in Britain, and contributed to marginalizing the socialists – who often sounded like a Gladstonian pressure group, rather than an alternative to liberalism.

From 1886 to 1895 both Liberalism and democracy in the British Isles were dominated by the debate on Home Rule, which involved fundamental

---

[33] Cooke and Vincent, *Governing passion*, 81–2.
[34] Vincent, 'Gladstone and Ireland'; A. Warren, 'Gladstone, land and social reconstruction in Ireland, 1881–1887, *Parliamentary History*, 2 (1983), 153–73.
[35] J. P. Parry, *Democracy and religion: Gladstone and the Liberal party, 1867–1875* (1986), 412–13. Cf. H. C. G. Matthew, *Gladstone, 1875–1898* (1995), 234–8.
[36] H. Tinker, *The foundations of local self-government in India, Pakistan and Burma* (1965); G. S. Georghallides, *A political and administrative history of Cyprus, 1918–1926, with a survey of the foundations of British rule* (1979), 41.
[37] Parry, *The rise and fall of Liberal government*, 302.   [38] Ibid., 306–11.

questions about sovereignty, citizenship and community, and forced people to redefine what they meant by 'liberty'. In Ireland, constitutional Nationalism became the dominant political discourse outside North-East Ulster. With British Liberalism it shared – among other things – a degree of ambiguity which allowed different social groups, ranging from the rural middle class to poorer peasants and farm workers, to appropriate and use it in defence of their own specific interests. While in Britain the complexity of Gladstonian Liberalism encouraged its adoption by the left, among Ulster Liberal Unionists it caused tension between Whigs and radicals such as T. W. Russell, who believed that, in order to survive in a political climate dominated by sectarian issues, the party must adopt radical land reform.[39]

Yet all these groups claimed to stand for 'national' causes independent of social and economic sectionalism, although the 'nation' they claimed to represent became increasingly indefinite, as the empire, England, Scotland, Wales, Southern Ireland and North-East Ulster each produced distinctive and sometimes antagonistic understandings of what the 'common good' required. Crucial in this respect was the fact that Gladstone and his followers developed a pluralistic understanding of the nation, one which was fully compatible with what he called 'local' patriotisms:

I hold that there is such a thing as local patriotism, which, in itself, is not bad, but good. The Welshman is full of local patriotism – the Scotchman is full of local patriotism; the Scotch nationality is as strong as it ever was, and should the occasion arise . . . it will be as ready to assert itself as in the days of Bannockburn. I do not believe that local patriotism is an evil. I believe it is stronger in Ireland even than in Scotland. Englishmen are eminently English, Scotchmen are profoundly Scotch . . . [t]he Irishman is more profoundly Irish; but it does not follow that, because his local patriotism is keen, he is incapable of Imperial patriotism.[40]

There were important areas in which the Conservatives were more responsive to Irish Nationalist demands than the Liberals: these included active support for peasant proprietorship from 1885 and, more importantly, a commitment to denominationalism in education. Moreover, the clash between Radicals and some of the Nationalists over the Bradlaugh

---

[39] G. Greenlee, 'Land, religion and community: the Liberal party in Ulster, 1868–1885', in E. F. Biagini (ed.), *Citizenship and community: liberals, radicals and collective identities in the British Isles, 1865–1931* (1996), 253–75; R. McMinn, 'The myth of "Route" liberalism in County Antrim, 1869–1900', *Éire–Ireland*, 17 (1982), 137–49.

[40] *Gladstone's speeches*, ed. by A. Tinley Basset (1916), 641–2. This pluralistic notion of the Britannic identity has been studied by J. S. Ellis, 'Reconciling the Celt: British national identity, empire and the 1911 investiture of the Prince of Wales', *Journal of British Studies*, 37, 4 (1998), 391–418.

case in the early 1880s – when the professing atheist MP for Northampton refused to take the biblical oath and was consequently ejected from Parliament – highlighted the extent to which Roman Catholics and Anglicans shared a vision of a Christian polity to be defended against militant secularism.[41] But these affinities amounted to little more than occasional encounters between strangers: they were not sufficient for building lasting political alliances, especially in view of the fact that Conservatives and Nationalists disagreed so radically in their understanding of social order and national loyalty. About the Christianity of the British Parliament, for example, the Nationalists seemed to have changed their minds by 1892, when they supported the Zoroastrian Parsi Dadabhai Naoroji in winning Finsbury Central for the Liberals. Moreover, Parnell himself entertained towards confessional politics a repugnance which distinguished him both from most of his own party and from the Liberal rank and file in Britain.[42]

The most serious flaw in Gladstone's Home Rule strategy was that it neglected the reality of Ulster.[43] The Northern Irish commitment to the Union proved a major stumbling block for the Liberals and further strengthened pro-Unionist feelings in Scotland and England. For the purposes of the present study, which is concerned more with the development of popular political ideas than with legislative schemes, it is important to bear in mind Loughlin's observation about Gladstone being guided by 'a preoccupation with the probity of social and political actions', more than with the human and material effects of such actions.[44] While this exasperated Irish Unionists, it was consistent with the climate of opinion created by the 1886 crisis in both Nationalist and Gladstonian circles – an ethos in which Home Rule was a statement of faith and the supreme assertion of political emancipation. 'It is really amazing what mad construction the peasantry and uneducated among the working class have put upon what is known as "Home Rule",' an Irish Unionist newspaper commented in 1886.[45] Home Rule was to the Irish working and lower middle classes what 'Reform' and free trade had been to their counterparts in Britain in 1864–85: it represented an atoning gesture which reassured them as to the acceptability and, in principle, legitimacy of the 'constitution'. Ultimately the latter was symbolized by Gladstone's

[41] A. O'Day, *Parnell and the First Home Rule Episode, 1884–87* (1986), 46; W. J. Arnstein, 'Parnell and the Bradlaugh case', *Irish Historical Studies*, 13, 51 (1963), 212–35.

[42] Jackson, *Home Rule*, 78. However, we should not forget that many Liberal intellectuals and parliamentarians were as horrified as he was by religious bigotry in politics.

[43] J. Loughlin, *Gladstone, Home Rule and the Ulster question, 1882–93* (1986); F. Thompson, *The end of Liberal Ulster: land agitation and land reform* (2001).

[44] Loughlin, *Ulster question*, 288.   [45] Cited in ibid., 112.

celebration of the Irish parliamentary tradition established by Henry Grattan in 1782. It is remarkable how far such Grattanian ideology became a source of political identity and focus of popular attention in both isles from 1886 to 1916.

Loughlin claims that by emphasizing the 'supposedly "constitutional" character of [Ireland's] historical development and ignoring the bloody struggles that more truly characterized it', Gladstone demonstrated 'a striking failure of historical perception'.[46] This may be true. However, we need to remember that Gladstone was involved not in an academic exercise intent on assessing major trends in Irish history, but in a political attempt to establish Home Rule and parliamentary politics as the corner-stone of a new Irish identity. Echoing Ernest Renan, R. Barry O'Brien wrote in *The Home Ruler's Manual* (1890) that a nation is 'a people bound together by historical associations'.[47] By promoting a certain vision of the Irish past Gladstone selected – perhaps even invented – the 'historical associations' which he regarded as 'binding' if politicians wanted to encourage the further development of popular constitutionalism. It was of course a *political* use of history, and Gladstone may have made the mistake of believing too much in his own rhetoric. However, such rhetoric propounded a self-fulfilling prophecy – whose aim was rooting parlia-mentary radicalism among Irish tenants, and, in the process, outbidding and marginalizing alternative political philosophies, which increasingly emphasized violence and the rejection of everything English. Thus, if Gladstone encouraged mere 'sentimental aspirations',[48] such hopes were formed around a solid core of political realism – at the time certainly more realistic and more political than either Fenian revolutionary dreams or the implausible visions of Celtic revivalists – and had an important impact on the Irish constitutional tradition.

Revisionisms

As Searle has noted, the Liberal party 'was a party of ideas and ideals, much given to discussion and argument'.[49] Its success, and that of the political style it embodied, was partly due to the fact that many Victorians were concerned about politics. I believe that the views articulated by these politically aware people – let us call them the activists – deserve as much attention as those of the parliamentary leaders for whom they wrote, voted and canvassed. Jon Lawrence is certainly right in stressing the importance for us of studying the 'gulf between the world of political

---

[46] Ibid., 289.   [47] Cited in ibid., 6.   [48] Ibid., 26.   [49] Searle, *The Liberal party*, 3.

activism ... and the everyday lives of potential voters', and the strategies which the activists adopted in trying to transcend it.[50] However, the starting point must surely remain the ideas of the 'organic' activists. The existence of the latter can be perceived as 'a romantic illusion' – in Lawrence's words – only if we take 'organic' to mean that they were 'indistinguishable in every respect from [their] fellow workers'.[51] But the very fact of their being 'activists' implies that they were 'distinct' from the rest, and the 'organic' simply signifies that they came from the group for which they claimed to be speaking. In this respect, if activism was an 'illusion' at all, it was one shared by the rather numerous, probably quite 'romantic' and certainly very 'organic' campaigners who made popular radicalism possible.[52]

The present work focuses on the verbal expression of ideas, values and aspirations, but is also deeply interested in both agency and causality from a perspective which has sometimes been described as 'new model' empiricism.[53] Like John Belchem, I am interested in 'context and conduct, in the way in which identity was affirmed, modified or subverted in collective political action'.[54] I focus on the way popular political ideas and ideologies (rather than simply languages) related to material interests, given the fact that genuinely held values of liberty and popular participation could, and were, also turned into ideologies of social control. This, in turn, involves two questions: how did perception, imagination, ideas and rhetoric relate to the actual pursuit of concrete political aims; and how did the latter (for example, Home Rule) acquire different meaning and relevance for different groups? Charisma, deference and party discipline created and sustained, but also reflected, a shared sense of purpose, which was thus a complex phenomenon. It partly relied on the actual common ground between these groups and their gentlemanly leaders,

---

[50] J. Lawrence, *Speaking for the people: party, language and popular politics in England, 1867–1914* (1998), 67; for a good example of a recent study inspired by this concern see K. Rix, 'The party agent and English electoral culture, 1880–1906', Ph.D. thesis, University of Cambridge, 2001.

[51] Lawrence, *Speaking for the people*, 61.

[52] Biagini, *Liberty*, 429–34; J. M. Bellamy and J. Saville, *Dictionary of Labour Biography* (1972–).

[53] J. Epstein, *In practice: studies in the language and culture of popular politics in modern Britain* (2003), 127. It certainly involves a strong endorsement of realism as a philosophical stance. The debates generated by the 'linguistic turn' and 'the problem' of cultural history are fascinating, but are not something with which I wish to engage here. For some recent developments see P. Mandler, 'The problem with cultural history', 94–117, C. Hesse, 'The new empiricism', 201–7, and P. Mandler, 'Problems in cultural history: a reply', 326–32, all *Cultural and Social History*, 1 (2004)

[54] John Belchem, 'Nationalism, republicanism and exile: Irish emigrants and the revolutions of 1848', *Past and Present*, 146 (1995), 134.

and partly was the product of propaganda and systematic self-deception. But finally, it was also – and to a large extent – the outcome of a strategy involving the appropriation of the rhetoric of liberty by subaltern groups who, in the process, could subvert the hegemonic strategies of the political elite. Here I selectively borrow Gramscian concepts to explain, for example, how the socially inclusive language of Nationalism could be used to foster the class interests of the better-off farmers and yet, at the same time, galvanize landless labourers into claiming their 'rights'; or how political women – another subaltern group – could adopt and adapt Gladstonian or Unionist ideas of liberty to their own specific and increasingly assertive vision of a gender-inclusive citizenship.

This leads us to consider the notion of 'the people', a notion of which I made extensive use in writing *Liberty, retrenchment and reform* as well as previous publications. Initially, I borrowed it from French and American historiography on late eighteenth- and early nineteenth-century radicalism.[55] Although vague, it was less so than Marxist concepts such as the 'labour aristocracy', and actually reflected the language in which generations of radical reformers had perceived and verbalized their own position and role in society. Like Stedman Jones,[56] I insisted on the importance of assessing radicals and reformers on their own terms and respecting the 'language' in which they conceptualized their particular world view. In the 1990s the 'people' became a more complex and widely used tool of historical analysis and was adopted by scholars such as Joyce and Vernon, influenced by the 'linguistic turn',[57] in response to what they saw as the final disintegration of the 'grand narrative' about the linear progression centred on the rise of 'class' and 'party'. In the present work I don't directly engage with this debate, although I do make a rather eclectic use of some of its results, as well as of the notion of 'class' and the related Marxist and Weberian traditions. However, I also propose a rehabilitation of the notion of 'party'.

Vernon has a point when he argues that electoral machines limit or 'discipline' popular participation, and that, as a consequence of the rise of mass parties, '[i]ncreasingly, if individuals were to matter as political

---

[55] A. M. Schlesinger Jr., *The age of Jackson* (1953), 42–3, 124–6; A. Soboul, *Les sansculottes parisiens en l'An II* (1962); E. Foner, *Free men, free soil and free land: the ideology of the Republican party on the eve of the Civil War* (1970).

[56] G. Stedman Jones, 'Rethinking Chartism', in Jones, *Languages of class: studies in English working class history, 1832–1982* (1983), 90–178; E. F. Biagini, 'Per uno studio del liberalismo popolare nell'età. di Gladstone', *Movimento operaio e socialista*, 5, 2(1982), 209–38.

[57] P. Joyce, *Visions of the people: industrial England and the question of class, 1840–1914* (1991); J. Vernon, *Politics and the People* (1993).

agents, they had to succumb to the disciplines and subjectivities of party politics, and therefore parties shaped the terms of their political participation.'[58] However, for both the Irish Nationalists and the British Radicals, political participation was not an end in itself, an opportunity to express one's 'subjectivity', but 'an instrument for the achievement of concrete aims, whose definition and control needed to be in the hand of organizations external to the dialectic of legislative assemblies'.[59] They *needed* to be, because the alternative was leaving them in the hands of the traditional social elites, that is, the notables who could afford effective participation *as individuals*. The latter were also those who most vocally expressed the concerns stressed by Vernon, as we shall see (chapter 6). Indeed, Vernon's 'Foucaldian' argument against mass parties is strangely reminiscent of J. A. Roebuck's contention, in the 1860s, that the trade unions 'suffocated' workers' individuality, and 'deprived' them of their 'freedom of choice'. Trade unionists replied that there was little 'freedom' of choice for non-unionized workers in the labour market. Was there any greater chance of freedom and participation for the workers – and for any other subaltern group – in the electoral process, without party organizations? Radical parties were the political equivalent of what trade unions (and land leagues) were in the economic sphere. In fact, historically – as Robert Michels pointed out at the beginning of the twentieth century[60] – such need was most acutely felt by democratic or socialist movements, which were the first to develop mass party organizations.

In this respect, within the broader European context the Irish party was less 'peculiar' than Cruise O'Brien has argued,[61] although it was certainly different from its rivals and competitors, the Conservatives and the Liberals. From 1885 it included a much higher proportion of farmers and provincial journalists than either of the main British parties. It was partly funded by the Irish diaspora overseas, including Americans, who had a revolutionary agenda,[62] and Canadians and Australians, who did not. Moreover, between 1885 and the 1890 split over the O'Shea divorce affair it was run in an autocratic way, like 'a regiment led by C. S. Parnell and by Michael Davitt'.[63] However, we must also bear in mind that the

---

[58] Vernon, *Politics and the People*, 337.

[59] P. Pombeni, *Partitie sisterri politici rella storia contemporare a* (1994), 249–50.

[60] R. Michels, *Political parties: A sociological study of the oligarchical tendencies of modern democracy* (1915).

[61] C. Cruise O'Brien, *Parnell and his party, 1880–90* (1957).

[62] Liberal Unionists made the most of it, denouncing the 'Irish members ... who ... are subsidised by American dollars contributed by the enemies of England' ('The future of Liberalism', *LW*, 5 June 1887, 1).

[63] Dr Kevin O'Doherty, cited in 'Meeting at Kells', *FJ*, 16 Nov. 1885, 7.

other parties in the United Kingdom were also 'different', each in its own way, especially in terms of the structure and role of their respective extra-parliamentary organizations, such as the Primrose League and the National Liberal Federation. Later, the foundation of the socialist ILP (1893) and of the trade-union-dominated Labour Representation Committee (1900) further added to the variety of experiences and experiments in party organizations in the UK.

In Britain there were similarities between the Labour and Liberal party *machines*, and they would need to be investigated.[64] For ultimately the question of party was not about a clash between popular 'spontaneity' and the 'caucus', or between 'communities' and 'elites', but a competition between what were – in most respects – rival types of 'caucuses'. Each was exclusive, 'elitist' and 'authoritarian' in its own way, though the one may have been more dominated by trade union bosses than the other. The question was simply one of power: the distribution of power within the local association or club and the relationship between the 'mass' organization and the parliamentary party.[65] In *Liberty, retrenchment and reform* I have examined the way in which such a question related to 'the politics of place', with particular reference to the rural caucus in mining districts where it was heavily infiltrated by the locally dominant and widely representative union.[66] The latter could influence the selection of the Liberal candidate in various constituencies in Northumberland, Durham, Yorkshire and South Wales. When this failed to happen, it was generally because the workers were either weakly organized or religiously divided. However, sometimes the labour leaders who indulged in anti-caucus rhetoric were simply those who lacked local trade union support. The fact this could happen not only to free-market radicals like George Howell but also to socialists like Keir Hardie indicates that it was not a question of ideology, but one of local support. Howell and Hardie were two of the many disgruntled radicals who felt constricted by 'the machine' and indulged in anti-caucus rhetoric. That the latter was often just that – mere rhetoric – has recently been confirmed by James Owen, in his work on three-cornered contests in English urban constituencies.[67]

In this context, a dimension which needs to be borne in mind is the *anti-parliamentary* orientation of much radical politics and ideology during the period 1877–1906. This, once again, went back to Chartism, eighteenth-century radicalism and beyond, to the army councils of

---

[64] Lawrence, *Speaking for the People*, 254–7.   [65] See chapter 4, and chapter 7, pp. 370–1.
[66] Biagini, *Liberty*, chapter 6.
[67] James Owen, 'The "caucus" and party organization in England in the 1880s', Ph.D. thesis, University of Cambridge, 2006.

those seventeenth-century Cromwellian revolutionaries who were often so warmly praised in Victorian Dissenting and Radical circles.[68] As far as the Liberals were concerned, the NLF was not only a machine for canvassing voters and winning elections, it was also a body whose aim was the representation of popular opinion – a 'Liberal Parliament outside the Imperial Parliament', as activists would continuously boast. Thus, provincial Liberals wanted, if not actually to 'legislate' for themselves, certainly to define the programme on which their MPs should act. Party leaders soon had reason to regret that such activists employed no empty rhetoric: the NLF meant business, and, especially between 1886 and 1895, caused havoc (as some said), or pushed forward the cause of party democracy (as others argued). The Nationalists had started with similar ideas of democratic county conventions and a national executive, but then conferred a sort of presidential trust on Parnell. The latter generated the most effective Victorian example of a caucus, in the shape of the INL, which relied on the strong sense of community engendered by nationalism and farming interests. Thus if the INL was 'a model of authoritarian control under democratic forms',[69] until 1890 Parnell exercised his power on the basis of what might be described as a popular mandate. However, in the wake of the divorce scandal he was perceived as betraying such trust and most of the party rejected his authority. As Cruise O'Brien has written, the crisis was a test which ensured 'the adherence of Ireland to parliamentary democracy', for which 'we have to thank not the principles of Parnell, but the example and conduct of the party which he formed'.[70]

The debates inspired by British 'revisionism' pale in comparison with the discussion elicited by its Irish equivalent. Of course, the latter has a completely different meaning, and concerns not methodological questions about the 'linguistic turn', but political ones about the national past.[71] I can only say that I approach such debate as an outsider. This does not mean that I am either more or less objective than anyone else,

---

[68] T. M. Parsinnen, 'Association, convention and anti-Parliament in British radical, politics, 1771–1848', *English Historical Review*, 88 (1973), 504–33; Biagini, *Liberty*, chapter 1. Interestingly, this 'anti-parliamentary' tradition lived on in the Liberal Party Organization of the twentieth century and was quite evident between the 1960s and 1981, especially with reference to the strategy called 'community politics': see B. Keith-Lucas, 'The Liberal party, local government and community politics', in V. Bogadnor (ed.), *Liberal party politics* (1983), 242–59.

[69] Cruise O'Brien, *Parnell and his party*, 354.   [70] Ibid., 355.

[71] B. Bradshaw, 'Nationalism and historical scholarship in modern Ireland', *Irish Historical Studies*, 26, 104 (1989), 329–51; R. F. Foster, *Paddy and Mr Punch: connections in Irish and English history* (1993), introduction and chapter 1; D. G. Boyce and A. O'Day (eds.), *The making of modern Irish history: revisionism and the revisionist controversy* (1996).

but simply that I consider the relationship between Nationalists and Liberals with the same degree of personal involvement (or lack thereof) with which I would approach, let us say, the relationship between Hungarian and Austrian liberals in the days of the Dual Monarchy (Arthur Griffith, the founder of Sinn Fein, would have approved of the comparison).[72] I do not play down the national question in Irish politics, but am not affected by the 'English obsession' in Irish historiography.

The present book approaches its subjects within two contexts – European history and the history of the British Isles. Any reference to 'the British Isles' may raise additional political questions: as Comerford has written, such a language 'has long posed problems for many Irish nationalists', who see it 'as implying a concession of political and/or cultural unity of the archipelago'.[73] It is a delicate question, but I should like to stress that at the time the whole of Ireland was an integral part of the United Kingdom and that the existence of a centralized parliamentary state had a major influence on Irish as much as on British politics and culture. If there was no cultural unity, there was at least, in Comerford's well-chosen words, an 'overlap between the cultures of modern Ireland and those of England'[74] – a most apposite observation both because of the notion of 'overlap' and because of the emphasis on the plurality of the cultures in question.

The European context is important, for *British democracy and Irish nationalism* is based on the rejection of 'exceptionalism', namely of interpretations which argue that the historical development of modern Ireland (or, for that matter, Britain) was 'exceptional', 'peculiar' or 'different' from that of other European countries. Far from suppressing national 'peculiarities', this approach stresses that *all* countries are 'peculiar' or 'exceptional', though each in its own way. But although each has its own *Sonderweg*, none is special to the extent of making essentially comparative and general concepts such as 'liberalism' or 'nationalism' inapplicable to its distinctive history. There was no 'exceptionalism' in Ireland's exceptionalism. The Irish *Sonderweg* was shaped, not by colonialism but by the Famine and mass emigration. Both had political implications and the latter continued to do so throughout the twentieth century. It operated as a safety valve, removing surplus labourers and potential class warriors who might otherwise have imperilled the stability of this religious, patriotic and agrarian country far more drastically than the Land League or the IRA ever did.

---

[72] A. Griffith, *The resurrection of Hungary: a parallel for Ireland* (1904); cf. T. Kadebo, *Ireland and Hungary: a study in parallels with an Arthur Griffith bibliography* (2001).
[73] R. V. Comerford, *Ireland* (2003), 12.   [74] Ibid., 49.

While the 'colonial paradigm' has firmly established itself in modern scholarship, historians looking at Ireland within the broader 'continental' context insist that a comparison with the situation within other European empires is at least as helpful.[75] Until 1919 most European 'small nationalities' were included in multinational empires, and unless we wish to describe the experiences of, let us say, the Czechs and the Slovenes – not to mention the Catalans – as 'colonial', we need to devise broader and less Anglo-centric models of historical analysis for Ireland. Furthermore, while aspects of that country's economic history may be interpreted through the 'colonial' lens, recent scholarship on the Irish involvement in the British Empire has shown the extent to which they were both protagonists and victims of imperial exploitation and expansion.[76]

Thus, my European bias is the main source of some reservations about the heuristic value of emphasizing Ireland's 'colonial' status and affinity with other parts of the empire. For example, let us consider the vexed question of the racialization of the Irish in *Punch* cartoons, some of which presented them as subhuman creatures similar to gorillas.[77] While the debate has recently been reappraised by Curtis – its chief originator – and a number of other scholars,[78] none of them has tried to examine the question within its European context. The latter is important because the racialization of the rebellious peasant was by no means an isolated Irish phenomenon. Subhuman, 'bestial' features were constantly ascribed to primitive rebels whose actions threatened not only property, but also the social order, and when their criminal activities endangered the lives of members of the ruling elite. Perhaps the most famous and widely illustrated nineteenth-century example is provided by the southern Italian 'brigands' in their protracted rebellion against the newly

---

[75] T. Garvin, *1922: the birth of Irish democracy* (1996), 1, 34–5, 193–302; S. Pašeta, *Before the revolution: nationalism, social change and Ireland's Catholic elite, 1879–1922* (1999); R. English, *Ernie O'Malley: IRA intellectual* (1998), 172–3; the editors' 'Introduction' to A. Gregory and S. Pašeta, *Ireland and the Great War* (2002); Comerford, *Ireland*, 12, 3, 28–9; P. Hart, *The IRA at war, 1916–1923* (2003), 240.

[76] S. B. Cook, 'The Irish Raj', Journal of Social History, 20, 3 (1987), 507–29; B. Crosbie, 'Collaboration and convergence: the Irish expatriate community in British India, c.1798–c.1898', Ph.D. thesis, University of Cambridge, 2005; J. Ridden, *Making good citizens* (2006).

[77] L. P. Curtis, *Anglo-Saxons and Celts: a Study of Anti-Irish Prejudice in Victorian England* (1968) and *Apes and Angels: the Irishman in Victorian caricature* (1971); S. Gilley, 'English attitudes to the Irish in England, 1780–1900', in C. Holmes (ed.), *Immigrants and minorities in British society* (1978), 81–110; Foster, *Paddy and Mr Punch*, 171–94; see also R. Romani, 'British views on the Irish national character, 1800–1846: an intellectual history', *History of European Ideas*, 23, 5–6 (1997), 193–219.

[78] See L. P. Curtis, J. Belchem, D. A. Wilson and G. K. Peatling, 'Roundtable', *Journal of British Studies*, 44, 1 (2005), 134–66; and M. de Nie, *The eternal Paddy: Irish identity and the British press, 1798–1882* (2004).

unified Italian state from 1861 onwards. Not only northern Italian observers, but also the southern bourgeoisie referred to them as a 'criminal class' – almost a race apart – and represented them as possessing physical features consistent with their moral degeneration.[79] In fact, Cesare Lombroso (1836–1909) built his academic career, reputation and a whole school of criminal anthropology by postulating the existence of a 'criminal type' distinguishable from a normal person by certain measurable physical features. He was neither a pioneer nor an exception, as Louis Chevalier and D. Pick have established with reference to the Parisian proletariat and 'faces of degeneration' elsewhere in Europe.[80] This was arguably the 'racialization' of crime (and poverty), but in fact had nothing to do with 'race' and instead owed everything to upper- and middle-class social fear and prejudice, and in particular to their shock and outrage against the Fenians, who 'dared to bring Irish violence, hitherto a remote phenomenon, into Britain itself'.[81] In conclusion, when the Fenian 'apes' are examined from a comparative European perspective it is difficult to escape Foster's conclusion that class – far more than 'race' – was the central preoccupation behind the alien identity of the Irish rural rebel.[82]

The limitations of the 'colonial' approach in the case of the history of Irish popular movements are perhaps best illustrated by Marylin Silverman's splendid work. Paradoxically, she escapes the insularity and Anglo-centrism of the colonial paradigm – which she accepts – because of her close focus on a *regional* reality (Thomastown, Co. Kilkenny). Far from being 'colonial', the picture which emerges from her study is eminently comparable to class (or class/status) realities in Britain and elsewhere in north-western Europe. Labour organizations, strikes and the struggle to modify the law, Christian morality as part of both the hegemonic discourse and the resistance movements of the workers, the emphasis on cleanliness, respectability and 'independence' are all aspects of social life and class conflict which the Irish shared with working classes in other national contexts. The legitimacy of the law was contested, not because it came from a 'colonial' power, but because it tended to enshrine

---

[79] A rich collection of cartoons and photographs describing the subhuman, bestial features of these primitive rebels is in *Brigantaggio lealismo repression nel Mezzogiorno, 1860–1870*, intro. by A. Scirocco (1984).

[80] L. Chevalier, *Classes laborieuses et classes dangereuses à Paris pendant la première moitié du XIXe siècle* (1958); D. Pick, *Faces of degeneration: a European disorder, c.1848–c.1918* (1989).

[81] O'Farrell, *England and Ireland*, 41.

[82] Foster, *Paddy and Mr Punch*, 193; see also Romani, 'British views on Irish National Character'.

landlord and farmer interests.[83] If anything, the imperial nature of the state helped to modify official attitudes to rural unrest: paternalist concession went hand in hand with coercion. If the latter feature seems to support the colonial comparison, it must be remembered that most other imperial states in contemporary Europe adopted a similarly paternalist approach (for example, the Austrians and Russians with their Polish peasants).

In contextualizing such traditions the present book operates on three parallel, but distinct levels: (1) ideas, values and rhetoric which were shared by radicals throughout the British Isles, including personal liberty, self-government and a non-confessional state; (2) geographical context and cultural meaning – for example, the rural setting of much Irish or Scottish Highland politics in contrast to the often urban focus of English radicalism – and the way this accounts for some of the differences and contrasts between these movements, including a commitment to sectarian education in Nationalist Ireland and Presbyterian Scotland; and (3) the interplay both between these two levels and between rhetoric and class interests. Gladstone, Chamberlain and Parnell were skilled at handling this dimension of popular politics, but, I argue, the task proved more difficult than any of them had anticipated.

Unlike *Liberty, retrenchment and reform*, the present study is not primarily concerned with *working-class* liberalism, but explores both the tension between elite and popular understandings of rights and liberties and the ambiguity between status- and class-based politics.[84] The latter was at the centre of Liberal practice and Gladstone himself encouraged it – as Jose Harris has noted – by moving 'enigmatically' between the rhetoric of party and that of social conflict.[85] It was a creative ambiguity and enabled liberalism to operate not only as a party language, but also as a set of cultural and ideological tools which reformers belonging to either gender and different social groups could appropriate to promote their own particular programmes. Thus political economy had been adopted by the trade unions from the 1850s, when another liberal orthodox creed, free trade, was being turned into an effective device for increasing the

---

[83] M. Silverman, *An Irish working class: explorations in political economy and hegemony, 1800–1950* (2001); see also F. Lane and D. Ó Drisceoil (eds.), *Politics and the Irish working class, 1830–1945* (2005).

[84] I use the expression 'status' politics in the Weberian sense highlighted by Peter Clarke ('Electoral sociology of modern Britain', *History*, 57, 189 (1972), 31–55), to denote a situation in which political alignment and allegiance were inspired by religion, ethnicity or locality, in contrast to economic differences.

[85] J. Harris, *Private lives, public spirit: Britain, 1870–1914* (1993), 16.

power of consumer pressure groups.[86] Later the extension of the parliamentary franchise was achieved by means of a gradualist strategy which incorporated the liberal discourse of respectability and independence, but insisted on the democratic, 'neo-roman' values of participatory citizenship. The fact that such values and related rhetoric were shared by many Liberal leaders further contributed to establishing a viable interclass alliance[87] and encouraged links with Irish nationalism – which itself emphasized a similar understanding of liberty.

This raises the question of whether the notion of 'popular liberalism' can be used at all in the Irish context. In the first place, were there in Ireland the preconditions for a democratic culture (whether liberal or not) to emerge? In the 1920s Kevin O'Higgins expressed the view – widely shared by British observers at the time and since – that behind Irish 'democracy' there was merely '[a] mixture of feudalism and brigandage ... and a deplorable amount of grabber and gombeen morality'.[88] This interpretation has been challenged by Bill Kissane, who has persuasively argued that throughout the nineteenth century 'the functional specialization of civil society, and an increasing pluralism in nationalist politics', 'regular local and national elections, administrative structures increasingly subject to popular control, and a parliament at times responsive to Irish public opinion', all contributed to the general politicization and democratization of Irish society.[89] Meanwhile, friendly societies effectively disseminated 'the rudiments of democratic practice' among a growing section of the Irish labouring population and promoted values 'such as thrift, self-reliance, reciprocity, self-government and civility'.[90] Theo Hoppen and others have made a good case for the strength of Catholic liberalism in Daniel O'Connell's days, and Vincent Comerford has established the extent to which it was still healthy during the election of 1868.[91]

---

[86] E. F. Biagini, 'British trade unions and popular political economy, 1860–1880', *Historical Journal*, 30, 4 (1987), 811–40 and 'Popular liberals, Gladstonian finance and the debate on taxation, 1860–1874', in E. F. Biagini and A. J. Reid (eds.), *Currents of Radicalism* (1991), 134–62.

[87] E. F. Biagini, 'Neo-Roman liberalism: "republican" values and British liberalism, ca. 1860–1875', *History of European Ideas*, 29 (2003), 55–72.

[88] B. Kissane, *Explaining Irish democracy* (2002), 79.   [89] Ibid., 113.

[90] Ibid., 87–8. For the role that similar developments had in the growth of popular liberalism in mid-Victorian Britain see A. Briggs, *Victorian people* (1954), chapters 5 and 7; T. Tholfsen, *Working class radicalism in mid-Victorian England* (1976), chapters 7–10; Biagini, *Liberty*, 'Introduction' and chapter 2.

[91] K. T. Hoppen, 'Riding a tiger: Daniel O'Connell, Reform and popular politics in Ireland, 1800–1847', *Proceedings of the British Academy*, 100 (1999), 121–43; R. V. Comerford, *The Fenians in context: Irish politics and society, 1848–82* (1985), 143, 162, 173–4.

However, most other scholars agree that Parnell was hardly a 'liberal', although few would go as far as Cruise O'Brien in crediting contemporary claims that he was a 'dictator' in the making.[92] He was certainly out of sympathy with Gladstonian sentimentalism and was a protectionist in commercial matters.[93] But this evidence only shows that he thought that Irish interests and needs were not served by English policies and that his first allegiance was to Ireland. More complex is the question whether or not, because he was out of touch with the sensibility and commercial policies of British Liberals, we should conclude that he was not a 'liberal' in the *Irish* context. In fact, if tested by this stringent criterion, most nineteenth-century French, American, German and Italian liberals would similarly fail to qualify. This leaves us with one of two options. Either we could apply this doubly insular test consistently across the board: then perhaps we should regard Depretis, Ferry, Naumann and the rest of the nationalist, protectionist supporters of indigenous industry as 'Parnellites', rather than liberals. Alternatively, we could abandon 'insularism' in all its varieties and accept that liberalism was a wider European and American cultural and political phenomenon which should not be defined by mere reference to the British experience. The latter is the approach adopted here. I agree with Tom Claydon that Parnell was 'an exponent of Atlantic principles', combining 'parliamentary liberalism and civic humanism' with a preference for small government.[94] As Roy Foster has put it, '[h]e represented a belief in the possibility of a future pluralist Irish identity' which 'reflected the variety, tolerance and depth of relationship to be found around his part of Wicklow'.[95]

In any case, the present book is concerned not with Parnell's ideas, but with those of his followers in the context of their times. Here we encounter a different historiographical problem: most scholars of Parnellism have emphasized the 'rejectionist' aspects of Irish nationalism and land agitation – that is, they have only been interested in what the Parnellites were *against*. But, in so doing, they have neglected what they actually stood *for* and how this compared with the aims and ideology of contemporary radical movements and groups in other parts of the British Isles. Yet the political views of the Irish tenant farmers and their leaders during

[92] Cruise O'Brien, *Parnell and his party*, 354–5.
[93] F. S. L. Lyons, 'The political; ideas of Parnell', *Historical Journal*, 16, 4 (1973), 749–75; Jackson, *Home Rule*, 77–8.
[94] T. Claydon, 'The political thought of Charles Stewart Parnell', in D. G. Boyce and A. O'Day (eds.), *Parnell in perspective* (1991), 165–6.
[95] Foster, *Paddy and Mr Punch*, 60; Foster, *Charles Stewart Parnell: the man and his family* (1979).

such a formative period – when the practice of democratic elections was established – are important if we want to understand how parliamentary democracy could become so deeply rooted in Ireland in the twentieth century. When the Nationalists' language and demands are studied in their own terms and context, what is most striking is not their anti-English rhetoric, but the ideological and cultural ground they shared with their British counterparts. For example, both insisted on radical land reform and civil rights under the 'constitution', both praised responsible local government in contrast to central control, and both were suspicious of militarized police forces and coercion laws. Moreover, both were inspired by the Chartist belief that political reform must precede social improvement.[96] If these were the values of popular liberalism in Wales and the Scottish Highlands, in Ireland they amounted to a distinctively liberal nationalist definition of Irishness. Like the Chartists in the 1840s, the National League criticized not the 'constitution' as such, but its 'corruption' and the way the law was allegedly 'manipulated' by the magistrates to safeguard the interests of the landowners. Far from being ephemeral products of propaganda from the days of the 'Union of Hearts', these convictions survived the Parnell split of 1891 and Gladstone's retirement in 1894. Nationalist commitment to the constitutional process and parliamentary democracy was not really endangered by the Gaelic cultural revival.[97] Renewed and reasserted from 1900–6, constitutionalism and parliamentary democracy slowly re-emerged from the violence of 1916–23 as central features of Irish political and cultural life.[98]

Popular liberalism in Britain consolidated the switch in post-Chartist democratic politics from quasi-revolutionary unrest for the extension of the constitution and fiscal reform, to a Parliament-centred, constitutional agitation for similar aims. The method, focus and parliamentary leadership, more than the aims and the democratic ideology, were the crucial changes. Ideologically, popular liberalism retained strong radical inclinations, with an emphasis on land reform, ranging from idealized visions of 'peasant proprietary' to support for Henry George's 'single tax' proposals.[99] The development of Irish rural radicalism followed a similar

---

[96] Comerford, *Fenians in context*, 40, 136.

[97] Jackson, *Home Rule*, 101; Pašeta, *Before the revolution*, 49, 75, 150.

[98] P. Maume, 'From deference to citizenship', in 'Republicanism in theory and practice', *The Republic*, no.2 (2001), 81–91; Garvin, *1922*; C. Townshend, 'The meaning of Irish freedom: constitutionalism in the Free State', *Transactions of the Royal Historical Society*, 6th series, 8 (1998), 45–70.

[99] Revd W. Tuckwell, *Reminiscences of a radical parson* (1905), 128–57. Cf. T. McBride, 'John Ferguson, Michael Davitt and Henry George: land for the people', *Irish Studies Review*, 14, 4 (2006), 421–30.

pattern, though with a different chronology: there was a movement away from Gladstonianism in 1874–81 and then, from 1882–3, a shift back to parliamentary politics.[100] In the 1880s the turning point came in the wake of Gladstone's Land Acts (1881, 1882 and the 1883 Labourers' Act) which satisfied basic demands, while the constitutional strategy offered hopeful prospects of further reform. Hitherto, historians have been prepared to admit that some Nationalist leaders shared with their British allies both 'civic humanism' and 'parliamentary liberalism'.[101] We know that many Home Rulers came from a Liberal background, to the extent that in the late 1870s it was felt that the epithet was a new word for Irish Liberal.[102] They revered W. E. H. Lecky's version of the Irish past, including 'Grattan's Parliament as a model of . . . self-government, concomitant with economic prosperity [and] increasing religious tolerance'.[103]

However, as far as the rank and file were concerned, scholarly accounts have emphasized either the pragmatism of the wirepullers and efficiency of the party machine or the resilience of the 'physical force' tradition.[104] On the whole, whereas the influence of the Irish Republican Brotherhood (IRB) and the anti-English culture nurtured by William O'Brien's *United Ireland* are widely recognized, the movement's more liberal aspects have been regarded either as a minority view – surviving in the 'blurred edges' between upper-class constitutionalism and Fenian militancy – or as one of the many facets of an intrinsically ambiguous movement.[105]

That the old account is not wholly satisfactory has been indicated by successive waves of 'revisionism' and 'post-revisionism'. On the one hand we know from Comerford that membership of the IRB was often of little more than social significance – a way of expressing 'individual identification with the national cause'.[106] On the other hand, it has long been

---

[100] Loughlin, *Gladstone, Home Rule and the Ulster question*, 9.

[101] Claydon, 'The political thought of Charles Stewart Parnell', 162–8; F. S. L. Lyons, *John Dillon: a biography* (1968), 322; L. W. Brady, *T. P. O'Connor and the Liverpool Irish* (1983), 54ff.

[102] E. O'Toole (1860–1922), *Whilst for your life, that's treason. Recollections of a long life* (2003), 26.

[103] R. V. Comerford, 'The land war and the politics of distress, 1877–82', in W. E. Vaughan (ed.), *A new history of Ireland*, vol. VI (1996), 26; Loughlin, *Gladstone, Home Rule and the Ulster question*, 9. 'Grattan's Parliament' was the old Irish Parliament in its supposed golden age, between 1782–1800, when it reached an unprecedented level of autonomy from British control. There is a certain irony in the fact that Lecky was a well-known Unionist: D. McCartney, *W. E. H. Lecky: historian and politician, 1838–1903* (1994).

[104] Cruise O'Brien, *Parnell and party*; Maume, *Long Gestation*.

[105] M. Hurst, 'Parnell in the spectrum of nationalisms', in Boyce and O'Day, *Parnell in perspective*, 81; Loughlin, *Gladstone, Home Rule and the Ulster Question*, 20; Comerford, 'The land war and the politics of distress', 28–31, 46–8; Maume, *Long Gestation*, 4, 11.

[106] Comerford, *Ireland*, 40. See also his *Fenians in context*.

accepted by scholars that the Irish in Britain were 'contaminated by Liberalism', and even that Gladstone 'replaced Parnell as the main object of Irish loyalty and affection' after 1891.[107] While Theo Hoppen has demonstrated the resilience of 'local', as opposed to 'national', identities and the 'normalcy' of electoral politics before 1885,[108] others have stressed the importance of reconsidering the history of democracy in Ireland in a comparative perspective. In particular, in his study on the 'birth' of Irish democracy, Tom Garvin has insisted on the ideological common ground between the Irish republican tradition and contemporary continental European, British and American liberal-democratic attitudes to citizenship, society and the state.[109]

The pre-1914 National party was in most respects ideologically closer to the liberal-democratic ideals in which Garvin is interested than any of the post-1922 Free State parties. The latter were shaped by the anti-individualist, majoritarian values of 1919–21 and tended to underplay what Garvin calls the 'positive connotations' of the European and American tradition – including the right to free speech and open government, and the positive value of individualism and minorities.[110] By contrast, late Victorian Nationalism went out of its way to assert its pluralist credentials and respect for minorities: indeed this was, according to the ageing John Dillon, the main difference between 'our independent lay party' – as he called it – and what he regarded as the 'clericalist' Sinn Fein.[111] The party of Parnell, Redmond and Dillon stood on an essentially secular platform, combined with constitutionalism and a libertarian critique of government coercion. It tried to harness revolutionary forces

---

[107] J. Denvir, *The Irish in Britain from the earliest times to the fall and death of Parnell* (1892), 381; S. Fielding, 'Irish politics in Manchester, 1890–1914', *International Review of Social History*, 23 (1988), 271–7; R. B. McCready, 'Irish Catholicism and nationalism in Scotland: the Dundee experience, 1865–1922', *Irish Studies Review*, 6, 3 (1998), 245–52.

[108] K. T. Hoppen, *Elections, politics and society in Ireland 1832–1885* (1984).

[109] Garvin, *1922*, 13–7, 22–5, 28–9, 64–5, 194, 200. See also T. J. White, 'Nationalism vs. liberalism in the Irish context: from a post-colonial past to a post-modern future', *Éire–Ireland*, 37, 3–4 (2002), 25–38 and J. M. Regan, *The Irish counter-revolution 1921–1936: treatyite politics and the settlement of independent Ireland (2001)*, 68–70.

[110] Garvin, *1922*, 16, 32–3; for a rather theoretical discussion of these concepts see White, 'Nationalism vs. liberalism'.

[111] As he wrote in a memorandum on Christmas Eve 1918: 'The fury of a large section of the priests, who are most dishonestly using S.[inn] F.[ein] to carry out a purpose they have long nursed – the destruction of our independent lay party and the recovery of their own [direct?] power over Irish politics, which the Parnellite movement had to a large extent destroyed.' Cited in Lyons, *Dillon*, 455. From the mid-1890s leading Nationalists had complained about 'the dead weight against which we have to struggle in the large body of clerics who support Healy' – the dissident Nationalist leader who had adopted sectarian politics after Gladstone's retirement (TS, Confidential, E. Blake to J. Dillon, Toronto, 7 Oct. 1895, in Blake Letters, P 4681, NLI).

to the chariot of parliamentary politics – which is what John Bright and other Radicals had done in Britain in the aftermath of the last national Chartist demonstration in 1848. The affinities between Nationalism and Chartism are particularly strong in the case of Michael Davitt even in the more radical phase of his career. For example, in 1878 '[t]he right of the Irish people to carry arms' was one of the planks of his creed, together with two other traditional republican demands, namely self-government and land reform with a view to establishing 'a system of small proprietorship similar to what at present obtains in France, Belgium, and Prussia'.[112] Each of these three demands had a Chartist pedigree and had been resurrected and 'domesticated' by mid-Victorian Liberals, especially those involved in the volunteer movement.[113] By the same token, to Irish nationalists all over the world, the story of Davitt's patient suffering in British prisons, as narrated by contemporary biographies,[114] must have read like Silvio Pellico's *Le mie prigioni* (1832) to an earlier generation of British Liberals.

Thus, what Loughlin has called 'the state of consciousness that the Irish National party's rhetoric was designed to inculcate'[115] was politically and functionally, as well as constitutionally, akin to what popular liberalism stood for in Britain. They both shared in a 'neo-roman' political culture interspersed with different religious and national traditions and enriched by contributions from the wider Anglophone world overseas. In particular American republicanism was influential among Irish nationalists, but was also widely echoed by British radicals, especially before 1877.[116] Canadian federalism inspired the debate on 'Home Rule All Round' together with the idea that Irish Nationalism was not inconsistent with the preservation of a purified Union – a view epitomized by Edward Blake, the former leader of the Canadian Liberal party and ex-Premier of Ontario, who became a leading Irish Nationalist MP at Westminster in the 1890s.[117]

---

[112] M. Davitt, 'The future policy of Irish Nationalists', speech delivered in the Mechanics Hall, Boston, 8 Dec. 1878, cited in D. B. Cashman, *Life of Michael Davitt with a History of the Rise and Development of the Irish National League* (1881), 90.

[113] Biagini, 'Neo-Roman liberalism'.   [114] E.g. Cashman, *Life of Michael Davitt*, 29–66.

[115] Loughlin, *Gladstone, Home Rule and the Ulster question*, 22.

[116] E.g. the cult of Abraham Lincoln in 1863–5 and the even more widespread ideal of the 'independent yeoman' celebrated by both Thomas Jefferson and Andrew Jackson: Biagini, *Liberty*, 69–79. As late as 1890 Lloyd George publicly referred to the USA as 'the great Republic of the West' (cited in J. H. Edwards, *David Lloyd George*, 2 vols. (1929), vol. I, 127).

[117] M. B. Banks *Edward Blake, Irish Nationalist: a Canadian statesman in Irish politics, 1892–1907* (1957).

In Ireland popular constitutionalism was 'liberal' in the sense in which this expression has been applied to the description of comparable movements in other agrarian countries in the nineteenth century. Liberalism – especially in its popular forms – encompassed both a method and a spectrum of opinions rather than a class or national ideology. It operated as a discourse with many elements that particular groups incorporated into their own language as the moment suited. If it prospered in urban settings around 1848, it was also highly compatible with the social and economic aspirations of peasants and farmers, as Roland Sarti, Alan Knight and other scholars have demonstrated.[118] Indeed, while 'the agrarian question was intimately connected with the rise of parliamentary democracy',[119] the 'independent peasant' was and remained a hero and a model citizen for liberals across the world of European culture, from Thomas Jefferson in the USA in the 1790s to Wilhelm Röpke in Germany in the 1950s. In the British Isles it had long been championed by John Bright, and it was later advocated by both the Irish Nationalists and the Liberal Unionists.[120]

The politics of humanitarianism

A. J. P. Taylor has coined the expression 'politics of emotionalism' to describe the Gladstonian approach to the Bulgarian atrocities in 1876. It consisted in the rhetorical exploitation of media reports to generate strong public reactions which could then translate into electoral results.[121] Emotionalism became even more prominent in British political debates from 1877–8, in response to the equally emotional Conservative politics of jingoism.[122]

In 1876 reports of indiscriminate, large-scale massacres of civilians by irregular Ottoman troops – deployed to repress a nationalist rising among

---

[118] A. Knight, *The Mexican Revolution, vol. I: Porfirians, liberals and peasants* (1986); R. Sarti, *Long live the strong: a history of rural society in the Apennine Mountains* (1985); V. Wahlin, 'The growth of bourgeois and popular movements in Denmark ca. 1830–1870', *Scandinavian Journal of History*, 5 (1980), 151–83.

[119] A. Hussain and K. Tribe, *Marxism and the agrarian question*, vol. I (1981), 133.

[120] T. MacKnight, *Ulster as it is or twenty-eight years experience as an Irish editor*, vol. I (1896), 79–82; J. Collings, *Land Reform. Occupying ownership, peasant proprietary and rural education* (1906).

[121] A. J. P. Taylor, *The trouble makers: dissent over foreign policy, 1792–1939* (1957; 1967), 75.

[122] The link between the two is explored in H. Cunningham, 'Jingoism in 1877–78', *Victorian Studies*, 14, 4 (1971), 419–53, and W. Fest, 'Jingoism and xenophobia in the electioneering strategies of British ruling elites before 1914', in P. Kennedy and A. Nicholls (eds.), *Nationalist and racialist movements in Britain and Germany before 1914* (1981), 171–89. For the emotional nature of Jingoism see J. A. Hobson's classical analysis, *The psychology of Jingoism* (1901).

Christian peasants – sparked off an outburst of popular indignation in Britain. The unashamedly pro-Ottoman stance of Disraeli, the then Prime Minister, contributed towards the swelling of this outburst into what Shannon has brilliantly described as a 'crisis of public conscience'.[123] There was widespread feeling that, as one Preston Liberal put it, 'Disraeli [had] deeply wounded the *moral sense* of the people.'[124] The latter – chiefly the Nonconformist people – now 'asserted that conscience rather than official and elite convenience should determine foreign policy, and that it was the responsibility of each voter to demand that those in charge of the State behaved in an appropriately Christian spirit'.[125] When Gladstone 'adopted' the movement – in September, following the publication of his famous pamphlet (which sold some 200,000 copies) – the protest grew into a popular front of moral outrage. Those involved in the agitation often stressed moral principles and the categorical imperatives of the Gospel, rather than debating the national interest in terms of *Realpolitik*.[126]

Rebecca Gill has produced an important revision of the widely accepted view that the origin of the agitation was in a spontaneous groundswell of indignation. In fact, far from being spontaneous, the agitation was carefully orchestrated by groups of elite liberal opinion makers (including W. T. Stead and E. A. Freeman), while the emphasis on natural outrage, the result of impulse rather than planning, helped to create the impression that politics was about 'real' humanitarianism.[127] The trick worked. Perhaps, as Gill writes, the Liberal newspaper coverage was 'Manichean' and unbalanced,[128] but public opinion and especially the Dissenters were genuinely shocked by the first media exposure of the systematic violation of what we now term 'human rights'. The Unitarians called for the government to take 'immediate steps ... to render the recurrence of similar atrocities impossible'.[129] Understandably less bellicose, the Workmen's Peace Association argued that 'justice demands that the Turkish Government ... be called upon to indemnify to the full extent of their losses, those whom they have so cruelly plundered and

---

[123] R. T. Shannon, *Gladstone and the Bulgarian Agitation, 1876* (1963), 42.
[124] An Admirer from Preston, n.d., Glynne–Gladstone papers, 702.
[125] J. P. Parry, 'Liberalism and liberty', in P. Mandler (ed.), *Liberty and authority (2006)*, 97.
[126] For two examples see W. Lake (a Devonshire farm labourer) to W. E. Gladstone, 24 Sep. 1874, in Glynne–Gladstone MSS 702; and Resolution of the Labour Representation League, 3 Nov. 1876, R(S. R.)61, Minute Book, f.215, in British Library of Political and Economic Science.
[127] Gill, 'Calculating compassion in war', 66, 78.   [128] Ibid., 80.
[129] Resolution passed by the Executive Committee of the British and Foreign Unitarian Association, 12 Sep. 1876, NA, FO 78/2551.

outraged'.[130] Although the protest was often couched in 'orientalist' language (contrasting 'the fatalism of Turkey' with 'the progressive [European] races of her Empire'[131]), it was not inspired by anti-Islamic bigotry. Even Gladstone, who did not mince his words, stressed that 'Mahometan ... does not mean the same as Turk'.[132] He wrote that Islam was a religion which had its noble manifestations, embodied by 'the mild Mahometans of India ... the chivalrous Saladins of Syria [and] ... the cultured Moors of Spain'.[133] The 'Turkish race' was, by contrast 'a tremendous incarnation of military power' and 'represented force as opposed to law'.[134] As Patrick Joyce has pointed out, drawing the distinction was important in order 'not to deny the brotherhood of man, existing under many versions of the Godhead'.[135]

Such a distinction was even more marked in the popular protest – and must be borne in mind as an important qualification of the oft-repeated link between the agitation and anti-Semitism or similar religious/ethnic animosities. Granted that what singled out the Bulgarians, Serbs and other rebel communities was their Christian culture (rather than their 'race'), the petitions routinely criticized not the religious but the *secular* authorities of the Ottoman Empire – both the 'soldiery and mercenaries' for what they had perpetrated, and the government for what they had allowed to happen. They supported the independence of the European nationalities in the Balkans not because the latter were under a 'Turkish' government, but because that government had proved 'cruel and oppressive'.[136] While demanding immediate British diplomatic action, the protest meetings also started a relief campaign, collecting 'money, and material of clothing, on behalf of the wounded and suffering in the Servian cause'.[137]

What is most remarkable about this episode is the scale of the popular mobilization, which Saab has explained in terms of the 'alienation from participation in the political process' felt by 'the newly enfranchised working classes'.[138] The 'working classes' is of course a very vague notion. However, if by it she means the organized labour movement,

---

[130] Council of the Workmen's Peace Association to the Right Hon. the Earl of Derby, NA, FO 78/2551.
[131] Ibid.
[132] W. E. Gladstone, *The Bulgarian horrors and the question of the East* (1876), 61.
[133] Ibid., 12.   [134] Ibid., 14, 15.
[135] P. Joyce, *Democratic subjects: the self and the social in nineteenth-century England* (1994), 209.
[136] Birmingham Women's Liberal Association to the Earl of Derby, n.d., NA, FO 78/2931.
[137] Meeting of the inhabitants of the Borough of Rochdale, convened by the Mayor, Rochdale, 4 Sep. 1876, NA, FO 78/2551.
[138] A. Pottinger Saab, *Reluctant icon: Gladstone, Bulgaria and the working classes, 1856–1878* (1991), 62.

then there was no obvious reason why they should have felt 'alienated' in 1876, given that they had just won (in 1875) a historic settlement of trade union rights and employment legislation. In any case, the TUC membership was then quite small and could not account for the agitation – whose effectiveness depended on 'the quantity of people who had been mobilized out-of-doors'.[139] Moreover, at the time the trade unions consisted almost entirely of the mature and established members of the relevant trades, while the agitation also involved the younger generation – as Saab has pointed out. Finally, the agitation was not exclusively or even predominantly working class: the middle classes were well represented and arguably comprised the bulk of the demonstrators (although we must bear in mind that boundaries between 'artisans' and the lower middle class were somewhat blurred).

With its emotionalism and emphasis on moral imperatives, the agitation was more like a religious revival than a social or political campaign. The idealism associated with it was one reason for the unusually high involvement not only of the youth of all social classes, but also of women. The politics of humanitarianism spanned the gap between the genders' 'separate spheres' and evoked strong responses among women of different social classes. As Saab has pointed out, '[p]ossibly because of the prominence of Nonconformists, and certainly because of the humanitarian focus of the movement, women played a large role'.[140] Indeed, from an early stage some women were assiduous in goading Gladstone himself into action.[141] Women's involvement had always been important in missionary work and anti-slavery campaigns, spheres within which their supposedly gender-specific responsiveness to human suffering was first mustered for purposes which had political, as well as religious and humanitarian, implications.[142] In his 1873 'Lectures to Women' the young Cambridge economist Alfred Marshall had insisted on the specifically feminine calling to moralize and ennoble society, claiming that the

---

[139] Pottinger Saab, *Reluctant icon*, 125. The largest anti-war meeting took place in Hyde Park at the end of February 1878 and involved some sixty or seventy thousand people while the largest petition, also against the war, contained 220,000 signatures (ibid., 181, 188–9). In 1884 the TUC had about 379,000 members (H. A. Clegg et al., *A history of British trade unions since 1889*, vol. I: 1889–1910 (1977), 3).

[140] Pottinger Saab, *Reluctant icon*, 101, 166, 188.

[141] 'Has Mr Gladstone so little to say while Bulgarian women and helpless maidens are foully [illegible] and children are horribly outraged? Has he lost his voice? Is he afraid of Disraeli?' Letter to Gladstone, from Birmingham, n.d. but before Sep. 1876, Glynne–Gladstone Papers, 702.

[142] C. Midgley, *Women against slavery: the British campaigns, 1780–1870* (1992); S. Thorne, *Congregational missions and the making of an imperial culture in 19th-century England* (1999), 97; C. Hall, *Civilising subjects: metropole and colony in the English imagination, 1830–1867* (2002), 332–3.

'new' women whom he sought to educate and motivate had a role to play in the 'public sphere'.[143] This strategy finds parallels in Gladstone's politicized humanitarianism and appeal to women during his 1879 Midlothian campaign. It was to women that he addressed one of the most famous passages in his speeches, when his indictment of Tory imperialism culminated in an emotional proclamation of rights – rights which were established by the Almighty and shared by all human beings, irrespective of national, religious, gender or race barriers:

Remember the rights of the savage, as we call him. Remember that the happiness of his humble house, remember that the sanctity of life in the hill villages of Afghanistan among the winter snows, is as inviolable in the eye of Almighty God as can be your own. Remember that He who has united you together as human beings in the same flesh and blood, has bound you by the laws of mutual love; that that mutual love is not limited by the shores of this island, it is not limited by the boundaries of Christian civilization; that it passes over the whole surface of the earth, and embraces the meanest along with the greatest in its unmeasured scope.[144]

As Patrick Joyce has shown, this was a significant development in Gladstone's rhetorical strategy and, more generally, in the definition of civic identity, the Liberal 'self', and the public conscience which needed to be stirred. Remarkably, in such a notion of the Liberal 'self', women 'represented the essential principle of ... human nature', 'the being of woman ... testified to humanity'.[145] Through their special religious sensitivity they were supposed to be particularly responsive to a sense of 'humanitarian duty' which extended, as Gladstone put it, 'beyond our shore'.[146] There is no reason to doubt his sincerity, but it is likely that, by trying to mobilize women, he also hoped to tap into a further source of support, through the influence which wives and daughters were supposed to wield on their male kinsfolk.[147] Whatever the case, his appeal to women was consistent with what Bebbington has described as

---

[143] E. F. Biagini, 'The Anglican ethic and the spirit of citizenship: the political and social context', in T. Raffaelli, E. Biagini and R. McWilliams Tullberg (eds.), *Alfred Marshall's 1873 lectures to women* (1995), 24–46.

[144] W. E. Gladstone, *Midlothian speeches 1879* (1971), 94.

[145] Joyce, *Democratic subjects*, 206, 210.

[146] Indeed, for Josephine Butler, in many ways the personification of the feminine Liberal self, 'liberty' was mainly about 'the fulfilment of altruistic and Christian duty' (H. Rogers, 'Women and liberty', in Mandler (ed.), *Liberty & authority*, 132).

[147] This assumption is exemplified by an imaginary dialogue in an 1886 electoral pamphlet: 'We must respect the rights o' property,' the 'owd parson' tells a farm labourer, trying to persuade him to vote Unionist. 'Yes', answers Polly, the labourer's wife, 'and so we must the happiness and lives o' men and women. Don't we know, Joe?' *Joe Jenkins on the Great Crisis. A Labourer's views on Home Rule* (1886), 11 (Bishopsgate Institute).

Gladstone's 'Christian liberalism'. The latter comprised three primary components: individual freedom from unnecessary government interference, the claims of 'communities' (local, national and international) and those of humanity, which qualified his nationalism and were central to his notions of international law and individual human rights.[148] These three primary principles informed also the way he was represented at the time by some of his supporters. As the veteran labour leader George Potter put it in 1885, 'Mr Gladstone's long and energetic labours in the cause of Suffering and Oppressed Nationalities show that his grand gifts have not been used exclusively for his own countrymen, but for common humanity.'[149]

This rhetoric was effective because it appealed to impulses deeply rooted in the British political tradition. In particular, when in his 1876 Blackheath speech he appealed to 'individual duty' and 'the recognized brotherhood of men',[150] Gladstone invoked three values which had been central to the British Protestant imagination since the seventeenth century – namely, the sovereignty of the individual conscience, the sanctity of life and the equality of human beings. Gladstone presented foreign politics as the arena for the exercise of 'non-partisan' Christian patriotism. As Bright had done with the abolitionist agitation during the US Civil War, the GOM seized on the Eastern question's human dimension and linked it to the passions, hopes and fears of zealous Nonconformists and pious High Churchmen and, as we shall see (below, chapter 3, pp. 163–6) at least some Irish Catholics. Among the Liberal rank and file his rhetoric was perceived as a powerful vindication of the suffering poor – not only in Bulgaria but also at home.[151] In its style and effect on the crowds, as well

---

[148] D. W. Bebbington, 'Gladstone's Christian liberalism', *Chf Bulletin*, (Summer 2005), 11–17.

[149] G. Potter, *Life of W. E. Gladstone*, reprinted in his 'Gladstone, the friend of the people', 'Leaflets for the new electors' (1885) (Bishopgate Institute).

[150] Pottinger Saab, *Reluctant icon*, 95.

[151] 'I am Glad to see you are making such a noble stand in the Cause of the poor Down Cast Christians in Bulgaria. I rejoice to know that we Have a statesman to whom the working Classes of England can trust on with the utmost Confidence and Honour Dear Sir in Sir S NorthCotes Address to the working men of Edinburgh He Had the Boldness to say that the working man of this Country did not understand the foreign policy of the present Government But Sir I Am Glad to find that they told Sir S NorthCote that they understand it Better than the Government. I hope Dear Sir you will still Go on in your Noble Cause till there is a Sound and a righteous Government for the poor Disregarded Christians in Servia But Sir I only wish you Could Comply with the request at BlackHeath to become again leader of the great liberal party in the House of Commons.' (William Lake, a Devonshire farm labourer, to Gladstone, 24 Sep. 1876, Glynne–Gladstone Papers, Hawarden, 702; spelling peculiarities in the original. Cf. the Secretary of the Amalgamated Labour League (farm labourers, Boston), to Gladstone, 9 Feb. 1878 in Glynne–Gladstone Papers, 714.)

as in its simple moral certainties, his rhetoric was reminiscent of the Moody and Sankey evangelistic campaigns of the previous three years.[152] Like the two American revivalists, he enthused large numbers of religious women and men, some of whom had recently been granted the vote, and whose perception of the broader world was shaped by the demanding universalist ethic of the Protestant Bible.

While Gladstone was at best an inconsistent champion of the primacy of humanitarianism, his speeches during the Bulgarian agitation and 1879 Midlothian campaign extended the scope and meaning of liberalism – and certainly made it more appealing to all those influenced by the internationalist and humanitarian ideas then typical of the left. The protest movement attracted radical intellectuals, artists and journalists including William Morris, D. G. Rossetti, H. Fawcett, E. A. Freeman and W. T. Stead. It enthused T. Motterhead, H. Broadhurst, T. Burt and many other influential labour leaders of the time. While a group of Liberal and pacifist MPs – including A. J. Mundella, H. Richard and S. Morley – established the Eastern Question Association, G. Howell and the other leaders of the Labour Representation League started to organize popular support on a large scale.[153] Their work also inspired the National Liberal League, which sought to unite trade unions and London radical clubs and focused on specific democratic reforms, as well as on Gladstone's foreign affairs programme.[154]

Of course there was no necessary or close correlation between Bulgaria and Ireland – notoriously, Joseph Cowen opposed Gladstone over the Eastern question although he was, already then, a strong supporter of Irish Home Rule.[155] However, in a way, the agitation became a trial run for the 1886 campaign for Home Rule. When the Nationalist party won the overwhelming majority of Irish seats at the 1885 election – the first to be fought under an extended and near-democratic franchise – Gladstone became convinced that Home Rule was a new 'crisis of public con- science'. He saw it in the same way as he had viewed the Eastern question in 1876, an issue 'transcending mere sectional interests'.[156] His overall

---

[152] J. Coffey, 'Democracy and popular religion: Moody and Sankey's mission to Britain, 1873–1875 campaign', in Biagini, *Citizenship and community*, 93–119.

[153] W. H. G. Armytage, *A. J. Mundella, 1825–1897: the Liberal background to the labour movement* (1951), 170–3; E. P. Thompson, *William Morris romantic to revolutionary* (1988), 202–25.

[154] Thompson, *William Morris*, 260–5.

[155] Although he was strongly criticized by some Newcastle radicals for doing so: see *Mr Cowen: apostle or apostate?* (1880), pamphlet in the Newcastle Central Library. For Cowen's attitudes to the Eastern question see *Joseph Cowen's speeches on the near Eastern question* (1909); for his attitudes to Home Rule see chapter 2, below.

[156] Pottinger Saab, *Reluctant icon*, 196–7.

rhetorical strategy was similar to the one he had adopted both in 1876 and 1879 – he linked Ireland to the broader politics of humanitarianism.

The way such politics developed after 1876 and its links with other humanitarian campaigns have been comparatively neglected by historians, although various studies have been devoted to specific pacifist and anti-imperialist pressure groups.[157] But the bigger picture – including not only Ireland, but also the various currents of radicalism within the British left – has been consistently neglected. In particular, in their studies on patriotism and internationalism, D. J. Newton, P. Ward and S. Howe have completely ignored the Lib-labs (trade union officials sitting as Liberal MPs), despite the fact that two of them, Randal Cremer and Arthur Henderson, were awarded the Nobel Peace Prize (in 1903 and 1934 respectively). And Blaazer's study on the 'popular front' overlooks the links between Ireland, anti-imperialism, peace, arbitration and disarmament.[158] Ward's argument that '[f]or most British socialists, internationalism was something desirable, but it was also something distant'[159] does not apply to Ireland. The latter was hardly 'distant' in any meaningful sense of the word – especially with the Irish National League of Great Britain campaigning in many constituencies throughout the country. Yet, Ireland is remarkable for its absence from Ward's analysis, and the related question of imperialism – which inspired so much of the European debate on democracy, socialism and patriotism at the time – receives merely a cursory reference in a footnote.[160]

Yet it is easy to show that popular radical concern for Irish social and constitutional demands was culturally deeper and politically more important than has hitherto been conceded. From the days of the Chartists the issue of Irish legislative autonomy was part of the broader question of democracy in the British Isles. As Dorothy Thompson has pointed out, the Chartists expected the repeal of the Act of Union to be one outcome

---

[157] E. W. Sager, 'The working-class peace movement in Victorian England', *Histoire Sociale–Social History*, 12, 23 (1979), 122–44; P. Laity, *The British peace movement 1870–1914* (2001); Peatling, *British opinion and Irish self-government*; M. Matikkala, 'Anti-imperialism, Englishness and empire in late-Victorian Britain', Ph.D. thesis, University of Cambridge, 2006.

[158] D. J. Newton, *British labour, European socialism and the struggle for peace, 1889–1914* (1989); S. Howe, *Anticolonialism in British politics: the left and the end of empire, 1918–1964* (1993); P. Ward, *Red flag and Union Jack: Englishness, patriotism and the British left, 1881–1924* (1998); D. Blaazer, *The Popular Front and the progressive tradition: socialists, liberals and the quest for unity, 1884–1939* (1992).

[159] Ward, *Red flag*, 52, n. 94.

[160] R. Gallissot, 'Nazione e nazionalità nei dibattiti del movimento operaio', in E. J. Hobsbawm, *Storia del marxismo, vol. II: Il marxismo nell'età della Seconda Internazionale* (1979), 787–867; F. Andreucci, 'La questione coloniale e l'imperialismo', in ibid., 868–96.

of the implementation of the demands contained in their celebrated 'Six Points'. Ernest Jones, the last Chartist leader of national repute, regarded Ireland as a sort of British Poland 'rightly struggling to be free' from English 'tsarism'.[161] The latter was the sobriquet applied to the Dublin Castle system, whose centralism and police powers were perceived as utterly 'un-English'. As early as 1833 – well before the promulgation of the Charter – the first popular demonstration in England against Earl Grey's Reform government was directed against its Coercion Act, which empowered both the Lord Lieutenant to prohibit public meetings and army officers to court martial offenders in 'proclaimed' counties. The radicals abhorred such measures in principle and feared that a government which was ready to use them against Irish peasants and town workers could easily do so against British artisans as well.[162] A later generation reached exactly the same conclusions, which were consistently expressed from the 1860s onwards by radical and labour leaders like George Howell, George Odger, A. A. Walton, Tom Burt and Joseph Cowen.[163] Well before 1886 such concern had developed into support for Home Rule. The latter was, by 1900, one of the few areas on which Lib-labs (the trade-union Liberal MPs), the ILP and the early Labour party all agreed. As Strauss has pointed out, both in principle and as a matter of expediency, British democracy could not ignore Irish Nationalism.[164]

Popular agitations inevitably involve both passion and populism, but the Home Rule crisis made post-1886 radicalism particularly passionate and emotional, and its leaders ruthlessly populistic. The 1886 Bill with the subsequent agitation and electoral campaigns polarized politics and increased political awareness among subaltern groups – including women – and helped to redefine and enlarge the notion of the public sphere in which it was 'appropriate' for them to be active. Although Gladstone was certainly shrewd in identifying humanitarianism as one of the distinctive features of 'feminine' liberalism,[165] he was wrong to

---

[161] D. Thompson, 'Ireland', in D. Thompson and J. Epstein (eds.), *The Chartist Experience: studies in working-class radicalism and culture, 1830–60*, (1982) 145; D. Thompson, *The Chartists*, 317, 325.

[162] Thompson, *The Chartists*, 19.

[163] G. Howell, 'Worst for the future', a lecture to the Pimlico branch of the Reform League, 28 March 1868, in Howell Collection (microfilm edition) IX/HC/LB, 379ff.; cf. his appeal 'To the electors of the Borough and Hundreds of Aylesbury', in ibid., 744; G. Odger, 'Address to the electors of Sothward', *The Bee Hive*, 8 Jan. 1868, 4; A. A. Walton, letter to the editor of *The Bee Hive*, 4 July 1868, 3.

[164] E. Strauss, *Irish nationalism and British democracy* (1951).

[165] Cf. J. Jordan, *Josephine Butler* (2001); J. Alberti, *Eleanor Rathbone* (London, 1996); and S. Pedersen, 'National bodies, unspeakable acts: the sexual politics of colonial policy-making', *Journal of Modern History*, 63 (1991), 647–80.

expect that women would be unaffected by either jingoism or Unionism. Animosity and partisanship under the recently enlarged franchise stimulated the rise of the party machine and caucus politics. The latter had contrasting effects on popular radicalism – simultaneously increasing and limiting effective participation in national politics – but became an essential device of mass mobilization. As years went by, the prolonged Home Rule crisis consolidated new identities, political cultures and party allegiances. In Ireland politics became less concerned with local issues and more influenced by a national debate sustained by both the Dublin and the provincial newspaper press and animated by the campaigns of Parnell's Irish National League (INL). As Hoppen has written, 'constitutional nationalism ... was at once able and obliged to provide a refuge for men who would as readily have declared themselves Whigs or Liberals in earlier days'.[166]

In Britain, John Vincent has claimed that the protracted agitation enabled the Liberals to 'absorb' Irish Nationalism electorally.[167] Even before Gladstone introduced his first Home Rule Bill in 1886 the Irish in Britain were grateful to their 'true friends' among the British Radical leaders, including Herbert Gladstone, the Prime Minister's son, and Joseph Cowen, in whose honour was named at least one Irish National League branch.[168] During the following years, 'many Irish men and women gained prominent positions within Liberal ward and divisional parties. Many became Liberal in both word and deed, strongly identifying with the party's Radical wing.'[169] Such trends were evident to contemporary observers, who actually thought that the 'liberal' side of nationalism was becoming so dominant that an eventual full merger between the Irish and British wings of Gladstonianism was a plausible scenario in 1890.[170] It was not merely a momentary impression: twenty years later, in 1910, J. L. Garvin, then editor of the *Observer*, perceived what he described as the danger of an Irish–Liberal–Socialist coalition.[171] Arguably, what was actually happening was a renewal of the old alliance between Chartist democracy, free-trade Cobdenites and latter-day O'Connellism in a popular front of moral outrage. Social radicalism had been a prominent concern in the 1890s, but from the turn of the

---

[166] Hoppen, *Elections, politics and society*, 485.   [167] Vincent, 'Gladstone and Ireland'.
[168] The Washington branch in County Durham: M. Roddy, on behalf of the INL, to J. Cowen, 14 Dec. 1885, in Cowen Papers, B343.
[169] Fielding, 'Irish politics in Manchester 271.
[170] As one Liberal Unionist observed, '[t]here will arise out of the fragments of the present Opposition, in time, a new party of which the Irish members will form a large portion'. (Arthur S. Elliott to J. Chamberlain, 12 Dec. 1890, JC 6/6/1B/4.)
[171] C. B. Shannon, *Arthur J. Balfour and Ireland, 1874–1922* (1988), 149.

century – in the days of Taff Vale, militarism and the importation of Asian workers in South Africa ('Chinese slavery') – radicals of all shades came together under a post-Gladstonian umbrella. The latter did its job fairly well until it was shattered by German and Fenian bullets in 1916.

A synopsis

British democracy and Irish nationalism relies on a variety of sources, including the papers of Lib-lab, Radical, Home Rule and Liberal Unionist parliamentarians, political autobiographies, party records, miscellaneous items from the John Johnson Collection and the local history collections of municipal libraries and county record offices, parliamentary debates, and the newspaper press. Most of these sources are examined in the conventional way: my method does not require any particular explanation here, apart from what I have already said about my approach to the study of 'language' and ideas. As for the newspaper press, I regard it as a collection of sources, rather than one source in any simple sense of the word.[172] It includes different literary genres, such as letters from the public and predominantly descriptive (although often tendentious) reports of meetings, popular demonstrations and other similar events.

Most newspapers regularly published letters from the public, but after 1887 such correspondence evolved into a special literary genre in the pages of the *Weekly Times and Echo*. Over the following few years this well-established radical newspaper – which in the 1860s had popularized J. S. Mill's ideas and in 1886 had espoused Chamberlain's Radical Unionism – set aside a full page (sometimes more) each week to allow its readers to discuss political ideas. Correspondents included H. M. Hyndman, Edward Aveling and Eleanor Marx, Tom Mann, Ben Tillett, J. Keir Hardie, and J. Ramsay MacDonald, as well as lesser-known Christian socialists, feminists and radicals of various political and party affiliations. It records the views of a variety of people, ranging from otherwise unknown activists to men and women who rose to national prominence.

The leading articles are of particular interest in the case of *Reynolds's Newspaper*, which must be regarded as an exception to what the authors of *Seems so!* wrote about the papers not forming political opinion and '[w]orking-class political opinion possess[ing] no newspapers'.[173] *Reynolds's* was, at any rate, a radical weekly with a Chartist pedigree and

[172] See detailed discussion in 'Introduction' to Biagini, *Liberty*.
[173] S. Reynolds, Bob and Tom Woolley, *Seems so! A working-class view of politics* (1911), 158.

a reputation for appealing to proletarian radicalism, among miners, soldiers and sailors, as well as artisans and labourers. It was unusual because
of its ability to sustain a close relationship with its highly politicized
readership, including a number who celebrated annual 'reunions' as
well as summer holiday excursions.[174] Its editor, W. M. Thompson,
called them 'the Reynoldsites' and thought that they were a democratic
movement. In 1899–1906 he actually demonstrated the accuracy of
his claim when he summoned his readers to form the short-lived but
highly successful National Democratic League (see below, chapter 6).
Therefore, the views expressed in *Reynolds's* are worth studying not only
because the newspaper was widely circulated and known to be influential,
but also because more than any other mass-circulated political weekly it
expressed the post-Chartist mind-set of popular liberalism.

Quite unusually for popular weeklies, we know much about the
editorial staff of *Reynolds's Newspaper*. The names of all the journalists –
together with their literary pseudonyms and short biographical sketches –
were published in an article in 1905.[175] Most of them were long-term
employees (one for more than forty years), a fact which helps to explain
the paper's remarkable continuity in terms of ideology, themes and
language. Thompson, chief editor from 1894 (when he replaced
Edward Reynolds, brother of the paper's founder), was born in Ireland
in 1857 and had long been involved in working-class causes and journalism. A founder of *The Radical*, described as 'the first Co-operative
Democratic paper in London', and a barrister specializing in issues
pertaining to the application of the Employers' Liability Act and
Workmen's Compensation Act, he was the standing counsel for a number
of trade unions and had acted in high-profile labour cases, defending
Burns, Hyndman, Champion, and Cunninghame Graham. He had been
a Radical parliamentary candidate and, like other *Reynolds's* staff, had sat
on the London County Council as a Progressive. With his solid middle-
class background Thompson was not an 'organic' intellectual. He was
rather the early twentieth-century equivalent of the gentleman-leader of
the Chartist and pre-Chartist radical tradition. Like his sub-editor,
F. H. Amphlett, he was active in the National Liberal Club. R. Wherry
Anderson (born 1865), who wrote under the pseudonym of 'Gracchus'
from 1880 (replacing Edward Reynolds when the latter became chief editor),
was a member of both the National Liberal Club and the Fabian Society,
but described himself as an 'Opportunist Socialist', that is, '[he] believed
in joint action between advanced Radicals, Progressives and Socialists'.

---

[174] '"Reynolds's" Reunion', *RN*, 20 Dec. 1903, 1 and 'Our reunion', *RN*, 27 Dec. 1903, 4.
[175] *RN*, 1 Jan. 1905, 1.

Other editors variously described themselves as humanists, anarchists, democrats and republicans. One, the 65-year-old John Morrison Davidson, had also been a columnist for the *Daily Chronicle* and the *Weekly Times* (see chapter 6). He was an organic intellectual, in Gramscian terms, having 'lived by the cause'. Despite describing himself as a pacifist anarchist, a republican and a Scottish nationalist, he was essentially inspired by Christian socialism.

How these diverse currents of radicalism could coalesce and prosper under the Gladstonian umbrella is explored in the rest of this book. Chapter 2 focuses on the arguments used by British supporters of Home Rule. The idea had been discussed already from the late 1860s and the 1870s. From 1882 the debate was radicalized by the anti-imperialists and the peace lobby, who drew parallels between the Irish question and the British invasion of Egypt. Interestingly, this resulted not in the 'othering' of Ireland, but in the rejection of the 'orientalist' stereo-types with regard to Egypt and in the application of Irish ('white' and European) models to India.[176] The groups most committed to Home Rule included miners, Nonconformists, the Women's Liberal Federation (WLF), and Scots and Welsh national revivalists. As one Durham miner put it, they saw Home Rule as a legitimate demand for the Irish 'to be let alone' – an improved version of collective self-help. The WLF – established in 1887, initially to campaign for Irish self-government – soon developed and articulated a sophisticated 'feminist' platform.[177] This chapter shows how such activism and self-confidence originated from the application of the new emphasis on moral imperatives and human sympathy generated by Home Rule to both gender roles and citizenship. In particular, emotionalism, which had traditionally been perceived as a specifically feminine *disability*, now became a *virtue*, something of which women boasted as adding to their fitness to be involved in the public sphere.

Chapter 3 discusses the liberal dimensions of Irish Nationalism with reference to the land agitation, the political role of the churches, the influence of British and continental European political thought, and the campaign for constitutional rights against coercion, culminating in the 'Union of Hearts'. It was not merely a tactical convergence, as illustrated by the Irish response to jingoism and the Armenian atrocities of the late 1890s, which is further discussed in chapter 6. Chapter 4 is about the

---

[176] C. A. Bayly, 'Ireland, India and the empire, 1780–1914', *Transactions of the Royal Historical Society*, 6th series, 10 (2000), 392–4.

[177] M. Pugh, *The march of the women: a revisionist analysis of the campaign for women's suffrage, 1866–1914* (2000), 70–1, 132–7.

popular party 'machines', primarily, the National Liberal Federation (NLF) and the Irish National League (INL). It was an issue of considerable importance: popular radicalism had always been about democracy, but from the 1880s the question became how to make democracy work. Moreover, the growing awareness of national politics created the question of how programmes should be developed and who should define the policies which Liberalism (or Nationalism in Ireland) was about. Claiming to be the general assembly of the Liberal party members, the NLF demanded policy-making powers, a claim which the parliamentary party was never prepared to accept. There was a similar clash going on in Ireland. Within the INL and its local conventions the activists' democratic ambitions were initially crushed by Parnell, but resurfaced after his fall in 1891 and again at the end of the century with the growth of the United Irish League (UIL), which more than any other previous development emphasized the tensions between rank-and-file democracy and the parliamentary elite.

The irony is that – for all their emphasis on 'democracy' – supporters of the NLF were reluctant to provide membership figures (the Women's Liberal Federation, by contrast, did so regularly). This was in part because in theory any Liberal elector or non-elector could attend local caucus meetings and vote for the local executive council. The number of representatives which each Liberal association would be allowed to send to the national council of the Federation was in proportion to the number of parliamentary *electors* in each constituency, irrespective of the total of party members. In this also the NLF tried to be like a 'parliament' for Liberal supporters nationwide, a representative assembly parallel to the British Parliament and claiming democratic legitimacy because, unlike Parliament, it was elected by universal male suffrage. Of course, this was only the *theory*, because *in practice* most people were insufficiently motivated to make use of their 'rights'.

Thus, if chapters 2 and 3 are about the politics of emotionalism and the populism of humanitarian imperatives, chapter 4 is about attempts to give organizational dependability and method to the politics of emotionalism or, as one apologist euphemistically put it, to 'give stability to popular opinion'. It was ironic that Joseph Chamberlain, one of the original architects of the NLF, was not only rejected by the organization he had created, but also was always completely out of touch with the politics of emotionalism. This is discussed in Chapter 5, which deals with Radical Unionism. The first section examines the transformation of Chamberlain, the rising hope of those 'stern and unbending' radicals until 1886, into their nemesis. Historians have often seen his defection as originally caused by a personality clash with Gladstone. This chapter argues that there were more fundamental causes, emerging in 1881–5 from Chamberlain's experience in government, social reform ambitions and the imperial crises in Egypt and India. From these he concluded that only a strong, united imperial government could deal with such crises and face both the problem of poverty at home and the Irish question across the channel. His Unionism originally represented a coherent form of liberalism, and was perceived as such by many at the time, especially by those who were concerned about relieving destitution, increasing literacy and popular education, and reforming land tenure.[178] He emphasized material, tangible results and was impatient with 'sentimental' humanitarianism and peasant nationalism. His clash with the Gladstonians about Ireland and collectivism was similar to the clash within the NLF between those who were primarily interested in electoral results and those who insisted that the citizens' active participation in the political process was more important.

There was no clear and uncomplicated 'liberal' answer to the questions raised by the Home Rule debate about individual liberty and participatory democracy or nationality and empire. But the fact that the large majority of both the caucus and the Liberal electors remained loyal to Gladstone placed Chamberlain and the other Liberal Unionist leaders in a situation of dependence on Conservative support. At some stage Chamberlain had to choose between his radicalism and the Conservative alliance. While he opted for the latter and went to the Colonial Office in 1895, his erstwhile close ally, the Northern Irish T. W. Russell, was himself ready to rock the Unionist boat in the pursuit of social reform. Perhaps not surprisingly, the Nationalists experienced similar dilemmas in their sometimes too close alliance with the Liberals. In the 1890s this resulted in a succession of groups breaking away from the anti-Parnellite Irish National Federation. Some of them, in order to maximize the benefits of land reform, were prepared to co-operate both with Unionist pressure groups and with the government.

Such tensions within both Radical Unionism and Nationalism are further discussed in chapter 6, which is about the recasting of popular radicalism in both Ireland and Britain between the general elections of 1895 and 1906. Social radical movements and pressure groups, including the ILP and the UIL, rejected the Liberal party and the official Irish nationalist organizations, feeling that they had betrayed their radical mandate. As one English Dissenter put it, 'the old Liberal party is still

---

[178] P. Bew, 'Liberalism, nationalism and religion in Britain and Ireland in the nineteenth century', in S. Groeveld and M. Wintle (eds.), *Britain and the Netherlands, vol. XII: Under the sign of liberalism* (1997), 93–101.

pledged to Adam Smith rather than Jesus Christ'.[179] But this quotation also suggests that Christian radicalism remained more effective in inspiring and galvanizing the radical 'people' than any secular version of socialism. Moreover, throughout this period it was not class, but various humanitarian concerns – such as the 1896 Armenian atrocities and the agitation against 'methods of barbarism' and Chinese slavery after the Second Boer War – that mobilized and united rank-and-file Liberals with various other currents of radicalism. Thus the last section of chapter 6 is devoted to the revival of a Chartist and Gladstonian movement in the shape of the National Democratic League. Although their demands were primarily concerned with domestic policy, they reasserted their support for Home Rule, which by then had become – together with free trade – one of the issues on which there was general agreement between Liberals, radicals, Labour, and the socialist societies.

[179] W. Jones Davies, 'The new party', *Primitive Methodist Quarterly Review*, Oct. 1895, 719.

2 'That great cause of justice': Home Rule in the context of domestic Liberal and radical politics

That the object of the League shall be. To enlighten the British Public as to the Political Condition and Relations of Foreign Countries; To disseminate the Principles of National Freedom and Progress; To embody and manifest an efficient Public Opinion in favour of the Right of every People to Self-government and the maintenance of their own Nationality; To promote a good understanding between the Peoples of all Countries.[1]

It is the custom to attribute the strength of the popular feeling [in favour of Home Rule] to the overwhelming personal popularity of Mr Gladstone, and there can be no doubt that his identification with the cause of justice to Ireland has contributed immediately to its creation. But not wholly. Nations are not moved to enthusiasm unless there is an undercurrent of strong motive. The truth is that the people have now been awakened for the first time to the enormity of the injustice which has been done to Ireland; and the popular mind is possessed with an intense and passionate desire to render generous, if tardy, justice. There is all the emotion of strongly-stirred sympathies; and the tide surges around the only man who can give legislative expression to popular sentiment.[2]

Before the 'Hawarden kite'

At the beginning of the Home Rule crisis Chamberlain expressed the view that '[i]n this great controversy there are three powerful influences all working in favour of the Gladstone's Bills'. These were: 'first ... the Liberal feeling in favour of self-government'; 'second ... the impatience generally felt at the Irish question & the hope to be rid of it once for all;

---

[1] 'The Peoples' International League', Minutes of the Provisional Committee, 5 June 1847, signed by Ashurst, Shaen, Stansfield [*sic*, sc. Stansfeld], Watson, Thornton Hunt, Hawkes, Linton and P. A. Taylor, Jun., in Archivio W. J. Linton, Biblioteca Feltrinelli, Milan, VI, 18.

[2] L.a., 'The classes against the masses', *The North-Eastern Daily Gazette*, 29 June 1886, 2.

and . . . third . . . the tremendous personality of Mr Gladstone himself'. He concluded that '[the] last of these three has had the greatest effect in causing Liberals to accept the proposals without careful personal invest-igation of them'.[3] Most historians agree with him. By contrast, the present chapter argues that in Britain, although Gladstone's charisma swayed many wavering voters during the 1886 general election, popular support for Home Rule antedated the events of that fateful year. It had been growing from the mid-1870s and especially in the early 1880s, shaped by enthusiasm for self-government and further strengthened by revulsion against coercion.

Like Chartism, popular liberalism had always been, above all, about democracy,[4] and many of its spokesmen were not the least embarrassed by the clash between parliamentary and popular sovereignty which the Home Rule agitation engendered. Indeed, the radical understanding of freedom was rooted in what Skinner calls 'neo-roman' liberty.[5] 'Self-government' implied more than a set of elected local authorities deriving their legitimacy from Bills passed by the imperial Parliament. It also implied that the legitimacy of Parliament itself depended on popular support and if the latter were to be permanently withdrawn, the former would collapse and government degenerate into despotism. This was the case in Ireland: the Union had to be amended because the overwhelming majority of the people rejected it. Moreover, from 1887 the notion that Home Rule was the only alternative to continuous coercion further reinforced the view that self-government *was* liberty. Without it there was only 'servitude' and 'tsarist' repression, which, if allowed to continue unchecked, would eventually corrupt not only the nature of government in Ireland, but also the whole fabric of the British constitution.[6]

Indeed Heyck has pointed out that a number of prominent Radicals were converted to Home Rule in 1881–2, when it appeared that not even a Liberal government could operate the Dublin Castle system without intro-ducing special repressive legislation.[7] Although this was an important turning point, Heyck's chronology is questionable, because some of the

[3] J. Chamberlain to T. Gee, 26 Apr. 1886, NLW, T. Gee MSS, 8305D, 15a.
[4] Biagini, *Liberty, retrenchment and reform* (1992).
[5] Q. Skinner, *Liberty before liberalism* (Cambridge, 1998). See E. F. Biagini, 'Liberalism and direct democracy: J. S. Mill and the model of ancient Athens', in Biagini (ed.) *Citizenship and community* (Cambridge, 1996), 21–44; and 'Neo-roman liberalism'.
[6] M. Matikkala, 'Anti-imperialism, Englishness and empire'; K. O. Morgan, *Keir Hardie, radical and socialist* (1984), 73.
[7] Heyck, *Dimensions*, 95. Cf. H. Labouchere, 'Radicals and Whigs', *Fortnightly Review*, 206 (Feb. 1884), 222–4; H. George, 'England and Ireland: an American view', *Fortnightly Review*, 186 (June 1882), 780–94; rep., 'East Leeds. Mr Lawrence Gane's candidature', *The Leeds Mercury*, 23 Nov. 1885.

MPs whom he identifies as 1882 converts to Home Rule had actually spoken in support of the cause as early as 1872–4, in response to Isaac Butt's first campaign. Moreover, many of the early converts to Home Rule – including Joseph Cowen, Patrick Lloyd Jones, A. J. Mundella and the editors of *Reynolds's Newspaper* – had been involved in Chartism in the 1840s, when the restoration of an Irish Parliament in Dublin was first debated in radical circles. Thus in 1842 a pamphlet proclaimed that 'SELF-LEGISLATION [*sic*] is the object of [both] Chartists and Repealers – in this consists their identity. Both stand up for the management of their own affairs.'[8] The idea was particularly popular in W. J. Linton's circle, which at one stage included liberals such as James Stansfeld and P. A. Taylor. To some of them, Ireland was an oppressed *nation*, like Italy or Poland,[9] and England was, like Russia, a 'great stronghold of despotism'.[10]

The Great Famine (1845–9) devastated the fabric of Irish society at the time when Chartism was finally defeated and ceased to be a national force in Britain. Moreover, mass emigration exported many of the discontents from both countries to North America and Australia. Not surprisingly after 1848 the cause languished in both Britain and Ireland, but, as G. K. Peatling has argued, it was gradually revived from the late 1860s. Peatling has focused on the Positivists, a group of intellectuals who played an important role in labour law reform and who championed many other radical causes at the time. Consistent anti-imperialists and proponents of international arbitration, they even defended the Paris Commune of 1871 as a legitimate democratic experiment.[11] Ireland had a stronger case than Paris, and from as early as 1866, men like Henry Crompton, Richard Congreve, Frederic Harrison, J. H. Bridges and E. S. Beesly voiced support for Irish self-government.[12] In 1868 Bridges was the first to argue that a separate Irish legislature would bring about a real 'union' between the two countries – a view later championed by Gladstone himself.[13] Bridges' argument relied on the Canadian precedent, but it is also

---

[8] [Anon.], *Chartism and Repeal. An address to the Repealers of Ireland, by a Member of the Irish Universal Suffrage Association* (1842), in Mitchell Library, Glagow, 14.

[9] William Bridges Adams to W. J. Linton, 31 Jan. 1847, in Archivio Linton, Biblioteca Feltrinelli, Milan, II-1.

[10] I. S. Varian from Cork, to W. J. Linton, Mar. 1848, ibid., IV-45. Thirty-six years later Linton, who had emigrated to America, retained his views, although the surviving correspondence contains only one reference to the Home Rule crisis. It appears in a letter to his son: 'So Gladstone is defeated. All right. Home Rule will come, and something better than [*sic*] GOM's muddlement.' (W. J. Linton to Will Linton, 14 June 1886, ibid., I-25.) This piece of evidence has been neglected by F. B. Smith, who argued that Linton became an unreconstructed Unionist: *Radical artisan: William James Linton, 1812–97* (1973), 209.

[11] R. Harrison, *The English defence of the Commune (1871)* (1971), 29–130.

[12] Peatling, *British opinion and Irish self-government*, 18.

[13] J. H. Bridges, *Irish disaffection: four letters addressed to the editor of the 'Bradford Review'* (1868).

interesting that he accepted the Chartist assumption that Ireland was a nation struggling to be free (he went as far as comparing the Fenians to Garibaldi).

Peatling has argued that the Positivists failed to influence the organized labour movement.[14] However, there is evidence that views similar to those which they propounded were widely echoed in popular radical circles. In 1869, in the context of the debate surrounding Gladstone's disestablishment of the Episcopal Church of Ireland, the London-based *Weekly Times* advocated the creation of an Irish Parliament subordinated to Westminster and similar to a state legislature in the USA. In 1871 the republican and secularist *National Reformer* hosted a discussion of Isaac Butt's Home Rule proposal, although Bradlaugh and other republican leaders were opposed to complete Irish separation. In 1872 the then influential trade union organ, *The Bee Hive*, came out in support of the principle of Home Rule.[15] In 1873, a number of prominent labour leaders followed suit. It was then that Joseph Arch was allegedly 'converted' to Home Rule, a cause which he supported for the rest of his life.[16] More significantly, that same year the two leading Lib-lab parliamentary candidates – Alexander McDonald (Stafford) and Thomas Burt (Morpeth) – successfully campaigned on platforms which included Irish Home Rule.[17] Recalling his early support for the cause in 1886, Burt said that by Home Rule he meant 'the establishment upon Irish soil of a Parliament to manage purely Irish affairs . . . I voted for Mr Butt [in 1874] and I voted for Mr Shaw and others who brought forward this question in the House of Commons.'[18] The 1874 debate on Home Rule was not a turning point, but the Irish party was pleased with the vote, which entailed fifty-three Irish MPs and ten British Liberals, including Sir Wilfred Lawson and Sir Charles Dilke, voting with them.[19]

---

[14] Peatling, *British opinion*, 33.

[15] E. Royle, *Radicals, secularists and republicans* (1980), 208; l.a., 'Home Rule', *The Bee Hive*, 17 Feb. 1872, 10.

[16] J. Arch, *The Autobiography of Joseph Arch*, ed. J. G. O'Leavy (1966), 174, 362–3, 371–2. Horn has shown that Arch's first involvement with Home Rule was based on a misunderstanding during a visit to Ireland: P. Horn, 'The National Agricultural Labourers' Union in Ireland, 1873–9', *Irish Historical Studies*, 17, 67 (1971), 340–52. His electoral platform did not include Home Rule until 1886, though in 1885 he did campaign for what he described as 'comprehensive measures' of local government for the whole of the United Kingdom: Horn, *Joseph Arch (1826–1919): the farm workers' leader* (1971), 234.

[17] See the reports 'The representation of Stafford. Speech by Mr McDonald', *Potteries Examiner*, 28 June 1873, 6; and 'Home Rule in the Potteries', ibid., 26 July 1873, 3; 'Representation of Morpeth. Mr Thos. Burt at Blyth', *NW*, 14 Nov. 1873, 3.

[18] T. Burt cited in *The Northern Echo*, 31 May 1886, 4.

[19] J. Martin to G. C. Mahon, 7 July 1874, NLI, MS 22, 203.

In January 1874, A. J. Mundella and Joseph Chamberlain in Sheffield and Joseph Cowen in Newcastle threw their weight behind the cause of Home Rule in the form then advocated by Isaac Butt. They all campaigned in constituencies where working-class radicalism was strong and included an Irish dimension. Though Cowen stressed that he did not support full Irish 'separation'[20] and Chamberlain was unclear about the retention of Irish MPs at Westminster, both politicians supported the establishment of a Parliament in Ireland to deal with purely Irish affairs. Whatever Chamberlain may have thought in private, his public stance at the Sheffield election of 1874 was emphatically 'in FAVOUR OF HOME RULE', one of his slogans being 'HOME RULE AND CHAMBERLAIN'.[21] The other Liberal candidate, A. J. Mundella, agreed, stating that 'he was an ardent supporter of Local Government and could see no reason why the Irish people should not have control of the internal affairs of Ireland . . . he would support by his vote the scheme propounded by Isaac Butt of Home Rule for Ireland',[22] a point which he again stressed the following evening (29 January) during a meeting which he and Chamberlain addressed together.

There is no reason to question the sincerity of their claims, especially in view of their repeated attempts to conciliate Butt's party in the late 1870s. However, their zeal in 1873–4 may have been partly inspired by their apprehension that in the forthcoming general election the Liberal party would be penalized by the Irish electors protesting against Gladstone's half-hearted 1870 Land Act.[23] At least as far as Irish constituencies were concerned, this preoccupation was well founded: in Ireland the Liberal party lost about sixty seats to the Home Rulers in February 1874. In England, Irish abstention may have been instrumental in securing Conservative victories in marginal constituencies. In Sheffield, Mundella won one of the seats, but Chamberlain was defeated in the other, perhaps

---

[20] Reps., 'Address by Mr Cowen', *NW*, 3 Jan. 1874, 3; and 'Representation of Newcastle – Mr Cowen's meetings', *NW*, 10 Jan. 1874, 2.

[21] Electoral leaflet addressed to the 'Irishmen of Sheffield', 1874, in Sheffield Archives, H. J. Wilson Letters and Papers, 5926.

[22] 'Our candidates on Ireland', electoral leaflet, 1874, in Sheffield Archives, H. J. Wilson Letters and Papers, 5927. In 1886 the Irish represented about 10 per cent of the electorate in Sheffield: J. Skinner to H. J. Wilson, 1 June 1886, in Wilson Papers, Sheffield University Library, 37P/21/8/i–ii.

[23] This was also the case with Chamberlain personally, to whom Charles Dilke wrote: 'I think that with Home Rule you could carry the Irish – & if you did you c[oul]d win the seat.' C. Dilke to J. Chamberlain, n.d. but from context likely to be 1874 rather than 1880, the date suggested by the Archivist (J. Chamberlain Papers, 5/24/12). In 1886 Chamberlain glossed his Home Ruler past as part of his support for the principle of 'Federation' (Chamberlain to Dilke, 3 May 1886, JC 5/24/485). For Chamberlain's conciliatory attitude in the late 1870s see Heyck, *Dimensions*, 39–40.

because of his hostility to Catholic and Anglican demands for denomina-tional education.[24] Partly because of the clash over education, after the election Mundella became more prudent about Home Rule.[25] In any case, it is significant that these Radicals adopted the cause at such an early stage and when it was not clear whether doing so would gain or lose them votes. In fact the anti-Catholic reaction among Protestant electors could outweigh the Liberal/Home Rule vote even in constituencies with large Irish communities such as Liverpool, as Lord Ramsay discovered to his cost in 1880.[26]

If electoral opportunism is not in itself an adequate explanation for this early spate of conversions to Home Rule, we should further explore the first of Chamberlain's 'powerful influences' – namely, the proposal's ideological consistency both with the principles of local government and decentralization and with the radicals' hostility towards heavy-handed bureaucracy, of which Dublin Castle was the most notorious example. As Hind has shown, considerations of this kind were crucial in shaping Henry Labouchere's support for Home Rule from the autumn of 1880.[27] As already noted, early English Home Rulers seem to have been influenced by Isaac Butt: in fact some of his early pamphlets were printed in Sheffield and copies have been preserved in the papers of H. J. Wilson, a leading Sheffield radical Nonconformist and himself an early convert to Home Rule. Butt's approach was pragmatic. He empha-sized the practical benefits of Home Rule as a system of government *within* the United Kingdom, to relieve pressure on Westminster and deliver more effective, better informed and more accountable government.[28] Crucial to the plausibility of his scheme was that it made provision for continued Irish representation in the imperial Parliament, so that there would be no question of 'taxation without representation' for Ireland (though Irish MPs would not be allowed to discuss or vote on questions pertaining solely to England, Scotland and Wales).

[24] R. Quinault, 'Joseph Chamberlain: a reassessment', in T. R. Gourvish and A. O'Day (eds.), *Later Victorian Britain, 1867–1900* (1988), 79–80.
[25] Mundella to Leader, 4 Aug. 1874, in Leader papers, Sheffield Univ. Library.
[26] See reports, 'The Liverpool election', *The Leeds Mercury*, 6 Feb. 1880, 8 and 7 Feb. 1880, 2; cf. J. P. Rossi, 'Home Rule and the Liverpool by-election of 1880', *Irish Historical Studies*, 19, 74 (1974), 156–68.
[27] R. J. Hind, *Henry Labouchere and the empire, 1880–1905* (1972), 59–60.
[28] *The Principles of Home Rule as explained by Isaac Butt, Esq., MP. Is it reasonable & what practical advantages are expected from it? By John G. MacCarthy, Esq.* (1873); see also *Rules of the Sheffield Branch of the Irish Home Government Association* (1873), both in H. J. Wilson Papers, Sheffield University Library. On H. J. Wilson see M. Anderson, *Henry Joseph Wilson: fighter for freedom* (1953), and W. S. Fowler, *A study in Radicalism and Dissent: the life and times of Henry Joseph Wilson, 1833–1914* (1961).

The Liberal defeat of 1874 and the Tory ascendancy thereafter delayed the issue from becoming one of practical politics for a few years. However, the Home Rule agitation continued to attract English advocates.[29] In 1875 'Gracchus' of *Reynolds's Newspaper*, attacked John Bright as a 'traitor' who had sold out to the Whigs, because he had 'dared' to denounce Home Rule as a 'mischievous dream'.[30] It was vintage *Reynolds's* hyperbole, but was in tune with the anti-imperialist line that the weekly paper had so consistently championed over the years. For 'Gracchus' Home Rule was about democracy and against 'autocracy' and was comparable to the Italian *Risorgimento* or the Bulgarian agitation. In 1879 'Ironside' (alias W. E. Adams, another ex-Chartist) wrote from Newcastle that there was little difference between the lot of the Irish under British rule and that of the Poles under the Russians, except that England – unlike Russia – was in the process of being democratized. He prophesied that soon illegitimate arrests of nationalist leaders and widespread social injustice would come to an end. However, the 'overburdened' Westminster Parliament could not effectively deal with Irish business, and Gladstone was already indicating that a measure of devolution would be advisable if not inevitable. Reading between the lines of Gladstone's Midlothian speeches, 'Ironside' concluded that these were '[i]mportant admissions in respect to what is called Home Rule'.[31] In the heady days of the second Midlothian campaign, the Irish Nationalist William Shaw suggested that justice to all classes was analogous to justice to all nations within the United Kingdom.[32] It sounded plausible and for a while even *Lloyd's Weekly* – which later became and remained consistently Unionist – advocated a measure of Home Rule under the motto 'Ireland for the Irish': it demanded 'the prompt satisfaction of just Irish claims for local government – such indeed as should be given to the various centres of the English people'.[33] Notably, 'home rule' was used in a rather vague sense and it is not clear how far any of its proponents would have been prepared to go and whether they envisaged the establishment of a whole Parliament in Dublin. Moreover, for these radicals Home Rule was not merely a proposal for solving specific Irish problems: it was also part of a broader humanitarian and emancipationist philosophy which they perceived as integral to Gladstonian liberalism.

[29] 'Ironside', 'The new Parliament', *Newcastle Weekly Chronicle*, 21 Feb. 1874, 4; l.a., 'The parliamentary week', *Lloyd's Weekly*, 5 July 1874, 6.
[30] Gracchus, *RN*, 14 Mar. 1875, 3.   [31] Ironside, 'Ireland', *NW*, 29 Nov. 1879, 4.
[32] W. Shaw, 'The general election', *FJ*, 19 Mar. 1880, 7.
[33] L.a., 'The Liberal programme', *LW*, 21 Mar. 1880, 1; and 'Ireland for the Irish', *LW*, 24 Oct. 1880, 1.

However, disillusionment followed in 1880–2, when the Gladstone government delivered not devolution, but more coercion in Ireland, Egypt and – for a while – South Africa. Moreover, Gladstone and Granville turned a blind eye to French imperialism in Madagascar, another issue which perturbed British anti-imperialists and humanitarians.[34] While the GOM managed to retain the allegiance of the party, frustration and dissatisfaction were voiced by some radicals. Chamberlain believed that, had John Bright started an agitation against the government (from which he resigned in protest), he would have caused its downfall.[35] In a pamphlet Frederick Harrison bluntly put their case in terms refreshingly free from 'orientalist' stereotypes:

Imagine your own feelings, if you had to send every year some forty millions sterling out of the taxes of the country to pay Turkish, or Arab or Chinese bond-holders; and then, having paid that regularly, that you had to keep a Turkish pasha and a Chinese mandarin in London to control your expenditure, so that every penny of the Budget had to get the sanction of their excellencies, and if Mr Gladstone or any other Chancellor of the Exchequer wished to put on or take off a tax, down would come a fleet of ironclads from the Bosphorus into the Thames, and train their 80-ton guns right in view of the Tower and Somerset House. That is the state of Egypt now.[36]

He reminded his readers that at the 1880 election the people had explicitly rejected Beaconsfieldism and its 'policy of aggression on weak countries, under the pretence of safeguarding British interests, a policy endeavoring [*sic*] to control the government of semi-barbarous States for our own advantage, and for the supposed protection of India'. He stressed that 'a war of aggression is wrong' even when 'covered by the justly-revered name of William Ewart Gladstone'.[37] Eventually, pressure for a stricter adherence to 'the principles of Midlothian' began to be felt, especially in regions such as urban Yorkshire and the north-east, where the trade unions were stronger and politically united. In April 1884 Mundella observed that 'Egypt is the rock ahead' and in June he feared that Gladstone might be brought down by Radical discontent over the whole affair.[38]

---

[34] K. von den Steinen, 'The harmless papers: Granville, Gladstone, and the censorship of the Madagascar Blue Books of 1884', *Victorian Studies*, 14 (1970), 165–76. For contemporary British anti-imperialism see Matikkala, 'Anti-imperialism, Englishness and empire'.

[35] Cited in A. J. P. Taylor, *The trouble makers: dissent over foreign policy, 1792–1939* (1957; 1985), 88.

[36] F. Harrison, *The crisis in Egypt*, Anti-Aggression League Pamphlet No. 2 (1882), 11.

[37] A. Besant, *Egypt* (1882), 1–2 (St Deiniol's pamphlet collection).

[38] Mundella to Leader, 17 Apr. and 21 June 1884, in Leader Papers.

Harrison presented the Egyptian crisis in 'class' terms – it was about peasants being oppressed by rentiers – at a time when radical opinion makers were describing the Irish agitation against the Coercion Act as the struggle of the 'toiling masses' against 'landlordism'. In both Egypt and Ireland political self-government was perceived as the key to social amelioration. For example, the original programme of the Democratic Federation – which targeted a working-class constituency – included 'National and Federal Parliaments' for the United Kingdom; indeed, according to Heyck, 'Ireland provided the adhesive to keep the Democratic Federation together.'[39] It may also have provided potential recruits: as a group of disenchanted Skye crofters pointed out to Chamberlain at the beginning of 1885, he was member of a government which was 'using the national forces to assist in extorting from labouring men the necessaries of life' by ruthlessly evicting Irish tenants unable to pay the rent.[40] It was hard for them to support such a man and his party. Aware of such unrest in Radical circles, Parnell himself tried to foster an Anglo-Irish Home Rule alliance in 1881, when he '[appealed] to the great masses of population of England and Scotland, who are much less represented in the House of Commons than the masses of Ireland'. He proposed '[a] junction between English democracy and Irish nationalism upon a basis of Ireland's right to make her own laws, the overthrow of territorialism in both countries and enfranchisement of labor [sic] from crushing taxes for maintenance of standing armies and navies'.[41] As Pelling has pointed out,[42] there is evidence to suggest that this situation generated tensions within popular radicalism and stimulated demands for the formation of an independent radical workers' party like those already existing in Italy, France and Germany. Indeed such alliance between the advocates of the working class and the champions of the national question was precisely part of the scenario which Karl Marx had envisaged when he thought about the conditions for the establishment of a successful independent socialist party in Britain.[43]

This hope that class solidarity would become a political force for justice remained one of the permanent features of British Radical support for

---

[39] Heyck, *Dimensions*, 66–7; Hamer, *Liberal politics*, 307; L. Barrow and I. Bullock, *Democratic ideas and the British labour movement, 1880–1914* (1996), 12.

[40] 'Resolution passed by the Skye Crofters at The Brae, Uig, and Glendale, at the meetings addressed by Mr Henry George', 3 Jan. 1885, printed resolutions in SLA, Meetings and Conference Agendas, NLS, Acc. 11765/35.

[41] Cited in M. Davitt, *The fall of feudalism in Ireland* (1904; 1970), 307–8.

[42] Pelling, *Origins of the Labour Party*, 15–21.

[43] Strauss, *Irish nationalism and British democracy* , 188.

Irish Nationalism, although some Lib-labs were characteristically uneasy about it and preferred to take a purely political view of the question. Thus in 1881 Tom Burt dismissed what he described as the 'narrow' class spirit behind Home Rule, arguing rather that it was about liberty and the constitution. He thought that the repeal of coercion required the establishment of legislative autonomy for Ireland and that the latter was compatible with the preservation of the Union.[44] Indeed, by then libertarian concerns had become more important than any 'class' alliance for both Burt and his Lib-lab colleague Henry Broadhurst. They remained consistent opponents of coercion – indeed, on occasion they were 'the only two radicals' to do so.[45]

If Britain and Ireland had become so completely alienated from each other that even a Liberal administration went so far as suspending constitutional liberty, then Ireland was entitled not only to Home Rule, but also to full independence. For British rule there had become merely a form of imperialism, '[that] sentiment that impels us to retain the possession of India in defiance of every moral law – it is that sentiment which forbids us even to entertain the claims of the sister island for independence',[46] as 'Ironside' put it in 1881. By then Home Rule was widely discussed in the north-east, as indicated by the proceedings of the Newcastle Debating Society. At the beginning of January 1882 the 'Irish Secretary' of the 'Government' in the society's mock parliament proposed 'to enquire into the relationship between England and Ireland and into the system of self-government now in practice in European and other countries'.[47] The member playing the 'Secretary of State for the Colonies' supported the proposal, arguing that '[there] are important matters of municipal management which are brought from Ireland to Westminster at great cost, and which, along with other matters of self-government, might, we think, be left to the Irish people'.[48] The debate continued over the following weeks with many 'MPs' supporting Home Rule and citing colonial examples of success and prosperity under that system of government.[49] The Newcastle area – with an Irish population of more than 50,000 – had become a Home Rule hotbed.[50] Not surprisingly

[44] L.a., 'County government', *NW*, 19 Nov. 1881, 4.
[45] G. O. Trevelyan to Lord Spencer, 16 Feb. 1883, in P. Gordon (ed.), *The Red Earl: the papers of the Fifth Earl Spencer, 1835–1910*, vol. I (1981), 241.
[46] Ironside, 'The two nations', *NW*, 22 Oct. 1881, 4.
[47] 'A Royal Commission on Home Rule', *Debater*, 9 Jan. 1882, 5, in Tyne and Wear Archives, 200/124.
[48] Ibid., 7.   [49] Ibid., 26 Jan. 1882, 5–7 and 2 Feb. 1882, 3–10.
[50] N. Todd, *The militant democracy: Joseph Cowen and Victorian radicalism* (1991), 128, 135, 141.

when the Home Rule Bill was discussed in the spring of 1886, the Newcastle Liberal Association voted in favour by a majority of 516 to 4 (the total membership was 600).[51]

It was one of the city's MPs, Joseph Cowen, who produced some of the clearest statements of the radical case for the establishment of a Parliament in Dublin. As early as 1880 he stressed the moral authority which should be recognized to the Home Rule MPs, arguing that the Irish Parliament had been suppressed in 1800 'by a combination of fraud and force' and the country ruled by Coercion Acts ever since. At the last election 'the Home Rule members returned for Irish constituencies [were] proportionately more numerous than the Liberals returned for English constituencies'. He concluded that 'if they [were] wise they [would] recognise it and deal with it'.[52] In 1881, in response to the Coercion Bill, he invited his fellow MPs to consider how they would feel if 'England had been conquered by France as Ireland had been by England', with a Parliament in Paris 'which contained some 550 Frenchmen and 100 Englishmen and that this Parliament of Frenchmen not only proposed to suspend the constitutional liberties of the English people but [also] the parliamentary liberties of the English representatives'.[53] Writing to a friend, Cowen observed:

Anything more inconsistent, or more suicidal, than the policy the liberal party [sic] have pursued on the Irish question it is impossible to conceive. If the liberals had been in opposition, instead of power, there would not have been two or three members, but two or three score, who would have done and said exactly what I have done and said in the House of Commons.[54]

Even so, the House sat continuously for more than forty hours to overcome Irish and radical opposition to the Bill – 'less the "ping-pong" recently experienced over Tony Blair's anti-terrorist legislation than Test Match cricket', as Tim Hames has commented.[55] In 1882, defending the Irish MPs against charges of 'moral responsibility' in acts of terrorism, Cowen reminded W. E. Forster that he had been an active supporter of English societies supporting the liberation of Italy from foreign occupation '[w]hen

---

[51] A. Keith Durham, Secretary of the Newcastle upon Tyne Liberal Association, to J. Cowen, 13 Apr. 1886, JC B374 (J. Cowen Papers).

[52] J. Cowen, House of Commons, 30 Aug. 1880, original TS in Cowen Papers, B207; HPD, CCLVI, 718–23.

[53] J. Cowen, House of Commons, 26 Jan. 1881, TS, in Cowen Papers, B211; HPD, CCLVII, 1477–8.

[54] Cowen to H. B. Thompson, from Newcastle, n.d. but winter 1881, in Cowen Papers, B415.

[55] T. Hames, review of R. Douglas, *Liberals*, in *Times Literary Supplement*, 8 Apr. 2005, 4. Cf. D. Thornley, 'The Irish Home Rule party and parliamentary obstruction, 1874–1887', *Irish Historical Studies*, 12, 45 (1960), 38–57.

the Austrians were occupying Lombardy and Venice, just like the English were now occupying the South of Ireland'. Yet, he had not been held responsible for the 'great many excesses' committed by the Italians in their struggle for independence, 'infinitely greater than any committed in Ireland'.[56]

He continued along these lines over the following years. In 1883, in a public speech he reminded Gladstone that, during the Midlothian campaign, he had condemned Tory coercion and declared that '[w]hen personal liberty is suspended we have arrived at a stage only short of civil war' – a reasoning which 'had not lost its cogency' only because repression was now implemented by the Liberals. If Gladstone's Crimes Act was necessary to prevent intimidation, it was remarkable that under its operation the Irish electors '[clung] all the closer to the alleged terrorists', whose parliamentary candidates were returned by large majorities 'in county and in borough, by farmers and by shopkeepers'. If the Nationalist MPs were in league with assassins, what about the people who elected them? 'When an entire people are against the law the law is wrong ... To convict the Irish representatives of being accessories to outrage is to convict the people of the same offence, and to convict the people is to condemn the Government.'[57] Parnell had then been recently rescued from bankruptcy by a popular subscription raised among the tenant farmers. Commenting on this episode, Cowen argued that such testimonial 'equals, or more than equals, that raised by the populous and wealthy England for Mr Cobden on the morrow of the great Free Trade victory'. It was 'the last, but not the least, striking proof of an intense and sustained national sentiment'. Such sentiment, Cowen argued, was 'plain enough to anyone but ourselves, but we cannot, or at least do not, see it. We would see it, however, clear enough and preach no end of homilies concerning it, if it occurred in a distant country and under foreign rule.'[58]

In Ireland there was a national revival demanding, but not receiving, recognition, and the resulting conflict deepened the political and cultural differences among the peoples of the British Isles: for, while British rule in Dublin was anti-national, Cowen was aware that the Irish themselves were divided between what he saw as the Protestant, 'mercantile', urbanized North-East and the Catholic, peasant and rural South and West. Blind to the complexity of the situation, the Gladstone government

---

[56] J. Cowen, House of Commons, 24 Feb. 1882, TS in B251 (Cowen Papers). This sentence is not included in HPD, CCLXVI, 1615, in which Cowen's speech was published.

[57] Cited in rep., 'Mr J. Cowen, MP, on Ireland', *FJ*, 24 Dec. 1883, 6.   [58] Ibid.

regarded the Irish problem in purely material terms: 'They conceive that all they want is money, and they throw a new Land Bill at them as they would throw a bone at a dog, and cry, "Take it and be content." The Irish do take it, and make the most of it, and are not content; and they won't be.' Cowen concluded that Home Rule was the only feasible way forward: 'Ireland is too big to be ruled for any length of time as we do the Mauritius or Fiji or Falkland Isles. If we tried remonstrances would come thick and fast from America and the colonies – remonstrances such as we sent to Turkey about Bulgaria, and to Russia about Poland.' By contrast, self-government would take the heat out of the question, and assimilate Ireland to other parts of the empire, including Canada, but also the Channel Islands and the Isle of Man. They worked well together, though each dealt in different ways with its specific, local or national problems. Paraphrasing one of John Bright's famous 1866 reform speeches, Cowen said: 'We have tried to rule Ireland by the army, by the Church, and by the landlords, and by the three combined. All these agencies have failed, and brought us only shame and humiliation. Let us now try to rule her by her own people.' He surmised that the empire would best be preserved 'by conceding to the divers nationalities within it liberty to work out their own national life in their own way. A genial diversity will give elasticity and strength, a procustian uniformity weakness.'[59]

The other MP for Newcastle, John Morley, was also an outspoken advocate of Home Rule. 'There is human nature even in Ireland,' he had claimed in an article in the *Nineteenth Century*. Self-government would provide 'institutions that shall give the manhood of Ireland' – those 'men of practical and independent character' which Englishmen regarded as 'the material of good citizenship' – 'a chance, and public spirit an outlet, and public opinion its fair measures of power and respectability'. This was what 'Home Rule' was really about.[60] Their ideas were given further prominence by Herbert Gladstone – the Premier's son – in a speech at Leeds on 12 February 1883. Significantly, he was one of the few Liberal candidates not to be opposed by the Nationalists in Britain in 1885, at the time of their pro-Tory campaign.[61]

---

[59] Ibid. Cf. Bright's Glasgow speech of 16 Oct. 1866: 'If a class has failed, let us try the nation' (cited in G. M. Trevelyan, *The life of John Bright*, (1925), 368). The notion that the divide in Ireland was between 'mercantile' and peasant interests was to become a recurrent theme in the post-1886 debate: 'Belfast Merchant' [R. Patterson], *Mercantile Ireland versus Home Rule* (Belfast, Liberal Unionist Association, 1888, in the Library of Queen's University Belfast).

[60] J. Morley, 'Irish revolution and English Liberals', *The Nineteenth Century*, Nov. 1882, reprinted in 'Mr John Morley on Ireland', *FJ*, 30 Oct. 1882, 6.

[61] MacKnight, *Ulster as it is*, vol.II (1896), 110.

It was in this context that Morley's close associate, Joseph Chamberlain, started to develop a Radical alternative to the government's policies, in the shape of a 'National Council Plan', which most observers perceived as very similar to actual Home Rule.[62] He firmly opposed any suggestion that Westminster's sovereignty could in any way be compromised. But this was not an issue for most British supporters of Home Rule because, as one Liberal candidate confessed, 'he [was] unable to see any difference between Elective County Boards in England and Home Rule in Ireland'.[63]

However, this was an area where deliberate equivocation blurred actual disagreement for, as Labouchere had pointed out as early as February 1882, 'Home Rule [could] be understood in any one of 100 senses, some of them perfectly acceptable and even desirable, others of them mischievous and revolutionary.'[64] While Harrison and other radicals insisted that Ireland was a distinct 'nation' and Home Rule was supposed to be a recognition of this fact,[65] many of the English Home Rulers were thinking only in terms of 'local government and no coercion'.[66] The latter's continuous application generated such revulsion in Britain that in October 1882 the main Nationalist paper, reviewing the policy recommendations voiced in the *Daily News* and *Birmingham Post*, declared that 'the chief difference between the Irish League and English Liberals [was] a point of detail'.[67] The confusion about the meaning and implications of Home Rule in contrast to local government may be a further aspect of the same radical 'anti-Parliament' culture already mentioned in chapter 1 (p. 22). For the parliamentary class – or at least for some of them – Home Rule and local government were clearly distinct and had different constitutional implications. By contrast, suspicion of both Parliament and the central government was a basic feature of English popular radicalism and Nonconformity and had various implications. In the economic sphere it sustained a preference for self-help and

---

[62] See below, chapter 5, pp. 233–4.
[63] Bowen Green, cited in 'The new political programme', *Pontypridd Chronicle*, 28 Aug. 1885, 5.
[64] Cited in Hind, *Labouchere*, 62.
[65] Rep., 'Mr Frederic Harrison and Home Rule' (at a 'crowded meeting' of the London Positivist Society), *FJ*, 31 May 1886, 5.
[66] J.L. Garvin, The life of Joseph *Chamberlain*, vol. I: 1836–1885 (1932), 612. As one radical elector wrote to Joseph Cowen during the Home Rule crisis, 'As an ardent Home Ruler in the sense of giving every province of the British Isles power to manage their own affairs with the utmost freedom (consistent with the ultimate supremacy of the Imperial Parliament) I regret to be unable to support Mr Gladstone's proposals.' ('A Native of Newcastle' to J. Cowen, 1 June 1886, in Cowen Papers, B376.)
[67] L.a., *FJ*, 19 Oct. 1882, 4.

free trade; in religious matters it inspired support for disestablishment and the separation of church and state; and in constitutional affairs, demanded that powers be devolved to locally elected assemblies. Furthermore, if (as some radicals insisted) sovereignty rested ultimately with 'the people', rather than Parliament, devolution was more than administrative decentralization – it was actually a claiming back of powers and rights which belonged to the people in the first place. Hence to many the difference between 'Home Rule' and 'self-government' was less important than we might have expected.

Yet, in the run up to the election of 1885, apart from in Newcastle and some other constituencies with a strong Irish presence, Home Rule was not a prominent issue with British Radicals. For example, William Abraham (Mabon) – who would soon become a Home Ruler – was mainly concerned about the various questions raised by Chamberlain's 'Unauthorised Programme', particularly disestablishment, allotments and homesteads for labourers.[68] George Howell, who stood for Bethnal Green, was implicitly against Home Rule in 1885, but adopted it in 1886.[69] The electoral programme of Joseph Arch – allegedly an old supporter of Irish self-government – demanded '[e]qual laws for all parts of the United Kingdom', which was quite the opposite of Home Rule.[70]

Another veteran Lib-lab, George Potter, who published a series of 'Leaflets for the new electors' in 1885, emphasized traditional Liberal ideas about religious equality, finance, taxation and electoral reform. Moreover, he recommended 'a sweeping and drastic reform of the land laws, so conceived as to secure the restoration to the community of the natural right to the common heritage of mankind, i.e., a right to share in the soil of their native land'.[71] In practice he recommended the extension of the Irish system of the 'three Fs' (Fixed tenure, Fair rents, Free sale) and the abolition of primogeniture and entail, which restricted the sale of land

[68] See rep., 'The Rhondda miners and the representation question – Great conference at Ton', *Pontypridd Chronicle*, 28 Jan. 1885, 5 and 'Mabon at Llynpia', ibid., 16 Oct. 1885, 5. See also 'The ideas of the new voters', *Fortnightly Review*, 37, 218, NS, 1 Feb. 1885, 148–67, contributions by H. Broadhurst, 'A Trade Union Official' and A. Simmons; and M. K. Ashby, *Joseph Ashby of Tysoe* (1974), 117.

[69] G. Howell, 'To the electors of the North-East Division of Bethnal Green', addresses for 1885 and 1886, both in the Howell Collection, microfilm edition, I/5, P6.

[70] Cited in Horn, *Joseph Arch*, 235. In June 1886 his programme explained that the adoption of Home Rule was due to 'the decisive voice of the Irish electors' who 'compelled the Liberal Party, as the truly Constitutional Party, to give their claims due consideration', the cause of Home Rule being 'the cause of justice and freedom' (ibid., 237).

[71] See, from G. Potter's 'Leaflets for the new electors', the following: 'Liberal v. Tory finance', 'The political situation' and 'The wants and claims of radicalism', in Nuffield Collection of Electoral Posters, Nuffield College, Oxford.

and helped to preserve the power and status of the large landowners. Even other radical candidates, who were already known supporters of Home Rule, did not raise the issue at the election. E. S. Beesly – who, as we have seen, had long been an advocate of Home Rule – stood for Westminster as a Radical candidate, but neither he nor Harrison, who supported his candidature, mentioned Irish self-government in his handbills. Instead they focused on the reform of parliamentary procedure, the relations between state and church, and international relations.[72] Beesly mentioned municipal government for London and allotments for farmworkers, and when he advised his electors 'not [to] be frightened by windy talk about danger to the Constitution', he meant the disestablishment of the church (which was actually advocated in other radical propaganda) rather than Home Rule.[73] In general, electoral propaganda addressed to working men emphasized traditional Liberal concerns, such as the benefits of free trade (in response to Tory calls for 'fair' trade), reform of the land laws, free elementary education, 'peace abroad', the national debt and municipal government for London.[74]

On the other hand, those radicals who *did* mention Irish self-government did not seem to regard it as more controversial than other radical causes, such as church disestablishment.[75] Thus Helen Taylor – J. S. Mill's stepdaughter, who took the extraordinary step of campaigning as a parliamentary candidate in North Camberwell – advocated legislative independence for Ireland as well as universal suffrage, free education, a graduated income tax and popular control over foreign policy and especially the right to declare war. She was enthusiastically supported by Anna Parnell and Michael Davitt, who praised her as 'the only English person . . . who looked on the Irish Question entirely from an Irish point of view'.[76]

[72] 'Professor E. S. Beesly' by Mr Frederic Harrison, and 'Westminster Town Hall Meeting', 6 Nov. 1885, handbills in John Johnson Collection, Bodleian Library, Oxford, 'Creeds, Parties, Policies'.

[73] E. S. Beesly, poster 'Electors of Westminster', 25 Nov. 1885; cf. 'The Disestablishment and disendowment of the Church of England essentially a working man's question', both handbills in Nuffield Collection of Electoral Posters, Nuffield College, Oxford.

[74] See, for example, 'Fair trade in America. Letter from a working man', handbill based on the report of a meeting of working men, Birmingham 14 Nov. 1885, published by the NLF, in Nuffield Collection of Electoral posters, Nuffield College, Oxford; F. A. Binney, *Why working men should be Liberals* n.d. [1885] pamphlet in J. Johnson Collection, Bodleian Library, 'Creeds, Parties, Policies', box 17.

[75] See E. H. Pickersgill to the 'Borough of Bethnal Green', handbill dated Oct. 1885, in ibid.

[76] *Ti*, 19 Nov. 1885, 7; handbills dated Dublin, 5 Nov. (Anna Parnell) and 12 Nov. 1885 (M. Davitt), in John Johnson Collection, Bodleian Library, Oxford, 'Ireland'. In the end Taylor was not able to stand because her nomination and deposit were rejected by the returning officer (P. Levine, 'Taylor, Helen (1831–1907)', *ODNB*, vol. LIII, 897–9).

However, neither of them mentioned Home Rule as an electoral issue, nor did Josephine Butler or the land reformer Henry George, who recommended Helen Taylor as the champion of 'the great idea of Justice'.[77]

It is not totally clear why they did not give more prominence to the cause, although quite naturally they were primarily concerned to secure Taylor's right to stand for Parliament, and with this purpose in mind focused on her broader radical credentials rather than a specific issue such as Irish Home Rule. On the other hand, at this point in time some radicals were under the impression that Home Rule, when it finally entered the realm of practical politics, would not be particularly controversial. After all, even a self-styled 'Progressive Conservative' like Colonel Hamilton in Southwark was prepared to support 'as large a measure of Local Self Government as is consistent with the Imperial interests of the United Kingdom'. This statement was like a feeble echo of the earnest advocacy of similar principles by his opponent, the radical R. Pankhurst.[78] The latter saw Home Rule as a question of local liberty – 'the oldest . . . the most solid, of our freedoms'. Together with '[t]he extension of *local self-government to London and the country*', it was 'a supreme duty, not merely for administrative efficiency and public economy, but for high moral and social ends'. Like 'local option' (empowering municipalities to prohibit the sale of alcohol), Home Rule would give 'to Ireland the opportunity of being governed with just regard to Irish ideas'. His peroration culminated with the motto '*local self-government on federal lines*'.[79] It was a good illustration not only of the fact that Home Rule remained a vague and malleable concept, but also of the exalted opinion that Victorian radicals had of local self-government.

[77] Handbills dated 20 Aug. (Butler), and New York, 25 Sep. 1885 (George), in John Johnson collection. For Butler's attitude to Home Rule see Jordan, *Josephine Butler*, 17–8, 277, and B. Caine, *Victorian feminists* (1993), 154.

[78] C. E. Hamilton, 'To the electors of Rotherhithe', Oct. 1885, and R. Pankhurst, 'To the electors of the Rotherhithe Division of the Borough of Southwark', 7 Oct. 1885, both in John Johnson collection. However, Hamilton made it clear that he would resist any proposal for a separate Parliament in Dublin. For this election see M. Pugh, *The Pankhursts* (2001), 40–2.

[79] Pankhurst, 'To the electors of the Rotherhithe Division' (emphasis in the original). Before 1885 this would have been enough to establish a strong claim to the Irish Nationalist vote – and to alienate moderate Liberals: in his previous attempt to enter Parliament, in Manchester, Pankhurst 'appears to have enjoyed the backing of . . . Parnell and Michael Davitt' (Pugh, *Pankhursts*, 28). In the end, Pankhurst's hostility to Catholic education and Parnell's nationwide appeal to the Irish electors to vote Tory were enough to secure the seat for Hamilton.

The politics of emotionalism

There is therefore evidence to argue that the 'Hawarden kite' (17 December 1885) did not *create* popular support for Irish self-government, but rather unexpectedly elevated the issue to the top of the Liberal party's agenda. As already indicated above, at the time it was not even clear that Home Rule would be more controversial than other radical causes. *Reynolds's*, for example, took it for granted that it would go ahead as a bipartisan proposal,[80] but urged its readers to 'rally around Mr Gladstone who is always ahead of his party'. In view of the fact that for months it had harassed Gladstone over the shortcomings of his land reform policy and the wanton bloodshed in the Sudan, this was a remarkable and indicative shift. Pointing out that the Irish 'voted for self-government in the proportion of eight to one so far as the electorate is concerned', it insisted that '[t]he solemn vote of a people, constitutionally taken, is not to be explained away like agrarian outrage or boycotting'.[81] Typically, it argued that the democratic awakening of the Irish was a good thing for the British Empire because 'the will of the people is the only legitimate source of power'. Home Rule would strengthen the real bonds holding it together, as it had 'for the Dominions, and for Australasia', countries which *Reynolds's* regarded as providing the blueprint for Irish liberty.[82]

On the day Gladstone was asked to form his third government the veteran Chartist journalist Lloyd Jones tackled Home Rule, which he now identified as the most urgent issue before the country. That the Act of Union was a sacred 'fundamental law' he dismissed as mere 'superstition'. To him

> Home Rule [was] as legitimate a subject for legislative action as Local Option or Sunday Closing ... The authority of Parliament is not self-derived; it exists and acts only by the will of the nation, as that may be more or less legitimately expressed; and should the nation to-morrow [*sic*] recognise the necessity of setting up a Parliament in each of the British islands, as well as in Ireland and Scotland, there is no constitutional authority by which such determination could be controlled.[83]

It also meant that, though Ireland was 'a nation', it was not more distinctive than any of the other three nations comprising the Kingdom.

[80] 'The prospects of political parties', *RN*, 3 Jan. 1886, 1.
[81] L.a., 'The legislative Union', *RN*, 10 Jan. 1886, 1.
[82] L.a., 'The dead-lock in Ireland', *RN*, 24 Jan. 1886, 1.
[83] Lloyd Jones, 'The Queen's Speech and Ireland', *NW*, 30 Jan. 1886, 4. Cf. l.a., 'The new government', *RN*, 7 Feb. 1886, 1: 'A political expedient eighty-five years old could only be called "a fundamental law" by a perversion of language'; see also l.a., 'The Church in Wales', *RN*, 14 Mar. 1886, 1.

Moreover, Lloyd Jones insisted that Ireland was not *two* nations, denying that Ulster had any special rights. This is quite interesting in view of Gladstone's similar inability to appreciate the strength of Unionism in the North-East. According to Lloyd Jones the latter was to be dismissed as a conspiracy and its English advocates as seditious: 'The policy of Lord Randolph is very simple, because it is a policy of rebellion of the North against the South. The Irish people are wrong in going to rebellion to obtain a parliament, but according to Lord Randoph Churchill a portion of the Irish people will be justified in rebellion because they have got a parliament.'[84]

By the same token and with few exceptions,[85] most radicals and Lib-labs did not appreciate the importance of Gladstone's proposal of land purchase as part of a policy of national reconciliation. On the contrary, they regarded it as an attempt to make the tax-payer bail out Irish 'land-robbers'.[86] In this respect it is interesting to follow the reactions of *Reynolds's* to the various stages of the crisis. The editors denounced the Land Bill and compared it to the 1833–8 compensation to slave owners for the emancipation of their bondservants, an outrageous ransom for a class of 'obnoxious rentiers'.[87] Gladstone was no longer the hero he had been in January, but a villain plotting to establish 'caucus dictator-ship' in Britain, a man as dangerous as Charles I had been in the seventeenth century. Gladstone's credibility was further undermined by Chamberlain's resignation from the government: if 'the rising hope of the Democratic party'[88] felt bound to leave the government there must be something sinister going on behind the scenes. However, all such doubts were dispelled once the Home Rule Bill was actually published and widely circulated both in the press and as a penny pamphlet.[89] Now Gladstone was (once again) 'the old man eloquent' who 'at seventy-seven

[84] L.a., 'The Irish parliament and Ulster', *RN*, 28 Feb. 1886, 1.

[85] E.g. the Durham miners' leader W. Crawford, who was also prepared to support the Land Purchase Bill, though the latter 'may need modification in committee': letter read at a meeting at the Colliery Institute, Brandeis Colliery, in rep., *The Durham Chronicle*, 7 May 1886, 8.

[86] G.O. Trevelyan to A.J. Mundella, 30 Sep. 1882, in Mundella Papers, Sheffield University Library, GP/15/241/i–ii/iii. Cf. the editorials in *WT*, 2 May 1886, 8–9; 'Irish land purchase', *RN*, 25 Nov. 1888, 1, and 'Buy or go: the new Tory policy', *RN*, 2 Dec. 1888, 1. On the wider debate within the party see G. D. Goodlad, 'The Liberal party and Gladstone's Land Purchase Bill of 1886', *Historical Journal*, 32, 3 (1989), 627–41.

[87] L.a., 'Breakers ahead', *RN*, 21 Mar. 1886, 1.

[88] L.a., 'The situation', *RN*, 4 Apr. 1886, 1.

[89] W. E. Gladstone, *The Government of Ireland Bill* (1886), Gladstone Library, Bristol Univ. Library 9579. GLA. By contrast, his pamphlet on *The Irish Land Bill* (1881) had been published at the comparatively high price of sixpence (ibid., DA 957.9).

set an example of lion-like courage to us all'.[90] He made 'the cause of the British and Irish Democracy his own, and challenge[d] the oligarchy to mortal combat'.[91]

Yet, even at this stage Chamberlain continued to attract radical sympathy on account of the flaws in the Bill, which proposed the withdrawal of Irish MPs from Westminster. This was unacceptable to radicals because it would have exposed Ireland to taxation without representation, and, as the Lib-lab MP Thomas Burt reminded his constituents, 'taxation without representation is tyranny'.[92] In order to defend the Home Rule *principle*, rather than the Bill itself, Burt downplayed the details of Gladstone's proposal. He said that he 'trusted' that the GOM would find a solution to the problem of imperial representation as he had already promised 'to call back the Irish members whenever there [was] to be any alteration in the taxation relating to Ireland, and also to adopt some means of giving them a voice in the discussion of Imperial affairs'. On the other hand, Burt criticized Chamberlain's 'preposterous' counter-proposal that Irish representation at Westminster should remain unchanged. Thus, while the Bill as it stood was 'unacceptable', it did provide the necessary starting point for a wider discussion about the future of both the Union and the empire as a whole. The latter could be turned into 'a confederated Empire with delegates from the Colonies to form an Imperial assembly in place of the House of Lords'.[93]

Imperial federationism helped to sideline the question of Irish representation at Westminster: Home Rule became a matter of principle and a vision for the future of the whole United Kingdom.[94] As Dilke wrote to Chamberlain on 7 April,

I believe from what I see of my caucus, and from the two large *public* meetings we have had for discussion, that the great mass of the party will go for Repeal [of the Union], though fiercely against the land [Bill]. Enough will go the other way to risk all the seats, but the party will go for Repeal, and sooner or later now Repeal will come, whether or not we have a dreary period of coercion first.[95]

When it became clear that the Premier was prepared to drop the Land Bill, the emotional tension surrounding Home Rule spiralled out of

---

[90] L.a., 'The Home Rule scheme', *RN*, 18 Apr. 1886, 1.
[91] L.a., 'Mr Gladstone's manifesto', *RN*, 9 May 1886, 1.
[92] Rep., *The Northern Echo*, 31 May 1886, 4, speech by T. Burt, MP.
[93] W. J. Rowlands to T. E. Ellis, 28 July 1888, in T. E. Ellis MSS, 1903; see also E. Richardson, 'The Federation of the British Empire', *Primitive Methodist Quarterly Review*, Oct. 1886, 672–83.
[94] See l.a., 'Federation', *RN*, 30 May 1886, 1.
[95] Cited in Jenkins, *Dilke*, 254. For similar reports about rank-and-file enthusiasm for Home Rule in 1886 see P. Lynch, *The Liberal party in rural England, 1885–1910* (2003), 48–50, 120.

control. While many Radicals and caucus members started to denounce the Birmingham leader as a 'Judas',[96] *Reynolds's* persisted in treating him with respect,[97] hoping that a reconciliation between the people's champions – the GOM and the 'Rising Hope of Democracy' – would still be possible. Indeed its editors decried the personal and emotional nature of the debate, which, besides causing unnecessary offence, pre-empted any rational discussion of Home Rule.[98]

There is evidence to suggest that it was not so much Chamberlain's 'betrayal' that incensed popular radicals, as his readiness to play the 'Orange card'. Thus in a scathing attack on his Ulster policy, Burt said that he was 'sorry that in connection with this question there should have been any attempt, direct or indirect, to foment religious bigotry ... I still more regret that any man who calls himself a Radical should have uttered a single word tending to increase religious animosity.' Pointing out that in Parliament there were five Protestant Nationalists who represented Irish Catholic constituencies, he concluded:

I have no special sympathy with the Roman Catholic hierarchy; but I will say this, because truth demands it, that the Irish people in the South of Ireland have shown less narrow-mindedness and bigotry than those in the Northern parts of Ireland, and I will add, much less than we in England, and Scotland, and Wales ... I would ask you to look at the fact that all the great popular leaders of the Irish party, from Grattan to Parnell ... with the exception of Daniel O'Connell, have been Protestants.[99]

Another miner 'ridiculed the fears of reprisals on the part of the Catholics towards their Protestant neighbours' and argued that the Irish question was social, not religious: '[t]he condition of Ireland in some parts was deplorable. The pigsties in this country were often superior to the dwellings of the Irish peasantry, and under Home Rule there would be some hope of improvement.'[100]

There was no question: the activists were on the war path. What remained unclear was the extent to which the intensity of the feelings they expressed affected the mass of the electors. Henry Labouchere thought that 'the masses care very little about Ireland ... [and] would be glad to have the question settled ... But justice to Ireland does not arouse their enthusiasm, unless it be wrapped up in what they regard as justice to

[96] Goodlad, 'Gladstone and his rivals', 163–83; Lynch, *Liberal party*, 122.
[97] L.a., 'Nearing the end', *RN*, 6 June 1886, 1.
[98] L.a., 'Solution or dissolution?', *RN*, 25 Apr. 1886, 1.
[99] Rep., *The Northern Echo*, 31 May 1886, 4, speech by T. Burt, MP.
[100] Rep., 'Sir Henry Havelock-Allan and his Constituents', *The Northern Echo*, 31 May 1886, 4, speech by trade union delegate Logan.

themselves.'[101] Linking Home Rule to justice for the English workers soon became one of the strategies adopted by Liberal spin doctors. As we have seen, Parnell had been the first to play the card as early as 1881, and later Michael Davitt refined this rhetorical device. Now Lib-lab leaders and Home Rule agitators appealed to the solidarity which British workers should feel with reportedly persecuted fellow-labourers in Ireland and claimed that Home Rule would improve their lot so much that they would no longer feel the need to emigrate – thus easing the pressure on the British labour market.[102] In any case, what A. J. Reid has defined as the central feature of the labour political tradition – namely, 'considerations of humanity and social justice' – came to dominate the Gladstonian gospel which was being preached to the poor.[103] Home Rule was a policy 'of justice, humanity and expediency'. It would 'restore law and order' and fulfil '[t]he principles of religious and civil liberty; of political morality and sound policy'.[104] Speaking at a meeting in Tysoe, South Warwickshire, Joseph Ashby highlighted the similarities between the plight of the Irish and that of English farm workers, including 'land hunger', resentment against squirearchy and the people's aspiration 'to manage their own affairs'. Home Rule was about '[letting] the Irish improve their own country, take their own problems in hand'. Who wanted to stop it? The same class that opposed land reform in the village of Tysoe.[105]

As Patricia Lynch has written, 'in the months preceding the 1886 election, it seemed as if the Liberal party might be able to survive the Home Rule crisis with its rural support intact'. Party officials observed considerable enthusiasm for the measure among the newly enfranchised electors: it was only in July that it emerged that such fervour was limited to 'a core of active Liberal supporters', with 'rural voters in general [being] sceptical of the idea'.[106] Whether the farm workers were sceptical or

---

[101] H. Labouchere to H. Gladstone, 9 July 1886, cited in M. Hurst, *Joseph Chamberlain and Liberal reunion: the round table conference of 1887* (1967), 378.

[102] Rep., 'Mr Davitt on Home Rule', a meeting in the Town Hall, Barrow-in-Furness, *FJ*, 31 May 1886, 5. The meeting demanded that the sitting MP for the borough vote for the second reading of the Home Rule Bill; Mr Woolanan cited in report, 'Mr Dillon in Cardiff', *Cardiff Times and South Wales Weekly News*, 10 July 1886, 2. Cf. J. Graham Jones, 'Michael Davitt, David Lloyd George and T. E. Ellis: the Welsh experience, 1886', *Welsh History Review*, 18 (1996–7), 450–82.

[103] A. J. Reid, 'Old Unionism reconsidered', in Biagini and Reid (eds.), *Currents of Radicalism*, 223. For a specific example see W. Crawford, letter read at a meeting at the Colliery Institute, Brandeis Colliery, in rep., *The Durham Chronicle*, 7 May 1886, 8.

[104] G. Howell, 'To the electors of the North-East division of Bethnal Green', 21 June 1886, in Howell Collection, microfilm edition, I/5, P6.

[105] M. K. Ashby, *Joseph Ashby of Tysoe, 1859–1899* (1974), 120–1. Cf. Lynch, *Liberal party*, 120.

[106] Lynch, *Liberal party*.

merely confused and intimidated, Ashby and his friends were unable
to mobilize them. By contrast, the efforts of the miners' leaders in
the north-east of England and in Wales were largely successful. They
relied on the discipline and loyalty of the largely unionized and predominantly Nonconformist pitmen. In Northumberland this was aided by pre-
existing feelings 'thoroughly and heartily in favour of the principle of
Home Rule', as Tom Burt put it.[107] On the other hand, in Yorkshire
observers commented that 'the boundless enthusiasm . . . everywhere . . .
displayed' for Home Rule constituted a new departure:

Had anyone a few months ago prophesied that now the English democracy would
be as enthusiastic in the cause of Home Rule for Ireland as the most devoted
Nationalists themselves, he would . . . have been scouted as a lunatic. But it is the
case. The masses are everywhere aroused . . . The popular success now means
much more than even the grant of justice to Ireland: it means nothing less than the
complete vindication of the popular cause, the splendid triumph of the popular
forces, the final victory of the popular power over that of opposing class [sic].[108]

Liberty was principally about self-government and the Durham miners
themselves were 'like Home Rule': '[they] like to manage their own
business and don't always submit to the powers that be'.[109] By contrast,
'[h]olding Ireland means the adoption of the principle that it is the business of the State to organise industry and apportion wealth'.[110] Thus,
Home Rule was interpreted as a general principle: it was like being 'let
alone' or being 'no longer governed by an oligarchy', but by 'men of their
own choice – by a Fenwick, a Wilson and a Crawford'.[111] Why should not
Irish tenants be similarly allowed to choose leaders from their own ranks?
Of course, the parallel was less than accurate (Durham county was not
demanding Home Rule, and the Lib-labs were content to sit at
Westminster), but it was one way of saying that 'the Democracy' should
not fear to endorse the claims of 'fellow toilers' in Ireland.

If in north-east England Home Rule was the miners' orthodoxy,
among pitmen north of the border it became an indispensable
weapon in the rhetorical arsenal of aspiring labour leaders. In 1888 in

---

[107] T. Burt cited in *The Northern Echo*, 31 May 1886, 4.
[108] L.a., 'The classes against the masses', *The North-Eastern Daily Gazette*, 29 June 1886.
    For evidence of popular enthusiasm for Home Rule in Yorkshire and Durham see the
    reports in *The North-Eastern Daily Gazette*, 1 July 1886 re. Stockton, York, the
    Hartlepools and Normanton (Benjamin Pickard's division).
[109] Newscutting, n.d. [1890 or 1891], 'Lecture by Mr John Wilson, MP for Mid-Durham',
    in John Wilson Papers.
[110] E. S. Beesly, *Socialists against the grain: or, the price of holding Ireland* (1887), 3, 6.
[111] C. Johnson in rep., 'Sir Henry Havelock-Allan and his Constituents', *The Northern Echo*,
    31 May 1886, 4. See also K. D. Brown, *John Burns* (1977), 75; Ashby, *Ashby of Tysoe*,
    119–21.

Mid-Lanark James Keir Hardie's political ambitions depended from the start on the creation of an improbable alliance centred on the Home Rule issue: '[the] Mining and Irish vote in Mid-Lanark [is] not less than 3500. If these, especially the Irish, can be secured, the seat is ours . . . I have the Irish leaders in Glasgow on my side, and will see Davitt on Monday evening. Some local miners [*sic*] agents, socialists too mark you, are in opposition.'[112] To the chairman of the local Liberal Association Hardie commended himself as 'a Radical of a somewhat advanced type', who 'from the first [had] supported Mr Gladstones [*sic*] Home Rule proposals'.[113] He was not selected and, refusing the NLF offer of an alternative constituency at the next general election, decided to contest Mid-Lanark as an independent radical and working-class candidate. Fearing the consequences of a split in the pro-Home Rule vote, the Irish refused to support him and endorsed instead the official Liberal candidate. Inevitably, Hardie was defeated.[114]

In Wales, the miners' and quarrymen's 'peasant' frame of mind was reportedly one of the reasons why they sympathized with the Irish.[115] The local trade union leaders' pro-Home Rule rhetoric combined 'class' and 'ethnic' arguments. At a meeting at Tonypandy one speaker urged: 'So now, boys, let us help Ireland to assert her rights. Ireland will help us when we need it. Let us join the Grand Old Man's army to fight for freedom for our Celtic race.'[116] Michael Davitt, who also addressed the meeting, promptly confirmed that the struggle was about class, and recommended a 'single tax' on mining royalties. He deplored Chamberlain's readiness to excite sectarian fears, but, rather inconsistently, let fly with an anti-Semitic tirade against Goschen, the Jew who 'represented that class of bond-holders, and usurers, and mostly money-lenders for whom that infamous Egyptian war was waged'. He did his best to reassure his hearers about Irish loyalty to the empire and the 'finality' of Home Rule, although someone in the audience did seem to be quite ready to contemplate that Ireland might in future become fully independent.[117]

---

[112] J. Keir Hardie to H. H. Champion, 15 Mar. 1888, National Library of Scotland, J. Keir Hardie Dep. 176, vol. 8, Letter Book, 104–5. For the general picture see I. G. C. Hutchison, *A political history of Scotland, 1832–1924* (1986), 181, 263 and T. C. Smout, *A century of the Scottish people, 1830–1950* (1986).

[113] James [Keir] Hardie to Bailie Burt Esq., 15 Mar. 1888, in NLS, J. Keir Hardie Dep. 176, vol. 8, Letter Book, 107.

[114] Morgan, *Keir Hardie*, 28–31.

[115] T. E. Ellis to A. Gyfaill, 1 July 1886, in Ellis Papers, 4733 and notes on the similarities between Ireland and Wales, n.d., ibid., 4647.

[116] Rep., 'The Rhondda electors and the Home Rule question: enormous mass meeting at Tonypandy', *Pontypridd Chronicle*, 7 May 1886, 8.

[117] Ibid.

At another meeting Mabon called the Liberals 'who had gone astray' to repentance, stressing that 'the 12 direct labour representatives now in Parliament voted altogether in one block for the scheme put forward [by] Mr Gladstone', and insisted that their vote 'was a true exposition of the feeling of the working men throughout the country'.[118] One speaker surmised that those who opposed Home Rule 'were mostly half-baked [sic] – religious fanatics, bigots, who had been preaching freedom for the protestants [sic] all their lifetime, but the moment that they saw the Catholics of Ireland were going to have a little freedom they came down with their foot on it and said, "We can't trust them."'[119] The miners' leader William Abraham ('Mabon') concluded that '[o]ur duty as working men is clear. The present to us is a golden opportunity – to say whether Ireland in future shall be governed by force or by constitutional means – by a policy of peace, or by that of coercion.'[120] He was returned unopposed for what was then described as the 'Rhondda Labour and Liberal seat', his grip on the constituency being such that his electoral expenses amounted to only sevenpence.[121]

Welsh support for Irish Home Rule and anger at Chamberlain's 'betrayal' of Gladstone was confirmed during the summer when Parnell, Dillon and, later, Chamberlain visited Cardiff. On 28 June Parnell brought large cheering crowds – including many women – on to the streets and eventually to a meeting in Park Hall, but those who sought admission were so numerous that a second, overflow open-air meeting was hastily arranged. On 5 July there was another 'great mass meeting' and scenes of '[t]he greatest enthusiasm' to welcome the Nationalist John Dillon to Cardiff. By contrast, when the leading Radical Unionist visited the city a day later, a reporter commented that it was 'a strange sight to see Mr Chamberlain, the man whom but a few months ago the working classes in England almost idolized, making his way through the streets of Cardiff protected only by the presence of the police from undoubted violence at the hands of a number of those same working men'.[122]

---

[118] Rep., 'The rent agitation in the Rhondda: mass meeting at Porth', *Pontypridd Chronicle*, 25 June 1886, 8.

[119] Ibid. For further examples see the report 'South Wales contests . . . important meeting at the docks', *Cardiff Times & South Wales Weekly News*, 2 July 1886, 8 and the speech (in Welsh) by J. Millward, in 'The Irish Home Rule question: open air meeting at Taff's Well', *Pontypridd Chronicle*, 16 July 1886, 5.

[120] W. Abraham, 'Mabon's manifesto: appeal to working-men voters', *Cardiff Times and South Wales Weekly News*, 10 July 1886, 2.

[121] Rep., 'Mabon's election expenses', *Cardiff Times & South Wales Weekly News*, 31 July 1886, 3.

[122] See the three reports: 'Mr Parnell in Cardiff', *Cardiff Times & South Wales Weekly News*, 3 July 1886, 6; 'Mr Dillon in Cardiff' and 'Mr Chamberlain in Cardiff', ibid., 10 July 1886, 2.

The Dissenters

Besides the miners, the other 'standing army' in the Gladstonian camp comprised the Nonconformists. As Bebbington and Goodlad have written, although Home Rule alienated a number of the more fervently Evangelical ministers, the large majority of the Dissenters remained loyal to the Premier.[123] Even in Calvinist Scotland, to the chagrin of hard-line Protestants, 'the bulk of the Free Church Voluntary ministers and elders [was] going dead for the Irish brigands and the Irish priesthood', becoming 'active supporters of Popery against Protestantism'.[124] Among the Wesleyans, traditionally less pro-Liberal than other Nonconformists, a contemporary survey suggested that no more than 30 per cent became Unionist as a consequence of the Home Rule Bill.[125] In Parliament, only two of the seventeen Methodist MPs opposed Home Rule in June 1886. *The Baptist Times*, which represented Irish as well as British churches and was Unionist in orientation, had to admit that a majority of the delegates at Baptist association meetings supported Gladstone.[126]

Bebbington and Goodlad have claimed that the Dissenters endorsed Home Rule as 'a matter not of prudential judgment but of moral principle'.[127] Part of the reason was that, in general, they were very sensitive about issues of civil liberty. In 1881 John Page Hopps, a pastor from Leicester, had written to Chamberlain to denounce the government's repression of the Land League, which he described as a legitimate organization campaigning to redress Irish grievances. His letter was published in *The Times* and various other newspapers and caused considerable concern to Chamberlain.[128] Home Rule was soon identified with civil liberty, but it is interesting that at the beginning of 1886 the Nonconformist response to Gladstone's Irish crusade was rather confused and hesitant. After all, the new proposal was in sharp contrast to the traditional Protestant view that the chief cause of troubles in Ireland was '*Popery*, which blights every portion of the globe where it is the predominant religion'.[129] Up until the

---

[123] D. W. Bebbington, *The Nonconformist conscience: chapel and politics, 1870–1914* (1982), 89–195; Goodlad, 'Gladstone and his rivals'.

[124] 'A Free Churchman', 'Free Church Humiliation', letter to *The Scotsman*, 7 July 1886, 10; see also 'A Free Church Elder', letter to *The Scotsman*, 8 July 1886, 10.

[125] D. W. Bebbington, 'Nonconformity and electoral sociology, 1867–1918', *Historical Journal*, 27, 3 (1984), 643.

[126] Heyck, 'Home Rule, radicalism and the Liberal party', 266–7; cf. Newman Hall, 'Nonconformists and Unionism', *Fortnightly Review*, 290 (1891), 320–3.

[127] Bebbington, *Nonconformist Conscience*, 89; Goodlad, 'Gladstone and his rivals', 180–3.

[128] Heyck, *Dimensions*, 73–5.

[129] J. Wood, 'Irish troubles and remedies', *The Primitive Methodist Quarterly Review and Christian Ambassador*, Oct. 1881, 647 (emphasis in the orginial).

eve of the 1886 election even the Gladstonian J. Guinness Rogers acknowledged that '[there] has not been within the memory of man a grave political issue in relation to which the opinions of Nonconformists have been so slowly formed and are still so much divided' as on Home Rule, 'which has up till a very recent period been so distinctly tabooed ... that Englishmen could not allow it even to be discussed'.[130] Both *The Baptist Magazine* and *The Congregationalist*, edited by J. Guinness Rogers, expressed concern about the radicalism of Gladstone's Irish plans and their likely pitfalls, especially in view of the potential risk of religious oppression of the Protestant minority.[131] *The Baptist Magazine* actually opposed and denounced Home Rule as a de facto repeal of the Union, a policy 'perilous to Great Britain, and not advantageous to Ireland', a reckless plan which was contemplated merely because of the general veneration for Gladstone's infallibility and which should teach Nonconformists 'the folly of having political popes'.[132]

Others, however, denied that the GOM's charisma had been decisive, pointing out that, after his snubbing of their demand for church disestablishment in 1885, Dissenters 'were not disposed to accept a policy of Irish Home Rule simply because Mr Gladstone was its author'. Instead, like Chamberlain, they objected to the way in which the measure had been forced upon the Liberal party: 'our [parliamentary] majority had been gathered for a very different purpose, and [was] not satisfied to see its strength shattered and broken in order to satisfy a body of men who had done it all the injury possible at the polls'.[133] Then, however, their attitude changed, partly in reaction against 'the virulent [Tory and Unionist] attacks upon Mr Gladstone' which 'not only roused [the Dissenters'] old loyalty', but also convinced them 'that the battle which is being waged around him is the battle for every principle we love and every cause in whose triumph we are interested'.[134] Some claimed that they were persuaded to support Home Rule by Bright and Chamberlain

---

[130] J. Guinness Rogers, 'The coming election: an address to Nonconformists', *The Congregationalist*, July 1886, 497.

[131] 'The Irish crisis', *The Congregationalist*, Feb. 1886, 146–53; 'The Liberal party and its leaders', *The Congregationalist*, Apr. 1886, 305; *The Baptist Magazine*, Apr. 1886, 183 and June 1886, 277.

[132] *The Baptist Magazine*, May 1886, 229–31.

[133] 'Mr Gladstone's Irish policy', *The Congregationalist*, May 1886, 383.

[134] Ibid., and 'The Liberal party and its Irish policy', *The Congregationalist*, June 1886, 467–73; cf. 'Politics', *The Primitive Methodist Quarterly Review*, Apr. 1886, 380. Even before the beginning of the Home Rule crisis, *The Congregationalist* deplored any personal attack upon the private character of politicians as one of the plagues of American democracy and utterly inconsistent with Christian ethics in politics: 'Religion in politics', *The Congregationalist*, Sep. 1885, 665.

more than by Gladstone because 'their opposing arguments were of the same type as those which have been urged against every reform in the past' and in fact were 'distinctly Tory'.[135] 'The reason underlying the Tory and Whig opposition ... is distrust of the Irish people ... [However, the] Irish are like other people; treat them unjustly, and they will be discontented, and disposed to rebel; treat them equitably, and repose a fair degree of trust in them, and they will be orderly and loyal.'[136]

British Dissenters were 'puzzled' by what they regarded as the sectarianism of the Irish Protestants[137] and contemptuous of Chamberlain's claim 'that the only Irishmen to be considered in the settlement of the question are the Irishmen of Ulster, or rather a section of them'.[138] Furthermore, the 'violence imported into the discussion by the Ulster Orangemen and their champions', Chamberlain and Churchill, discredited their cause.[139] Orangemen were no freedom fighters: instead, they feared the separation of religion from political power as much as English and Welsh Anglicans hated disestablishment. Their reasons were similar: they tried to preserve both privilege and discrimination 'and took refuge in blatant imperialism'.[140] In any case, they were misguided, for they did not realize that 'Home Rule would not make the country one whit more Catholic than it is at present'. The priests would not have greater influence over their flocks than under the Dublin Castle system, because they already 'exercise a paternal authority at present' and the British government 'would never dream of hindering the Irish people from obeying their chosen spiritual guides ... The power they possess to-day is not due to religious terrorism.'[141] In fact, the one thing likely to increase their power was Protestant sectarianism and in particular the activities of the Orange Order, who, 'with the watchwords of freedom on their lips, have ever proved themselves [Protestantism's] worst enemies'.[142]

In contrast to the Orange interpretation of the religious conflict, which focused on the allegedly inherently intolerant nature of Roman Catholicism, British Nonconformists argued that it was the link between church and state – not the teaching of any particular church – which had

[135] 'The plebiscite', *The Congregationalist*, Aug. 1886, 604.
[136] 'Politics', *Primitive Methodist Quarterly Review*, July 1886, 572.
[137] J. Y. Calladine (North Bucks. Liberal Registration Association) to E. Blake, 20 May 1893, inquiring about the Irish Baptists, in NLI, Blake Letters, [993] 4685.
[138] 'Politics', *Primitive Methodist Quarterly Review*, June 1887, 571.
[139] 'The Liberal party and its Irish policy', *The Congregationalist*, June 1886, 467–73.
[140] J. M.[orrison] D.[avidson], 'The Book of Erin', *RN*, 6 May 1888, 5.
[141] 'The future of Ireland', *Primitive Methodist Quarterly Review*, Apr. 1893, 315.
[142] 'Nonconformist Liberals and Unionists', *The Congregational Review*, May 1888, 470–1.

caused religious persecution in the past.[143] In Ireland such a link had been removed in 1869. Before that date, persecution had targeted Catholics more than Dissenters. Disestablishment 'was not done to gratify the vanity of a few, – but on account of its justice' for, although '[t]he natives of Ireland are Papists ... they form the greater part of a noble nation'.[144] It was precisely '[the Dissenters'] Protestantism ... because of its very thoroughness ... [that] inclined [them] to the side of the Nationalists, for it ... taught [them] faith in liberty and right'.[145] The same sense of fair play had moved these pious Christians to support the claims of the atheist Bradlaugh in his struggle against religious tests.[146] Thus, while true Protestantism led to true Liberalism, the latter's primary object '[was] to guard the rights of the weak ... give them better chances in life ... that none shall be forced to the wall'; and 'Home Rule [was] a consistent application of this fundamental maxim of Liberalism to Ireland.'[147]

If the law was sufficient to protect religious liberty in Italy, where the Pope (the 'Triple Tyrant') resided, surely it would be adequate in Ireland. Not only were the Irish no different from the Italians, but also they were no different from the British working men, nor were they more difficult to 'pacify', despite the English notion that they 'changed the question' every time the government came up with an answer. '[I]s it any wonder that partial reforms have made the Irish people resolve to have reforms more complete?' The British had done exactly the same with parliamentary reform:

In 1867 household suffrage was granted to a part of the people of Great Britain; but did that satisfy the people? Nothing of the kind; they were more dissatisfied than ever, and did not rest till household suffrage was granted in borough and country. This has now been done; but are the people satisfied? Not they. A more equitable state of the franchise still is demanded, so that men every way qualified to vote may not be excluded.

Therefore, '[if] Ireland has to be pacified, and if our old methods have proved unsuitable to secure this end, it is at least time to try some other

---

[143] 'If they would refer to the Bible they would find that ... Daniel was thrown into the den of lions simply because he would not obey the State religion. Religious persecution was the offspring of that unholy alliance of Church and State.' (A. Thomas, MP, in 'The Irish Home Rule question: Open air meeting at Taff's Well', *Pontypridd Chronicle*, 16 July 1886, 5.)

[144] L.a., 'Mr Balfour sick of coercion', *Glamorgan Free Press*, 6 June 1891, 4.

[145] 'Nonconformist Liberals and Unionists', *The Congregational Review*, May 1888, 470–1; F. V. Williams ('A Cornish Quaker') to E. Blake, 16 Mar. 1893, NLI, Blake Letters [823] 4685. For the Liberal Unionist answer to this particular argument see chapter 5, pp. 239–44. For the background see T. Larsen, *Friends of religious equality* (1999), 228–9.

[146] C. Leach, 'Democracy and religion', *The Congregational Review*, Nov. 1885, 844.

[147] 'A plea for union', *The Congregational Review*, Mar. 1887, 274–5.

method; and what other method can be tried than that of allowing Irishmen to have the management of their own affairs, and placing upon them the responsibility of directing their own local government'.[148] The Parliamentary Union was founded 'upon the idea that the Irish people are qualified for self-government; that they are amenable to reason, and that they, like the great mass of mankind, will under fair conditions organize themselves for common action and a common purpose – the protection of life and property against the selfishness of individuals and the other objects to be attained by political action'.[149]

The empire required 'the maintenance of law and order'. But 'where the form of government is democratic', as in Ireland, law and order could only be maintained by 'the creation of the law-abiding character' among the people. This, in turn, required the fulfilment of three conditions: 'That the laws are substantially just according to the current standard of ethics', '[t]hat the body which creates the laws and is the source of their authority commands the confidence of the people', and '[t]hat the executive and judicial officers who administer and enforce the law are regarded with respect as the trusted agents of the community, and not with hatred or fear as the servants of a hostile power'. In Ireland the Dublin Castle system signally failed to meet these 'conditions': in fact, on each count it produced the opposite, resulting in '[w]idespread disaffection to English rule, hatred for the officers of the law, contempt for the decisions of the courts, the use of fraudulent means for controlling the verdict of juries, and general disorder'.[150] Was this merely owing to the 'terrorism' of the National League which intimidated and coerced the law-abiding majority, as the Unionists argued?

Assuming that the picture is not overdrawn, one cannot help remarking in the first place that the existence of such a body implies political capacity of a high order in the Irish mind ... In the next place one notices that the relations between the governing body of such a League and its members or those who are controlled by it, are precisely such as are found, when the three conditions I have mentioned are fulfilled, to subsist between a regular government and its subjects. The decrees of the National League are according to the moral standard of those they control substantially just; the governing body commands the confidence of is members; and its officers are their friends and not their foes ... The power of such a society must be derived from the sympathy of the larger part of the people.[151]

---

[148] 'Politics', *Primitive Methodist Quarterly Review*, Apr. 1886, 382.
[149] D. Mabellan, *Home Rule and imperial unity, an argument for the Gladstone–Morley scheme* (1886), 67.
[150] Ibid., 60–1 and 16 (for the 'three conditions').   [151] Ibid., 62.

In other words, these Nonconformist spokesmen espoused a notion of political legitimacy similar to the old Chartist view, namely that sovereignty resided in the nation and that the United Kingdom was a multinational state within which the people of each nation were, or ought to be, sovereign.[152]

This argument elaborated on Gladstone's insistence that three of the four nationalities of which the Kingdom consisted '[had] spoken for Irish autonomy in a tone yet more decided than the tone in which the fourth [England] has forbidden it'. To him the 1886 election had been contested 'upon the question of nationality', a fact which in itself gave new prominence to that issue 'as an element of our political thought', especially if 'these nationalities will be inclined to help one another'.[153] The 'four nation' argument sank deep into British radicalism, and was unwittingly confirmed by the Unionist government's 1888 county council scheme. Because the latter excluded Scotland and Ireland, 'the Tories practically recognize the existence of nationalities they are endeavouring to ignore': 'Nationality, as Edmund Burke said, and as Burns felt, is a "moral essence" which cannot be suppressed by any form of county or local government, however comprehensive or democratic ... Hence the argument in favour of Home Rule first and Local Government afterwards.'[154]

Coercion and 'slavery'

As we have seen (chapter 1, pp. 10–11), the defeat of the Home Rule Bill and subsequent Liberal rout at the general election of 1886 created a political context within which the Unionists could implement their Irish strategy without any need to compromise with the Home Rulers. As far as the British public was concerned, the weakest part of such a strategy was the government's recourse to repressive legislation. This strengthened the Liberal claim that the Union itself was the cause of the people's unrest in Ireland and that it would be unsustainable without destroying their liberties.[155] Unlike previous measures, which had been temporary and designed to lapse unless renewed periodically, the 1887 Coercion Bill was 'part of the permanent statute law, without any limitation of time'.[156] As Barker has argued, the resulting erosion of personal and political rights in

---

[152] 'The political situation', *The Congregational Review*, Apr. 1887, 860.
[153] W. E. Gladstone, *The Irish question* (1886), 15 (pamphlet in the Gladstone Library, Bristol Univ. Library). This view was broadly echoed within the NLF.
[154] L.a., 'Ritchie's revolution', *RN*, 25 Mar. 1888, 1.
[155] 'Politics', *Primitive Methodist Quarterly Review*, Jan. 1887, 189.
[156] 'Politics', *Primitive Methodist Quarterly Review*, June 1887, 573.

a constituent part of the United Kingdom 'did more to engender the celebrated "union of hearts" than any commitment to establish a Parliament on College Green'.[157] It also encouraged Dissenters to indulge in an apocalyptic rhetoric reminiscent of their campaign to stop the Bulgarian atrocities in 1876, while the Liberal propaganda machine further stirred up popular emotion with the use of the visual aids provided by contemporary technology to illustrate the suffering of the evicted tenants.[158]

Gladstone himself was largely responsible for the resulting rhetorical climate. In 1887 after listening to one of his speech, the leading Baptist minister John Clifford commented that '[t]he hearer felt he was witnessing a fight for righteousness, for humanity, for God'.[159] It is easy to see that people steeped in the culture of Dissent and the values of labour were likely to hold strong views about the use of repression, the 'cruel conduct' of the 'heartless' evictors, and their readiness to demolish and burn the homesteads of a panic-stricken peasantry. A town meeting in the Workmen's Hall, Walthamstow (Essex) invoked 'the condemnation of the civilized world' on those who perpetrated 'such infamous and wicked proceedings'.[160] Even in Somerset and Dorset – solid Unionist heartlands – crowds of 'many more' than fifteen thousand (according to one Unionist estimate) attended demonstrations to condemn the 'blind, indiscriminate, blundering force' used by the government: 'They had suppressed meetings, they had imprisoned ... members of Parliament, they were going to lock up the clergy, they were proceeding against the freedom of the Press.'[161]

The plight of the Irish reminded Nonconformists and trade unionists of their own past history of suffering persecution for the sake of conscience and the right of association. Coercion relied on 'deceit – a species of political fraud' because it professed to target crime, but in reality '[was]

---

[157] Barker, *Gladstone and radicalism*, 78. See for a few examples the reports in *WT*, 17 Apr. 1887, 9, 'The coercion agitation', about the meetings in Derby and London. For the Irish enthusiastic response see 'Mr Herbert Gladstone on the Irish party and their traducers', *FJ*, 5 May 1887, 5; and 'The government and Ireland: the right of public meeting', *Cork Examiner*, 28 Sep. 1887, 3.

[158] Rep., 'Extraordinary eviction scene', *RN*, 17 Apr. 1887, 1. At the 1887 Northwich by-election '[the] mural literature was of extraordinary abundance. The Gladstonians displayed in large numbers photographs and cartoons illustrative of Irish evictions.' ('The Northwich election', *FJ*, 15 Aug. 1887, 5.)

[159] Cited in J. F. Glaser, 'Parnell's fall and the Nonconformist conscience', *Irish Historical Studies*, 12, 46 (1960), 120.

[160] Rep., 'English sympathy with the evicted', *Cork Examiner*, 21 Jan. 1887, 3.

[161] John Morley speaking at Templecombe, at a meeting said to have numbered fifteen thousand: 'Great Liberal demonstration in the West', *WT&E*, 2 Oct. 1887, 16; and 'Mr. Morley on Ireland', *LW*, 2 Oct. 1887, 1.

directed against political combination, and … associations for [the] protection of the poor and oppressed'. It gave power to the 'Castle party' to suppress 'all constitutional agitation such as we in England are allowed to conduct freely' and to 'strike down, not criminals, but political opponents'.[162] It was altogether unconstitutional in so far as '[t]he liberty of the subject is the first object of the British constitution'.[163] Commenting on a petition signed by more than 3,200 Nonconformist ministers, *The Congregational Review* insisted that '[w]hether "political discontent" should be put down by force, is a matter of principle about which ministers of the gospel have a title and … a special fitness to speak' because of their own historical experience.

> It has been said that the law is only made for the disobedient, and that an Irishman can escape its penalties by not violating its provisions. Of course, if those provisions had relation to actual crime this would be true enough. But this Bill will fail of its object if it does not prevent the formation of political associations and the expression of political opinions … There was a law once passed by the ancestors of the party now in power which made it criminal to attend a conventicle. Will it be maintained that the law was unobjectionable inasmuch as no Dissenter needed to incur its penalties, and all might be perfectly free by abstaining from conventicles altogether?[164]

While some Nonconformists celebrated the Irish as 'a [fellow] subject race',[165] the class-conscious *Reynolds's* saw Fenianism as a reaction not to 'racial', but to social oppression, as the equivalent of nihilism in Russia and socialism in Germany.[166] In this sense Fenianism was indeed the product not of a Nationalist plot, but of a conspiracy 'of English, Irish and Scottish land robbers against the honest toilers of the three nations. Nay, more, it is a foul conspiracy against the God-given rights of man', resulting in a class war in which the British working man had a stake, for 'the cause of Ireland is the cause of universal democracy'.[167] Therefore, for both Michael Davitt and Frederic Harrison, resistance to coercion was a *labour* question; it was the Irish equivalent of the struggle that British trade unions had fought from 1824 to 1875 to secure the repeal of 'the obscure and sinister law of conspiracy'.[168] Under the Coercion

---

[162] 'Politics', *Primitive Methodist Quarterly Review*, June 1887, 572–3.

[163] L.a., 'Liberty and law', *RN*, 4 Sep. 1887, 4.

[164] 'The Nonconformist protest', *The Congregational Review*, May 1887, 403–4.

[165] 'Nonconformist politics: Home Rule and disestablishment', *The Congregational Review*, July 1889, 273.

[166] Gracchus, 'Oppression, repression and assassination', *RN*, 27 Mar. 1887, 3; Northumbrian, 'What is law?', *RN*, 3 Apr. 1887, 2.

[167] L.a., 'Coercion once more', *RN*, 27 Mar. 1887, 1.

[168] Rep., 'Mr Frederic Harrison on the Irish question', *Cork Examiner*, 5 Jan. 1887, 3; M. Davitt to W. J. Parry, 28 Dec. 1885, in Parry MSS, 8823 C, 5–5(d). Thomas Burt

Act, as under the old Conspiracy Law, convictions were based on circumstantial evidence and the arbitrary decisions of socially biased
magistrates:

> It is this loose definition of conspiracy which constitutes the Coercion Bill into an
> Act of the most oppressive character ... The right allowed to English workmen to
> say that they will not work for less than a certain price is not allowed to be
> exercised by Irish tenants, who are in this position, that rent stands to them in
> the same relation as wages do to working men in England. As Mr Gladstone put it,
> working men in England are paid in wages, and working men in Ireland have their
> earnings reduced by the payment of exorbitant rents, so that it practically comes
> to a reduction of wages in the end. The right of combination peaceably and quietly
> is therefore the same in both countries, and subject only to the preservation of
> public peace.[169]

If, as Cooke and Vincent have argued, 'with his rediscovery of class war
in his manifesto of 1 May [1886] ... Gladstone firmly occupied the whole
left of politics', his task was greatly facilitated by the police adopting
heavy-handed tactics to repress unrest not only in Ireland, but also in
England.[170] The agitation against coercion culminated with the Hyde
Park demonstration of April 1887. A considerable effort had gone into
the canvassing of working-class opinion, with more than a hundred
thousand copies of a handbill about coercion being distributed.[171] In
the run up to the demonstration, preliminary meetings of the London
radical clubs were held with the participation of labour and Home Rule
leaders including George Howell, Randall Cremer, T. P. O'Connor and
H. Labouchere. Coercion was described as a class device for making land
purchase inevitable, 'throw[ing] upon the English taxpayer the cost of
buying out the Irish landlords',[172] and 'a desperate effort of the oligarchy
to stifle the splendid possibilities of the democracy'.[173] Over the next few

---

held serious reservations, however. He agreed that '[the] tenants are right in uniting &
they should do whatever they can to assist each other against being compelled to pay
impossible rents.' Nevertheless, he dismissed the claim that 'the "Plan of Campaign" is
in principle "identical with a strike"', as the latter 'is not necessarily a breach of contract.
When it is ... it is illegal and punishable. Nor do I think the action of the government
bears any analogy to the attack on trade unions in the country some years ago. Unions
were then illegal.' (T. Burt to W. T. Stead, 20 Dec. 1886, in W. T. Stead Papers, 1/12.)
For the official Liberal line see D. A. Hamer, *John Morley: Liberal intellectual in politics*
(1969), 237–8 and Barker, *Gladstone and radicalism*, 91.

[169] L.a., 'The mark of the Coercion Bill', *RN*, 28 May 1887, 4.
[170] Cooke and Vincent, *The governing passion*, 79; cf. L. M. Geary, *The Plan of Campaign,*
1886–1891 (1986), 94.
[171] Rep., 'The Hyde Park demonstration', *Cork Examiner*, 7 Apr. 1887, 2.
[172] Rep., 'Hyde Park demonstration against Coercion', *RN*, 3 Apr. 1887, 1.
[173] L.a., 'To your tents, o Israel', *RN*, 8 Apr. 1887, 1.

days preparations for a large protest meeting were reported at great length as the London Trades Council joined the agitation.[174]

Eventually, on 11 April, a bank holiday Monday, '[f]avoured by brilliant weather, no less than by a firm faith in the justice of their cause, the working men of the metropolis successfully carried through a gigantic demonstration'. Combined Radical, Irish and socialist demonstrations – an estimated total of about a hundred thousand people, although newspapers reported radically different figures[175] – marched through London. For an hour and a half a stream of societies, sporting colourful banners and stirring mottoes, moved along Pall Mall, St James's Street and Piccadilly to Hyde Park Corner; while other contingents from the western suburbs entered the park through the Marble Arch.

The bands played democratic tunes such as 'La Marseillaise', 'Garry Owen' and 'God save Ireland' ('Tramp, tramp'), reflecting the ideological outlook of the protesters who hailed from a number of different radical and socialist societies. Their banners proclaimed 'No coercion' and 'Justice to Ireland' and the demonstrators paraded portraits and statuettes of Gladstone, while the red flags of the socialist clubs were interspersed with the more elaborate silk banners of trade unions such as the stevedores and labour guilds of the East End, as well as with green flags with Irish harps. Other mottoes 'denounc[ed] coercion, rack rents, privilege, tyranny, and oppression' and stated 'Salisbury is the symbol of death'. One banner portrayed 'Salisbury's union' – 'two hands, un-joined and fettered at the wrist' – and 'Gladstone's Union', showing 'two hands joined in a grip of friendship'.[176] The speakers included G. W. Foote the secularist, Sexton for the Irish Nationalists, Henry Labouchere, Michael Davitt and other radicals. Henry Broadhurst was the most eminent labour spokesman. In his address he said that the people of London 'had sympathized with the oppressed in all parts of the world – with Poles and Bulgarians, and with the Negroes when they were held in slavery in the Southern States of America. That was because they knew more of them than they knew about Ireland, but now they knew about the

---

[174] Rep., 'The Coercion Bill: the Hyde Park demonstration', *RN*, 10 Apr. 1887, 1.

[175] 'I wonder how many people there really were in Hyde-park last Monday? The *Daily News* says it was the largest demonstration of its kind ever held in London; the *Daily Telegraph*, with a caution commendable in itself, but hardly tending to accurate information, says there were between one and two hundred thousand present; the *Times* declares fifty thousand a fair estimate; the *Morning Post* admits there were several thousand there; and the *Daily Chronicle* affirms that the nucleus of the gathering was small and thin.' ('Powder and shot', *WT*, 17 Apr. 1887, 9).

[176] Rep., 'The anti-coercion meeting in London', *RN*, 17 Apr. 1887, 1.

wrongs of Ireland, and were determined to redress them.' Introducing the 'ministers of the Gospel' on the platform, he said that:

> He's true to God who's true to man
> Wherever wrong is done,
> To the humblest and the weakest
> 'Neath the all-beholding sun.
>
> The wrong is also done to us
> And they are slaves and base
> Whose love of right is for themselves,
> And not for all their race.[177]

Reynolds's hoped that the agitation would signal the beginning of the end for landlordism not only in Ireland, but indeed throughout the British Isles and world-wide. From being solely on behalf of justice for Ireland, the Home Rule campaign was now expected to usher in 'the future British republic, federal, social and democratic'.[178] In their usual hyperbolic style, the editors boasted that the Home Rule agitation was the most 'fateful' movement 'since the martyrdom of Tiberius and Caius Gracchus. It is a step towards the realization of the splendid day-dreams of Kant, Mazzini, Victor Hugo, and Garibaldi, "the United States of Europe" ... The peoples are brothers, and nothing but the rascality of their rulers keeps them apart.'[179] The next step would be 'a vast English-speaking Federation embracing enormous territories and populations in every quarter of the inhabitable world', not as a centralized empire but as a 'true fraternal democratic idea'. For *Reynolds's* this would eventually result in a republican federation of Great Britain and Ireland, with Home Rule for India and a wider confederation of 'Greater Britain' overseas, including the USA, which continued to be romanticized as the land of equality and democracy. Britain would transform its foreign policy, cease to be a European Power and concentrate on its 'trans-oceanic interests'.[180] Paradoxically, while celebrating the intercontinental nature of Britishness and British interests, these democratic isolationists claimed that their ultimate ideal was the Swiss Confederation, a tiny land-locked country.[181]

---

[177] Ibid.   [178] L.a., 'Before and after', *RN*, 17 Apr. 1887, 1.

[179] Ibid. This remained for a long time the hope expressed by *Reynolds's*: cf. l.a., 'Balfourism challenged', *RN*, 1 July 1888, 1: 'What the Tories and the Dissentient Liberals fail to recognise is that the solidarity of the English, Scottish, Welsh and Irish democracies is now an accomplished fact. The masses of the four Nationalities have been quick to learn that their cause is one and indivisible, and that Ireland is the standard-bearer of a universal crusade.'

[180] L.a., 'Greater Britain and federation', *RN*, 15 May 1887, 1; Gracchus, 'India for the Indians', *RN*, 2 Sep. 1888, 2.

[181] L.a., 'Liberal Unionism at Liverpool', *RN*, 22 Dec. 1888, 1.

Gladstone's eventual endorsement (1888) of a continued Irish presence at Westminster, which Parnell publicly accepted, further increased radical interest in ideas of colonial federation. It is interesting that, while contemporary Radical Unionists, especially in Scotland, shared many of these ideas, they disagreed on the means to bring them about. What to them were 'agitators', to the Home Rule imperial federalists were 'Leaders of the democracy'. These included Gavan Duffy and John Dillon, but also, posthumously, the Young Irelander Thomas Davis.[182] They praised Parnell as the Gladstone or Cavour of Ireland, pointing out that '[w]hile any National upheaval is too often accompanied with crime and disorder', Parnell '[had] striven to establish fair and Constitutional methods of expressing the National desire'.[183] Edward Blake was another of their heroes.[184] It was because Blake really believed in 'Home Rule all round' that he was in high demand as a speaker at Liberal meetings in England – especially in London,[185] but also in Birmingham (where he was regarded as an 'antidote' to Chamberlain) and Scotland.[186] John Morley summoned his help in Newcastle, explaining that 'we are likely to be very hard pressed there, & a speech . . . from you would be of immense service to me'.[187] Another correspondent confirmed that Blake had considerable appeal also in Yorkshire: '[your] letter of consenting to come has raised the spirit of our party considerably . . . the fact of your name, influence and presence could arouse an additional interest in the Labour party to hear you'.[188] One Mrs M. S. Reid of the Women's Liberal Association for South Kensington wrote: 'I believe that an address from you would

[182] 'Demon', 'Leaders of the democracy', *RN*, 10 Apr. 1887, 2. At a meeting in Dublin Mr Clancy, MP, declared that 'except Mr Gladstone, there was no more popular man in England than John Dillon' (rep., 'The National League', *Cork Examiner*, 5 Jan. 1887, 3).

[183] Dunbartonshire Liberal Association, 11 July 1889, NLS, Acc. 11765, 37.

[184] E. L. Gales, Liberal Association for the Frome Division, Bath, to E. Blake, 11 Nov. 1892, in NLI, Blake Letters, [436] 4685. Canada was the model for Home Rule not because of its imperial connection to Britain, but because of the autonomy which each of the provinces enjoyed in its relationship with Ottawa: E. Gales to Blake, 30 Apr. 1892, ibid., [274] 4684. On Blake see Introduction, p. 33 and chapter 3, p. 123.

[185] In the Blake Letters see those by F. Aylett, Hon. Sec. Peckham Liberal and Radical Association, 8 Feb. 1893 [653] 4685; H. Morgan, Clapham Reform Club, 10 Feb. 1893 [666] 4685; Mrs E. C. Fellows for the Hampstead Liberals, 19 Feb. 1893 [710] 4685.

[186] See Blake Letters, NLI, [868], [869] and [977] 4685 (all for 1893).

[187] J. Morley to E. Blake, 11 Aug. 1892, ibid., [2] 4683. Blake accepted immediately (14 Aug. 1892, [4] ibid.,). J. F. X. O'Brien, Executive Officer of the Irish National League of Great Britain, invited him to speak in Newcastle again in 1895, adding that 'you would have a magnificent meeting there' (4 Feb. 1895, ibid., [26]4683). But this did not save Morley from the ire of Joseph Cowen and his new SDF/ILP friends.

[188] Alfred Walker, Borough of Huddersfield Parliamentary Election, Mr Wodehead's Candidature, Central Committee Rooms, 21 Jan. 1893, ibid., [607] 4685.

attract a large audience & be of great value.'[189] C. P. Trevelyan was even
more enthusiastic, and writing to Blake about a speech which the latter had
given in Cambridge, reported that 'you seriously shook the faith of three
Tory friends ... One of them became a member of the Liberal Club on the
spot.'[190] At least one correspondent specified that it was Blake's 'moderation of demand and argument' which was so appreciated, and stated
that 'Home Rule all round' would have been 'logical' from the start, and
hoped that the Irish MPs would not be withdrawn from Westminster
anyway.[191] The latter point was strongly endorsed by Michael Davitt.[192]

J. F. X. O'Brien and E. Blake encouraged the Irish in Britain to
get involved in the Liberal party and organize joint demonstrations
with them. The invitation was often accepted with enthusiasm. Close
co-operation between the Irish National League of Great Britain
(INLGB) and the Liberals was commonplace, and some INLGB members – both men and women – rose to prominent leadership roles in local
Liberal caucuses. A good example was the president of the Clapham
branch of the INLGB, E. W. McGuinness, who believed that Liberal
demonstrations were more useful than Irish ones and 'acted upon [this
view] ... on every occasion. As a matter of fact I am a member of the
Liberal and Radical Association and a Vice President of the Council of
300 [i.e. the local caucus assembly].'[193]

At the end of August 1887 another demonstration was called in
London to protest against the proclamation of the National League, but
it was not as successful as the previous events.[194] The radical campaign
was rekindled by the Mitchelstown 'massacre' (9 September 1887), in
which three people were killed when the police opened fire to stem a riot.
In England the episode renewed memory of the 1817 'Peterloo massacre'
and further contributed to strengthening the 'class' dimension of the
agitation against Balfour's 'sanguinary reign of terror'.[195] Gladstone
famously denounced the behaviour of the constabulary, who 'ought to

---

[189] Mrs M. S. Reid to E. Blake, 22 Feb. 1893, ibid., [733] 4685.
[190] C.P. Trevelyan to E. Blake, 22 Feb. 1893 (from Dublin Castle), ibid., [734] 4685.
[191] E. L. Gales, Liberal Association for the Frome Division, to E. Blake, 15 Feb. 1893, ibid., 4685.
[192] Davitt, *The settlement of the Irish question. A speech by Mr Michael Davitt, MP, on Apr. 11th, 1893 in the House of Commons*, 'Authorised edition' as a penny pamphlet (1893), 11–2 (Gladstone Library, Bristol Univ. Library).
[193] E. W. McGuinness to E. Blake, 3 Feb. 1893, in NLI, Blake Letters [637] 4685.
[194] For contrasting accounts see 'Monster demonstration of London radicals in Trafalgar-square', *FJ*, 29 Aug. 1887, 5 and 'Demonstration in Trafalgar-square', *LW*, 28 Aug. 1887, 1.
[195] L.a., 'The reign of terror in Ireland', *RN*, 18 Sept. 1887, 1 and 'Remember Mitchelstown and Peterloo', *RN*, 16 Oct. 1887, 4.

have been given into custody', while the people acted – so he insisted – 'with perfect legality and propriety, and in the defence of law and order'.[196] The arrest of eminent English Home Rulers, including Sir Wilfrid and Lady Anne Blunt and the Radical MP Charles Conybeare, was a godsend for Liberal propaganda, which predicted that coercionist methods would corrupt the English constitution and that England itself would soon be consigned to 'Cossack'-style discipline.[197] The theme of government brutality and arbitrary repression was shared across the board by the opposition, from the Liberals and the Lib-labs to social radicals such as R. B. Cunninghame-Graham, and the popular press and the Trades Union Congress (TUC).

The meeting at Mitchelstown had been called to protest against the imprisonment of William O'Brien, MP. He was denied the status of 'political prisoner' despite his bad health, a treatment which was perceived as being unnecessarily severe and exposing an elected representative of the people to indignities comparable to those suffered by the Neapolitan prisoners of 'Bomba' (the King of Naples who bombarded his own rebellious subjects into submission) and famously denounced by Gladstone in 1851.[198] In London, on Sunday 13 November a further large demonstration, demanding his release, clashed with the police and army. The episode was taken as evidence of the impending collapse of English liberty: 'Coercion in London: a Radical meeting proclaimed', headed one handbill. 'We want free speech,' the demonstrators were reported to have shouted. 'We are all true Englishmen, Irishmen and Scotchmen, and we only want our legal rights as citizens of London.'[199]

The 'feminization' of Gladstonianism

In July 1887 the Lady Mayoress of Dublin received a deputation led by Miss Cobden and Mrs W. McLaren, who presented her with a document

---

[196] Gladstone, *Coercion in Ireland. Speech delivered by the Right Hon. W. E. Gladstone, MP, in the House of Commons, on Friday, Feb. 17th, 1888,* Liberal Publications Department (1888), 12–13 (Gladstone Library, Bristol Univ. Library).

[197] W. E. Gladstone, *The Treatment of the Irish Members and the Irish Political Prisoners, a speech by the Right Hon. W. E. Gladstone, MP, to the Staffordshire Liberals,* penny pamphlet of the Liberal Publications Department (1888), 1 (Gladstone Library, Bristol Univ. Library); l.a., 'The unemployed and Warren's ukase', *RN,* 13 Nov. 1887, 1; cf. l.a., 'Toryism and tyranny', *RN,* 9 Oct. 1887, 4; W. T. Stead, 'Memo. of a conversation with Cardinal Manning', 4 Oct. 1890, in W. T. Stead Papers. Cf. L. M. Geary, 'John Mandeville and the Irish Crimes Act of 1887', *Irish Historical Studies,* 25, 100 (1987), 364.

[198] L.a., 'Balfour's brutality', *RN,* 15 Nov. 1887, 4; rep., 'National Liberal Federation', annual meeting of the Council (Birmingham), *FJ,* 7 Nov. 1887, 6.

[199] Rep., 'Serious riots in London: monster procession to Trafalgar-square', *RN,* 20 Nov. 1887, 6.

signed by more than forty thousand British women, expressing 'sympathy' with their sisters in Ireland 'in their sorrow over the troubles of their country'.[200] Despite the almost non-partisan wording of their speech, both Cobden and McLaren were active Gladstonian campaigners and were effectively using Home Rule to bridge the gap between the 'separate spheres' – namely the male preserve of constitutional affairs and the female sphere of family and moral concerns. To them Ireland was a cause with social and humanitarian implications and therefore could be construed as 'a woman's issue'. For Josephine Butler the consequences of the Coercion and Crimes Acts were 'inhuman' – causing the eviction of thousands of families and exposing women and children to police brutality – and 'touched closely upon their hearts, their maternal feelings, their deepest emotions [and] their most profound convictions'.[201] She compared coercion to the forcible medical examination of women suspected of prostitution under the Contagious Diseases Acts, repealed in 1886 after a long campaign in which Butler herself had played a leading role.[202]

Like Margaret Thatcher a century later, Butler argued that national affairs were best understood through the prism of domesticity: thus the Unionist contention that Home Rule would undermine imperial unity was similar to arguing that judicial separation in an unhappy marriage, 'brought about by a mixture of force and guile', should not be allowed, because doing so might encourage happily married couples to divorce. She insisted that imperial politics was like relationships between partners: each marriage depended on the will of the partners. In the same way it was 'clear' to her that 'it is the will of the nation which must decide in each case its form of Government', for 'the Government of a nation against the will of the people is the very definition of slavery'.[203] The 'household' metaphor was taken up by other campaigners, including Hannah Cheetham, who told the Southport Women's Liberal Association in 1886 that 'the same sympathy, the same refinement, the same emotional insight' which sustained a well-run household 'are needed to purify and ennoble the government of the larger home – our country'.[204] Party

---

[200] 'London correspondece', *Cork Examiner*, 6 July 1887, 2.
[201] 'L. Walker, 'Party political women: a comparative study of Liberal women and the Primrose League', in J. Rendall (ed.), *Equal or different: Women's politics, 1800–1914* (1987), 175, and Josephine Butler speaking at the Portsmouth Women's Liberal Association, cited in ibid.
[202] P. McHugh, *Prostitution and Victorian social reform* (1980); J. Walkowitz, *Prostitution and Victorian society* (1990).
[203] J. E. Butler, *Our Christianity tested by the Irish question*, (n.d. [1886]), 57.
[204] Cited in Walker, 'Party political women', 176.

politics became akin in character to the philanthropic work in which many women found it natural to be involved: as one Wyndford Phillips put it in her *Appeal to Women* (c.1890), 'Women: your duty is your home! Yes, but you have a double duty. First of all to your family, and secondly to the wider family, the world of human beings outside.'[205] It seemed that '[t]he Irish question has done more in the last two or three years to settle definitely the contested question of women's mission and women's place in politics than the patient and laborious efforts of twenty years past had done'.[206] One area in which this was most obvious was public speaking on issues of national relevance – that is, pertaining to the male 'public sphere'. While women had been active in local politics, particularly from 1870 (when some of them were given the vote and became eligible for school boards),[207] constitutional reform or foreign policy was not something about which they were expected to have anything 'sensible' to say. Although a number of them had been involved in Chartism and had spoken at Chartist camp meetings in the 1830s, their expertise in addressing popular demonstrations was largely limited to Nonconformist revival gatherings.[208] To the chagrin of some traditionalists,[209] the Home Rule agitation was to change that from the 1880s.

Exploiting the newly blurred divide between public policy and the private sphere, women started to address with confidence and authority predominantly male political meetings. At the London agitation of April 1887 one of the main orators was Mrs Ashton Dilke, of the Women's Suffrage Society. She claimed to be speaking 'for thousands and millions of the women of England who were on the side of liberty, and who, like Mr Gladstone, desired home rule and justice for all alike'.[210] Like other Liberal women, she developed a distinctive agenda, which was formally consistent with contemporary expectations about women's duties in society, and yet subversive of such roles and tasks.

Allegedly, the 'subversion' was only temporary and was justified by the emergency which the nation was facing. But, as we shall see (chapter 4),

---

[205] Cited in ibid., 174.   [206] Cited in Walker, 'Party political women', 175–6.
[207] P. Hollis, *Ladies elect: women in English local government, 1865–1914* (1987).
[208] For example, Alice Cambridge (1762–1829) and Anne Lutton (1791–1881), coincidentally both Irish: C. H. Crookshank, *Memorable women of Irish Methodism in the last century* (1882); C. Murphy, 'The religious context of the women's suffrage campaign in Ireland', *Women's History Review*, 6, 4 (1997), 549–62. The other important exceptions were the Parnell sisters and the Ladies' Land League in 1881.
[209] Such as Lady Londonderry, who preferred to exert her influence in less direct ways: M. Pugh, *The Tories and the people, 1880–1935* (1985), 58.
[210] Rep., 'The anti-coercion meeting in London', *RN*, 17 Apr. 1887, 1. For other examples of women addressing political meetings see 'Loughborough Reform Club', *LW*, 28 Aug. 1887, 1, and 'Political meeting in Regent's Park', *LW*, 4 Sep. 1887, 1.

the establishment of a party 'machine' turned this 'exception' into something permanent. This process was further encouraged by what Margot
Asquith called 'Gladstone worship',[211] in which women were prominent.
'[N]urtured under the shadow of [his] high idealism, [women] were at
one in believing ... that those who take service under [Liberalism's]
banner must apply its principles to all relations of life, both public and
private.'[212]

Their leaders exploited the ever closer link between politics, morality
and religion to expand their sphere of social action. Morality and religion
had long been perceived as the twin pillars of their 'duty to society', and
the association between these concepts acquired a more political and
institutional prominence in the aftermath of the 1870–1 Franco-
Prussian War, as Gill has demonstrated.[213] However, from 1886, under
the combined pressure of Gladstone's haunting rhetoric and the dictates
of the 'Nonconformist conscience', they also became central to politics.
As one leaflet proclaimed, 'religion is not more important to our spiritual
wants than politics to our material wants ... Religion tells us we should be
helpful to one another, and politics shows us how to be helpful, wisely and
effectively.'[214] This line of argument was effectively summarized by Lady
Aberdeen when she declared that 'Liberalism was the Christianity of
politics.'[215] There was no longer any legitimate room for the selfish pursuit of naked national interest, because politics had become the arena in
which moral standards were upheld and religious imperatives applied to
the solution of social and constitutional problems. By the same token,
humanitarianism, both at home and overseas, emerged as the defining
feature of the Gladstonian faith. It appealed both to the politically aware
section of the population – irrespective of class and gender differences –
and to those who lacked political training and sophistication.

As politics became more religious and religion more political, some of
the traditional arguments against the extension of political rights to
women, that is, that they were 'emotional' or 'priest ridden', lost much
of their rhetorical power: as May Dilke pointed out, '[the] influence of the
priest is at least as respectable as ... [that] of the publican' to which many

[211] M. Asquith (Lady Oxford), *More Memoirs* (1933), 148.
[212] Lady Aberdeen, *'We Twa'. Reminiscences of Lord and Lady Aberdeen*, vol. I (1925), 272.
[213] Biagini, 'The Anglican ethic and the spirit of citizenship'; (1995) Gill, 'Calculating
compassion in war', 13; B. Taithe, *Defeated flesh: welfare, warfare and the makings of
modern France* (Manchester, 1999).
[214] From a leaflet of the Warwick and Leamington Women's Liberal Association, 1890,
cited in Walker, 'Party political women', 177.
[215] Lady Aberdeen, *'We Twa'*, 278.

male electors were supposedly highly susceptible.[216] To the horror of many intellectuals[217] and some of the more conventionally 'masculine' parliamentary Liberals, such as Hartington and Chamberlain, the role of emotions in Liberal politics had steadily grown since the Bulgarian agitation of 1876. In fact, Gladstone's own style of revivalist politics created among Liberal women a new pride in their supposedly innate emotionalism. If the ideology of 'separate spheres' included the notion of women's moral superiority based on their 'freedom from debasing habits' and preference for virtue and uprightness over expediency, now their 'higher moral enthusiasm' was trumpeted as one of the reasons why they should be listened to in the public sphere. In 1879, Gladstone had famously called on women to 'open [their] feelings and bear [their] own part in a political crisis like this'. He stressed that this was 'no inappropriate demand' but rather a duty fully consistent with their character as women.[218] As Eliza Orme noted, 'many people, women as well as men, who had been accustomed to hold themselves aloof from party politics', now felt that they should '[take] an active part in the struggle'.[219] Progress, in politics as much as in missionary or temperance work, demanded women to act as 'a combined body' with crusading zeal. Thus, as Linda Walker has pointed out, '[a]ll the arguments for women's involvement in politics – moral, religious, educational, maternal, legislative – rested on a powerful new notion that . . . [w]omen who wanted to work for the Liberal cause could do so . . . using direct rather than backstairs influence'.[220]

This upsurge in female participation corresponded to the Liberal party's apparent eagerness to enlist their support. Local women's Liberal associations began to appear from 1880, but the nation-wide Women's Liberal Federation (WLF) was founded only in 1887, largely in response to the Home Rule crisis. Despite its upper-class leadership, the WLF's original membership was socially mixed and included schoolteachers, wives and daughters of tradespeople and artisans, and even factory workers – reflecting both the broad social appeal of Gladstone's rhetoric and the lack of competition from other left-wing organizations before the foundation of the ILP in 1893. These groups were targeted by Liberal propaganda on the assumption that wives played a special role in the shaping of their husbands' political views, especially over Home

---

[216] May Dilke, unfinished manuscript on 'Women's suffrage', n.d. [1885], 25, in C. Dilke Papers, Churchill Archives.
[217] C. Harvie, 'Ideology and Home Rule: James Bryce, A.V. Dicey and Ireland, 1880–1887', *English Historical Review*, 91, 359 (1976), 298–314.
[218] *Midlothian Speeches*, Second speech, 89–90.
[219] Walker, 'Party political women', 167.   [220] Ibid., 177.

Rule.[221] In numerical terms the WLF rose rapidly from 16,500 members and 63 branches in 1887, to 82,000 and 448 branches in 1895.[222] This was not as impressive as the contemporaneous development of the Primrose League's female membership, but, in contrast to the latter, the women in the WLF 'enjoyed effective control of their own organization from the outset, with their own council, executive [and] annual conference'.[223] Even more important was that each local association was able to deliberate and put forward its own political programme, a fact which further contributed to making such associations 'more decentralized and less socially hierarchical than the Primrose League Habitations'.[224]

Thus, while ostensibly the WLF's role was simply to inspire and organize canvassers, 'it also provided a convenient means of bringing wives, mothers and sisters into regular contact with feminist ideas and recruiting activists for suffragism'.[225] Mrs Gladstone was not keen on the idea, but women from younger generations insisted on the link between Irish Home Rule and votes for women. In itself even their public advocacy of Home Rule was intended as a statement of their political rights:

'But what tom-foolery is this!' some will say, as they hear or read of our meeting. What do we want with women coming with their sickly sentimentality, mixing themselves up in politics, talking about matters they cannot understand, when they rely only on their own feelings to guide them? And yet we here presume to think that it is just because we can assert the fact that this resolution represents the feeling of many thousands of thinking, high-minded women, that it possesses a significance of its own. We believe that when we ask our president [Mrs Gladstone] to convey the expression of this meeting to her husband that he will attach a special value to it because it comes from women.[226]

North of the border, from the start the Federation of Scottish Women's Liberal Associations combined social activism with political radicalism, demanding (in this order) independence from the WLF, Home Rule and no coercion for Ireland, the rejection of Irish land purchase, the party's adoption of both women's suffrage and right to be elected as county councillors, municipal control of liquor traffic and international arbitration. They gave special emphasis to the call for trade union organization

---

[221] For an example of how women were supposed to influence their partners see *A labourer's views on Home Rule* (1886), a penny pamphlet in the Bishopsgate Institute Library.
[222] Walker, 'Party political women', 168; Pugh, *March of the women*, 133.
[223] Pugh, *March of the women*, 133.   [224] Walker, 'Party political women', 169.
[225] Pugh, *March of the women*, 133.
[226] The Countess of Aberdeen moving the Home Rule Resolution at the 1888 meeting of the Women's Liberal Federation, 6 Nov. 1888, in *The Women's Liberal Federation Annual Reports*, 1888, 123.

among working-class women, a demand whose urgency depended on the whole question of female oppression within the labour market. In particular, while 'a large number of women must maintain themselves . . . these, as a rule, are compelled to work very long hours for most inadequate pay', and this induced some of them to seek relief through the pursuit of 'vice' – '[prostitution] among women [being] caused by poverty due to the difficulty of earning a livelihood'.[227] Thus there emerged a feeling that Home Rule and women's political rights were the twin pillars of a new and inclusively democratic liberalism,[228] as humanitarianism was applied to social reform and the campaign against sweated labour.

The power of this mixture of moralism and politics was illustrated by the party's response to the sexual scandals involving Sir Charles Dilke and C. S. Parnell. When each was convicted of adultery – the former in 1886, the latter in 1890 – Liberal women felt they had a special responsibility to purify the party and '[uplift] the standards of morality in a way that never has been done before'.[229] Rejecting Parnell's leadership became tantamount to asserting a universal moral principle, namely that '[a] man with stained character . . . can never hold high public office in this country again'.[230] Women stood to gain from a campaign which took sexual purity as the standard, and the scandals both highlighted the extent to which the core values of feminine liberalism had wide currency within the party, especially its Nonconformist wing,[231] and fuelled Liberal women's self-confidence and assertiveness.

Over the following three years a new radicalism swept the WLF and transformed its leadership. Catherine Gladstone resigned from the office of president in 1893, as she felt unable to reconcile herself with the rising tide of suffragism. She was replaced, in turn, by two pro-suffragists: Lady Aberdeen and Lady Carlisle. Eventually the WLF split over the issue of women's political rights, with a minority anti-suffrage Women's National Liberal Association breaking away with 10,000 members and 5,060 branches, but leaving behind an even more militant WLF. The latter's

---

[227] Women's Liberal Association for Glasgow and The West of Scotland Conference of Delegates from Women's Liberal Associations, 20 Oct. 1890, SLA Papers, NLS, Acc. 11765/35.

[228] The Aberdare Women's Liberal Association to Mrs T. E. Ellis, 14 Apr. 1899, NLW, T. E. Ellis MSS, A. C. 3182; J. D. T., 'Women and politics', *Primitive Methodist Quarterly Review*, July 1886, 532–46; l.a., 'Women to the front!', *RN*, 22 Apr. 1888, 4.

[229] J. E. Ellis to T. E. Ellis, 22 Jan. 1891, in Ellis MSS. 5141. Similar feelings were expressed publicly in 'The Right Hon. W. E. Gladstone, MP', printed leaflet dated 6 Dec. 1890, from the Liberal Association of the Constituency of Midlothian, SLA Papers, NLS, Acc. 11765/35.

[230] J. E. Ellis to T. E. Ellis, 22 Jan. 1891, in Ellis MSS, 5141.

[231] Glaser, 'Parnell's fall and the Nonconformist conscience', 138.

commitment to the women's cause was apparently restrained only by their even more complete dedication to Home Rule. As Aberdeen wrote to Edward Blake, 'We represent some 80,000 women, the majority of whom are terribly in earnest.'[232]

Meanwhile feminine liberalism also tackled the sphere of social reform, showing an interest in the Poor Law system, with the demand for equal pay for officers, irrespective of sex differences.[233] Concern about equality in the workplace inspired the Scottish Women's Liberal Federation (SWLF) to campaign for causes ranging from equal access to university education to the reduction of shop assistants' working hours and the formation of trade unions for working women, which they advocated under the heading 'Home Rule apart from Politics'.[234] The SWLF was bound by its constitution not only '[t]o secure just and equal legislation and representation for women, especially with reference to the Parliamentary Franchise, and the removal of all legal disabilities on account of sex', but also 'to protect the interest of children'.[235] In England, the WLF supported such aims and also developed a new interest in collectivism and state intervention. Though their reformist attitude was shaped more by their practical experience in local government than collectivist theory, as Pugh has pointed out, '[t]hey were one of several movements leading the party towards the "New Liberalism" around the turn of the century'.[236] For the politics of humanitarianism was as applicable to social reform as it was to either the Irish question or international relations.

The Celtic fringe

In 1886 the Liberals in Scotland achieved their worst result since 1832, with the Tories securing ten seats and the Liberal Unionists seventeen. If these figures indicate the strength of Unionism north of the border – a subject which has attracted much scholarly attention in recent years[237] – we

---

[232] Ishbel Aberdeen to Edward Blake, 27 Mar. 1893, in Blake Papers, NLI, 4685; see also Rosalind Carlisle, President of he Women's Liberal Federation, to E. Blake, 31 Jan. 1897, in ibid., [1927] 4687. For the context see Pugh, *March of the women*, 135; C. Roberts, *The radical countess: the history of the life of Rosalind Countess of Carlisle* (1962), 117.

[233] Rep., 'Pontypridd Women's Liberal Association', 17 Feb. 1893, 6.

[234] Exec. C.ttee, 26 Jan. 1892, SWLF, Minute Book No. 1, 30–3, NLS, Acc. 11765/20; Literature Committee, 13 May 1891, 41, SWLF, Minute Book No. 1, ibid.

[235] Constitution and Rules of the Scottish Women's Liberal Federation, SLA Papers, 21, SWLF, Minute Book No. 1, 1891–5, 1–2, ibid.

[236] Pugh, *March of the Women*, 136.

[237] Hutchison, *A political history of Scotland*, 162ff. Cf. C. MacDonald (ed.), *Unionist Scotland, 1800–1997* (Edinburgh,1998) and C. Burness, *Strange associations: the Irish question and the making of Scottish Unionism, 1886–1918* (2003).

should not lose sight of the fact that they also show that two-thirds of the Scottish constituencies remained in Gladstonian hands. Cooke and Vincent have argued that this was achieved only because of the GOM's personal popularity and charisma,[238] while Hutchison has surmised that Unionism acquired considerable following even within radical Liberalism. On the other hand, Scottish Liberal Unionists were themselves in some ways 'nationalist'. Many of them opposed Home Rule partly because it was limited to Ireland, but would have been ready to contemplate devolution as part of a federal or 'Home Rule all round' programme.[239]

In any case, it is remarkable that right from the start the Scottish 'caucus' was ready to endorse Gladstone's proposal: in fact, the Scottish Liberal Association (SLA) took the lead, adopting Home Rule at the end of April, a week before the NLF took a similar decision.[240] Home Rule had its attractions for the SLA. In particular, it was perceived as implying a broad set of policies and principles affecting the rights and prospects of the rural poor (of which northern Scotland had its share). Coercion was 'revolutionary in character ... and ... subversive of any real union between Great Britain and Ireland', because it manipulated the law and was 'directed against political opinion in the interests of a dominant minority'.[241] In this respect it was 'a menace to the rights and liberties of a free people' and 'destructive of any real union between Great Britain and Ireland': 'it declares to be criminal what has hitherto been regarded as a lawful and fundamental civil right; and ... it deprives the Irish people of vital constitutional safeguards against the despotic abuse of criminal law'.[242]

These views were further strengthened by the report of the SLA committee which visited Ireland in 1887 – one of the many Liberal 'fact-finding missions' on the effects of coercion.[243] En route to Dublin from Belfast, the Scottish delegates were met at the main stations by 'crowds' and presented with welcome addresses. In Dublin they 'were received by

---

[238] Cooke and Vincent, *Governing passion*, 435–6.
[239] E. A. Cameron, *The life and times of Fraser Mackintosh Crofter MP* (2000), 165–7.
[240] Barker, *Gladstone and radicalism*, 107.
[241] Meeting of General Council, SLA, 20 Apr. 1887, 30, NLS, Acc. 11765/4.
[242] The Scottish Liberal Association, National Conference of Liberal Associations in the Waterloo Room, Glasgow, 3 June 1887, resolution proposed by T. C. Hedderwick, South Lanarkshire, seconded by R. Cunninghame-Graham, MP, West Perthshire (vol. XL, SLA Meeting and Conference Agendas 1885–91), NLS, Acc. 11765/35. Cunninghame-Graham was involved in the Trafalgar Square riots of November 1887, when he was arrested by the police (Rep., 'Serious riots in London', *RN*, 20 Nov. 1887, 6).
[243] Heyck, *Dimensions*, 191–5; cf. G. Shaw Lefevre, *Incidents of coercion: a journal of visits to Ireland in 1882 and 1888* (1889); Shaw Lefevre, *Mr John Morley, MP, in Tipperary. Why he went and what he saw* (1890).

the lord Mayor, the leaders of the Nationalist party, and a prodigious concourse of people, who conveyed them, with bands of music and much cheering, to the Imperial Hotel, Sackville Street'.[244] Over the following days the delegation met with similarly enthusiastic receptions and large meetings in Mitchelstown, Cork and Limerick.[245] They were impressed. On returning to Scotland, they produced a report which described the National League as 'a lawful and orderly combination of the people for mutual defence', one which 'invariably exercises its powerful influence for the maintenance of social order and the suppression of violence and crime'. The League was a truly 'national' organization, with 'branches everywhere, [and] includ[ed] in its membership the best men of each district, and usually the Priest of the Parish'. Even more important was what the report said about the politics of the National League: '[this] great national organisation ... virtually [carries] into practice the great Liberal principle of "Government by the people for the people"'. Both its methods and its programme were deemed to be consistent with Gladstonian Liberalism: 'It has taught the people that moral influences, directed within constitutional limits, are the most powerful instruments of defence against agrarian injustice and oppression – the root cause, as everyone knows, of Ireland's miseries.'[246] 'The deputies had opportunities of examining the operation of the Plan of Campaign' which was 'another organisation for mutual defence, but not associated with the National League'. They were impressed with 'the absolute necessity of some such method of defence, if the tenantry on rackrented estates were to be saved from ruin and dispersion at the hands of semi-bankrupt landlords'. The aim of government coercion was 'the suppression of all such combinations in the interest of the landowning class and of the holders of land bonds ... the position amounts to nothing short of civil war in Ireland'. Yet, '[t]he National League opposes a fierce defiance to the Coercion raids of Dublin Castle, and counsels the people to maintain stolid resistance and patient endurance of consequences, be these what they may'.[247] As for the Catholic clergy, the Presbyterian Scots took a remarkably generous view of their social and political role:

Being constitutionally Conservative, they [the priests] refrained, as a body, from helping actively the development of the National League, until the progress of events made it expedient and necessary in the interest of their country that they

---

[244] Report of deputies commissioned to visit Ireland by the Executive of the Scottish Liberal Association, 16 Nov. 1887 (these were G. Beith, C.J. Kerr, JP, J. MacPherson, H. Smith and Angus Sutherland, the crafters' MP), 1, in NLS, Acc. 11765/35.
[245] Ibid., 3.   [246] Ibid., 3–4.   [247] Ibid.

should do so. Their great influence is invariably exercised in the interest of social order, and the suppression of crime. They manifest a marked anxiety as to the pernicious effect of Government by coercion, and maintain that Mr Gladstone's Home Rule policy can alone bring peace and prosperity. The deputies were much impressed with the culture and superiority of the Clergymen with whom they came in contact, and they cannot speak too highly of the hospitality and kindness which they experienced at their hands.[248]

Moreover, the deputies were sanguine about Ireland's material prospects under Home Rule. The latter would also lead to economic and demographic growth, with ever closer links with Britain and the rest of the empire, because, in contrast to Unionist talk about the commercial rivalry which might plague the relationship between Dublin and London, quite accurately they pointed out that 'England would be the nearest and almost the only outlet for her [Ireland's] produce, and the British Empire the great field for her enterprising sons.' They considered it 'a moral certainty' that under Home Rule the Union 'would rest on the sure basis of mutual interest . . . and would be clung to by the Irish people as an element vital to their prosperity and their very existence as a nation'.[249]

MacKnight, the great Ulster chronicler, commented that 'those political tourists . . . [saw] what they wish[ed] to see, and they endeavour[ed] to see nothing else'.[250] However, it is also true both that they managed to look at the situation from the Nationalist point of view and that their enthusiasm for Home Rule was genuine. Indeed, so persuaded were they about its potential beneficial effect, that they advocated its extension to both Scotland and Wales. Their report further strengthened the pre-existing devolutionist tendency among Scottish Liberals. For, although Hutchison has argued that the party adopted devolution only in 1888, the SLA passed resolutions demanding Home Rule for *both* Ireland and Scotland as early as June 1887.[251] In October, they argued that the urgency of applying Home Rule to all component parts of the United Kingdom, 'and especially to Scotland', derived from the fact that 'questions closely touching the welfare of the people, and long ripe for settlement, are from year to year superseded by the dominating influence of

---

[248] Ibid., 5. For similar praises for Irish Catholic priests and their social influence see report of the Leeds Deputation in 'Politics', *Primitive Methodist Quarterly Review*, Oct. 1890, 755.

[249] Report of deputies commissioned to visit Ireland by the Executive of the Scottish Liberal Association, 5–6.

[250] MacKnight, *Ulster as it is*, 215.

[251] SLA, National Conference of Liberal Associations, 3 June 1887, resolutions III and V, NLS, Acc. 11765/35. Cf. Hutchison, *Political history of Scotland*.

English interests and opinions in the Imperial Parliament'.[252] The
Scottish revivalist Professor J. Stuart Blackie supported Scottish devolution for three sets of reasons, which he described as 'Utilitarian' (in the
sense of better government), 'Patriotic' (in the sense of Scottish national
pride) and 'Imperial', affirming his belief that 'the strength of Britain lies
not in the overgrowth of a monstrous centralisation in the English section
of the empire, but in the harmonious balance of a well-calculated strength
in all the separate social units of which the empire is composed'.[253]

Hutchison has claimed that, in contrast to the NLF, the SLA was never
controlled by the radicals. However, as we have already seen, the SLA did
espouse Home Rule for Scotland at an early stage: this was in fact quite a
'radical' step, and its political significance was emphasized by the fact that
the caucus also adopted a series of other reform proposals generally
associated with radicalism. These included a Liquor Traffic Local Veto
Bill and the drastic democratization of the electoral and franchise system,
'excluding University representation . . . embodying the principle of "one-
man-one-vote" and reducing the period of residence required to obtain
that vote' in order to procure 'the true representation of all classes in the
Imperial Parliament'.[254] Moreover, the SLA demanded the payment
of Members of Parliament 'out of the Imperial Exchequer' and that of
'the returning officers' expenses out of the local rates'.[255]

The debate on social policies was often initiated by local branches. At
the beginning of 1889 the Ross and Cromarty Liberal Association promoted a reform of the Crofters' Act, demanding the extension of its
provisions to all tenants 'paying an annual rent of not more than £50',
the enlargement of the crofters' existing holdings and the creation of new
ones by the Crofters' Commission. They further requested '[that] the
people be directly represented on [that body] by qualified assessors
chosen by the people themselves', that financial aid be provided for the
erection of new buildings and 'stocking new and enlarged holdings' and,
finally, '[that] in order to develop the national resources of the Highlands,
and to relieve immediate wants of certain sections of the people, harbour,

---

[252] Resolution adopted at a District Conference of Liberal Associations, 20 Oct. 1887,
NLS, Acc. 11765/35. Over the next few years this remained standard argument for
Scottish devolution: cf. l.a., *The Scottish Highlander*, 8 Oct. 1891, 4.

[253] Blackie, *Home Rule and political parties in Scotland. A review* (1889), 11.

[254] Resolution IV, adopted at a District Conference of Liberal Associations, 20 Oct. 1887,
NLS, Acc. 11765/35.

[255] From the Glasgow Junior Liberal Association, Resolutions Adopted at a District
Conference of Liberal Associations, 20 Oct. 1887, ibid. See also Resolutions adopted
at a National Conference, res. 3, Edinburgh 9 May 1888, in ibid.

roads, railways, and other works of public utility be commenced by the Government without unnecessary delay'.[256]

From 1889 the SLA programme included an Eight-Hour Bill for the miners, the compulsory sale of land 'for the erection of public buildings and dwelling houses in the immediate vicinity of towns', allotments for the agricultural labourers and an increase in smallholdings, complete religious equality through church disestablishment, free education, reform of registration, payment of MPs and triennial parliaments. In 1889 the Scottish caucus 'initiated a movement to secure Free Education for Scotland out of the Probate Duty' through door-to-door canvassing with pamphlets.[257]

As it happened, English hostility to 'landlordism', which years of public discussion and exposure by government commissions had identified as the root cause of the social question in both Ireland and the Highlands, was rekindled by Unionist plans to buy off the Irish landowners.[258] Land purchase was cited as a further argument for Scottish Home Rule, because the SLA claimed that, if such a buying-up occurred, Scotland would be made to pay heavier taxes in order to redress centuries of English misgovernment in Ireland, thus compounding the existing disadvantages of the already intrinsically inequitable fiscal arrangement under the unreformed Union.[259]

For the SLA Home Rule was part of a programme for the federal reconstruction of the United Kingdom,[260] a cause pursued with particular energy by the Scottish Home Rule Association (SHRA). In 1892 its secretary, James Reith, proposed to the Irish Nationalist leader, Edward Blake, the formation of a 'Joint Parliamentary Party of the Representation of Scotland, Ireland and Wales', to demand 'Home Rule all round' as the only just solution to the Home Rule question.[261] Several of Blake's other Scottish and English correspondents strongly supported such a

---

[256] Resolution received from Mr G. G. Macleod, President, Ross and Cromarty Liberal Association, in Materials for the preparation of the Annual Meeting of General Council, Edinburgh, 19 Feb. 1889, vol. XL, SLA Meeting and Conference Agendas 1885–91, Acc. 11765/35.

[257] Circular to Secretaries of Liberal Associations in connection with the distribution of Free Education Pamphlets, Manuscript circular signed A. Macdougall, 29 Mar. 1889, XL, National Conference Programme, 22 Nov. 1889, in Acc. 11765/35, NLS.

[258] The Scottish Liberal Association, Conference of the Western Associations, Glasgow, 4 June 1890, ibid.

[259] Scottish Home Rule Association, 11 Sep. 1890, SLA Meeting and Conference Agendas 1885–91, ibid.

[260] Resolutions Adopted at a National Conference, Glasgow, 22 Nov. 1889, vol. XL, SLA Meeting and Conference Agendas 1885–91; see also District Conference of Liberal Associations, Kilmarnock, 6 Nov. 1890, ibid.

[261] J. Reith to E. Blake, 9 Aug. 1892, in NLI, Blake Letters, [221] 4684. Enclosed with the letter Reith sent an 'Outline of a Federal Union League for the British Empire'.

solution,[262] which was also advocated by some Scottish Liberal Unionists (hence the SHRA's claim that 'all parties' in Scotland endorsed the cause).[263] Although Blake himself agreed, his Irish colleagues were not prepared to throw their lot in with the British federalists.[264] As C. P. Scott of the *Manchester Guardian* wrote to Blake in 1895, there was widespread concern that an effect of any attempt 'to grant Home Rule to Ireland as part of a measure for granting it to England, Scotland & Wales w[oul]d be to postpone it to the Greek Kalendas'. Scott concluded: 'you appear to think that a general scheme might be advanced and yet the partial scheme alone passed. I think this w[oul]d be excessively dangerous', indeed '[it] would be folly ... to make Home Rule for Ireland in any degree contingent on a larger scheme. No doubt both in Scotland & in Wales there is need for some considerable measure of devolution of legislative powers, but their need is a different & a smaller one than that of Ireland and it w[oul]d be well to keep it entirely distinct.' For, whatever the new party leader Lord Rosebery thought of federal schemes, Scott concluded, 'I am certain that in England, which makes up so very much of the greater part of the whole, there is no desire or demand for anything of the kind.'[265]

There were good reasons for being cautious. Different and sometimes contrasting radical agendas came under the general umbrella of 'Home Rule all round', which many radicals associated with church disestablishment. The latter meant different things to different people. While in Wales disestablishment was part of a *nationalist* platform which culminated in the demand for Home Rule for Wales,[266] in England it was a

---

[262] See E. L. Gales (Frome Division, Bath), 30 Aug. 1892, NLI, Blake Letters, [274] 4684; J. Milne Watts (Glasgow) to E. Blake, 9 Aug. 1892, ibid., [222] 4684, and H. French (Taunton) to E. Blake, 10 Aug. 1892, ibid., [228] 4684. Cf. J. M.[orrison] D.[avidson], 'The Book of Erin', *RN*, 6 May 1888, 5. The views of Morrison Davidson are further discussed in chapter 6, 287–91.

[263] Printed circular dated 15 Oct. 1890, addressed to the Secretary of the Liberal Association, conveying the resolution of the 3rd Annual Conference of the Scottish Home Rule Association (which had taken place on 24 Sep. 1890). Signed: John S. Blackie, Chairman, John Romans, Vice-Chairman (one of the conveners of Gladstone's Midlothian Committee), Ch. Weddie, Hon. Sec., Th. McNaught, Hon. Sec., W. Mitchell, Hon. Treasurer, Scottish Home Rule Association, NLS, Acc. 11765, 35; printed letter/leaflet signed Ch. Waddie, addressed to The Secretary of the Liberal Association, dated 13 Nov. 1890, NLS, Acc. 11735.

[264] E. Blake to Sir J. Leng, MP for Dundee, 26 Jan. 1896, in NLI, Blake Letters [1644] 4687. Blake believed that 'a great general policy [to be taken up along with Irish Home Rule] ... has the incidental merits of minimizing the evils of the Lords, & removing the difficulties inherent in the scheme of partial Home Rule now before the Country'.

[265] C. P. Scott to E. Blake, 28 Jan. 1895, in NLI, Blake Letters, [1647], 4687.

[266] Andrew Reid to T. Gee, 8 Feb. 1890, NLW, T. Gee MSS, 8308D, 250; I. Dorricott, 'Disestablishment in Wales and Monmouthshire', *Primitive Methodist Quarterly Review*, Apr. 1887, 307–16. Cf. D. W. Bebbington, 'Religion and national feeling in nineteenth-century Wales and Scotland', in S. Mews (ed.), *Religion and national identity* (1982), 489–503.

democratic proposal to replace the traditional hierarchical relationship between church and society with an American-style 'free market' within which all religious groups would compete for converts.[267] Finally, for the Scots disestablishment was a controversial *ecclesiastical* issue, not only dividing the Church from the Dissenters, but also splitting the latter between those who wanted separation between church and state and the supporters of a reformed but established Presbyterianism.

The issue was further complicated by the overlap between ecclesiastical and class divides in the Highlands, where the Land League regarded the established church as the crofters' enemy, an organization which 'supported the lairds and was the bulwark of landlordism and the refuge of Toryism'.[268] *The Scottish Highlander*, 'the poor crofter's paper', was particularly scathing about the economic cost of the established church and what it dismissed as 'state Christians'.[269] The clearances and Disruption were defining episodes for the culture and class identity of many of its readers. While at the time the Highland Free Church enjoyed a reputation of social and political radicalism – 'those Fenians of ours', according to an embittered churchman[270] – the 'state church' was perceived as a class institution. One Dissenter asked rhetorically: what did the Kirk do during the Highland clearances, when the crofters, 'as well-behaved and God-fearing a class of men as ever the world looked upon', were forced to abandon their holdings? 'Dumb dogs every one of them; or if they did speak, it was in favour of the landlords.' Again the established church did not show any sympathy for the Highlanders at the time of the Great Disruption, 'when, in 1843, the people and their ministers had to forsake churches and manses for loyalty to their Master . . . Had they been loyal too, we know the issue might have been very different then.'[271]

[267] G. Howell, Letter Book, Spring 1878, in Howell Collection, IX; 'The Church and the Working Classes', Durham Miners' Association, *Monthly Report*, no. 44, Jan. 1884, pp. 4–6, in Durham Co. Record Office, D/DMA 7.

[268] Councillor Gunn (Inverness) in report, 'The Lentran oppression case', *The Scottish Highlander*, 17 Sep. 1891, 6.

[269] L.a., 'State Christians in the Highlands and what they cost', *The Scottish Highlander*, 26 Feb. 1891, 4; the definition of the newspaper as 'the poor crofter's paper, without subsidy or aid from landlords', appears in a letter signed 'The Highlands First', ibid., 19 Mar. 1891, 3.

[270] Devine and others have claimed that, over the issue of the clearances, the Free Church was actually as supine and pro-landlord as the established church, a view which has been recently subjected to substantial revisionism: A. W. MacColl, *Land, faith and the crofting community: Christianity and social criticism in the Highlands of Scotland, 1843–1893* (2006), 19–57.

[271] Free Churchman, 'The state church in the Highlands', *The Scottish Highlander*, 5 Mar. 1891, 5.

However, as already indicated above, the Free Church as a whole had long been divided over the issue. Some, led by the Highland minister John Kennedy, accepted that the existing connection between church and state was unscriptural, but were adamant that the confessional principles of historic Presbyterianism 'bound [the Free Church] to seek, not the annihilation of that connection, but its rectification'.[272] Non-ministerial, non-party political lobbies such as the Laymen's League also articulated opposition towards the disestablishment and secularization of the endowments of the Church of Scotland. The League promoted the reunion of all the Scottish Presbyterians but wanted to reform and so preserve the principle of the establishment as the embodiment of Scottish national identity. They insisted that 'from time immemorial the Scottish People have maintained the principle that Religion should be recognised by the State', and that the church was now under threat from 'the British Parliament, contrary to the wishes of the people of Scotland'.[273]

Not surprisingly, some Welsh Liberals suspected that '[there] is no *urgency* whatever in the Scotch grievance. There is no *national* movement behind it. There is much *religious* sentiment against the notion of secularization of religious endowment. There is substantial division in Scotch *Liberal* ranks.'[274] In fact, they feared that the campaign for Scottish disestablishment would delay, rather than help, the cause of Wales, in particular because 'Mr Gladstone has been from the first a little playfully perverse on this point': being a Scottish MP, he claimed special interest in the disestablishment of the Church of Scotland, but used this to stop Welsh disestablishment.[275] By the same token, they were eager to avoid any involvement with the movement against the Church of England, insisting that disestablishment should be pursued as 'a Welsh question pure and simple', rather than 'the thin end of the wedge of the Liberation Society'.[276] Wales should fight as Wales, seeking all the allies it could find, but always insisting that the church question was a national, not an ecclesiastical issue.

---

[272] A. Auld, *Life of John Kennedy, DD.* (1887; 1997), 106–7; see also the 'Petition', ibid., 151–3.

[273] Laymen's League, leaflet, n.d. [*c*.1890], SLA Papers, NLS, Acc. 11765/35.

[274] Stuart Rendel to T. Gee, 30 Oct. 1892, in NLW, T. Gee MS 8308D, 274a (emphasis in the original).

[275] Ibid. For Gladstone's attitude 'from the first' see W. E. Gladstone to T. E. Ellis, 2 July 1890, in NLW, T. E. Ellis MSS, 8306D, 92a, in which the Liberal leader refused either to commit himself to disestablishment in Scotland and Wales, or to say which of the two should be dealt with first.

[276] Stuart Rendel to T. Gee, 16 Mar. 1889, in NLW, T. Gee MS, 8308 D, 257; see also S. Kendall to T. Gee, 18 Mar. 1889, ibid., 258.

In this respect the Principality was supposed to be more similar to Ireland than to either England or Scotland, particularly because its Episcopal Establishment, like the Church of Ireland before 1869, was perceived not just as unscriptural, but also as an 'alien' institution symbolizing the English conquest.[277] Disestablishment was thus 'a measure designed not alone to remove religious inequality, but to initiate a scheme of social reconstruction and to secure the effective recognition of Welsh nationality'.[278] Further affinities between the two 'Celtic' nations included the people's attachment to both the soil and the ideal of a national farming community, the problem of rural poverty and the desire to revive the national language.[279] In both countries agriculture was dominated by a large number of small tenants with comparatively few farm workers. Such a situation encouraged contacts and co-operation between Welsh and Irish land agitators and led to the formation of a Welsh Land League at the end of 1886 under the leadership of the fierce Nonconformist preacher Thomas Gee of Denbigh, the publisher of the intensely political *Baner ac Amserau Cymru*.[280]

In Wales as much as in Ireland the social divide between farmers and landlords coincided with a contested religious frontier, to the extent that it was difficult to say which of the two problems was more important in sustaining the Welsh 'Tithe War' of 1886–91 – land hunger or sectarian animosity. Rural unrest reached Irish levels of intensity.[281] The extensive evidence collected by the Revd Robert Lewis – himself involved in the 'war' as a church bailiff – vividly conveys the strength of the resistance, the role played by women and how resistance was encouraged by some Nonconformist ministers (to the dismay of many of their colleagues), some of whom took upon themselves the role of national liberators (one

---

[277] Notes for speeches in the Ellis papers, suggesting parallels between the Welsh, Irish and Italian national movements, in which he compared the Anglican Bishop of St Asaph to Prince Metternich (the architect of Austrian rule in Italy between 1815–48): 'Notes on decentralization', n.d., NLW, T. E. Ellis MSS, 3022.

[278] From T. E. Ellis' 1895 electoral manifesto, in NLW, Ellis MSS, 2963.

[279] See NLW, T. E. Ellis MSS, 4647, containing notes on the similarities between Ireland and Wales, based on quotations from political speeches by contemporary politicians; and 'Some considerations affecting the home language of the Cymry', Notes, n.d., in ibid., 3022.

[280] M. Davitt to W. J. Parry, 28 Dec. 1885, in NLW, W. J. Parry MSS, 8823 C, 5–5(d); and M. Davitt to W. J. Parry, 7 Jan. 1886, in ibid., 7: 'Mr O'Brien has promised to me to speak to Mr Parnell and advise him to send one or two prominent members of his party to address the projected meeting at Caernarvon.' For the Land League see K. O. Morgan, *Rebirth of a nation: Wales, 1880–1980* (1982), 38–9, 50.

[281] E. G. Griffith to T. E. Ellis, 11 Oct. 1886, in NLW, T. E. Ellis MSS, 8306D, 94a.

of them was aptly named Garibaldi Thomas).[282] The government found it necessary to provide bailiffs with strong police and military escort, often amounting to hundreds of men. As columns of constables and soldiers paraded throughout rural Wales, incidents were frequent and sometimes serious. Even when none occurred, the deployment of the military 'was felt as an insult to our humanity, loyalty and Christianity'.[283]

In both Ireland and Wales there was a close alliance between national and land reform movement and the locally predominant religious denominations, the National League with rural Catholicism and Cymru Fydd/the Welsh Liberals with Dissent.[284] This came with comparable class/political cleavages: if the Irish gentry dreaded the Nationalist farmers, in Wales rich landowners had the reputation of 'hat[ing] small freeholders' because the latter 'voted Liberal'.[285] Even in the sphere of education – often the main cause of the 'disunity of hearts' within the Home Rule camp – the differences between Welsh and Irish nationalists actually reflected a common pattern, namely the close alliance enjoyed by each movement with its national religious culture, which demanded, respectively, secular and denominational schooling. While in Wales the education problem was largely solved from 1870 onwards through the operation of the school board system,[286] in the late 1880s the clash over the tithes indicated the need for further reform. As Ellis wrote in 1889, '[it] is humiliating for us to be ruled in Wales by Home Secretary Matthews and Major Bassett Lewis. I can understand why Irishmen denounce their Castle rulers as brutal and mean. I often feel I should like some good thumping, reeling blow dealt at the tithe system and police brutality.'[287]

Such perceived affinities help us to understand why Welsh caucuses were solidly on the side of Irish Home Rule from 1886, despite the fact that until 1885 Chamberlain had been very popular in Wales, where he was identified with disestablishment, drink control, education and land reform.[288] Pressure from constituency parties soon forced the few

---

[282] Revd R. Lewis, 'Reminiscences of the Tithe War in West Wales', NLW, MS 15321 D. Cf. K. O. Morgan, *Wales in British politics, 1868–1922* (1980), 84–94 and J. Davies, *A History of Wales* (1994), 452–3.

[283] R. Morris from Pentre to T. E. Ellis, 19 Aug. 1893, in NLW, T. E. Ellis MSS, 1524.

[284] For an example see Resolution enclosed with Amlwch Reform Club to T. E. Ellis, 9 Mar. 1894, in NLW, T. E. Ellis MSS, 63.

[285] W. P. Davies, a smallholder, in a letter to his MP, T. E. Ellis, 23 Feb. 1892, in NLW, T. E. Ellis Papers, 313.

[286] T. M. Bassett, *The Welsh Baptists* (1977), 327; cf. Biagini, *Liberty*, chapter 3.

[287] T. E. Ellis to Mr Gibson, n.d. [1889], in NLW, Ellis MSS, 2755, Letter Book, 22. Major Bassett Lewis was chief Constable of Cardiganshire (15321 D, ibid.).

[288] Stuart Rendel's notes from interviews with local Liberal party activists in Feb. 1886 indicate substantial support for Home Rule, which was expected to give the Irish the

remaining Chamberlainite Radicals – including the young Lloyd George – to forsake Unionism.[289] In fact from an early stage some resented Gladstone's unwillingness to treat Wales 'in the spirit of the proposed Irish legislation',[290] which would involve 'freeing' the country from the constraints of Westminster politics and granting it an assembly to deal with purely Welsh matters according to Welsh ideas. When a motion along these lines was put to a meeting of two thousand dock workers in Cardiff, in July 1886, it was carried with only four dissentient voices.[291] Thus the Welsh did not so much complain about past oppression under the Union, as focus on the future: theirs was 'a much less romantic and much more prosaic standpoint [than the Irish]' for, as they put it, 'we do not feel so much that we are writhing under a wrong done to us 180 years ago; we feel rather that we are suffering from a disability at this very moment'.[292]

For Tom Ellis – a farmer's son, the rising star of Welsh Liberalism and 'the Parnell of Wales' – 'the Irish question [was] so huge, fierce, volcanic that it fills the public mind to the exception of all other topics … so comprehensive that in fighting on its various issues we fight on principles which will have application far and outside Ireland, and not the least [in] Wales'.[293] He regarded Home Rule as by 'far the noblest effort of modern Liberalism. It is the touchstone of Liberalism. I believe in Home Rule for its intrinsic value to a nation and to the sum total of human good.'[294] In both countries Home Rule was 'a policy of prudence for labour … a policy of hope, of promise, of growth'.[295] It was not only a device for

power to solve their internal difficulties: interviews with J. Hamer Jones, 15 Feb. 1886, and with D. Jones, 15 Feb. 1886, both in Stuart Rendel MSS, 19448, VII 1. For further examples see the reports 'East Glamorgan Liberal Three Hundred', *Pontypridd Chronicle*, 23 Apr. 1886, 3, and 'Meeting of Swansea Liberals', *Cardiff Times & South Wales Weekly News*, 12 June 1886, 2.

[289] Graham Jones, 'Welsh experience, 1886', 450, 465–70; R. Price, 'Lloyd George and Merioneth politics, 1885, 1886 – a failure to effect a breakthrough', *Journal of Merioneth History and Record Society*, 8 (1975), 301–3.

[290] Dr I. Davies to A. J. Williams MP, 6 June 1886, in Ellis Papers, 4007.

[291] Rep., 'Sir E. J. Reed at the docks', *Cardiff Times & South Wales Weekly News*, 3 July 1886, 3.

[292] J. W. Crombie speaking at the 'Conference with the Aberdeen Liberal Association', in rep., 'Scottish Home Rule Conference at Aberdeen', *The Scottish Highlander*, 1 Oct. 1891, 5. For further examples see the reports 'Meeting of the South Glamorgan Liberal 300', *Cardiff Times & South Wales Weekly News*, 19 June 1886, 3; 'Mr W. Abraham, MP, at Mountain Ash', ibid., 9 Oct. 1886, 3; 'Cymry Fydd: the South Wales Liberal Federation: annual meeting at Swansea', ibid., 22 Feb. 1889; and Abraham's article 'Home Rule for Wales', ibid., 9 Feb. 1889, 1.

[293] T. E. Ellis to Gibson, Letter Book, 22, 3 Apr. 1889, in Ellis Papers, 2755. For Ellis as 'the Parnell of Wales' see rep., 'National demonstration at Navan', *FJ*, 2 Nov. 1888, 5.

[294] Notebook, n.d. [1893–4], in Ellis Papers, 3019.

[295] Notebook on Switzerland, n.d., Ellis Papers, 4375.

national self-determination, but also a Liberal safeguard against the evils
of centralized government and a step towards federalism, which he
regarded as a superior constitutional system.

As a student at Oxford Ellis had been influenced by Arnold Toynbee's
critique of the evils of unlimited competition and laissez-faire as well as by
J. S. Mill's claim that the distribution of wealth offered ample scope for
state intervention and 'socialist' experiments.[296] He argued that '[the]
first duty of a State is to see that every child born therein shall be well
housed, clothed, fed and educated, till he attains the years of discretion'.
His vision of nationalism was deeply religious – the political translation
of the Methodist revival, – and he wanted to see *'all denominations'*
involved in '[the] nation making its own way to truth and light and self-
reliance'.[297] A Mazzini enthusiast and admirer of the *Risorgimento*, he
shared the Italian patriot's vision that citizenship should entail both social
and political rights and that it should be religiously inspired. Like Davitt,
he was a supporter of women's rights and of the kind of social nationalism
inspired by both Ruskin and Walt Whitman.[298] Ellis championed an ideal
of nationality which included a linguistic, literary, artistic and academic
revival. One of his models was Switzerland, 'the sacred home of republican freedom', with twenty-three cantons 'each sovereign', where '[the]
advocate of parish councils finds the strength of his argument in the
working of the Commune'.[299] Another was the Tyrol, whose size and
population were smaller, though comparable to those of Wales. In the
Tyrol a 'Home Rule' parliament had 'an unbroken history of over 500
years' during which it had been 'the centre of their national life'. 'Its land
system has been modified to suit the necessities of its people. Of the tillers
of the soil 100,000 are freeholders and 10,000 tenants. The Tyrolese have
had native bishops and priests. They have had their University, their
National Museum, and a native School of Art.' As a result, they had
always been very loyal to Austria.[300] His dream was a nation of independent farmers, one of the many ideals which he shared with the Irish
nationalists.

---

[296] Notes on Political Economy, Oxford 1882–4 ('Lectures on politico-economical questions, by Arnold Toynbee'), Ellis Papers, 3193.
[297] T. Ellis Papers, 3019 (emphasis in the original).
[298] Aberdare Women's Liberal Association to Mrs T. E. Ellis, 15 Apr. 1899, in Ellis Papers,
AC 3182.
[299] Notebook on Switzerland, Tyrol and Home Rule for Wales, n.d. [but 1893] in Ellis
Papers, 4375.
[300] Notebook on Switzerland.

3   Constitutional Nationalism and popular liberalism in Ireland

I am not sure at all that the Parnellites elected next Autumn will hang together. The Labourers won't pull with them and though these are a weak body in Ireland they may be enough to form a New party in alliance with Landlords of a Liberal type.[1]

When, said Mr Parnell, it was conceded to us as one of the principles of the Irish Party that it was the right of the Irish people to be governed by the people, for the people and in accordance with the will of the majority of the people, we gladly recognised that that was our principle, and 'upon that principle we cordially shake hands with you, and we wish long life to the Liberal Party in their career of self-Government for Ireland, and justice to the English people'.[2]

The roots of Irish 'popular liberalism'

'Legislative and administrative decentralization is one Irish idea', *Reynolds's* commented in 1888, 'and the abolition of landlordism is another. We cannot advocate them as beneficial to Ireland without feeling that they have the strongest significance for ourselves.' 'Indeed,' it concluded, 'it is not the British Democracy that is absorbing the Irish – it is the Irish that is absorbing the British.'[3] Few scholars would be prepared to endorse such a view, but many would admit that there were at least parallels between constitutional nationalism and British radicalism.[4] The question is whether such parallels depended merely on temporary alliances between individual leaders, or whether they reflected ideological affinities more widely shared by the rank and file as well. As already

---

[1] Lord Spencer to Lord Lansdowne, 16 Aug. 1885, in P. Gordon (ed.), *The Red Earl: the papers of the Fifth Earl Spencer, 1835–1910*, vol. II (1986), 73.
[2] L.a., *FJ*, 21 July 1887, 4, summarizing Parnell's speech at the banquet held in honour of the Irish party at the National Liberal Club.
[3] L.a., 'Senators in harness', *RN*, 19 Feb. 1888, 1.
[4] Heyck, *Dimension*, 18–21; Brady, *T. P. O'Connor*, 54–6, 69–71.

indicated (pp. 28–30) my argument here is that the relationship between the two movements was characterized, if not by 'absorption', certainly by cross-fertilization and by a common emphasis on both democracy and constitutional liberty.

Some agrarian radicals were obviously very close to their British colleagues. The chief inspirer of the Land League and the greatest hero of popular nationalism – Michael Davitt – was basically a social radical in the Tom Paine tradition, a crusader against 'feudalism'.[5] Contemporary biographies stressed his commitment to the establishment of peasant proprietorship, the '[e]xclusion of all sectarian issues from the [Nationalist] platform' and the '[a]dvocacy of all struggling nationalities in the British Empire and elsewhere'.[6] Following in the footsteps of many British land reformers, in 1880 he visited France and Belgium to collect firsthand evidence about yeoman farming in those countries, which J. S. Mill and others had upheld as models of land tenure.[7] In prison in 1881–2, Davitt had the opportunity of reading extensively. Besides Henry George, he devoted his attention almost exclusively to French, British and Irish Liberal historians and social scientists: Thiers, Thierry, Guizot, Macaulay, Lecky, Herbert Spencer, Thorold Rogers, Émile de Laveleye, Joseph Kay (about free trade in land) and especially John Stuart Mill.[8] His views were reflected in Land League publications and rhetoric, which cited Herbert Spencer, Henry Fawcett and even Bonamy Price in support of subversive land reform.[9] Both Mill and other liberal thinkers – in particular the Prussian von Hardenberg – were important influences on other Land League agitators, such as T. Brennan.[10]

Moreover, with the mass of Irish Nationalists Davitt shared a commitment to temperance, artisan education,[11] self-help and the individualist virtues of the independent farmer. Here, again, there was common ground between British and Irish radicals. All held that the golden rule

---

[5] See his speech in the report of the Land Law Reform meeting at St James's Hall in February 1880 and the speeches delivered by A. Besant and C. Bradlaugh, in *The National Reformer*, 22 Feb. 1880, 114–16; and newscutting from *DN*, 28 Feb. 1882, in J. Chamberlain Papers, B253; cf. Davitt, *The fall of feudalism*.

[6] Cashman, *Michael Davitt*, 72.

[7] T. W. Moody, *Davitt and the Irish revolution, 1846–82* (1981), 509–12, 515; Cashman, *Michael Davitt*, 219; cf. L. Kennedy, 'The economic thought of the nation's lost leader: Charles Stewart Parnell', in Boyce and O'Day, *Parnell in Perspective*, 174.

[8] Moody, *Davitt*, 504; M. Davitt, *Leaves from a prison diary* (1885; 1972), 105–12; Davitt, *Fall of feudalism*, 161.

[9] Moody, *Davitt*, 522–8. National League Poster in Hefferman Papers, NAI, MS 21,910. The Spencer text was *Social Statics*, chapter 9, section 2; Bonamy Price was cited on rent, and Henry Fawcett on freedom of contract.

[10] Davitt, *Fall of feudalism*, 410.

[11] Rep., 'Mr Davitt and Mr Healy, MP, on social reform', *FJ*, 11 Oct. 1882, 3.

of good government was its cheapness, and accepted the Gladstonian 'moral duty' of meeting deficits with adequate revenue.[12] All were fiercely critical of the National Debt as well as 'over-taxation' – which the British perceived as a consequence of 'class legislation', and the Irish in terms of national oppression.[13] Both identified the cause of these financial and fiscal evils with that old bogey of all radicals, the 'Norman yoke' and the iniquitous effects of 'baronial' primogeniture.[14] The abolition of 'land-lordism' was going to be the first step towards the building of a fairer society for the man who worked for his living; it would usher in peasant proprietorship, the ultimate utopia of self-help economics. In Oliver MacDonagh's words, the Irish small farmer emerged as 'the final convert and devotee of Political Economy'.[15]

Thus, though the Nationalist agrarian programme implied an unprecedented degree of state interference with property rights, such intervention was not perceived as a first step towards a new 'socialist' philosophy of government. Rather, it was 'intervention to end all intervention' – a mere 'exception' to the otherwise staunchly upheld rule of laissez-faire – and would create the conditions for effective self-help. The 'exception' was justified by the argument that 'landlordism', the last embodiment of feudalism, was a problem of a *political* – rather than merely *social* and *economic* – nature. Its solution required not only an alteration of the land laws, but also a series of political and constitutional reforms. In Britain these included the 'mending or ending' of the House of Lords; in Ireland, a Home Rule Parliament; in both countries, the extension of political rights to all 'independent' adult men. While insisting on the 'constitutional rights' of the Irish people – the right of free speech and meeting, for example, against coercion and special police powers – the Nationalists demanded participation and self-government as ends in themselves, as well as the means whereby good government could be ensured. Like the Chartists in Britain in the late 1830s, Irish Nationalists in the 1880s expected all sorts of economic and social improvements from the establishment of a government 'of the people, by the people and for

---

[12] L.a., *FJ*, 12 Mar. 1880, 4.

[13] T. M. Healy, 'The Irish parliamentary party', *Fortnightly Review*, 32, NS (July–December (1882)), 629; Cashman, *Life of Michael Davitt*, 137.

[14] E.g. Cashman, *Life of Michael Davitt*, 127–8; cf. C. Hill, 'The Norman yoke', in J. Saville (ed.), *Democracy and the labour movement* (London, 1954), 15–46; Biagini, *Liberty*, 50–60.

[15] O. MacDonagh, *States of mind: a study of Anglo-Irish conflict 1780–1930* (London, 1983), 42; D. Jordan, 'The Irish National League and the "unwritten law": rural protest and nation building in Ireland, 1882–1890', *Past & Present*, no. 158 (1998), 149; for the importance of the culture of self-help, see Kissane, *Explaining Irish democracy*, 88–9.

the people'.[16] They were adamant that such government should aim at 'the parliamentary regeneration of the country'.[17] Not surprisingly, as early as 1880–1 Henry Labouchere thought that the Nationalists were 'sound on most radical issues' and that 'the Democracy of England and Ireland ought to unite' in a campaign for land reform and devolution and to drive the Whigs from the Liberal party.[18]

James Loughlin has rightly stressed the role of extremist nationalism in confusing moderate opinion in both Ireland and Britain and has criticized the Irish party's 'reluctance, or inability, to define exactly what Home Rule meant'.[19] Indeed as late as Christmas 1885 Parnell complained that 'public expression of opinion on our side ... has been tending to show that we ourselves are not agreed on what we want'.[20] However, as D. George Boyce has shown, the main problem was not really lack of 'definition', but that different, competing definitions of Home Rule were presented by different spokesmen at different times, to serve the rhetorical needs of the moment.[21] At one level this was hardly surprising: as T. M. Healy pointed out in 1882, the Irish party saw little scope in producing a draft Home Rule Bill if the government was not prepared even to discuss the issue in principle. Moreover, the defenders of the Union were equally vague, and their cry against the 'Dismemberment of the Empire' served to cloud the issue, as much as to clarify their stance.[22]

Yet, among the pre-1886 definitions of Home Rule, the notion of parliamentary self-government within the British Empire had been elaborated as early as 1873 and popularized by Isaac Butt. It was further discussed in 1880 by William Shaw, then leader of the Irish party, in response to Lord Beaconsfield's manifesto. Anticipating a line which would be adopted by the Liberals in 1886, Shaw argued that '[w]e mean by Home Rule not that the connections between the two countries should be destroyed, but that the relationship may be based on a healthy and natural and honest basis'. In his view, '[t]he country wants a Government that will preserve the integrity of the Empire, not by attempted repression and reaction, but by dispensing strict and impartial justice to all classes, and to all parts of the Empire'.[23] Though in 1880–2 the Parnellites voiced a far more robust and oppositional political *style*,

---

[16] Rep., 'Nationalist Convention in Farmagh', *FJ*, 10 Jan. 1885, 6, speech by F. Mayne, MP.
[17] From the first resolution, 'Nationalist Convention in Farmagh', *FJ*, 10 Jan. 1885, 6.
[18] Hind, *Henry Labouchere*, 86, 88–9.   [19] Loughlin, *Gladstone*, 31–4.
[20] C. S. Parnell to E. Dwyer Gray, 24 Dec. 1885, in T. W. Moody, 'Select documents: Parnell and the Galway election of 1886', *Irish Historical Studies*, 8, 33 (1954), 332.
[21] D. G. Boyce, *Nationalism in Ireland* (1991), 216.
[22] T. M. Healy, 'The Irish parliamentary party', *Fortnightly Reivew*, 32, n.s. (1882), 627.
[23] W. Shaw, 'The general election', *FJ*, 19 Mar. 1880, 5.

the *substance* of their programme was little different, focusing on 'Parliamentary, Municipal, Poor Law, Grand Jury, and Registration reforms, the development of the Land Act, and some species of Self-government',[24] the latter consisting of elected county councils and a 'National Assembly' on the model of colonial Parliaments.[25] Such understanding of Home Rule combined an old tradition (the revival of 'Grattan's Parliament') with the Canadian example and more recent 'Britannic liberties' – the latter embodied by the American republican tradition, with which emigration had long established strong links.[26] It was precisely this understanding of Home Rule that was supported by the Lib-labs and a few Radical MPs from as early as 1874 – as we have seen in the previous chapter. In fact, contemporaries were aware that there was much common ground between Liberals and Nationalists. As T. M. Healy argued in 1883, at a meeting in Newcastle upon Tyne,

the connection between Ireland and the Liberal party had always been a close one. Indeed he might say that all the great measures which had been passed for the benefit of the English people had been caused by means of the Irish alliance, the alliance between the Liberals and the Irish members. When he mentioned the Liberal party he had to make a distinction . . . There were a number of Liberals at the head of affairs who had no claim whatever to the distinction of leading Parliament . . . Then there was Mr Chamberlain, a gentleman for whom he had the highest possible respect, and who if he continued to be assaulted by the calumny of his enemies and continued to deserve the enmity of those by whom he was antagonised, would, he (Mr Healy) ventured to say, be the future Premier of England . . . the Liberal party was not directed by those who ought to govern it, and . . . the men who were sincerely anxious to do justice to the people of Ireland, whose hearts pulsated with the masses of the people were completely outweighted. It was because of this state of affairs that the Irish party was at war with the Liberal party, and he ventured to say they should continue to be at war until there was infused into the Liberal Cabinet a few more men of the same type as Mr Chamberlain.[27]

While this rhetoric was partly motivated by Healy's wish to propitiate Chamberlain – then perceived as one of the most pro-Home Rule Liberal leaders – its content was consistent with that emanating from other Nationalist sources and statements. Healy concluded that, '[w]ith the exception of Coercion, there is scarcely any measure that the Liberals may force through with which the Irish party will not be in political

---

[24] Healy, 'The Irish parliamentary party', 626.
[25] Ibid., 630–1; Davitt, *Leaves from a prison diary*, 251–4.
[26] C. B. Shannon, *Arthur J. Balfour and Ireland, 1874–1922* (1988), 14.
[27] T. M. Healy, cited in rep., 'Mr Healy, MP, and the Liberal Party', *FJ*, 14. Sep. 1883, 2.

sympathy . . . So far as concerns legislation . . . the only principle dividing the Liberals and the Irish is Home Rule.'[28]

Though Nationalist commitment to denominational education in schools and universities was actually a further major issue of disagreement with *English* Liberals, Healy did have a point here: after all, *Scottish* Liberals were divided over the issue, as we have seen in the previous chapter, and Gladstone had reformed, not abolished, denominational (Presbyterian) education in Scottish schools in 1872. In principle, at least, the case of Catholic education was similar. Moreover, for the Nationalists the introduction of sectarian education was not tantamount to the creation of a new ecclesiastical establishment because their commitment to such education also included the defence and preservation of Presbyterian and other Protestant institutions, such as the Queen's Colleges.[29] And if the Nationalists assumed a close link between Catholicism and the people of Ireland, as Boyce has pointed out, 'it was the liberal Gladstone who . . . described the Nonconformists of Wales as "the people of Wales"'.[30] On the other hand, the INL, as much as the Land League before it, was careful to present the Nationalist movement 'in secular and non-sectarian terms'.[31] In this endeavour, they were helped by the fact that from 1869 church and state in Ireland were actually independent of one another, a constitutional feature that had important political and ideological implications.

As Gladstone had anticipated, disestablishment was a blessing in disguise for the Episcopalian Church, also because the tithe issue – which was to cause serious unrest in Wales in the 1880s – had long been settled in Ireland.[32] Thus, when the land agitation began in 1879, it was directed against *secular* landlords – whether Roman Catholic or Protestant – and did not develop a sectarian, anti-Anglican agenda. Of course, both before and after 1869, claims of clerical interference in Irish elections were frequent and well documented, but involved the Catholic, rather than the Anglican, clergy.[33] However, the situation in Ireland was very

---

[28] Healy, 'The Irish parliamentary party', 625, 627.

[29] L.a., *United Ireland*, 17 July 1886, 4.   [30] Boyce, *Nationalism in Ireland*, 220.

[31] P. Bull, *Land, politics and nationalism* (1996), 74.

[32] A. Jackson, 'Irish Unionism, 1870–1922', in D. George Boyce and A. O'Day (eds.), *Defenders of the Union* (2001), 118.

[33] Hoppen, *Elections, politics and society*, 158–60, 232–56. On the other hand, Protestant tenants in the North-East, although famously self-assertive in dealing with their landlords, did not generally identify with the Land League, which they perceived as a Catholic and Nationalist organization. And, of course, the polarization of Irish society which followed the land agitation was based on confessional allegiances: D. Haire, 'In aid of the civil power, 1868–1890', in F. S. L. Lyons and R. A. J. Hawkins (eds.), *Ireland under the Union: varieties of tension* (1980), 115–48.

different from that in either France or Italy – the two countries where anti-clericalism was at the time most virulent – or indeed in Britain. In both Italy and France the Roman Catholic Church was associated with the *ancien régime* by means of personal and political links between members of the hierarchy and the 'black' or legitimist aristocracy. Moreover, even after the sale of monastic lands, the church retained considerable wealth and influence, and in fact was establishing itself in the world of banking and insurance. In Britain the Church of England was both part of the 'constitution' and a powerful landowner, while many of its ministers behaved as village squires who felt confident of their role at the centre of the national establishment. These social and political attributes were resented by the Nonconformists, especially in Wales. In fact, as we have seen in the previous chapter, the Welsh 'tithe war' gave rise to scenes of total alienation between the people and those expected to enforce the law, with army and police columns patrolling the Welsh countryside, in the attempt to enforce the payment of tithes from a rebellious peasantry.

By contrast, in Ireland the Roman Catholic Church was not a collective landlord, and was as yet devoid of the institutional and material attributes of power. It presented itself as the church of the poor and in this way acquired a social and political status comparable to that of the Nonconformist denominations in England and Wales, or the Free Church in the Scottish Highlands.[34] The latter were convulsed by a land agitation which nearly escalated into a 'war'. In particular, after the harvest failure of 1881 there were serious disputes in the west of Skye (February 1882), ultimately requiring the intervention of the army. Then in April 1882 a sheriff's officer was prevented from evicting a few tenants by a crowd of crofters in the Braes district. The crofters, who had adopted the Irish tactic of withholding rent payments from the landlords, eventually clashed with the police and chased them away in the 'Battle of the Braes'. As Allan MacColl has demonstrated, the Free Church ministers were generally behind the crofters, although always eager to avoid violence (as most of their Catholic colleagues were in Ireland).[35]

Fundamental to this ambiguous attitude was the question of the legitimacy of both the law and the existing land tenure system, which, in the

---

[34] T. Garvin, *The evolution of Irish nationalist politics* (1981), 215; cf. A. G. Newby, ' "Shoulder to shoulder"? Scottish and Irish land reformers in the Highlands of Scotland, 1878–1894', Ph.D. thesis, Unversity of Edinburgh, 2001.

[35] A. W. MacColl, 'The churches and the land question in the Highlands of Scotland, 1843–1888', Ph.D. thesis, University of Cambridge, 2002, 105–10, 188–9; MacColl, *Land, faith and the crofting community*; E. A. Cameron, ' "Alas, Skyemen are imitating the Irish": a note on Alexander Nicolson's "Little leaflet" concerning the crofters' agitation', *The Innes Review*, 55, 1 (2004), 83–92.

Highlands as much as in Ireland, was now widely contested.[36] Although Jordan has suggested that the alienation felt by Irish tenants in relation to both land laws and the gentry found no parallels in Britain, the fact is that from the 1880s until 1914 Scottish crofters, Welsh farmers, English labourers and radicals everywhere in Britain denounced and tried to subvert 'landlordism', which they saw as 'the Norman yoke', an 'alien' feudal institution, in contrast to a lost (and largely mythical) Celtic or Saxon democracy of free peasants.[37] Victorians were aware of these parallels: one farmer complained to the Napier Commission – appointed in 1883 to 'enquire into the condition of the crofters and cottars' in the Highlands – that the crofters '[are] inspired by the Free Church, and that these are the Fenians we have – not the Free Church of the south, but the Free Church north of the Caledonian Canal [which] ... sent ignorant, unlettered men about the place to spread discontent among the people'.[38] Some of the Free Church ministers reciprocated in kind. James Cumming, minister of Melness (Sutherland) and the elected delegate of the crofters in his parish, protested that 'we are, in fact, under an absolute despotism'.[39] The most militant of the clerical 'Fenians' was the Revd Donald MacCallum – a minister in the established Kirk – who was eventually put into prison 'like John the Baptist', his admirers said,[40] for his relentlessly subversive activities among the poor.

In any case, it was true that the crofters and various land agitators, such as John Murdoch of *The Highlander*, were influenced by Michael Davitt and Irish nationalism (in fact, Murdoch himself had dealings even with John Devoy and the Fenians). Not surprisingly, the alliance between church and land reformers resulted in quasi-nationalist agrarian radicalism.[41] Irish Nationalist MPs co-operated with the crofter MPs in an unsuccessful attempt to radicalize the 1886 Scottish Land Bill,[42] and by 1889 Parnell was a Highland hero. When he visited Scotland N. MacPhail and D. Cowan of the Highland Land Law Reform Association welcomed him 'as Celts of the same race and speaking the same language as your fellow countrymen. We thank you for what you have done for the peasantry of Ireland ... because in resisting landlord

---

[36] Jordan, 'Irish National League and the "unwritten law"', 146, 158; MacColl, *Land, faith and the crofting community*, 95–155.

[37] Jordan, 'Irish National League and the "unwritten law"', 149; cf. Biagini, *Liberty*, 54–5, 90, 189; I. Packer, *Lloyd George, liberalism and the land: the land issue and party politics in England, 1906–1914* (2001).

[38] D. C. Cameron, cited in MacColl, 'Churches', 115.   [39] Cited in ibid., 119.

[40] J. Cameron, *The old and the new Highland and Hebrides* (1912), 104.

[41] D. W. Kemp, *The Sutherland Democracy* (1890); Davitt, *The fall of feudalism in Ireland*, 228–9.

[42] T. M. Devine, *Clanship to crofters' war* (1994), 223, 231.

oppression you have been fighting our battle as well as theirs.'[43] 'To you and the Irish agitation', declared the Sutherlandshire Association, 'Scotland, and more especially the Highlands, is indebted for the Crofter Commission' – the first step towards justice to 'the Celt'.[44] It is not surprising, then, that when Irish Home Rule became an issue, the pro-crofter ministers of the Highland Free Church, despite their fierce Calvinism, were far from unanimously opposed to the Bill.[45]

In both countries, ministers and priests were influential because they enjoyed mass support in their parishes, not because of the institutional position of their respective churches, and were often regarded as the 'natural' spokesmen for their flock. Contemporaries were aware of this elective affinity: thus, in 1895 Edward Blake struck a responsive chord among his Edinburgh audience when he presented the Irish Catholic Church as distinctively 'nonconformist':

When it was said that what the Irish Roman Catholic priests really wanted was an opportunity to endow and establish the Roman Catholic Church, he, as a Protestant, declared that there was no greater example in the history of the world of the capacity of a Church to stand without endowment, without establishment, as the church of the poor, kept impoverished to assist the church of the rich, than the Roman Catholic Church of Ireland (cheers), and there were no people within his knowledge who were more disposed to ignore religious distinctions in secular affairs than the people who belonged to the Church in Ireland (cheers).[46]

Liberalism had as long a tradition among Irish Roman Catholics as among Presbyterians. It stretched back to Daniel O'Connell, and Irish Catholic MPs were among the first to appropriate the label 'Liberal' in a political sense,[47] at a time when 'Reformers', 'Radicals' and 'Whigs' were the labels preferred by British MPs. As Kissane has pointed out, the alliance between O'Connell and the Catholic church 'gave deeper

---

[43] In [Anon.], *Scotland's welcome to Mr Parnell: A souvenir of his first political visit to Scotland, containing 146 addresses of Congratulations*, 20 July 1889, 44–5.

[44] Edinburgh Branch, Sutherlandshire Association, ibid., 45.

[45] MacColl, 'Churches', 199–200.

[46] Cited in rep., 'Nationalist demonstration in Edinburgh: Splendid speech by the Hon. Mr Blake, MP', *FJ*, 21 Mar. 1895, 5. The meeting was organized by two branches of the Irish National League – one of them named 'W. E. Gladstone'. On Blake see Banks, *Edward Blake*.

[47] E.g. R. M. O'Farrell, (Keldare) and John O'Brien (Limerick City) (*Dod's Parliamentary companion*, 1844). O. MacDonagh, *The life of Daniel O'Connell, 1775–1847* (1991), 389–90; on O'Connell's own liberal ideology see ibid., 305–6 and Hoppen, 'Riding a tiger'. See G. C. Mahon to J. Martin, 29 Dec. 1874: 'The Irish priests . . . in their open advocacy of democratic principles during the O'Connell agitation . . . took good *Protestant* ground and if only in 1848 they only stuck to the principles, which for 20 years previously they had publicly inculcated, I should really expect much good from them' (NLI MS 22, 203).

democratic resonance' to 'the liberal idea of the public sphere', as 'Catholic politicians from the 1820s on were able to construct political movements that were expansive, rather than restrictive in their attitude towards membership, geared towards politicising the people rather than excluding them, and seeing mass participation as the most effective proof that they represented public opinion.'[48] While O'Connell's Catholic Association continued to inspire nationalist political ideology in parts of Ireland for years after the 'Liberator's' death,[49] at a national level Irish support for the Liberal party revived from 1865, after the death of Palmerston, who had been very unpopular with the Catholics for his 'Orange' views. By contrast, his successors, Gladstone and even Russell, enjoyed a much better reputation. In particular, Gladstone's promise to do justice to Ireland, in December 1867, galvanized the Irish Catholics. As Larkin has put it, 'the bishops succeeded in enlisting their clergy in what can only be described as a religious crusade in the constituencies on behalf of Gladstone and the Liberal party', particularly because the 'People's William' had not only 'promised to remedy the outstanding Irish grievances about the established Church, Tenant Right, and educational reform', but also that he would legislate on those matters according to the Irish ideas about what was necessary, rather than 'according to what the English thought might be good for them'.[50]

Apart from disestablishment, there is evidence that at least some priests were responsive both to liberal ideas of land reform, and to liberal humanitarian policies in general. Thus the Revd John Hacket in 'an excited speech off the altar before concluding mass' at Lisvernane (Co. Tipperary) in October 1869 compared the People's William to Joshua 'and prayed that W. E. Gladstone, the leader of the people, like Joshua of the Israelites would lead them to liberty'.[51] Canon Bourke, parish priest of Claremorris (Co. Mayo) and the mentor of the nationalist leader John O'Connor Power, 'had been much influenced by the writings of John Stuart Mill'.[52] Perhaps because of Mill's influence, he was one of the supporters of the Ladies' Land League. After the disappointment

---

[48] Kissane, *Explaining Irish democracy*, 95.
[49] D. Jordan, 'John O'Connor Power, Charles Stewart Parnell and the centralization of popular politics in Ireland', *Irish Historical Studies*, 25, 97 (1986), 46–7.
[50] E. Larkin, *The consolidation of the Roman Catholic Church in Ireland, 1860–1870* (Chapel Hill, N. C. and London, 1987), 690, 691; Larkin, *The Roman Catholic Church and the Home Rule movement, 1870–1875* (1990), 81–2, 391.
[51] Cited in Boyce, *Nationalism in Ireland*, 186.
[52] J. McL. Côté, *Fanny and Anna Parnell: Ireland's patriot sisters* (1991), 4; Bull, *Land*, 97; Jordan, 'John O'Connor Power', 63. Bourke was former president of St Jarlath's College and a close friend of Archbishop MacHale, himself a strong supporter of Home Rule.

associated with the 1870 Land Act (although Cullen liked it) and the 1873 University Bill, the 1879–80 Midlothian campaigns revived clerical support for the Liberal party, which stood for land reform and an end to coercion.[53] Later the Gladstone government's record on these two issues affected clerical attitudes to the Liberal party. In the early 1880s, though there were priests who dared to assert their loyalty to Gladstone even if this meant antagonizing part of their flock,[54] the response exemplified by a Revd Father Trainor was more common. At a meeting in 1883, he declared that he had believed in Gladstone and supported the Liberal candidate in 1880, but had since lost 'his political faith', because 'Mr Gladstone ... instead of giving his whole strength to the Land Act was all the time manufacturing Coercion Acts'.[55]

If many priests 'lost' their faith in the People's William during Forster's 'coercion rule', they found it anew from 1886 – as we shall see in the next section – when Gladstone raised his voice *against* coercion and *for* Home Rule: thus, at a meeting in Clonakilty (Co. Cork) in 1887, a Father Lucy referred to him as 'the greatest statesman the world has ever seen'.[56] But even from 1880 to 1885 some priests saw little difference between Liberalism and Land League militancy. T. W. Crooke, Roman Catholic Archbishop of Cashel, referred to '[the] great statesman [Gladstone] ... who stands at the head of Her Majesty's Ministers, and whose good will to Ireland has been abundantly made manifest...'. The Revd Maurice Mooney, parish priest at Cahir (Co. Tipperary), was heard to '[pass] an eulogium' on Gladstone at a meeting in 1882, and, quoting John Bright, exhorted his parishioners 'to agitate constitutionally for their rights, but to keep strictly within the constitution and not break the peace'.[57] Interestingly, to him 'constitutional agitation' also included the with-holding and reduction of rent payments, tactics which he boasted of having personally adopted in his capacity as one of the local leaders of the land campaign. During the same meeting, the Revd Mr Foran, parish priest of Ballooly (Co. Down) 'spoke of Mr Gladstone as the greatest intellect of the age, who would have made the Land Act better than it was, but he had a hostile Lords and Commons to conciliate'.[58] This meeting passed a resolution in support of 'peasant proprietary' as the only solution

---

[53] In 1880 T. W. Crooke, Roman Catholic Archbishop of Cashel, praised '[the] great statesman [Gladstone] ... who stands at the head of Her Majesty's Ministers, and whose good will to Ireland has been abundantly made manifest...' (Hefferman Papers, NAI, MS 21,910).

[54] Cited in Moody, *Davitt and the Irish revolution*, 423.

[55] Cited in rep., 'Meeting at Greenan Cross', *FJ*, 25 June 1883, 6.

[56] Cited in rep., 'The National League', *Cork Examiner*, 1 Nov. 1887, 4.

[57] Cited in rep., 'Demonstration at Cahir', *FJ*, 30 Oct. 1882, 6.   [58] Ibid.

which would satisfy both farmers and labourers, and reduce state intervention in Ireland's land economy – an interference which was criticized
as expensive, 'suspicious and untrustworthy', and conducive to 'discontent and dissension'. Such words could not have been more consistent
with traditional liberalism had they been uttered at a Durham miners'
meeting by some regular readers of the *Weekly Times* or *Reynolds's
Newspaper*. They came with the pledge of the local 'tenant farmers, artisans
and labouring classes' to support Parnell and his party in their effort 'to
procure for the people of Ireland the blessings of Home Rule, the extension
and assimilation of the Irish parliamentary and municipal franchise to
those of England, the substitution of elective county boards for the present
grand jury system', as well as 'the payment by the constituencies of the
popular Irish members of Parliament'.[59] Although the priests supported
constitutional liberties and were opposed to coercion, they were often
autocratic and domineering. But also in this respect – as authoritarian
advocates of the rights of 'society' against the state – they resembled their
colleagues, the Free Church ministers in the Scottish Highlands.

Like their Calvinist counterparts, the Irish priests derived their power
from the fact that they were rooted in the communities which they served.
On the other hand, popular devotion to the Irish clergy did not necessarily
imply blind submission either to their dictates or to those of the hierarchy.
After 1874 the bishops came to support Home Rule because they felt they
needed to do so if they wanted to recover their political power and influence in the constituencies, which had been weakened by their close
association with Gladstone and the Liberals during the previous
years.[60] Later Isaac Butt skilfully negotiated with the bishops the terms
of a future Catholic University Bill and in the process strengthened both
his authority and that of the Irish party, and exposed the lack of unity
among the bishops.[61] In the early 1880s, Nationalist loyalty to the
bishops was conditional on the latter's support for Parnellism: whenever
they contradicted or criticized the League, they elicited reactions which
in continental Europe would have been described as 'anti-clerical'. Thus
in 1883, when the Pope vetoed the public subscription to relieve Parnell
of his debts, his interference had the effect of boosting the plan: the
fund, which stood at £7,000 when the papal rescript was received,
reached £40,000, as pious Catholic peasants taxed themselves to rescue

---

[59] Ibid.
[60] Larkin, *Consolidation of the Roman Catholic Church*, 693; O'Farrell, *Ireland's English
question*, 163.
[61] E. Larkin, *The Roman Catholic Church and the emergence of the modern Irish political system,
1874–1878* (1996), 558–60.

a Protestant landlord from bankruptcy.[62] Again in 1888, when the Unionist government successfully sought papal support against the Nationalists, Davitt said publicly that '[t]he Vatican has its politics as well as Ireland has, but Ireland, even in the days of O'Connell, declared through him that she would prefer to take political lessons from Stanboul than from Rome'.[63] As he wrote in his account of the nationalist agitation, '[a] feeling of intense indignation swept through the country at this attack upon the Protestant leader of a people whose Catholicity was being used as a cover for an unwarranted interference in their political and national concerns'.[64]

Nationalists were not usually anti-clerical in the French sense of the word – with few exceptions, T. P. O'Connor being one – although many priests supported Nationalism without fully exploring the possible implications of its political platform.[65] However, after the 1891 party split, the Parnellite minority became more assertive in their rejection of clerical interference: 'I don't desire to deprive a priest of his rights as a citizen because he is a priest,' argued Redmond in 1895, 'but what I say is that when he comes into the political arena as a citizen his influence must be the influence of a citizen and not what I may call the supernatural influence which he exercises as a clergyman.'[66] His point was somehow conceded: William Walsh, the Archbishop of Dublin, responded that bishops and priests had the right 'to exercise to the fullest extent their natural and legitimate influence in all public affairs', but subject to certain guidelines, including being '[r]egardful of the right of all to think and act for themselves in every matter that stands clear of the line of Christian duty'.[67] The latter was a principle which Nonconformist pastors – and certainly Presbyterian ministers in Scotland – would have regarded as altogether acceptable.

In any case, the Nationalists presented their cause as non-sectarian and 'patriotic' in the sense of being inspired by love for the common good:

---

[62] J. L. Hammond, *Gladstone and the Irish nation* (1938), 364.

[63] Cited in rep., 'Mr Michael Davitt on the papal circular', *FJ*, 30 Apr. 1888, 5. See also S. O'Mara about the Bishop of Kerry in 'National League – branch meeting', *Cork Examiner*, 1 Jan. 1887, 3. On Nationalist anti-clericalism see Cruise O'Brien, *Parnell and his Party*, 28 and n. 3, and 50; O'Farrell, *England and Ireland*, 137; T. Garvin, *Nationalist revolutionaries in Ireland, 1858–1928* (1987), 18, 27–8, 126–30; and A. Macaulay, *The Holy See, British policy and the Plan of Campaign in Ireland, 1885–93* (2002), 182–3. See also chapter 4, below.

[64] Davitt, *Fall of feudalism*, 398.

[65] Brady, *T. P. O'Connor*, 10; O'Farrell, *Ireland's English question*, 189.

[66] Newscutting 1 May 1895 in J. Redmond Papers, 45, MS 7421, 15.

[67] 'The election contest in East Wicklow – The duty of the clergy – Letter of the Archbishop of Dublin', *FJ*, 15 Apr. 1895, 5.

'We claim for all equal rights before the law.'[68] This was a cause which not only the Catholics, but also, as they hoped, 'a large mass' of the Protestant population could support.[69] Parnell insisted on 'the high importance of acting with every possible regard and consideration for the susceptibilities of our Orange fellow Countrymen . . . Our policy is one of generous toleration and consideration for all sections of the Irish nation.'[70] T. M. Healy, who from the mid-1890s would espouse intransigently sectarian politics, in 1883 insisted that '[h]e would put his foot on the neck of oppression and injustice (cheers), whether he found it in a Protestant landlord or a Catholic landlord (cheers). He would meddle with no man's creed. He would interfere with no man's conscience (cheers).'[71] The *Freeman's Journal*, commenting on meetings where declarations of this kind had been made, stressed that such demonstrations 'were attended by Protestants and Catholics – clergymen and lay electors. The true Liberals and the true tenant-righters are equal to the occasion . . . Protestant shakes hand with Catholic, over a question which is not one of Creed but which is one of class – the people *versus* the few – the substantial democracy against an effete and worthless aristocracy.'[72] According to these nationalists, the issue at stake was between 'popular rights' and 'democracy' (whether Catholic, Presbyterian or Episcopalian)[73] on the one hand, and aristocratic privilege on the other. It was a crusade for constitutional rights and freedoms, and against 'coercion tyranny'. It was a struggle of 'labour' *versus* landlordism. '[T]he landlords of Ireland are all of one religion,' claimed Michael Davitt in 1881 – 'their God is mammon, and rack-rents, and evictions their only morality, while the toilers of the field, whether Orangemen, Catholics, Presbyterians, or Methodists are the victims whom they desire to see fling themselves under the juggernaut of landlordism.'[74]

Throughout the period of the agitation for the first two Home Rule Bills, Protestant Nationalist opinion was given a high profile in press

---

[68] Cited in rep., 'Proposed National demonstration in Derry: address to the People', *FJ*, 10 Dec. 1883, 6.

[69] From the speech of the Lord Mayor of Dublin, cited in rep., 'The National League: the Irish Bills', *FJ*, 21 Apr. 1886, 6.

[70] C. S. Parnell to T. Harrington, 9 June 1884, Parnell Letters, NLI, MS 8581 (1).

[71] T. M. Healy cited in rep., 'Meeting at Ballytrain', *FJ*, 25 June 1883, 6. For Healy's emphasis on religious toleration and the non-sectarian nature of Nationalism in the early 1880s see F. Callanan, *T. M. Healy* (1996), 110. For his latent, and, later, militant, clericalism and bigotry see ibid., 264, 372, 374–81.

[72] L.a., *FJ*, 25 June 1883, 4.

[73] T. M. Healy cited in rep., 'The Monaghan election', *FJ*, 25 June 1883, 6.

[74] Cited in F. Campbell, *The dissenting voice: Protestant democracy in Ulster from Plantation to Partition* (1991), 285; for similar statements by W. Redmond and others, see Boyce, *Nationalism in Ireland*, 220, n. 134, 227.

reports.[75] The latter provided full coverage both of the meetings of the Protestant Home Rule Association[76] and of any Presbyterian support Nationalist leaders could muster in the North.[77] The few Protestant notables ready to come out and be counted were proudly introduced at local meetings by the Catholic parish priests, who stressed that 'it was a mistaken idea that because they differed at the altar they could not unite for their motherland'.[78] On the one hand, although only a small number of ministers of various Protestant denominations were found to speak up for the tenants by the 1881 Royal Commission,[79] Protestant Nationalists and Liberals like John Pinkerton and the Reverends Isaac Nelson and Matthew Macaulay shared the radical agrarianism of their Catholic opposite numbers, as did Alexander Bowman, a Belfast-based trade union leader and a Gladstonian.[80] Indeed, as we shall see in chapters 5 and 6, agrarian radicalism was an important component of Liberal Unionism in both Ulster and Scotland. On the other hand, some Protestant notables – including Jeremiah Jordan (Methodist), Isaac Nelson (Presbyterian) and several others – moved from tenant rights agitation to membership of the National party at Westminster, where, in 1891, they numbered thirteen

---

[75] 'A Presbyterian Irishman', letter on 'Presbyterians and Home Rule', *FJ*, 23 Jan. 1886, 7; and 'A Protestant Nationalist', letter on 'Protestant Nationalism – its existence and duties', *FJ*, 11 Feb. 1886, 3. For Presbyterian arguments in support of Home Rule see the penny pamphlet by J. D. Craig, *Are Irish Protestants afraid of Home Rule? Two speeches delivered by Rev. J. D. Craig Houston and Professor Dougherty at the General Assembly of the Presbyterian Church, held in Belfast, on June 9th, 1893*, The Liberal Publications Department (London, 1893), in National Liberal Club Collection.

[76] E.g. the reports, 'Protestant Home Rule Association', *FJ*, 11 Jan. 1887, 3; and 'The Protestant Home Rule Association and coercion: enthusiastic demonstration last night [in Dublin]', *FJ*, 13 Apr. 1887, 6. For the activities and ideology of this organization see J. Loughlin, 'The Irish Protestant Home Rule Association and nationalist politics, 1886–93', *Irish Historical Studies*, 24, 95 (1985), 341–61.

[77] E.g. 'The land question in the North: demonstration in North Antrim', *FJ*, 13 Apr. 1887, 6: the reporter stressed the 'Orange' component of the crowds who listened 'with the greatest attention' to John Dillon's speech. See also Craig, *Are Irish Protestants afraid of Home Rule?*

[78] Cited in rep., 'The National League: meeting at Queenstown', *The Cork Examiner*, 6 Nov. 1887, 3.

[79] *Report of Her Majesty's Commissioners of Inquiry into the Working of the Landlord and Tenant (Ireland) Act*, PP, xviii and xix (1881), better known as the Bessborough Commission Report.

[80] Cited in 'The representation of the County Leitrim', *FJ*, 19 Mar. 1880, 7. Eventually Nelson entered Parliament for County Mayo as a follower of Parnell, and in 1885 became president of the Protestant Home Rule Association in Belfast: Campbell, *Dissenting Voice*, 289, 294; G. Moran, 'James Daly and the rise and fall of the Land League in the west of Ireland, 1879–82', *Irish Historical Studies*, 29, 114 (1994), 199–200; T. Bowman, *People's champion: the life of Alexander Bowman, pioneer of labour politics in Ireland* (1997), 48–86; Geary, *The Plan of Campaign*, 53.

(including Parnell).[81] The post-Parnell party continued this tradition, and counted among its leading members Quakers such as Alfred Webb and Episcopalians like Edward Blake. The latter, a Canadian-Irish Evangelical and former Liberal Prime Minister of Ontario, was elected by Longford with strong clerical support in July 1892.[82] His platform was 'in general politics, decided[ly] Liberal'.[83] One of the points Blake and his Protestant Nationalist friends tried (unsuccessfully) to impress on Ulster Protestant opinion was that '[i]t is utter rubbish to talk of the "tyranny of the Catholics" '.[84] This was stressed also by Michael Davitt, who, speaking on the second Home Rule Bill, pointed out that 'Catholics and Protestants live in political harmony together in the colonies, without any attempted interference with religious rights ... the Prime Minister of Canada is a Catholic, and two of the chief Orangemen of Ontario are members of his Government.'[85]

While Nationalists and Liberals shared significant ideological ground, the former complained about the latter's hypocrisy: '[t]he Liberals are with the Irish Party in everything save Home Rule, having got rid of all controversy by the process of promising everything required and never giving it'.[86] Of course, this criticism was not totally fair, especially with regard to constitutional obstacles to reform. For example, Gladstone's 1880 Compensation of Disturbance Bill (which the Nationalists welcomed) was killed in the Lords by a large majority.[87] The popularity of the demand for Home Rule was partly a reaction to such institutional constraints to reform, and partly reflected the fact that a growing number

[81] Campbell, *Dissenting Voice*, 294; O'Brien, *Parnell and his Party*, 261, and 333 n. 1.
[82] For the support of the Roman Catholic clergy see C. Casey to Blake, 10 Mar. 1894 [1391], Blake Correspondence, 4686. For his religious views see M. B. Faughner to H. de F. Montgomery, 13 July 1892, PRONI, D/627/428/188. Blake, retired in July 1907 on health grounds. His correspondence attests to his personal popularity not only with his constituents – who tried to dissuade him from resigning – but also generally with his colleagues and with supporters and admirers in both Britain and Canada. For his resignation see Blake, 'To the Nationalist electors of South Longford', 19 July 1907, and subsequent exchanges in Blake Correspondence, 2538, 2548 and 2551, NLI, 4688.
[83] E. Blake, 'To the electors of South Longford', in *Election Addresses, 1892, vol. II: Counties, Scotland, Ireland and Wales*, Gladstone Library Collection, Bristol University Library.
[84] A. S. Loghill (a Protestant admirer) to Blake, 11 Aug. 1892, Blake Correspondence, NLI, 4684 [233].
[85] *Davitt, The settlement of the Irish Question. A speech by Mr Michael Davitt, MP, on April 11th, 1893, in the House of Commons*, penny pamphlet of the Liberal Publications Department (London, 1893), 18. Exactly the same point was made by Gladstone himself in a speech to Ulster Protestants: ibid., 5 (Belfast, 1893), 12–13. Both pamphlets are in the National Liberal Club Collection.
[86] L.a., *FJ*, 6 Nov. 1882, 4. This paraphrased one of the points made by T. M. Healy in the article, in n. 13.
[87] E.g. Cashman, *Davitt*, 232–3.

of people were aware that in many areas Ireland had interests and priorities which could hardly be accommodated within the parliamentary Union. The latter was of course the main source of differences between British Liberals and Irish Nationalists. It was ultimately a difference of *national* interests and as such had nothing to do with universalist ideologies such as liberalism.

Here we have the parameters and limits of the Nationalist claim to 'independence' from Gladstone's Liberal party.[88] On the one hand, if in Ireland the 1880s saw the 'birth of popular liberalism', it was an *Irish* movement – not the 'western' branch of a British one. In other words, the rise of Irish 'popular liberalism' cannot be assessed by simple reference to any British model, because Ireland and Britain were two different countries as much as Austria and Hungary. In particular, in Ireland as in Hungary the question of full citizenship was complicated by the overlap between national, ethnic, religious and social conflicts.

On the other hand, though the 'constitution' which was staunchly defended by the Nationalists was 'the Constitution of Ireland', the latter was modelled on notions of the *British* 'constitution' to such an extent that Nationalism as a movement for constitutional reform reflected 'the absorption of British and American values'.[89] As the USA influenced British radicalism as well as Irish nationalism, it is hardly surprising that eventually the two movements came to share demands and aspirations, including the 'reform of the grand jury law' – that is, the creation of democratically elected local authorities – the extension of the franchise, and the democratization of the electoral system for Poor Law guardians.[90] Likewise, much of the negative press which Dublin Castle received, especially in the years of 'coercion rule', replicated contemporary British hostility to anything smacking of a 'police state' and government unresponsive to public opinion.

Home Rule aimed precisely at the solution of this last problem: an Irish Parliament was the only guarantee of an executive which would respond to Irish public opinion, ensuring a government 'by its own people and for its own people'.[91] On this basis, the Nationalists claimed to be 'the popular party' (a label which British Liberals frequently applied to themselves) and indeed managed to attract a large share of the vote which formerly had gone to the Irish Liberals, sometimes cast by electors who

---

[88] See, e.g., l.a., *FJ*, 30 Oct. 1882, 4.   [89] Kissane, *Explaining Irish democracy*, 113.
[90] Resolutions cited in rep., 'The Ballinasloe Tenants Reform Association', *FJ*, 18 Mar. 1880, 5.
[91] L.a., *FJ*, 18 Apr. 1882, 4.

still professed to be Liberal.[92] As Nationalism became more and more 'constitutional' after 1882, the proposed alternatives to the Union were consistently drawn from the imperial experience, and were accompanied by the claim that Australia and Canada also supported the cause of Home Rule for Ireland.[93] This implied that Home Rule was 'safe', loyal and fully compatible with the British constitutional tradition and ongoing membership of the empire.

As Kissane has noted, 'the wide range of demands besides Home Rule that the party now made of the British state' is both important and revealing.[94] In particular, from 1882 the Irish National League (INL) provided for its supporters what could be described as a programme of 'homely' liberalism. The League's constitution consisted of six long articles, the first of which concerned Home Rule. The others dealt with land laws, local government, parliamentary and local franchises, and 'the development and encouragement of the Labour and Industrial Interests of Ireland'.[95] The land reform clauses – periodically updated in later editions of this document in response to government legislation – included the establishment of 'an occupying ownership or Peasant Proprietary' by means of Treasury loans, compulsory purchase of 'waste' lands, better compensation for improvements, and 'the admission of leaseholders to the benefits of the 1881 Land Act'. Under the heading 'Local Government', the INL asked for the creation of elected County Boards with extensive powers over education, public works, police and local magistrates, together with '[t]he transfer to County Boards of the management of union workhouses, lunatic asylums and other institutions supported by local rates'. With regard to the parliamentary franchise, the INL demanded full equality with Britain. As for the defence of 'Labour and Industrial Interests', pride of place was given to the erection of dwellings for farm labourers (a demand tentatively addressed by the 1883 Act), and 'out-door relief for labourers during illness'. Moreover, the League asked for the creation of an Industrial Committee with representatives from all branches of industry, trade and agriculture, for the purpose of 'encouraging the use and sale of Irish products', the organization of industrial exhibitions and the production of 'scientific reports of the industrial capacities' of the various regions around the country.

---

[92] See rep., 'County Dublin election: the nominations – meeting at Kingstown', *FJ*, 25 Feb. 1883, 2; l.a., *FJ*, 8 Mar. 1883, 4.
[93] L.a., *FJ*, 20 Dec. 1882, 4.   [94] Kissane, *Explaining Irish democracy*, 100.
[95] *Constitution of the Irish National League*, Heffernan Papers, NLI, MS 21,910, acc. 1921. The constitution was published in *FJ*, 16 Oct. 1882. For a contemporary commentary see l.a., *FJ*, 16 Oct. 1882, 4.

This radical catechism represented a systematic expression of Irish 'popular liberalism'. Like Gladstonian liberalism in Britain, the INL aimed at attracting working-class support while retaining its hold on the 'middle-class' farming vote. As Hoppen has shown, to a large extent it was successful.[96] Branch after branch of the Labour and Industrial Union decided to merge with Parnell's organization, which, they thought, 'embrace[d] in its programme all the forms necessary for constituting a free, contented and prosperous nation'.[97]

Constitutional rights and social tensions

The mist of night had scarcely disappeared over the valley of the Suir this (Saturday) morning, when Head Constable Ward and 15 fully-armed constables paraded in front of their barracks at Carrick-on-Suir [Co. Tipperary]. After the inspection of their pouches, in which were ammunition ... the men formed fours, and a bailiff marched within with writs. The bailiff was acting for Thomas Lalor JP ... Mr Lalor is a Catholic, and lives amidst his tenantry. In recent years he added to the small property of Cregg – to which on his father's death he succeeded – the townlands of Ballinagrana, Figlash, Mainstown, and Newton. On acquiring these latter places, which he purchased in the Encumbered Courts, he raised the rents, and kept them at this standard until the Land Courts altered some, a proceeding which so displeased him that in all cases he appealed against the fair rent.[98]

Without waiting for the outcome of the appeal, Lalor sought and obtained writs of eviction, after rejecting his tenants' compromise proposals (involving a rent reduction of 15 per cent). As the constables approached Newton, the scene was set for a violent confrontation, ultimately caused by Lalor's ability to 'circumvent' the law, which a weak or allegedly biased Irish government was unable to enforce. Despite the fact that few peasants were awake in the early hours of a November morning, the constables were sighted before they had reached the first house. 'Then from every house along the mountain side, up the glen, and away on the far hills shrill cries and like-sounding horns' alerted the whole community. The church bells were rung and before long were echoed by the bells of the villages nearby. As the constables struggled to overcome the resistance of the first farmhouse, large crowds – eventually numbering about one

---

[96] Hoppen, *Elections, politics and society*, 477–8.

[97] Rep., 'Meeting at Mulligar', *FJ*, 1 Nov. 1882, 5; for other similar statements see the reports of meetings at Clonoulty (*FJ*, 4 Nov. 1882, 3) and Newbridge (*FJ*, 6 Nov. 1882, 6).

[98] Rep., 'Writ-serving near Carrick-on-Suir', *FJ*, 16 Nov. 1885, 7. The landowning class in nineteenth-century Ireland was by no means entirely Protestant: in 1861 43 per cent of landlords were Roman Catholic, in comparison with 48 per cent belonging to the Church of Ireland: F. Campbell, *Land and revolution: nationalist politics in the west of Ireland, 1891–1921* (2005), 288. About 10 per cent of the great landowners were Catholic.

thousand men and women – gathered around them. The climax was reached when the constables, in their attempt to arrest a farmer, 'almost bayoneted a woman. At this the crowd closed on the police, who were forced to wade waist-deep the river', constantly pursued by the peasants.[99]

Irrespective of whether Lalor was 'representative' of Catholic landlords, this incident conveys the extent to which nationalism and the land question encompassed a multi-layered social and political conflict, with associated, and sometimes competing, forms of legitimacy. If, as one Nationalist leader put it, '[t]he agrarian war was ... the landlord enforcing his legal rights, and the tenant standing by his natural rights',[100] such conflict between 'rights' did not necessarily reflect the Protestant/Catholic divide. In the episode reported above, the landlord (himself a member of the local community) refused to abide by legally defined 'fair rents', and rejected the compromise offered by his tenants. A riot ensued, and eventually the police came to grief when they seemed to be ready to use their weapons against women – thus violating another 'natural right', namely, the respect and protection due to the female members of the community.

On the whole, 'the union of all classes ... and ranks in this country'[101] claimed by Parnell was almost as problematic and elusive as that other plank of the Nationalist creed – 'the union of all creeds'. While the 'social-integrationist' ideology was largely the product of urban agitators, in rural constituencies class conflict split both the Catholic and the Protestant communities.[102] The demands of various groups had to be negotiated again and again, as the movement for land reform achieved new successes from 1881. There was continuous tension between different social groups – not only between landlords and farmers, but also and increasingly between large graziers, smaller tenant farmers and farm labourers.[103] Though the INL interceded for the concession of rent-free

---

[99] 'Writ-serving near Carrick-on-Suir'. This episode is reminiscent of the 'Battle of Carraroe' of January 1880, and suggests that the police had not learned the lesson quite as well as Paul Bew has suggested in *Land and the national question in Ireland, 1858–82* (1978), 92–3.

[100] T. D. Sullivan, MP, cited in rep., 'The National League', *FJ*, 29 Mar. 1883, 2.

[101] C. S. Parnell, cited in rep., 'The representation of the County Tipperary', *FJ*, 24 Mar. 1880, 7.

[102] S. Clarke, 'The social composition of the Land League', *Irish Historical Studies*, 17, 68 (1971), 447–69; J. R. B. McMinn, 'Liberalism in North-Antrim, 1900–1914', *Irish Historical Studies*, 13, 89 (1982), 28–9; Geary, *The Plan of Campaign*, 49; see also chapter 6, pp. 291–8.

[103] See D. E. Jordan, *Land and popular politics in Ireland: county Mayo from the Plantation to the Land War* (1994), 8–9, 262–3; P. Bew and F. Wright, 'The agrarian opposition in Ulster politics, 1848–87', in S. Clark and J. D. Donnelly (eds.), *Irish peasants, violence and political unrest, 1780–1914* (1986), 223–4; J. W. Boyle, 'A marginal figure: the Irish

plots of land for the labourers, and tried to act as a mediator between farmers and farm workers, the latter often felt neglected and manipulated, especially after Gladstone's legislation of 1881–2.[104]

As some Nationalist leaders feared,[105] the second Land Act, supplemented by the Arrears Act in 1882, had a considerable impact on the targeted social groups,[106] to the extent that 'Mayo – the cradle of the Land League, was the principal county ... to swamp the courts with petitions to have the rents judicially fixed.'[107] These reforms did not 'pacify' Ireland, but brought about the 'constitutionalization' of popular protest. If Peelite reforms and Gladstonian free trade undermined the revolutionary potential of Chartist ideology, the reforms of 1881–2 started a similar process in Ireland. However, the two Land Acts made no provision for a minority of embittered small farmers and the whole of the labourers. These groups had provided much of the manpower for the agitation, but, like British artisans after the 1832 Reform Act, felt bypassed, if not betrayed, by 1881–2. As the farmers basked in the 'three Fs', which had no relevance for the poorer social groups, the farm workers began to wonder about the aims and purposes of the agitation they had supported.[108] Characteristically, both Parnell and Gladstone were responsive to their plight. In order to provide organization and support for such a rural 'proletariat', the Labour and Industrial Union was formed in August 1882 under Parnell's auspices. In October, the INL, reviving part of the more radical features of the old Land

rural labourer', in ibid., 311–38; D. S. Jones, 'The cleavage between graziers and peasants in the land struggle, 1890–1910', in ibid., 374–413; G. Moran, 'Land League in the west of Ireland, 1879–82', in ibid., 205.

[104] E.g. the reports of meetings in *FJ*, 27 Dec. 1882, 6 and in *FJ*, 3 Jan. 1883, 6 (Rathvilly, Co. Carlow). Cf. P. Bew and F. Wright, 'The agrarian opposition in Ulster', in Clark and Donnelly, *Irish peasants*, 193.

[105] 'Gladstone by his acceptance of the Lords amendments has killed the Land Bill but yet the d—d whigs and miserable traitors must be watched or they will try and bamboozle the people into putting some reliance in it.' (P. Egar to Dunn, Paris, 17 Aug. 1881, in Harrington papers, NLI, MS 8577 (ii).)

[106] Cruise O'Brien, *Parnell and his Party*, 127; Comerford, 'The land war and the politics of distress', 47–8; Comerford, *Fenians*, 238; Jordan, *Land and popular politics*, 306–10; Silverman, *An Irish working class*, 172, 211; Moody, *Davitt*, 498–9, 528–31. The Land Act 'produced a general reduction in rent of nearly 20 per cent ... The balance of opinion among ministers principally involved was in favour of true fair rents fixed from time to time in court, with freedom of contract thrown overboard.' Vincent, 'Gladstone and Ireland', 216.

[107] After the passing of the 1881 Act, '[a]pplications from tenants [for legal revision of their rent] poured in at the rate of several thousand a day' (B. Lewis Solow, *The land question and the Irish economy, 1870–1903* (1971), 161). Cf. Moran, 'James Daly', 202.

[108] 'That as the labourers of Ireland have proved faithful to the tenants during the last agitation, resulting in two remedial measures for the latter, we now call on them to share with the labourers some of the benefits conferred by the Land Act.' Cited in rep., 'The Irish National League ... meeting in Kilrush', *FJ*, 18 Dec. 1882, 7.

League's programme,[109] adopted some of the farm workers' demands in a successful bid for their support. Then in 1883 the Liberal government passed the Labourers' (Ireland) Act, virtually an attempt to outbid Parnell. The Act transferred part of the responsibility for the erection of adequate working-class housing to the boards of Poor Law guardians. Though this was an important step, and was well received by the labourers, Gladstone's Act was only partly successful, as the farmers were reluctant to fund working-class housing out of the poor rates.[110]

However, from Gladstone's point of view, the Labourers' Act served at least a *political* purpose. Like the 1881 Land Act for the farmers, the 1883 Act provided the labourers with an alternative to agrarian radicalism – that is, a legal framework within which they could claim their rights. It conveyed the impression that the government cared and was responsive to popular protest. Furthermore, by throwing the financial burden of working-class housing on to the rate-payers, the Labourers' Act fuelled class conflict and political tension between farmers and labourers, thus compounding the difficulties of the Nationalists. If the aim of the Liberal strategy was to defuse the Nationalist threat by institutionalizing class conflict – a tactic which belied the INL ideology of 'national' unity – there was evidence that concessions to the labourers would do the trick. Thus at an INL meeting in Dunlavin (Co. Wicklow) in 1883, when the chairman, Edward O'Kelly, appealed to national unity, he discovered that his audience were of a different opinion:

They had assembled to obtain a Land Act. The Land Act that had been given had completely failed to give justice to the farmers. They were also assembled to agitate for the amelioration of the condition of the agricultural labourer.

---

[109] Cf. 'Irish National Land League – National Convention, 15th September, 1881' in Lalor Papers, NAI, MS 8574 (4), Clause 8: 'That each farmer be recommended to set aside land for the use of the labourer or labourers, members of the League, employed on his holding, in the proportion of at least half an acre of tilled land for each thirty acres of tilled land in his occupation (or the grass of a cow for each labourer), pending further legislation for enabling labourers to become owners of the land; and that the direct or indirect payment made by the labourer for such plot shall not exceed the rent payable for it by the farmer.'

[110] Boyle, 'Irish rural labourer', 332. For an example see J. Dillon to E. Blake, 8 Apr. 1895, and enclosed letter by William McDonnell, a labourer who intended to appeal to the Irish Chief Secretary (Morley) to overrule the Longford board of guardians. 'The Guardians and farmers of this Division – McDonnell argued – seem to think anything in the way of housing was good enough for the poor. They compel their labourers to reside in houses they would consider unsafe and unfit for their cattle ... It is a fact that the Act of Parliament passed for the benefit of such men as me. [*sic*] Can be made nil and void by the opposition of unprincipled Guardians to gratify their friends.' (Blake Letters, NLI, 4681[110].)

A Voice – That is what we want.

The Chairman trusted they would all unite until that was obtained – farmer, shopkeeper, labourer –

A Voice – All but the farmers, Mr O'Kelly, and down with them.[111]

As O'Farrell has pointed out, the INL was quick to adapt Liberal rhetoric to its own needs.[112] This is true of their anti-coercion rhetoric, as we have seen, but is also relevant to their attitudes to 'class' struggle: whenever necessary and politic, INL speakers invoked the law against the tenant-dominated Poor Law guardians and demanded the full implementation of the Labourers' Act 'with a comfortable house and half an acre of land'.[113] Yet, on the whole, class conflict was a potentially embarrassing issue for the Nationalists, as it diverted attention away from the question of Home Rule, and exposed the extent to which the problems of the rural poor were a result of social inequality rather than national oppression. These tensions might have exploded into open conflict similar to that which periodically affected the relations between farmers and labourers in Britain, had it not been for the imperial (rather than national) context of Irish politics.[114] The deep-seated, widespread distrust of the government and especially of Dublin Castle engendered an attitude with which, as we have seen in the previous chapter, British radicals of an older generation were able to sympathize. This was the 'Chartist' conviction that no economic or social reforms would be possible without prior constitutional change – that 'the true remedy for Irish discontent [was] that the people should be governed by Laws made by their own representatives in a native Parliament'.[115]

Thus even such a sincere agrarian radical as Michael Davitt felt constrained to preach class harmony, exhorting 'the tenant farmers and the labourers not to look upon each other as occupying antagonistic positions in the land movement. The one common enemy you have to struggle against – he argued – [was] the principle of monopoly.'[116] Once 'monopoly' was overthrown, and Ireland had parliamentary self-government, 'then the right of the agricultural labourer to his share of the land [would] be recognised as much and as fully as the right of the tenant

---

[111] Rep., 'The National League', *FJ*, 23 July 1883, 7.

[112] O'Farrell, *England and Ireland*, 26.

[113] Rep., 'Meeting at Ashbourne, County Meath', *FJ*, 16 Nov. 1885, 7.

[114] At a popular meeting in Limerick, in preparation for the Prince of Wales' visit to Ireland, John O'Connor, MP, complained that the prince 'came as if to hunt elephants, as he did in India', while neither he nor 'any other scion of the Royal Family of England ever came in Ireland's day of trial and trouble' (rep., 'Great Nationalist demonstration in Limerick', *FJ*, 7 Apr. 1885, 6).

[115] From the first resolution, cited in rep., 'Great demonstration at Killucan', 5 Nov. 1883, 6.

[116] Cited in rep., 'Great land meeting in Wexford', *FJ*, 9 Oct. 1882, 6.

farmer (loud cheers)'.[117] To Davitt 'monopoly' was, of course, 'land-lordism' – the main social evil against which both the Nationalists and the Liberals inveighed at the time. Allegedly, 'landlordism' in Ireland was even more 'monopolistic' than in the rest of the United Kingdom, because the landlords controlled not only the land, but also the police, the courts of justice and ultimately Dublin Castle.[118] It was 'responsible for the arbitrary attempt made by the Irish Government to suppress legally convened constitutional meetings',[119] as well as for the judicial 'misconstruction' of the Land Act, for the purpose of making its provisions ineffective.[120] It operated 'a system of the most merciless coercion ever invented', and one 'of jury packing and judicial murder in operation – one of the most iniquitous that ever disgraced the judgement seat (cheers)'.[121]

In Nationalist ideology the law and the state were 'alien' institutions, a description which wealthy farmers must have found socially reassuring, because it ruled out questions of 'class', which, at the time, was poisoning farmer/labourer relations in Britain. In this context, the National League claimed to be the only institution which could provide 'the Irish' (that is, the temporary alliance between farmers and labourers) with some of the protection normally provided by the law. Likewise, only the Irish party '[was] strong enough to bring the meaters and superiors of the police to their senses (cheers)'.[122] This fostered a special sense of solidarity among all those who happened to be at the receiving end of Coercion Acts, irrespective of social background. Whatever other purpose 'coercion' actually served, it certainly helped the INL to overcome the embarrassment of class struggle by an appeal to civil liberties and national self-government. In this way it enabled the Nationalists to present moderate policy aims as a major challenge to the government. The 'radical moderation' of this strategy had the additional advantage of uniting all the fringes and factions of the movement: the

---

[117] Ibid. Quite unusually, one of the resolutions passed called for land nationalization, and the meeting endorsed the programme of the Labour and Industrial Union. For the link between Home Rule and the labourers' question in Nationalist rhetoric cf. rep., 'R. Lalor, MP, and Mr A. O'Connor, MP [addressing a meeting at Ballylinan]', *FJ*, 23 Oct. 1882, 6.

[118] M. Davitt, cited in rep., 'Messrs Davitt and M'Carthy, MP, at Edgeworthstown', *FJ*, 16 Oct. 1882, 7.

[119] From the first resolution, cited in rep., 'The Killimore-Daly meeting', *FJ*, 5 Nov. 1883, 6.

[120] T. Healy in rep., 'The Monaghan election', 22 June 1883, 3; see also the lively debate at the Kilkenny Board of Guardians between Lord Ormonde and the Nationalist guardians in rep., 'Lord Ormonde and the Land Act', 29 Dec. 1883, 3.

[121] Mr O'Brien, MP, cited in rep., 'Great demonstration at Killucan', 5 Nov. 1883, 6.

[122] T. Sexton, MP, and a man from the crowd, cited in rep., 'The representation of Sligo. the nominations: popular demonstration at Tubber Curry', *FJ*, 15 Aug. 1883, 3.

priests and well-off farmers liked its contents, the Fenians liked its results and the labourers were given yet another scapegoat for their frustration.

That the interests of the property holders could be defended without discarding the ideological framework of the liberal tradition was a further bonus for the Nationalists. They could reassure their electors and at the same time challenge British public opinion by attacking the government with arguments which were plainly drawn from the familiar Gladstonian rhetorical arsenal:

They well remembered – an Irish MP told his Newcastle audience – that before the general election of 1881 [*sic*, sc. 1880] every Liberal sounded the doctrine of hatred of coercion and the love of liberty, and whenever any high-handed action was perpetrated by the Government in office, denunciations were raised from every Liberal platform throughout the length and breadth of the land, and the country was called upon to rise up and put an end to this state of things; but when the Liberals came into power there was an end to these headstrong declarations about liberty and progress, and they found those who professed to be their friends in Opposition turn upon them as soon as they held the reins of power.[123]

While the INL claimed to stand by the rights of the people, 'unconstitutional' government repression reached an initial climax with the 1881 and 1882 Coercion Acts. The former made provision, among other things, for the arrest and detention, without trial or appeal, of any person 'reasonably suspected' of being involved in seditious activities. The latter Act, which was to continue in force for three years, conferred wide-ranging powers on the magistrates, interfered with the liberty of the press and suspended trial by jury.[124] Particularly objectionable was the imprisonment of MPs, 'confined under . . . sham accusation[s]' and ' compelled . . . to wear the convict uniform, just like any other person confined in . . . jail'. A Liberal government persecuted 'the elected representatives of the people' in Ireland, yet, 'if . . . a popular leader was arrested in France or Italy, or any other European country, some serious event would have followed'.[125] Indeed, '[i]f any other country in the world had maintained such a struggle against foreign domination as Ireland, English statesmen, poets, and writers would be loud in their praises of that country'.[126]

Michael Davitt was not an MP when he was arrested in February 1881, but was definitely a popular leader. Though the British government ensured that he would be granted privileged treatment while in prison,

[123] J. Barry, MP, cited in rep., 'Mr Healy, MP, and the Liberal Party', *FJ*, 14. Sep. 1883, 2.
[124] V. Crossman, *Politics, law and order in nineteenth-century Ireland* (1996), 224–6. See also L. P. Curtis, *Coercion and conciliation in Ireland, 1880–1892* (1963).
[125] T. D. Sullivan, MP, cited in rep., 'The National League', *FJ*, 29 Mar. 1883, 2.
[126] 'Democratic Ireland: lecture by Mr Edmund Leamy, MP', *FJ*, 7 Jan. 1886, 8.

in Ireland his arrest generated considerable emotion.[127] It was a '[viola-tion] of the spirit of English law' by an irresponsible authority, bent on pleasing a group of selfish landlords.[128] Once released, Davitt proceeded to address meetings in both Ireland and Britain, and argued that he had been imprisoned because his speeches had tried to 'provoke' the govern-ment 'to perform their duty', to act in time and prevent famine, distress and starvation in the west of Ireland. He elicited '[l]oud and prolonged cheers' from an English crowd at Bermondsey in December 1882, when he declared that '[i]f I could prevent starvation from entering the hovels of my people – if I could prevent one death during this coming winter – I would make twenty inflammatory speeches and would go to prison in the bargain'.[129] Having explained his motives, Davitt challenged his English audience to say whether in Britain they would tolerate an inquisitorial system and penal law based on circumstantial evidence and administered by 'crown prosecutors with seats on the bench' and 'special' juries. He denounced and ridiculed Forster's repressive methods, arguing that – far from providing an effective check on rural crime – they alienated the 'strong conservative' classes in Ireland and brought the law and the police into disrepute by showing that both were ineffective and biased against the public.

In their actual practice, the constabulary occasionally made things worse by lack of tact and discretion. Thus in Sligo, in August 1883, the chairman of a meeting about to be held at Riverstown was seized 'with an amount of violence which I never saw exceeded – wrote a reporter – [and] dragged ... to the police station'. Thomas Sexton, the main speaker at the meeting, tried to find out the charge against his friend, but the constable in charge refused to answer, first declaring that he '[knew] nothing about it', and then that the charges were '[his] busi-ness'. The arrest of a town 'notable' in such a way, in the presence of an MP and a large number of Nationalists assembled for a lawful meeting, was something which tested the patience of an already excited crowd. However, Sexton managed to prevent the deterioration of the situation into a riot. He 'urged [the crowd] to bear with any amount of provocation rather than give a handle to their enemies, and advised them to return home peacefully'.[130]

The Irish point of view was that the people were being deprived of their rights 'under the constitution', which was constantly being tampered with

---

[127] Cashman, *Davitt*, 239.   [128] Moody, *Davitt*, 471.
[129] Cited in rep., 'The pacification of Ireland', *FJ*, 23 Dec. 1883, 5.
[130] Rep., 'The representation of Sligo – extraordinary scene – strange arrest', *FJ*, 16 Aug. 1883, 6.

to serve class and sectarian purposes, while Nationalist leaders were imprisoned 'for language which might have been uttered with impunity on any English platform'.[131] That similar convictions were voiced not only by newspaper editors and parliamentarians, but also by farmers and their Catholic clergy,[132] conveys the extent to which the notion of constitutional rights was rooted in Irish political culture. Even before the 'Kilmainham Treaty' there was a strong link between the tenants' agitation and claims of constitutional rights, particularly freedom of speech.[133] After the 'treaty' this liberal rhetoric became the staple of Nationalist protest meetings. Voiced by the leaders at the hustings, it was echoed by ordinary people in the streets and squares when confronted with police violence. A good example is provided by the following episode, at a banned meeting in Galway, in December 1882. Following a typical Victorian custom, '[t]he various contingents [of the demonstrators] marched to the place of meeting in military order, wearing laurel leaves in their hats. There was a very large attendance of ladies.'[134] Everything was calculated to convey the impression of order and respectability. However, at 2 p.m. the police intervened to disperse the meeting, which had been prohibited earlier in the morning. At 3 p.m. 'an excited scene took place':

A farmer said in a loud voice – Who rules this island who could tolerate such tyranny – constitutional liberty suspended at the bidding of landlords? (Cries of 'Because we would not allow them hunt over our lands. We never will.')

Here a policeman proceeded towards the farmer and told him as the Lord Lieutenant's proclamation was read he should arrest him if he did not leave, and cease addressing the people.

Farmer – You can shoot me, but I will not leave. I can hardly believe Mr Gladstone would allow this devilish tyranny to be practised in his name.[135]

The conflict – as the people in this crowd saw it – was about the law and constitutional legitimacy:

Another tenant farmer stepped forward to where some police were staying in a large field. Addressing the police he said – Leave this place, ye are trespassers. I am paying a heavy rent for this place . . . I require each policeman's name.

Police – We won't leave; nor will we give our names.

Sub-Inspector Bell – Do you know that we have a legal right to be here? An offence against the law has been committed, and it is our duty to get evidence. Don't interfere with me and my men.

---

[131] L.a., 9 Feb. 1883, 4.

[132] E. Larkin, *The Roman Catholic Church and the Plan of Campaign in Ireland, 1886–1888* (1978), 75.

[133] Rep., 'The land question: freedom of speech' (a tenant farmers' meeting at Portsdown), *FJ*, 16 Mar. 1880, 5.

[134] Rep., 'Another meeting suppressed', *FJ*, 19 Dec. 1882, 6.   [135] Ibid.

Farmer – I am within my right, sir, here on my own land. I have broken no law.[136]

Eventually at four o'clock the police left, having taken the names of all the ladies and some three hundred young men, to be prosecuted at petty sessions. The people – about two thousand of them – then moved to another field and held the meeting anyway. Addressed by an Irish American, the gathering passed a resolution calling for 'complete national independence', though the spirit of the event was better captured by another resolution, which decried 'the unwarrantable and unconstitutional attempt made to suppress our legally constituted meeting' and express 'pity [for] the statesman who could trample under foot the last shred of the so-called Constitution to satisfy the vindictive and corrupt minds of the rack-renting, foxhunting landlords of Galway'.[137]

The government's justification for coercion was that it was necessary in order to preserve life and property against agrarian outrage and the organized terrorism of secret societies. With such aims Nationalist leaders and the INL fully concurred, but they regarded the government's methods as worse than useless for they failed to distinguish between passive resistance and social solidarity against eviction (including boycotting)[138] on the one hand, and actual violence on the other. By outlawing both forms of protest, the government brought about the very evils which coercion was supposed to avoid.

The reality was of course more complex, but there in no doubt that constitutional nationalists loathed political and rural crime and rejected it on both moral and political grounds. At least in this they were similar to the leaders of the 'New Model Unions' in Britain at the time of the 'Sheffield outrages' in the 1860s, having tried to establish the 'respectable' character of their movement. From this standpoint 'moonlighting' was the equivalent of what the terrorist trade union practices had been to the mid-Victorian labour movement. For example in 1882 Davitt denounced the Maamtrasna murders in Co. Galway (where five members of one family were murdered in August 1882) as a crime 'almost without a parallel for its atrocity in the annals of agrarian outrage'.[139] In 1885 he denounced moonlighting as 'a species of cowardly terrorism which would

---

[136] Ibid.   [137] Ibid.

[138] However, from 1886 boycotting was also forbidden by the INL, and offending branches were threatened with expulsion: see T. C. Harrington, secretary of the INL, to W. Kennedy, Kildorrery, 3 Feb. 1886, in Harrington Papers, MS 9454.

[139] Cited in Hammond, *Gladstone and the Irish nation*, 315. Of course later the Parnellites would denounce Spencer and Trevelyan (the Viceroy and the Chief Secretary) for 'judicial murder' once it emerged that one of the suspected assassins, Myles Joyce, was convicted and executed on spurious evidence (Heyck, *Dimensions*, 87).

do irreparable injury to Ireland and bring deserved disaster to any movement that would lend the slightest sanction to it'.[140] Justin McCarthy complained that the moonlighters 'care no more for the Land League or Home Rule or the political agitation than they did about the Eastern Question'.[141] T. C. Harrington, secretary of the INL, went as far as turning down applications for grants in support of tenants evicted in districts where serious outrages had occurred.[142] As Joseph O'Brien has written, not only did they '[take] every opportunity to denounce agrarian crime', but also they 'were as fervent in upholding the rights of private property as an English landlord'.[143]

The most infamous episode in the saga of political violence was the murder of T. H. Burke and Lord Frederick Cavendish in May 1882. If Parnell panicked, Davitt was horrified: the ex-convict offered his assistance to the police, and, jointly with other Nationalist leaders, issued a manifesto against terrorism. The latter was so strongly worded that, it was feared, it would imperil the lives of its signatories, although the Irish Republican Brotherhood repudiated the murders in the vain attempt to stem the decline in its popular influence, which, according to one member, 'became very feeble if it did not die out altogether'.[144] After the Phoenix Park murders, even violent language at demonstrations became intolerable to Davitt: once at a meeting when someone in the crowd shouted 'Down with the landlords', Davitt's response was prompt and decisive. Interrupting his speech he said: 'If I hear any more such voices as "Down with them", I shall order whoever utters such language to be ejected from the meeting (cheers).'[145] Davitt disagreed with the government not in his attitude to crime, but in his views of the best way to deal with it. For example, he denounced the 1881–5 bombing campaign – organized by Jeremiah O'Donovan Rossa and Irish American militants – as 'a method of injuring the Irish cause', a strategy which had few sympathizers in Ireland. Coercion, however, was not the right way to deal with terrorists:

---

[140] Cited in 'Meeting at Kells', *FJ*, 16 Nov. 1885, 7; for more comments along the same line see rep., 'Mr Michael Davitt again denounces outrages', *FJ*, 22 Feb. 1886, 6.

[141] Memo 'Dictated by Mr McCarthy, dated Aug. 17th 1886', concerning an interview between Parnell, Morley and McCarthy, NLI, MS 24,958 (7).

[142] Though the local branch was apparently not involved in any illegal action: Harrington to J. J. MacMahon (Co. Kerry), 5 Feb. 1886, in Harrington Papers, MS 9454.

[143] J. V. O'Brien, *William O'Brien and the cause of Irish politics, 1881–1918* (1976) 51; Macaulay, *The Holy See*, 26.

[144] Moody, *Davitt*, 536–7; the citation is from O'Toole, *Whist for your life*, 52.

[145] M. Davitt, cited in rep., 'Messrs Davitt and M'Carthy, MP, at Edgeworthstown', *FJ*, 16 Oct. 1882, 7; Moody, *Davitt*, 459.

Take Russia. Take Austria. Look at the case of Ireland. Coercion is one of the Anarchists' trump cards. Suppose Rossa and a number of his friends were given up to the English Government [by the American government], do you think the conspiracy, the outrages, would stop? No, indeed. The cause would receive a fresh impetus. Rossa and his men would be converted into martyrs, with sympathisers in America, in Ireland, in England ... You can't stamp them out as you would a snake with the heel of your boot. The effect of any coercive method would be to create a band of men, devoted and fanatical, reckless of danger and careless of life.[146]

As implied by the comparison with 'autocratic' and 'despotic' Russia and Austria, there remained, beyond the question of which strategy was best in order to 'stamp out' terrorism, Dublin Castle's persistent lack of national legitimacy. In what Callanan has described as an 'exercise in polemical ingratiation', Nationalist spokesmen conceded that after so many important reforms and the 1881–3 Land Acts in particular, there was no doubt that the Gladstone government '[meant] well toward Ireland'. However, 'the very fact that it does mean well, and that it has so completely failed, and that it is driven to such methods as the Crimes Act to maintain itself, is the clearest possible demonstration of the incapacity of any English Government satisfactorily to administer Irish affairs'.[147] Continued agitation by the INL was justified by results, as the government, by its remedial legislation, acknowledged that there were 'legitimate grievances in the working of the Irish land system'.[148] Would such legislation have been forthcoming without agitation? Once more the GOM's words were quoted against his own practice: 'Mr Gladstone has very often, and very recently, shown that he knows there are many and great Irish interests to be legislated for, and honourable Irish sentiments to be gratified, but does he not also know that even he is powerless to do that, of which both his head and his heart approve, without healthy agitation?'[149] Nationalist agitation, almost the Irish equivalent of the Midlothian campaign, had to continue, because Ireland, unlike Britain, had not really experienced the benefits accompanying the fall of 'Beaconsfieldism'. Indeed, an editorial in the *Freeman's Journal* argued,

The Government, which in England is Liberal, in Ireland disregards every canon of the Liberal creed. The politicians who in Ireland call themselves Liberal would in England be called Conservatives. It is through not comprehending this that English politicians make so many mistakes. They come into contact with so-called Irish 'Liberals', and they imagine that these men are real Liberals. But they are

---

[146] Cited in interview, 'Mr Davitt on the explosions of Saturday', *FJ*, 27 Jan. 1885, 6.
[147] L.a., *FJ*, 1 Dec. 1882, 4; Callanan, *Healy*, 95.
[148] Crossman, *Politics, law and order*, 151.   [149] L.a., 10 Nov. 1882, 4.

nothing of the kind. Speak to them in private and you will discover that they have no conception of the real principles of Liberal policy.[150]

If Liberalism was about civil rights, '[w]hich clause of the Coercion Code would a true Liberal identify himself with? That under which public meetings are suppressed, that under which the ex-mayor of Wexford has just been sent to prison, that under which newspapers are seized, that under which Messrs Davitt and Healy are going to jail – the Curfew Clauses, or the blood tax?'[151] Thus, the *Freeman's* concluded, Liberalism was a creed which, in Ireland, only the Nationalists upheld and championed: 'The essence of Liberalism is the abolition of class privileges and giving to the people full power over their own affairs. The essence of the creed of the Irish "Liberals" is distrust of the people and the retention of class privileges.' Irish 'liberalism' was first and foremost about Home Rule because '[t]here are but two living powers in Irish politics – that which aims at the maintenance through English power of the ascendency [*sic*] of a class in Ireland, and the other which claims for Irishmen the right to manage their own affairs'.[152] The latter – Parnell's party – was thus to be regarded as the real equivalent of what the Liberal party stood for in Britain: indeed, it was to be wondered whether 'there existed real "Liberals" outside the National ranks in Ireland'. In another leading article the *Freeman's* criticized Forster for his reservations about extending the franchise and representative local government to Ireland, and exposed what it perceived as the affinities between Forster's attitude and the old 'Adullamite' arguments against the extension of the franchise to the British working classes in 1866–7:

'First he would and then he wouldn't!' [Forster] said that if the franchise in England were given to the masses, Ireland also should have a Reform of the Franchise. But then the Government should see that power was not given into the hands of agitators. Ireland is not as well educated as England and Scotland, and though he disliked to use the word, there is a 'residuum' in Ireland. What does all this mean? What but that Mr Forster would only give such franchises into Irish hands as would suit the English Government's cards! What but that with all his professions of liberality he would not be influenced by motives of justice, by the principles of liberty, equality and fraternity between the countries in his legislation, but rather by the promptings of expediency and the lust of power! ... Mr Forster treats the County Government question in a similar strain. He would have a County Government Bill for Ireland as well as for England; but then suddenly bethinks him that we are wholly unaccustomed to local self-government, and above all, he would not give us control over our police.[153]

---

[150] L.a., *FJ*, 26 Jan. 1883, 4.   [151] Ibid.   [152] Ibid.   [153] Ibid.

The Royal Irish Constabulary (RIC), with its paramilitary structure and separate barracks, was the equivalent of the despised *gendarmeries* typical of France, Spain and Italy (and of the much more popular Royal Canadian Mounted Police). Such armed paramilitary forces were viewed by English radicals as incompatible with liberty. Ironically, consistency with 'English' police practice became a Nationalist battle cry. Although the RIC was actually widely respected among the ordinary people and seen as 'an attractive source of careers and husbands' by the less politicized peasants,[154] Nationalists denounced it as a symbol not only of Ireland's persistent inferiority within the Union, but also of the assumption that 'the Irish are a residuum – are, to put it in plain English – dregs!' Demanding its reform was a consequence of the fact that 'the Celt loves liberty and security as much as the Saxon does'.[155] From this point of view, Parnell's wish to replace it with a civil and unarmed police force was the most 'English' of his demands.[156]

The Union of Hearts

The movements of the Welsh people in connection with the recent distraint for tithes are very embarrassing for those Liberals who are urging forward the Coercion Act. The quondam Liberal *Spectator* ... endeavours to comfort itself by declaring that 'the Welsh have always been liable, from time to time, to outbreaks of crime of the Irish kind,' which it accounts for by their having 'the Celtic proneness to, and aptitude for, the organisation of common actions by mobs and half-constituted and tumultuous assemblies.' We suppose the phenomena of the Scottish Crofters, rising and defying the law, would be accounted for by the fact of their being Highlanders, and therefore, too, partaking of the disorderly Celtic blood. English riots are mere free fights, and, therefore, as it may be assumed, easily put down. But we think our contemporary is not quite as sagacious in drawing these distinctions as it used to be before enlisting under the banner of injustice. English riots are not, as a rule, political. We do not call an election row a political riot or disorder. It is too trivial and too temporary in its causes. But riots arising out of some great and general popular feeling are rare. But it is not for the reason the *Spectator* would have us believe. They are put down, we grant, but there is unusually [*sic, sc.* usually] no occasion for the people to repeat them. The massacre of Peterloo was followed by the first Reform Bill; the tearing down the rails of Hyde Park ensured the passing of the second. They are easily put down and they are not organised, because the people are not permanently alienated

---

[154] Maume, *Long gestation*, 7; E. A. Cameron, 'Communication or separation? Reactions to Irish land agitation and legislation in the Highlands of Scotland, c.1870–1910', *English Historical Review*, 120, 487 (2005), 649.

[155] M. Davitt cited in l.a., *FJ*, 24 Oct. 1882, 4.

[156] Annotation in Parnell's handwriting on 'Confidential – memorandum of O'Brien's suggestions', n.d. [1886], 24(8,9), Parnell Letters, MS 8581 (2).

from the Government, as they know well enough that no Government could long subsist which was in chronic hostility to popular feeling. When the *Spectator* was Liberal it would have seen this; since it has become Unionist it has to descend to the theory of race in order to explain away the phenomena brought about by misgovernment. Riots are rarer and less systematic in Scotland and Wales than in Ireland, for the simple reason that the occasions less frequently arise, and when they occur the grievances from which they sprung are certain to be remedied. Scotland received prompt justice – or at least a prompt instalment of it; Wales assuredly will do so, too; Ireland would only get a mockery of justice, which would be used at the same time as an excuse for a Coercion Act.[157]

Thus commented the *Cork Examiner* in 1887, in a perceptive deconstruction of Victorian 'national character' stereotypes and the unequal partnership within the Union. One of the effects of Gladstone's decision to adopt Home Rule was to bring to an end the sense that Ireland was fighting alone against the rest of the UK. As the Liberals took up a distinctively 'Celtic' complexion, the Irish struggle became the central feature of a broader democratic project. Moderate Irish nationalists had always longed for such recognition.

As early as 1866 the welcome granted by Dublin to John Bright – who, together with J. S. Mill, had then just earned Irish gratitude by opposing the suspension of *habeas corpus* – showed how responsive the country was to constitutionalist rhetoric even in times of threatened revolutionary risings. His visit personified the links between the Radicals and the National Association of Ireland, established in 1864 and part of an influential Irish movement to emulate the English Liberation Society. According to Comerford, 'it was evident that Bright commanded the support of a far wider spectrum of Irish opinion and interests than any living Irishman'.[158] Barry O'Brien may not have been the only supporter of 'physical force' nationalism to be converted to parliamentary politics by reading John Bright's speeches.[159] Not surprisingly, during the

---

[157] L.a., *Cork Examiner*, 7 June 1887, 2.

[158] Comerford, *Fenians*, 143. See R. Barry O'Brien, *John Bright* (1910), 31: 'Why should I write a monograph on John Bright? What is there in common between the English Puritan statesman and an Irish Catholic Nationalist? Had a stranger entered my father's house in the West of Ireland forty years ago [i.e. in 1860], the first object which would have met his eye was a bust of John Bright. Why was it there? Because alone among leading English statesmen, at that time, Bright fearlessly identified himself with the Irish popular cause.'

[159] This was the beginning of a long relationship with the Liberals. His *parliamentary history of the Irish land question* (1880) was praised by both Bright and Gladstone for its contribution to the debate on the Land Bill. In the 1890s he was a sub-editor and later acting editor of the Gladstonian *The Speaker*. Yet, O'Brien remained always a loyal Parnellite and in 1899 published Parnell's official biography: P. Maume, 'O'Brien, Richard Barry (1847–1918)', *ODNB*, 41, 381–2.

following few years popular liberalism, which Bright had done so much to generate and Gladstone came to lead, seemed to achieve a virtual 'incorporation' of Irish nationalist politics into a pan-Britannic crusade for reform. Gladstone offered to the Irish what he was also offering to both Welsh and Scottish reformers: 'an alternative to nationalism'.[160] At the election of 1868, disestablishment and the claim of 'constitutional liberties' ensured that 'anyone seriously seeking catholic [sic] votes was obliged to promise support for Gladstone'.[161] For the Liberals it was a triumph.

Yet, only a few months later the question of the Fenian prisoners generated widespread popular protest, which culminated in the Cabra demonstration organized by the Amnesty Association in October 1869. The farmers were no friends of the Fenians, but the prisoners were 'adopted' as symbols of all popular grievances. It has been argued that the 200,000 people who took part 'were not . . . rejecting Gladstone: they were, rather, letting him know how much they expected of him'.[162] Whatever the case, this agitation induced a number of Irish Liberal MPs – including Sir John Gray of the *Freeman's Journal* – and many 'Gladstonian' Catholic priests, to '[jump] on a bandwagon which they feared to ignore'.[163] Though allegiances had not changed, it was already evident that land reform – the crucial political issue – would determine the fortunes of liberalism in Ireland.

It was frustration about Gladstone's first Land Act which led both to the foundation of the Home Government Association in May 1870, and to the rekindling of agrarian unrest.[164] The latter forced the government to renew the Peace Preservation Act (April 1870), which in turn disappointed Irish expectations about 'constitutional liberties', and compounded the irritation already felt about the continued suspension of the Habeas Corpus Act (from 1866). On the one hand, agrarian outrages were serious enough to prevent the Liberal government from proceeding to grant an early release of the prisoners and to mitigate coercion: in fact, the number of incidents had increased and continued to do so (from 160 in 1868 to 767 in 1869). On the other hand, violent episodes were largely confined to a few counties[165] and Irish opinion resented coercion as excessive and unjustifiable. Already in March 1869, even normally conservative Protestant newspapers argued that '[i]f the power of the Imperial Parliament be used only to suspend the Constitution in the whole of

---

[160] D. Thornley, *Isaac Butt and Home Rule* (1964), 21; Bull, *Land*, (1996), 91–2; Maume, *Long gestation*, 3.
[161] Comerford, *Fenians*, 162.   [162] Ibid., 173.   [163] Ibid., 174.
[164] Thornley, *Butt*, 83–137; Comerford, *Fenians*, 181, 187–8.
[165] Crossman, *Politics, law and order*, 117.

Ireland, it may well be questioned whether the model of a free Legislature might not be advantageously borrowed, for Irish use, from Canada'.[166]

In this context, the first victory for a Home Rule candidate came in 1871, at a by-election in County Meath, traditionally a constitutional Nationalist stronghold. Though this result was due to the abstention of the previously Liberal farmers (the turn-out was only 28 per cent), other nationalist successes soon followed, sparking off a mass exodus of Gladstonian voters and candidates towards the Home Rule party. The latter was attractively moderate in political terms, and firmly identified with the tenant rights movement. As a consequence, by 1874 the Liberal party, which had held 66 seats (out of 105), had been reduced to 10. By contrast, Home Rule now occupied 60 (out of 103 – two seats having been disenfranchised).[167] However, of these, about 30 were held either by former Liberals who had changed colours, or by MPs who had been elected for the first time and had similar allegiances.

As the previous two sections of the present chapter have shown, such fundamental loyalties proved more resilient than election results would suggest, and were shared by the non-revolutionary nationalists who supported Parnell after 1882. This post-liberal cultural environment was ready for Gladstone's conversion to Home Rule. Well before the 'Hawarden Kite' was flown by the Liberal leader's son, Herbert, in December 1885, it had repeatedly been rumoured that Gladstone was 'secretly' in favour of Home Rule. In March, commenting on Gladstone's manifesto to his Midlothian electors, the *Freeman's Journal* claimed to detect 'between the lines of Mr Gladstone's proclamation the restraining hand of men who are behind him'. The latter were animated by opportunistic considerations: 'It is obvious that the Liberal Party fears that in the English Elections it would lose by an apparent yielding to the Home Rule Party more than it would gain by conceding to Ireland her desire, and that Mr Gladstone is held back from a more specific *pronounciamiento* by that general and party loyalty.'[168] Perhaps these expectations were not

---

[166] *Dublin Evening Mail*, 11 Mar. 1869; cf. *The Irish Times*, 10 Mar. 1869, both quoted in Thornley, *Butt*, 86. On coercion see Crossman, *Politics, law and order*, 114–52, 218–20.

[167] P. J. Corish, 'Cardinal Cullen and the National Association of Ireland', in *Reactions to Irish Nationalism* (1987), 163; Comerford, *Fenians*, 197–8.

[168] L.a., *FJ*, 12 Mar. 1880, 4. Indeed, already in February 1880, in the Commons, Gladstone's speech upon the Obstruction Resolution had been cheered by the Irish party, who interpreted it as 'the most weighty parliamentary pronouncement in favour of the principle and spirit of the Home Rule cause' (*FJ*, 28 Feb. 1880, 4). Gladstone had argued that Parliament was over-stretched and could not cope with the legislative demands of the various parts of the empire. For sympathetic Nationalist attitudes to Gladstone in 1880 cf. Callanan, *Healy*, 44.

unrelated to the enthusiastic reception accorded to Gladstone during his second visit to Ireland, in August 1880. When he landed,

On the quay a considerable crowd had collected, by whom the Premier was cheered. Rough working men, grey-haired priests, and railway porters came forward and shook him by the hand, some of them crying out, 'You are a friend to Ireland.' ... [After visiting Dublin] Mr Gladstone walked back to the station, being greeted with great enthusiasm on the way. The station was crowded and so was that at Kingstown, where the ticket collectors were too much engaged in cheering, and waving their caps to attend to their business of taking tickets.[169]

Over the next few years these hopes, shared by Parnell himself in May 1882,[170] were periodically strengthened by the Prime Minister's son, Herbert. In November 1882 the *Freeman's Journal* rightly sensed that a conversion was taking place, and reported that 'in theory he is ready to accept the idea of Self-Government for Ireland, so long as the supremacy of the Imperial Parliament is maintained'.[171] This was of course a concession which moderate nationalists were only too eager to make. The only thorny issue was the question of import duties. The *Freeman's* claimed that the status of Australia and Canada (entailing control over trade legislation) would be best for Ireland and compatible with the principles of free trade, but that Ireland was prepared to forfeit its claims in this area and accept a more limited autonomy, similar to the one enjoyed by the states of the American Union.[172]

Speculations as to Gladstone's 'secret' intentions continued over the next few years. In January 1883, at a National League meeting in Wexford, Herbert Gladstone was quoted as having said '[t]hat the British Government in its rule of Ireland was the worst government in all Europe'. How should such a statement be read? 'Mr Herbert Gladstone was a very young man, but they had it on words of authority that wisdom often comes from the mouth of babes; and he hoped that the old man would take heed to the words of his son, and act on them.'[173] About a month later, the *Freeman's Journal* devoted a lengthy commentary to another speech by the GOM's son, in which he advocated full representative equality for Ireland within the UK, but stopped short of Home Rule and rejected separation as an option. Stressing the high esteem in which both Herbert and his father were held by the Irish, the

---

[169] *Ti*, 30 Aug. 1880, 8.   [170] Cited in Moody, *Davitt*, 532.
[171] L.a., *FJ*, 30 Nov. 1882, 4. See A. B. Cooke and J. R. Vincent, 'Herbert Gladstone, Forster and Ireland (I)', *Irish Historical Studies*, 17, 68 (1971), 526; and *Irish Historical Studies*, 18, 69 (1973), 74–89.
[172] L.a., *FJ*, 30 Nov. 1882, 4.
[173] T. D. Sullivan, MP, cited in 'Meeting at Gorey', *FJ*, 8 Jan. 1883, 6.

editorialist pointed out that, in so far as constitutional government was government by the majority of the people, and the majority of the Irish wanted Home Rule, Home Rule was the only solution to the Irish question. Herbert Gladstone

> [was] avoiding the conclusions of his own premises. They do not lead to the granting of separation, which the majority of the Irishmen does not demand, and which, therefore, we reject with him. But they do lead to Home Rule, and to Home Rule in its fullest as well as its fairest extent consistent with the integrity of the Empire ... If a people have the right to judge for themselves what is good for them, and if they judge that to be Home Rule, then they should be let give Home Rule a fair trial.[174]

It was against the background of such expectations and rumours, and in the context of a long-standing Irish tradition of support for liberalism, that the impact in Ireland of Gladstone's adoption of Home Rule must be seen. In 1884 the extension of the franchise added about half a million to the Irish electorate, which now grew to about 700,000.[175] At the ensuing election, in the forty-nine contested elections outside Ulster the Nationalist candidates were elected with 80 per cent of the popular vote or more: Jeremiah Sheehan in East Kerry secured 3,069 votes to his opponent's 30 and J. F. X. O'Brien in South Mayo received 4,953 to 75.[176] Most of the newly elected Parnellites were resident in Ireland, though less than one-half of them resided in the constituency to which they were elected: in other words, many of them were 'party' men, rather than local politicians, the product of the double screen of clergy and party managers which operated the selection.[177] Socially they have been described as representing the first Irish 'labour' party: they were farmers, small tradesmen and provincial journalists. Only nine of them had university education.[178] Most were ardent nationalists and ex-Land Leaguers or ex-Fenians, to such an extent that Cruise O'Brien has suggested that '[a] party composed of such men as these would, if it had existed in 1881–2, have made the evolution into constitutionalism

---

[174] L.a., *FJ*, 13 Feb. 1883, 4. For Herbert Gladstone's vigorous disclaimer see his letter to William Haley, dated 20 Feb. 1883, in William Haley Papers, NLI, MS 3905.

[175] Shannon, *Balfour*, 18; K. T. Hoppen, *Elections politics and society in Ireland, 1834–1885* (Oxford, 1984).

[176] Cruise O'Brien, *Parnell and his Party*, 150, n. 2.

[177] Ibid., 157. Cf below, chapter 7.

[178] Cruise O'Brien, *Parnell and his Party*, 154–5. After 1885, the party reverted to more prosperous candidates (ibid., 269). For evidence of urban working-class support for the Nationalists see rep., 'Workmen's club', *FJ*, 4 Jan. 1886, 6 and speech by the Revd Thomas Phelan, in rep., 'Demonstration in the Co. Kilkenny', *FJ*, 4 Jan. 1886, 6.

decidedly more difficult.'[179] This can perhaps be borne in mind as we assess the extent of Gladstone's political achievement in converting 'physical force' people to parliamentary politics – a success which compares well with the 'conversion' between 1848 and 1868 of the ex-Chartists to Liberalism.

It is not clear to what extent rank-and-file Nationalists had a view of the first Home Rule Bill, but it is obvious that in their response to Gladstone's Bill they were deeply influenced by the leaders of the National party,[180] as well as by their tendency to react against the Conservatives. In this sense the old claim that 'the Irish Question was an invention of British politicians'[181] is correct – because they helped to polarize the terms of the debate. In any case, from the beginning of 1886, Gladstone's adoption of Home Rule was celebrated at Nationalist meetings as the natural culmination of a long career of truly and consistently Liberal reforms, many of which had benefited Ireland.[182] However, the actual Home Rule Bill at first received a mixed welcome,[183] which only changed into outright enthusiasm when people began to appreciate the difficulty of the political situation in Parliament. Apparently, the Nationalists originally expected that 'if the Grand Old Man were allowed to form a cabinet, he would easily get over the kickers in the Liberal ranks who are now shying at Home Rule, and once in power, if his Bill were accepted in Ireland, the only obstacle to its passing would be the House of Lords'.[184] A straight constitutional struggle would then follow, with the Radicals 'mending or ending' the Lords. In other words, the main problem was supposed to be the nature of the Bill, which might not satisfy Irish demands, rather than Gladstone's ability to carry whatever Bill he chose to adopt. As a consequence, the predominant initial feature in the popular response both in Ireland and among the Irish in America focused on the intrinsic merits of the Bills,[185] which were limited and led some – who had not forgotten the

---

[179] Cruise O'Brien, *Parnell and his Party*, 156.
[180] E.g. speech by Alfred Webb, MP, cited in rep., 'The National League', *FJ*, 17 Mar. 1886, 2.
[181] D. G. Bayce, *The Irish question and British politics, 1886–1996* (Basingstoke, 1996), 34.
[182] Thomas Sexton, MP, and the Right Hon. T. D. Sullivan, Lord Mayor of Dublin, cited in 'The Irish National League', *FJ*, 3 Feb. 1886, 2. For more examples see reports of branch meetings of the INL published regularly in *United Ireland* (6–7), especially April–June 1886.
[183] E.g. l.a., *FJ*, 9 Apr. 1886, 4. Cf. Loughlin, *Gladstone*, Appendix I, 293–4.
[184] L.a., *United Ireland*, 2 Jan. 1886, 2.
[185] Cf. T. M. Healy, MP, cited in rep., 'The National League: the Irish Bills' (a meeting of the Central branch of the INL to comment upon the 1886 Bills), *FJ*, 21 Apr. 1886, 6; and rep. 'Irish-American opinion of the measure of Home Rule – Gladstone's Bill acceptable', *FJ*, 24 Apr. 1886, 6.

disappointments of 1870–3 and 1881–5 – to warn that Gladstone was not to be trusted.[186]

The question of taxation – and, implicitly, free trade and protection of Irish industry – was an issue on which Nationalist opposition focused. The 'revival of Irish industries' had long been one of Parnell's most cherished dreams.[187] In 1886 his protectionist dream was echoed and discussed by various speakers and newspapers.[188] However, quite apart from Liberal hostility to the very idea of protection, the latter was hardly feasible given the fact that most Irish industries were concentrated in the North-East, which was staunchly free trader. It is not clear whether protection could ever have brought about industrialization in the South, but in any case, the farmers showed no interest in subsidizing inefficient Irish industries by paying higher prices for locally manufactured goods. Of course, complaints about the effects of foreign competition on the price of Irish *agricultural* products were widespread, but were usually accompanied by a prescription for purely agrarian solutions: namely, adequate reductions in the rents and land reform.[189] The latter was consistent with the Nationalist message of unity across the class divide; by contrast, agricultural protection would alienate urban consumers and workers, who supported the free importation of cheap American goods.[190]

This and other problems – such as the control of the constabulary – would have been more controversial had it not been for the rapid deterioration of the parliamentary prospects of Home Rule in any form or shape. The split in the Liberal party, the resolute hostility of the

---

[186] Amendment by Mr John McEvoy to the (pro-Gladstone) resolution proposed by C. Dennehy, in rep., 'The Dublin Corporation and Home Rule', *FJ*, 15 Feb. 1886, 2. Significantly, this amendment obtained only four votes out of forty. In a private conversation with McCarthy, Parnell said, 'he [was] sure we shall be able to accept Gladstones [*sic*] scheme as a complete settlement of the Home Rule Question' (J. Mccarthy to Rose C. M. Praed, n.d. [March 1886], *c*. two weeks before the introduction of the first Home Rule Bill, NLI, MS 24,958 (5)).

[187] Strauss, *Irish nationalism and British democracy*, 174; Kennedy, 'Economic thought', 185. In 1882 a meeting at Ballylinan adopted a resolution aimed at encouraging 'native industry' by purchasing 'nothing that has not been manufactured in Ireland': rep., 'Mr R. Lalor, MP, and Mr A. O'Connor, MP', *FJ*, 23 Oct. 1882, 6.

[188] Sir Thomas Esmonde, MP, cited in *FJ*, 4 Jan. 1886, 6; 'The influence of an Irish Parliament on Irish industries: a lecture by Mr Charles Dawson', *FJ*, 5 Jan. 1886, 6; cf. *United Ireland*, 2 Jan. 1886, 6.

[189] Speech by the Very Revd N. Keena, PP, in rep., 'Sheriff's sale at Kells', *FJ*, 4 Jan. 1886, 6. After the Parnell split and in the run up to the 1892 election, the Nationalists tended to emphasize the extent to which the Bank of Ireland regarded the prospect of a Home Rule victory with equanimity: no surprises, 'business as usual' seemed to be the Nationalist approach to financial matters: l.a., *FJ*, 16 July 1892, 4.

[190] Rep., 'The City of Dublin Workingmen's Club', *FJ*, 16 Feb. 1883, 4.

Conservatives and the dramatic struggle in Parliament ensured that popular debate shifted rapidly from details to general principles, and from rational analysis to the emotional assertion of moral imperatives. To some extent this 'chain reaction' followed a pattern reminiscent of English responses to the 1866–7 Reform crisis: at that time working-class radicals had rallied round the doomed Reform Bill introduced by Russell and Gladstone more for the principles at stake and to affirm their own 'respectability', than out of any commitment to the Bill as such.[191] In 1886 the Conservatives and Liberal Unionists did for the Home Rule Bill what the Tories and Liberal 'Adullamites' had done for the Reform Bill twenty years before: they converted a moderate proposal into a symbol, a touchstone and *the* solution to the Irish question. In Ireland the GOM began to be represented in ways reminiscent of the hero worship lavished on him by British working-class radicals in 1864–7, as the first statesman to protest against 'the whole system of exaggeration and caricature directed ... towards the Irish character',[192] the emancipator of 'humble "working [men]" ' whom the Conservatives had declared 'incompetent and unworthy to enjoy the benefit of the Franchise'.[193] With their denunciations of the Liberal leader, in 1886 Salisbury, Hartington and Chamberlain, more than anyone or anything else, persuaded Irish Nationalist opinion that Gladstone was, indeed, their liberator.

In June the inauguration of the new Midlothian campaign was celebrated by *United Ireland* in an article entitled 'Mr Gladstone's departure for the front'.[194] By then the GOM seemed to have overtaken even Parnell as the new recipient of popular adulation in both Ireland and America. Two of the three resolutions of sympathy forwarded by 'Chicago citizens in mass meeting assembled' praised the Prime Minister and 'the services rendered by him to liberty and humanity'. His ability 'to overcome prejudice ... and his manifest desire to undo the wrongs and remove the dissensions' between Ireland and Britain 'do honour not only to his head and heart, but also to the nation and the age of which he is so conspicuous a citizen and leader'.[195] He was the friend of the people who did not consider personal costs when 'justice and truth' were at stake. A leading article in the *Freeman's Journal* compared Gladstone to 'the resolute hero of the "Pilgrim's Progress" [who] will

[191] Biagini, *Liberty*, 257–64.
[192] T. M. Healy, MP, cited in 'The Irish National League', *FJ*, 6 May 1886, 6.
[193] James Woods, a working man, in a letter to Gladstone enclosed with his pamphlet on *Ancient and Modern Sketches of the County of Westmeath*, Dublin, 1890. The letter was not dated. St Deiniol's Library, Hawarden, 'Pamphlets on Ireland', 5/D/10.
[194] *United Ireland*, 17 June 1886, 1.
[195] Cited in rep., 'American sympathy with Home Rule', *FJ*, 5 June 1886, 5.

push on, undaunted by difficulties'.[196] At the end of April 'the Archbishop and clergy of the archdiocese of Cashel and Emly, in Conference assembled' produced a powerful endorsement of the GOM, shaped along similarly Bunyanesque lines:

We ... desire to express our deep sense of gratitude to the Right Hon. William Ewart Gladstone ... for the many signal services he has from time to time rendered to our country during his distinguished career as a statesman, notably for the disestablishment of the Protestant Church, for the Land and Franchise Acts, and, in general, for the great and abiding interest he has for many years evinced in everything that could tend to the progress and pacification of Ireland. But at this, perhaps the most critical period of our history, we feel called upon to declare, in a very special manner, that we have been profoundly moved by the heroic fortitude, the utter forgetfulness of self, and the fearless devotion to high principle which he has manifested by the framing of those measures for the better government of Ireland quite recently proposed by him and read a first time under his auspices in the House of Commons.[197]

This 'politics of martyrdom' culminated with the election of 1886. As Callanan has written, '[t]he Liberal-nationalist alliance was sealed as much by the defeat of Gladstone's home rule bill as by its introduction ... the *éclat* of Gladstone's embrace of home rule was perpetuated through a sentimental solidarity in defeat.' After the election '[a] sense of unrequited moral purpose suffused what had been a parliamentary alliance to achieve a defined end'.[198] To Healy, Gladstone 'appeared to unite in his person a timeless integrity with modern enlightenment'.[199] His enthusiasm for the GOM was echoed all over the country. Nationalist agitators and MPs, travelling by train to a demonstration at Nenagh (Co. Tipperary) in January 1887 were met 'at the different stations after Ballybrophy ... by large crowds of people who cheered repeatedly for the members of the Irish party, Mr Gladstone, and the Plan of Campaign'.[200] In October the *Freeman's Journal* referred to

This veteran statesman, whose name and work reflect so much lustre upon the Empire to which his genius has been devoted, has all but completed his fourscore years, and yet the series of wonderful speeches which he has delivered during the present week ... are a perfect marvel of keen, masterful, and enthusiastic intellectual force. His almost unequal [sic] abilities are a tower of strength to any party, but the whole man, as he stands to-day, great alike in his unconquerable vitality,

---

[196] L.a., *FJ*, 16 Feb. 1886, 4.
[197] 'The Archbishop and clergy of Cashel and the Prime Minister', *FJ*, 30 Apr. 1886, 5. Cf. rep., 'The hierarchy, clergy and people, and coercion', *FJ*, 13 Apr. 1887, 6.
[198] Callanan, *Healy*, 232.   [199] Ibid., 233.
[200] Rep., 'Magnificent demonstration at Nenagh', *FJ*, 7 Jan. 1887, 2.

and in the brilliant record of the service which he has rendered to his country, lends an inspiring and consecrating spirit to the cause which he espouses.[201]

While Hawarden became 'a sort of Mecca or Lourdes' for the Nationalists, the GOM was eulogized by his Irish supporters in terms which even his most enthusiastic constituents in Midlothian might have found extravagant: Davitt noted that 'Gloria Gladstone in Excelsis' seemed to be the text of the new Nationalist anthem.[202] Enthusiasm for the GOM rebounded on his supporters and backbenchers. In September, English and Scottish Liberal party delegates visiting Ireland were given a triumphal welcome in both Dublin and the provinces.[203] Earlier, in August, there had been popular demonstrations, including public speeches and processions, in Limerick, Mitchelstown and Kanturk, Co. Cork, to celebrate the news that the Liberal candidate had won the Nantwich by-election, in Cheshire. In Kanturk 'the band of the town turned out and played through the streets. Quite a demonstration was made, and much enthusiasm and rejoicing was manifested at these tidings.'[204]

As early as December 1885 Healy had claimed that the Liberal party's adoption of Home Rule would ensure that the Nationalists 'would regard [themselves] as member [sic] of the Liberal party'.[205] Now his prophecy was almost literally fulfilled: Liberals and Nationalists shared a constitutional programme, an interpretation of the Irish past and a vision of the empire's future which was to be spearheaded by 'the great combined movement of Liberalism and Irish nationality'.[206] According to Alan O'Day, Justin McCarthy was 'a genuine Gladstonian' by August 1886,[207] and Healy had acquired a similar reputation.[208] Michael Hurst

---

[201] L.a., *FJ*, 21 Oct. 1887, 4.   [202] Callanan, *Healy*, 232, 234.

[203] See rep., 'Visit of the English delegates to Tralee: great demonstration en route: enthusiastic reception in the capital of the Kingdom', *Cork Examiner*, 20 Sep. 1887, 3; and rep., 'The Scotch delegates in Cork', ibid., 25 Sep. 1887, 2.

[204] Rep., 'The great victory in Nortwich', *Cork Examiner*, 18 Aug. 1887, 2; for Mitchelstown's reaction see ibid., 17 Aug. 1887, 3.

[205] Cited in Callanan, *Healy*, 139. As early as 1882 rumours to that same effect had been circulated by Captain O'Shea, who claimed to be speaking on Parnell's behalf in the run-up to the 'Kilmainham Treaty': T. Wemyss Reid, *The life of the Rt Hon. W. E. Forster*, 2 vols. (1888; 1970 edn), vol. II, 437.

[206] L.a., *Cork Examiner*, 1 Jan. 1887, 2.

[207] O'Day, *Parnell and the first Home Rule episode*, 210. Before becoming a Nationalist MP, McCarthy had worked as a London Liberal journalist and author of popular history books. For the development of his attitude to Gladstone see McCarthy to Rose C. M. Praed, n.d.[February (?) 1886], NLI, MS 24,958 (5) and McCarthy to Rose C. M. Praed, 23 Apr. 1888: 'Gladstone made a splendid speech, magnificent in voice, magnificent in his advanced and advancing Radicalism.'

[208] Cited in Callanan, *Healy*, 351.

has suggested that Parnell himself had become 'if not a Liberal, then an Irish nationalist deviously striving to maintain synchronised beats in the Union of Hearts'.[209] While in 1874–5 Isaac Butt and several other Home Rulers had refused to join Liberal clubs as they had perceived membership to be 'a breach of the Home Rule pledge',[210] in the aftermath of the 1886 election Parnell, the two Redmonds and thirty-three other Nationalist MPs joined the National Liberal Club.[211] The 1887 Parnell banquet at the National Liberal Club was described by the *Freeman's Journal* as

unique in the history of the two countries. It gives the social seal . . . to the political friendliness of the Liberal and the Irish parties in Parliament; it typifies the kindly and ardent feeling which has sprung up between the two peoples as the first fruit of Mr Gladstone's great policy, and it is the symbol of the union of heart which is the object of that policy to substitute for the union of force which has been so long the scandal of England and the degradation of Ireland.[212]

This apotheosis of the 'Union of Hearts' was repeated the following year, when the National Reform Union gave a banquet in honour of the so-called 'Balfour's criminals' – Nationalists imprisoned under the Coercion Act – in the Manchester Free Trade Hall.[213] As we have seen in the previous chapter, this banquet was a joint Liberal–Nationalist act of defiance against Unionist coercion. The latter had played a considerable role in consolidating pro-Liberal feelings among the Nationalists, as much as it had helped the Liberals in Britain to sympathize with Parnell's party and Home Rule. Newspaper reports projected the image of a popular struggle for the restoration of constitutional rights. They described police heavy-handedness in the impossible task of preventing demonstrations and speeches, and clashes between constables and crowds. The latter, under the leadership of Irish Nationalist and British Liberal MPs, with the blessing of the parish clergy, insisted on the right of public meeting, and stood by the Liberal interpretation of 'the constitution'.[214] The government had allegedly adopted 'Peterloo' methods, alluding to the 1817 'massacre' of peaceful demonstrators: meetings, platforms and squares were cleared by force, with MPs, journalists,

---

[209] Hurst, 'Parnell in the spectrum of nationalisms', 97.   [210] Thornley, *Butt*, 217.
[211] Cruise O'Brien, *Parnell and his Party*, 331. On the other hand, a number of Liberal MPs joined the (by then officially suppressed) INL (ibid., 209). The tradition continued after the split: see receipt for membership subscription in Edward Blake's Papers, NLI, [465], 4685. The receipt is undated, but Blake was first elected to the House of Commons in 1892.
[212] L.a., *FJ*, 21 July 1887, 4.   [213] See the commentary in l.a., *FJ*, 15 Mar. 1888, 4.
[214] Rep., 'Large assemblies dispersed: the police let loose on the people: bayonet and baton charges . . .', *FJ*, 9 Apr. 1888, 5.

town 'notables' and Catholic priests occasionally being beaten up in the process. Eventually, in 1887, the Mitchelstown 'massacre' – when the police fired on the crowd after an unsuccessful attempt to disperse a meeting – brought about almost a latter-day repetition of Peterloo. We have already seen the response in Britain. In Ireland the public outcry was enormous, and the actions of the police and the Balfour administration denounced as the ultimate expression of 'the system of [government] terrorism which existed in this country'.[215] That even in the days of Mitchelstown the Nationalist leaders, priests and press consistently condemned agrarian outrages and 'moonlighting',[216] while Balfour was defending police violence, further emphasized the crisis of legitimacy experienced by Dublin Castle.

However, the fact that the Liberal party was up in arms against this 'shocking result of the Government's interference with the right of public meeting',[217] created the feeling that constitutional strategies were really working. The old sense of isolation – based on the impression that Ireland had to fend for itself and could count on no friends in Britain – had gone, and with it the residual legitimacy of revolutionary nationalism. All over the United Kingdom it was a battle of 'masses against classes', of '[t]he democracies of Great Britain and Ireland ... now for the first time fighting shoulder to shoulder', against aristocratic privilege and 'Tory despotism'. The government had to reckon 'not with the Irish people merely, but with the masses in England as well'.[218] The credit for this new situation was given to Gladstone, who had masterminded the people's emancipation by first enfranchising the householders, and then starting the Home Rule campaign. 'The working classes are the rulers of England now, and their liberator is their leader and our best friend. They will not suffer their brethren in Ireland to be sacrificed to the cold platitudes of doctrinaires or the brutal greed and bigotry of a dominant class.'[219] For '[t]he poor love the poor. A double bond of interest and sympathy binds the working classes of the two countries together.'[220] Every fresh 'coercion outrage' – like the Glebeigh evictions (Co. Kerry), when in the depth of winter, forty people, including infants, were forcibly

[215] Rep., 'The Lord Mayor on the Mitchelstown meeting', *Cork Examiner*, 13 Sep. 1887, 4.
[216] E.g. 'Shocking tragedy in Clare: encounter between police and moonlighters', *Cork Examiner*, 13 Sep. 1887, 2.
[217] L.a. paraphrasing a speech by Sir William Harcourt in the Commons, *Cork Examiner*, 13 Sep. 1887, 2.
[218] L.a., *FJ*, 2 Feb. 1887, 4.
[219] '*United Ireland* and the outrages', cited. in *Cork Examiner*, 21 Jan. 1887, 3.
[220] Ibid. For the British side of this story of class solidarity cf. chapter 5.

expelled from their cottages by the police and left homeless – cemented the Nationalist–Gladstonian solidarity. This was based on the assumption that any other consideration ought to be overridden by the dictates of humanity and natural rights.[221]

The effectiveness of such rhetoric was greatly increased by Gladstone himself. His speeches against coercion and in defence of '[the] legitimate combination which is allowed [to] the people in England and denied [to] the people in Ireland' were elaborated upon in leading articles[222] and reported verbatim not only by the national press, but also in some provincial newspapers.[223] The daily spectacle – in its newspaper rendition – of the parliamentary debate on the latest Coercion Bill, with vigorous speeches by Gladstone, John Morley and others, helped to consolidate these feelings. The deliberations of dozens of meetings throughout the land indicated both the strength of the popular feeling against coercion, and the extent to which the 'Union of Hearts' was affecting the culture of popular Nationalism. On the one hand, coercion was condemned in liberal terms: it was 'cruelly oppressive ... and absolutely subversive of our civil rights',[224] 'violating our constitutional rights as free citizens, insulting the dignity of our nation',[225] and ultimately inspired by the aim of 'coerc[ing] the Irish tenants into paying impossible rents'.[226] On the other, popular discussions did not seem to be complete unless they were concluded by a vote of thanks 'to the Right Hon. W. E. Gladstone and the great Liberal party in England for their able advocacy of the rights of the Irish people to National self-government'.[227] At a meeting at St Margaret (Co. Dublin) a speaker declared that '[t]he terms of the Coercion Bill were degrading and provocative, but the palliative influence of Gladstone's statesmanship furnished a rampart of passive

---

[221] '*United Ireland* and the outrages', cited in *Cork Examiner*, 21 Jan. 1887, 3. Cf. reports in *Cork Examiner*, 12 Jan. 1887, 3, and 14 Jan. 1887, 3. Despite his scepticism about Gladstone worship, Michael Davitt was one of the spokesmen for this naive faith in democracy: see rep., 'Mr Michael Davitt in England: meeting at Radcliffe', *FJ*, 26 Sep. 1888, 6.

[222] L.a., *FJ*, 8 Nov. 1888, 4.

[223] Thus on 20th October 1887 the *Cork Examiner* devoted two of its four pages to a report of Gladstone's Nottingham speech, which relaunched the Home Rule campaign in England.

[224] 'Meeting in Enniskillen', *FJ*, 18 Apr. 1887, 6. Years later, John Redmond – by then leader of the break-away Parnellite group – quoted J. S. Mill, J. Fitzjames Stephen and Mazzini to show that Balfour's prisoners (whom Gladstone refused to release) were being punished for 'political' offences: newscutting dated 13 Nov. 1893, in J. Redmond Papers, NAI, MS 7419.

[225] 'Meeting in Monaghan', *FJ*, 18 Apr. 1887, 6.   [226] 'Meeting at Rathfarnham', ibid.

[227] Cited in rep., The National League: Meeting at Queenstown', *Cork Examiner*, 6 Sep. 1887, 3, third resolution.

resistance behind which the people were invincible (cheers)'.[228] At the same meeting – and at many others – resolutions were passed to affirm that 'Mr Gladstone's Bill for the Government of Ireland is the only solution of the Irish difficulty'.[229] Even speakers who had not lost their anti-English panache had good words for the Liberal leader: 'When Mr Gladstone – fine old man, grand old man (great cheering) – got up to speak a few nights before he was insulted as if he had been a mere Irish Nationalist member by these Tories.'[230]

In one sense at least, Gladstone had achieved the most complete form of 'unionism' in nineteenth-century politics. In 1886 Healy had asserted the existence of a 'dual leadership' in the Liberal–Nationalist alliance, and – prophetically, in view of the outcome of the 1890 split – had acknowledged a divided allegiance.[231] In March 1887 the GOM was said to have 'formally taken command of the forces opposed to Coercion',[232] which was a threat to British as much as to Irish liberty. The Nationalist press was proud to take its line against the government from Liberal speeches,[233] and the anti-tithe agitation in Wales – another popular rising for farmers' rights – was closely and sympathetically reviewed in Irish newspapers. As Liberalism developed a distinctive 'Celtic' image, Nationalism drew closer to this pan-Britannic phenomenon. The *Cork Examiner* reported the proposed extension to Wales of the Home Rule principle that people should be governed according to local ideas and that Home Rule should become the cornerstone of the Liberal empire.[234] In Ireland Protestant speakers insisted on Home Rule as a programme of national liberty and imperial solidarity, and alluded to

---

[228] 'Meeting at St Margaret's', *FJ*, 18 Apr. 1887, 6, speech by T. O'Sullivan.

[229] Ibid., first resolution, and third resolution, 'Meeting at Waterford', ibid.; see also rep., 'The National League in West Cork', *Cork Examiner*, 30 Jan. 1888, 3.

[230] Speech by Dr Tanner, cited in rep., 'National League meeting at Donoughmore', *Cork Examiner*, 7 June 1887, 4.

[231] Callanan, *Healy*, 233; cf. 350–1.

[232] L.a., *FJ*, 25 Mar. 1887, 4; J. McCarthy to Caroline M. Praed, 24 Mar. 1887 and 2 Apr. 1887, in NLI, MS 24,958 (8).

[233] For example, in Mar. 1888 a leader quoted Campbell-Bannerman on the latest Coercion Bill, under which 'offences of a political or at least a semi-political kind involving points of great nicety are sent to be tried, without a jury, by men whose appointment involves executive as well as judicial functions, and who are not only judges but servants of the Executive' (l.a., *FJ*, 2 Mar. 1888, 4). For another example see rep., *Cork Examiner*, 1 June 1887, 2.

[234] Rep., 'The great demonstration at Swansea: "imperial, Welsh & Irish" – a monstre procession', *Cork Examiner*, 6 June 1887, 3; see also 'Demonstration at Drogheda', ibid., 3 July 1887, 3; the resolution adopted by the Thomastown branch of the INL, *FJ*, 14 Apr. 1887, 6; and 'Mr Gladstone's visit to South Wales', ibid., 3 July. 1887, 3.

a Nonconformist support which cut across national, confessional and gender barriers.[235]

The imprisonment of Charles Conybeare, a Radical MP, and of the eccentric poet and anti-imperialist campaigner Wilfrid Blunt added two English martyrs to the Nationalist cause. Blunt was reported as receiving 'a vast number of resolutions and private letters of congratulations and sympathy'.[236] At popular meetings he was eulogized by parish priests as 'an Englishman of wealth and rank and station, of great courage and ability, who like several others of his compatriots, has come over to Ireland to aid the oppressed against the oppressor, as he aided Arabi against his persecutors'.[237] Though of course Arabi's chief 'persecutor' had been Gladstone himself, the latter was reputed to have since mended his ways. Likewise, Liberal coercion under Forster was now seen as not quite as bad as Balfour's 'bloody' regime: while the Liberals 'drifted into the employment of the more despotic provisions of their Coercion Act', the Unionists 'are deliberately directing their operations against political opponents as such'.[238] Now Nationalists compared Balfour's coercion system with 'King Bomba's rule', alluding to the brutal repression of the 1848–9 revolution in Sicily.[239]

The zenith of the Union of Hearts was reached in 1887–90, as the 'Piggott case'[240] brought about a further strengthening of the links between Liberals and Nationalists. When the Liverpool Reform Club decided to start a subscription to help Parnell defray the legal costs of fighting the case, Liberal clubs from London and elsewhere joined the campaign, which generated considerable emotional response among Nationalists.[241] In 1889 two nationalist novels – Samuel Strahan's *The resident magistrate* and Hester Sigerson's *A ruined race* – were dedicated to Mr and Mrs Gladstone respectively. In a letter *To the clergy and laity of the Diocese of Meath*, the Roman Catholic bishop, Thomas Nulty, acknowledged that '[t]he masses of the English people love justice, truth, and fair

---

[235] Cited in rep., 'The National League: meeting at Queenstown', ibid., 6 Sep. 1887, 3, speech by the County High Sheriff of Cork, Mr Ledlie.

[236] Rep., 'Mr Blunt and Lord Randolph Churchill', ibid., 1 Nov. 1887, 4.

[237] Father J. Lucy, cited in rep., 'The National League ... Clonakilty', *Cork Examiner*, 1 Nov. 1887, 4.

[238] L.a., *FJ*, 27 Aug. 1887, 4.

[239] E.g. rep., 'Mr Gladstone in Wrexham ... the "Bomba rule" parallel', *FJ*, 5 Sep. 1888, 5.

[240] On 7 March 1887 *The Times* started a series of articles on 'Parnellism and crime', which included the notorious claim that Parnell approved of the 1882 Phoenix Park murders. The London newspaper was sued for libel and eventually a special commission established that a letter in which Parnell apparently expressed approval of the murder had actually been forged by Richard Piggott, himself a journalist.

[241] L.a., *FJ*, 17 Aug. 1888, 4.

play above and beyond any nation on earth'. Therefore Parnell, by proving the falsehood of the charges and convicting his enemies 'of falsehood, forgery and deliberate slander', would win the case for Home Rule.[242]

From 1890 the divorce scandal and subsequent split of the Nationalist party undermined such enthusiastic 'Union of Hearts'. Many rank and file, including the executive of the INL, rejected the alliance and stayed loyal to Parnell, their fallen leader.[243] Working-class votes were decisive in enabling the Parnellite Redmond to defeat Michael Davitt at the Waterford by-election in December 1891.[244] However, as McCarthy and others had anticipated, soon public opinion turned against Parnell.[245] Their frustration was further exasperated by the incident which brought about his downfall: 'You can imagine what the feeling is with these men who have sacrificed these 12 years: & now when victory is so near, to see all lost by the leader they had trusted. One man spoke of the frightful levity of a leader, who had imperilled the Cause for the sake of a woman "Where have you brought us" he said "Into the Divorce Court".'[246]

In his last two years Parnell had been pursuing 'a pan-British radical alliance' of the left,[247] and after 1891 most of the Nationalist party and their constituents maintained their pro-Gladstone orientation. For the anti-Parnell majority the Union of Hearts survived, and indeed, as Callanan has put it, Nationalists displayed 'excessive susceptibility ... to Gladstone's charisma'.[248] In 1891 Michael Davitt seemed unable to perceive ideological or political conflict between Irish Nationalism and Gladstonian Liberalism – something which annoyed enormously his opponent, John Redmond.[249] But for Davitt the Liberal–Nationalist alliance was 'a concordat of conciliation and justice', and the Union of Hearts was a coming together of classes fostering radical democracy in both countries.[250] Davitt celebrated the workers' brotherhood sealed

---

[242] T. Nulty, *To the clergy and laity of the Diocese of Meath* (1888), 12–13; in St Deinol's Library, Hawarden, 'Pamphlets on Ireland', 5/E/2.

[243] As McCarthy complained, 'the Dublin mob is all Parnellite': letter to R. C. M. Praed, 20 Sep. 1891, in NLI, MS 29.458 (40).

[244] Newscutting of an interview with J. Redmond, 29 Dec. 1891, in NLI, MS 7414, 12–13.

[245] J. McCarthy to R. C. M. Praed, 1 Jan. 1890, NLI, MS 29,458 (26); and 18 Dec. 1890, in ibid., MS 24,958 (32).

[246] McCarthy reporting the words of J. (John Dillon?), in a letter to R. C. M. Praed, 4 Dec. 1890, in ibid.

[247] D. George Boyce, 'Parnell and Bagehot', in Boyce and O'Day, *Parnell in Perspective*, 126.

[248] Callanan, *Healy*, 232.

[249] Newscutting of an interview with J. Redmond, 29 Dec. 1891, NLI, MS 7414.

[250] Cited in Callanan, *Healy*, 390.

in blood at Mitchelstown as much as at Peterloo in a previous generation. On one occasion he underscored this point by reciting a poem which declared that

> The people's cause is one alone
> Through all the world wide;
> By foreign name or foreign tongue
> That cause you can't divide!
>
> Two races do I only see
> Upon this globe of ours:
> The cheated sons of woe and toil,
> The juggling 'higher powers'!
>
> One master crushes both alike,
> The Saxon and the Celt –
> For all the pomp of lords and pride,
> *Our* bone and substance melt.
>
> Then hand in hand we'll face the foe
> And grapple with the wrong,
> And show to the Tyrant and the Slave
> A people's will is strong.[251]

A couple of months later he wrote to Edward Blake – on his way to the USA on a speaking tour – suggesting to him that in his speeches he should stress '[t]he part played by the British working class ("Democracy" would mean something else, possibly in Chicago) in the triumph of the Home Rule cause in the Commons ... together with the part that the Irish Representatives will play in keeping forward labour legislation &c.'[252] This internationalist vision of democratic solidarity may have been due – as Callanan has argued – to Davitt's 'superimposition of a simplistic radical paradigm on nationalist politics', in the expectation that Irish politics would follow the conventional left–right divide. However wrong he may have been on this last point, Davitt was not alone in voicing such a 'simplistic radical paradigm' at the time. Indeed, granted that Home Rule remained 'the priority over all other things', under the leadership of Justin McCarthy and John Dillon the party moved further towards an understanding of Nationalist politics in 'conventional' terms. Nationalism involved a non-sectarian campaign in which the Irish party and the Liberals were aligned against the Conservatives.

---

[251] M. Davitt, cited in 'The National Federation: meeting of the Central branch', *FJ*, 28 July 1892, 5.
[252] Davitt to Blake, 12 Sep. 1893, in Blake Letters, 4681, NLI.

It was a struggle of 'democracy' *versus* the House of Lords and aimed at establishing 'liberty' in a country disfigured by 'Castle rule' and confused by unfounded sectarian scares.[253] Likewise, after his accession to both the House of Commons and the party's committee in 1892, Edward Blake stressed that '[i]n general politics I am a decided Liberal, ready to co-operate in all well considered measures of reform'.[254] He insisted on the relevance for Ireland of the Canadian social and constitutional experiment – a view which, as we have seen, was widely shared at the time. This was indeed one of the reasons why so much expectation was invested in Blake by both his constituents and the leaders of the Irish party. In a telegram sent by Michael Davitt to the organizers of a meeting at which Blake was due to speak, he 'respectfully advise[d] [that] he [Blake] should deal with beneficial effect Home Rule Canada upon religious rights and feeling and maintenance of imperial integrity. Also development loyal feeling after agitation which won Canadian autonomy.'[255] Blake was only too happy to comply. In a speech given by him at the Eighty Club in August 1892, he insisted that Ireland was not 'exceptional'. Indeed, Canada, like Ireland, had 'a powerful Orange party ... bigoted men in the Roman Catholic Church and in the Protestant denominations', and many who – before Home Rule – prophesied that 'the majority in race and creed would use their power to oppress the so-called loyal minority which posed as the English party, and argued that the connection [with the UK] depended upon its continued ascendancy, or on the continued deprivation of the popular rights demanded'. Yet, concluded Blake, these prophets had proved wrong. For Canada had also

good men with nerves (laughter) ... the sober and settled thought of the great majority of our people of each creed and race had shown itself superior to the efforts of bigots, the cries of alarmists, the aims of extremists of whatever creed or race, and has satisfactorily proven our adhesion to the principles of civil and religious liberty and equal rights (hear, hear). Markedly have we shown the efficacy of covenanted organic guarantees and restrictions, which have ever been sacredly observed.[256]

---

[253] John Dillon to E. Blake, 6 Oct. 1894, and 'Confidential note on affairs of Irish party', typescript memo, attached to Blake to J. Dillon, 7 Nov. 1894, both in Blake Letters, 4681 [86 and 92], NLI; A. Webb, MP, *An address to the electors of Waterford* (1888), 9, 11.

[254] Blake's electoral address to the electors of Longford, Dublin, 7 July 1892, in Blake Letters, NLI, 4684 [84].

[255] Telegram, Davitt to Knox or O'Connor, McCarthy Committee Rooms, Derry, n.d. [probably early July 1892], Blake Letters, 4681.

[256] Cited in rep., 'The Hon. Edward Blake, MP – banquet at the Eighty Club', *FJ*, 5 Aug. 1892, 3.

This speech – welcomed by the *Freeman's Journal* as 'moderate, forcible and eloquent'[257] – followed Blake's election to the Nationalist party's committee, and confirmed the party's intention 'to give Mr Gladstone a free hand in the pending struggle'. Partly as a reaction against the break-away Parnellite group, which was fiercely critical of Gladstone and the Liberal alliance,[258] mainstream Nationalists were pushed towards positions which could be perceived as hardly distinguishable from those of the Liberal party itself. They were contemptuously labelled 'the Irish Whigs' by the frustrated Parnellites[259] – who, in turn, were regarded as Unionists in disguise by the Nationalists.[260] Yet, the Parnellites too were arguing their case in strictly 'liberal' terms:

Our object is to confer on the whole of the Irish people, without distinction of religion or politics, the blessings of freedom. To secure to the humblest man the same liberty in the exercise of his political rights as enjoyed by the richest and most powerful in the land. We have not struggled to put down one tyranny in order to set up another. We demand for ourselves and for all other men, though they may be opposed to us in politics and in religion, liberty to think and to act. Our motto is liberty for all, licence for none.[261]

To a large extent the GOM's personal prestige and charisma remained unaffected. Even Redmond continued to admit that the Liberal leader was a true Home Ruler – though one of the very few in the Liberal party[262] – and that '[i]t [was] to the interest of every Irishman that Mr Gladstone should return to power, and that as soon as possible'.[263] Not only were 'Gladstone Prints' used as propaganda material in Longford in 1892,[264] but the electoral campaign that year provided opportunities for Nationalist leaders to praise repeatedly 'that eminent and venerable statesman', whose 'liberal mind and the sense of what was fair' had 'always carried him in the direction of justice and right'. As soon as Ireland returned a majority of representatives pledged to Home Rule 'Mr Gladstone seized the opportunity, and said that he, as a constitutional

[257] L.a., *FJ*, 5 Aug. 1892, 4.
[258] J. Redmond in newscutting of a speech at Elphin, 12 Jan. 1896, in J. Redmond Papers, MS 7422.
[259] J. Redmond, MP and Sweetman (the candidate) in rep., 'The public meeting', *FJ*, 15 Apr. 1895, 6.
[260] The 'Factionists' – as the Parnellites were nicknamed by the Nationalists – were regarded as almost more dangerous than the Unionists: l.a., *FJ*, 18 July 1892, 4.
[261] J. Redmond: newscutting dated 11 Oct. 1895, in J. Redmond Papers, MS 7421.
[262] The other two being Morley and Labouchere: newscutting dated 7 July 1892, in J. Redmond Papers, NAI, Ms 7417.
[263] J. Redmond in a newscutting from the *New York Herald*, 16 June 1892, in J. Redmond Papers, NLI, MS 7418.
[264] T. W. Delany to E. Blake, 16 Aug. 1892, in Blake Correspondence, NLI, 4684.

Minister, would give Ireland Home Rule because a majority of her representatives demanded it'. Although the Bill had been defeated, 'Mr Gladstone had not surrendered or gone back in his word to Ireland (cheers). Mr Gladstone was faithful and true.'[265]

Eventually such expectations were not fulfilled, but Nationalists remained fascinated by the Liberal leader to the end. Justin McCarthy – who was present in the House when Gladstone delivered his last speech – wrote in a private letter: '[The speech] was splendidly delivered – it was a call to the country to do battle against the tyranny of the House of Lords. I cannot tell you what an emotional time it was when he was speaking – that last speech. One's mind went back & back: and it seemed like the sin[k]-ing for some sun. At last the sun went out in a blaze of light & splendour.'[266] In Ireland, even after his retirement, the mention of Gladstone's name at public meetings frequently elicited enthusiastic reactions.[267] Nationalist novels continued to be dedicated to the GOM – as in the case of Ada Ellen Bayly's *Doreen: the story of a singer* (1894). Among the Irish in Britain his name became a battle cry and guarantee of the reliability of the Liberal alliance.[268] Behind this persistent enthusiasm for the GOM there were sentimental and emotional factors, as in 1886. Despite, or because of, the ultimate defeat of the second Home Rule Bill, the Nationalists were deeply moved by Gladstone's loyalty to 'the Cause': 'If Mr Gladstone has never faltered in his services to Ireland, Ireland has not faltered in the confidence with which she has repaid him.'[269] The statesman's retirement added weight to his words and deeds, which continued to attract the reverent comment of the anti-Parnellite press:

He is still the great missionary power, preaching Home Rule to the people of Great Britain . . . He was the first great apostle of National Brotherhood to the two great democracies and he brought that glorious gospel home to hearts of both people

---

[265] Mr. T. D. Sullivan, MP, in rep., 'The Irish National Federation: bohern Abreena Branch', *FJ*, 25 Apr. 1892, 5. Cf. l.a., *FJ*, 24 June 1892, 4; see also John Deasy, MP, in rep., 'The Nationalist Convention in Louth', 23 June 1892, 6.

[266] McCarthy to R. C. M. Praed, 2 Mar. 1894, NLI, MS 24,958 (39).

[267] 'Mr Gladstone (cheers) had devoted the last years of his magnificent life to the work of undoing all the injustice which his country had inflicted on Ireland in the past, and to his (Mr Dillon's) own knowledge . . . he was in his retirement thinking more of Ireland than of any other subject.' (John Dillon cited in rep., 'The National movement: great meeting in Co. Wexford', *Cork Examiner*, 2 Jan. 1895, 6. See also rep., 'Nationalist meeting in the North [Magherafelt, Co. Derry]', ibid., 18 Jan. 1895, 5.)

[268] 'Go to the polls and support only the candidates who are in favour of Mr Gladstone's Irish policy, to the return of the Liberal party – the party of Home Rule – the party which has never taken up any great cause without ultimately carrying it to victory.' From the Manifesto of the Irish National League of Great Britain, signed by T. P. O'Connor, in *FJ*, 11 July 1895, 5.

[269] L.a., 'Mr Gladstone's eighty-fifth birthday', *FJ*, 29 Dec. 1894, 4.

[*sic*]. In the old days it was the reproach of the Coercionists that he had single-handedly converted the Liberal party and the people of Great Britain to the principles of Home Rule.

And the *Freeman's Journal* continued, quoting 'Gerald Massy, the poet of the people':

> Well they may call him the one man power,
> Standing alone where there's room but for one,
> In his pride of place like a mountain tower
> That catches the rays of the rising sun.
>
> We in the valley of final decision
> Gather around him as close as we can
> To see what he sees from his summit of vision –
> The triumph that beckons the Grand Old Man.[270]

By 1895 Gladstone had been elevated to the status of a lay saint in Nationalist hearts – 'he is a miracle, not a man'.[271] The 'Friendly Sons of St Patrick' – an organization of Irish Americans – forwarded to Gladstone a farewell address, which was 'finely engrossed on vellum and bound in morocco leather, beautifully embossed with gold'. It celebrated and testified to the success of Gladstone's own interpretation of Home Rule and the Irish national cause. The eulogy started by stating that '[t]he civilized world sees with equal regret and admiration the close of an unusually long career as a leader, devoted alike to the best interest of his native country and to those of humanity.' It went on to praise Gladstone's 'heroic and persistent endeavour' to secure for the people of Ireland 'the simple meed of political and social justice enjoyed by Great Britain and her colonies' – for example, Canada, 'and the colonies of South Africa, Australia, New Zealand, and the West Indies'. And it concluded by expressing to Gladstone the 'admiration, respect and gratitude' of 'Americans of every race and creed'.[272] Blake wrote in similar terms: 'Among the peoples of that Continent [America] your personality has become identified with the cause of freedom, and you are to them the embodiment of their highest ideal of the statesman.'[273]

---

[270] 'Mr Gladstone will doubtless receive many messages of congratulation. But none will be warmer than those that well, pure and warm, from the hearts of every Irishman worthy of the name.' (L.a., 'Mr Gladstone's eighty-fifth birthday', *FJ*, 29 Dec. 1894, 4.)

[271] Ibid.   [272] Rep., 'Irish-Americans and Mr Gladstone', *FJ*, 8 Jan. 1895, 5.

[273] Blake to W. E. Gladstone, 2 Mar. 1894, in Blake Letters, [612], 4683. For a Canadian 'ode' to Gladstone, Blake, Laurier, Cleveland and Henry George see letter by Thomas Harris, 'a poor farmer', to Blake, 28 Jan. 1893 in ibid., 4685. For prose versions of similar panegyrics about the GOM and Irish freedom see M. E. Keep, Mayor of Halifax and former President of the Irish Charitable Society, to Blake, 24 Feb. 1893 [740], and M. D. McEniry to Blake, 28 Feb. 1893 [793], both in ibid.

Commenting on Gladstone's 1845 aborted tour of Ireland, the *Freeman's Journal* wrote:

How different might have been the story of Ireland had the Gladstone of 1845 known even as much as of Ireland as the Gladstone of 1870! When the light came, however, this friend of justice did not sin against it. He followed it bravely and loyally to the end, and made it a beacon to those who had been ignorant of Ireland's story and blind to her rights. The beacon will never cease to burn as long as British history contains the name of Gladstone.[274]

Empire and jingoism

The 'Union of Hearts' popularized a psuedo-'Burkean' interpretation of the links between national self-government and the empire.[275] Centred around the notion of the compatibility between 'local patriotism' and 'imperial loyalism', which Gladstone had championed from 1886,[276] such a view was endorsed by the strong pro-Home Rule lobbies in the settlement colonies and especially Canada. Already in May 1882 the Canadian Parliament had written to the Queen, commending the advantages of federalism and its applicability to Ireland.[277] In February 1886 the Assembly of Quebec – a province comparable to Ireland in that it was divided along religious and language lines – commended the imperial dimension of Home Rule.[278] These moves were widely echoed in Ireland. In January 1887, the Nationalist MP T. P. Gill surveyed the events which led – through rebellion and reform – to Canada's 'home rule' in 1867,

---

[274] L.a., *FJ*, 8 Jan. 1895, 4. For responses in the USA, Australia and New Zealand see E. L. Godkin, 'American opinion and the Irish question', *Nineteenth century*, 22 (Au. 1887), 285–92; J. F. Hogan, *The Irish in Australia* (1887) and the modern studies J. P. O'Farrell, *The Irish in Australia: 1788 to the present* (2001) and R. P. Davis, *Irish issues in New Zealand politics, 1868–1922* (1974).

[275] J. E. Redmond cited 'the great Irishman Edmund Burke' as a leading authority on the matter of how to rule Ireland: rep., 'The National League: the Irish Bills' (a meeting of the Central branch of the INL to comment upon the 1886 Bills), *FJ*, 21 Apr. 1886, 6. As early as October 1885 the *Freeman's Journal* had run a series on 'Colonial constitutions' by Sir Charles Gavan Duffy (*FJ*, 8 Oct. 1885, 5).

[276] W. E. Gladstone, 'The first Home Rule Bill, April 8, 1886' in Gladstone's speeches ed. by A. Tinley Bassett (1916), 640–3; rep., 'Mr Gladstone in Wrexham', *FJ*, 5 Sep. 1888, 5. For the success of this vision in Liberal and Nationalist circles see Ellis, 'Reconciling the Celt'.

[277] *Address of the Canadian Parliament to Her Majesty in relation to the condition of Ireland, based on resolutions moved by the Hon. John Cadigan in May, 1882*, signed by the Speakers of the Senate and the House of Commons in *Scraps about Ireland No. 2, called from the Utterances of 'Men of Light and Learning'*, (1886) (St Deiniol's Library, Hawarden, Gladstone Tracts, M/F, 6/44).

[278] Quebec Legislative Assembly, Home Rule Resolution, 17 Feb. 1886, in ibid.

which turned rebels into loyalists.[279] Looking at the British Empire within the context not of colonial empires, but, significantly, of the contemporary European experience, Gill argued that there were two main modern approaches to empire. One required centralization, authoritarian government, constant coercion and military repression whenever necessary. However, this was bound to backfire, as it had done in the Thirteen Colonies in 1774–6, in Italy and Hungary from 1848, in Canada before 1867. As a consequence of these failures and revolutions, even the Austrians – the traditional advocates of autocratic imperialism – had moved towards 'Home Rule' in their relationship with Hungary. Home Rule was the only system which reconciled unity with diversity, freedom with strong government. To the delight of the British proponents of 'Home Rule All Round', in 1888 Parnell himself seemed to advocate a system under which Ireland would continue to be represented at Westminster.[280] As one of Tom Ellis' correspondents concluded, 'the tendency of the Home Rule question is towards Federalism'.[281]

Irish Nationalists were prepared to apply this vision of the empire not only to the 'white' dominions, but also to India. In 1895 great emphasis was given to the election of the Quaker Nationalist Alfred Webb to the presidency of the Indian National Congress.[282] His inaugural speech was a consistent statement of liberal nationalism. It must have struck a responsive chord among his Indian audience – many of whom were, like Webb, influenced by ideas adapted from Gladstone, as well as from other advocates of national rights, including Mazzini and J. S. Mill:

My nationality is the principal ground for having been elected ... However, I do not question the fitness of your choice , for I am responsible in several respects. I was nurtured in the conflict against American slavery. In the words of William Lloyd Garrison, the founder of that movement, 'My country is the world; my countrymen are all mankind.' To aid in the elevation of my native country has been the endeavour of my riper years. In the words of Daniel O'Connell, 'My sympathies are not confined to my own green island. I am a friend of civil and religious liberty all over the world.' I hate tyranny and oppression wherever practised, more especially if practised by my own Government, for then I am in a measure responsible. I have felt the bitterness of subjection in my own country.

---

[279] T. P. Gill, MP, 'The Home Rule constitutions of the British crown', republished in *FJ*, 25 Jan. 1887, 5. For the view of the Confederation held by the French Canadians see A. I. Silver, *The French-Canadian idea of confederation, 1864–1900* (1982).
[280] W. J. Rowlands to T. E. Ellis, 28 July 1888, in Ellis Papers, 1903.
[281] T. E. Ellis to unnamed correspondent, 21 June 1889, ibid., 2882.
[282] Such as Franck Hugh O'Donnell: D. Fitzpatrick, 'Ireland and the empire', in A. Porter (ed.), *The Oxford History of the British Empire, vol. XXX: The Nineteenth Century* (1999), 505–6. For O'Donnell's involvement in other democratic campaigns see chapter 6, p. 334.

I am a member of the Irish parliamentary Party. I am one of the Indian parliamentary Committee. I am a Dissenter, proud of the struggles of my Quaker forefathers for freedom of thought and action; a Protestant returned by a Catholic constituency; a Protestant living in a Catholic country, testifying against craven fears of a return to obsolete religious bitterness and intolerance – fears in your country and in mine worked upon to impede the progress of liberty. To be placed in this chair is the highest honour to which I can ever aspire . . . In our efforts for reform and constitutional liberty, much will depend upon individual character and training; upon the extent to which we wisely administer the powers we have.[283]

Webb's completion of tenure as Congress President was fêted at the National Liberal Club at a banquet attended by, among others, Justin M'Carthy, J. F. X. O'Brien, John Dillon and Dadhabhoi Naoroji, the first Asian MP, soon to become the icon of Indian constitutional nationalism. The chair was occupied by J. Stansfeld, the Mazzinian enthusiast. In his speech Webb argued that 'the happiness and contentment of India', as much as of Ireland and indeed Britain itself, depended on the establishment of parliamentary self-government – though he suggested that Indian representation at Westminster could be an alternative to Home Rule for India. Justin M'Carthy argued that the Congress 'showed them . . . what form the future government of India was to take'.[284] Obviously Irish Nationalism had moved a long way from 1883, when Parnell felt it strategically necessary to oppose Charles Bradlaugh on account of his religious views,[285] while the *Freeman's Journal* had sarcastically commented that Westminster would one day count, among its members, even 'Fire-Worshippers',[286] the latter being a derogatory nickname for the Zoroastrian Parsees. Dadabhai Naoroji was indeed a leading Parsee, and his election for Finsbury in 1892 was partly a result of the support he had received from the local Irish Nationalists.

Nationalist attitudes to foreign and imperial affairs were informed by a form of anti-imperialism reminiscent of Gladstone's 1879 Midlothian gospel. Shannon and Pottinger Saab have commented on the lack of Nationalist responses to the 1876 Bulgarian agitation.[287] It is true that, while the Irish Nonconformists echoed the indignation of their brethren

---

[283] Cited in rep., 'Mr Alfred Webb, MP – address to the Indian National Congress: Ireland and India', *FJ*, 16 Jan. 1895, 6. For the influence of Gladstonian Liberalism on the early National Congress see S. R. Bakshi, *Home Rule Movement* (New Delhi, 1984), 1–3, 15; for the context see W. Wedderburn, *Allan Octavian Hume*, ed. by E. C. Moulton (2002), 76–7.
[284] Cited in rep., 'The Indian National Congress', *FJ*, 20 Feb. 1895,5.
[285] Although the party was divided, with anti-clericals such as M. Davitt, T. P. O'Connor, Lysaght Finigan and Parnell himself being to various degrees sympathetic to Bradlaugh: Arnstein, 'Parnell and the Bradlaugh case'.
[286] L.a., *FJ*, 2 May 1883, 4. Cf. Arnstein, 'Parnell and the Bradlaugh case'.
[287] Shannon, *Bulgarian agitation*, 80, 150, 158–60; Pottinger Saab, *Reluctant icon*, 159–60.

in Britain, some Nationalists tended to dismiss atrocities in the East as 'not more cruel than the deeds of oppression and injustice perpetrated by the landlords of Ireland, with the sanction of the laws and Constitution of England'.[288] Yet, there is some evidence of Nationalist anti-Ottoman feeling. On 5 September the *Freeman's Journal* argued that

> The matter is not between Turkey and Servia, or Turkey and her revolted provinces, but between the Christian and civilized world and a power which has outraged law and trampled upon humanity . . . If the powers decide in accordance with the public opinion of Europe, they will cut down and annihilate the authority of the Turk in those lands which are Christian and civilized; and if Christianity and civilization are to be regarded, then the whole fabric of rottenness will be swept away altogether.[289]

On 8 September, the Dublin newspaper welcomed the publication of Gladstone's *Bulgarian horrors* as a mark of his 'conversion' from the line he took at the time of the Crimean War. On the 9th, commenting on the protest meetings in Cork and Belfast, it argued that '[t]he feeling as to the Bulgarian atrocities . . . and the indignation against the Government is clear'.[290] The same day the *Cork Examiner* gave notice of another forthcoming protest meeting, which would be supported by local worthies including the parish priest. 'Public feeling on the subject has been stimulated by the knowledge that the unutterable atrocities perpetrated in Bulgaria are not an isolated tragedy, but the natural and inevitable outcome of the barbarous and fanatical spirit in which the government of the Sultan deals with its Christian subjects.' The *Cork Examiner* proposed a radical solution to the problem: 'So long as the Turks are permitted to rule over millions of disarmed and helpless Christians there can be no security against the repetition of these iniquities . . . It has become the duty of every civilised community not merely to express horror at the enormities that have already occurred, but to take effective means to render such crises impossible in the future.'[291] Far from regarding the British agitation as 'hypocritical',[292] the *Examiner* viewed it as a redeeming factor: 'To their honour, it must be said, the people of England appear to have become fully sensible of their obligation . . . Englishmen have cast off their national prejudices.'[293]

---

[288] 'Kildare branch of the Irish National League', Heffernan Papers, NLI, MS 21,910, acc. 1921. For an example of the Irish Nonconformist attitude see Resolution passed by the members and friends of the Free Congregational Union (Ireland) at their Quarterly conference and public meeting held at Moneyrea, Co. Down, 31 Oct. 1876, NA, FO78/2556.

[289] L.a., *FJ*, 5 Sep. 1876, 5.   [290] L.a., *FJ*, 9 Sep. 1876, 5.

[291] L.a., *Cork Examiner*, 9 Sep. 1876, 2.   [292] Shannon, *Bulgarian agitation*, 80.

[293] L.a., *Cork Examiner*, 9 Sep. 1876, 2.

On 10 September a large, though chaotic, popular meeting took place in Dublin with the participation of about ten thousand people, including, apparently, a noisy Fenian contingent. The protesters refrained from flying Ireland's green flag because it was felt to be reminiscent of the Turkish colours: instead they used the Stars and Stripes.[294] One speaker denounced 'the atrocities of the Turk, and also of the Turkish ally – England'. Another, R. J. Dunne, drew parallels between the Bulgarians and the Irish, arguing that the '[s]cenes of pillage, outrage and murder' in Bulgaria and Servia 'were never equalled, except in Ireland in '98'. As people from the crowd cheered 'the Irish Americans' and 'O'Donovan Rossa', Dunne went on to say that

All this time . . . we were keeping an ambassador in Constantinople . . . living there in luxury and idleness while Christians were being butchered by the Turk, and that because England is the ally of the Turk . . . ruffianly blackguards both . . . The originators of this meeting do not want in the least to back Gladstone (hear, hear). He is as much a matter of indifference to us as Bright, or Disraeli, or any other Englishman . . . It is for us to take an independent stand on the question. I believe that to-morrow in 'Rebel Cork' . . . they will hold an indignation meeting, and do what we are doing to-day – denounce the Turk for oppressing the Servians; for they feel as we do that the Servians are an oppressed nationality like ourselves.[295]

Moderate, liberal-minded Home Rulers were appalled by both the disorderly proceedings and the Fenian views expressed by the demonstrators.[296] Yet, from the historian's viewpoint, the meeting is interesting precisely because it showed the extent to which the 'horrors in the East' and Gladstone's demand for a foreign policy inspired by respect for 'peoples struggling to be free' had resonance at different levels within the nationalist movement. The Irish response was consistently anti-jingoistic, but, despite the Fenians, did not necessarily indicate hostility to the empire. As Comerford has written, 'insofar as there was widespread popular feeling on the matter in Ireland that owed less to nationalist instincts than to Gladstone's calculated and highly orchestrated exposure of infidel Turkish atrocities against Balkan Christians'. In other words, 'Irish popular opinion on the subject was moved in much the same way as British popular opinion.'[297] In this as in many other respects, Parnell's coolness and detached contempt for 'English' politics was atypical. In foreign affairs there was an 'elective affinity' between Nationalism and the humanitarian liberalism embodied by Gladstone, whose 'voice and pen concentrated the

---

[294] Rep., 'Meeting at Harold's Cross', *FJ*, 11 Sep. 1876, 2–3.   [295] Ibid.
[296] The *Freeman's Journal* in particular: see the leaders in 11 Sep. 1876, 5, which also eulogized Gladstone for his Greenwich speech.
[297] Comerford, *Fenians*, 220.

sympathy of humane Europe upon the mean and heartless tyrannies of Bombaism in Naples. Again were his tongue and pen turned with most effective force upon the shrinking horrors under the brutal regime of the Unspeakable Turk in Bulgaria.'[298] His support for Irish Home Rule was regarded from this internationalist point of view.

Thus, far from being an insignificant aspect of the Irish movement, anti-jingoism and internationalism were two of its central features and help to explain why the Nationalists became so attached to the GOM. A concern for moral imperatives was what 'singled out' Gladstone 'personally' from 'what is known as the Liberal party'. Unlike Lord Hartington, the 'sincere and genuine Gladstone' was 'a man with a heart as well as a mind. His sympathies are progressive, and we owe to this personal ardour of his all the good work that has been done for Ireland as well as England in these latter days.'[299] While at the 1880 election the Nationalist manifesto was completely dominated by internal Irish matters, the *Freeman's Journal* took a broader view of Ireland's interests, adopting a consistently Gladstonian tone in financial and imperial affairs. Its editorials decried Tory financial profligacy, deploring jingoism and the government 'who spill our blood futilely in Zululand or Afghanistan ... [and] squander our money'.[300] Its editorial line was in favour of the preservation of the empire, but against jingoism – a view broadly shared by Nationalist leaders both then and throughout the period up to 1914.[301] The Irish vote in Britain went to the Liberals.[302]

As we have seen, it was between 1880 and 1882 that Forster's coercion brought about a general disillusionment with the Liberals, a feeling compounded by the invasion of Egypt. The latter was regarded as the overseas version of 'Forsterism'. The parallels between Egypt and Ireland, both victims of Liberal 'duplicity', were striking. Egypt was being 'coerced' in ways similar to Ireland and for comparable reasons – the interests of a small group of privileged and ruthless men. The landlords were to the one what the corrupt Khedive and foreign bondholders were to the other.[303] In both cases the result was the spoliation of the people. Arabi's rebellion, which expressed 'the national feeling of the Egyptians', had elicited contrasting responses from democratic France and aristocratic England. 'France had the humanity and uprightness to back out, and England went in and did the work ... Thus begins another phase of the

---

[298] L.a., *FJ*, 8 Nov. 1888, 4.   [299] L.a., *FJ*, 12 Mar. 1880, 4.
[300] Ibid.: three leading articles devoted to these subjects.
[301] Banks, *Edward Blake*, 333–5; N. Mansergh, 'John Redmond', in D. Mansergh (ed.) *Nationalism and Independence* (1997), 24.
[302] T. M. Healy, *Letters and leaders of my day*, 2 vols. (n.d. 1928), vol. I, 79.
[303] L.a., *FJ*, 9 Oct. 1882, 4; l.a., *FJ*, 15 Nov. 1882, 4.

role of the Liberal Government of England.'[304] Like John Bright and other anti-imperialists, the *Freeman's Journal* referred to the invasion as 'the Egyptian crime'.[305] Its critique followed the typical radical interpretation of the Egyptian expedition as a ploy to satisfy the cravings of greedy capitalists at the expense of the tax-payer, whose interests were neglected by both government and opposition. Yet, jingoism and the Conservative party were ultimately responsible, as 'the whole Egyptian complication springs out of the Beaconsfield–Salisbury Bondholder policy, and . . . Mr Gladstone did no more than to undertake the obligation bequeathed to him by his predecessors'.[306] The Irish party as such adopted a similar line. In the Commons, T. P. O'Connor argued that Egypt's financial problems derived from the exorbitant interest rates charged by the European negotiators of the loans,[307] while J. O'Kelly (Roscommon) maintained that the bombardment of Alexandria 'was not an act of war', but rather 'assassination upon a large scale'.[308] The riots and 'massacres' – whose suppression had been invoked as one of the reasons for the invasion – were grounds for Gladstone to protest to the Egyptian government, but could not legitimate direct British military action.[309]

In their 1885 manifesto, the Nationalists claimed that their political distinctiveness consisted in a principled and disinterested advocacy of ideals and policies which the Liberals also proposed, but hypocritically betrayed whenever they seemed incompatible with economic interests and imperial aims.[310] Nationalist 'honesty' was contrasted not only with Liberal pusillanimity, but also with the reckless and shallow idealism of the British radicals. For T. M. Healy the Irish party embodied national common sense, in contrast to what he regarded as Saxon vacuous idealism. Moreover, the Nationalists were both more 'loyal' and more effective in all spheres of public policy than the radicals. For example, in terms of the running of the national finances, while the Irish party was second to none in its zeal for retrenchment, it rejected as 'extravagant or alarming'

---

[304] L.a., *FJ*, 10 Nov. 1882, 4.   [305] L.a., *FJ*, 13 Jan. 1883, 4.
[306] L.a., *FJ*, 14 Oct. 1882, 4.
[307] T. P. O'Connor, HPD, 3rd series, 28 CCLXXXVIII (19 May 1884), 673.
[308] HPD, 3rd series, 277 (12 July 1882), 182–3.   [309] Ibid.
[310] '[T]he Liberal Party promised peace, and it afterwards made unjust war; economy, and its Budget reached the highest point yet attained; justice to aspiring nationalities, and it mercilessly crushed the National movement of Egypt under Arabi Pasha, and murdered thousands of Arabs rightly struggling to be free. [In Ireland] Twelve hundred men were imprisoned without trial. Ladies were convicted under an obsolete act, directed against the degraded of their sex; and for a period every utterance of the popular Press and of popular meeting was as completely suppressed as if Ireland were Poland and the administration of England a Russian autocracy.' ('Manifesto to the Irish Electors in Great Britain', signed by T. P. O'Connor, T. M. Healy, J. McCarthy and others, *FJ*, 23 Nov. 1885, 4.)

the radicals' critique of the Civil List, and pointed out that those who proposed 'to cut down these little pickings' were prepared, 'at the same time, [to] vote hundreds of thousands of pounds for Irish informers, and millions for the prosecution of unjust wars against people "rightly struggling to be free"'.[311] While making allowance for some Liberals whom the Executive of the League thought deserving of support, the manifesto asked Irish electors 'to vote against the men who coerced Ireland, deluged Egypt with blood, menaced religious liberty in the school, [and] freedom of speech in Parliament'.[312]

That such 'Gladstonian' features of Irish constitutional nationalism were emphasized in the age of the 'Union of Hearts' is perhaps not surprising. More remarkable is the fact that they became increasingly pronounced after Gladstone retired and the Liberal party distanced itself from Home Rule. Nevertheless, the nationalism professed by many of the Irish leaders and MPs of both factions was 'Gladstonian' in its rejection of jingoism not because it was 'British', but because it was morally deplorable in that it subordinated the claims of humanity to those of a misguided national self-interest.[313]

---

[311] T. M. Healy, MP, cited in 'The National League', *FJ*, 8 Apr. 1885, 3. Healy stressed the Nationalists' loyalty to the Crown and their willingness to pay for the financial burdens it involved – a sort of 'fire risk' as the monarchy secured 'a stable, prosperous, and peaceful Government'.
[312] L.a., *FJ*, 8 Nov. 1888, 4.
[313] L.a., 'The civilisers in Burmah', *United Ireland*, 30 Jan. 1886, 1.

4   'Giving stability to popular opinion'? Radicalism and the caucus in Britain and Ireland

There is nothing incongruous in the union of [classical] democratic doctrines with representative institutions. Ancient order and modern progress are not incompatible.[1]

Those which are ineffective without each other must be united . . .[2]

[The caucus] appears to be a necessary outcome of democracy. In a small community, such as the Canton of Uri, all the freemen may meet in a meadow to pass laws. In larger societies direct government by the people gives place to representative government; and when constituencies consist of thousands, associations which aid the birth of popular opinion and give it strength, stability and homogeneity seem indispensable.[3]

'Athenian democracy' or 'American caucus'?

After Gladstone's retirement, the last bastion of the alliance between the Nationalists and the Liberals was the National Liberal Federation (NLF). The Irish perceived the NLF as embodying the solidarity between 'the peoples' of Britain and Ireland, allegedly united in their support for 'the cause of democratic reform'.[4] Yet, as both contemporaries and modern historians have always pointed out, the democratic legitimacy and the popularity of the 'caucus' were questionable. While in popular circles 'suspicion of party ran deep',[5] politicians earnestly debated whether the

---

[1] 'Political address by Mr Cowen, MP', *NC*, 18 Feb. 1885, 2–3.
[2] Aristotle, *The Politics*, Book 1, chapter 2.
[3] J. Macdonnell, 'Is the caucus a necessity?', *Fortnightly Review*, 44 o.s., 38 n.s. (Dec. 1885), 790.
[4] L.a., *Cork Examiner*, 18 Jan. 1895, 4.
[5] Lawrence, *Speaking for the People*, 91, and 'Popular politics and the limitations of party: Wolverhampton, 1867–1900', in Biagini and Reid, *Currents of radicalism*, 65–85.

'machines' were at all compatible with either liberalism or parliamentary government.[6]

By contrast with the intellectual debate generated by the NLF from the 1880s, there was little theoretical preparation for its establishment in 1877: no blueprint had been drawn up by 'the lights of liberalism'. Even John Stuart Mill – whose writings and personal involvement in various radical agitations set standards for generations of liberals – had been comparatively silent on the question of mass party politics.[7] This omission is somewhat surprising when we consider that during his life-time there flourished well-organized pressure groups, including the National Education League, with which he was well acquainted, and the Land Tenure Reform Association, of which he was a member. The NLF, launched only four years after Mill's death, drew heavily on the experience of such leagues and associations, some of which it tried to co-ordinate.[8] It has sometimes been suggested that, for all his intellectual prestige, Mill was actually unable to understand either the reality or the needs of party politics in his day. This impression is strengthened by the fact that, even in his last major works on representative government, he gave no account of the role of parties.[9] Yet, he was not in principle hostile to them, and in 1865–8, as a parliamentarian, he generally behaved like a disciplined and loyal 'party man',[10] without showing anything like the restless individualism which Joseph Cowen and James Keir Hardie – the

---

[6]   P. Pombeni, 'Starting in reason, ending in passion: Bryce, Lowell, Ostrogorski and the problem of democracy', *Historical Journal*, 37, 2 (1994), 319–41; for Minghetti's hostility to the caucus see Pombeni, 'Trasformismo e questione del partito', in Pombeni (ed.), *La trasformazione politica nell'Europa liberale, 1870–1890* (Bologna, 1986), 247; for Bluntschli's attitude see J. Sheehan, *German liberalism in the nineteenth century* (1982), 17, 150–1.

[7]   With the exception of a few remarks, in connection with his discussion of Thomas Hare's proportional representation scheme. Most of his criticism focused on the 'first-past-the-post' system. The American Caucus did not attract his attention, but he wrote that 'in America electors vote for the party ticket because the election goes by a simple majority' (*CW*, XIX, 464): again, the problem was with the first-past-the-post system, not with parties. However, in *Considerations on representative government* he indicted the British party system of the time on the ground that candidatures were selected by small cliques – 'the attorney, the parliamentary agent, or the half-dozen party leaders', or even worse, 'three or four tradesmen or attorneys'. (*CW*, XIX, 362 and 456 respectively; see also *CW*, XXVIII, 12.) Of course, this was precisely one of the problems which Chamberlain boasted to have solved with his broadly representative Liberal association: see pp. 181–3.

[8]   R. Spence Watson, *The National Liberal Federation: from its commencement to the general election of 1906* (1907), 6.

[9]   P. Pombeni, *Introduzione alla storia dei partiti politici* (1990), 136.

[10]   J. Vincent, *Formation of the British Liberal party* (1972), 183–95; B. L. Kinzer, A. Robson and J. M. Robson, *A moralist In and out of Parliament: John Stuart Mill at Westminster, 1865–1868*, Toronto and London, 1992, 92–4.

populist champions of 'political opinion' against the caucus's 'undue supremacy'[11] – were to display in the 1880s and 1890s respectively.

It would be tempting to explain away these problems as illustrations of Mill's inconsistency, or maybe of the fact that his works described an ideal, while his deeds reflected the needs of real politics, identified experientially, though not elaborated theoretically. Nevertheless, there is evidence to suggest that the problem is broader and more complex. The already mentioned hostility to the very idea of a 'caucus' was shared by both the popular and intellectual representatives of liberalism. Bearing this in mind, we may wonder whether Mill's silence on the party issue was really a consequence of his defective understanding of contemporary political realities, or whether it reflected well-established features in Liberal culture, amounting to a rejection of the very idea of party 'machines'.

Despite his familiarity with Tocqueville's analysis of American trends, Mill's ideal of democracy and mass politics was inspired more by *classical* models then by modern models, with a typical emphasis on both participatory citizenship and charismatic leadership. Throughout his career, he repeatedly expressed his preference for the ancient *polis*, based on face-to-face relationships and virtually co-extensive with a local community. In it, participation and debate would spontaneously arise from the awareness of common interests, and from the feeling of belonging to a socio-cultural entity to which one felt a positive emotional commitment. He waxed lyrical about Athens in the days of Pericles, which he regarded almost as a liberal paradise, where each citizen was continually invested with some public magistracy: the *polis* had not only universal suffrage, but also 'the liberty of the bema, of the dicastery, the portico, the palestra, and the stage'.[12] The perpetually deliberating Demos allowed intellectual minorities – 'public moralists' such as Themistocles, Aristides, Pericles and Demosthenes – to emerge as the guides of public opinion. That depended on the fact that '[t]he multitude have often a true instinct for distinguishing an able man, when he has the means for displaying his ability in a fair field before them'.[13] In the context of the *polis*, elitism and participatory democracy coincided; and what linked them together was charismatic rhetoric.

The present chapter does not address Mill's lack of theoretical concern for party organization. Rather, by standing such a question on its head, it

---

[11] From the minutes of the Hatton Henry Colliery, an appeal to J. Cowen not to withdraw from politics, signed by W. J. Bird, T. Willis, C. Bowhill, M. Cook, W. Fleetham and J. Turnbill, 27 Jan. 1886, in Cowen Papers, B 357.

[12] Mill, *Considerations*, 324.   [13] Ibid., 458.

tests the hypothesis that the NLF – in its activists' perception – reflected Mill's position in at least two respects. First, the NLF shared Mill's reluctance to accept the implications of mass party politics, while actually making use of mass organization. Second, it proclaimed ideals similar to those of Mill's utopia, with its dream of participatory citizenship, and of infusing the spirit of classical democracy – the ancient Athenian *ekklesia* – into modern parliamentary government.[14] Being steeped in this classical tradition of 'republican virtue', British Liberals manifested symptoms of a curious kind of schizophrenia. On the one hand, like their continental namesakes, they showed distrust for the 'caucus' and other features of 'Yankee' politics. On the other, the NLF derived both its ideological justification and its practical weaknesses, not from the model of the American party machine,[15] but from classical notions of direct democracy akin to the ones which, on the continent, inspired left-wing opponents of Liberalism and, in particular, hindered the organization of modern party politics among French radical democrats.

In this context, it is interesting to compare the British Liberal experience with that of Irish Nationalism. The Irish National League (INL) was much more than a party 'machine': it had close, organic links with the land reform agitation and was deeply rooted in the reality of local life. Moreover, as Jordan has shown, its functions and ambitions were complex, in fact far more complex than those of the NLF or any other British radical organization.[16] Yet, in so far as it provided, among other things, the 'mass party' organization of parliamentary Nationalism, the debates surrounding its operation and development offer interesting parallels with the contemporary arguments about the NLF. In both countries such discussions reflected concerns about accountability, policy making and participation. In Ireland it all came to a head in the 1890s, with the party's rejection of Parnell's leadership, followed by the formation of the Irish National Federation (INF) as a rival to the INL and, eventually, after further splits, the rise of the United Irish League (UIL). The latter aimed at recreating party unity *from the bottom up*, an operation which the parliamentary leaders of all factions did not welcome, but had to accept in 1900. In Britain accountability, policy making and participation were what the NLF constitution was all about. This constitution was frequently amended, often with important consequences for the party's

[14] Cf. Biagini, 'Liberalism and direct democracy'; Biagini, *Liberty*, 313–15; Harris, *Private lives, public spirit*, 248; and M. Daunton, *Trusting Leviathan: the politics of taxation in Britain, 1799–1914* (2001), 256–301.

[15] Pombeni, 'Starting in reason, ending in passion', 322.

[16] Jordan, 'Irish National League and the "unwritten law"', 146–71.

identity: indeed it went through at least sixteen major revisions between 1877 and 1935. During 1877–1907 it was as much an internal battleground between members championing contrasting visions of the party, as a constitution, with major changes in 1880, 1885, 1886, 1887, 1890, annually between 1895 and 1897, and more drastically at various stages between 1903 and 1907. Whether or not comfortable with the principle of a mass organization, Liberals were not sure of what role it ought to play. Thus an analysis of the constitution is helpful to comprehend the members' perception of the party identity and the way it changed over time, and provides a template for understanding 'the distribution of power and functions'[17] within the party as a whole. The latter is significant not only in itself, but also because a party's internal authority structure – such as the relationship between 'mass organization' and parliamentary party, rank-and-file representation and central authority – reflects its ideological profile.

From the beginning, the NLF had generated misgivings among both rank and file and national leaders, though for different reasons. Of the ninety-five associations which had originally accepted Chamberlain's invitation, only forty-six actually sent delegates to Birmingham. Arguably, the actual formation of the Federation itself owed more to the Bulgarian agitation,[18] than to any grand plan of reform of popular politics. The then party leader, Lord Hartington, far from welcoming the new development, rightly saw it as a challenge from the periphery to the power at the centre.[19] Moreover, many MPs and candidates feared that their 'independence' was now being threatened in the constituencies, having already been curtailed at Westminster.[20] Critics of the NLF included several working-class leaders, such as George Howell, who complained that the 'caucus' was an exclusive, elitist device which destroyed the 'open' system of the traditional 'constitution' and the 'independence' of the electors.[21] However, Howell had been one of the

---

[17] Pombeni, *Introduzione alla storia dei partiti politici*, 23.

[18] See *The MP for Russia: reminiscences and correspondence of Madame O. Novikoff*, vol. I, ed. by W. T. Stead, 1909 vol. I, 275–8.

[19] Garvin, *Joseph Chamberlain*, vol. I, 14; B. McGill, 'Schnadhorst and Liberal party organization', *Journal of Modern History* (1962), 19–39.

[20] M. Ostrogorski, *Democracy and the Organization of Political Parties* (1902; reprinted 1964), 97–8; see also S. M. Lipset's 'Introduction' to Ostrogorski, *Democracy* and P. Pombeni, 'Ritorno a Birmingham. La "nuova organizzazione politica" di Joseph Chamberlain e l'origine della forma partito contemporanea (1874–1880)', *Ricerche di storia politica*, 3 (1988), 52, 55, 57; D. E. D. Beales, 'Parliamentary parties and the "independent" member, 1810–1860', in R. Robson (ed.), *Ideas and institutions of Victorian Britain* (1967).

[21] G. Howell, 'The caucus system and the Liberal party', *The Quarterly Magazine*, 10 (1878). Cf. W. T. Merriott, 'The Birmingham caucus', *Nineteenth Century*, 11 (1882),

first advocates of a democratic reorganization of the Liberal party to provide working men with a forum to discuss their views[22] – which is one of the aims the NLF tried to achieve.

'Independence' seemed to be what Liberals were most concerned about. Not only were MPs jealous of their right to vote according to conviction, sometimes against the wishes of their leaders and constituents, but also local Liberal associations were keen to safeguard their own freedom from interference by the whips. Furthermore, Liberal activists and voters in general were jealous of their own independence from local associations or anybody else. Independence was indeed a key word in Victorian Liberalism. J. S. Mill, as an MP for the borough of Westminster in 1865–8, insisted on his own rights and prerogatives against all sorts of external interference. The Liberal party which he joined in the House of Commons was structurally similar to its Conservative counterpart: a coalition of MPs and peers, held together by shared opinions and prejudices, patronage and tradition. At the time there was no such a thing as an official 'mass organization'. Of course, there were various local Liberal associations rooted in the realities and culture of the town or county in which they operated, and electoral committees with professional agents. Moreover, there were several popular radical organizations, two of which – the Reform League and the National Reform Union – had established a quasi-national reputation. However, so far as there was any national co-ordination, it came from the whips and the Liberal Central Association (LCA). Established in 1860 and controlled by the whips,[23] the LCA was the closest equivalent to a party bureaucracy. Originally, its purpose was limited to the preparation of the electoral registers.[24] Later it began to try to harmonize the work of local agents and Liberal associations, but did not have any influence on MPs. The latter continued to be co-ordinated by the whips in the House, and – socially, outside the House – by various London clubs, including the Reform and eventually the National Liberal Club.[25]

953, 954–7; and J. Davis, 'Radical clubs and London politics, 1870–1900', in D. Feldman and G. Stedman Jones (eds.), *Between neighbourhood and nation: histories and representations of London since 1800* (1989), 106.

[22] Pottinger Saab, *Reluctant icon*, 51.

[23] D. Kavanagh, 'Organization and power in the Liberal party', in V. Bogdanor (ed.), *Liberal party politics*, (1988), 124, 130, 133; C. Cook, *A short history of the Liberal party*, 1900–2001 (2002), 12.

[24] J. Scott Rasmussen, *The Liberal party: a study of retrenchment and revival* (1965), 51 n. 68.

[25] National Liberal Club. Objects and Rules, London, n.d., 1, National Liberal Club Collection in Bristol University Library. In the 'provinces' local Liberal clubs organized dinners, demonstrations and public meetings, lectures, concerts, luncheons in the town hall, and picnics for the rank and file. See the papers of the Newcastle-upon-Tyne Liberal Club, in Tyne and Wear Archives, 200/104.

Yet, as the electorate expanded after the 1867 Reform Act, the move towards greater organization – which implied some degree of discipline at all levels – was inevitable. It was propelled by the various pressure groups of popular liberalism – including the labour movement – and spurred on by electoral struggles for the control of local government.[26] Particularly interesting in this respect is the evolution of the Birmingham Liberal Association. Building on a long tradition of political unions,[27] this association was established in 1867. It resulted from the merger of two pre-existing organizations, one of which was the local working-class reform league.[28] Boosted by the challenges posed by the 'minority clause' of the 1867 Reform Act and, even more, by the 'cumulative vote' introduced by the 1870 Education Act, it gave rise to a new model of party politics, which contemporary critics dubbed 'the caucus'.

Generations of scholars – from Moisei Ostrogorski to Jon Lawrence and James Vernon – have been worried about the 'coercion' allegedly exercised by the caucus and its large-scale version, the NLF. These organizations sapped 'liberty' – according to some – by exchanging blind partisanship for educated public opinion;[29] or – according to others – by undermining the viability of traditional working-class politics by bourgeois professionalism;[30] or – finally – by caging customary and spontaneous expressions of community politics in a Foucaultian panopticon.[31] Interestingly enough, arguments similar to these were used at the time by disgruntled Liberals and Radicals, including town notables and old-fashioned artisan politicians.[32]

On one issue there seemed to be agreement: the caucus and the NLF tried to stand on its head the understanding of 'party' which had been shared by liberal political thinkers from Edmund Burke to Benjamin

---

[26] F. H. Herrick, 'The origins of the National Liberal Federation', *Journal of Modern History*, 17 (1945), 116–29.

[27] Garvin, *Joseph Chamberlain*, vol. I, 253.

[28] Cf. Birmingham Liberal Association, Objects, Constitution and Laws, Birmingham, 1878, in Birmingham Liberal Association Collection, Birmingham City Libraries.

[29] For example, Ostrogorski: Pombeni, *Partiti e sistemi politici*, 163.

[30] Lawrence, 'Popular politics'.   [31] Vernon, *Politics and the people*, 182, 192, 337.

[32] Cf. Sir Wemyss Reid's comments on the rejection of Sir Edward Baines by the Leeds caucus in 1874: in H. J. Hanham, *Elections and party management: politics in the age of Disraeli and Gladstone* (1978), 126. In 1874 Baines was defeated despite the fact that he had some trade union support (see letter by 'A Unionist', *The Leeds Mercury*, 2 Feb. 1874, 3). It is noteworthy that J. S. Mill had criticized the party system of his time on similar grounds: see above, note 7. By contrast, NLF activists and leaders, including major trade union bosses, emphasized its democratic impact and potential: they maintained that, thanks to the Liberal associations, candidatures were now decided by the party rank and file, rather than by a clique of self-selecting worthies: Frank Schnadhorst in a letter to *The Times* in 1878: cited in Hanham, *Elections and party management*, 133; cf. Biagini, *Liberty*, 332–3, 360–8.

Constant and J. S. Mill,[33] for it seemed that while '[f]ormerly the issues made the parties; now the parties [made] the issues'.[34] The traditional Liberal emphasis on 'ideas opened to enlightened spirits'[35] and the spiritual character of their movement was hardly conducive to enthusiasm for the practical implications of political organization. Thus '[t]he term party ... took on a negative connotation when it was used to refer to something other than an ideological community.'[36] Not surprisingly, in Britain as in the rest of Europe there were Liberals who were unable to accept this development of the concept of party.[37] There is no doubt that, with the establishment of the NLF in 1877, 'Chamberlain was opening many questions for contemporary liberalism.'[38]

What is remarkable is that both critics and supporters tended to exaggerate the effectiveness of the new organization. For, as Colin Matthew has shown, the caucus was 'chaotic and incapable of prolonged organizational effort, since it was devoid of the bureaucratic structures typical of the twentieth century'.[39] Thus, despite the fact that it has often been suggested that the caucus 'was determinant in the general elections of the 1880s, fifty per cent of these caucuses had disappeared after two or three years'.[40] As late as 1880 Joseph Cowen could confidently write to one of his American correspondents:

The process of popular agitation is very simple. A number of men satisfy themselves that a certain Legislative or social change is required. They form themselves into a society, collect as much money as they are capable, and try to influence public opinion by means of lectures, tracts, public meetings, conferences, and other political mechanisms. There is not much mystery about the business, and there is no settled plan of proceeding ... There has been an attempt recently to establish what are called Liberal associations ... but ... the movement has been a failure ... Mr Linton has [sic] considerable experience in the Chartist agitation in England ... Matters have not much altered since he was engaged in public affairs.[41]

---

[33] Pombeni, 'Trasformismo e questione del partito', 233–4; Sheehan, *German liberalism*, 15–16.
[34] Lowell to Bryce in 1905, complaining about one of the effects of the NLF: cited in Pombeni, 'Starting in reason, ending in passion', 323.
[35] Pombeni, 'Starting in reason, ending in passion', 326.
[36] Sheehan, *German liberalism*, 17.
[37] Pombeni, 'Trasformismo e questione del partito', 246–7.
[38] Pombeni, 'Starting in reason, ending in passion', 326.
[39] H. C. G. Matthew, 'Moisei Ostrogorski e la tradizione inglese di studi politici', in G. Orsina (a cura di), *Contro i partiti. Saggi sul pensiero di Moisei Ostrogroski* (1993), 53.
[40] Ibid.
[41] J. Cowen to Revd J. Harwood Pattison, New Haven, Connecticut, n.d. [1880], in Cowen Papers, B414, Letter Book, 7–9.

The weakness of the 'machine' was compounded by the fact that the NLF as a whole was financially independent of the LCA.[42] This arrangement had two consequences: on the one hand, it meant that the whips had little institutional influence on the mass party, a restriction which was indeed a matter of pride for the NLF.[43] On the other hand, it implied that the financial resources of the NLF were severely limited, and this affected its performance as an electoral organization. In the long run, real problems were to arise not from the efficiency of the mass party and its allegedly coercive powers, but from its endemic anarchy and ineffectiveness.

While critics described the NLF and its branches as the last stage in the 'Americanization' of Liberal politics, in reality there was neither the desire nor the opportunity to turn it into a British Tammany Hall.[44] Far from creating a national machine, the long-lasting effect of the NLF was to perpetuate Liberal localism – that is, what Spence Watson proudly described as 'the independence' of the local associations.[45] This aspect of the NLF was strengthened by the Nonconformist culture of so many of its members, with its typical emphasis on local government and congregational autonomy. Liberal localism, despite Watson's pride, was a questionable asset for the party's electoral performance and prospects. It meant, for instance, that the NLF was unable to control candidatures,[46] a fact that frustrated attempts to accommodate trade union demands for political recognition, and arguably contributed to hastening the rise of independent Labour politics. Gladstone himself was so frustrated about the NLF's inability to select working-class candidates that he 'astonishingly shared the opinion that labour was perfectly justified in organizing on an independent basis in order to compel Liberals to translate official sympathy into positive action'.[47]

Yet, from the beginning the NLF did have a working-class component, both in terms of individual membership and in terms of corporate

---

[42] Watson, *The National Liberal Federation*, 195.

[43] First Session of the Council, Thursday, 18 March 18 1897, in, National Liberal Federation, Annual Reports and Council Proceedings, 1877–1936, Microfilm edition (Harvester Press) in Cambridge University Library (henceforward cited as NLFAR), 37.

[44] Watson, *The National Liberal Federation*, 16. Cf. *National Liberal Federation. Constitution Submitted to the Conference of 1877*, V, 'Special General Meetings of Council', in NLFAR. Cf. J. Bryce's preface to Ostrogorski, *Democracy*.

[45] Watson, *The National Liberal Federation*, 16. Watson was the president of the NLF from 1890 to 1902. Besides being one of the most influential Liberal 'wirepullers', he enjoyed a measure of personal support, and was described by the *Co-operative News* (5 June 1880, 381) as 'one of the most popular men on Tyneside'.

[46] Watson, *The National Liberal Federation*, 195.

[47] Barker, *Gladstone and Radicalism*, 134. Cf. H. Pelling, *Popular politics and society in late Victorian Britain* (1979), 101–20.

representation on the executives of federated caucuses.[48] Later it pursued a strategy of incorporation from the top, co-opting successful labour leaders. Newcastle upon Tyne was always in the forefront of Liberalism: already in October 1880 Thomas Burt was listed among the officers and members of the committee of the Junior Liberal Club (which included also Joseph Cowen, the then sitting MP).[49] In 1895 Burt, as well as the other most influential miners' leader, Charles Fenwick, were listed as members of the Newcastle upon Tyne Liberal Club.[50] In 1884 among the 'Additional Members of the General Committee' were Henry Broadhurst and Joseph Arch. In 1886 the NLF vice-presidents included Lib-lab worthies such as Henry Broadhurst, Thomas Burt, William Crawford, Charles Fenwick, Benjamin Pickard, Joseph Arch, and even George Howell,[51] who, only a few years earlier, had been one of the bitterest labour critics of the 'caucus'. In 1891 it was Thomas Burt who was chosen to deliver the welcome address to Gladstone at the commencement of the famous Newcastle meeting of the NLF.[52]

However significant some of these personalities were, to the labour movement as a whole it was of little use that the NLF was ready to bestow honours on those of their representatives who were already successful anyway. On the other hand, this attitude was not specific to the NLF, but reflected common practice at the time. In a letter to Conor Cruise O'Brien, Henry Harrison, a veteran Nationalist MP, stated that in Parnell's days 'a rich as well as politically robust' parliamentary candidate would be preferred to a poor one, on the grounds not of class, but of costs to the party funds.[53] This is precisely the reason why the Liberal caucuses preferred 'bourgeois' candidates and were reluctant to nominate penniless and expensive working men. The difference was that while in Ireland this social bias was missed in the general nationalist fervour, in Britain it was interpreted along 'class exclusion' lines by ambitious and disappointed labour candidates. However, this strategy amounted to laissez-faire in the politics of party organization, a free-market approach to power relations within the party. It was totally inadequate, for what the

---

[48] Admittedly, it was only a marginal component: for example, the list of delegates nominated to attend the 1877 conference included representatives of only one working men's club, that of Banbury. Resolutions passed at the Conference, 31 May 1877, 9, in NLFAR. The representatives were Thomas Olds and Israel Bunton.

[49] Newcastle upon Tyne Junior Liberal Club, *List of Officers and Committee for 1880*, 14 Oct. 1880: in Tyne and Wear Archives, 200/104.

[50] Ibid.   [51] Meeting of the Council, Stoke-on-Trent, 7 Oct. 1884, in NLFAR.

[52] Cf. Proceedings of the Annual Meeting of the Council, Tyne Theatre, Newcastle upon Tyne, 2 Oct. 1891, in NLFAR.

[53] Cruise O'Brien, *Parnell and his party*, 139, n.1. The letter was written in 1943 and Harrison had become a candidate in 1890.

labour movement needed was a political machine for the fostering of working-class interests through a much wider parliamentary representation. That some form of mass organization was a necessity for popular liberals is confirmed by the fact that, from the early 1880s, some of the most interesting tensions in the Liberal/radical camp took place not between individual candidates and the 'machine', or the latter and 'free-born' artisans, but between two competing 'machines'. Again, Newcastle upon Tyne offered various examples of this phenomenon in the early 1880s, when Joseph Cowen set up his own anti-caucus caucus in order to prevent the election of John Morley.[54] A similar case occurred in Sheffield in 1885, when the United Committee of Radical and Labour Associations challenged the official Liberal association in order to impose its candidate on one of the new city constituencies.[55] The irony was that one of the aims of the founders of the Sheffield caucus had been to avoid any future splitting of the Liberal vote.[56]

What divided these people were not issues of principle, but personality clashes and power relations: this is well illustrated by William Abraham, 'Mabon', in South Wales. In 1885, at the beginning of his parliamentary career, when 'Mabon' was struggling against the local Liberal Three Hundred, he branded it as a 'conspiracy' against working-class representation.[57] Ten years later, when he had become a successful and established Lib-lab politician, he accepted invitations to be the main guest at the inauguration of Liberal clubs,[58] and was a speaker (and a singer) at the 1895 NLF Council meeting.[59] Meanwhile the miners' union in South Wales had become the most effective caucus in its region. While some of these 'organic' caucuses eventually incorporated, or were incorporated into, the local official Liberal associations, the fact is that they, rather than the Liberal associations, were the real answer to the new needs of working-class electoral politics. Trade union caucuses, which dominated local Liberal party councils with their 'block vote', can be seen as the first

[54] Biagini, *Liberty*, chapter 6.
[55] See the 'Memo' dated 28 Mar. 1885, H. J. Wilson Papers, 37P/20/46, in Sheffield University Library. For a few other examples see Biagini, *Liberty*, chapter 6.
[56] R. Leader to H. J. Wilson, 1 Jan. 1885, in H. J. Wilson Papers, 37P/20/9/i–ii.
[57] See Mabon's speech in 'Representation of the Rhondda', *Cardiff Times and South Wales Weekly News*, 1 Aug. 1885, 8.
[58] Rep. 'Liberalism at Ferndale, opening of a working men's club', *Glamorgan Free Press*, 2 Nov. 1895, 5.
[59] W. Abraham (Mabon), motions on labour legislation and administration, in Sixteenth Annual Meeting of the Council, Cardiff, 16–19 Jan. 1895, 103, in NLFAR; on 18 January Mabon opened the meeting by leading the council in the singing of Welsh hymns and songs: see ibid., 107.

experiments in what would become the constitutional framework and 'machine' of post-1918 Labour politics.

These developments took place, not because of, but despite the efforts of the Liberal associations directly involved, and independent of the NLF. Indeed the latter's passion for decentralization, besides antagonizing frustrated labour Liberals, thus reducing the NLF's electoral effectiveness, hampered the formulation of coherent policies based on broad strategies. Moreover, localism did not help the party to deal with 'faddism', one of the problems which the NLF had set out to solve in the first place.[60] While tensions among parallel but unco-ordinated 'currents of radicalism' were common to all liberal and democratic movements in Europe,[61] faddism was potentially more disruptive in Britain than in any other country, as British liberalism was more vigorous and popular than elsewhere in Europe. The application of the representative principle to popular liberalism aimed at creating for all Liberal and Radical pressure groups an overarching 'civic community', which would encompass pre-existing allegiances within a federal hierarchy of assemblies. Such an aim was moderately successful in certain contexts, such as Birmingham. Given the Victorian enthusiasm for discussion and political meetings, its potential should not be underestimated, especially as we bear in mind the extraordinary clubbability of the Victorians, a passion which did not know barriers of either class or gender. In particular, the contemporary blossoming of parliamentary debating societies offers a further indication of the general passion for political participation and debate in the country at the time.[62]

However, in general the caucus model of party politics did not work because, on the one hand, it was based on unrealistically high expectations of civic 'virtue' and participation,[63] while, on the other, pre-

---

[60] Watson, *The National Liberal Federation*, 6. Cf. Report of the Committee, 11th Annual Meeting, Birmingham, 6–7 Nov. 1888, 26–7, in NLFAR: 'The associations ... cover the whole ground, so far as England and Wales are concerned, and it is hoped they will prevent that multiplication of organizations for special purposes which in times past have wasted the means and energy of the Liberal party with no commensurate beneficial results.'

[61] Cf. Pombeni, 'Trasformismo e questione del partito', 215–28.

[62] Some of these societies counted more than a thousand members: the one in Newcastle had 1,100 in 1882 (*The Debater. A Weekly Record of the Newcastle Parliamentary Debating Society* (Tyne and Wear Archives 200/124, 16 Mar. 1882, 4)). Seventy-five debating societies sent delegates to the 1882 national conference: *The Debater*, 20 Apr. 1882, 3. This article argued that most of these societies had been established between 1879 and 1882: this was the period when the NLF took off as a more permanent feature of Liberal politics; it was also the age of the Midlothian campaigns and the great duels between Gladstone and Disraeli.

[63] For an example see Lawrence, 'Popular politics', 76.

existing community allegiances proved too strong for the caucus to absorb them. Though a degree of 'democratic centralism'[64] was supposed to characterize the Federation, it was hardly comparable with what the Labour party was to achieve after 1918,[65] or, as we shall see, with the degree of centralism achieved by the Irish Nationalists after 1885. Liberal energies could be focused on a single long-term effort only when either a charismatic leader took over (as happened, in 1886–94, with Irish Home Rule, under Gladstone), or when a spontaneous rising of the rank and file occurred to defend some threatened Liberal dogma (as in 1903–6 with free trade).

The claim that the caucus was the forum for popular Liberalism[66] was rather inaccurate, in view of the comparatively small size of the NLF and the fact that local Liberal associations were often resented, or even resisted, by working-class radicals. Nevertheless, it was an interesting claim, because it involved a repudiation of the caucus in Ostrogorski's sense of the word – that is, as a 'machine' to deliver electoral victory. To NLF activists, as much as to their critics, such a caucus would have been incompatible with the spirit and principles of Liberalism. In short, the main point in the Liberal apologia for their mass organization was that it was *not* a 'party' organization.

There was some truth in this apologia. For, as Michael Barker has observed,[67] unfortunately for the Liberals, the NLF could not really operate like that party 'machine' which it was expected to be and which the labour left needed in order to assert its influence in the party and in Parliament. The NLF fell altogether short of such requirements, combining, as it did, exasperated localism with inadequate support from the centre: indeed, as Hanham has pointed out, 'its resources were small. Its income (and consequently its expenditure) remained well below that of the great nonconformist propaganda agencies.'[68] The Liberal machine relied on voluntary work and the support offered by social and religious groups on the basis of local allegiances. From this point of view the structure of NLF politics was rather similar to the pattern of traditional, pre-1877, popular agitations. Features of this continuity included both the emphasis on locality and grass-roots democracy, and the extra-parliamentary aspect. While the relationship between the NLF and the

---

[64] T. Marsh, *Joseph Chamberlain: entrepreneur in politics* (1994), 120.

[65] K. O. Morgan, 'The high and low politics of Labour: Keir Hardie to Michael Foot', in M. Bentley and J. Stevenson (eds.), *High and low politics in modern Britain* (1983), 291.

[66] J. Chamberlain, 'A New Political Organization', *Fortnightly Review*, n.s., 22 (July 1877), 126.

[67] Barker, *Gladstone and radicalism*, 153–4.

[68] Hanham, *Elections and party management*, 140.

parliamentary party was not clearly defined until 1907 at least, all the Victorian editions of its constitution focused on the democratic nature of the extra-parliamentary party. Thus the 1877 constitution proclaimed that '[t]he essential feature of the proposed Federation is . . . the direct participation of all members of the party in the direction of its policy, and in the selection of those particular measures of reform and of progress to which priority shall be given.' It went on to say that '[t]his object can be secured only by the organization of the party upon a representative basis: that is, by popularly elected committees of local associations, by means of their freely chosen representatives, in a general federation.'[69]

Though the ultimate aim was to reorganize the party as a whole on a federal, representative basis,[70] the means of achieving this result were not specified by the constitution. Nor was it clear how it would affect the internal authority structure as between the parliamentary party and the leader on the one hand, and the mass party on the other. By contrast, the political aims of mass agitation were discussed in detail. In 1880 they included a seven-point programme asking for the extension of the household franchise to the counties, the redistribution of seats, the prevention of corrupt practices at elections, county councils, the curbing of the powers of the House of Lords, and 'comprehensive schemes of land law reform for Great Britain and Ireland'. The last would consist of four parallel and concomitant strategies: abolition of primogeniture and entail, free sale, tenant rights and land purchase. In order to achieve such a programme the federated associations committed themselves 'to take united action, whenever it may be deemed desirable, in defence or support of the Liberal Policy and Government'.[71]

The typically rural emphasis of this programme was both a memento of a democratic tradition stretching back to Chartism and evidence of the enduring Radical concern with land reform, which would culminate with the Lloyd George campaign in 1914.[72] The last point, the plan of campaign by popular agitation, amounted to a proclamation of loyalty to Gladstone's government and foreshadowed the post-1886 alliance between the mass party organization and a leader whose power depended on his ability to use the media and popular radicalism as 'sounding boards' for his rhetoric. If the Reform League had idolized Bright, Gladstone and indeed Mill, the NLF needed Gladstone as an icon and national 'platform

---

[69] National Liberal Federation, Constitution Submitted to the Conference of 1877, V, 'Special General Meetings of Council', in NLFAR.

[70] Cf. National Liberal Federation, Its General Objects, and Its Immediate Work, Autumn 1880, 'Constitution', 35–6; Annual Reports and Council Proceedings of the Conference of 1886, 'Objects', in NLFAR.

[71] NLF, 'Immediate Work', 37, ibid.   [72] Packer, Lloyd George.

orator'.[73] What was remarkable was that the NLF combined the temperament of an old radical organization with the functions of a 'national'
electoral machine.[74] Its novelty lay in the adoption of the principle of
rank-and-file sovereignty by a party whose primary expression remained
the parliamentary group. For the first time the rank and file of a major party
were able to challenge not only the system of aristocratic patronage at
constituency level, but also the authority of their leaders in Parliament,
and claimed the right to define party policy and priorities.

The dream of party democracy, 1886–95

The decision to endorse Home Rule was a turning point in the history of
the NLF. 'Not a single constituency organization, save in Birmingham,
rejected a Gladstonian candidate. They stuck as one with Gladstone.'[75]
Terry Jenkins has suggested that support for Gladstone came from the
NLF 'wirepullers' rather than from the ordinary Liberal voters. He argues
that the caucus men were concerned only with winning elections, and that
any challenge to Gladstone's authority was seen as a threat to the performance of the party.[76] This interpretation reproduces a contemporary
analysis by the *Pall Mall Gazette*, and, like that, suffers from two main
problems. First, Home Rule was not a vote winner, and this quickly
became evident. On the contrary, it was an extremely divisive issue,
which immediately deprived the party of important assets, including
many of its wealthy supporters, much of the front bench and most of
the newspaper press. Yet, despite the electoral defeat in 1886 and
repeated frustrations, leading to the debacles of 1895 and 1900, the
NLF remained loyal to Home Rule with an almost religious zeal. The
second problem with Jenkins' explanation is that, far from being a step
inspired by cynical electoral calculations, the decision to support Home
Rule was largely influenced by *emotional* responses to perceived injustices
and to the GOM's appeal, as well as by entrenched support for Home
Rule in some radical circles, particularly influential at a regional level.[77]

---

[73] Cf.'Presentation by the Artisans of Birmingham', in Proceedings of the Annual Meeting
of the Council, Birmingham, 6 Nov. 1888, 164, in NLFAR.
[74] National Liberal Federation, Constitution Submitted to the Conference of 1877, I, in
NLFAR.
[75] Lubenow, *Parliamentary politics and the Home Rule crisis*, 246.
[76] T. A. Jenkins, *The Liberal ascendancy, 1830–1886* (London, 1994), 216.
[77] Goodlad, 'Gladstone and his rivals'; J. Shepherd, 'Labour and Parliament: the Lib-labs
as the first working-class MPs, 1885–1906', Biagini and Reid, *Currents of radicalism*, 198.
See chapter 2, above, pp. 50–75.

Jenkins' interpretation is reminiscent of Max Weber's classical thesis, namely, that the NLF's decision was of 'crucial importance'[78] in re-establishing Gladstone's control over the party. However, there is evidence to suggest that it would be more accurate to say that it was crucial in establishing the authority of the NLF itself within the party as a whole. For it was only then that the NLF became a focal point for Gladstonian loyalism, growing in size with the accession of fifty additional Liberal associations and seventy MPs.[79] Part of this growth was due to the multiplication of the number of parliamentary constituencies after the adoption of the single-member system in 1885. However, the redistribution of seats is not of itself sufficient to account for the growth in federated associations: for, even after the loss of the Unionist vote and membership, the proliferation of federated Liberal associations continued after 1886, reaching 850 in 1890.[80] In 1897, in spite of the disarray caused by the 1895 electoral disaster, the number of federated associations was still above the 1888 level.[81] Furthermore, the secession of most of the Whigs cleared the way for the Federation's burgeoning as a power within the party as a whole. For, on the one hand, it forced the party further to develop its electoral machine in order to compensate for the loss of wealth,[82] patronage and influence. On the other, it purged the party of most of its non-radical components, thus increasing the scope for the adoption of those policies with which the NLF was identified. These developments reached their climax during the years 1888–95.

The 1888 report of the General Committee left unchanged the ambiguous relationship between the NLF and the party leaders. It claimed loyalty to the party leaders, but at the same time reasserted the independence of the mass organization.[83] The latter's general assembly was supposed to be, or to become, the truly sovereign body within the party, thus implicitly challenging the authority of those leaders to whom loyalty had been pledged. Throughout its many versions, the NLF constitution

---

[78] Cook, *A short history of the Liberal party*, 23; cf. M. Weber, 'Politics as a vocation', in H. H. Gerth and C. Wright Mills, *From Max Weber: essays in sociology* (1948), 77–128.
[79] Cook, *A short history of the Liberal party*, 23.
[80] Barker, *Gladstone and radicalism*, 114.
[81] Proceedings of the 1897 Meeting, Norwich, 18 Mar. 1897, 5, in NLFAR.
[82] Barker, *Gladstone and radicalism*, 113–14.
[83] Report of the Committee, 11th Annual Meeting, Birmingham, 6–7 Nov. 1888, 26–7, in NLFAR: 'The Federation embodies and expresses the profound and unshaken loyalty of the Liberal party to its great chief, and the confidence felt in his colleagues. At the same time, the Federation has never been ... a merely official organization. It receives its inspiration from the people; one of its chief functions is to ascertain the will of the party, to give expression to that will, and to unite all leaders as well as followers, in serving the objects which the party desires.'

invariably proclaimed that 'the essential nature' of the Federation was 'the direct participation of all members of the party in the direction of its policy' *and* 'in the selection of those particular measures of reform and of progress to which priority shall be given'.[84] These two points deserve further discussion. Though historians entertain legitimate misgivings about how 'essential' this alleged 'nature' really was,[85] it must at least be recognized that the most prominent feature in the self-perception of NLF's activists was the emphasis on the Federation's 'popular basis'. According to the 1877 constitution:

1. The whole body of Liberals in the borough is recognized as the constituency of the Association; and every Liberal has a vote in the election of its committees.
2. Political responsibility, and the ultimate power of control, belong to the largest representative body, and the policy of the Association is loyally guided by its decision.
3. The decision of the majority, in the selection of candidates and other matters of practical business, is regarded as binding upon those who consent to be nominated, as well as upon the general body of members.[86]

While critics charged the caucus with usurping the electors' rights, the caucus' advocates retorted that the NLF and its branches were expressions of the citizens' right of self-government,[87] and reflected their public spirit, rather than their will to electoral power.[88] The party's general assembly, the council, was primarily presented and described not as a component of the electoral 'machine', but as the 'parliament' of rank-and-file opinion. As such it was supposed to be instrumental in bringing the people's views to bear on the parliamentary party: '[w]e hope that the time is not distant when we may see a meeting of what will be a really Liberal Parliament outside the Imperial Legislature, and, unlike it, elected by universal suffrage.'[89] Similar feelings about the purpose of the

---

[84] National Liberal Federation, Constitution Submitted to the Conference of 1877, V, 'Special General Meetings of Council', in NLFAR.

[85] Hanham, *Elections and party management*, 141.

[86] National Liberal Federation, Constitution Submitted to the Conference of 1877, V, 'Special General Meetings of Council', paragraphs (1), (2), (3) and (4), 30, in NLFAR.

[87] H. W. Crosskey, 'The Liberal association – the "600" – of Birmingham', *Macmillan's Magazine*, 35 (1876–7), 307; J. Chamberlain, 'The caucus', *Fortnightly Review*, 24 n.s. (1878), 724, 734.

[88] Chamberlain, 'The caucus', 740; cf. H. J. Hanham, 'Tra l'individuo e lo stato', in P. Pombeni (ed.), *La trasformazione politica nell'Europa liberale 1870–1890* (1986), 93–102.

[89] Report of the Conference, 31 May 1877, 16, in NLFAR. See also National Liberal Federation, Constitution Submitted to the Conference of 1877, III, 'Council', and IV, 'General Committee', in NLFAR, in a sort of 'TUC' of rank-and-file Liberalism, J. L. Garvin's words. Garvin, *Joseph Chamberlain*, vol. I, 236.

mass organization were expressed at the 1885 conference of Scottish Liberal associations (to which more than 160 associations sent delegates).[90]

This resulted in the foundation of the Scottish Liberal Association (SLA), which, like the NLF, opted for 'a purely Representative' structure.[91] In the early 1880s, even among Scottish Liberals '[t]he key question was whether or not the SLA could make policy' – a question so divisive that eventually the radicals – who supported policy-making powers – broke away in 1885 to form the Scottish Liberal Federation (SLF).[92] In England the NLF amended its constitution and increased the representative nature of the council by introducing a stricter form of proportionality in the allocation of delegates.[93] This produced a rather large representative assembly. In practice, however, councils were attended by only a minority of delegates, except when Gladstone was speaking, as at the 1888 council. The latter was attended by 3,300 delegates,[94] numbers being boosted by the attraction of personal contact with the leader, a further reminder of the importance of the charismatic factor.

The federated associations were similarly built on representative principles, so that at both the national and the local level the structure of the NLF tried to parallel the British system of representative government. In the 1880s and 1890s this representative edifice was strengthened by the introduction of the NLF equivalent of 'Home Rule All Round'. This involved the establishment of regional associations for the Home Counties, the Midlands and the West Country (1890), the North and East of Scotland Association and the Scottish Liberal Federation (1880; the latter two merged in 1887). In 1887 regional branches active in a campaign of radical agitations included divisions for the Midland Counties, Cheshire, Cornwall, Staffordshire, Huntingdonshire, Norfolk, Suffolk, the Home Counties and London, besides the London Liberal and Radical Union, the North Wales Federation and the South Wales Federation.[95] Part of the aim of the new regional organizations was to bring the Federation 'closer to the people', but there was also the more

---

[90] Cited in rep., 'Conference of Scotch Liberals', *FJ*, 16 Sep. 1885, 6.
[91] Appeal for funds, a circular dated October 1887 and signed 'Alex. MacDougall, Secretary', SLA Papers, NLS, Acc.11765/35. However, the list of 'Donations and Subscriptions, 1888' comes to only about £1,300: see printed list, ibid., unnumbered page.
[92] Burgess, '*Strange Associations*', 35.
[93] Council Proceedings of 1887, III. 'Council', 36, in NLFAR. For the previous system of representation see Council Proceedings of 1886, 'Council', 29, ibid.
[94] Proceedings of the Annual Meeting of the Council, 6–7 Nov. 1888, 87 in NLFAR.
[95] Ibid., 17ff.

practical and modern concern to reach out to those who were politically indifferent or uncertain.[96] Such a concern could well be seen as contributing towards the subsequent formation of the Women's Liberal Federation (WLF, in 1887, with 20,000 members by 1888),[97] though the end result was in this case the empowering of women and the gradual winning over to suffragism of rank-and-file female Liberals.[98]

At the 1890 meeting the constitution was amended again, this time with a view to allowing a more frequent and timely convocation of the council.[99] In addition, the General Committee was deprived of its power to co-opt members, and this meant that the executive would then be completely controlled by the elected representatives of the local associations. To some extent the 1891 'Newcastle Programme' was a product of this approach to the running of the party. For the first time a programme was imposed on the parliamentary party by the mass organization.[100] The programme insisted on Irish Home Rule, but also included a number of democratic and social reforms such as the disestablishment of the church in both Scotland and Wales, arbitration in international disputes, increased death duties and taxation of land values, and the 'mending or ending' of the House of Lords.[101]

Though Barker has suggested that the caucus was run by 'wirepullers' such as Schnadhorst and his authoritarian successor, James Kitson,[102] even he has found it difficult to propose an unequivocal answer to the question of who 'controlled' the NLF. There are several reasons for this difficulty. First, some of these wirepullers – including Spence Watson – had a genuine democratic following, and, at least at a regional level, were popular irrespective of their role in the party machine.[103] Second, there is evidence that at least a few of the 'wirepullers' actually believed in party democracy (perhaps more than their bosses, the elected representatives of the people). Thus, while Chamberlain's own papers and correspondence

---

[96] 'A recent article in the *Times* newspaper says that "the people whose votes really turn elections, and ultimately govern the destinies of the country, are not the people who go to the great meetings", and it should be one of the great works of a Liberal organization to reach this class.' (Meeting of the Council, Nottingham, 18–19 Oct. 1887, 27–8, in NLFAR.)

[97] The Women's Liberal Federation, in Proceedings of the Annual Meeting of the Council, Birmingham, 6 Nov. 1888, 126, in NLFAR and the Women's Liberal Association (1893).

[98] Pugh, *The march of the women*, 131–5.

[99] NLF, Proceedings in Connection with the Annual Meeting of 1890, 7.

[100] Cook, *A short history of the Liberal party*, 26.

[101] 'The programme of the Gladstonian party', *Ti*, 2 Oct. 1891, 9.

[102] Barker, *Gladstone and radicalism*, 138ff., 158.

[103] According to the *Co-operative News* (5 June 1880, 6) 'Mr Robert Spence Watson ... is one of the most popular men on Tyneside.'

contain substantial evidence of effective 'wirepulling', the correspondence of the chief party manager, F. W. Schnadhorst, indicates an obsession with policy making and accountability, and a concern to establish the
'constitutional' rights of the NLF to shape the agenda of Liberalism (to
Chamberlain's annoyance). Furthermore, the situation and the balance
of power within the NLF evolved with political vicissitudes and the
election of new presidents. Finally, the interventions of defiant delegates
at the annual councils and ongoing constitutional instability suggest a
picture more complicated than a wirepuller's paradise. This is confirmed
also by Gladstone's prudent handling of the 'Newcastle Programme'
when addressing the 1891 council. Then, as Barker has pointed out, far
from assuming that the 'wirepullers' would sort things out for him,
Gladstone spoke to the general assembly of the NLF with great caution,
fully aware of the importance of the council: 'he ... realized that the
democratic forces which had recently transformed the party made it
impossible for the parliamentary leaders to ignore the wishes of the
popular organization'.[104] Instead, he preferred to give a lead to it, by
establishing an order of priority among the various points of the programme and by encouraging further debate on issues in which he was
personally interested, including old age pensions as a part of a plan to
reform and replace the Poor Law system.[105]

However, at a local level limited popular participation and aggressive
lobbying by a few highly committed activists could often stifle internal
debate and present assemblies with a *fait accompli*. As one A. Hulan
complained, 'A practically self-constituted executive (for they spring
their names suddenly by resolution on the assembly and allow no speaking on it except by their own nominees, and no amendments to the
proposal), a practically self-constituted executive, I say, frame a report
and yearly, in secret conclave, determine the resolutions that are to be
voted at the great annual assembly.'[106] He proposed a series of amendments to encourage and allow effective debate and to encourage the
submission of competing diverse proposals. Similar concerns were shared
by many other radicals within and without the NLF, including the post-
Chartist Morrison Davidson, who advocated the introduction of the 'second ballot'. The latter would allow electors to choose between candidates

---

[104] Barker, *Gladstone and radicalism*, 163. Cf. W. E Gladstone, 'The future policy of the
Liberal party, Newcastle, October 2, 1891', in A. W. Hutton and H. J. Cohen (eds.), *The
speeches of the Right Hon. W. E. Gladstone* (1902), esp. 383–5.
[105] Barker, *Gladstone and radicalism*, 197–8; see Gladstone's speech (at an NLF meeting in
London) in *Ti*, 12 Dec. 1891, 7; he alluded to the issue the following year: HPD, 4th
series, 24 Mar. 1892, 1711.
[106] Letter, 'The National Liberal Federation', *WT&E*, 10 Oct. 1891, 6.

in preparation for an election and would obviate 'any necessity for the anti-Democratic institution of the Caucus, which usurps the functions of the constituencies by limiting their choice of candidates'.[107]

They had a point, especially in so far as the proceedings and operation of local caucuses were often dominated by an elite of notables and professional party agents. For example, the address presented to Gladstone in 1890 by the Dunbartonshire Liberal Association (DLA) was prepared by the secretary (a paid official) and approved by two other members of the Executive Committee.[108] The rules of the association were modified to ensure that wealthy party benefactors would sit on the General Committee. The latter now consisted not only of elected representatives, but also of an indefinite number of 'gentlemen who are liberal subscribers to the [party] funds' co-opted by the Executive Committee.[109] While this rule made the association more elitist, it is interesting that it was introduced in 1889 to compensate for the allegedly excessive internal democracy, which excluded the very men on whose money the DLA survived.[110] The association's General Council consisted of about 190 representatives (in 1889), elected by the Liberals throughout the county. At their general meeting they selected the constituency's parliamentary candidate on the recommendation of the selection and executive committees.[111] There is little evidence of popular participation in the proceedings, except in times of crisis such as the Parnell split: the Special General Meeting convened to reassert confidence in Gladstone's leadership and Irish policy attracted 'a large attendance of delegates [and] specially appointed delegates from nearly every part of the County'.[112] However, the DLA did not devote much time to discussion and was primarily a registration machine, operating in a highly competitive environment within which the Unionists seemed to have the advantage of more numerous and better-funded agents.[113] In 1889–92 its officials worked hard to improve its funding, management and propaganda activities, turning it into an even more professional organization, within which the party agents played an

---

[107] J. Morrison Davidson, 'Progressive programme', *WT&E*, 7 July 1895, 6.
[108] DLA, 14 Oct. 1890, NLS, Acc.11765/37.
[109] DLA, Report of the Executive Committee at the Annual Meeting, 29 Jan. 1889, ibid.
[110] The clause seems to have achieved its aim (the DLA accounts improved steadily), but was quietly repealed in the 1890s, when the DLA reverted to a system under which all members of the executive were to be elected: 'Constitution and rules', printed text included in DLA, Minutes of the Annual general Meeting, 14 Mar. 1898, NLS, Acc. 11765/37.
[111] DLA, Meeting of the Annual Meeting of the General Committee, 29 Jan. 1889, ibid.
[112] DLA, Minutes of Special General Meeting of the General Committee, 15 Oct. 1891, ibid.
[113] Report of the Registration Committee, 28 Jan. 1889, ibid.

important role under the close scrutiny of the Executive Committee. The kind of popular involvement which was increasingly desired was for the purpose of canvassing and 'proselytizing' electors.[114] The reality of local caucus politics was quite different from the national rhetoric of the party as the Liberal *ekklesia* outside the imperial Parliament.

The Irish model

It is proposed to form an association to be known as 'The Irish National League', an association which is . . . to concentrate into a single movement the scattered and various lines of action by which it has hitherto sought to advance the national cause. This body is to have what in the convenient American phrase we may describe as a platform resting on five planks – National Self-Government, Land Law Reform, Local Self-Government, extension of the Parliamentary and Municipal Franchises, the development and encouragement of the Labour and Industrial Interests of Ireland.[115]

With these words in October 1882 the *Freeman's Journal* announced the foundation of the Irish National League (INL), the first modern 'mass organization' of the Irish National party. It replaced the Land League and tried to incorporate other popular organizations, such as the Labour and Industrial Union and the Home Rule League. The constitution allowed for the formation of branches 'in parishes in the country, and in wards in the cities and towns', run by a committee elected annually. Branches would collect subscriptions ('1s. for every £5 valuation') and 75 per cent of all subscriptions would be forwarded to the Central Council. By secret ballots local delegates would be elected to annual county conventions,[116] which would select parliamentary candidates and discuss (or rather ratify) proposals. The ruling council would consist of forty-eight members: 'thirty-two to be elected by county conventions, one for each county, and sixteen by the Irish parliamentary party'.[117]

With its emphasis on county conventions, the INL drew on a long Irish tradition, stretching back into the eighteenth century and especially to the O'Connell movement before the Famine. But in the context of the 1880s, the railway network and the printing press allowed for a degree of

---

[114] See the Secretary's Annual Reports, General Meeting of the General Committee, DLA, 23 Feb. 1892 and 6 Feb. 1896, ibid. For the situation in England cf. Rix, 'The party agent and English electoral culture', 258–9 and Moore, *Transformation of urban liberalism*.

[115] L.a., *FJ*, 16 Oct. 1882, 4. Cf. *Address of the Irish National League:to the People of Ireland*, in Heffernan Papers, NLI, MS 21,910, acc. 1921 and drafts in Parnell letters 8581 (3).

[116] The Irish National League, 'Rules for branches', in Heffernan Papers, MS 21,910, acc. 1921.

[117] 'The constitution of the Irish National League', ibid.

organization and centralization which were quite unprecedented. The INL transformed the Home Rule movement 'from a loose conglomeration of independent and sometimes discrepant elements into a well-knit political party of a modern type, existing at four levels – the local branch, the county convention, the organising committee, and the parliamentary party – and effectively monopolizing the political expression of the national sentiment'.[118] In this respect it succeeded in achieving effective national co-ordination, one of the aims that the leaders of the NLF had always unsuccessfully pursued. Success was consolidated by the INL's rapid growth – from 242 branches in January 1884, to 592 branches in 1885, and 1,286 branches in 1886, equivalent to one branch for every Roman Catholic parish in Ireland.[119] However, the cost of this achievement – in terms of democratic deficit and internal party strife – was considerable, and confirmed the difficulty of combining a democratic, participatory ideology with the requirements of a mass party organization.

Until the INL was established, Ireland did not have any equivalent of a real 'party machine'. In the general elections of 1874 and 1880 the selection of candidates had been carried out in different ways according to local customs. These included, in some constituencies, 'ad hoc meetings of "the clergy and laity" summoned by the bishop or some other influential ecclesiastic; in others . . . meetings of electors convened by the lord mayor . . . in a third category, the nomination was decided, provisionally or finally, by some permanent political body representing nationalist opinion'.[120] There was no co-ordination between such local clubs and associations: they were all autonomous and unaccountable to any central headquarters. They could, if they so wished, involve themselves in the preparation and revision of the register of electors, in the organization of meetings, and in other electoral activities. However, they could also limit themselves to endorsing local candidates, towards whom the system continued to be biased.[121] The Irish National Land League – which was established in Dublin in October 1879, with Parnell as its first president – was far from being the party's mass organization. In fact, it refused to provide either financial help (except within very limited terms) or organizational support in the constituencies. Though in 1880 it helped to create enthusiasm for Parnell, it was not committed to, or even primarily interested in, Home Rule as a programme. Rather, it was always eager to assert its independence from the parliamentary party, which it suspected

---

[118] Cruise O'Brien, *Parnell and his Party*, 133.
[119] Garvin, *Evolution of Irish nationalist politics*, 89.
[120] Cruise O'Brien, *Parnell and his Party*, 125.   [121] Ibid., 126.

of 'Whiggism' (from a Fenian, revolutionary standpoint), because of its devotion to constitutionalism.

However, while the Land League had been almost revolutionary in its methods, the INL rested – at least in theory, and in the opinions expressed by the rank and file – on a radical programme not dissimilar from that which inspired popular liberals in Britain. With popular liberalism it shared not only the radical agrarian ideal – embodied in the commitment to the establishment of peasant proprietorship[122] – and the democratic outlook discussed in the previous chapter, but also a strong emphasis on parliamentary politics. It was based on an internal representative system consisting of branches, county conventions and a national council. As in the case of the NLF, the definition of the constitutional relationship between the parliamentary party and the representatives of the local constituency parties was a permanently contentious issue.

At the inaugural conference, which met in Dublin on 17 October, two positions emerged quite distinctly. The radical democrat Michael Davitt, supported by several county delegates and a few MPs, demanded a popularly elected council. The parliamentary elite – represented by T. M. Healy, T. P. O'Connor and Parnell himself – demanded that ten out of thirty council seats be reserved to MPs, chosen by their peers.[123] Healy argued that county representation would not provide an adequate composition of the council, because 'there [were] many counties ... in which you would not be able to get one man fit to sit in the executive'. Such 'backward counties' should not have imposed on them the 'burden' of representation, which was best if left in the hands of 'men trained to public affairs'.[124] Surprisingly, Healy's elitist statement – uttered only two years before the extension of the franchise to farm labourers – did not generate any uproar.[125] However, a lively debate ensued a little later, when Davitt put what might be regarded as the opposite view. Concerned about the representative legitimacy and the accountability of the INL, and hoping to achieve the integration of the Protestant counties in the movement through equal representation, Davitt proposed that the council should consist of thirty-two popularly elected county representatives,

---

[122] O'Day, *Parnell and the first Home Rule episode*, 43.
[123] 'Thirty members, twenty to be elected by county conventions, and ten by the Irish Parliamentary party. The branches in each county shall send delegates to the County Convention; and each delegate shall cast his vote for the candidate nominated to the Central Council in manner provided by the rules. Members of Parliament shall be ineligible for election to the Council by a County Convention.' ('The National Conference,' *FJ*, 16 Oct. 1882, 3.)
[124] Ibid., 6.
[125] Though others insisted that 'we should leave nothing [i.e. indirect parliamentary election] between the people and their representatives' (Mr Metge, MP, ibid.).

one for each Irish county. MPs could stand for election, if they so wished, but were not entitled to any seats *qua* MPs. Davitt stressed that it was important that 'all distinctions between non-members and members of Parliament will be ended'. His proposal, if adopted, would have made the National League fairly similar to the NLF: a popularly elected extra-parliamentary body, constitutionally weighed with a view to defending local rights and minorities, and entrusted with the power to discuss and even formulate party policies. His proposal proved unacceptable to the majority of the parliamentarians. While localism was anathema to Healy, who 'relentlessly championed a centralised nationalism against the claims of local organisations and favourite sons',[126] both Parnell and Healy were determined to preserve the leader's authority.

At this stage one of the clerical delegates (the Revd O'Leary) shifted the focus of the discussion by objecting to *equal* county representation on what purported to be democratic grounds:

I was astonished that Mr Davitt, who has travelled in America, would ask for representation for every county as being for Republican and Democratic reasons . . . In the Congress of the United States were all States represented by the same number of delegates? Surely they are not. Let the system of representation be . . . according to branches, and if there be say 100 branches in one, and 300 in another, let there be three men selected in the latter case and one in the former. I call that democratic and republican.[127]

However, it soon became clear that O'Leary's real aim was to limit Protestant influence and strengthen the parliamentary – as against the direct representation – option: 'The selection made in this matter should be representative and efficient. If we allow the Irish parliamentary party to select ten members to be on that council, neither Mr O'Donnell, nor Mr Davitt, nor any other can say they are not a representative body. This secures at least a fair representation.' Eventually, another delegate proposed a compromise: council should consist of thirty-two popularly elected county representatives, plus sixteen MPs nominated by the parliamentary party. While the assembly deliberated the pros and cons of these competing proposals, and many voiced their admiration for

---

[126] Callanan, *Healy*, 96. Thus, as late as 1885 Healy could publicly proclaim that the electoral aim of the nationalists was 'to efface and blot out every local distinction and recognise only the interests of the country at large'. Such an attitude would have been rejected as outrageous if anyone had dared to propose it at an NLF meeting. It was less controversial in the Irish party, both because Ireland was a much smaller country than Britain, and because the INL was comparatively homogeneous – in political and social terms – so long as the overarching aim was the achievement of a Parliament in Dublin.

[127] Revd O'Leary, 'The National Conference,' *FJ*, 16 Oct. 1882, 3.

Davitt, T. P. O'Connor rose to speak. He turned the tables by transforming the issue of parliamentary nominations into one of confidence:

Will you not, by refusing to give to the Parliamentary party this right of nominating one-third of the members of the council – will you not give to those calumniators and enemies of the Parliamentary party the idea that they are not calumniators and that their charges are sanctioned by a National Conference of the Irish people? (Hear, hear, and applause) . . . I will never consent to occupy a false position. I will bear no responsibility when I have no consultation. I will never be a member of any body where everything can be done in spite of my judgement and the judgement of my colleagues (hear, hear). Heaven knows it is a sufficiently thankless task to stand up in the House of Commons, a member of a miserable minority numerically, speaking in the face of some of the ablest orators in the world, meeting the combined efforts of the Whig and Tory enmity to Ireland; but bad as that task is . . . it is far less difficult than to be in the House of Commons, compelled to bear silent approval when your heart bleeds for the follies that were being committed (cries of 'oh' and hear, hear). You may enforce responsibility on your Parliamentary representatives where you give them power, but you have no right to give them responsibility without power. I say again, if you give them responsibility, you ought to give them powers; and therefore, I call upon you to vote for the resolution (applause).[128]

This emotional appeal worked wonders. Though Davitt forcefully rejected the insinuation that he did not trust the parliamentary party, he felt compelled to withdraw his amendment.

Though the outcome of the conference hardly strengthened the cause of internal party democracy, the lively debate, in which so many voices were represented, indicated the extent of the ambitions of the party activists. O'Connor's claim that Davitt's proposed structure would indicate lack of trust in the party was questionable. However, there is no doubt that Davitt's purely democratic and extra-parliamentary council would have provided a source of legitimacy and authority alternative to those of the leader and the parliamentary group.[129] With the support of some ecclesiastical delegates, the parliamentary leaders were able to manipulate the emotions and loyalties of the assembly and achieved a constitutional settlement in which popular democracy was effectively tamed. Under this constitution, the representatives of the parliamentary party would need the support of only nine of the thirty-two popular representatives in order to dominate the council.[130] Even this was a purely hypothetical prospect, because, as a matter of fact, the council never met.[131] Until 1891 all the important decisions continued to be taken by Parnell and a few of his closest colleagues, whom he consulted

---

[128] Ibid.   [129] Callanan, *Healy*, 96.
[130] Strauss, *Irish nationalism and British democracy*, 167.   [131] Callanan, *Healy*, 78.

as he pleased. The INL became 'an autocratically controlled body, ruled by a committee which it had not elected, and whose powers were undefined'.[132] Thus, having been born for the purpose of 'representing opinion' and defining the party programme, the INL immediately evolved towards a top-down structure whose purpose was winning elections.

Such an outcome was extraordinary, given the democratic zeal of many among the rank and file. It had various different causes, linked to the unique features of contemporary Irish politics. There was, first, the notion that '[t]he struggle for Home Rule was a form of warfare ... Indiscipline and insubordination in the face of the enemy – that is to say in the presence of English parties – was a form of treason.'[133] For this purpose discussion was restricted to generalities 'to which no interest group could take exception'.[134] Second, there was what in Gramscian terms we could describe as the hegemony of Parnell and the elite of upper-class and university-educated MPs, with a visible Protestant component, over the provincial rural middle classes and clergy.[135] Parnell's personal prestige was partly owing to each of the previously mentioned factors, and was compounded by his control over the 'Paris funds' – the Irish equivalent of what the Lloyd George fund was to become to a later generation of British radicals[136] – and by his effectively charismatic

---

[132] Cruise O'Brien , *Parnell and his Party*, 128.

[133] F. S. L Lyons, *The Irish parliamentary party, 1890–1910* (n.d. [*c.* 1951]) 41.

[134] M. Laffan, *The resurrection of Ireland: the Sinn Féin party, 1916–1923* (1999), 5; Cruise O'Brien, *Parnell and his party*, 47.

[135] In 1880–5 the allegedly 'lower-class' nature of the party was a matter of contemporary perception. Although the replacement of about ten landlords by new MPs who had brains but no land seemed 'cataclysmic' to some Nationalists, the party remained 79 per cent upper class: Cruise O'Brien, *Parnell and his party*, 18–21, 27.

[136] Thanks to their American friends, the Parnellites fared better than any other political organization in the whole of the UK. Between November 1879 and October 1882 (when the INL was founded), the Land League received £250,000 from benefactors in the USA. Following the constitutional turn in Parnell's politics, the American contribution dwindled, but when the Land League was dissolved the balance was not passed on to the INL, but to a special bank account in France – the 'Paris funds' – under the direct control of Parnell and two other party leaders. It amounted to £30,000 (Cruise O'Brien, *Parnell and his party*, 133–5). The second apex in subscription was reached in 1886, as a result of Gladstone's 'conversion' to Home Rule. At the beginning of that year, after fighting the 1885 election, the balance was £3,000. By the end of 1886 receipts had reached £100,000 (though they decreased again afterwards). Of this money, £48,000 was spent on salaries of MPs, £11,500 on registration expenses and £13,000 on propaganda in Britain (ibid., 267). The latter went mainly to print literature which would then be distributed by the Home Rule Union, a Liberal organization to which more than sixty local Liberal associations were affiliated in 1888 (ibid., 266; cf. *Journal of the Home Rule Union*, 1, March 1888).

leadership.[137] Indeed, in the aftermath of the National Conference, enthusiasm for Parnell was enormous. When he visited Cork in December, he 'was welcomed . . . by a demonstration of gigantic proportions . . . An enormous concourse of people, accompanied by several bands, awaited his arrival at the railway station, and his reception on alighting from the train was of the most enthusiastic description.'[138] His appeal to popular emotions was comparable to the one Gladstone generated among his popular supporters in Britain, though, unlike the GOM, Parnell was not a great platform speaker. But, as Sexton put it, he was believed to have achieved '[t]he most that a leader can do', that is, 'to discipline and organise the public mind; to teach the people how to use the power they have'.[139]

The INL achieved a considerable success, and, according to police reports, by 1 July 1886 1,285 local branches had affiliated to it.[140] These were established at popular meetings all over the country in the aftermath of the 1882 conference,[141] or derived from the affiliation of already existing national organizations to the INL.[142] At a local level, branch meetings were frequently reported for the first year, then became less prominent in the pages of the *Freeman's Journal* (from the spring of 1883). County conventions operated effectively in preparation for local by-elections and the general elections of 1885 and 1886. Parnell – whose words were spin-doctored by the press – professed great respect for local branch opinion, but on the rare occasions when his views about the selection of a candidate were rejected – as happened in Tipperary in early January 1885 – he summoned again the county convention, in this case on the grounds that forty branches were unrepresented at the first meeting. The second convention duly selected the party man.[143]

Thus, county conventions were far from giving 'free' expression to local political views. As Strauss put it, Parnell 'distrusted the popular element in the League constitution to such an extent that . . . [b]y a small scale *coup*

---

[137] R. V. Comerford, 'The Parnell era, 1883–91', in W. E. Vaughan (ed.), *A new history of Ireland*, vol. VI (1996), 80; P. Bew, *Charles Stewart Parnell* (1991), 22, 66–8, 75.
[138] 'Mr Parnell, MP, in Cork', *FJ*, 18 Dec. 1882, 6.
[139] Ibid.   [140] Cruise O'Brien, *Parnell and his party*, 133.
[141] E.g. 'Meeting in Kilrush', *FJ*, 18 Dec. 1882, 7.
[142] E.g. 'The Irish Labour and Industrial Union', *FJ*, 18 Dec. 1882, 3.
[143] 'The course that is being taken is in no sense a derogation of the authority of the body which selected Mr O'Ryan; but Mr Parnell acts with his usual wisdom in asking the delegates to afford him an opportunity of laying his views before them, so that it cannot be charged that so important an office as that of Member of Parliament has been filled up through some momentary impulse or parochial pique. The delegates, we are sure, will rejoice at being able to learn the views of the Irish leader, and after hearing them will be in a much better position to arrive at a fitting conclusion.' (L.a., *FJ*, 5 Jan. 1885, 4. Cf. Cruise O'Brien, *Parnell and his party*, 132 and n. 2.)

d'état ... [he] "packed" the League conventions from top to bottom by appointing all priests *ex officio* delegates'.[144] Such clerical delegates were not provided for in the League's constitution, but became a regular feature of INL activities from the Wicklow convention of 1885. County conventions consisted of about 150 laymen and 50 priests,[145] the latter providing also the chairman, when he was not an MP. Through the active support of its priests, the Catholic clergy became for Parnell an equivalent of the trade union 'block vote' in Lib-lab and, later, Labour politics: namely, the pillar of the leader's authority. Archbishop Walsh had laid down clear principles for clerical participation, which amounted to a careful sifting of the candidates in order both to ascertain that they had 'satisfactory antecedents', and to avoid 'surprise' candidates.[146] Convention chairmen had clear instructions from Dublin as to the nominations, which were decided by Parnell in consultation with some of his colleagues. Thus, the selection of parliamentary candidates, which before 1882 had been in the hands of constituency meetings and local clubs, was now centrally controlled and locally ratified by county conventions, sometimes in contexts which attested to what – in Weberian terms – could be described as Parnell's 'Caesarist' ascendancy.[147] Party democracy was affirmed, but was reduced to a mere façade.[148]

On the whole, the INL became 'Parnell's way of reasserting his grip both inside Westminster and beyond',[149] and helped local notables and ecclesiastics to recover their ascendancy in democratic politics.[150] Despite the protests of anti-clerical MPs such as L. Finigan, the clerical delegates were accepted and even welcomed by their lay colleagues –

---

[144] Strauss, *Irish nationalism and British democracy*, 167.

[145] Cruise O'Brien, *Parnell and his party*, 128–31. For an example see 'County Meath convention', *FJ*, 9 Oct. 1885, 5 At this particular convention there were 105 lay delegates and 60 priests. At the Wicklow convention, there were '40 of the clergy of the county, and 80 elected delegates': 'The Wicklow convention', *FJ*, 6 Oct. 1885, 5. It was on the latter occasion that the 'rules for the guidance of conventions' were published. For the operation of the 'block vote' in Lib-lab elections see Biagini, *Liberty*, chapter 7, 328–68.

[146] Davitt, *Fall of feudalism*, 469; Cruise O'Brien , *Parnell and his party*, 129.

[147] For one example see the address of the Clonmel Branch of the INL to Parnell, in 'The Tipperary election: unopposed return of Mr John O'Connor', *FJ*, 10 Jan. 1885, 6: 'We congratulate you on the loyalty to you of magnificent Tipperary, which, in deference to your wish and to that of your powerful and faithful ally, the great Archbishop of Cashel (cheers), has given to you the man of your choice as a parliamentary auxiliary. We believe that he will be true to you, and we know that only on the condition of being true to you can he retain the confidence of Tipperary (cheers).'

[148] Lyons, *Irish parliamentary party*, 142.

[149] D. M. MacRaild, *Irish migrants in modern Britain, 1750–1922* (1996), 144; cf. Cruise O'Brien, *Parnell and his party*, 128.

[150] Comerford, 'Parnell era', 54. Cf. Pašeta, *Before the revolution*.

more or less as the representatives of the Durham Miners' Union were welcomed by the local Liberal party associations[151] – and the nationalist press was ecstatic about the results. Commenting on the Meath convention, the *Freeman's Journal* praised 'the perfect harmony of its deliberations, and the absolute unanimity of its decisions': '[a]t no previous epoch in our annals has anything approaching the same combination of the whole priesthood and the whole people, of their undivided unity in political action, and their capacity for the practical work of calm deliberative consultation, been witnessed'.[152] More prosaically and accurately, Strauss has described the change as the INL achieving the 'domination of the movement by the Irish middle-class'.[153]

These developments strengthened a trend towards centralization which had been noticeable from as early as 1880. In December 1880, at a meeting in the City Hall, Dublin, Parnell proposed a resolution, which was passed, to the effect that 'the parliamentary committee, *acting as a cabinet of the party*, shall have the power to shape and direct the policy of the party in any emergency or in any particular measure or proposal in reference to which the party has not already met and decided and to arrange the details for carrying out the general policy decided upon by the party'.[154] As Cruise O'Brien has pointed out, '[t]he importance of this resolution was not so much the powers conferred, which are not very precisely defined, as the claim that a committee originally set up as an organisational convenience was now "acting as a cabinet"'.[155] However, the committee never really worked like a 'cabinet': 'emergency' decisions were taken by Parnell himself (as in the case of the Kilmainham Treaty) after consulting only with those colleagues whom he chose to consult.[156] As Parnell said years later, his system was based on the following principle: 'Get the advice . . . of everybody whose advice is worth having – they are very few – and then do what you think best yourself.'[157] It was these 'very few' people whose advice mattered, rather than the parliamentary committee, who acted as the 'cabinet' of the party. If it was a cabinet, 'it was a "cabinet" in the American rather than the British sense; its

---

[151] Cf. Biagini, *Liberty*, 364–5.   [152] L.a., *FJ*, 9 Oct. 1885, 4.
[153] Strauss, *Irish nationalism and British democarcy*, 167.
[154] Cited in Cruise O'Brien, *Parnell and his party*, 144 (my italics). The parliamentary Committee – which consisted of sixteen members, including the chairman, the treasurer and two whips – 'was elected for the session, and empowered to convene party meetings, summon members to attend the House, and collect subscriptions'.
[155] Ibid.   [156] Ibid., 145; Lyons, *Irish parliamentary party*, 142.
[157] Cited in Cruise O' Brien, *Parnell and his party*, 145, n. 1. The group of those 'whose advice was worth having' consisted of T. M. Healy, T. Sexton and J. J. O'Kelly, and was later expanded to include also J. E. Kenny, T. Harrington and W. O'Brien.

members derived their powers from a leader who did not share his responsibility with them'.[158]

Until 1891–5 the Nationalist party was comparatively free from the soul-searching and constitutional dilemmas faced by the NLF, despite the discrepancy between the participatory ideals of the rank and file and the reality of Parnell's domination of the party. For, as Tim Healy put it in 1883,

What is it to them whom Mr Parnell nominates for county or town, so long as the work they want done is performed? The interests of the people and its leader being one, and the purposes the same, so long as he gives them results, so long will they give him the means which he declares necessary to obtain them. It is not merely Mr Parnell the Irish people are following, but their own proper interests, the gratification of their national pride, the humiliation of their oppressors, the achievement of the full measure of their rights.[159]

But the test for the leader's actual power came in 1890–1. The divorce crisis has often been examined in terms of a clash between Parnell's autocratic, aristocratic outlook and the hard realities of both clerical influence in Ireland and the 'Nonconformist conscience' in Britain. However, it contains important constitutional aspects, which had wide-ranging implications for Irish nationalism and party democracy. When the party split, the issue at stake was ultimately the question of where authority resided: whether in the leader, as had been de facto the case for the past few years, or in the parliamentary party.[160] In constitutional terms, the debate was about the meaning of the party pledge. As Sexton put it for the anti-Parnellites,

they heard a great deal about a pledge to follow their leader. They never pledged themselves to follow an imaginary leader. (Hear.) The leader was selected every year; he was the sessional chairman, and what was the meaning of suggesting that they were bound to a certain leader when they had to elect him at the beginning of every session, and when they might supersede him at any time? (Hear.) But there was a pledge – a pledge that was intended to guard the union of the Home Rule party – a pledge without which the Parliamentary cause of Ireland would be in danger of destruction – the pledge that bound every member of the party to submit to the vote of the majority, and they had not broken that pledge.[161]

More than ever before, during the crisis Parnell seemed to behave like a 'dictator',[162] abusing his powers as party chairman at the meeting in

---

[158] Ibid., 147.   [159] T. M. Healy, 'The causes of Mr Parnell's power', *FJ*, 29 Dec. 1883, 3.
[160] This dimension has been mentioned, but not fully explored, by Cruise O'Brien, *Parnell and his party*, 241–2.
[161] T. Sexton, *The Irish Times*, 11 Mar. 1891, 7; on the pledge cf. Lyons, *Irish parliamentary party*, 142–3.
[162] Cruise O'Brien, *Parnell and his party*, 354–5.

Committee Room 15 (when he secured his own re-election despite the looming disaster of his divorce), and then following a line which was sanctioned neither by the party nor by the electors. In the early 1880s his style had elicited loyalty and admiration, as it was felt that 'dictatorial' powers were necessary to resist the might of the British 'coercionist' government. However, from 1886 Gladstone's adoption of Home Rule and the ensuing Liberal alliance created a less partisan atmosphere within Nationalist circles. In this context both the parliamentary party and the rank and file felt freer to assess the relative merits of Parnell and his critics. Ironically, in view of his imminent loss of power and subsequent death, Parnell began *now* to be denounced as 'the Dictator'. His rule – it was argued – could only be conducive to 'Tyranny'.[163]

Because the INL remained loyal to Parnell, the anti-Parnellites claimed that it had 'ceased to be the league of the people and become the instrument and the agent of personal rule'.[164] In March 1891 they set up a new organization, the Irish National Federation (INF). Its policy aims were defined by the constitution, and the means to be used were those typical of any party 'machine'.[165] The INF's provisional executive committee was completely dominated by parliamentarians: it consisted of fourteen MPs plus Michael Davitt, 'with power to add to their number'. The final constitution and relative rules for the new executive were adopted only eighteen months after the foundation, in November 1892. Firm safeguards were in place to allow for the control of the popular organization by the parliamentary party. The INF council consisted of forty-five elected delegates (thirty-two county and thirteen civic delegates, elected by the municipal corporations) and '[t]he members for the time being of the Irish Parliamentary party'.[166] The last group, consisting of seventy to eighty MPs, was obviously in a position to dominate the council. This was crucial, for the INF executive (consisting of 'not more than' twenty-five members of the council) was to be elected by the council itself. To make things more easily manageable (in both senses of the word) the quorum for the council was only fifteen, and the quorum of the executive was to be fixed by the council.[167] One delegate pointed out that no provision was

---

[163] A voice from the crowd at the inaugural meeting of the INF, in *The Irish Times*, 11 Mar. 1891, 7.

[164] T. Sexton, *The Irish Times*, 11 Mar. 1891, 7.

[165] 'The establishment and extension of branches; the cultivation of public opinion; the organization of the elective franchise; the rerun to Parliament of members bound by the pledge of the Irish party . . .' (*The Irish Times*, 11 Mar. 1891, 7).

[166] The constitution was published in the report of the meeting of 'The National Convention', *FJ*, 16 Nov. 1892, 5.

[167] Ibid.

made in the constitution for an annual convention – the equivalent of the NLF assembly, which embodied the sovereignty of the rank and file. To this question the chairman (Justin McCarthy, who was also chairman of the parliamentary party) responded that '[i]t has not appeared that an annual convention may be necessary.'[168] Despite such a heavy-handed approach, the debate at this convention was lively, with many questions and comments from the floor.

As it had been for the INL, the popular basis of the INF was the system of the county conventions, the gatherings of clergy and elected delegates from local branches. Candidates continued to be selected by these conventions, first in secret sessions chaired by MPs (a post-Parnellite innovation to fend off the danger of convention-led party democracy),[169] and then ratified in open meetings. However, while under Parnell the actual choice had been made by the leader in consultation with a few colleagues, in 1892 it was arranged by an election committee consisting mainly – but not exclusively – of MPs. This committee had wide-ranging powers,[170] but it paid more attention to local wishes than had been usual in the past: this reflected both the weakened legitimacy of the party after the split, and the need to compete for popular support against the Parnellites.[171]

Tension about internal party democracy was restrained by the delegates' awareness of the double pressure (from both Unionists and Parnellites) under which the party now operated. However, the rank-and-file demand for a greater say was soon to cause further troubles and splits. The INF constitutional settlement – not being legitimized by either charismatic leadership or a democratic system – really depended on, and would ultimately be justified only by, political success. When the latter became less and less likely, troubles began. In the first place there was a sharp decline in membership – a decline which affected also the old INL: by 1894 both associations combined had only 765 branches,[172] down from 1,286 in 1886. Furthermore the leadership effectively lost control over the nominations, while the party became more decentralized.[173] Any parliamentary 'dictatorship' over the constituencies would now be intolerable: as a consequence, as William O'Brien put it, '[o]ne man's power was replaced by eighty men's powerlessness.'[174] The turning point had

---

[168] Ibid.   [169] Lyons, *Irish parliamentary party*, 145.

[170] Including 'arranging the dates at which the conventions were to be held, choosing the chairmen to preside over them and considering the claims of the various candidates for selection'. (F. S. L. Lyons, 'The machinery of the Irish parliamentary party in the general election of 1895', *Irish Historical Studies*, 8 (1952–3), 117.)

[171] Ibid., 117–18; Lyons, *Irish parliamentary party*, 146.

[172] Garvin, *Evolution of Irish nationalist politics*, 87.   [173] Ibid., 90.

[174] Lyons, *Irish parliamentary party*, 40.

taken place already in 1893, after the defeat of the second Home Rule Bill, when in the name of 'freedom of the constituencies', T. M. Healy and his faction began 'to break the long established control of the party over the selection of the candidates'.[175] As the Healyite *Irish Catholic* put it on 5 August 1893,

What we denounce is the monstrous and intolerable theory that because the committee of the Irish party, consisting only of eight members, and deciding upon their action by a paltry majority, think fit to sanction the candidature of a particular gentleman, he is to be forced upon the constituency whether its electors wish to receive him or not ... What we stand by today is the broad constitutional principle that the people of West Mayo, and they alone, have the right to say who shall be, and who shall not be, their member.[176]

The Healyites were apparently standing – at least in *this* case – within a broadly defined liberal tradition. Healy's 'liberalism' was, however, unwelcome to the majority of the party, led by John Dillon (on most issues, himself a better 'liberal' than Healy), who managed to impose a London-based candidate over the local man. Dillon believed that the only way forward consisted in the restoration of parliamentary centralism. Accordingly, in 1895 it was decided that the management of the electoral campaign would be entrusted to the party chairman and the parliamentary committee (elected annually at the beginning of the parliamentary session), rather than to an especially elected committee. This decision, which was taken at a meeting attended by only forty-five of the seventy anti-Parnellite MPs, was strongly resisted by T. M. Healy, who effectively split the party again.

Despite Healy's rhetoric, the new split was not primarily about 'party democracy', and had more to do with the Liberal alliance, which Healy was now questioning, while Dillon and William O'Brien continued to support it. Whatever his ulterior motives, Healy's attack on the legitimacy of the way parliamentary candidates were selected was widely echoed among the party rank and file. The Dublin branches of the INF demanded 'perfect freedom of election and selection of representatives',[177] and the summoning of a national convention. The latter was important because a national convention could claim an authority and a legitimacy to which county conventions could not aspire. It would also provide an appropriate institutional setting for the definition of policy aims, in the way the Newcastle Convention of the NLF had done in 1891. Hence the importance of party 'democracy' for those who were dissatisfied with the policies of the official leaders. These demands were rejected, as the leaders refused to countenance any decrease of their powers. Indeed, in response to Healyite

---

[175] Ibid., 47.   [176] Cited in ibid.   [177] *FJ*, 28 June 1895, 5.

resolutions passed by the executive of the INF in 1895, Justin McCarthy declared that the executive 'was elected for the internal management of the Federation, and the Irish party cannot recognise any right in such a body to control or overrule the work of the party'.[178]

That the rank and file were not prepared to accept this line without a fight was shown by the county conventions: open hostility was frequently voiced, several conventions asserted their independence by choosing their own chairman, and others demanded the convocation of a national convention. This struggle culminated in the 'Omagh scandal' at the Tyrone convention of 8 July 1895, when Healy revealed that the party leaders had 'made over' to the Liberal party four Irish seats in Ulster, for £200 each.[179] Although the claim was not quite correct,[180] and caused a storm of indignation in the party and the press,[181] there was some truth in it, particularly in so far as it revealed a severe shortage of party funds and the close alliance between the National party and the post-Gladstonian Liberal party. The real problem behind the incident was again a constitutional one: while Dillon and McCarthy maintained the right of the parliamentary committee to direct electoral campaigns, Healy claimed that this system was unrepresentative and deprived the constituencies of the freedom to select candidates.[182] In electoral terms, the 'scandal' was very embarrassing and shattered public trust in a less than transparent party machinery.

This and other mishaps did not prevent Dillon from remodelling the constitution along lines which would allow even fuller control of the INF by the parliamentary party.[183] The latter was now a self-perpetuating body with effective powers to co-opt new members. Yet, it was a pyrrhic victory. After the disastrous results of the 1895 election, the machinery and the methods of the Nationalist party were discredited, and their embarrassment was compounded by the fact that the INF – unlike the NLF – was dominated by the MPs,[184] who were thus fully responsible for policies and political outcomes. 'Freedom for the constituencies' was

---

[178] Cited in Lyons, 'The machinery of the Irish parliamentary party', 123–4.
[179] Ibid., 131.
[180] F. S. L. Lyons, 'The Irish parliamentary party and the Liberals in mid-Ulster, 1894', *Irish Historical Studies*, 8, 27 (1951), 191–5.
[181] 'Mr Healy's campaign against his colleagues: his extraordinary conduct at Omagh', *FJ*, 11 July 1895, 11.
[182] Lyons, 'Irish parliamentary party and the Liberals', 191.
[183] Lyons, *Irish parliamentary party*, 66; cf. E. F. V. Knox's letter in *FJ*, 26 Jan. 1897, 4.
[184] It consisted of thirty-two county delegates, thirteen civic delegates and all the Irish MPs. Furthermore, 'the real controlling authority' within the INF was its executive committee, consisting of twelve delegates, thirteen MPs and five ex-officio members (secretaries and treasurers), with a quorum of only five: Lyons, 'The machinery of the Irish parliamentary party', 122, n. 17.

now a battle cry whose appeal reached well beyond Healy and his followers. Such groundswell of opinion found an outlet in the foundation of
the UIL.

The internal party diplomacy and the conventions which led to reunification under the chairmanship of the Parnellite John Redmond have
been fully discussed by Lyons and Bull.[185] Here it is important to point
out that unity was achieved *despite* the hostility of many party leaders,
rather than thanks to their joint efforts.[186] The explanation of this apparent paradox is to be found in the ongoing struggle between the parliamentary party and the rank-and-file organizations, which had
representative ambitions and claims. The decisive factor was the electors'
response to the UIL, which spread like wildfire in both counties and
boroughs, and gained substantial victories in the local elections of 1898
and 1899. These and later successes confirmed that the UIL was in tune
with the demands of the electorate, who were tired of divisions and the
personal feuds of the parliamentarians, and demanded reunion.

However, the latter came so suddenly after these developments, that
UIL leaders saw it as a 'desperate intrigue' for the purpose of stemming
the League's further growth. Indeed, the question – as both Healy and
Redmond now saw it – was quite clear. Either the parliamentarians seized
the initiative and reunited the party, or the UIL and the supporters of
internal party democracy (such as O'Brien)[187] might do so, and in the
process ensure a power shift away from Parliament towards the conventions and the 'mass organization'. Most Nationalist MPs feared this
prospect as much as their Liberal colleagues feared a revival of the
NLF's claims after 1895. The game was further complicated by the
changing role of the clerical delegates: in Parnell's days the priests had
provided the leader with a reliable 'block vote', which dominated INL
conventions. Now the leaders of the parliamentary party could no longer
take clerical support for granted, and in fact it was the UIL that welcomed
priests at its conventions, and indeed made 'the clergy of *all* denominations'[188] ex officio members.

The national convention which met at the end of June 1900 seemed to
fulfil the aspirations of those who wanted political power vested in the
UIL. The latter replaced both the Healyite and the anti-Parnellite

[185] Lyons, *Irish parliamentary party*, 67–109, and Bull, 'The United Irish League and the
reunion of the Irish parliamentary party, 1898–1900', *Irish Historical Studies*, 26, 101
(1988), 51–78. See also below, 301–4.
[186] Bull, 'The United Irish League', 62; W. B. Wells, *John Redmond. A biography*, (1919) 62.
[187] Lyons, *Irish parliamentary party*, 109.   [188] Ibid., 151 (my italics).

organizations as 'the sole official organisation of the nationalist party',[189] while the UIL was in a position to claim control over electoral strategy.[190] However, as a matter of fact, the composition of the parliamentary party was not drastically affected: the old guard remained firmly entrenched and new voices from the rank and file were limited to six new MPs.[191] The end result was thus a compromise: on the one hand, the party was *formally* more democratic than ever before. On the other, the readiness with which the old elite adopted the demands of the popular organization meant that the Nationalist leaders were able to retain effective power by 'riding the tiger' of internal democracy. The UIL's very insistence on party discipline, which led to the expulsion of Healy and J. L. Carew at another convention later in 1900, meant that the 'supremacy' of the mass organization would strengthen, rather than challenge, Redmond and the other party leaders. The main political change was a shift away from Parliament as the effective seat of power, towards party structures. For now the leaders' influence depended no longer on the fact that they were MPs, but sprang 'from the fact that some of them were also members of the National Directory – the supreme executive authority of the league'.[192]

'Direct democracy' and the representative principle in the NLF political theory

The period 1886–91 was one of the most exciting in the history of the NLF, when the latter, rather than the liberal leadership, had claimed the right to shape party policy.[193] Yet, in electoral terms the outcome of the changes which took place in those years was a mixed blessing for the Liberals. Despite victory at the 1892 election, the Newcastle Programme as such was too ambitious to be implemented by any one government. At any rate, most of the reforms it proposed could not be implemented by Gladstone's fourth administration (1892–4), with its slim majority in the Commons and hopeless minority in the Lords. Later, the crushing electoral defeat of 1895 was regarded by some as an indication of the shortcomings of party democracy, and led to a new constitutional debate in 1895–7. In 1895, in his addresses to the council, the new party leader, Lord Rosebery, argued that the NLF should limit itself to thrashing out

---

[189] Bull, 'The United Irish League', 75.
[190] Lyons, *Irish parliamentary party*, 153–4. See also contemporary comments in *The Irish People*, 23–30 Apr. 1900 and in Lyons, *John Dillon*, 207–14.
[191] Bull, 'The United Irish League', 76–7.
[192] Lyons, 'The machinery of the Irish parliamentary party', 138.
[193] H. V. Emy, *Liberals, radicals and social politics, 1892–1914* (1973), 40, 42.

'the various issues that lie before the Liberal Party',[194] and thus leave to the parliamentary front bench and the Cabinet the actual decisions about which policies to implement and in what order. This was the model of the mass party as 'a great educational assembly',[195] which Rosebery's colleague and rival, Vernon Harcourt, had already aired at the Council of 1889. However, the reactions of the Council and the ensuing debate showed no sign of the rank and file having become more amenable to the leadership's wishes.

Although Barker has suggested that by 1895 the NLF was humiliated and ready to defer to leaders,[196] the draft of the new constitution which the General Purpose Committee submitted to the council was – rather than a surrender – a compromise between rank-and-file democracy and parliamentary centralism. It proposed the reshaping of the three governing bodies of the Federation, namely the committee itself, the General Committee and the council.

Firstly, the General Purpose Committee was to be renamed the Executive Committee. It would consist of twenty elected members and the three Federation officers (president, chairman of committee and treasurer). It was elected by the General Committee, upon nominations by local Liberal associations. The election was to be guided by 'two special considerations': 'namely, that the different districts of the country should all be represented, and next, that a very considerable proportion of the Committee should be Presidents, or other Officers, of the affiliated associations, of which the Federation is merely a united embodiment'.[197]

Second, this principle of regional representation was further strengthened in the General Committee. The latter was to be elected by the local associations, each of which would have the same number of delegates (three), rather than, as hitherto, a variable number proportional to the population of each parliamentary constituency.[198] The General Committee was thus to represent not members, but associations and constituencies, irrespective of demographic considerations (a principle reminiscent of the system for the election of the federal Senate in the USA).

---

[194] Proceedings of the Annual Meeting, Portsmouth, 13–14 Feb. 1895, 111, in NLFAR. Cf. also Rosebery's speech in Proceedings of the Annual Meeting, Huddersfield, 26 Mar. 1896, 109–10, in NLFAR.
[195] V. Harcourt, in Proceedings of the Annual Meeting of the Council, Manchester, 3 Dec. 1889, 120, in NLFAR.
[196] Barker, *Gladstone and radicalism*, 164.
[197] 'The Constitution and functions of the federation', NLFAR, 1896, 34.
[198] See 1880 Report, 'Constitution', clause IV, 28, in NLFAR.

Third, the council was to retain the old representative principle of one delegate per one thousand electors. It was still supposed to be 'the meeting of the whole Federation'; however, the idea that it was just a 'sounding board' for the leaders' rhetoric and for decisions taken elsewhere was institutionalized. Members were to be mere delegates, rather than representatives.

This in itself was a double-edged move. Through the emphasis on the principle of delegation, rather than representation, the NLF apparently drew closer to the continental democratic tradition, particularly to French radical democracy and socialism. However, without the glue of either the social homogeneity or of Marxist ideology which held together continental socialist parties, and without corporate trade-union representation, the outcome of the change to delegation was an additional increase of the power of the party notables. Such an outcome was further favoured by the fact that Liberal MPs were now ex officio members of both the council and the General Committee. Since only a minority of the elected representatives and delegates either cared, or were able, to attend meetings,[199] MPs would represent a sizeable proportion especially of the General Committee. In conclusion, these reforms implied a dramatic shift of the party's internal balance of power towards both the parliamentary party and the local notables. In fact, the General Committee was to become the forum for any discussion. As the report explained:

It must be obvious that, in the future as in the past, adequate discussion of debating points can only take place at the meetings of the General Committee. To seek to turn an assembly, like the Federation Council, of perhaps 2,000 people, sitting at most for 10 or 12 hours, into an open conference for the debate of multitudinous questions about which the party has come to no agreement, is impossible. The less unwieldy General Committee, equally representative of the Affiliated Associations, is the body at which discussion should take place. The Council must remain largely an assembly of a declaratory character; a great Annual Demonstration of the rank and file of the Party to ratify, emphasise and give forcible public expression to the ascertained wishes of the Party on matters of agreed and settled policy.[200]

The apologists of such constitutional change presented it as a step towards greater democracy, particularly through the extension of the powers of the NLF's 'federal senate', the General Committee, which would meet more often and control the party more effectively. Moreover, 'as circumstances arose they might have open conferences and free discussion upon the questions before the country'.[201]

---

[199] For concerns about attendance see ibid., 35–6.   [200] Ibid.
[201] Edward Evans, chairman of the General Purpose Committee, ibid., 71.

However, on the whole the new constitution meant a major departure from the 1877 rhetoric of participatory citizenship and a 'parliament outside the Imperial Parliament'.[202] It seemed that the old dream of a free assembly ruling the Liberal party – almost reminiscent of Mill's dream of the *ekklesia* of a Victorian Athens – was abandoned.

Yet there is evidence to show that the situation was rather more complex than this summary would suggest. First, the outcome of the constitutional changes of 1895–7 may have been at variance more with the Victorian *ideal* of direct democracy than with its actual *practice*. Direct democracy was, and still is, *less* radical than commonly supposed. For, as Mogens Herman Hansen has demonstrated, even the ancient Athenian *ekklesia* – which did in fact consist, like the NLF council, of more than 2,000 people[203] – could deliberate effectively only because most ordinary citizens limited themselves to ratifying or rejecting proposals, which were usually passed by a unanimous vote.[204] A similar procedure is still nowadays common in the Swiss cantons which have retained their ancient system of direct democracy.[205] As for the real discussion, both in the Athenian *ekklesia* and in the Swiss *Landsgemeinde*, it involved only a minority of *rhetores* and their retinue.[206] They dominated the debate not as modern parties dominate parliamentary debates, but rather in a way reminiscent of regional bosses and national charismatic leaders at the councils of the NLF.

More generally, it is significant that, as we look back on the continental scene – to which Victorian politicians referred to contextualize and understand their own experiences[207] – we find parallels between the

---

[202] Report of the Conference, 31 May 1877, 16, in NLFAR: 'We hope that the time is not distant when we may see a meeting of what will be a really Liberal Parliament outside the Imperial Legislature, and, unlike it, elected by universal suffrage.'

[203] M. H. Hansen, *The Athenian Ecclesia* (1983), 212–13.   [204] Ibid., 215–16.

[205] Namely Glarus, Obwalden, Nidwalden and the two Appenzell half-cantons: while the *Landsgemeinde* is the sovereign body, deliberations are prepared in advance by the *Landamann* (the president) and the *Regierungsrat* (the government), and then discussed in all their details by the *Kantonsrat* or parliament (ibid., 209–10, 212). Only then are proposals submitted to the *Landsgemeinde*. Furthermore, '[n]o law or decree can be moved directly in the Landsgemeinde. All proposals must be sent to the parliament several months in advance.' (210) A further similarity with what happened at NLF Councils in the 1890s is that '[m]ost items on the agenda attract no debate whatsoever and the vote can be taken immediately (Obwalden) or the bill is declared accepted without any show of hands (Glarus)' (211).

[206] Where 'only a negligible minority of the citizens make use of their right to address the people. The speakers are mostly officials or politicians, but not always' (Hansen, *The Athenian Ecclesia*, 210–11, 216–17, 222): the practice at NLF Councils in the 1890s was very similar.

[207] E.g. J. Macdonnell, 'Is the caucus a necessity?' *Fortnightly Review*, 44 (1885), 780–90, 782–5.

vicissitudes of the NLF and, not so much those of continental liberalism, but of the tradition associated with radical democracy. For example, in Germany the SPD was the only party which ascribed to rank-and-file congresses a constitutional role comparable to that of the council in the NLF, namely that of a legislative assembly for the parliamentary front bench.[208] Like the NLF, the SPD took pride in representing a democratic Parliament 'outside the Imperial parliament', indeed 'a political society in its own right'.[209]

Though the NLF was not homogenized by a class-separatist ideology, it too espoused something similar to their notion of the party as 'a parallel state within a state', a vision they shared, in various degrees, with both continental socialists and the old INL.[210] In fact they claimed to be the parliament of the 'Liberal nation' in Britain. Inherited from the tradition of popular 'anti-Parliament' politics, stretching back beyond Chartism to early nineteenth-century radicalism, this notion was reinforced by the NLF's commitment to Home Rule, which created a sort of surrogate of the socialist ideology of 'separatism', and may have been cherished for similar reasons. For, as German and Swedish social democrat bosses had discovered, a 'separatist' ideology was 'an instrument to mould participants and members into greater loyalty'.[211] Further parallels between the NLF and the SPD emerged at the beginning of the new century, when the German socialists experienced a power struggle between the parliamentary delegation and the rank-and-file assembly similar to the one which affected the British Liberals, with similar outcomes. After 1905, SPD 'party congresses ceased to be the supreme legislative assembly and became a symbol of ritual celebration of political ideology ... from which participants would disperse refreshed and capable of disseminating ideological refreshment'.[212] Dillon, Redmond, Rosebery and Harcourt would surely have approved of such an arrangement.

France too offers interesting parallels. There the ideal of ancient direct democracy had been extolled and popularized during the Great Revolution, but French liberals rejected it for the reasons put forward by Benjamin Constant in his famous 1819 lecture on the 'Liberty of the Moderns'. While the liberals became converts to Napoleonic centralism,

---

[208] J. P. Nettl, 'The German Social Democratic party 1890–1914 as a political model', *Past & Present*, no. 30 (1965), 72; cf. D. Groh, *Negative Integration und revolutionarer Attentismus. Die deutsche Sozialdemokratie am Vorabend des Ersten Weltkrieges* (Frankfurt/ an Main, Berlin and Vienna), 1973.

[209] Nettl, 'The German Social Democratic party', 71, 78.

[210] Pombeni, *Partiti e sistemi politici*, 249; Jordan, 'The Irish National League and the "unwritten law"', 171.

[211] Nettl, 'The German Social Democratic party', 80.   [212] Ibid.

radical democrats and socialists – as much as British radicals – remained enthusiastic supporters of both direct democracy and local self-government. If the NLF struggled with the inevitable contradictions between the desire to establish a national party organization, and the aspiration to strengthen participation and the local dimension, in France both democrats and socialists found their attachment to direct democracy to constitute a major 'practical and ideological'[213] hindrance to the formation of a modern party. The latter implied delegation of sovereignty and a certain degree of centralization, both bureaucratic and political. Although the French too were acquainted with forms of local electoral societies structurally similar to the Birmingham 'caucus',[214] their main problem was how to integrate regional associations into a national political organization. This involved subordinating the inclinations and practices of local, spontaneous political sociability to the needs of electoral action.[215] It was only in 1905, with the foundation of the French Socialist party, that they developed a working definition of the relationship between deputies in the National Assembly, local clubs – always extremely jealous of their autonomy – and the party leader. Both British radicals and French socialists were hesitant to accept the full implications of the representative principle: namely, that the power of the people should be parted with, and given over, for a limited period, to an elected deputy. Obviously, in the case of the NLF the problem derived not from any *sans-culotte* heritage, but from the old British emphasis on participatory citizenship and community self-government, as well as a reluctance to tolerate intermediaries between MPs and their constituents.

Thus, in a comparative perspective the NLF does not look much less democratic – or more oligarchic – than other left-wing organizations in contemporary continental Europe, let alone Ireland. In fact, as the powers of the council were curtailed in 1895, delegates became more aggressive and outspoken than they had ever been in the past. It was clear that centralization could not be carried out without generating considerable attrition with local associations. In particular, the reaction of the rank and file became vocal at the 1897 council, when the Kingston delegates demanded more power in policy making and the introduction of a postal ballot for the election of the executive. The latter request aimed at ensuring larger and more representative polls by maximizing members' participation and by making the executive more accountable and more

---

[213] R. Huard, 'La genesi dei partiti democratici moderni in Francia', in M. Brigaglia (ed.), *L'origine dei partiti nell' Europa contemporanea, 1870–1915* (Bologna, 1985), 131.

[214] P. Polivka, 'L'elezione senatoriale di Fallières nel 1906. Militanti e notabili radicali al tempo del "Blocco delle sinistre"', in Brigaglia, *L'origine dei partiti*, 165–80.

[215] Ibid.

authoritative in its dealings with both the parliamentary party and the allied pressure groups.[216]

At present some 200 people met at some place in the north or the south, and that small body elected the Executive Committee, which had to control the destiny of the Liberal party. The principle now suggested was … a sound democratic principle. Let them not be humbugged, but stand to their principles and support popular representation. Take control from the hands of the few and place it in the hands of the many. Instead of putting power in the hands of 200 people, put the power in the hands of the delegates of the associations … Their organization needed to be much more decentralized than it was. They now had an opportunity to make the Federation democratic, but if they would not do so, don't let them go about the country and talk about one man and one vote and popular representation, which their leaders, without consulting them, dropped into the background.[217]

The proposal was supported by the delegates of several provincial associations, including a working man, George Markam (East St Pancras), who complained that 'the Liberal party … had to some extent got out of touch with the Labour party'[218] (that is, with its labour supporters). By contrast, among the main opponents were Herbert Samuel and Professor Massie of the Oxford association,[219] both arguably closer to the London leaders than to provincial radicalism. They expressed a view which was effectively summarized by Haldane, when he wrote that '[the] future programme could not be fashioned by the officials of the National Liberal Federation, but only by a statesman with an outlook which was fresh and appreciative of this country as the centre of an Empire'.[220] Eventually it was decided to appoint a committee to inquire into the matter.[221] This was little more than a procrastinating tactic, but, as a concession to the NLF's 'democratic' wing, it was agreed that at the council 'on the motion for the adoption of the Annual Report, there may be "free discussion of any matter affecting the policy and principle of the Liberal Party". This will afford an opportunity for the ventilation of views upon subjects not dealt with in the Resolutions.'[222] For the rest, it

---

[216] Alderman W. Thompson (Kingston Division), in First Session of the Council, Thursday, March 18th [1897], in NLFAR, 75–6. The problem of the 'allied associations' as factors of excessive 'enthusiasm' and 'instability' had already been raised at the 1896 council (Proceedings of the Annual Meeting, Portsmouth, 26 Mar. 1896, 88, in NLFAR).

[217] W. Thompson in First Session of the Council, 18 Mar. 1897, in NLFAR, 76–7.

[218] Ibid.

[219] H. Samuel (Hon. Secretary of the Home Counties Division of the National Liberal Federation), ibid., 78 and J. Massie, ibid., 77.

[220] R. B. Haldane, An Autobiography (1929), 100; he alluded to Rosebery.

[221] NLFAR, 1897, 80.   [222] Ibid., 36.

was argued that '[t]he real work must be done by the local organizations',[223] rather than by the council.

After twelve years of radical rhetoric and the Newcastle Programme, it
was difficult to reject the democratic dream of a 'Liberal Parliament
outside the Imperial legislature' without risking a split or defections.
Both leaders and delegates acknowledged the seriousness of the division
within the party. Speaking for the NLF executive, Sir James Woodhouse
said that

> He did not share the view of his hon. colleague Sir James Kitson as to letting those
> who differed from them go out from them and form another association. He did
> not want anybody to go out of the Federation ... He wanted the Federation to be
> representative, as it always had been, not of one shade, but of all shades of opinion
> in the party. The representatives of the various shades would assemble at the
> annual conference, and would thrash out any points which might arise.[224]

His words were echoed, from the party left, by one delegate from a
Radical association, who stressed that internal differences ought to be
tolerated if the party was to survive as a democratic institution.[225]

The executive's *Report* conceded the extent of internal controversy and
criticism, but at least tried to define the relationship between the NLF
and the party leaders. This came down to two basic principles, or rather
customs and traditions, which had never previously been recorded in any
clause of the constitution. First, the report denied that the party leaders
tried to influence or interfere with the operation and deliberations of the
NLF – an implicit affirmation of the illegitimacy of such behaviour.
Second, it reasserted that 'one object of the Federation must still be to
get its views and decisions adopted by the leaders of our Party'.[226] It was
an emphatic restatement of the democratic view that the NLF ought to
be the sovereign policy-making institution within British Liberalism. When
the council began to discuss the new rules *seriatim*, the debate focused on
the role and importance of the MPs within the NLF. The feelings aired
suggest the extent to which the 'mass party organization' stood in the old
tradition of popular 'anti-Parliament' politics.[227] Alderman Winfrey from
Lincolnshire, and Booth, the Eccles delegate, demanded that the executive be elected by the council rather than by the General Committee. To
Winfrey it was a question of participation and democratic control: he
argued that '[d]elegates were attracted to the annual meeting who did not

---

[223] Sir J. Woodhouse, ibid., 72.   [224] Ibid., 72.
[225] George R. Thorne, President of the West Wolverhampton Liberal Association, ibid., 91.
[226] Ibid., 36.
[227] Parsinnen, 'Association, convention and anti-Parliament'. For the persistence of
Chartist traditions and outlooks in the 1880s, cf. Davis, 'Radical clubs', 105.

attend the meetings of the General Committee, and it would be an easy matter to conduct the ballot between the two sessions of the annual meeting'.[228] Woodhouse answered that '[a]t the last meeting of the General Committee there were 400 delegates present, so that the various associations were fairly well represented'. However, he was promptly contradicted by a delegate from Portsmouth, one Mr Morris, who said that 'he represented an association which always sent sixteen members to the annual meeting and only one to the General Committee'. He concluded by declaring that '[t]he Women's Liberal Federation found no difficulty in electing their executive at the annual meeting, and he could not see why the men should not do it'.[229] Morris was supported by the delegates from Bermondsey and Cardiff. After further exchanges, the amendment was withdrawn on the understanding that it 'should be brought up for consideration next year'[230] in order to allow time for the General Committee to consider its effects on other aspects of the constitution.

The vehemence of the feelings generated by the constitutional debate was further confirmed when C. P. Scott denounced as 'perfectly monstrous' the proposal 'that the remaining rules be adopted as they stood', en bloc.[231] Indeed many other clauses excited considerable discussion, and most of them dealt with the issue of internal party democracy. For example, George Cooper of the London County Council, a delegate from Bermondsey, moved that 'the suggestions received from the federated associations should be discussed and decided upon by the General Committee, and not by the Executive Committee'.[232] Another amendment aimed at depriving the Executive Committee of the power to co-opt candidates for re-election, in addition to those nominated by the federated associations. Both amendments were lost, but they provided illustrations of how deep-seated was rank-and-file diffidence towards the executive and central officials of the party.

The rule which explicitly excluded MPs from the Executive Committee was unanimously endorsed, and the chairman emphasized 'that they should be free from all thought of outside influence'.[233] At the 1897 meeting R. Winfrey moved again that the Executive Commitee 'should be elected by the annual assembly and not by the General

---

[228] Winfrey, in NLFAR, 1897, 73.   [229] Speech by Morris, ibid., 74.
[230] Interventions by Percy Bunting and the chairman, ibid.   [231] Ibid., 75.
[232] Speech by G. Cooper, ibid., 76. The main argument against that seemed to be 'the difficulty and expense of annual meetings' which would be compounded 'by holding a few months prior to such gatherings another meeting to consider the same resolutions as were afterwards to be submitted to the annual meeting' (Speech by Evans, ibid., 76).
[233] Ibid., 77.

Committee'.[234] The motion generated such strong feelings within the Executive Committee that during the preliminary debate one of its members resigned. Massie again opposed the change, claiming that the committee was actually *more* representative than the council, which 'although ... larger, was less evenly representative of all parts of the country'. He pointed out that the district in which the Federation happened to meet would be unduly favoured. 'Norfolk was represented to-day by a larger number of delegates than Lancashire; that was to say, a population of 500,000 was represented by a larger number of delegates than a population of three and a half millions. That was very nice for Norfolk, but if next year's meeting took place in Lancashire, where would Norfolk be?'[235] Obviously this problem would have been to a large extent obviated if the Kingston amendment about the postal ballot had been accepted, but Massie did not seem to realize that his position could be perceived as inconsistent, or worse. In fact, when it came to a vote on the motion to refer both resolutions to the Executive Committee, the council was almost evenly split: 201 voted in favour, 173 against.

It is not surprising that the NLF claimed extensive powers, when we consider the traditional Liberal emphasis on community self-government. The paradox is that the intensity of this radical democratic ideology was reinforced, rather than undermined, by the NLF's weakness, and particularly by its failure to dominate the party as a whole. Especially from 1891 the incipient tripartition of power among NLF, MPs and leader created a margin of uncertainty as to where ultimate authority did actually lie. Like the constitution of the German Empire, the internal structure of authority in the Liberal party seemed to be based on reciprocal irresponsibility. The party leader, like the German Chancellor, was not responsible to the representative assembly, though the latter could censure policies and MPs, thus embarrassing the leader and even jeopardizing electoral prospects. Since the leader could exercise only limited control over the deliberations of the council, this system encouraged radicalism without responsibility within the NLF. Before 1894 a constitutional impasse was avoided thanks to Gladstone's charisma, to which the NLF, like all other branches of popular liberalism, was very responsive. As a result, even at the height of its power and prestige, the mass organization remained the party leader's 'sounding board', thus further increasing his charisma.[236] In this sense Gladstone's rhetoric was neither

---

[234] Alderman R. Winfrey, Spalding Division of the Lincolnshire Liberal Council, ibid., 79.
[235] Massie, ibid., 79–80.
[236] Barker, *Gladstone and radicalism*, 156. Cf. A. Cyr, *Liberal party politics in Britain* (1977), 158, 164.

a development from, nor a counterbalance to, the 'caucus' system.[237] Rather the NLF was an instrument of Gladstone's style of political communication, in which party discipline seemed to rely mainly on the leader's charisma.

It may seem strange that charismatic leadership was so important to NLF Liberals, given, on the one hand, their reputation for bureaucratic organization, and, on the other, their passion for decentralization and liberty, and emphasis on rational discussion. Yet, the political space and the need for a charismatic leader were created by their very hatred of authoritarianism: charismatic authority – that is, authority as an 'exception'[238] – was more acceptable than an institutionalized, hierarchical structure.

Such an attitude to charismatic leadership was facilitated by the fact that 'platform' politics was part of both the liberal heritage and the popular radical one.[239] The 'orator', like the philosopher in the Athenian *ekklesia*,[240] was crucial to Mill's idea of informed citizenship. He hoped that '[m]odern democracies would have their occasional Pericles',[241] and Gladstone could be perceived as one of them. Indeed Mill himself, like the philosophers in the *ekklesia*, played the role of the 'public moralist' in the Westminster assembly in 1865–8.[242] Far from eschewing the challenges of mass politics, Mill could be an effective orator both in and out of Parliament. After his defeat in November 1868, he did not seek re-election and declined the offer of other constituencies. However, he remained in great demand as a popular speaker, to the extent that, as Stefan Collini has put it, 'the 66-year-old philosopher on the stump [threatened] to out-Gladstone Gladstone'.[243] Like the latter in his post-1876 mood, Mill believed that platform speech-making was the most effective way whereby the modern 'philosopher' could address the national '*ekklesia*' of public opinion, fully exploiting both the press and the suggestibility of mass demonstrations. To him this had nothing to do with demagogy: the contemporary liberal conviction was that rhetoric was the midwife of truth and the counterpart of logic, a

---

[237] Matthew, *Gladstone 1875–1898*, 50.
[238] W. J. Mommsen, *The age of bureaucracy: perspectives on the political sociology of Max Weber* (1974), 91.
[239] G. Watson, *The English ideology: studies in the language of Victorian politics* (1973), 115–24.
[240] Mill, *Considerations*, 458.   [241] Ibid., 460.
[242] Kinzer *et al.*, *A moralist in and out of parliament*.
[243] S. Collini, *Public moralists: political thought and intellectual life in Britain, 1850–1890* (1991), 167–9.

view consonant with Mill's Aristotelian understanding of active citizenship.[244]

The NLF was steeped in this frame of mind. Indeed if Home Rule contributed to NLF discipline, rhetoric and charisma were the elements which cemented together the various components of the party.[245] If the problem of political communication admitted of two types of solution – either organizational or rhetorical[246] – the NLF managed to combine both. As a party *organization* it tried to embody the ideal of a civically minded, permanently deliberating Demos. Within the party, as in the Athenian *ekklesia*, emphasis on equality and independence, and the rejection of both deference and bureaucratic encroachment, meant that only 'the magic of direct rhetoric' could 'engage mass opinion'.[247] Anarchistic and restless like the ancient *ekklesia*, the Liberal party organization required its Themistocles and Pericles. Internal cohesion depended on the leader's personal prestige and powers of persuasion,[248] the only means whereby he could win over both MPs and the 'mass party' assembly. This also meant that non-charismatic leaders, or divisions within the leadership, could affect the Liberals much more seriously than any other party, as was illustrated by the electoral disasters of 1895–1900 and, on a larger scale, of 1916–23. Despite the NLF's reputation as the cutting edge in 'caucus' and 'machine' politics, the real problem with the Liberal party was not lack of ideas and programmes, but inadequate organization.

---

[244] H. C. G Matthew, 'Gladstone, rhetoric and politics', 34; in P. J. Jagger (ed.) *Gladstone* (1998), 213–34, Biagini, 'Liberalism and direct democracy'.
[245] Matthew, *Gladstone*, 93.   [246] Ibid., 43.
[247] C. S. Meier, 'Democracy since the French Revolution', in J. Dunn (ed.), *Democracy: the unfinished journey, 508 BC to AD 1993* (1992), 150.
[248] Matthew, *Gladstone*, 93.

[S]urely it were better to regard these islands as forming but one nation
and let each man, whatever his nationality, have such share of the
common inheritance as he shows himself fitted for.[1]

The loss of Chamberlain alone was an immeasurable disaster; his
influence with the democracy had for some time past exceeded
Gladstone's ... In any case, the energy of a Parliament created for social
reform was to be spent on prolonged struggle over a subject which had
formed no part of the election programme. Working men would find
that their devotion had been thrown away, their confidence abused, the
promised reforms to which they gave their votes postponed indefinitely,
if not altogether sacrificed, to a measure of which no one among them
had ever heard.[2]

The rising hope of those stern and unbending Radicals, 1882–6

Chamberlain's 1885 pre-election tour of Scotland was a triumph. In the
electoral campaign itself he 'out-Midlothianed' Gladstone.[3] Although he
avoided the open-air speeches at which the GOM excelled, preferring
carefully stage-managed meetings in public halls, his rhetoric was
'electrifying' and left an indelible mark on the then rising generation of
radicals such as Augustine Birrell and Lloyd George. 'I still remember' –
wrote Ramsay MacDonald in 1914, recalling Chamberlain's speech in
Glasgow of 15 September 1885 'as if it were but yesterday' the thrill of
pleasure which went through Radical Scotland ... Its bold audacity
struck the imagination of the country.'[4] Perhaps the most memorable

---

[1] 'A Congregationalist minister', *The Liberal Unionist*, 4 May 1887, 93.
[2] Tuckwell, *Reminiscences of a Radical parson*, 59–60.
[3] D. Judd, *Radical Joe* (1977), 123; cf. Garvin, *Joseph Chamberlain*, vol. I, 391, 393, 395, vol. II, 106; Marsh, *Chamberlain*, 167, 174, 203, 206.
[4] J. Ramsay MacDonald, in Lord Milner et al., *Life of Joseph Chamberlain* (1914), 164.

description of his hold on the crowd was recorded by Beatrice Webb (then Beatrice Potter):

As he rose slowly, and stood silently before his people, his whole face and form seemed transformed. The crowd became wild with enthusiasm . . . Perfectly still stood the people's Tribune, till the people, exhausted and expectant, gradually subsided into fitful and murmuring cries. At the first sound of his voice they became as one man. Into the tone of his voice he threw the warmth of feeling, which was lacking in his words; and every thought, every feeling, the slightest intonation of irony and contempt was reflected on the face of the crowd. It might have been a woman listening to the words of her lover! Perfect response and unquestioning receptivity.[5]

Obviously Chamberlain knew how to 'work' the crowds, but this 'unquestioning receptivity' was not simply the result of his charisma. It was also a response to his gospel of popular emancipation, which seemed consistent with Gladstonian liberalism while going beyond it, almost its natural extension and the fulfilment of the expectations of justice and fair play which Gladstone had aroused.[6] Ultimately, Chamberlain's credibility depended on the solid reality of municipal democracy in Birmingham – then widely regarded by many radicals as a model for the rest of the country. It was a city which was 'Radical to its very centre . . . here artisans have seats on the governing bodies, including the Town Council, the School Board, and the Board of Guardians. If anywhere, surely in Birmingham the democracy is all powerful. John Bright once said, "As the sea is salt [*sic*] wherever you taste it, so Birmingham is Liberal wherever touched."'[7]

It is tempting to see that city's 'municipal socialism' as an anticipation of Chamberlain's later demands for state-sponsored social reform, and therefore inevitably incompatible with Gladstone's unrelenting zeal for retrenchment at the Treasury, a suggestion in fact made by Chamberlain himself in 1886.[8] In 1880–5 there were occasional divergences of opinion between the two, and Chamberlain was generally on the side of state intervention. Indeed, in 1880, and again in 1882, he proposed a plan of public works to relieve distress in Ireland: it was inspired by contemporary French social reform, particularly the so-called Freycinet scheme, and included demands for improved communications, help for industrial enterprise, and drainage and reclamation of lands.[9] He also supported

---

[5] B. Webb, *My Apprenticeship* (1950), 109.   [6] Ashby, *Joseph Ashby of Tysoe*, 117–18.
[7] C. Leach, 'Democracy and religion', *The Congregationalist*, Nov. 1885, 841.
[8] In a conversation with A. J. Balfour in Mar. 1886, cited in Judd, *Radical Joe*, 150–1.
[9] Memos dated 18 Aug. 1880, JC 8/5/1/1 and 21 Apr. 1882, the latter in J. Chamberlain, *A political memoir, 1880–92*, ed. by C. H. D. Howard (1953), 55. Charles de Freycinet, Minister of Public Works in 1877–9. His scheme involved the investment of 350 million francs of government money in the development of infrastructures such as harbour

John Bright's proposal for the creation of peasant proprietorship in Ireland, a scheme which at the time Gladstone turned down as wildly expensive[10] – although, as we have already seen (see chapter 1, p. 9), eventually he proposed an even more expensive plan in 1886.

However, it is important to observe that both examples concern Ireland, which was then entering a period of spiralling social and political crisis, and which, in any case, was hardly indicative of any politician's 'normal' inclinations (certainly it was not usual for Bright to advocate ambitious plans of social engineering). As Marsh has pointed out, in most other cases, and especially as far as the problems of urban England were concerned, '[t]he contrast between laissez-faire Gladstonian Liberalism and Chamberlain's constructive variety was more rhetorical than substantive'.[11] The Victorian 'constitution' recognized different roles for local authorities and the central government. The latter could preach and implement drastic cuts to public expenditure in the areas for which it was directly responsible – such as the army, navy and servicing of the National Debt – while the former could expand its functions and related budgets. This must be borne in mind if one is to explain the apparent paradox that Chamberlain 'remained . . . throughout a consistent disciple of J. S. Mill in matters of social and economic doctrine',[12] while Gladstone himself was responsible for the growth of local government, most significantly as a result of the 1870 Education Act – perhaps the single most expensive social reform passed by any British government in the nineteenth century.

Yet, in other respects Chamberlain was indeed 'different' from both Gladstone and most other Liberal leaders. By 1880, together with John Bright, he was one of only two Dissenters to have risen to a position of national leadership. A generation younger than Bright, he was more self-confident and assertive. Partly as a consequence, Chamberlain, like Gladstone, possessed the temperament and outlook of the executive politician. Although both Bright and Chamberlain reflected the Nonconformist tradition of 'conviction' politics, Chamberlain's Dissenting principles did not include peace, and indeed his family had made a fortune out of Britain's past wars. The uncompromising part of his Dissenting background reflected his debt to Utilitarianism and

facilities, railways and canals. He was then Foreign Minister in 1882, in the days of the invasion of Egypt. Freycinet was one of the many Protestants holding high office under the Third Republic.

[10] Marsh, *Chamberlain*, 150; K. Robbins, *John Bright* (1979), 241.

[11] Marsh, *Chamberlain*, 181.

[12] P. S. Fraser, *Joseph Chamberlain: radicalism and empire, 1868–1914* (1966), xiii, 46; Quinault, 'Joseph Chamberlain', 71, 73, 75.

Philosophical Radicalism, traditions which prized individual liberty of judgement, and scrutinized religious as well as social practices in the cold light of reason. In this respect, Chamberlain was the political heir of Joseph Priestley, as much as of Tom Paine and Richard Price.[13]

For a Radical and 'a man of the people', this heritage came with obvious benefits, but also some disadvantages. Among the latter, 'the emotional impoverishment of strictly rational religion' was critical, since this cut him off from the other Dissenters, and indeed from much of the rest of British culture,[14] then dominated by a powerfully emotional form of Christianity – Evangelicalism. This 'disability' was compounded by the fact that '[he had] received his formal education in schools which stressed modern rather than classical subjects: mathematics, some science, and French as well as Latin'.[15] Like that of J. S. Mill, Chamberlain's education did not include any particular emphasis on sentiment or the poetic imagination. While Mill had moved away from dry Utilitarian rationalism in the aftermath of his famous 'mental crisis', Chamberlain's emotional development was complicated by his loss of faith in 1875 after his second wife's tragic death.[16] The anger and deep anguish associated with this experience further weakened his ability to relate to the predominant Evangelical mood of the country – and especially to the famous 'Nonconformist Conscience'. This was bound to generate misunderstandings, which originated not in the sphere of *political difference*, but in the deeper and extra-rational one of *emotional incompatibility*. An example is provided by the events of 1876, when Chamberlain supported the Bulgarian agitation, but without sharing the related emotionalism. To most Dissenters it was a question of moral imperatives whose urgency overruled alleged national interests. To Chamberlain, however, it was a matter of party politics, and entailed a situation in which national interests were not really at stake, because Britain's virtual control of the Suez Canal made its route to India safe, irrespective of Constantinople's power and attitudes. Later, when he changed his mind, he repudiated the policy.[17]

Real political differences between Chamberlain and Gladstone began to emerge only in late 1885, in the aftermath of the famous 'Ransom'

---

[13] J. Loughlin, 'Joseph Chamberlain, English nationalism and the Ulster question', *History*, 77 (1992), 209.

[14] Marsh, *Chamberlain*, 7.   [15] Ibid., 8.   [16] Ibid., 92.

[17] In 1886 he wrote that 'Mr Gladstone's Bulgarian Agitation ... was a gigantic mistake – almost as great as his Home Rule proposals', not because of Constantinople's strategic importance, but because he thought that Britain needed Turkish support to stop the Russians in the Balkans (Chamberlain to Dilke, 2 Dec. 1886, JC 5/24/501). For his views in 1876 see Marsh, *Chamberlain*, 115. At the time the 'emotionalism' of the agitation alienated some Utilitarians and social reformers, including J. Fitzjames Stephen and F. Harrison (Shannon, *Bulgarian agitation*, 207).

speech. With its emphasis on land reform, its aggressive critique of the landed aristocracy and quasi-republican rhetoric, this speech stretched the remit of social reform to include both constitutional and fiscal policies, thus trespassing on two highly sensitive political areas. His 1885 *Radical Manifesto* alluded to the 'socialist' legislation which the times demanded, and his electoral speeches stressed that 'Government of the people, and by the people' now meant 'of course . . . Socialism'.[18] In other words, Chamberlain's new approach involved the *politicization* of social reform. In future radicalism was to be about improving the people's material conditions. Gradually he was rejecting the old Peelite and Cobdenite doctrine of the state's economic and social 'neutrality' in favour of a new interventionist philosophy which saw the government as ultimately responsible for progress.

Besides being intrinsically novel, this approach had important, albeit indirect, implications for both the impending debate on Irish Home Rule and the relationship between the state and society. One implication was that if poverty was to be reduced by state intervention, then what Britain required was not devolution and the weakening of Parliament, but the rational reconstruction and empowerment of the imperial executive at its centre. As Chamberlain told Balfour, 'a democratic government should be the strongest government . . . in the world, for it has the people behind it . . . My radicalism, at all events, desires to see established a strong government and an Imperial government.'[19] Although he was then in the process of parting company from Gladstone, conceptually the greater break was really rather with Bright. For, while the strong government which Chamberlain proposed could be seen as a mere development of Gladstone's pragmatic and *dirigiste* style in both domestic and imperial affairs, it was fundamentally incompatible with Bright's understanding of the role of the state. Unlike Gladstone, Bright was not prepared to compromise on the traditional free-trade principle of state neutrality in economic affairs, namely that the state should not 'succour' any particular interest, whether landed or industrial.[20]

---

[18] J. Chamberlain et al., *The Radical programme* (1885; ed. by D. A. Hamer, 1971), 12, 59; see also G. L. Goodman, 'The Liberal Unionist party, 1886–1895', unpublished D.Phil. thesis, University of Chicago, 1956, 5. See also E. A. Cameron, ' "A far cry from London": Joseph Chamberlain in Inverness, September 1885', *The Innes Review*, 57, 1 (2006), 36–53.

[19] During the famous dinner with A. J. Balfour on 22 Mar. 1886, cited in Garvin, *Chamberlain*, vol. II, 191.

[20] While in 1886 both Gladstone and Chamberlain contemplated further land reform in Ireland, Bright thought that the 1881 Land Act had 'settled' the question: he now objected to land purchase, despite the fact that he had proposed it in 1880

That Chamberlain was closer to Gladstone than to Bright had already emerged in 1881–2 in the course of the two African crises, the first of which concerned the Transvaal. During the Midlothian campaigns the Boers understood Gladstone to promise that a future Liberal government would restore their independence. Chamberlain had no doubt that this was indeed the right policy, both morally and politically.[21] Like Gladstone, he assessed foreign policy in terms of 'right and wrong'. In his speeches and in correspondence with John Bright, he seemed prepared to accept that British imperial ambition ought to be subordinate to both liberal principles and the 'true interests' of subject races. The virtual convergence between Chamberlain and Gladstone on this matter became evident after the formation of the government in March 1880. At this time Chamberlain urged a prompt British withdrawal from the Transvaal, while Gladstone supported annexation. Yet, he appointed Chamberlain as the cabinet's parliamentary spokesman on South African matters. When Kruger's insurrection resulted in British defeats, Chamberlain insisted on appeasement rather than repression and appealed 'to the impartial public opinion of Europe and America' in support of a policy which preferred 'justice to revenge and the best interests of South Africa to the vain pursuit of military glory'.[22] Gladstone agreed, and Britain withdrew. Bright was delighted. Chamberlain's only reservation about withdrawal was the fate of the natives, whom the Boers had a reputation for maltreating, and towards whom Britain was supposed to have a moral obligation.[23] While this crisis was settled to the satisfaction of the three leaders, it is important to observe that, like Gladstone but in contrast to Bright, Chamberlain dealt with the problem from the standpoint of an executive politician, prepared to accept the compromises which power demanded. Moreover, his concern for the Africans' welfare was a reminder that – again unlike Bright – he was not committed to non-intervention but was prepared to assess each case on its own merits.

(R. A. J. Walling (ed.), *The diaries of John Bright* (1930), entry for 12 Mar. 1886, 535). On this aspect of the relationship between state and society in Victorian Britain see Daunton, *Trusting Leviathan*, 63ff.

[21] D. M. Schreuder, *Gladstone and Kruger: Liberal government and colonial 'Home Rule', 1880–85* (1969), 91, 94.

[22] From a speech in Birmingham, 7 June 1882, cited in Garvin, *Chamberlain*, vol. I, 441.

[23] 'I have always hoped that as the natives enormously outnumber the Boers ... the latter when left alone would be compelled to come to terms with their neighbours & treat them with ordinary fairness. If this should not be the case our position is a serious one, and although I do not say that we are necessarily bound to stand aloof, still the greatest caution ought to be observed, and I should be reluctant to press the matters to the utmost unless it became imperatively necessary; and even then I would feel the greatest anxiety as to the result.' (J. Chamberlain to R. W. Dale, 14 Sep. 1882, in JC 5/20/41.)

This was fully illustrated by the outcome of the second African crisis, in Egypt. Chamberlain, like Gladstone, 'misliked' the Egyptian imbroglio 'quite as much as the Transvaal entanglement or the Irish misery'.[24] And once again he sided with him and thus against John Bright – though, of course, both professed the greatest respect and veneration for the old Quaker.[25] At first, again like Gladstone, Chamberlain regarded Arabi and 'the so-called revolutionary movement' as possibly 'the legitimate expression of discontent and of resistance to oppression. If so, it ought to be guided and not repressed.'[26] However, he soon became more cautious in his assessment of the Egyptian colonel. Interestingly, popular liberal reaction was similarly perplexed and divided. In Parliament, Henry Broadhurst – the former secretary of the TUC and one of the leading Lib-labs – inquired anxiously about the government's intention, indicating his disapproval for both the use of force and the related expenditure 'in order to secure the British bondholders from anticipated losses'.[27]

While some of these fears and anxieties could be assuaged by Gladstone's magic influence, it is remarkable that so few radicals protested against the bombardment.[28] In any case, popular liberalism had an imperialist side as well. For example, always eager to reflect the line which was more likely to 'sell to the million', *Lloyd's Weekly* took a 'muscular' approach to the Egyptian difficulty, arguing that the British should 'hold themselves in readiness to act as a police', and that '[their] admirals are messengers of love and peace to the Egyptians, if the sons of the Desert will only remain quiet, and allow their Khedive to follow the advice of the English and French Consuls-General'.[29]

Eventually, in June news of riots in Alexandria convinced Chamberlain not only that 'the sons of the Desert' would not remain quiet, but also that 'Arabi was only a buccaneer and that there was no "national" party behind him.'[30] The time for Britain to act – and to do so swiftly – had come. Again the similarity with Gladstone is striking. Like the latter, Chamberlain thought that 'intervention should be directed not to impose on Egypt institutions of our choice but to secure for the Egyptian people a free choice for themselves *so far as this may not be inconsistent with the*

---

[24] Garvin, *Chamberlain*, vol. I, 444.
[25] For Gladstone's handling of the Quaker leader see his three letters to Bright, dated 12, 13 and 14 July 1882, in *The Gladstone diaries*, vol. x (1990), 296–8.
[26] On 7 Jan. 1882: Garvin, *Chamberlain*, vol. I, 445.
[27] HPD, 3rd Series, vol. CCLXXI, 29 June 1882, 773–4.
[28] Laity, *The British peace movement*, 97, 99–100; P. Horn, *Joseph Arch (1826–1919)* (1971), 165.
[29] L.a., 'Our Egyptian patchwork', *LW*, 21 May 1882, 6.
[30] Garvin, *Chamberlain*, vol. I, 447; Chamberlain, *Political memoir*, 71.

permanent interests of other Powers'.[31] Obviously this qualification was to prove of overriding importance, but, for the time being, Chamberlain insisted on the programmatic statement in the quotation's main clause. Indeed, in a memo of June 1882 he highlighted the contrast between the allegedly sinister interest of international finance and 'the rights of the Egyptian people to manage their own affairs'. On the other hand, at no stage did such rights mean British non-intervention, because, once law and order had collapsed and anarchy reigned under Arabi, further 'change' was inevitable. Moreover,

if a change has to be made in a system which has the sanction of International agreement it should be on the demand of some body entitled to speak for the Egyptian people, and not at the dictation of a military adventurer supported by an army which he is forced to keep in good temper by bribes of pay and promotion & whose action compromises the welfare and liberties as well as the interest of foreigners.[32]

Between pursuing the latter and fostering 'the further development of Representative institutions which have been swallowed up in the military movement of Arabi Bey', there was thus a happy coincidence. Chamberlain claimed that Britain had a mission in the East: 'The duty cast upon us, as the Liberal Government of a free nation, is to secure to the Egyptian people the greatest possible development of representative institutions.'[33] Or, in Gladstone's words, it was that of 'exporting western and beneficient [*sic*] institutions' to Muslim countries.[34]

In radical, as much as in Whig, political thought civilization, progress and individual liberty were the essential prerequisites of self-government.[35] Hence Britain was justified in enforcing law and order, retrenchment and financial accountability among reluctant or corrupt subjects. Ireland and

---

[31] Chamberlain's minute of 21 June 1882, cited in Garvin, *Chamberlain*, vol. I, 448. My italics.

[32] Memo, June 1882, in JC, 7/1/3/1. This was indeed Gladstone's official policy: see printed memo, signed W. E. Gladstone, dated 15 Sep. 1882, in *Cabinet Papers: Confidential*, 'The Settlement of Egypt', point 3 (in JC 7/1/3/2): 'Subject to all due provisions for the fulfilment of international engagements, it is presumed that England will make a firm stand for the reasonable development of self-governing institutions in Egypt ... Little sympathy could be expected from the Powers in promoting the development of securities for liberty; while in England they will be demanded, and will be hailed with satisfaction.' For Gladstone's attitudes see E. F. Biagini, 'Exporting "Western and beneficent institutions": Gladstone and empire, 1880–1885', in D. Bebbington and R. Swift (eds.), *Gladstone centenary essays* (2000), 211.

[33] Chamberlain's minute of 18 Oct. 1882, in JC 7/1/3/3.

[34] Gladstone to Lord Rosebery, 15 Nov. 1883, in *Gladstone diaries*, vol. XI, 59.

[35] F. Rosen, *Bentham, Byron and Greece: constitutionalism, nationalism and early liberal political thought* (1992), 292–4; see also I. Bradley, *The optimists: themes and personalities in Victorian liberalism* (1980), 20.

Egypt from 1882 were cases in point – negative illustrations of what Romani has described as 'the relationship between a free constitution and the moral adequacy of its citizens'.[36] In such instances, irrespective of ethnic or religious differences, people ought to be *coerced* into being 'free' – an old 'republican' or neo-roman notion which acquired new significance in Britain's imperial heyday. Political rights could be granted later and would be consequent on the people's ability to care for the 'public interest'. Time and again Chamberlain appealed to the latter in his defence of government intervention in areas such as municipal socialism, education and land reform. During the Egyptian crisis he was eager to be perceived as standing up for the public interest, rather than for the sectional concerns of the bondholders. He argued that there could be 'no doubt' that European control was to Egypt's public advantage.

The question was whether this 'rational' consideration should be allowed to override the 'emotional', 'sentimental' inclination of the misguided Egyptian people, who 'prefer[red] native administration with all its consequences to the inflexible severity & honesty of European control'.[37] It was no easy choice and he wavered. In June, despite having recently espoused interventionism, he was still ready to admit that if the Egyptians preferred self-government to good government, 'it is not Englands [*sic*] business nor right to force on them an unpopular system which could only be permanently maintained against their wishes by practically assuming the Government of the country'.[38] In July, however, he changed his mind, but on condition that temporary, 'good' British imperial rule became a stepping stone to better Egyptian self-government. Once again, he echoed Gladstone, who was anxious to show that British intervention was devoid 'of any selfish purpose and design' and that its only aims were 'to put down tyranny and to favour law and freedom'.[39] The dichotomy between public and sectional interest was paramount in his mind, especially 'in reference to the development of

---

[36] Romani, 'British views on the Irish national character', 193.
[37] Chamberlain, Minute of 21 June, in *Political memoir*, 72; Gladstone struggled with the same dilemma: see Biagini, 'Exporting', 214–15. Somewhat inconsistently for the man who invaded Egypt, in February 1884 he concluded that '[f]ew ... are the peoples so degraded and so lost to every noble sentiment that it shall be a matter of indifference to them whether they are governed by persons who belong to the same political constitution with themselves, or whether they are governed by those who come from a remote quarter, with foreign instincts, foreign sympathies, and foreign objects'. (*Egypt and the Soudan*, a parliamentary speech republished as a penny pamphlet by the Liberal Central Association, 1884, 15.)
[38] Chamberlain, Minute of 21 June 1882, cited in Garvin, *Chamberlain*, vol. I, 448.
[39] Gladstone on 27 July 1882, HPD, 3rd Series, CCLXII, 1590.

Egyptian liberties and popular institutions', in order to 'avoid the general conclusion that the interests of the bondholders have been the first if not the only care of Her Majesty's Government'.[40] The same day, in a separate minute he admitted that there was 'an uneasy feeling among Liberals with respect to Egyptian questions'. The main reason was 'the civil reorganization of the country': 'There is a great anxiety lest after all the bondholders should too evidently be the only persons who have profited from the war, and lest phrases which have been used concerning the extension of Egyptian liberties, and Egypt for the Egyptians should prove to have no practical meaning.'[41] A few days later, in a letter to another leading radical, Sir Charles Dilke, he admitted that

The interference, the confusion of interests remain . . . Nothing is done to 'develop the institutions' to 'promote the liberties' to give 'Egypt to the Egyptians' – in fact to carry out a single word of the fine phrases with which we went to war . . . English Liberal opinion will say you have made Finance and the interests of the creditors the key note of your policy – you have sacrificed the liberties and the independence of Egypt to the security of the bondholders and you have done nothing to relieve this country from the embarrassment in which the unrighteous interference with the internal affairs of Egypt has involved us.[42]

However, he was ready to reassure himself that '[t]he difficulty of the situation consists in the apparent impossibility of conciliating the natural intentions and wishes of English Liberalism with the privileges claimed by *other* European Powers and especially France'.[43] It was a remarkable feat of self-deception and on a Gladstonian scale. Having played a leading role in the British decision to invade, Chamberlain could now contrast the 'benevolence' and 'disinterestedness' of his government, with the 'self-ishness' of the French, who had refused to take part in the invasion. As Bright pointed out,[44] it was a rather paradoxical and hypocritical stance. Although the written correspondence between the representatives of Birmingham radicalism fully reflected their disagreement, they managed to remain on friendly terms with each other. 'I never thought that any word of yours was directed against me, but what you said at Ashton shows

[40] J. Chamberlain, Memo on Lord Granville's Draft of 18 Oct. 1882, in JC 7/1/3/4; see also Chamberlain to Sir C. Dilke, 22 Oct. 1882, in JC 5/24/327.
[41] J. Chamberlain's minute of 18 Oct. 1882, in JC 7/1/3/3.
[42] Chamberlain to Sir C. Dilke, 22 Oct. 1882, in JC 5/24/327.
[43] Chamberlain's minute of 18 Oct. 1882, in JC 7/1/3/4.
[44] 'But the French did not think it their duty to attack the Forts, & they are now not obliged to justify their conduct by false statements such as our Govt. is driven to when its members say the bombardment was not war but a necessary act of self-defence . . . the war was bad enough, but the statements made in its defence were monstrous . . .' (John Bright to J. Chamberlain, 4 January 1883, in JC 5/7/20.)

how great is the difference between us,' Bright wrote to Chamberlain in one of the clearest critical analyses of the government's policy in Egypt:

You join together 'the policy of non intervention & peace at any price', as if one had necessarily any connection with the other. A man may be absolutely against intervention, & yet ready & eager to fight against any one attacking himself or his Country. And further you claim the policy of non intervention 'to be an unworthy and ignoble doctrine'. This is a doctrine held by Washington, & to which Civilization & Christianity are evidently tending. You speak of the 'honour and interest of England' as justifying intervention, and you refer, further on, to 'certain stock arguments of defeatism'. Are not your words of the stock arguments of the Jingo school? I have heard them for 40 years in the House of Commons. They are words of Palmerston throughout his mischievous career, & from William 3rd to our own time they have been spoken in defence of all the crimes which have built up the Debt & wasted the wealth & the blood of the people.[45]

Chamberlain argued that '[e]verything turns in my opinion on the probabilities of what would have happened if we had not interfered. I think that anarchy in Egypt and the massacre of European[s] would have ensued and that this in turn would have been followed by European intervention and very likely by European war.'[46] In defence of government policy he argued that '[we] see now the evils of interference, but it is impossible to say what the result of a different course would have been, both in Egypt & public opinion here.'[47] Meanwhile he continued to urge Gladstone to produce 'an expression of opinion in reference to Egyptian liberty and popular institutions', in particular 'First, with regard to the establishment or reform of native tribunals and the general administration of justice in the country, and Secondly, the creation of some kind of national representative assembly' – although not a democratically elected one.[48] Bright's assessment was radically different: he insisted that the war was no more justifiable when the decision to invade was taken than it was in hindsight. And, directly contradicting Chamberlain, he added that it was easy to see what the situation would have been without the invasion: 'there would have been for the moment a bloodless revolution & England, France and Turkey would have discussed the future of Egypt, but there would have been no war – no bombardment – no city in flames – no

[45] J. Bright to J. Chamberlain, 4 Jan. 1883, in JC 5/7/20.
[46] J. Chamberlain to J. Bright, 31 Dec. 1882, in JC 5/7/37. This view was widely disseminated among British policy makers at the time as a justification for the invasion: A. L. Al-Sayyid-Marsot, 'The British occupation of Egypt from 1882', in A. Porter (ed.), *The Oxford history of the British Empire*, vol. III: *The nineteenth century* (1999), 651.
[47] J. Chamberlain to J. Bright, 14 Jan. 1884, in JC 5/7/39.
[48] J. Chamberlain to W. E. Gladstone, 18 Oct. 1883, in Gladstone Papers, Add. MSS 44125, ff.166–7.

thousands of men slaughtered'.[49] Eventually Chamberlain seemed to concede Bright's point: 'I am afraid you were right and we were wrong . . . I think I shall end by joining the Peace Society after all, though it will go against the grain of my unregenerate nature.'[50]

Obviously, it was his 'unregenerate nature' which carried the day in the end. Far from joining the Peace Society, Chamberlain moved further towards the idea of a strong, decisive government as essential to the pursuit of the public interest. This trend was further encouraged by his enthusiasm for a more interventionist approach to social reform, again from 1882–3 when he was much taken by Henry George's *Progress and poverty*.[51] In December 1884, in the aftermath of the Third Reform Act, he considered that democracy would now require a strengthening of the executive in the United Kingdom, because 'a democratic House of Commons cannot attend to administrative details',[52] and because, as he would put it to Balfour in 1886, the gravity of its social problems suggested that the country might come to face a revolution which only resolute government intervention would be able to avert.[53]

About the future of the empire, he argued that democratic Britain should follow in America's footsteps and move towards isolationism, 'retir[ing] more & more from European politics' and consolidating its empire. Devolution, especially in India, made no sense:

The future of our rule in this great dependency is to me a matter of speculation & even of anxiety. I do not suppose that we can obtain the affection of the people. As far as I know there is no instance in history of one nations [*sic*] having ruled another with its full consent & approval. If the people of India were of one race & one mind they could drive us into the sea & rule themselves. But is this ever likely to be the case? If not can we safely give any considerable extension of liberties?[54]

This was in a letter to C. P. Albert, a Legal Member of the Council of India. It is interesting to note that even as Chamberlain reached the apex of his democratic reputation, he came to share the views articulated by that distinguished but remorselessly authoritarian body of Indian bureaucrats. Sir Henry Maine, another Legal Member of the Council, denied that the quality or legitimacy of a government rested on popular participation. India was 'divided into a vast number of independent, self-acting, organised social groups' – and this entailed sectionalism, the very opposite

[49] J. Bright to J. Chamberlain, 18 Jan. 1884, in JC 5/7/21.
[50] J. Chamberlain to J. Bright, 14 Jan. 1884, in JC 5/7/39.
[51] Garvin, *Chamberlain*, vol. I, 385–6.
[52] JC to C. P. Albert, Legal member of the Council of India, 19 Dec. 1884, in JC 9/1/2/1.
[53] From Balfour's account of his famous convivial discussion with Chamberlain, on 22 Mar. 1886, cited in Judd, *Radical Joe*, 151.
[54] JC to C. P. Albert, Legal member of the Council of India, 19 Dec. 1884, in JC 9/1/2/1.

of Chamberlain's 'public' interest, a view at the time shared by other Liberals. He rejected the idea that the role and justification of British rule included training Indians in nation-building and self-government.[55] Because only authority could enforce the pursuit of public interest and the 'greatest happiness of the greatest number', he was not embarrassed by the authoritarian implications of his Utilitarianism. Neither was Chamberlain, apparently not even in 1884. Furthermore, unlike his Birmingham associate and fellow-Nonconformist R. W. Dale, his attitude was not inspired by the then commonplace notion that the Indians were 'not yet ready' for self-government. In fact, in 1882 he had ridiculed this view, both as a general argument and with regard to the Egyptians.[56] Rather, it was a question of national interest and imperial survival: '[e]xcept as a preparation for entire self-government a mixed system is productive of grave embarrassment. Look at the case of the Cape & South African colonies! Australia & Canada afford no guide. There we have practically conceded independence and nothing but the sentimental tie remains.'[57]

This reasoning was applicable to Ireland. The question was not simply whether Home Rule was consistent with the then current British colonial policy, because, while the latter was in itself conducive to imperial disintegration, the former contained the germs of a lethal nationalist 'contagion'.[58] Chamberlain's prescriptions involved a proactive role for the British executive and for Parliament, whose sovereignty could not be questioned. In 1880 he considered land reform in conjunction with local government, for example 'elective County Boards [which] will be formed to exercise a qualified Home Rule within the limits of the

---

[55] H. Maine, *Village communities in the East and the West* (1876), 56–7; J. M. Burrow, 'Henry Maine and the mid-Victorian idea of progress', in A. Diamond (ed.), *The Victorian achievement of Sir Henry Maine* (1991), 68; cf. A. S. Kirshner, 'Character and the administration of empires in the political thought of Henry Maine', unpublished M.Phil. dissertation, University of Cambridge, 2002, 62. For sectionalism allegedly preventing nation-building in both India and Ireland see MacKnight, *Ulster as it is*, 140, 237.

[56] 'As regards representative government the opinions of all authorities are tainted by the incoherent distrust of authorities of the capacity of the people to govern themselves. Macaulay's illustration of the man who would not go into the water until he had learned to swim is the type of all the objections raised by the extension of self-government among the people. It is said the fellaheen are not fitted for representation. I should like to know any case in the history of any nation when the unrepresented classes have not been met with the same objection by those who have arrogated to themselves the right of disposing of their destinies. At the present moment it is the stock argument of Tories with regard to the agricultural labourer.' (Chamberlain's minute of 18 Oct. 1882, in JC 7/1/3/3.) For R. W. Dale's attitude see Hall, *Civilising subjects*, 383–4.

[57] JC to C. P. Albert, Legal member of the Council of India, 19 Dec. 1884, in JC 9/1/2/1.

[58] S. H. Zebel, 'Joseph Chamberlain and the genesis of tariff reform', *Journal of British Studies*, 7, 1 (1987), 132–3.

county'.[59] In 1881, in correspondence with the Irish MP Charles Dawson, he expressed his reservations about the consequences of assimilation of the electoral laws of Britain and Ireland. Moreover, in connection with Home Rule, he stated: 'I am not prepared to offer to Ireland State rights similar in all respects to those possessed by the States of the American Union. These rights caused the Civil War & their concession in Ireland would, I have no doubt, lead to a similar catastrophe.' In vain did Dawson suggest that – in his view, which had been that of the Radicals in 1861–5 – the Civil War had been caused by slavery, not by state rights. All that Chamberlain was prepared to concede was 'devolving on local government in G[rea]t. Britain as well as in Ireland some of the duties now performed by an Imperial Parl[iamen]t'.[60] 'I say to Ireland what the Liberals and the Republicans of the North said to the Southern States of America – "The Union must be preserved (cheers); you cannot and you shall not destroy it (cheers)." Within these limits there is nothing that you may not ask and hope to obtain – equal laws, equal justice, equal opportunities, equal prosperity.'[61]

The parallel with the US Civil War, with its epic struggle between 'good' and 'evil', held a central place in the British Radical imagination.[62] The attraction of applying it to the Home Rule crisis was evident: in particular, it helped to present the Liberal Unionist cause as perfectly consistent with the Anglo-American and European liberal tradition, which sought improvement by means of the consolidation of regions and provinces into larger and economically feasible nations – according to Friedrich List's 'threshold' theory of nation-building. Separatism, especially when it came with the request for privileges by the Catholic Church, was regarded as the very opposite of both nation-building and progress. This was particularly the case with Ireland, because, as liberals and democrats of the calibre of Tocqueville and Mazzini had argued in the 1840s, its problems were not those of an oppressed nation: rather,

---

[59] H. Labouchere to J. Chamberlain, 17 Dec. 1880, forwarded to Gladstone on 22 Dec. 1880, in Gladstone Papers, Add. MSS 44125, ff. 55–6.

[60] J. Chamberlain to C. Dawson, 31 Oct. 1881 and C. Dawson to J. Chamberlain, 2 Nov. 1881, respectively in JC 8/6/32/2 and JC 8/6/36/3.

[61] J. Chamberlain, *Home Rule and the Irish Question: A collection of speeches delivered between 1881 and 1887* (1887), 27.

[62] A. G. Gardiner, *The life of Sir William Harcourt*, vol. II, (New York, n.d.), 48. For parallels in the contemporary debate see J. M. Horton Jr.,'The case of the American Civil War in the debate over Irish Home Rule', *American Historical Review*, 69 (1964), 1022–6; K. M. Foster, 'The intellectual duke: George Douglas Campbell, 8th Duke of Argyll, 1823–1900', Ph.D. thesis, University of Edinburgh, 2005, 149, 161 (in this respect Argyll deserved the sobriquet of 'the radical duke' – at any rate his attitude was closer to Bright than to those of other Liberal leaders).

they were social and political, and their solution was to be sought in the establishment of full constitutional equality for all British subjects throughout the United Kingdom, without distinctions of creed, ethnicity or other criteria.

In this context it is instructive to compare the attitudes of Chamberlain, Gladstone and Bright towards the politics of law and order. In principle, all three were against coercion. However, from as early as 1880 Chamberlain was prepared to endorse it on both pragmatic and opportunistic grounds: 'there [was] no alternative' and '[t]he workmen here [did] not like to see law set at defiance'.[63] Whatever Birmingham artisans actually thought (and there is evidence of virulent anti-Catholicism in the town[64]), Bright, the other radical MP for the city, agreed that coercion was necessary. Like A. J. Mundella (an erstwhile and future Home Ruler), both Chamberlain and Bright felt that with coercion and the closure '[t]he Government is really making a fight for *representative institutions*'.[65] It seemed that Bright was almost eager to see the Habeas Corpus Act suspended, having reached the conclusion that the Irish Nationalists – supported, as they were, by Britain's enemies in America – were 'not only a *foreign* element ... but a *rebel* party, with whom we must reckon'.[66] Chamberlain, who was continuously involved in negotiations with the 'rebels', was more ambiguous. When the Irish Secretary W. E. Forster demanded the suspension of the Habeas Corpus Act, he threatened to resign. At the NLF meeting of 1881 he described it as 'a blot upon our civilization', although he concluded that 'the ultimate duty of a Liberal was to support and assert the law'.[67] This sense of 'ultimate duty' was compounded, in the summer of 1881, by the news of the shooting and subsequent death of J. A. Garfield, the president of the USA, an appalling crime which strengthened the general revulsion against terrorism and political violence felt by the British public.

---

[63] J.Chamberlain to Sir C. Dilke, 27 Oct. 1880, JC 5/24/296. For the reluctance of the three Liberal leaders to adopt coercion see Chamberlain to Gladstone, 14 Dec. 1881, and Gladstone's reply to Chamberlain, 15 Dec. 1881, in Gladstone Papers, Add. MSS. 44125, respectively ff. 102–3, 104–5, 106. While rejecting 'coercion', Gladstone concluded: 'but without doubt there is great & formidable mischief to deal with, and the Government will act free and boldly in support of the law as it is now doing, and with any additional improvement of means which experience may suggest'.

[64] Hall, *Civilising subjects*, 428–30.

[65] Mundella to Leader, 12 Mar. 1881, in Leader papers, Sheffield Univ. Library (emphasis in the original).

[66] Cited in Robbins, *John Bright*, 242. This view was shared by Mundella and other radicals: Mundella to Leader, 15 Jan. 1881, in Leader Papers, Sheffield Univ. Library.

[67] Chamberlain, *Home Rule and the Irish question*, 27.

The twin pillars of Chamberlain's alternative strategy for the pacification of Ireland were further land reform and local government. Radical land reform was a policy with impeccable liberal credentials, going back to J. S. Mill's 1868 pamphlet *England and Ireland*, in which the philosopher had indicated that nothing else could avert the spread of nationalism among the peasants. Likewise, in 1880–1 Chamberlain demanded drastic reform both as a means to an end – in his case, Parnell's defeat – and as an end in itself. Eventually he was persuaded to accept further coercion, but only in response to Parnell's open defiance of the law and challenge to the unity of the kingdom. As he wrote to Dilke, he had reached the conclusion 'that Parnell has now gone beyond us. He acts for No Rent and Separation, and I am not prepared to say that the refusal of such terms as these constitutes an Irish grievance.'[68] The passing of the 1881 Land Act had removed '[t]he chief grievance' – now the agitators' object was to create 'sentimental' ones for subversive purposes, pursued through terrorism and intimidation. 'It is, therefore, war to the knife between a despotism created to re-establish constitutional law, and a despotism not less complete elaborated to subvert law and produce anarchy as a precedent to revolutionary changes.'[69] However, he felt that the Liberal government was in a quandary. On the one hand, it could get away with further coercion in the short term for '[t]he parties aimed at are not very popular anywhere, and infernal machines, [US President] Garfield's assassination, Fenianism, etc., will all be so mixed up in people's minds with what is proposed, that I think it would pass without objection'. On the other, he saw little prospect of coercion succeeding in the medium term, because putting down the League 'would involve so many questions affecting public agitation in this country that the radicals would surely be up in arms'. Significantly he concluded: 'the Tories might do it, if they were in office, which I wish to God they were'.[70]

Over the next few years Chamberlain's outlook continued to be dominated by the tension between his determination to preserve the unity of the kingdom, and his genuine wish to reform and democratize Ireland. For example, in 1882 he suggested to Gladstone that he appoint an Irishman, W. Shaw, to the position of Chief Secretary, and added: 'I know it may be objected that he was the former leader of the Home Rule Party but I do not attach much weight to this. Home Rule may mean

[68] J. Chamberlain to C. Dilke, 4 Oct. 1881, in JC 5/24/304.
[69] J. Chamberlain to J. Morley, 18 Oct. 1881, in Chamberlain, *Political memoir*, 18.
[70] J. Chamberlain to C. Dilke, 4 Oct. 1881, in JC 5/24/304.

anything – including local government.'[71] And as late as 1885 he denounced Dublin Castle rule as a system 'founded on the bayonets of 30,000 soldiers encamped permanently as in a hostile country' and comparable to Russian government over Poland. He demanded 'the concession to Ireland of the right to govern itself in matters of its purely domestic business'.[72] Moreover, despite his later, and largely correct, claim that the Home Rule question played no role in the general election, in February 1885 he had actually stressed that the reform of the Irish system of government was part of *the work to which the new Parliament will be called*.[73] As we have seen (chapter 1, pp. 7–8), this was a widely held view within the Liberal leadership in 1885.

The real question, however, concerned the extent and purpose of reform. In December 1884 Chamberlain outlined an Irish Board with wide-ranging powers and allowed W. H. Duignan to circulate its details informally. In January 1885, through O'Shea, he discussed Parnell's proposal for county councils and a Central Board.[74] In March of that year he produced a memorandum envisaging a different scheme, with the creation of two 'Provincial Legislative Assemblies' for Ireland, '[o]ne to represent the three Southern Provinces of Munster, Connaught, & Leinster, and to sit in Dublin' and the other 'such part of Ulster as may choose to be so represented, & to sit in Belfast'. Fully aware of the complexities of Ulster's religious and political geography, he suggested that '[t]he Counties of Ulster might be allowed to vote whether they would be represented in the Belfast or the Dublin Assembly', and reflected on the question as to whether 'any of the Counties in Connaught or Leinster have a right to be represented at Belfast if they prefer it'.[75]

It was a detailed and carefully thought-out proposal, which specified the functions of the assemblies and imposed rigid limits to their powers chiefly with regard to the preservation of religious equality and civil rights. In some respects, Chamberlain relied for a model on the 1867 British North America Act, but made it clear beyond any doubt that the imperial Parliament would remain sovereign: for example, it could make 'remedial legislation for the due execution of this Act' if 'any Provincial law is

---

[71] J. Chamberlain to Gladstone, 2 May 1882, in Gladstone Papers, Add. MSS. 44125, ff. 136–7.
[72] MS report of a speech delivered on 17 June 1886, in Gladstone Papers, Add. MSS 44126, ff. 91–2 and *Birmingham Daily Post*, 22 May 1885.
[73] Gladstone Papers, Add. MSS 44126, ff. 91–92 (underlined in the original).
[74] Hammond, *Gladstone and the Irish nation*, 366.
[75] 'Secret. Extension of local government in Ireland', n.d. [probably March 1885], JC 8/5/1/16.

declared to be illegal or ultra vires, and in case Provincial Legislatures fail to take the necessary steps to give effects to the decisions, or to carry out this Act'. Although he relinquished this plan in April in favour of the better-known Central Board scheme – which Chamberlain was misled to believe would be more acceptable to Parnell – the March proposal was remarkable for its clarity and internal consistency, as well as for its compatibility with the preservation of imperial sovereignty, and indeed for the extent to which it anticipated partition as the logical consequence of self-government. In both cases it was evident that Chamberlain regarded Irish self-government as 'the only hope of ultimately securing better relations between the two countries'.[76] It was also clear that his proposed Irish authorities would only 'deal with what may be called *local national questions*; as, for instance, Education in all its forms including endowed schools; -public works; -lunatic asylums &c &c'.[77]

Hence the yawning chasm between his and Gladstone's approach to the question. For Gladstone Irish self-government was about undoing the wrong caused by Pitt's Union which had '[*destroyed] the national life of Ireland*'; he thought of the future of Britain and Ireland in terms of a dual monarchy – linking different nations, like Austria and Hungary.[78] While it is not accurate to say that Chamberlain had always been against Home Rule, the latter had long been an ambiguous concept and, at least from 1880, for him it was a useful one only in so far as it could help in consolidating the national life and purpose of the United Kingdom as a whole by means of adequate devolution to *provincial* authorities.[79]

Yet, when the two leaders met at Hawarden on 7–8 October 1885, Gladstone was vague and 'very sweet on National Councils'.[80] Here was a grey area in their policy plans, but it was one which allowed for misunderstanding rather than compromise and conciliation. This was indicated by the fact that while the GOM found Parnell's last speech 'satisfactory', or at least 'more moderate', Chamberlain thought that the Irish leader 'was not to be depended upon. He will not stick to any minimum . . . he must go for a separate independent Parliament.'[81] Temperamentally, the two men could hardly have been more different, with Gladstone looking

[76] Memo dated 11 Apr. 1885, JC 8/5/1/11. For the Irish MPs' response see T. P. O'Connor, *Memoirs of an old parliamentarian* (1929), vol. I, 350–1.

[77] JC 8/5/1/11 (emphasis in the original). On the making of the scheme cf. C. H. D. Howard, 'Joseph Chamberlain, Parnell and the Irish "central board" scheme, 1884–5', *Irish Historical Studies*, 8 (1953), 324–63.

[78] In conversation with Lord Derby, cited in Garvin, *Chamberlain*, vol. II, 111 (emphasis in the orginal).

[79] J. Loughlin, 'Joseph Chamberlain', 211.

[80] Chamberlain to Dilke, 7 Oct. 1885, Garvin, *Chamberlain*, vol. II, 107.

[81] Ibid., 107–8, and Chamberlain to Gladstone, 26 Oct. 1885, ibid., 114.

(in Garvin's words) 'prophetic' and 'blazing', while his junior colleague was 'hardy and cool'. Where the former saw a historic opportunity, the latter saw a major threat.

It was not simply, as Garvin wrote, that '[o]ne was full of the Irish Question and hardly considered the social question', while the other was 'full of the social question', regarding Ireland as secondary. It was also that for Chamberlain's strategy to solve both the Irish and the social question demanded the preservation of the Union, which Gladstone now regarded as a constitutional quagmire. As Chamberlain wrote to John Morley, 'I do not believe that there is anything between National Councils and absolute Separation . . . it seems to be most mischievous and inexpedient to raise false hopes by vague generalities and to talk of maintaining the Unity of the Empire while granting Home Rule.'[82] And to Labouchere he expressed his conviction that '[t]here is only one way of giving *bona fide* Home Rule, which is the adoption of the American Constitution', with '[s]eparate legislatures for England, Scotland, Wales and possibly Ulster. The other three Irish provinces might combine', as he had already suggested in his memorandum about Provincial Legislatures. Westminster would continue to control 'Foreign and Colonial affairs, Army, Navy, Post Office and Customs'. Finally, he envisaged '[a] Supreme Court to arbitrate on respective limits of authority'.[83] It was the clearest and boldest plan of constitutional reform to be conceived by a British statesman in the nineteenth or, for that matter, the twentieth century. Britain adopting 'the American Constitution' could be a drastic and revolutionary step quite uncalled for except to appease the Irish Nationalists.[84] Yet the notion that Home Rule implied the creation of a 'Supreme Court . . . master of both Parliaments . . . humiliating our Imperial Parliament . . . and depriving it of the power it exercises for the general good of the State', remained part of the Liberal Unionist case.[85]

Of particular importance, again, was Chamberlain's concern for Ulster, one which he shared with both John Bright and Lord Spencer.[86] In particular, Chamberlain reckoned that without the Union there was no future for either civil and religious liberty or economic progress in Ireland, and indeed for the United Kingdom if it allowed a vocal but insignificant minority of short-sighted farmers and self-interested politicians on the periphery to break away. Other leading Liberals – including the

---

[82] On 24 Dec. 1885, ibid., 147. [83] On 26 Dec. 1885, ibid., 145.
[84] Chamberlain to C. Dilke, 28 Dec. 1885, JC 5/24/446.
[85] 'A working man's appeal to his fellow-workmen', *The Liberal Unionist*, Aug. 1888, 4–5. On the debate see Collini, *Public moralists*, 287–301.
[86] Lord Spencer to C. Boyle, 20 Sep. 1885, in Gordon, *The Red Earl*, vol. II, 75.

anti-imperialist Leonard Courtney and John Bright – fully agreed: national interest, individual liberty, the cause of progress in Ireland and the greatness of Britain in the world, all depended on the preservation of the Union.[87]

Chamberlain's doctrine amounted to something like secularized Erastianism, the traditional Whig approach to ecclesiastical matters, which insisted on parliamentary control as the only guarantee against the rise of religious fanaticism. For Chamberlain Parliament was to be the adjudicator between rival sectarian and sectionalist claims in the social and economic conflict between classes. The weakness of his approach was that, although he identified correctly the direction in which British politics was moving, his intuition was relevant only in the long run. In general, at the time '[t]he urban working classes were apparently less socialistic in their appetites than he had assumed'.[88] Even in the case of 'free' education – an old radical mantra – rate-payers were afraid that it would actually result in a major increase in the burden of local taxation. On the whole, however, Chamberlain turned out to be 'ahead' of popular radicalism not only in 1885, but also during the following years, when he outlined his old age pensions proposal.[89] Although the latter might be expected to have been a vote winner, popular responses highlighted the extent to which self-help – and in particular the friendly societies as providers of relief – continued to define public expectations in matters of social reform.[90] To some extent Gladstone's 1886 Irish Land Purchase Bill suffered from a similar problem, namely persistent popular horror at state expenditure, compounded, in his case, by the impression that the proposed Bill would involve 'a gigantic piece of class legislation', whose primary aim was to rescue the Irish landowners from the revengeful

---

[87] 'I am against anything in the shape or taking the name of a Parlt. in Dublin, & will not go to the Colonies for an example for us. The Canadian Confederation is even now showing symptoms of breaking down – and I wish to maintain the unity of the Govt.' (J. Bright to J. Chamberlain, 9 June 1886, in JC 5/7/30.) Cf. L. Courtney to John Scott in 1887, cited in E. Stokes, 'Milnerism', *Historical Journal*, 5, 1 (1962), 47–8: 'I see the contagion of Home Rule is extending to India as we know it must. How you on the spot must groan over such premature encouragement to foolhardiness. I don't fancy this trouble will become serious in our time; but the working man voter would think no more of giving up India than of giving up Ireland, not caring to inquire seriously what would be the fate of either when abandoned.'

[88] Marsh, *Chamberlain*, 209, 213.

[89] From April 1891, and developed in a series of publications including his 'Favourable aspects of state socialism', *North American Review*, May 1891; 'Old age pensions', *The Liberal Unionist*, July 1891, 228; 'Old age pensions', *National Review*, 18 February 1892, 721–39; 'The labour question', *Nineteenth Century*, 32, November 1892, 677–710; and 'Old age pensions and friendly societies', *National Review*, 24 January 1895, 592–615.

[90] Rep., 'Mr Chamberlain and the pension system', *WT&E*, 17 May 1891, 9; 'Social reforms', *LW*, 14 Oct. 1894, 8.

legislation likely to be enacted by a Nationalist Parliament in case Home Rule was passed.[91] Eventually the 1903 Wyndham Act together with the previous land purchase measures passed between 1885 and 1896 proved even more expensive. Nevertheless, in the short run at least, Salisbury offered the old, reassuring Gladstonian mixture of constitutional consolidation and financial retrenchment, reversing the 'profligate expenditure' of the last Liberal government 'without the services being impoverished'.[92]

Chamberlain was closer to the prevalent mood of popular Unionist Radicals in the area of more conventional domestic reforms, which were consistent with self-help and could provide a platform around which all 'true Liberals' could unite. In particular the land laws could be reformed: through 'free trade in land', 'the number of the owners of the soil must be largely increased; the conditions of the agricultural labourers must be improved; charities and endowments require to be overhauled in respect of the rights of the poor [and] there must be an extension of local government on a popular basis'.[93] Again, after 1886 such demands were no longer specifically Liberal: indeed Chamberlain insisted that there was 'a better chance of really popular reform from a Unionist Government than from the Parnell–Gladstone [alliance]'.[94] He was echoed not only by the Unionist quality press, but more significantly by the London penny weeklies, which expressed their confidence that, provided 'the Tory party sees that it must keep its bargain with the Liberal Unionists', 'Englishmen of ordinary common sense . . . have no objection . . . to secure by Tory aid solid legislative benefits which are apparently not worth the consideration of those Liberals who . . . see nothing worth living [for] but the accomplishment of the separation of the three kingdoms.'[95]

There was the promise that other 'solid fruits of true Liberal legislation' would follow – reforms 'likely to work silent revolutions', such as the 1887 Tithes Bill and the Land Transfer Bill, which was expected to abolish primogeniture, 'making land transfer as easy as that of

[91] 'A working man', 'A working man's reasons', and 'Reformer of 1832', 'Mr Gladstone on Home Rule and temperance', in *The Scotsman*, 3 July 1886, 12; for similar views see also l.a., '£150,000,000', *WT*, 2 May 1886, 8–9.

[92] L.a., 'Mr Gladstone at Nottingham', *WT&E*, 23 Oct. 1887, 8. For the cost of the Unionist land purchase policy see B. Solow, *Land question and the Irish economy, 1870–1903* (1971).

[93] L.a., 'Who are true Liberals?', *LW*, 19 June 1887, 1; l.a., 'Allotments for labourers', *WT&E*, 10 July 1887, 6.

[94] Cited in M. C. Hurst, 'Joseph Chamberlain, the Conservatives and the succession to John Bright, 1886–89', *Historical Journal*, 7, 1 (1964), 91.

[95] L.a., 'The fruits of Liberal-Unionism', *WT&E*, 17 Apr. 1887, 9.

Consols'.[96] However, these disappeared in the so-called 'Massacre of the Innocents' at the end of the 1887 parliamentary session – being crowded out by more urgent and less radical Bills. Eventually the 1888 and 1889 Local Government Acts achieved what was described as practical 'Home Rule' for Scotland, as well as for England and Wales.[97] Indeed in Scotland there was a feeling among members of the Land Law Reform Association that Chamberlain remained more interested in their griev-ances than the Gladstonian Liberals were.[98] Free education was actually introduced in 1891, and, although it failed to impress some Nonconformists, it did provide some evidence that Liberal Unionism was working for the people.[99] On balance, however, in the early 1890s Radical Unionism continued to be about traditional 'popular liberal' causes.

Coercion, for the sake of civil and religious liberty

Thus, although there was no consensus on the specifics of the radical agenda, there was a link between the Union and social reform: as 'A Scottish Workman' commented in 1886, '[w]e are all yet living under some unequal laws, but these will be removed more speedily and more fairly by one united democracy as a first motive power, with a simple sense of justice springing from the bosom of the people.'[100] While in the second half of the 1880s even the USA was reputed to be abandoning states' rights for 'consolidated institutions' at its centre, '[t]he fatal blot in Mr Gladstone's new policy is … his false admission that the United Parliament has at last proved a failure; that whatever we owe Ireland is far too great a debt to be discharged by the united wisdom and the united resources of the three Kingdoms'.[101] In particular, Ireland needed 'the concentration of the attention of the people in the pursuit of industry, and time for the remedial measures of last session to work. Substantial justice

---

[96] 'The fruits of Liberal Unionism', *WT&E*, 17 Apr. 1887, 8; l.a., 'The session and the Union', *LW*, 24 July 1887, 1.

[97] 'Home Rule for England', *WT&E*, 25 Mar. 1888, 9; 'Home Rule for Scotland', *WT&E*, 14 Apr. 1889, 9. The measures alluded to were the County Councils Act of 1888 and the equivalent Bill for Scotland, passed in 1889.

[98] See reports by the secretaries of the Caithnesshire Liberal Association and of the Kingussie Liberal Association, meeting of the Western Committee of the Scottish Liberal Association, Glasgow, 26 June 1889, in Scottish Liberal Association, Minutes, vol. I, 219–21.

[99] 'What the Unionist government has done for the working man', *The Liberal Unionist*, June 1891, 205. For a Gladstonian Nonconformist dismissal of Unionist free education see 'Politics', *Primitive Methodist Quarterly Review*, July 1891, 567–8.

[100] 'What the Unionist government has done'.

[101] L.a., 'Surrender and despair', *WT&E*, 2 Feb. 1890, 8.

has been done by the Imperial Parliament, thereby taking away the strongest pretext for the Home Rule cry.'[102]

From this point of view, even 'Home Rule All Round' was undesirable, for it would turn the United Kingdom into a 'nineteenth-century Heptarchy', saddling Ireland with an 'insignificant' national Parliament which would represent the interests of a class (the farmers) rather than a 'nationality'.[103] Indeed 'Home Rule All Round' might be even worse than simple Irish Home Rule, for the latter was like '[inoculating] the United Kingdom with a mild virus . . . in the hope of thus preventing the disease from becoming more dangerous', while the former amounted to inoculating the 'virus' 'with the special purpose of developing and intensifying the disease all round'.[104] Likewise, while Chamberlain declared himself in favour of imperial federation as early as 1888, the idea was dismissed in the *Liberal Unionist* on the basis of all sorts of practical objections – from reluctance to meddle with an imperial system which worked well as it stood, to scepticism as to whether the colonial governments would really tolerate any pooling of legislative powers.[105]

Liberalism stood for 'independence', both national and individual, but also insisted on civil and religious liberty, the rule of law, and peaceful and ordered progress. The last three were the values stressed by the Radical Unionists. The view that they ought to be enforced at all costs was linked to the 'muscular' trend in Victorian culture, with its admiration for the Spartan 'democratic' features of contemporary Germany as a well-ordered society with its peasant farmers and popular militia.[106] Chamberlain, despite having built his career and reputation as an advocate of participatory democracy, had no time for those like Schnadhorst

---

[102] L.a., 'This vexed Irish question', *LW*, 2 Oct. 1887, 1

[103] E. Myers, 'The nationalities of the United Kingdom', *The Liberal Unionist*, 27 Apr. 1887, 66–7; and letter from 'A Congregationalist Minister', ibid., 4 May 1887, 93 (opening quotation for this chapter) which proposes an interesting conceptual distinction between 'nation' (the UK) and 'nationalities'. Home Rule All Round was more popular in Scotland, among both Gladstonians and Unionists; see Hutchison, *A political history of Scotland*, 173 and Cameron, *Mackintosh*, 3. See also pp. 96, 100–1. George Canning's claim that the repeal of the Union would bring about a regression to the anarchy and impotence of the Heptarchy had been reintroduced into the Home Rule debate by Thomas MacKnight of the *Northern Whig* in October 1885: MacKnight, *Ulster as it is*, vol. II, 98–9.

[104] E. Dawson, 'Home Rule All Round', *The Liberal Unionist*, June 1890, 204–5.

[105] Hurst, 'Chamberlain and Bright', 90. Cf. T. Raleigh, 'Imperial federation and Home Rule', *The Liberal Unionist*, Sep. 1888, 17–18 and l.a., 'Imperial federation', ibid., July 1891, 226–7.

[106] L.a., 'Landed tenure: tenant farmers versus landed proprietors', *RN*, 29 Sep. 1867, 4; l.a., 'The Irish Land Commission', *NW*, 24 July 1880, 4; but see also *FJ*, 17 Feb. 1880, 4.

or the Lib-labs, let alone Gladstone, who seemed to regard the process as more important than the actual result. He compared politics, including its parliamentary variety, to a profession, such as the medical one,[107] which required the centralization of power in the hands of men of proven ability and integrity (a further way in which he was closer to the high Utilitarianism of the Indian Council than to those operating within the J. S. Mill tradition).

Although Chamberlain himself embodied such 'muscular' radicalism, the latter was most effectively articulated for the benefit of the artisan classes by *Lloyd's Weekly* and the *Weekly Times & Echo*. These two widely circulated penny papers were already pursuing a no-nonsense approach to the agitation in Ireland in 1881–5 when they dismissed both the 'land war' and Home Rule as 'seditious agitations' brought about by Tory misrule and Liberal timidity with regard to helping the country to 'progress out of distress'.[108] They advocated a two-pronged strategy consisting of repression and equitable land reform, in the conviction that, although the Land Leaguers were a reckless minority to be put down, the social grievances which they exploited to subvert the tenant farmers were genuine and should be redressed. They also echoed the widespread notion that reforms should not precede the restoration of order, because the British government could not 'stoop to make terms with law-breakers'. As one Nonconformist Unionist put it, this was '[the] just and Christian way' of dealing with Ireland.[109] Chamberlain argued that coercion was about protecting, indeed *freeing* the law-abiding majority from the terror of the moonlighters: '[a] law of this kind ... becomes tyranny in the hands of tyrants, but in the hands of men who are liberal and just may be a law of protection and of great mercy to Ireland'.[110]

The Phoenix Park assassinations in May 1882, the even more atrocious Maamtrasna murders in August (when a whole family was slaughtered), further assassinations and murder attempts, and finally the publication of the results of the police inquiries all contributed to consolidating, even within Liberal circles, the impression that coercion was inevitable for the defeat of a large-scale criminal conspiracy.[111] British public opinion was both genuinely shocked by the extent to which rural Ireland appeared to be in the grip of organized criminal gangs and perplexed by the utter

---

[107] E. E. Gullie, *Joseph Chamberlain and English social politics* (1926), 252–3. Cf. J. Chamberlain in *The Nineteenth Century*, 32 (1892), 688–9.

[108] L.a., 'The end of Tory rule', *WT&E*, 4 Apr. 1880, 4.

[109] *The Baptist Magazine*, May 1886, 230.

[110] John Bright's words, cited as conclusive evidence in l.a., 'Coercion', *LW*, 30 Jan. 1881, 6.

[111] T. Corfe, *The Phoenix Park murders* (1968), 230–64. Cf. Davitt, *Fall of feudalism*, 381–2.

exoticism and mystery of it all.[112] The reports and telegrams from the troubled areas regularly published in the metropolitan press, the parliamentary debates which filled column upon column in the newspapers, the extraordinary difficulties encountered by the Irish Secretary W. E. Forster in his well-meaning but ill-fated attempts to improve the country's situation – all suggested that Britain was dealing with an alien and inexplicable reality: '[t]he very air', wrote Lord Carlingford in 1885, 'seems charged with hostility and hatred towards England and towards Irishmen also of my class'.[113] Two years earlier, the Liberal Chief Secretary, G. O. Trevelyan, had similarly observed that '[t]he effect of getting used to what is bad in Ireland is that you get more and more disgusted with the whole thing. The perversity of everybody who either writes or speaks is something inconceivable.' He concluded that '[i]f these people were left to themselves, we should have a mutual massacre'.[114] Even Parnell was said to be living in fear that he would be assassinated if he did not appear to 'deliver' concessions from the government.[115] Could the 'Resources of Civilization' yet stop the terror through which the Invincibles and other Fenian sects endeavoured to frustrate the normal operation of civil government and defeat all hopes of peace and progress? Or was Liberalism so 'soft' as to back away from force as a means of executing justice, preserving the peace, protecting life and property, and enforcing the law? Indeed, in 1884–5 the Gordon massacre in Khartoum created the impression that Gladstone could not be trusted in an emergency.[116]

In 1886 the worst type of crisis overwhelmed the Liberal party. For those members in both Parliament and the country who followed Chamberlain, it was not difficult to continue to find plausible reasons to justify further coercion. First, the National League's claim to be the equivalent of a 'trade union' was highly questionable and indeed rejected by members of the British labour movement. Second, even if one wanted to maintain the parallel, there was the fact that under the 1875 Trade

---

[112] Especially in the Maamtrasna case, '[t]he victims, and most of the men accused of the crime, were all called Joyce; those not called Joyce were all called Casey. None of them spoke English.' (Hammond, *Gladstone and the Irish nation*, 316.)

[113] Cited in Geary, *Plan of Campaign*, 8. Forster's honesty and good intentions were acknowledged even by the Nationalists: Davitt, *The fall of feudalism*, 346. For the long-term effects of these reports about episodes of 'cruelty and lawlessness on the English temper' see Hammond, *Gladstone and the Irish nation*, 37–48.

[114] Cited, in O'Farrell, *England and Ireland*, 177.

[115] H. Labouchere to J. Chamberlain, n.d. [June(?) 1882], in Gladstone Papers, Add. MSS 44125, f. 150.

[116] Chamberlain, *Political memoir*, 83. Chamberlain to C. Dilke, 12 Sep. 1884, in JC 5/24/368.

Union Act intimidation and violence were illegal; therefore, in this respect, the Irish Crimes Act was hardly exceptional.[117] Third, despite Nationalist propaganda, only a tiny minority of the farmers – 2–4 per cent[118] – joined the Plan of Campaign: it was possible to claim that they were not 'the masses', but if anything 'the classes', that is, the *criminal* groups intent on terrifying and manipulating public opinion. The case for coercion was constantly kept in the public eye by the steady flow of press reports about 'outrages', including murder and terrorism.[119]

The fact that Roman Catholic priests were occasionally involved in instances of intimidation added to the alarm, irritation and disgust felt by a predominantly Protestant and often anti-clerical readership towards the Nationalists. Dismissing the specifically sectarian dimension of the conflict as marginal, the Liberal Unionists emphasized the allegedly broader aspect of the problem: Ireland was part of a Catholic Europe struggling to free itself from clerical domination. 'When Frenchmen and Italians protest against *Cléricalisme*, no one is so stupid to accuse them of ... "appealing to bigotry". It is in fact against ... the political priest that their protest is made.'[120] Thus some of the men who had supported the Italian *Risorgimento* in the 1860s were attracted by Radical Unionism after 1886.[121]

Indeed, both before and after the Parnell split – which was followed by an upsurge in clerical influence on elections – Mazzini's and Cavour's 'opinion' on Home Rule was posthumously canvassed and quoted with approval (both had been strongly against).[122] By the same token, somewhat inconsistently, the cause of Ulster's freedom was often compared to

---

[117] These points were made, respectively, by 'One of the masses', 'The National League and trade unionism', *The Liberal Unionist*, 22 June 1887, 199; and by G. Pitt Lewis, QC, MP, 'Trade unionism and the National League', ibid., 27 Apr. 1887, 65–6.

[118] O'Brien, *William O'Brien*, 48. Although this glossed over the fact that the Plan was only put into operation on selected estates.

[119] See the reports 'Ireland: the reign of terror in Tipperary: the killing of Captain Plunkett: inhumanity of the Nationalist press', *The Liberal Unionist*, Jan. 1890, 106–7; and 'The Cronin murder trial', ibid., 107–9.

[120] An Irish Liberal, 'The clerical conspiracy in Ireland', *The Liberal Unionist*, May 1891, 181; Isabella Tod, 'The Orange cry', ibid., Aug. 1891, 2–4.

[121] A good example is Bennet Burleigh, a well-known *Daily Telegraph* correspondent who had served with Garibaldi in Sicily in 1860 (throughout the rest of his life he continued to be interested in the Garibaldian movement, reporting the operation of the Italian Legion in the 1896 Greek-Turkish war). In 1886 Burleigh stood unsuccessfully as a Liberal Unionist candidate. However, this was not a sign of incipient Conservatism: on the contrary, in 1892 he stood as a Labour candidate, proclaiming himself a radical and a socialist. (*ODNB*, vol. VIII, 866–8, A. Viotti, *Garibaldi: the revolutionary and his men* (Poole, 1979), 196–7, and information in the author's personal possession.)

[122] 'Mazzini and the Irish question, by one of his friends [P. A. Taylor]', *The Liberal Unionist*, Dec. 1887, 77; 'Cavour's opinion as to Home Rule', ibid., Aug. 1892, 13.

that of Italian independence from the Austrians: the Irish Protestant horror at the idea of subjection to a Home Rule Parliament was 'the same feeling that would make the people of Lombardy or Venice quiver at the bare idea of a revival of Austrian dominion'.[123] Elsewhere in Ireland what was at stake was whether the modern state would be replaced by a latter-day theocracy turning 'Leinster, Munster and Connaught . . . into a new "State of the Church" governed by a secret conclave of bishops in the heart of the British Empire.'[124]

The popular impact of these press reports was compounded by the itinerant propaganda of the Liberal Unionist vans. The latter had been organized in emulation of the Liberal anti-coercion vans, and – like their counterparts – emphasized the emotional side of the Irish question: while the Gladstonians insisted on the inhumanity and brutality of the evictions, the Liberal Unionists depicted the identical aspects of the Nationalist outrages (sometimes with the help of a stereoptican projector and slides).[125] Given that ordinary law was not obeyed in Ireland, it was pointless for Liberals to shut their eyes to the violent reality that impelled the government to introduce special criminal laws. The latter 'can only affect the guilty . . . all others are perfectly safe and exempt from its provisions . . . It simply affords protection to the law abiding, and provides the machinery of justice, which is now lacking, for criminals.'[126] Besides Chamberlain, other leading Nonconformist Liberals such as R. W. Dale and John Bright – who had supported Gladstonian coercion in 1881–2 – now stressed again that 'it [was] one of the elementary duties of Government to provide for the detection and punishment of crime' and confirmed their support for 'measures of repression for the sake of law and order'.[127] In September 1887 and again in October 1888 Bright publicly denounced Gladstone's duplicity, pointing out that his government had implemented equally arbitrary and severe coercion Bills in 1881–2 – measures which Bright had endorsed in the same spirit in

---

For the impact of the Nationalist split on this aspect of Liberal Unionism see 'An Irish Unionist', 'McCarthytes and imperial supremacy', ibid., Aug. 1891, 161, and E. Dawson, ' "Popery" and "clericalism" ', ibid., Dec. 1891, 8.

[123] E. Dawson, 'The shadow of the sword', *The Liberal Unionist*, Sep. 1890, 21.

[124] An Irish Liberal, 'The clerical conspiracy in Ireland: II.', *The Liberal Unionist*, June 1891, 201–3. Cf. J. Loughlin, 'Imagining "Ulster": the north of Ireland and British national identity, 1880–1921', in S. J. Connolly (ed.), *Kingdoms united? Great Britain and Ireland since 1500* (Dublin, 1999).

[125] Rep., 'Union Jack vans', *The Liberal Unionist*, June 1890, 217; on their role see Goodman, 'The Liberal Unionist party',121.

[126] L.a., 'Ireland, Parliament and the Speaker', *LW*, 10 Apr. 1887, 1.

[127] 'Dr Dale on the Crimes Bill', *The Liberal Unionist*, 27 Apr. 1887, 70; 'Mr Bright and coercion', ibid., 4 May 1887, 87.

which he endorsed Balfour's Crimes Act in 1887.[128] Gladstone's own words of 1882 – when he denounced boycotting as 'combined intimidation made use of for the purpose of destroying private liberty' – were now quoted against him to show the inconsistency and opportunism of his stance, in contrast to Liberal Unionist integrity and high-mindedness.[129]

Viewed in this context of continuity, and sanctioned as it was by the authority of reputedly incorruptible and disinterested Liberal leaders, Gladstone's anti-coercion agitation appeared foolish and naive: 'How is it that the coercion or punishment of criminals raises such pious horror in England and there is not a word of sympathy for the honest labourer, tradesman or farmer coerced grievously by the National League? (For, recollect, it is hardly the wealthy aristocrat that is boycotted).'[130] Gladstone '[had] thrown the aegis of his great name over anarchy and disorder',[131] having himself lost all respect for the law. His arguments in defence of the League could be 'as legitimately applied to the defence of the Gunpowder Plot, or of any other attempt at rebellion or assassination recorded in our history', and amounted to a 'new doctrine that a man may choose which laws he would obey', a doctrine which was 'a treason to democracy'.[132]

Thus, as Judd has pointed out, the Radical Unionists played the 'anti-terrorist card' in the attempt to generate an emotional response and the cry of 'no surrender' – namely, that Britain would never submit to 'the dagger of the assassin . . . and the threats of conspirators and rebels'.[133] By contrast, what Gladstone proposed was, allegedly, unconditional surrender. The age believed, as Romani has put it, in 'the primacy, logical and historical, of national character over institutions'[134] and rural unrest was taken as evidence of sad deficiencies in the Irish character. How could any true lover of liberty seriously consider the establishment of a separate Parliament in a country disgraced by 'scenes of inhuman outrage . . . when scoundrels shoot old men in the legs' and 'mock and jeer at the widow of

---

[128] See 'Mr Bright and the North Hunts election', *The Liberal Unionist*, Sep. 1887; and his letter of 9 Dec. 1887, published in ibid., January 1888, 87.

[129] 'The Liberal Unionist party and coercion', *The Liberal Unionist*, July 1888, 177; it was an editorial and included a reprint of a Unionist leaflet endorsed by Lord Hartington.

[130] Letter by 'An Irish Radical', *The Scotsman*, 29 Apr. 1886, 7.

[131] L.a., 'Recruiting at Nottingham', *LW*, 23 Oct. 1887, 1.

[132] 'The coercion debate', *WT&E*, 1 July 1888, 8; 'Mr Chamberlain and the work of reform', *LW*, 24 Feb. 1889, 1.

[133] Judd, *Radical Joe*, 155.

[134] Romani, 'British views on the Irish national character', 195, 206. See also S. Collini, 'The idea of "character" in Victorian thought', *Transactions of the Royal Historical Society*, 5th series, 35 (1985), 29–50, and H. A. McDougall, *Racial myth in English history* (1982).

the man whom they have assassinated'?[135] Such a Parliament would inevitably consist of terrorists like O'Donovan Rossa, the man who had directed the first nationalist bombing campaign in mainland Britain in 1881–5.[136]

Yet, from the Radical Unionists' point of view these arguments were uncomfortably double edged because they implied that the terrorists enjoyed actual *democratic* support and legitimacy in Ireland. If that was granted, then it was difficult to escape the Gladstonian conclusion that only Home Rule could pacify Ireland. One way around this embarrassing conclusion was to stress that the Irish party did not consist *entirely* of terrorists, but of three distinct groups: first, there was a 'genuine' constitutional section, including 'some honest and able men, smitten with the dual Parliament craze'; then there were the 'malcontents' and 'blind partisans' of all descriptions; and finally there were 'Michael Davitt and his more or less unscrupulous associates' closely linked to 'the violent Fenian section of the irreconcilables'.[137] In other words, terrorists could 'infiltrate' the National party and mislead – or intimidate – electors into supporting them. This analysis had a further important implication. If the Nationalists were either easily gullible idealists or separatists and rebels, then, in the event of a future European war, the country over which they held sway would be a potential enemy, as it had been in 1798 when the rebels tried to stab Britain in the back as the latter was facing a French invasion. Thus, if such was the case, coercion was a question of national security, rather than merely a matter of law and order.[138]

This 'patriotic' argument was particularly endorsed by John Bright. From as early as October 1881 he had warned that Parnell's 'main object [was] a break-up of the United Kingdom for he hates us & England even more than he loves Ireland'. Bright was despondent about the prospects of democracy in Ireland where he saw little opposition to 'the rebel faction led by Parnell', and 'no expression of opinion in support of public law & public order' – a situation which he attributed to the absence of a 'middle class as there [was] in England'. Partly as a consequence, he was more inclined to endorse the use of military force in Ireland than in Egypt, his main qualification being that '[u]nfortunately when disaffection takes the shape of passive resistance it cannot be successfully met by troops and

---

[135] 'The prospects of Liberal re-union', *LW*, 13 Mar. 1887, 1.
[136] Letter by 'A Dumfriesshire Liberal' to *The Scotsman*, 8 July 1886, 10.
[137] 'The end of Parnellism', *WT&E*, 16 Sep. 1888, 8.
[138] L.a, 'Mr Balfour and Ireland', *LW*, 18 Dec. 1887, 1; l.a., 'Irish facts and fiction', *LW*, 2 Sep. 1888, 1; l.a., 'What is meant by Home Rule?', *LW*, 2 Dec. 1888, 1; W. Morrison, 'A vital question', *The Liberal Unionist*, 1 June 1887, 145–6.

constabulary'.[139] In 1884, during the discussions which preceded the
Redistribution Bill, he urged Gladstone to keep the Irish representation
at over one hundred MPs, as in the Act of Union, and to retain two-
member constituencies.[140] The first measure would counteract the
Nationalist claim that Ireland was powerless within the Union; hopefully
the second would provide a measure of 'proportionality' in the parliamentary representation of political opinion – helping to preserve Irish Liberals
from the electoral extinction anticipated by Lord Spencer, on the basis of
his detailed knowledge of the country.[141] With the 1885 Redistribution
Act, Ireland did not lose seats, despite being over-represented in relation to
its population. Thus in 1886 Bright could claim that, within the Union, the
Irish had no reasonable constitutional grievance to complain of: in fact they
were as well represented at Westminster as the southern states had been in
the US Congress before the Civil War.

This was a historical parallel of which Bright was particularly fond. In
rejecting Home Rule, he repeated the arguments which in 1861 he had
already used to denounce the Confederates as 'rebels' against the
American Union, within which they had enjoyed all the privileges of full
and equal representation. Accordingly, he also rejected 'any scheme of
federation as shadowed forth by Mr Chamberlain' and objected even
more strongly to Home Rule, which he regarded as 'a surrender all
along the line' to the 'Rebel Party', consigning the hapless Irish, 'including Ulster and all her Protestant families, to what there is of justice and
wisdom in the Irish party now sitting in the Parliament at Westminster'.
Moreover, he argued that Home Rule would create insoluble constitutional difficulties for London, by enabling 'the Rebels' 'to war with
greater effect against the unity of the three kingdoms with no increase of
good to the Irish people'.[142] He believed that '[a] Dublin Parl[iamen]t
would work with constant friction, and would press against any barrier
[Gladstone] might create to keep up the unity of the 3 Kingdoms'.[143] If
Home Rule was granted, he saw no chance of a permanent subordination
of Dublin to London, for '[a] Parliament is a great weapon if once created

[139] Bright to Gladstone, 4 Oct. 1881, in Gladstone Papers, Add. MSS 44113, ff. 160–3.
[140] Bright to Gladstone, 26 Nov. 1884, ibid., ff. 208–9.
[141] It is interesting that at this stage Spencer was actually more optimistic than Bright about
     the results of franchise reform, hoping that, even if the Liberals faced defeat in the short
     term, they would eventually 'again find their place among Irish MPs' and that the
     admission of the labourers would 'moderate' the farmer vote, as well as reduce the
     recruiting pull of the 'outrage mongers' 'if they felt that some of them had a
     Constitutional voice in Public Affairs'. Lord Spencer to Lord Hartington, 21 Oct.
     1883, in Gordon , The Red Earl, vol. I, 254.
[142] Bright to Gladstone, 13 May 1886, in Gladstone Papers, Add. MSS 44113, ff. 224–7.
[143] Walling, The diaries of John Bright, entries for 12 and 20 Mar. 1886, 535–6.

and opened'. This weapon would largely be controlled by foreigners, the Fenian 'gang' of New York, 'by whom outrage and murder were and are deemed patriotism in Ireland, and who collect the funds out of which more than half of the Irish party in the Parliament at Westminster received their weekly and monthly pay'.[144]

As for Gladstone's 'historical' case against the Union as an inequitable arrangement fraudulently imposed on a recalcitrant Ireland, Bright thought it was 'somewhat one-sided, leaving out of view the important minority and the views and feelings of the Protestant and loyal portion of the people'.[145] While most modern historians agree with him against Gladstone on this particular point, Bright's real objection was ultimately that he could not believe the Irish party to consist of men who were either 'honourable' or 'truthful'.

As we have already seen, the link between 'character' and capability for political self-government ran deep in Liberal Unionist arguments: the real Irish question consisted ultimately in the allegedly 'childish' character of the Irish people.[146] This contemptuous attitude was sometimes framed within the language of 'race' – especially in contrasting Irish barbarism and cruelty with Anglo-Saxon loyalty and chivalry. For example, a recurrent Radical Unionist argument consisted in pointing out that, despite the parallels one could trace between the Irish Nationalists and the secessionists of the rebel states, the Confederates were never 'assassins' like the Fenians[147] – a claim which would probably have come as a surprise to William Quantrill and his infamous Raiders.[148] The 'racial' dimension of the Unionist discourse reflected both the influence of pseudo-biological determinism on the post-Darwinian generations and the old fear about peasant 'fanaticism' and violence.

As Catherine Hall has shown, often social and 'racial' concerns were compounded by imperial angst.[149] The extent to which the British identity

---

[144] J. Bright, 'A Parliament in Dublin', *The Liberal Unionist*, Nov. 1887, 50.

[145] Walling, *The diaries of John Bright*, 20 Mar. 1886, 536.

[146] Heyck, *Dimensions*, 29. Robert Lowe and other opponents of electoral reform had said exactly the same about the English working man in 1866.

[147] 'It is something for the English-speaking race to say, that the darkest conspiracy against human liberty the world has ever witnessed [the rebellion of the southern states] was unsullied by the crimes of the assassin, or the dark and tortuous alliance which have been the most formidable resources of Irish conspirators and their allies.' L.a., 'State rights and Home Rule', *WT&E*, 17 Feb. 1889, 8; for the 'innate' murderous proclivities of the Irish peasant see 'The Clan-Na-Gael: alleged murder of Mr M'Inery', *WT&E*, 7 July 1889, 18.

[148] Among their exploits there was the massacre of some two hundred men and boys in Lawrence, Kansas, in August 1863. On the topic see R. S. Brownlee, *Gray ghosts of the Confederacy: guerrilla warfare in the West, 1861–1865* (1986).

[149] Hall, *Civilising subjects*.

was shaped by the empire is controversial, but in the late 1880s concern for its preservation was growing even in Radical circles, especially in England and Scotland.[150] As Chamberlain argued in a speech at Ayr in April 1887, Home Rule was 'a programme which, if successful, [would] overthrow the supremacy of Parliament, destroy the authority of the law, break up the unity of the kingdom, and thus pave the way for the dissolution of the Great Empire which has been the envy and admiration of the world'.[151] Even the otherwise staunchly Gladstonian Nonconformist press was occasionally excited by imperial issues, often displaying ambiguous attitudes to the whole enterprise.[152] Although Dissenter imperialism was primarily motivated by missionary concerns and the anti-slave trade campaign in Africa,[153] their press sometimes covered a wide range of cultural themes. The latter were assessed – even in the most uncompromisingly Gladstonian denominational journals – in ways which revealed not only sectarian prejudice, but also an 'orientalist' outlook, a confident imperialism and a patronizing attitude to other races and creeds.[154] They betrayed a firm belief in the baleful consequences of Catholic culture on national character, and especially on the character of 'inferior' races.[155] Ultimately, they confirm Rebecca Gill's conclusion that the agenda of many (though not all) liberal-humanitarian organizations was based on the conviction that British civilization was the engine of progress and was thus linked to nationalism as much as internationalism and universalism.[156]

---

[150] G. Walker, 'Empire, religion and nationality in Scotland and Ulster before the First World War', in I.S. Wood (ed.), *Scotland and Ulster* (1994), 98–9; Cameron, *Mackintosh*, 165.

[151] L.a., 'Not the way to help Ireland', *LW*, 17 Apr. 1887, 1.

[152] Although scholars disagree on this point: Bebbington, *The Nonconformist conscience*, 106–26; D. Fitzpatrick, 'Ireland and the empire', in Porter, *The Oxford history of the British Empire: the Nineteenth century*, 499; A. Porter, *Religion versus empire? British Protestant missionaries and overseas expansion, 1700–1914* (2004), 280–1, 316–30; Thorne, *Congregational missions*, 89–124; and the splendid analysis of the colonial and missionary 'imagination' of Birmingham Nonconformity in Hall, *Civilising subjects*.

[153] B. Porter, *Critics of empire: British attitudes to colonialism in Africa, 1895–1914* (London, 1968); K. Grant, *A civilised savagery: Britain and the new slaveries in Africa, 1884–1926* (London, 2005).

[154] J. Smith, 'Central Africa and its mission fields', *Primitive Methodist Quarterly Review*, Jan. 1888, 98–108; M. Clarke, 'Australian Aborigines', ibid., Oct. 1889, 623–32; J. Ashworth, 'Mohammedanism in relation to Christian missions', ibid., Jan. 1890, 40–53; G. Lansing Taylor, 'The new Africa', ibid., Apr. 1890, 222–38. Even commentaries on apparently less political topics, such as archaeology in Egypt, displayed this unabashed 'orientalism': for example, the pyramids were dismissed as nothing more than 'the most frightful monuments of despotism to be found anywhere in the world' (W. F. Adeney in *The Congregationalist*, May 1885, 395).

[155] For example see 'Politics', *Primitive Methodist Quarterly Review*, Apr. 1883, 191, and 'Madagascar and France', *The Congregationalist*, Mar. 1885, 226.

[156] Gill, 'Calculating compassion in war', 26–7.

Bearing in mind that Victorian Liberals and Nonconformists often adopted 'culturist', rather than biological, understandings of racial differences, it is not surprising that the Radical Unionist case against Home Rule was partly based on the claim that there were 'great distinctions ... in race and religion between the South and the North'.[157] Jesse Ashworth, in a rare Unionist contribution to the *Primitive Methodist Quarterly*, argued that 'the wide extremes which are found among the population of Ireland in race and creed, temperament and character' would certainly prevent an Irish Parliament from functioning 'with harmony and success'.[158] The Irish displayed a tendency to use 'coercion mixed with cruelty' on each other through boycotting and terrorism.[159]

The cartoonists of *Punch*, *Judy* and other journals developed a full range of ape-like representations of drunk, violent, unruly, irrational Celtic peasants intent on spreading misery and death among their unfortunate compatriots. Claim that this reaction was informed by 'racial' stereotypes has generated considerable heat among historians. In any case it finds parallels in other similarly religious-inspired conflicts: for example, it is reminiscent of the cultural stereotypes which informed German Protestant Liberals in their attitude to Polish Catholic peasants in the religious border regions of the *Kaiserreich*, and, as we have seen, cartoons of southern brigands in the Italian bourgeois press.[160] Moreover, it was neither consistent nor necessarily associated with the imperialist mind-set. For example, in December 1880 General Gordon took issue with the denigrators of the Irish peasants and wrote to *The Times* that 'these people are made as we are, they are patient beyond belief, loyal, but, at the same time, broken spirited and desperate, living on the verge of starvation in places in which we would not keep our cattle'.[161] It is not always easy to assess the evidence, especially in the

---

[157] Cited in rep., 'Mr Chamberlain and the Irish question', *NW*, 24 Apr. 1886, 2. For cultural racism see Hall, *Civilising subjects*, 125–33, 364–6; and B. Porter, *The absentminded imperialists: empire, society and culture in Britain* (2004), 100.

[158] J. Ashworth, 'Symposium: the government of Ireland, especially with reference to Home Rule: third paper', *Primitive Methodist Quarterly Review and Christian Ambassador*, July 1887, 468–8.

[159] 'The new Coercion Bill', *WT&E*, 8 Apr 1887, 8.

[160] H. W. Smith, *German nationalism and religious conflict: culture, ideology, politics, 1870–1914* (1995), 174–5. For the Italian comparison see Scirocco (intro.), *Brigantaggio lealismo repression nel Mezzogiorno*. For the debate on 'racism' and the 'Celts' see R. C. K. Ensor, 'Some political and economic interactions in later Victorian England', in L. Schuyler and H. Ausbel (eds.), *The making of English history* (1952), 534–42; Curtis, *Anglo-Saxons and Celts* and *Apes and angels*; Fitzpatrick, 'Ireland and the empire', 499; and the revisionists critiques of Gilley, 'English attitudes to the Irish in England' and Foster, *Paddy and Mr Punch*, chapter 9.

[161] Cited in Hammond, *Gladstone and the Irish nation*, 196–7.

period 1882–93 when rhetorical hyperbole was the staple diet of each side's description of the other.

Despite the ambiguities of the case, the fact remains that racial differences and related tensions were often mentioned as one of the reasons why North American federalism could not be successfully introduced to the British Isles. Moreover, whether based on 'national character' or on 'race', this dismissal of Irish political integrity was accompanied by a parallel ideology about 'inferior European races' such as the Portuguese who, as one Radical Unionist commentator confidently argued, the British could crush as 'a cleanly man' crushes 'an insect'.[162] Obviously Chamberlain was not the only Nonconformist to have discovered the appeal of new racial theories, nor was Dilke the only Radical to celebrate the triumphs of Anglo-Saxon civilization.[163]

For those of Chamberlain's generation, the defence of religious and ethnic minority rights was also partly linked to this 'racial' aspect of Radical Unionism. They saw the 'Ulster Scots' as a distinct group within Ireland, one with its own views and rights to self-determination to be sheltered from what a Radical elector, writing to Cowen to express his opposition to Home Rule, described as 'the ignorant and fanatical Celts of the South and West of Ireland'.[164] Moreover, they demanded and deserved protection under the Union, especially in view of the fact that they were threatened not only by religious intolerance, but also by Nationalist commercial bigotry in the form of protectionism – a blasphemy for all right-minded Liberals.[165] Ulster stood for all that British popular liberalism had always espoused, including 'independence', resourcefulness, honesty and determination. 'Industrious and prosperous', Anglo-Saxon Ulster should not be 'handed over', 'bound hand and foot', to a bunch of law-breakers and quasi-anarchist Celts, who were agitators today but would be legislators tomorrow.[166]

---

[162] See the leaders 'True Liberal patriotism', *WT&E*, 7 July 1887, 8 and 'The struggle in Africa', ibid., 9 (an article about the Delagoa Bay railway incident); and 'One step more in Africa', *WT&E*, 19 Jan. 1890, 8.

[163] By 1883 Chamberlain had become a reader and an admirer of John Seeley, *The expansion of England* (1882), and, under the influence of his close friend Sir Charles Dilke, he had developed a lively interest in 'Greater Britain'. Dilke and Seeley were two of the influences in the making of Chamberlain's vision of a wider British national identity which would unite English speakers throughout the world (Chamberlain to Dilke, Sep. 1881, cited in S. Gwynn and G. M. Tuckerwell, *The Life of Sir Charles Dilke, MP* (1917), 501). For the Nonconformists see Bebbington, *Nonconformist Conscience*, 106–26.

[164] 'A Native of Newcastle' to J. Cowen, 1 June 1886, in Cowen Papers, B376.

[165] 'Some facts about Home Rule', *WT&E*, 30 Dec. 1888, 9.

[166] Walker, 'Empire, religion and nationality', 103.

Ulster's Liberty

If the Irish people will stand by the English people the hold of the landlords (the real curse of the country) will be reduced in a very few years to a rent charge and a rent charge can be made to disappear in 40 years. That is my remedy to which all others are subsidiary. I dread Ireland being led off on false trails after 'Home Rule', 'Catholic Education' or any other of the cries which false patriots and cunning English politicians will attempt to raise – 'Home Rule' will *never* set the Irish peasants free and 'Catholic Education' will be their curse.[167]

Thus Froude laid out in 1872 what was to remain the Liberal Unionist attitude to the Irish question for the next thirty years. Froude's correspondent was G. C. Mahon, a Protestant Home Ruler who detested Catholic nationalism as consisting of 'Romanism & communism',[168] but abhorred the Union even more. He believed that 'if Home Rule succeeds it will place us Protestants absolutely under the heel of Irish RC priests' and 'nothing but the bad faith, the extortion and violence of England would make the prospect endurable for a moment'. Irish Protestants should therefore work for Home Rule 'but more from good honest detestation of England and from good honest love of Ireland than from any prospect of benefit to themselves'.[169] Ultimately what made Home Rule bearable was '*the nature of the people*, from whom both priests and laity are taken' – alluding to their traditionally deferential attitude towards men of property. If the 'nature of the people' changed, then 'the utmost' that one could hope for was that Protestant landlords would have 'time to "sell out" and leave the country, which [was] to be governed by a majority devoted to Rome and but slightly influenced by abstract ideas of "Civil and religious liberty" '.[170] By 1886 the Land League first and then the National League had deeply changed the way people like

---

[167] J. A. Froude to G. C. Mahon, 29 Oct. 1872 from Ithaca, in NLI, MS 22,201 (emphasis in the original). To Mahon this was tantamount to trying to appease Ireland by implementing legislation based '*on Communist principles* – spoiling one class ostensibly for the benefit of another but really for the sake of the lucre in the shape of political capital which might stick to English fingers in the manipulation of the scheme' (G. Mahon to J. Martin, 4 Nov. 1872, MS 22,201(emphasis in the orginal). Mahon's nationalist correspondent, J. Martin, commented: 'the fun is that you, naturally empathizing, from family connection and education, with the Protestant-Ascendancy Landlord class in Ireland, should write in accord with such sympathy to Froude and should receive from him an answer in which, with cynical candour and true English disdain, he confides to you his desire and policy to ruin the Irish landlords, because they no longer are a support to the English interest' (J. Martin to G. C. Mahon, 21 Nov. 1872, NAI, MS 22,201). This exchange gives an idea of the distrust with which Irish landlords had come to view 'English rule'.
[168] G. C. Mahon to J. Martin, 10 Jan. 1874, NLI, MS 22,203.
[169] G. C. Mahon to J. Martin, 29 Dec. 1874, NAI, MS 22,203 (emphasis in the original).
[170] G. C. Mahon to J. Martin, 10 Jan. 1874, NAI, MS 22,203.

Mahon perceived and assessed 'the nature' of the people, and 'the character of the men to whom power would be given in an Irish parliament' became one of the principal Liberal Unionist objections to Home Rule.[171] As Mahon had prophesied, the consequence was that not only the landowners, but also all the Irish Protestant denominations, including Nonconformist bodies such as the Primitive Methodists and Moravians, became seriously worried about their future under Home Rule.[172] Indeed, the preservation of religious liberty was converted into one of the central tenets of Liberal Unionism in both countries.

Yet, there were important differences between the ways in which the issue was handled, respectively, by the British and by the Irish. The former were eager to stress the dangers of religious persecution and gave prominence to actual episodes of intolerance in south-west Ireland, claiming that they were but a foretaste of a more general hostility.[173] Believing that the Catholic priests exerted 'absolute' control over the minds of the populace, Nonconformist leaders such as John Bright, C. H. Spurgeon, Newman Hall[174] and in particular Joseph Chamberlain[175] felt that under Home Rule Parnell would be unable to control the popish mobs composed of his followers. It is remarkable that such anxieties were shared by people of different social, educational and denominational backgrounds throughout Britain.[176] What is even more surprising is that similar concerns were privately expressed even

---

[171] McCartney, *Lecky*, 124.

[172] They thought that it was 'indisputable' that Home Rule would be *Rome* Rule as a majority of the Nationalist MPs were 'but tools of the Roman Catholic hierarchy'. 'Brief Notes', *The Baptist Magazine*, April 1886, 184; Revd W. Nicholas, *Why are the Methodists of Ireland opposed to Home Rule* (1893), 18.

[173] E.g. rep., 'Religious intolerance in the west of Ireland', *The Liberal Unionist*, 27 July 1887, 283.

[174] Liberal Unionist Association Pamphlets No. 33. *Mr Bright and Mr Spurgeon on the Home Rule Bill* (1886); C. Newman Hall to Gladstone, 21 Jan. 1887, in Gladstone Papers Add. MSS 44188, ff.193–5.

[175] For a few examples see Chamberlain, *Political memoir*, 252 (letter to *The Baptist*, 25 Feb. 1887); and the reports 'Mr Chamberlain's visit to Ulster', *FJ*, 17 Oct. 1887, 5; 'Mr Chamberlain in Edinburgh', *The Liberal Unionist*, Jan. 1892, 105–6; 'Mr Chamberlain and the Nonconformists', ibid., May 1892, 185–6.

[176] Hutchison, *A political history of Scotland*, 162–3; C. M. M MacDonald, 'Locality, tradition and language in the evolution of Scottish Unionism: a case study, Paisley 1886–1910', in Macdonald (ed.), *Unionist Scotland, 1800–1997* (1998), 59; D. Wormell, *Sir John Seeley and the uses of history* (1980), 175; and C. Harvie, *The lights of liberalism: university liberals and the challenge of democracy, 1860–86* (1976), 218ff.; T. Dunne, '*La trahison des clercs*: British intellectuals and the first home-rule crisis', *Irish Historical Studies*, 23, 9 (1982), 134–73; G. Jones, 'Scientists against Home Rule', in D. G. Boyce and A. O'Day (eds.), *Defenders of the Union: survey of British and Irish Unionism since 1801* (2001), 188–208.

by some Gladstonians[177] and indeed by at least one prominent Irish Nationalist leader.[178] As late as 1893 C. P. Trevelyan concluded that 'the retrogressive influence of Catholicism commercially and educationally cannot be exaggerated'.[179] Particularly galling was the charge that the Roman Catholic bishops were imposing 'ecclesiastical government' in Ireland, through their interference in by-elections. Of course, the church had been involved in Irish elections for ages. Although the hierarchy's main victims were the breakaway Parnellites, rejection of 'clerical dictatorship' enabled Chamberlain and others to play off a little rhetorical *Kulturkampf* in the hope of attracting Nonconformist votes.[180]

By contrast, in Ireland, some Liberal Unionists were clearly upset and disgusted by Chamberlain's anti-Catholic antics,[181] while others campaigned to dismantle sectarian segregation, complaining that Home Rule would strengthen it.[182] Even those who in England indulged in sectarian

---

[177] H. Labouchere to J. McCarthy, n.d. [early 1886], NLI, MS 24,958 (5); L. A. Waterman, from Detroit (Michigan) to E. Blake, 2 Mar. 1893, Blake Letters, NLI [779] 4685; A. Drummond and W. Galbraith, Provincial Grand Orange Lodge of Quebec, to E. Blake, 13 Mar. 1893, ibid., [809] 4685.

[178] The latter advised against the abolition of an upper house in the second Home Rule Bill, in view of the fact that Ireland had neither statesmen of 'moderate and cautious views', nor '[a] fine class of yeomanry', and as a consequence there was justified 'anxiety as to partial, unjust and confiscatory proceedings by the Irish Legislature' (E. Blake to J. Bryce, 24 Oct. 1892, in NLI, Blake Letters, [5] 4681). Not surprisingly, Radical Unionists made the same point about the legitimacy of the House of Lords' decision to reject the Bill in 1893: l.a., 'The country and the Lords', *LW*, 1 Oct. 1893, 8.

[179] C. P. Trevelyan from Dublin Castle, to E. Blake, 22 Feb. 1893, in NLI, Blake Letters, 734,4685; rep., 'Mr Chamberlain on the political situation', *WT&E*, Jan. 1893, 9.

[180] L. P. Curtis, Jr., 'Government policy and the Irish party crisis, 1890–92', *Irish Historical Studies*, 13, 52 (1963), 313; A. Jackson, *Colonel Edward Saunderson: land and loyalty in Victorian Ireland* (Oxford, 1995) 131; Lyons, *The Irish Parliamentary Party*, 37; B. M. Walker, *Ulster politics: the formative years, 1868–86* (1989), 193–4. For the more sectarian and militant rhetoric of Ulster Conservatives see J. Anderson, 'Ideological variations in Ulster during Ireland's first Home Rule crisis: an analysis of local newspapers', in C. H. Williams and E. Kofman (eds.), *Community conflict, partition and nationalism* (1989), 149.

[181] 'In his Clogher speech [J. Chamberlain] rails against Catholics & shows me clearly what an intolerant man he is.' (W. Kenny to H. de F. Montgomery, 29 Oct. 1894, D/627/428/ 259.) As well as being a Catholic himself, when he wrote this letter William Kenny was Unionist MP for the marginal Dublin constituency of St Stephen's Green, which included a significant number of middle-class Catholic Unionists. This added to the sensitivity of the subject. (I am grateful to Paul Bew for these details.) For Chamberlain's anti-Catholic rhetoric see his speech in 'Mr Chamberlain in Dundee', *Birmingham Daily Post*, 15 Feb. 1889, 5.

[182] For example, a Miss Richardson described the hierarchy's decision that girls from convents should no longer be entered for the public system of intermediate examination as a foretaste of the sectarian divide that a Home Rule Parliament would foster: rep., 'National Liberal Union: women's meeting in the Town Hall', *Birmingham Daily Post*, 27 Apr. 1889, 5.

rhetoric when addressing public meetings, in Ireland claimed to be championing the unity of 'all classes and creeds'.[183] In Ulster, the Liberals – in contrast to the Conservatives – seemed to be primarily worried about the economic and commercial, rather than religious, implications of Home Rule. It made electoral sense: in a society where sectarian issues were explosive and likely to polarize opinion between Nationalists and Conservatives, for the Liberals a 'secular' or non-sectarian platform was a question of electoral life or death. In 1880 they had secured nine seats by campaigning on tenant rights and land reform, an issue which had also been prominent during the previous general election, in 1874.[184] At the election of 1885 many candidates adopted a radical line on land reform as well as on other social issues, such as temperance and better housing for the labourers. They emphasized their support for free trade, in contrast to Parnell's call for protection. Some of them went as far as endorsing women's suffrage: Thomas Shillington (a Gladstonian, North Armagh), John Workman (South Belfast), Alexander Bowman (Independent Labour candidate for North Belfast), William Johnston and of course Isabella M. Tod – for whom women's political rights were inextricably linked to the Union.[185]

In Ulster all the Liberal candidates were defeated in 1885, when sixteen Conservatives and seventeen Nationalists were elected in a poll dominated by sectarian divisions. This result was not unexpected – in fact during the debate for the Reform and Redistribution Bills of 1884–5 Ulster Liberals had expressed their fear that the farm worker's vote in single-member constituencies would drown them in a sea of Orange and Nationalist votes.[186] Yet the apparent growth of sectarianism persuaded more and

---

[183] W. C. Trimble to H. de F. Montgomery, 12 Mar. 1894, D/627/428/235; for Trimble's propaganda among the Nonconformists in Britain see G. Litton Falkiner, Irish Unionist Alliance, Dublin to H. de F. Montgomery, 14 Mar. 1894, D/627/428/239. Trimble was the editor of the Enniskillen *Impartial Reporter*, and had supported the Land League in the early 1880s. His paper was seen as pro-tenant contrast to the Conservative and pro-landlord *Fermanagh Times*. (I am grateful to Paul Bew for these details.) Trimble was not selected and complained about the 'caste' prejudice against him, an allusion to the hostility of the gentry (see his letter on 28 Mar. 1894, D. 627/428/259). However, Montgomery regarded him as a sort of charlatan.

[184] L. J. McCafrey, 'Home Rule and the general election of 1874 in Ireland', *Irish Historical Studies*, 9, 33 (1954), 190–212; G. Greenlee, 'Land, religion and community', 253–75.

[185] Walker, *Ulster politics*, 213. On Tod's politics see M. Luddy, 'Isabella M. S. Tod, 1836–1896', in M. Cullen and M. Luddy (eds.), *Women, power and consciousness in nineteenth-century Ireland* (1995); H. Brown, 'An alternative imperialism: Isabella Tod, internationalist and "Good Liberal Unionist"', *Gender and History*, 10, 4 (1998), 358–80; and N. Armour, 'Isabella Tod and Liberal Unionism in Ulster, 1886–1896', in A. Hayes and D. Urquhart (eds.), *New perspective on Irish women* (2004), 72–87.

[186] MacKnight, *Ulster as it is*, 76–7.

more Liberals to seek an alliance with the Conservatives,[187] but did not affect the ideology and strategy of most of those who decided to remain independent. The latter hoped that political trends and electoral fortunes would change again, as had happened so often in the past, but the Whig leader, Hugh de Fellenberg Montgomery feared that the increasingly sectarian nature of Ulster politics world marginalize the liberals.[188] R. J. Bryce commented on the risk that the debate could become dominated by the Presbyterians' concern for the preservation of religious liberty. The latter was 'a precious cause, no doubt', but its rise as an electoral factor was 'proof of the urgent necessity for all Liberals, of whatever religious denomination, to stand forth on the broad ground of their citizenship in denouncing the slightest hesitation on the part of any Government in leaving Ireland to be torn in pieces by the dissentions which would be the inevitable results of a separate and independent Parliament'.[189] A similar concern was shared by W. E. H. Lecky.[190] For T. A. Dickson, a Radical who opted for Home Rule in 1886, the way forward was root-and-branch reform to make the Union fairer to Ireland. He recommended the abandoning of coercion, the passing of a land purchase act, 'a Scheme of Local and County Government on the widest and most comprehensive basis', the abolition of the role of the viceroy and the establishment of a royal residence in Ireland 'accompanied by an entirely new departure in the administration of Irish affairs'.[191] He was a Presbyterian 'ready to resist any encroachment upon [his denominational rights]', but entertaining no sectarian fears. Rather, he said, 'I fully recognise that my lot is cast in a country where Roman Catholicism guides and controls the lives of the vast majority of the people; and that much misgovernment in the past has arisen from ignoring or disregarding this important fact.'[192]

---

[187] D. C. Savage, 'The origins of the Ulster Unionist party, 1885–6', *Irish Historical Studies*, 12, 47 (1961), 189.

[188] H. de F. Montgomery in rep., 'County Tyrone Liberal Association', *The Northern Whig*, 2, Jan. 1886, 7. Montgomery was one of the leading Ulster Liberals, a key figure for understanding the events of this period, and one who left a remarkably extensive collection of political correspondence. On the family's involvement in Northern Irish politics in the twentieth century see P. Bew, K. Darwin and G. Gillespie (eds.), *Passion and prejudice: Nationalist–Unionist conflict in Ulster in the 1930s and the founding of the Irish Association* (1993).

[189] Letter by R. J. Bryce, 'The Ulster Liberals and the Union', *The Northern Whig*, 8 Feb. 1886, 8.

[190] McCartney, *Lecky*, 125.

[191] T. A. Dickson, *An Irish policy for a Liberal government* (1885), 21.   [192] Ibid., 14.

Despite the sectarian violence dominating Belfast – culminating in the riots of the summer of 1886[193] – a similarly 'secular' mind-set was shared by Liberal Unionist rank and file. This was illustrated by the resolutions passed by local Liberal associations, which focused on issues such as the economic prosperity of both Ireland and Britain, and concern that Parnell would drive 'trade and industry' from the country, his protectionism indicating that economic bigotry was more dangerous than the religious intolerance of the Catholic Church.[194] The Nationalists did not realize – 'a Belfast delegate' told a Birmingham audience – that '[s]ome things legislation can do for a people, other things it cannot do. The average Irish belief is that a Government can and may support a people. The working people of Belfast know that a people must support a Government.'[195]

Irish Liberal Unionists stressed not only free trade and the advantages which the island had gained and would continue to derive from it, but also land purchase schemes (like the 1885 Ashbourne Act), which depended on imperial credit, available only if Ireland remained within the Union. Throughout the period 1886–93 they contrasted the businesslike common sense characterizing Ulster Liberal objections to Home Rule with Gladstone's unreasonable and obsessive commitment to a principle based on a fantastic interpretation of Irish history.[196] In terms of constitutional change, they recommended the creation of elective county councils to achieve the legitimate (as against the revolutionary) aims of Home Rule. Again, local government would serve primarily economic objectives: '[it] would stimulate agriculture and industry alike', as Isabella Tod put it.[197] By contrast, Home Rule, she argued, would penalize the socially weaker groups such as farm workers and female householders. Appropriating Unionist rhetoric about minority rights, she claimed that, as an oppressed minority, women ought to be enfranchised and pointed out that they were not 'party politicians', but reasonable and rational citizens who would vote for 'the party, whichever it is, that does them

---

[193] The worst of the century, claiming the lives of 32 people, with 371 others being injured: C. Hirst, *Religion, politics and violence in nineteenth-century Belfast: the Pound and Sandy Row* (2002), 174–9. For a graphic account of the severity of one of these riots see rep., 'The rioting in Belfast', *The Northern Whig*, 9 Aug. 1886, 5. According to MacKnight the violence reflected the fear of an impending Liberal/Home Rule repression, following rumours of large bodies of Southern Catholic police concentrating around Belfast 'to shoot down the loyal Protestants' (MacKnight, *Ulster as it is*, 150).

[194] Letter by 'A Belfast Liberal', 'Ulster Liberals', *The Northern Whig*, 3 Feb. 1886, 8; a similar point had been made in a leader two weeks before (ibid., 2 Jan. 1886, 4); rep., 'North Antrim Liberal association', ibid., 8 Feb. 1886, 8.

[195] Rep., 'A Belfast delegate on Home Rule', *The Northern Whig*, 7 June 1886, 8.

[196] For a good example see MacKnight, *Ulster as it is*, 230–1, 322–7.

[197] Cited in rep., 'Ulster and Home Rule', *The Northern Whig*, 25 May 1886, 8.

justice'.[198] Indeed she felt 'quite certain' that a Nationalist government 'would relegate Catholic women in Ireland to a permanently inferior position; and take away from Protestants all hope of public usefulness. The same forces which have kept back the majority of women in Ireland, and would, if parted from England, keep them down permanently, would of course have retrogressive effects in other directions.'[199]

As well as being the instigator of the first Irish Women's Unionist, a founding member of the Ulster Liberal Unionist Association (ULUA), and the only woman to be listed in that otherwise all-male list of notables.[200] Thus she was an influential Liberal Unionist as well as a leading women's rights campaigner, and her views were widely echoed by the party rank and file and officially endorsed by the ULUA.[201] For, although the male leaders of Liberal Unionism were not sympathetic to women's demands, the party did attract a number of prominent feminists *avant la lettre*, including Lydia Becker, Millicent Fawcett and Kate Courtney.[202] They were motivated by different reasons, including personal antipathy to Gladstone and hostility to what they regarded as the Liberal party's flirtation with 'socialist' policies. While the Women's Liberal Unionist Association was started in 1888, it is well known that women were strongly represented within the Primrose League, an organization which, according to the staunchly Radical Unionist *Weekly Times*, was so completely permeated by their presence that it had become 'feminine in [its] methods and instincts'.[203]

While the economic and material case for the Union was thus being continually emphasized, the Liberal Unionists initially denied that the Home Rule controversy involved class conflict. Indeed, according to 'A Working Man', Gladstone was totally mistaken in presenting the issue as a question of 'the masses against the classes': certainly in North-East Ulster working men were not in favour of it. He personally opposed the proposal, fearing that, if implemented, 'capital would be driven from our shores, and we will be forced to break up our homes and seek

---

[198] I. M. S. Tod, 'Lord Salisbury and women's suffrage', *The Liberal Unionist*, Sep. 1891, 26.

[199] I. M. S. Tod, *The Northern Whig*, 1 May 1886, 8.

[200] *[Anon.] The Ulster Liberal Unionist Association. A sketch of its history 1885–1914. How it has opposed Home Rule, and what it has done for remedial legislation for Ireland*, introduction by Mr J. R. Fisher, published by the authority of the Executive Committee of the Ulster Liberal Association, Ulster Reform Club (1913), 18–20. Interestingly, the list did not include either T. Lea or T. W. Russell, who were soon to be elected as Liberal Unionist MPs for Ulster constituencies. Lea was admitted in June 1886 (ibid., 20).

[201] Ibid., 15.

[202] Pugh, *March of the women*, 132; G. Sutherland, *Faith, duty and the power of mind: the Cloughs and their circle, 1820–1960* (2006), 117.

[203] 'Powder and shot', *WT&E*, 17 April 1887, 9.

employment elsewhere'. Home Rule would 'kick the bread from our shores'.[204] Should the Southern majority of the electorate be allowed to ruin the country? 'It is impossible to build a nation on such foundations', 'A Presbyterian Liberal' argued. 'In fighting for our own individual liberties and rights we are really fighting for the best portion of even the Catholic South.'[205]

More fundamentally, for the Ulster Liberals at this stage Home Rule was a question of identity and belonging. It concerned whether or not Ireland should remain within the Union – rather than religious liberty. This persuaded E. T. Herdman, president of the Tyrone Liberal Association, to write to the press as early as January 1886, advocating an alliance between Liberals and Conservatives in Ireland. His initiative sparked off a furious debate which continued for months. At a stormy meeting the association censored him, passing a motion of confidence in Gladstone, conditional on both the preservation of the Union and the reform of local government.[206]

As the Home Rule Bill took shape, Ulster Liberal criticism focused on its specific features, and in particular on the exclusion of the Irish MPs from Westminster, a move which, had it been implemented, would have turned Ireland from a partner in empire into a 'contributory nation' and a 'vassal'. In June 1886 the 'Ulster Liberal Unionist Committee' published an 'Address to the people of the United Kingdom', in which, as usual, the religious issue was ignored, although the question of law and order was stressed. At stake was 'the repression of crime and the maintenance at all hazards of the rights of freemen to exercise their liberties, and live their lives secure from intimidation and outrage'. The National League was denounced for its intolerance. The address emphasized the expected economic disadvantages of Home Rule, which '[was] already breaking up mercantile confidence amongst us, depreciating Irish securities to a degree unprecedented even in times of commercial panic, and driving capital wholesale out of our country'. The measure would 'inevitably increase poverty and pauperism in Ireland' and 'flood the labour markets of manufacturing Ulster and of English and Scottish industrial centres, with hosts of Irish unemployed'. They criticized Gladstone's complacent and cavalier attitude towards Ulster, insisting that a permanent solution

---

[204] Letter by 'A Working Man', 'Working man and Home Rule', *The Northern Whig*, 10 May 1886, 8.

[205] Letter by 'A Presbyterian Liberal', 'Liberal duties', *The Northern Whig*, 8 Mar. 1886, 8.

[206] Rep., 'County Tyrone Liberal Association: important meeting', *The Northern Whig*, 21 Jan. 1886, 7. Despite their opposition to Home Rule, most Ulster Liberals rejected Gladstone's leadership only at the end of April (the Home Rule Bill was introduced on the 8th of that month): Walker, *Ulster politics*, 235–6.

to the Irish question required the gradual establishment of 'a widespread system of occupying owners' in the country. Once the land question was settled, local government could be established.[207]

As we have seen, Chamberlain had been toying with the idea of an Ulster Protestant assembly as early as March 1885. In this respect he differed from Bright, who insisted that 'any plan for dealing only with the Protestants of Ulster by themselves & not associated with the rest of the population of the Province, is an impossible plan & is not worth one moment's consideration'.[208] In 1886–7, however, Bright was a more consistent 'Unionist', largely because he distrusted the Irish Nationalists even more than Chamberlain did and insisted on the iniquity of abandoning 'five millions of our population to the rule of a conspiracy which is represented by men who sit in the House of Commons by virtue of contributions from America'.[209] He also distrusted Gladstone's rhetoric about the claims of the distinct nationalities within the United Kingdom. Particularly galling, he thought, was the GOM's readiness to accord to Wales the privileges and status of a nation, while ignoring the equally strong claims of Ulster to be so regarded:

Mr Gladstone ... speaks as if there were no province of Ulster or loyal Catholic population in Ireland. He seems ignorant or unconscious of the fact that the whole of Wales had a population in 1881 of only 1,360,000, which is, I think, less than that of Ulster by something like 300,000. Ulster may be a nationality differing from the rest of Ireland at least as much as Wales differs from England, but Wales is treated to a flattery which, if not insincere, seems to me childish, and Ulster is forgotten in the discussion of the Irish question.

Moreover, he questioned the wisdom of artificially fostering ethnic revivalism, noting that Gladstone spoke 'as if it were a good thing to make Wales almost as un-English as he assumes all Ireland to be. He conceals the fact that there are more loyal men and women in Ireland than the whole population of men and women in Wales.'[210] When Gladstone remonstrated with Bright, the latter vented his exasperation:

You say 'if there is a desire, a well considered desire on the part of the Protestant population in the portion of Ulster capable to be dealt with separately, we were perfectly agreed to consider any plan for the purpose.' But can anything be more unsatisfactory than this sentence? You ask for a 'well considered desire' on the part of the 'Protestant population'. Has it not been known to all men that the desire has been 'well considered', & that it has been expressed in the loudest

[207] *The Northern Whig*, 28 June 1886, 8.
[208] Bright to Gladstone, 14 June 1887, Gladstone Papers, Add. MSS 44113, ff. 230–1
[209] Bright as reported in 'The Crimes Bill through the Commons', *LW*, 10 July 1887, 6.
[210] 'Mr Bright on Mr Gladstone's Welsh speeches', *The Liberal Unionist*, 15 June 1887, 180.

terms by those who are entitled to speak for the Protestant inhabitants of the Province?[211]

As we have already seen, this was the line long since adopted by Chamberlain, who in private conversation as much as in his public speeches insisted that Ulster should not have to submit to 'a servitude and subjection which they detested. They must, if they were consistent, concede the claim of Ulster as a separate, and individual, and independent claim, at the same time as they conceded the claim of the three southern provinces.'[212]

This requirement, amounting to partition, began to be taken on board by Gladstone and his party as the 1892 election drew near. However, throughout the period between the first and the second Home Rule Bills, Irish Liberal Unionists were appalled at the idea of 'separate treatment' for Ulster.[213] Whatever the larger picture for the Unionists as a whole, the Liberals fitted in with Loughlin's integrationist hypothesis, with its emphasis on absolute and undivided parliamentary sovereignty, in contrast to Miller's 'contractarian' model (according to which Ulster's 'loyalism' was conditional on England's support for Irish Protestantism).[214] Particularly vocal was Isabella Tod, for whom all that was needed was the establishment throughout the UK of representative county councils, without discrimination or special treatment for the Irish who would be allowed to stay within the Union, 'as free as we are now, and with all our ties to the rest of the Empire unbroken. Whoever else may be attracted by little paltry Councils, legislating on narrow provincial grounds, we are not.' In her view 'what Ireland most needs [was] a larger outlet to the world' rather than 'a smaller and poorer life, spiritual, intellectual and material'.[215] When, at a meeting of Liberal working men in England, Tod was asked why the Irish people should not be allowed to decide their affairs in Ireland instead of in London, she replied: 'What affairs?' In

---

[211] Bright to Gladstone, 14 June 1887, Gladstone Papers, Add. MSS 44113, ff. 230–1. This letter was published in *The Liberal Unionist*, 22 June 1887, 196 ('Mr Bright and Mr Gladstone').

[212] MacKnight, *Ulster as it is*, 186; Chamberlain in rep., 'Mr Chamberlain in Scotland', *LW*, 17 Feb. 1889, 1.

[213] L.a., 'The convention in Dublin', *The Liberal Unionist*, July 1892, 222–3. Cf. A. Jackson, *The Ulster party: Irish Unionists in the House of Commons, 1884–1911* (1989), 14. However, a few weeks earlier Isabella Tod had publicly claimed that Ulster was ready to stand up for itself and wanted only to be left alone (rep., 'Women's Liberal Unionist Association', *The Liberal Unionist*, June 1892, 209).

[214] Loughlin, *Gladstone*', 157–8; D. W. Miller, *Queen's rebels: Ulster loyalism in perspective* (1978).

[215] Isabella M. Tod, 'The "separate treatment" of Ulster', *The Liberal Unionist*, Sep. 1887, 28–9.

Ireland as much as in Britain local affairs should certainly be handled by elected county authorities. But she urged them not to forget that there was a wider world out there, one for which more or less parochial assemblies were not adequate, and insisted that '[w]e had duties to the whole world, and it was only through an Imperial Parliament that we could perform them'. What she dismissed out of hand was the relevance of national councils:

While there were undoubtedly local interests which the manufacturing, the agricultural, and the fishing districts of Ireland might attend to by themselves, there were actually no interests or affairs whatsoever that concerned the whole island of Ireland and not equally England and Scotland . . . There was nothing which could be decided by itself for Ireland as a whole; but there was very much indeed that could be done by the Imperial Parliament on the one hand, and, on the other, by the spread of local governments for which she argued. It was, therefore, quite a fallacy to talk of giving to Ireland a Parliament to manage Irish affairs.[216]

Likewise, Tod also dismissed the religious fanaticism of the Orangemen – who had turned 'religion [into] a tabooed subject between most Protestants and Catholics' – and insisted that 'the great principle of liberty cannot be preserved except by preserving the one United legislature'.[217] For Tod Ireland was the result of a mixture of Danish, Norman, Spanish, English, Scottish and Celtic peoples, while millions of Irish people lived overseas. Furthermore, she insisted that this was a feature that Ireland shared with both England and other modern 'successful' countries, showing 'how valuable to civilization is the steady accretion of new powers, brought about by the frequent admixture of different races'.[218] Tod rejected the 'fundamentalist' Gaelic account of Irish history and defended the value of a socially and culturally diverse Ireland. She denied that the Celts had ever formed either a national Irish state or had even filled up the country in which they themselves were 'immigrants'. She also denied the Gaelicist claim 'that all comers after the Celts were intruders into a regular State, and should have conformed to its ways. On the contrary, from the earliest times there was full intercourse and frequent colonisation between Ireland and the other countries, and no sharp line of demarcation.'[219] Therefore, Ireland was historically a melting pot and this had always been its strength. By contrast, a purely Celtic state could not create 'a framework of life large enough for other races to share'. Her reasoning relied heavily on the importance of

[216] Rep., 'Miss Tod in England', *The Northern Whig*, 6 July 1886, 7; see also letter by Samuel Black, 'Home Rule', ibid., 24 Aug. 1886, 8.
[217] I. M. S. Tod, 'The Orange cry', *The Liberal Unionist*, Aug. 1891, 3.   [218] Ibid.
[219] I. M. S. Tod, 'Some historical fallacies', *The Liberal Unionist*, Aug. 1892, 3–4.

encouraging variety and diversity of 'human types' within Ireland in order to encourage progress. By contrast, '[t]he dangers of merely Celtic life are an intensifying and stereotyping of the narrowness, and adherence to tradition, and indifference to the rest of the world, which makes all improvement so slow as it is'. And she concluded by highlighting the contrast between ideal and reality in Parnellism: 'Terrible as the tyranny of the National League is from the point of view of individual liberty, it is almost ludicrous from this other point of view, in its painful endeavour to prevent movement, variety, and natural expansion.'[220]

Tod contrasted the entrepreneurial open-mindedness of the 'pioneers of industry' in Ulster with 'the monotonous toil of a community of land cultivators' in the South and concluded that 'the different sections of the [Irish] people ... can only work well together in settled equality and independence of each other; that is, under an Imperial Parliament, in which all races, creeds and classes are equal'.[221] Thus, while in general the Radical Unionist response was characterized by an emphasis on the material – rather than national or religious – nature of both liberty and the Irish crisis, in so far as they discussed the spiritual side of the crisis they stressed themes from the J. S. Mill tradition, rather than sectarian issues.

In 1886 one notable exception to this Irish Liberal preference for 'secular' policies and moderate style was T. W. Russell. He was a Scot and in some respects an outsider: far from being a member of the political elite, he was the son of a stonemason and the grandson of an evicted crofter, and he had moved to County Tyrone when he was eighteen. He had been a Sunday school pupil of T. A. Dickson, the radical MP. Later, with the encouragement of his employer, Russell himself entered politics as a temperance campaigner, and such 'faddism' provided him with political training and a radical reputation.[222] He always remained a Radical Liberal of sorts, eventually rejoining the Liberal party in 1907. In 1886–95 he was Chamberlain's protégé and political adviser, at first operating through Jesse Collings – a Radical Unionist of similarly plebeian origins – as an intermediary. With Chamberlain and Collings he shared a strong commitment to land reform, to the distinctiveness of Liberal Unionism within the anti-Home Rule coalition, and to

---

[220] Ibid.   [221] I. M. S. Tod, 'Myth and fact', *The Liberal Unionist*, June 1887, 146–7.
[222] MacKnight, *Ulster as it is*, 158–9; J. Loughlin, 'T. W. Russell, the tenant-farmer interest, and progressive Unionism in Ulster, 1886–1900', *Éire–Ireland*, 25, 1(1990), 44. Russell was Liberal Unionist and then Liberal MP for South Tyrone (1886–1910) and eventually North Tyrone (1910–18). In 1886 he was one of only two Liberal Unionists to secure a seat in Ulster (the other was Thomas Lea). A third Liberal Unionist was elected in 1892 for West Belfast: H. O. Arnold-Forster, W. E. Forster's adopted son.

democracy.[223] A frequent speaker at Liberal Unionist gatherings in Britain,[224] he argued his case vigorously in a series of articles and pamphlets. Although he opposed and denounced the Plan of Campaign as both unacceptable in principle and counterproductive in practice,[225] he pursued radical social reform by legal and parliamentary means and conducted his own fierce anti-landlord campaign, often embarrassing his fellow Liberal Unionists and annoying the Conservatives. Fully exploiting the fall-out from the land war – which had turned Ulster Liberalism into 'a substantial political movement, giving the Protestant tenant farmers the means and opportunity to further their interests by independent action'[226] – he insisted that Presbyterian tenant allegiance to Liberal Unionism was conditional on land reform, a view which was credible at the time.[227] Russell pressed his case to the point of formally resigning (temporarily) from the party in 1887, rejoining it when the Salisbury government took action with the passing of another Land Bill.[228] Unappeased, Russell continued to campaign for justice for the farmers and in 1889 his devastating denunciation of Lord Clanricarde provoked the indignation of the Earl of Erne and considerable tension within Irish Unionism.[229]

Here a comparison with both his colleague Jesse Collings and his mentor, Joseph Chamberlain, is instructive. They were all animated by

---

[223] T. W. Russell, 'The Irish question from the standpoint of a Liberal', *Dublin University Review*, 2 (1886), pp. 105–14; HPD, 3, CCCXVII (12 July 1887), 540.

[224] See, for example, the reports 'Women's associations', *The Liberal Unionist*, Feb. 1890, 137–8 and 'Liberal Unionism in Leeds and the West Riding of Yorkshire', ibid., Apr. 1890, 167. See also Russell, 'The Irish question'; and HPD, 3, CCCXVII (12 July 1887), 540.

[225] E.g. 'Mr T. W. Russell on the O'Brien episode', *Birmingham Daily Post*, 8 Feb. 1889, 4; T. W. Russell, *Disturbed Ireland: the Plan of Campaign estates* (1889), 7–9; and his two articles in *The Liberal Unionist*, Oct. 1890, 'Affairs in Ireland', 41–2 and 'The war in Tipperary', 48–9.

[226] Bew and Wright, 'The agrarian opposition in Ulster politic', 193.

[227] 'We all stand in a difficult position at present, and it is hard to tell which is the right road; even the much lower and less important question, of which is the "expedient" road, is not easy to answer. I agree with you in thinking that Russell has done a good deal which is calculated to irritate and offend. At bottom I believe he is right, and that we should really be much weaker in Ulster if no Unionist took the line he does. He is very extreme no doubt in some matters, but he does much to atone for any errors in that direction by his great ability and zeal in the cause of the union. There are people equally extreme on the other side, who certainly do not possess the compensating qualities I have spoken of.' (H. O. Arnold-Forster to H. de F. Montgomery, 9 Dec. 1894, D627/428/266.)

[228] Loughlin, 'Russell', 49. Despite his resignations he '[continued] to work – though independently – with the Liberal Unionists' (*The Liberal Unionist*, Sept. 1887, 26).

[229] See T. W. Russell, *The Plan of Campaign illustrated* (1889) and the response of the Earl of Erne, in P. Buckland (ed.), *Irish Unionism, 1885–1923* (1973), 24–6; for the tensions that this caused within Ulster Unionism see G. Walker, *A history of the Ulster Unionist party* (2004), 15–16.

a zeal for radical reform. However, from as early as 1887 Chamberlain reached the conclusion that the continuation of the Unionist alliance was worth major compromises with the Conservatives – for example, over coercion and Church disestablishment,[230] but also over the comparative merits of social paternalism over popular agitation.[231] Aware of his subordinate position and debt to Chamberlain, Collings remained what the *Oxford Dictionary of National Biography* describes as 'a loyal colleague and a good party servant'.[232] When in office with the Salisbury and Balfour governments (1895–1902) he devoted his time and energy to administrative work, although he published extensively on the question of land reform.[233] By contrast, as we shall see in the next chapter, Russell was not prepared to water down his agrarian radicalism for the sake of the Unionist alliance and continued to rely on his regional power base in South Tyrone to affirm his de facto independence from both the Ulster Liberal Unionists and the Salisbury government, even at the cost of enhanced tensions within Unionism. While this resulted in a bitter split within the ULUA, in 1892 his own majority increased from 99 to 372.[234]

Russell's readiness to adopt sectarian rhetoric reflected his peculiar relation to Ulster Liberalism as well as his faddist background and related tendency to exaggerate a case in order to provoke a strong emotional response. It also reflected his awareness that he needed the votes of both Conservatives and Orangemen in order to defeat William O'Brien – who was likely to gain the bulk of the Catholic vote, irrespective of whether Russell played the sectarian card or not. Thus his 1886 electoral address elaborated on emblematic cases of National League violence and moonlighter cruelty – although the victims mentioned in some of his examples were Catholic farmers – and enlarged upon seventeenth-century episodes of religious persecution, recalling 'how Tyrconnell's forces drove the scattered Protestants of Ulster before them until a stand was finally made "behind the bulwarks of the city of refuge"' in Londonderry.[235]

---

[230] For an early example see J. Chamberlain to J. Craig Brown, 5 July 1887, JC 6/6/1A/3, about the adoption of his son Austen by the Burghs constituency.

[231] As early as October 1887, in a speech he delivered at Coleraine, he started to 'undo' the work which Ulster Liberals had carried out from 1880, arguing that 'it was not necessary [for the tenant farmers] to engage in autonomous activity', but that they should instead rely on 'elite initiative' (Bew and Wright, 'The agrarian opposition in Ulster politics', 226). See T. A. Jenkins, 'Hartington, Chamberlain and the Unionist alliance, 1886–1895', *Parliamentary History*, 2, 1 (1992), 108–38.

[232] *ODNB*, vol. XII, 668.

[233] Collings, *Land reform* and *The colonization of rural Britain* (1914). Cf. J. Collings and J. L. Green, *Life of the Right Hon. Jesse Collings* (London, 1920).

[234] H. de F. Montgomery to J. Chamberlain, 31 July 1895, D/627/428/273. Cf. Loughlin, 'Russell', 51, 54, 57.

[235] Rep., 'The representation of South Tyrone', *The Northern Whig*, 18 June 1886, 7.

If in 1886 'political reputations in Ireland were built upon spectacular extremism',[236] Russell showed that he could play the game as well as any Conservative, allegedly '[convincing] thousands of Non-conformists [in England] that the Roman Catholic savage will persecute the Protestants'.[237]

While this was also what Chamberlain and arguably many other Nonconformist leaders actually believed anyway, it would seem that Russell opportunistically *used*, rather than actually shared their prejudice.[238] His ideology was more sophisticated: in particular, he insisted on the link between urbanization and the question of religious liberty in Catholic countries. He argued that in Ireland the problem was compounded by the overwhelmingly rural nature of society: 'Ireland is not a country of large cities and towns where free thought and intellectual life combine to defeat clerical intolerance. Ireland – at least three-fourths of it – is dominated by peasants ... [who] are to a large extent, illiterate ... Over these men the Church rules, and would rule.'[239] To the question of whether religious freedom would not be as safe in Home Rule Ireland as in Catholic France, Belgium or Italy, he answered that the comparison simply confirmed his concern: 'I maintain that in these countries minorities are safe and free, just in proportion as the political power of the Church has been destroyed by Liberalism. In Ireland, men, no matter what the patriots say, are Catholics first, and Irishmen after.'[240] Moreover, he feared that the urbanized and industrial North-East would be fiscally exploited and economically ruined by the peasantry of the South and West, who 'had no knowledge of the laws which governed commercial pursuits'.[241] This clash between city and countryside was serious enough to contain 'a distinct menace of civil war. This is undoubtedly what it may come to.'[242]

Such allusions to civil war were commonplace among the most intransigent Protestant preachers, like the Revd Hanna,[243] but not so popular

---

[236] A. Jackson, 'Irish Unionism and the Russellite threat', *Irish Historical Studies*, 25, 100 (1987), 404.

[237] In W. H. Smith's words, 20 Sep. 1889, cited in ibid., 378.

[238] Loughlin, 'Russell', 46–7; cf. Quinault, 'Joseph Chamberlain', 79–80; and Loughlin, 'Joseph Chamberlain', 215.

[239] T. W. Russell, *Ireland. No. XXIX. The case for Irish Loyalists*, published by the Irish Loyal and Patriotic Union (1886), 10–11.

[240] Ibid., 11; for a vigorous attack on 'priestly rule' see his speech in 'Mr T. W. Russell, MP, in Ulster', *The Liberal Unionist*, Oct. 1891, 44.

[241] 'Mr T. W. Russell, MP, on the Irish question', *The Northern Whig*, 11 Apr. 1889, 8.

[242] Rep., 'Mr T. W. Russell on the Ulster question', *The Liberal Unionist*, May 1892, 189.

[243] See his speech in 'Unionist demonstration in the Ulster Hall', *The Northern Whig*, 16 Feb. 1889, 8.

with Ulster Liberal Unionists at the time – although Isabella Tod compared the 1892 Ulster Convention to the 1782 Volunteers' Convention at Dungannon 'which, created on a sudden emergency to meet a great danger, practically ruled Ireland for nearly a decade by its pressure upon the otherwise weak "Grattan's Parliament"'. The comparison implied an allusion to the Unionists' potential military might and she underscored this point by repeatedly referring to 'the duty laid upon them by the Providence of God' and the sovereign binding power of their individual conscience at a stage when the struggle was about '[r]eligious liberty (not mere toleration, but freedom of personal and associated action) [as] the condition of civil liberty'.[244] As we have already seen, until then Tod had consistently dismissed sectarianism and other emotional celebrations of the past and it is possible that her allusions to them in 1892 reflected an attempt to recapture part of the shrinking Liberal Unionist constituency in Ulster.

By contrast, as Russell became more confident about his grip on South Tyrone, he argued that the danger was based not on sectarian divides, but rather on specific material grievances. By the same token, he denied that the fierce Unionism of the Ulster Presbyterians reflected either the strength of the Orange Order or an ingrained sectarianism of the Belfast merchants and artisans; instead, it was a function of their capitalist mind-set and resolve to cling to that 'commercial society' which had made Ulster prosperity originally possible.[245]

Thus, in contrast to what Loughlin has argued, in the early 1890s there was little evidence of Russell espousing an 'opportunist' approach to Unionism – that is, one which depended on his expectation that the Ulster farmers were more likely to obtain landownership from Westminster than from a Parliament in Dublin.[246] In fact, the opposite was true: he was one of the earliest proponents of the consistently integrationist view, resurrected by Enoch Powell in the 1970s, according to which the sovereign British Parliament had the right to cut Ireland off from the imperial connection, but not the right to transfer the allegiance of the Ulster Unionists to another Parliament 'and say in such a case who our masters are to be'.[247]

---

[244] I. M. S. Tod, 'Ulster Convention: preliminary meeting', *The Liberal Unionist*, May 1892, 1–2.
[245] Ibid. A fortnight later the same point was made by a Miss Richardson, BA – another Ulster Liberal Unionist – again speaking in Birmingham at a women's meeting: *Birmingham Daily Post*, 27 Apr. 1889, 5.
[246] Loughlin, 'Russell', 47.
[247] Letter, 'Mr T. W. Russell on the Ulster question', *The Liberal Unionist*, May 1892, 189.

The impotence of being earnest

The English people '[had] always been known for their sound, practical common sense', conducive to 'systematic and practical progress'.[248] 'Honest Men' concerned about the common good would reject Gladstone's 'sentimental Liberalism' and flock to Chamberlain, the 'manly' patriot.[249] This was the Liberal Unionists' plea from 1887. By 1892, however, the insistence with which it was repeated belied a massive erosion of confidence within the party. Whether or not their analysis of the English 'national character' was accurate, it was clear that Chamberlain's contempt for sentimentalism was not shared by traditional Liberal voters. Already in April 1886 a caucus official had observed with dismay that 'most men are moved through their emotions rather than through their reason, & the very name of Gladstone is a most potent instrument to conquer with. The creed of the majority seems to be – "If you cannot see eye to eye with Mr Gladstone in this Irish matter, you are no Liberal." To criticize is impudence, to oppose, treason.'[250] Coercion in Ireland made things worse. As a Liberal Unionist working man admitted in frustration, the Gladstonians shirked all the economic and constitutional complications attending their Home Rule proposals, '[t]he chief point they dwell upon is that of what they call Coercion', but '[t]his seems to raise enthusiasm at Radical meetings'.[251]

Sentimentalism about coercion – what Peter Clarke and Patrick Joyce have described as the 'politics of conscience' and 'the primacy of a religious over an intellectual sensibility'[252] – was further excited by itinerant Nationalist propagandists, who stirred English sensitivity with lurid accounts of government oppression (see chapter 2, above). In order to counteract their influence, the ULUA decided to develop its own brand of sentimentalist propaganda by sending over to England and Scotland a number of its own 'missionaries'. They were hand-picked: 'good men – Methodists if possible, and working men – to assist at the by-elections, and to help to stem the torrent of Nationalist misstatements which are

---

[248] H. Huth, Hon. Sec. Huddersfield Liberal Unionist Association, and Yorkshire Liberal Unionist Federation, 'The future of Liberal Unionism', *The Liberal Unionist*, Nov. 1890, 73.

[249] F. Cammarano, *'To save England from decline': the national party of common sense: British Conservatism and the challenge of democracy (1885–1892)* (2001), 32.

[250] John Borastin, Secretary of the East Cornwall Liberal Association, to Jesse Collings, 16 Apr. 1886, JC 8/5/3/12.

[251] Letter by 'A working man', 'A working man's appeal to his fellow-workmen', *The Liberal Unionist*, Aug. 1888, 5.

[252] P. Clarke, *A question of leadership* (1991), 28; Joyce, *Democratic subjects*, 217.

poured out on every election platform'.[253] With the help of the chairman of the Belfast Trades Council they carefully selected seventeen such men and dispatched them across the channel. Their success and effectiveness forced the Liberals to organize 'speaking corps' of *Protestant* working-class Home Rulers.[254] The resulting competition between two varieties of bleeding-heart evangelists provided the fullest possible demonstration of the English susceptibility to sentimentalist politics.

Although in December 1885 Chamberlain had claimed that '[t]he English working classes ... are distinctly hostile to Home Rule',[255] his hopes of a bright radical future without Gladstonianism were soon quashed: by 1892 Liberal Unionists everywhere were struggling to retain working-class support, falling behind both Conservatives and Gladstonians in the populist competition for the vote of the masses. This decline was reflected in the sphere of political debate and ideas. For example, *The Liberal Unionist*, the party's official journal, germinated, briefly blossomed and then withered in the short space of five years: started as a penny weekly on 30 March 1887, it became a monthly in August, and ceased publication, abruptly, in September 1892, with little explanation except that Home Rule had ceased to be an imminent danger.[256] During the final two years of its life the number of letters to the editor shrunk and the advertisements – always an important source of income for a periodical – had halved to only one page.

The main problem of the Liberal Unionists was the vulnerability of their electoral base – especially affecting their Radical wing. While before June 1886 there were thirty-two Radical MPs who had opposed Home Rule, after the election their number dropped to about twenty, which further dwindled to eleven in 1892. The Parnell divorce scandal merely slowed down the Home Rule advance, which, however, was enough to turn the 1886 Unionist majority of 118 into an 1892 Home Rule one of 40. By then the Gladstonians were the single largest party in the

---

[253] R MacGeah to H. de F. Montgomery, 14 Feb. 1890, D. 627/428/130; 19 Feb. 1890, D. 627/428/131; and 5 Mar. 1890, D. 627/428/132.

[254] 'Scores of constituencies were lost to the Liberal Party by the operation of the Protestant working men sent from this country to frighten English working men against Home Rule.' (W. Hastings, from Dublin, to Rosebery, 18 Aug. 1895, in Ellis Papers, 4039.)

[255] J. Chamberlain to W. E. Gladstone, 19 Dec. 1885, in Chamberlain, *Political memoir*, 171.

[256] Valedictory by the editor St Loe Strachey in *The Liberal Unionist*, Sep. 1892, 1. The decision was taken by the Liberal Unionist Association after the general election. There was no prior warning. About the prospective Second Home Rule Bill Strachey said that Gladstone had already accepted the retention of the Irish MPs at Westminster, and that this would make his proposal far less threatening, although, in any case, it was hopeless in view of the government's small majority.

Commons and had secured 49 per cent of the English vote, and a majority of both the Scottish and the Welsh vote.[257]

Under the circumstances, the question as to whether there should be a merger with the Conservatives was 'in the air'. Those who argued in favour suggested that the operation would not be like joining the old enemy because '[t]here are no Tories now. The Conservative of to-day is, to all intents, the modern representative of the Liberalism of twenty years ago.' In any case, the relationship between the two parties 'must either become more intimate or end in rupture' – which would result in Liberal Unionist extinction.[258] Those who were opposed to the merger pointed out that the formation of a 'National party' would be strongly resisted in the constituencies and would inevitably lead to the alienation of many party activists and the demise of the popular liberal vote, in particular that 'of the Liberal and Radical workmen of the country at the next general election. *Though they are deaf to us now*, the working classes will listen to us at a general election when the facts are clearer. They did so before.'[259]

Not all working men were 'deaf' to Liberal Unionism, but there was a general expectation that they would soon become so even in the strongholds of Radical Unionism. The Conservatives were fully aware of their allies' embarrassment and – especially at a constituency level – increasingly intolerant of Radical Unionist claims on parliamentary seats which could only be held with the aid of Conservative votes. Even in Birmingham the truce between the Chamberlain and the Tory caucus came under threat repeatedly in 1889–95. There the Liberal schism had been experienced as a crisis of quasi-religious proportions, with 'political aversions ... breaking everywhere old friendships and severing old allies'.[260] Although the Liberals were not to secure a seat there for generations, the Radical Unionists were painfully aware of the vulnerability of their own position and felt very nervous every time an electoral contest approached. This is well illustrated by the 1889 by-election in Central Birmingham, the seat formerly held by John Bright. Like Chamberlain, he had long personified the radical domination of the city, a hegemony deeply resented by the local Conservatives. When the veteran Radical tribune fell ill in 1888, discussions about selecting a successor for him were started between Chamberlain and Palmer on behalf of the

---

[257] E. D. Steele, 'Gladstone and Ireland', *Irish Historical Studies*, 17, 65 (1970), 61.

[258] Letter by James Couper Jr. (Glasgow), 'A National party', *The Liberal Unionist*, Apr. 1891, 175.

[259] Letter by R. Bird (Glasgow), *The Liberal Unionist*, Mar. 1891, 155 (my emphasis). See also W. L. Blench (Derby), 'A National party', *The Liberal Unionist*, Feb. 1891, 128.

[260] Tuckwell, *Reminiscences*, 70.

Conservatives, who hoped to secure the seat. Chamberlain seemed ready to contemplate a deal.[261]

There were various reasons why Chamberlain felt unsure of his hold over Central Birmingham. Bright had been a loyal supporter of the Unionist cause, but also uncompromising in his anti-imperialism. If the latter was shared by his electors, the seat might be lost to the Gladstonians, whose strength in the town was difficult to assess. After all, late in 1888 they had held a triumphant demonstration at Bingley Hall, where the GOM addressed the annual meeting of the NLF. He had attracted large crowds, up to 'twenty-five thousand men and women', eliciting unprecedented demonstrations of support for the cause of constitutional reform.[262] The threat of a Gladstonian breakthrough was, however, only part of the problem. In view of the Chamberlain–Palmer discussions of 1888, a crucial question concerned the proportion of the Unionist vote which was actually Conservative rather than Radical. Chamberlain needed to be able to show to their Conservative ally-competitors that 'the democracy' was still with 'Joe', so that there would be no question of a Tory, rather than a Liberal Unionist, candidature in future.[263]

When the seat eventually became vacant, the Radical Unionists selected John Albert Bright, a son of the late MP, to contest it. He was neither gifted nor committed as a politician, and gave a rather condescending electoral address, indicating that he would have preferred to be elected without having to speak to his constituents.[264] Despite this, caucus officials had reason to believe that 'a real live Bright' would be 'an amazingly strong candidate'.[265] Yet, Austen Chamberlain, J. Powell Williams and other Radical Unionist party leaders canvassed the constituency anxiously. When the early results looked too good to be true, they counter-canvassed by sending round a Radical Unionist farm labourer who pretended to be touting for the Gladstonians, to see whether people would make indifferent promises of support to whoever turned up.[266] To their great relief, reports came in to indicate that 'the L[iberal]

---

[261] 'Synopsis of a conversation on Friday September 11 – 1888 between Mr Chamberlain and Mr Palmer', JC, 6/2/1/23. The notes were taken by Palmer, the Conservative agent, who later asked Chamberlain for permission to publish them; the permission was denied as Chamberlain had 'no recollection of the details of the private interview' (Chamberlain to Palmer of *Birmingham Gazette*, 20 Apr. 1889, JC 6/2/1/24).

[262] According to one eye-witness: Tuckwell, *Reminiscences*, 78–83.

[263] Hurst, 'Joseph Chamberlain', 90–1.

[264] Rep., 'Mr Bright's candidature', *Birmingham Daily Post*, 11 Apr. 1889, 5.

[265] J. Powell Williams to J. Chamberlain, 11 Apr. 1889, JC 6/2/1/19.

[266] Austen Chamberlain to J. Chamberlain 10 Apr. 1889, JC 6/2/1/17; J. Powell Williams to J. Chamberlain, 10 Apr. 1889, JC 6/2/1/18.

U[nionist]s [were] much stronger than [was] generally supposed'.[267] J. Powell Williams, an old caucus hand, agreed: 'One thing comes out most clearly, and in a way that cannot be really controverted, namely that there are an immense number of Liberal Unionists in the Division, and that the Tory estimate of the [?] relative strength of the sections of the unionist forces is all fudge.'[268]

Eventually the result was a triumph, with more than a two-to-one victory for the Radical Unionist candidate on 15 April 1889. However, the election continued to foment bad blood within the Unionist camp. Albert Bright felt undermined by the virulent hostility of the Conservative caucus and their chief 'wirepuller', Satchell Hopkins. By November he had already considered resigning and retiring from politics.[269] Although he did not do so but actually stayed on to win the seat in 1892, his weakness forced Chamberlain to negotiate with the Conservatives. The ensuing correspondence between Chamberlain, Powell Williams and Hopkins provides a classic example of how 'wirepulling' bypassed the formal democratic process of candidate selection by local caucuses. Moreover, old animosities resurfaced and the discussion became embarrassingly confrontational and public.[270] The Tories demanded a larger share of the Birmingham constituencies and threatened to field Lord Randolph Churchill without further consultation with the Liberal Unionists.[271] Throughout the episode and subsequent developments the Conservatives were remarkably arrogant and aggressive while Chamberlain was atypically diplomatic and accommodating.[272]

It was but a foretaste of things to come and an example of the general Liberal Unionist predicament. All over the country, as Liberal Unionist

---

[267] A. Chamberlain to J. Chamberlain, 10 Apr. 1889, JC 6/2/1/17.

[268] J. Powell Williams to J. Chamberlain, 11 Apr. 1889, JC 6/2/1/19.

[269] John Albert Bright to J. Chamberlain, 5 Nov. 1889, JC 6/2/1/26; John Albert Bright to J. Chamberlain 8 Nov. 1889, JC 6/2/1/27.

[270] See newscutting about this from the *Birmingham Times*, 28 Apr. 1889: 'A call to Conservatives: Stirring letter by Mr J Owlands: three seats demanded: Lord R. Churchill's meeting', in JC 6/2/6/2; J. Chamberlain to J. S. Hopkins, 1 Aug. 1889, JC 6/2/5/2; J. Chamberlain to J. S. Hopkins, 29 Oct. 1889, JC 6/2/5/5; memo of a meeting with J. Powell Williams, G. Dixon and J. Satchell Hopkins, 23 Feb. 1891, JC 6/2/3/2; memo by Chamberlain of his meeting with Hopkins, n.d., JC 6/2/3/1; Chamberlain to Hopkins, 17 Apr. 1891, JC 6/2/5/13.

[271] J. Chamberlain to J. S. Hopkins, 1 Aug. 1889, JC 6/2/5/2; C. A. Vince to J. Chamberlain, 25 May 1895, JC 6/2/7/7.

[272] 'Central Birmingham Parliamentary Division – Resume of Events and Proceedings, 23 Mar. 1895', JC 6/2/7/3; C. A. Vince to J. Chamberlain, 25 May 1895, JC 6/2/7/7; C. A. Vince to J. Chamberlain, 7 June 1895, JC 6/2/7/11. See also correspondence in JC 6/2/7/20–26 showing the power of 'wirepullers' and local leaders in the period 1886–95, with some minor qualification in terms of what the rank and file would accept, but little reference to the wishes of ordinary electors.

seats became vacant, local Conservative associations bullied their allies to secure a Tory candidature or to exact favourable terms from them. For example, in 1892 when Austen Chamberlain proposed his own candidature for East Worcestershire, the local Conservative association refused to endorse him 'unless he [was] prepared to pledge that he [would] not support the Disestablishment of any branch of the State Church'. This prompted the Birmingham Liberal Unionists to threaten to withdraw their endorsement of the Conservative candidate for East Birmingham unless he promised to back disestablishment.[273] It was not the only incident of its kind. In 1894–5 there were serious disputes between the Liberal Unionist and Conservative associations for the selection of the Unionist candidate for Hythe (Sussex) and Warwick and Leamington.[274] Instead of appealing confidently to the electors, the Liberal Unionists pleaded with their allies to respect the 1886 'treaty obligations'. But the Conservatives pressed for the creation of a joint Unionist association – which would have involved the stronger group effectively absorbing the weaker. The reality was that, '[l]ooking at the state of the two parties – the Conservatives outnumber the Liberal Unionists by at least nine to one, and that a Liberal Unionist candidate will have no chance whatever of being returned without the support of the greater number of the Conservatives in the borough'.[275]

These conflicts also reflected both the ideological tensions between the two branches of the Unionist coalition and the extent to which Liberal Unionists continued to be sensitive about their own 'Liberal' identity even at this late stage and with the prospect of a Gladstonian electoral victory. Despite confident predictions that the GOM's 'extremism' would soon drive recalcitrant moderate voters into the arms of the Liberal Unionists,[276] it was the latter who felt increasingly squeezed out of the political game. With the Gladstonian party virtually dominating the left, the Liberal Unionists needed to draw closer to the Tories in the hope that they would thus be able to attract the moderate vote.[277] But they

---

[273] J. Chamberlain to A J Balfour, 18 Jan. 1892, JC 6/6/1C/3.
[274] See correspondence and newscuttings in JC 6/6/1E/1 and JC 6/6/1E/2, including a letter by John Sherwood, chairman of the local branch of the Liberal Unionist association to the *Folkestone Express*, 1 Sep. 1894 and the reply from from the leader of the local Conservative caucus; and G. Peel to J. Chamberlain, 12 Mar. 1895, JC 6/6/1F/1.
[275] See JC 6/6/1E/1, JC 6/6/1E/3 and in particular JC 6/6/1E/2, 'The Borough representation', newscutting from the *Folkestone Express*, 22 Nov. 1894, letter sent by General Sir J. Bevan Edwards, selected Conservative candidate to A. H. Gardner, Secretary of the Conservative association. See also the correspondence between J. Borastin, the Duke of Devonshire, Lord Salisbury and J. Chamberlain (early 1895) in JC 6/6/1E/5–8.
[276] C. A. Vince to J. Chamberlain, 1 Apr. 1895, JC 6/6/1F/21.
[277] C. A. Vince to J. Chamberlain, 1 Apr. 1895, in JC 6/6/1F/21.

found it increasingly difficult to reconcile their Liberal or Radical identity with the compromises which coalition politics demanded, especially in the sphere of ecclesiastical and religious questions – including the Salisbury government soliciting the Pope's intervention against Irish Nationalism and the Tory opposition to the Welsh church disestablishment campaign.[278]

The crisis culminated in the case of the 1895 Warwick and Leamington by-election, when George Peel, the Liberal Unionist candidate, was humiliated after a long controversy about the selection of a Unionist to represent the constituency. Again some party enthusiasts and wirepullers started by boasting of their strength among the electors and especially the working men, while being well aware that they were playing 'a game of bluff'.[279] Chamberlain still hoped to be able to rely on the working-class vote, at least in his Midlands stronghold. In the end this proved insufficient – a further instance of the fact that his advocacy of social reform was a questionable asset when it came to deciding how the urban working class would vote.[280]

Although embittered, in 1895 the Radical Unionists again had to put up with further Conservative demands in Central Birmingham when Albert Bright finally stood down. They came to an agreement with the Tories but the bitterness remained: 'I wish all Birm[ingha]m Tories were in Sheol!' exclaimed Powell Williams, in utter frustration.[281] '[I]f we are to continue to be treated by the Conservative Party just as now, we shall give up supporting them,' complained one official of another Liberal Unionist association.[282] Even at the turn of the century there remained pockets of die-hard popular Radical Unionism, impervious to

---

[278] L.a., 'The Pope, Ireland, and Great Britain', *WT&E*, 25 Dec. 1887, 8. Aware of Ulster Protestant opinion, A. J. Balfour in April 1887 refused to consider this mission, but he later changed his mind, although the issue remained problematic: see Loughlin, 'Russell', 50; Macaulay, *The Holy See, British policy and the Plan of Campaign*, 254, 293, 359. On the Welsh disestablishment issue see J. Chamberlain to T. Gee, 16 Apr. 1890, in NLW, T. Gee MSS, 8305D, 17; and R. W. Dale to T. Gee, 25 May 1890, in ibid., 8305D, ff. 30–30f.

[279] See correspondence between G. Peel, C. A. Vince, secretary of the National Liberal Union and J. Chamberlain in JC 6/6/1F/1–2 and J. Powell Williams to Akers-Douglas, 11 Apr. 1895, JC 6/6/1F/34.

[280] Pelling, *Popular politics*, 17; Cooke and Vincent, *Governing passion*, 33.

[281] J. Powell Williams to J. Chamberlain, May 1895, JC 6/2/7/10.

[282] J. H. Cooke of the Cheshire Liberal Unionist Association to J. Borastin, 25 Mar. 1895, JC 6/6/1F/17. For the bitterness in Liberal Unionists ranks see also J. Borastin to J. Chamberlain, 26 Mar. 1895, JC 6/6/1F/18 and J. Powell Williams to Akers-Douglas, 11 Apr. 1895, JC 6/6/1F/34.

the grand strategy of the party and jealously suspicious of the electoral trustworthiness of their Conservative allies, feeling great pride in their *Liberal* identity and traditions.[283]

[283] Annual Report for 1897 and 1898 (submitted to the council on 9 May 1898), in Archives of the Birmingham Central Library, Birmingham Liberal Unionist Association, Minute Book of the All Souls Ward Executive Committee, March 1897–1914, MS 814; Meeting of the Executive Committee held at the Club 364 Lodge Rd, 16 July [19]03, Min. No. 159, ibid.

6   Social radicalism and the revival of the Gladstonian 'popular front'

Gladstone in his old age seems to partake of the super-natural. I have seen him intimately during the last week, and I am daily more and more impressed with the greatness of his mind and character.[1]

The BUDGET was a FAIR BUDGET. It was an HONEST Budget – it paid its way. It laid down the important and far-reaching principle that extra taxation ought to fall on THOSE WHO CAN AFFORD TO PAY. It removed the unjust PRIVILEGES which landlords have possessed in the past. SUPPORT THE PARTY WHICH CARRIED THIS DEMOCRATIC BUDGET.[2]

Liberalism must re-unite itself with the Labour interest. Until that is done we cannot look for much success . . . The programme of the Liberal party must, therefore, be so altered as to include those items of legislation for which the industrial classes are striving.[3]

Radicals parting ways

Although Chamberlain was rapidly marginalized within the radical left after 1892, his 'materialist' approach to politics – the priority of social reform – and emphasis on parliamentary centralism, in the conviction 'that the day of Local Parliaments and of small nationalities is past',[4] were to have enormous impact on twentieth-century radical politics. If 'modern' radicalism was about 'the social question', and if poverty was to be reduced by government action, then the country needed the rational reconstruction and empowerment of the imperial executive at its centre, rather than legislative devolution. The example for Britain to follow was not Austria-Hungary, which Gladstone had studied and Sinn Fein's

---

[1] A. J. Mundella to R. Leader, 30 Mar. 1891, in Leader Papers, Sheffield Univ. Library.
[2] 'The Budget of 1894: what it was and how it was carried', handbill, James Bryce Papers, Bodleian Library, Oxford.
[3] 'The liberalism of the future', *The Liberal*, 27 July 1895, 182.
[4] L.a., 'Mr Chamberlain and the work of reform', *LW*, 17 Feb. 1889, 1.

Arthur Griffiths was to celebrate, but the German Empire. The then fastest-growing industrial power in Europe was also a model in terms of social reform and national efficiency. There the social democratic party (SPD) goaded Bismarck towards a 'reasonable and orderly Collectivism', while he repressed and contained both Catholic clericalism and regional separatism in the Polish provinces and Alsace-Lorraine.[5] The Anglophile German radical Karl Blind recommended a similar strategy for the United Kingdom: 'the strict upholding of the Legislative Union' was 'the only guarantee for the security of England, for the intellectual progress of the masses in Ireland, and for the general furtherance of popular freedom and welfare'.[6]

However persuasive to some Radical Unionists at the time, there were three main problems with this analysis. The first was that the *Kaiserreich* involved a relationship between state and society which both British and Irish liberals and democrats found alarming and objectionable. The second was that both Bismarck and Chamberlain were mistaken in their belief that the social question was more urgent or 'real' than the national question; in any case, the latter was far more politically explosive and intractable both in Germany and in the United Kingdom, and would bring about a drastic downsizing of both countries by 1921. And, finally, the third was that Radical Unionism was no equivalent of the SPD, not only ideologically, but also in terms of its electoral muscle: while the SPD was a cohesive mass party with a distinctive political philosophy and a growing popular constituency, Radical Unionism was small and shrinking, its grass-root support was unstable and its ideas, far from being a unifying force, reproduced all the tensions and divergences which had bedevilled the pre-1886 Gladstonian Liberal party.

If Radical Unionism's long-term strategy was flawed, its short-term analysis would soon prove mistaken. In 1886 part of its appeal depended on three assumptions: that democracy demanded social reform, which Gladstone was accused of wilfully neglecting; that the Liberal schism would soon be healed; and that for as long as the latter lasted the Liberal Unionists would retain the will and ability to pursue a radical agenda. Each of these three assumptions proved wrong: the Gladstonians – especially the younger generation – soon adopted social radicalism, including old age

---

[5] See the leading articles 'Prince Bismarck and socialism', 1 Dec. 1887, 8; 'German socialism', 26 May 1889, 6; and 'German socialism', 2 Feb. 1890, 8; cf. Hammond, *Gladstone and the Irish nation*, 465–7.

[6] Karl Blind, 'Irish disruption and German union', *The Liberal Unionist*, 13 Apr. 1887, 34.

pensions.[7] The Liberal schism proved permanent. And finally, Chamberlain began to feel uneasy about 'socialism' once the latter was actually adopted by sections of the trade union movement, and he was unable to press on with reforms which Hartington and Salisbury found unacceptable, and was unwilling to contemplate other progressive demands which might have given a distinctive cutting edge to Radical Unionism, such as the extension of political rights to women.

Peter Fraser has produced the best analysis of Chamberlain's attitude to socialism and the reasons why, when faced with the challenge of class struggle, he opted for radical imperialism.[8] In the post-Darwinian climate of the 1880s collectivist rhetoric reflected more new academic and cultural trends – in sociology, anthropology and philosophy – than any precise awareness of the meaning of socialism as it was then articulated by Marx and Engels and the Second International. Later, as socialism became less exotic and esoteric, it elicited stronger opposition: thus from 1890 *The Liberal Unionist* hosted articles which took a strong anti-socialist line, even attacking the Eight-Hour Bill as a form of 'protectionism', and providing party canvassers and activists with a sort of catechism of free trade and economic individualism.[9]

In any case, Chamberlain's collectivism 'was by no means a progression towards socialism. It had much closer affinities with imperialism. The nation was its natural unit and community.' More importantly, Chamberlain's vision 'had no place for the idea of class war, the materialism or the suppression of individuality which, rightly or wrongly, were associated with socialism'.[10] His Radical Unionism involved promoting social unity at home and British power abroad. By the same token, in two famous speeches (at Birmingham on 23 January and in the Commons on 29 July 1889) he denounced the 'new Radicals' who represented 'the class jealousies, the petty spite, the enmities which they do their utmost to stimulate'. They were 'the Nihilists of English politics' preaching a gospel of 'universal disintegration'.[11] He was persuaded that 'the electors [were] much more interested . . . in social questions and the problems connected

---

[7] A. Roberts, secretary of the Merionethshire Liberal Association to T. E. Ellis, 29 June 1895, in Ellis Papers, 1781. The proposal was more popular in rural than in urban constituencies: Minute of the meeting of Literature Committee, 20 Oct. 1898, 435, in SLA Papers, NLS, Acc. 11765/6.

[8] Fraser, *Chamberlain*.

[9] M. Crackanthorpe, 'Unionism and state socialism', *The Liberal Unionist*, Jan. 1890, 1–2. 'A defence of individualism', *The Liberal Unionist*, Feb. 1890, 134; 'Plain words on socialistic problems: II', ibid., July 1891, 222 and Aug. 1891, 2; 'Plain words on socialistic problems: IV: protection does not protect', ibid., Oct. 1891, 42; 'Socialism tested by facts', ibid., Sep. 1892, 38.

[10] Fraser, *Chamberlain*, 140.   [11] Cited in Loughlin, 'Chamberlain', 213.

with the agitation of the Labour Party than they [were] with either the House of Lords or any constitutional subject'. But from 1893–4 he reached the conclusion that the TUC was preaching 'universal confiscation in order to create a Collectivist State' – an unacceptable prospect. He feared that the Gladstonians '[would] yield to the demands of the New [Trade] Unionism just as they [had] previously yielded to the claims of the Irish Nationalists, the Local Veto fanatics, and the Radical opponents of the House of Lords'. He felt that '[t]he Independent Labour Party [was] proceeding on this assumption'.[12]

By the same token, he was aware that Unionist coercion in Ireland could be seen as a form of class struggle in which his party was aligned on the 'wrong' side. Even for the rabidly Unionist *Weekly Times*, the eviction of 'many poor tenants . . . including old men and women and children . . . without providing any other shelter, but rather burn[ing] the houses to the ground rather than they should be re-entered' appeared 'so unnecessary, so heartless, so cruel, so inhuman', nothing but 'acts of Vandalism'.[13] Chamberlain himself was shocked and thought that it was 'suicidal' for the Liberal Unionists to support such policies.[14] He voted against the proclamation of the INL and urged Hartington and Randolph Churchill to consider a more 'constructive' approach. Hartington replied that this would undermine the alliance with the Tories and bring the Liberal Unionists to a schism, and Chamberlain desisted.[15]

Liberal Unionist cohesion was also ruffled by the new politics of gender. As Martin Pugh has pointed out, while the party's male leaders 'proved highly unsympathetic' to women's demands, Liberal Unionism attracted a number of prominent female suffragists, including Lydia Becker, Millicent Fawcett, Kate Courtney and Isabella M. S. Tod.[16] As we have already seen in the previous chapter, their Liberal Unionism had a variety of different motivations and different outcomes – with, for example, Fawcett supporting and Courtney opposing the Boer War at the turn of the century.[17] Paradoxically, as Liberal Unionism lost popular support, it became more amenable to the demands of its

[12] Memo., 13 Nov. 1894, cited in Fraser, *Chamberlain*, 152. For the increasingly collectivist attitudes within the TUC see J. Keir Hardie, 'The Trades Congress, special report', *WT&E*, 10 Sep. 1893, 9; Ben Tillett, 'The Trades Union Congress', *WT&E*, 16 Sep. 1894, 6; and F. G. Jones, 'Socialism and capital', ibid., which preached class struggle from an aggressively Marxist standpoint. See also Morgan, *Keir Hardie*, 69.
[13] L.a., 'The government losing ground', *WT&E*, 23 Jan. 1887, 8.
[14] Gardiner, *Harcourt*, vol. II, 45.
[15] Garvin, *Chamberlain*, vol. II, 313–14; Gardiner, *Harcourt*, vol. II, 46.
[16] Pugh, *March of the women*, 132.   [17] Laity, *British peace movement*, 154.

radical fringes, among which the women were prominent and increasingly vocal. They were able to achieve a higher profile within a shrinking
movement.[18] In particular, the Women's Liberal Unionist Association
was as assertive as the Gladstonian Women's Liberal Federation.[19]
Moreover, their importance within the party as a whole was recognized
at the 1891 Conference of Liberal Unionist Associations, when the
fifty delegates from the women's associations were 'admitted for the
first time ... to share the counsels of their masculine colleagues' –
something which the women of the WLF had also tried, unsuccessfully,
to achieve. This success was further highlighted by the fact that Kate
Courtney was asked to write the conference report for *The Liberal
Unionist*, and thus acted as the official spokesperson on behalf of the
male as well as female members.[20] A few months later it was Isabella
M. S. Tod who reported about the Ulster Unionist convention.[21] In this
context, in 1891–2 the Scottish Liberal Unionists demanded women's
suffrage as part of a broader and truly radical programme, which
included, among other issues, graduated taxation and the reform of
the House of Lords.[22]

Among the cause's advocates were the two most widely circulated
Liberal Unionist penny weeklies. In particular, the *Weekly Times* combined 'class' and gender analysis in its advocacy of 'womanhood suffrage,
as well as manhood suffrage, [as] the ultimate best condition of a really
free people'.[23] Women were workers and tax-payers and as such had
'earned' the vote. 'To-day every man, to-morrow, let us hope, *every
woman* – for the worker's battle cannot be won while women but look
on – who earns his or her living, or is willing to do so, is bound to fight
to get it – *a living*, mind, not mere existence. Theirs is the party of the
future – the true Commonwealth.'[24] The vote for all adult women became

---

[18] Electoral prospects were so bad that Kate Courtney considered quite bluntly the possibility that 'every Liberal Unionist member [would lose] his seat at the next election': 'The
Manchester conference', *The Liberal Unionist*, Dec. 1891, 81.

[19] Pugh, *March of the women*, 132.   [20] Courtney, 'The Manchester conference'.

[21] I. M. S. Tod, 'Ulster convention: preliminary meeting', *The Liberal Unionist*, May 1892,
1–2. It is indicative of Liberal Unionist women's ambitions that, despite all these tangible
marks of recognition, Millicent Fawcett felt it necessary to write a scathing letter to the
editors of the party's monthly magazine complaining about what she perceived as their
'reactionary' attitude to women's rights, resenting the fact that they did not enthusiastically endorse the cause (M. Garrett Fawcett, 'Women and politics', *The Liberal Unionist*,
Jan. 1892, 109).

[22] Burgess, *'Strange alliances'*, 75.

[23] See the editorials 'Women's right to labour', *LW*, 26 June 1887, 6; 'Ladies to the front',
WT&E, 26 May 1889, 6; and 'Women suffrage', *WT&E*, 12 July 1891, 8.

[24] L.a., 'The new political party', *WT&E*, 19 Nov. 1893, 8.

the newspaper's official policy from 1894, when, as we shall see, the newspaper was at the height of its enthusiasm for socialism.[25] Even then it did not advocate the vote for women because they were equal with men, but because they had distinctive feminine gifts from which society would benefit. In particular, it credited women with special powers of 'intuition' which would enable them to detect 'sham Liberalism'. Moreover, their help and co-operation 'on equal terms' with men was needed in order to achieve any real improvement in society, including 'stemming the dreadful increase of gambling and betting ... redressing the unequal laws governing the relations of men and women which make so disastrously for immorality', bringing about the revival of 'real religion in the Churches', and especially establishing socialism.[26]

The *Weekly Times* was then at the beginning of an unusual ideological development which was to bring it from Radical Unionism to socialism and back to New Liberalism by the turn of the century. In many ways its trajectory symbolized the dilemmas of the left in the 1890s. For, on the one hand, the latter was attracted by Chamberlain's version of liberalism, with its emphasis on social justice and the relief of poverty. On the other, no one who took democracy seriously could permanently ignore the issues raised by Home Rule – including national self-determination versus imperialism – and the parallel humanitarian questions associated with Gladstonian politics.

From Radical Unionism to socialism: the strange trajectory of the *Weekly Times*

Surprisingly, despite the richness of its political texture and connections, this remarkable newspaper has been little studied.[27] Established in 1847, for forty years it consistently voiced the claims of metropolitan radicalism until the Home Rule crisis forced its editors to reassess their view of Gladstonian Liberalism. While one of its main competitors, *Reynolds's News*, renewed its well-established commitment to Home Rule, and another, *Lloyd's Weekly*, became Unionist out of commercial considerations, in 1886 the *Weekly Times* espoused Radical Unionism on the basis

---

[25] L.a., 'How many have the vote, and use it?', *WT&E*, 22 Apr. 1894, 8.
[26] L.a., 'Women's suffrage and the Registration Bill', *WT&E*, 17 June 1894, 8; for enthusiastic endorsement by a reader see letter by H. H. Hopkins, 'Women and the suffrage', *WT&E*, 24 June 1894, 6.
[27] The only study is V. Berridge's unpublished Ph.D. thesis, 'Popular journalism and working-class attitudes', University of London, 1976. Very few historians have taken any notice of the *Weekly Times*: two rare exception are Barrow and Bullock, *Democratic ideas*, 40, 92.

of political conviction. Moreover, precisely because it arose from conviction, Unionism motivated the editors to rethink the purposes and aims of radicalism. Consequently, the newspaper's ideological outlook and range of contributors changed several times during the following twenty years. In 1886 the editors sacked the long-serving 'Littlejohn', because he was a Home Ruler. Later, by the end of the 1880s, they opened up their columns to contributors and correspondents from the socialist and anarchist left. The newspaper's advertisement and self-presentation in the *Press Directory* changed accordingly: between 1886 and 1893 it was described as 'Liberal' in politics and advocating 'all measures of political and social progress and an abolition of all the distinctive privileges in the Universities, Church, etc.'.[28] From 1894 it was described as 'Democratic. Advocates, irrespective of party, the claims of the workers, and all social reforms, especially Labour questions.'[29] Even the new wording understated the extent of the change, for the *Weekly Times* had become a forum for socialist and feminist ideas, playing a role similar to that of *The Bee Hive* in its heyday in the early 1860s. But, unlike *The Bee Hive*, which had always been constrained by its small circulation, the *Weekly Times & Echo* claimed an 'enormous sale' in the mid-1890s and a growing distribution, reaching 'more than Two Million Readers'.[30]

In this respect, a comparison with the equally mass-circulated *Lloyd's Weekly* is instructive. In the aftermath of the Home Rule split, both newspapers defended their Unionist stance by claiming that Gladstone was distracting radical energies from the struggle against poverty and widespread sickness. However, both newspapers were anti-socialist, claiming that state intervention ought to support – rather than replace – traditional self-help, for example by providing loans to working men wishing to buy their homes and by involving the friendly societies in a national old age pensions scheme.[31] In fact they were rather complacent about the urban poor: Britain was already providing for them 'bountifully', although the system could be improved by discriminating more carefully in favour of the elderly and sick 'from whom no labour can be expected'. As for the able-bodied unemployed, they should be sent to labour colonies, where, as 'inmates', they would be made to perform

---

[28] *Newspaper Press Directory* (1886), 46.   [29] Ibid. (1894), 74.

[30] Ibid., advertisement section, 241. This may have implied a much smaller circulation, perhaps below 500,000 copies – on the assumption that each copy was read by at least four people. It was certainly lower than the circulation of its main Liberal Unionist competitor, the *Lloyd's Weekly*, which boasted 'the largest circulation in the world', in excess of two million *copies*.

[31] L.a., 'Social reforms', *LW*, 14 Oct. 1894, 8.

useful tasks, such as reclaiming waste lands.[32] As in the 1860s, these newspapers insisted that the country's principal need was 'for retrenchment in our national expenditure'.[33] On Irish and imperial affairs they advocated Chamberlain's views,[34] but hoped for Liberal reunion and refused to accept the Conservative alliance as anything more than a temporary arrangement serving contingent political emergencies. They were both 'old Free Traders' and denounced 'the fallacies of Fair Trade', including the delusion that protection would increase employment at home: 'the only people who would benefit would be the landlords'.[35] 'Fair trade' was nothing less than a '[conspiracy] against the commercial supremacy of England' and in 1889 the *Weekly Times* dismissed the Sugar Bounties Bill – the aim of which was to limit the importation of bounty-fed, artificially cheap European sugar, which was replacing British West Indian cane sugar – as the product of 'folly'.[36]

The two papers started to diverge when Radical Unionism began to run out of steam in 1889–90. *Lloyd's Weekly* chose to dilute its political content and coverage and eventually came back to the Liberal fold by 1906, under the editorship of Robert Donald, who had written for T. P. O'Connor's *Star* in the late 1880s.[37] The *Weekly Times* adopted the opposite course and became more militant, and more serious about social reform. Moreover, each in its own way tried to respond not only to changed political circumstances, but also to the growing specialization of the popular press. One of the most interesting developments of the late 1880s was the rise of 'non-political' working-class newspapers like the *Cotton Factory Times* (Manchester), the *Yorkshire Factory Times* (Barnsley) and the *Labour Tribune* (West Bromwich). They were concerned with issues such as strikes, wages, rents and land reform and supported direct labour representation,[38] but neither reported nor discussed party political matters in the way traditional radical weeklies had

---

[32] L.a., 'The unemployed, and why?', *WT&E*, 23 October 1887, 8.

[33] L.a., 'Free trade in America, and what it means', *WT&E*, 11 Dec. 1887, 8.

[34] 'The British Empire must be the Empire of the many, and the many must take the trouble to learn to govern it if it is to be of permanent advantage to the many.' (L.a., 'The colonial question', *WT&E*, 1 Sep. 1889, 8.)

[35] L.a., 'Free trade in America, and what it means', *WT&E*, 11 Dec. 1887, 8.

[36] L.a., 'parliamentary prospects', *WT&E*, 26 May 1889, 8. See A. Howe, *Free trade and liberal England, 1846–1946* (1997), 204.

[37] O'Connor, *Memoirs of an old parliamentarian*, vol. II, 256; A. J. Lee, 'The radical press', in A. J. A. Morris (ed.), *Edwardian radicalism, 1900–1914* (London, 1974), 52; A. J. A. Morris, 'Donald, Sir Robert (1860–1933)', in *ODNB*.

[38] However, the *Cotton Factory Times* opposed the formation of the Labour Representation Committee (LRC) in 1900: the editors regarded an independent Labour party as a useless addition to the 'burdens of labour': l.a., 'Parliamentary labour representation', 13 Jan. 1900, 1.

done for generations since the heyday of Chartism. For example, from the outset they steered clear of the whole Home Rule controversy, paying no attention whatever to Irish issues.[39] Partly as a reaction to the 'eviction' of party politics from the new working-class press, there was the emergence of strictly political, local penny papers, which targeted specific working-class communities, reporting only the parliamentary divisions which were of local interest and broadcasting local news and what the proprietors saw as 'instructive political articles, social notes & (as an additional attraction) a social novel'.[40] Finally, in view of the fact that more than ever before reading was becoming part of the burgeoning leisure industry, we should remember that the decade saw the success of non-political, leisure-oriented publications like *Titbits*.[41] *Lloyd's Weekly* successfully steered a middle course between leisure, information and its traditional political vocation. Although it continued to be described as 'Advanced-Liberal and popular progressive', it endeavoured to renew its appeal 'to the million' by exploiting what it described as 'the two great principles of quantity and cheapness'. Besides offering value for money in terms of news coverage, it claimed that 'its contents [were] far more creditable and comprise far more of light and literary character, than might be conceived. Certainly it present[ed] an immense mass of matter; with a little of everything, and a good deal of many things.'[42] Finally, although not stated in its advertisements, the newspaper remained alert to market demands, wishing to *reflect*, rather than *form*, public opinion. For example, despite its consistent Unionism, *Lloyd's Weekly* was ready to capitalize on the widespread popular veneration of Gladstone as the national icon of a past age. It hosted articles by him and interviews with him,

[39] In June 1886 the *Labour Tribune* simply published a manifesto approved by the Labour MPs and signed by Arch and Joseph Leicester, and invited the reader to vote for the labour representatives irrespective of any other consideration: *Labour Tribune*, 19 June 1886, 4. The *Cotton Factory Times* expressed no views on the general election of 1886, but then celebrated Broadhurst's appointment in the Home Office as a great opportunity for the labour movement, in view of the fact that that department controlled the inspection of factory and mines (l.a., *Cotton Factory Times*, 5 Mar. 1886, 3). This has sometimes been construed as evidence that working men had no time for Home Rule, which was just another Liberal fad that 'blocked the way' to practical social reform. However, even scholars like Henry Pelling, who suggested this view, had to admit that somehow the Labour party too adopted Irish Home Rule by 1900, as either an electoral necessity or a matter of principle (Pelling, *Origins of the Labour party*, 30). This is an implicit admission of the fact that political parties with the ambition of appealing to the working men had no way of avoiding the Home Rule question.

[40] D. Rees from the *Chronicle*, Northwich, to T. E. Ellis, 14 May 1888, about the proposal to establish a new newspaper, in NLW, T. E. Ellis MSS, 1723.

[41] H. Friederichs, *The life of Sir George Newnes* (1911), 48–103.

[42] *Newspaper Press Directory* (1894), 66.

illustrated with portraits and autographs (obviously the GOM was happy to be published in the 'largest circulated newspaper of the world').[43]

The *Weekly Times'* strategy was totally different. Far from responding to the demand for leisure-oriented and light-hearted journalism, it adhered to the secularized puritanism of the J. S. Mill tradition to the extent of taking pride in its refusal to publish any 'sporting or other objectionable news'.[44] Throughout the period it was published by one E. J. Kibblewhite.[45] It claimed to be speaking for '[the] daily-growing myriads of our people' who were concerned about how to apply 'the principle of Brotherhood' to national government, but '[were] not interested in Home Rule, or Disestablishment, or any one of the shibboleths by means of which rival sets of self-seeking statesmen strive for office'.[46]

However, as we have seen, its politics were at first rather conventional and unreceptive of the new social radicalism: for example, as late as 1887–8 it was sceptical about Bismarck's proposals for 'the general insurance of the German working classes', dismissing them as 'undoubtedly Socialistic' and too expensive to be practical.[47] The ideological turning point apparently came as a reaction to labour unrest from 1888, which led to growing disenchantment with Liberal Unionism and disgust for the other alternatives facing 'the English Democracy'.[48] In response to the great strikes of 1888–9 the editor started to make space for external contributors of a more or less socialist orientation. The newspaper rapidly moved from recommending soup kitchens and 'five acres and a cow', to demanding alternative employment for starving dockers,[49] and, finally, to hosting high-powered discussions of new radical ideas. This took the shape of the regular publication of a large number of 'letters to the editor', including contributions from socialists of various schools. Such correspondence occupied a whole page of each issue – certainly more than might have been commercially viable; it must have reflected a deliberate editorial policy which the proprietors were prepared to subsidize. An

---

[43] *LW*, 4 May 1890, 8–9.   [44] *Newspaper Press Directory* (1894), 74.

[45] About whom very little is known. The *Weekly Times* company was voluntarily wound up in 1911: National Archives, BT31/12277/9714.

[46] L.a., 'German Socialism', *WT&E*, 26 May 1889, 8. However, it strongly supported Welsh disestablishment in 1895, when it was introduced by Asquith, and strongly criticized the Liberal Unionists for opposing the Bill: 'Liberalism worthy of the name', whether Unionist or not, '*must* destroy such excrescences as the Welsh Establishment ...' (L.a., 'Welsh disestablishment', *WT&E*, 3 Mar. 1895, 8 (emphasis in the original)).

[47] L.a., 'Prince Bismarck and socialism', *WT&E*, 11 Dec. 1887, 8. Although it regarded the English Poor Law also as both 'socialist' and expensive.

[48] L.a., 'Humbug all round', *WT&E*, 14 July 1889, 8.

[49] See the long letter by A. Johnson, a frequent contributor, on 'Socialism and its critics', *WT&E*, 28 July 1889, 11; 'The cry of the unemployed', *WT&E*, 16 Oct. 1887, 6; 'The great dock labourers' strike', *WT&E*, 1 Sep. 1889, 9.

important new development was the weekly column of John Morrison Davidson, a former and future editor of *Reynolds's* and the author of a number of works on radicalism.[50] The fact that his Christian socialist rhetoric was sometimes echoed in the leading articles was in itself a new departure for a newspaper which had traditionally been militantly anti-clerical, and which, in its criticism of Home Rule, appeared to be more concerned to roll back 'priestism', than to safeguard the empire.[51] But it is difficult to draw conclusions about this aspect of the editorial line because the newspaper was really an open forum for the left as a whole. By 1894 its correspondents included H. M. Hyndman, Edward Aveling and Eleanor Marx, Tom Mann, Ben Tillett, J. Keir Hardie, J. Ramsay MacDonald and various feminists.[52] Other correspondents advocated anarchism rather than socialism, boasting links with illustrious continental exiles such as Kropotkin, Merlino and Yanovsky.[53]

Their proposals were very 'advanced', as one might have expected from such a group, and ranged from land nationalization and the right to work (the county councils should provide work for the unemployed), to rudimentary forms of planned economy to replace competition and the market and – remarkably – the proto-Keynesian notion that unemployment derived from idle capital, or 'the refusal of capitalists to allow their

---

[50] Such as *Eminent radicals in and out of Parliament* (1879): cf. Shannon, *Bulgarian agitation*, 227–8. He described himself as a Scottish 'Barrister-at-Law': 'The old order and the new: from individualism to collectivism', *WT&E*, 16 June 1889, 10. A Christian socialist standpoint was also expressed by other contributors: John Howie, 'Jesus and socialism', *WT&E*, 7 July 1889, 12. For the change in the editorials see 'The great dock labourers' strike', *WT&E*, 1 Sep. 1889, 9.

[51] See the letter by Agnostic, 'Home Rule and toleration', *WT&E*, 12 Mar. 1893, 6, and the editorials 'Mr Gladstone and Protestantism', 12 Mar. 1893, 6 and 'The Home Rule Bill postponed', 19 Mar. 1893, 8; see also the strongly anti-Evangelical l.a., 'Queer co-religionists', 23 Mar. 1891, 8. Another article concluded that 'the ultra-religious of all sects are much alike' ending up in clericalism and bigotry ('The "distinctive religious teaching" difficulty', 19 Nov. 1893, 8).

[52] E.g. Mrs Warner Snoad, 'The Women's Progressive Society', *WT&E*, 2 Apr. 1893, 12; Katharine St. John Conway, 'A new A B C', *WT&E*, 24 June 1894, 6 and 1 July 1894, 6; and H. A. Hopkins, 'Women and the suffrage', *WT&E*, 24 June 1894, 6. See also the leaders 'Voteless women slaves', *WT&E*, 23 Apr. 1893, 8 (about the exploitation of women's labour); and 'Woman in battle', *WT&E*, 29 Oct. 1893, 8 (about equality of dignity and opportunity); 'Women's trade unions', *WT&E*, 4 Nov. 1894, 8; and the plea for married women's suffrage, which would improve turn-out. The latter was a consideration of some importance, in view of the fact that one million electors did not vote in 1892 and another million were not registered, huge figures when compared with the government's majority of only 232,000. But then 'both political parties are afraid of women's suffrage' ('How many have the vote and use it?', *WT&E*, 22 Apr. 1894, 8).

[53] See letters about women's education, socialism and anarchism in *WT&E*, 8 April 1894, 6, and 30 June 1895, 6, and in particular J. Hunter Watts, 'Anarchism and social democracy', *WT&E*, 14 Jan. 1894, 6.

capital to be used unless they see fit'.[54] Yet, most of the policies advocated by both correspondents and editors were not incompatible with the views expressed by the radical wing of the NLF. Indeed the ultimate aims proclaimed by most *Weekly Times* correspondents were worded in such a way as to appear consistent with the old ideology of the 'free-born Englishman': they included an emphasis on personal 'independence', freedom from monopolies and privilege, and a commitment to the electoral process and parliamentary politics.[55] For some, socialism was 'the only method of securing the largest measure of liberty to the greatest number, of satisfactorily dealing with tyrannism [*sic*], and of respecting as far as is humanly possible the apparently sole want of the Anarchist, viz., his personal freedom – in fact it is . . . the best basis for freedom that can be devised'.[56] In this way socialism embodied 'the best tendencies . . . of the Democratic Movement' – a concept which may have reflected the influence of Eduard Bernstein (whose name, however, was never cited).[57] For others 'anarchism' was summed up in

The abolition of artificial monopoly and privilege; a society of free men, each one enjoying the fruits of his own labour, and being free to dispose of it as he pleases; each one being free to associate with his own fellows, or to decline; the production and distribution of wealth, organized and carried out by free individuals; a perfectly free market, a sound monetary system, free credit, free land – in short, a free life.[58]

Although officially the newspaper was not committed to any of the views published,[59] leading articles consistently upheld radical causes and occasionally flirted with anarchism, for example inciting its readers to fiscal rebellion.[60] Insisting that Liberalism should adopt social democracy, the

---

[54] See George Field, 'The right and the duty to work', *WT&E*, 26 Mar. 1893, 12. See also T. L. McCready, 'Single tax v. freedom', and R. Stevens, 'Human nature and poverty', in *WT&E*, 9 Sep. 1894, 6; A. Withy, 'Single tax and free money' and G. Standring, 'Christianity and social reform', in *WT&E*, 21 Oct. 1894, 6; Adrian Forr, 'What is socialism?', *WT&E*, 27 July 1890, 6.

[55] See J. Hunter Watts, 'Anarchism and social democracy', *WT&E*, 14 Jan. 1894, 6, who claimed that the anarchists dismissed electoral democracy and were mere individualists.

[56] See letters by J. B. Shipley and 'Another socialist' in *WT&E*, 7 Jan. 1894, 6.

[57] J. C. Kenworthy, 'Men of the movement: X – Ben Tillett', *WT&E*, 12 Aug. 1894, 4. Cf. I. Fetscher, 'Bernstein e la sfida all'ortodossia', in E. J. Hobsbawm, *Storia del marxismo*, vol. II (1979), 260. For Bernstein's influence in England see D. Tanner, 'Ideological debates in Edwardian Labour politics: radicalism, revisionism and socialism', in Biagini and Reid, *Currents of radicalism* (1991), 271–93.

[58] R. Stevens, 'Anarchism', *WT&E*, 14 Jan. 1894, 6.

[59] As one contributor admitted, 'it is well known that the Editor of this paper allows an open field of discussion' (J. Hunter Watts, 'Anarchism and social democracy', *WT&E*, 14 Jan. 1894, 6).

[60] L.a., 'Why should we pay taxes?', *WT&E*, 4 Feb. 1894, 8.

newspaper advertised Fabian tracts as embodying the best way forward in social reform and in particular popular education.[61] By July 1894 it regarded itself as belonging to the same league as *Clarion* and the *Labour Leader*. It fundraised for the ILP,[62] campaigned for Tom Mann[63] and deplored sectarian divisions among the various socialist schools, wishing that it were possible 'for us of the Movement ... to work as MEN and WOMEN bound to each other by the common tie of Humanity'.[64]

By 1893–4, for the first time since 1886, and perhaps because of the influence of Morrison Davidson, the *Weekly Times* expressed a more positive view of the Liberal party: in 1893 a leading article drew its readers' attention to the difference between 'the old' and 'the new' radicalism. The former 'kept a sharp eye upon the public purse and showed a laudable jealousy at every fresh demand upon its resources'. By contrast '[t]he new Radicalism hardly troubles itself to contend against the clamour of the generals and admirals ... being too much occupied in enforcing claims to increased outlay upon education, factory inspection and other expenditure of a more productive character'.[65] In 1894 the newspaper welcomed Harcourt's famous budget as 'the thin end of the wedge as regards the graduation of the Death Duties'.[66]

These changes were accompanied by the gradual adoption of a more nuanced attitude to the Irish question, in particular through the espousal of the notion of imperial federation – 'which is so dear to large-minded patriots both here and beyond the sea'.[67] Home Rule for Ireland featured prominently only in J. Keir Hardie's 1892 electoral programme, printed in full,[68] but the editor was tolerant enough to allow Morrison Davidson to advocate 'Home Rule All Round'.[69] As a Scot, his views echoed the debate within the radical wings of both parties north of the border,[70] but

---

[61] L.a., 'State education at home and abroad', *WT&E*, 15 July 1894, 8.

[62] L.a., 'Wanted at once – £500', *WT&E*, 15 July 1894, 8.

[63] 'Every Trade Unionist should, by every means in his power, forward Tom Mann's candidature.' ('Powder and shot', *WT&E*, 12 Aug. 1894, 9.)

[64] L.a., 'The SDF and the ILP', *WT&E*, 12 Aug. 1894, 8–9; l.a., 'The "larger hope" of socialism', *WT&E*, 19 Aug. 1894, 8. This article commented upon and endorsed a letter from H. M. Hyndman published in the same issue.

[65] L.a., 'The disappointing Budget', *WT&E*, 30 Apr. 1893, 8.

[66] L.a., 'The Budget', *WT&E*, 22 Apr. 1894, 8.

[67] L.a., 'Imperial penny postage', *WT&E*, 30 Apr. 1893, 8.

[68] Rep., 'Mr Keir Hardie and his programme', *WT&E*, 10 July 1892, 6. However, the same page contained a report about Daniel O'Connell's son supporting a Unionist candidate and rejecting Home Rule as 'not only ... injurious to this country, but most disastrous to Ireland'.

[69] J. Morrison Davidson, 'Scotland and Home Rule', *WT&E*, 8 Apr. 1894, 6.

[70] E. g. J. Milne Watts (Glasgow) to E. Blake, 9 Aug. 1892, NLI, Blake Letters [222] 4684; Cameron, *Mackintosh*, 3.

there was little doubt that on Irish affairs Morrison Davidson was close to the Gladstonians. Indeed, in 1888 he had fervently advocated Irish Home Rule in *Reynolds's*, a newspaper for which he wrote again from 1900.[71] In 1895 he used the columns of the *Weekly Times* to defend the Liberal government, which he saw as locked in a mortal struggle against privilege and on behalf of labour.[72] Surveying Gladstone's last campaign, Davidson argued that the GOM's mistake was not to make the second Home Rule Bill the issue of 'an informal *Referendum*', seeking a mandate from the people instead of proceeding as he did by 'his crafty policy of concealment'.[73] He eulogized his successor Rosebery as a fearless fighter against the 'most unholy Trinity' (peer, publican and parson). The fall of the Rosebery government was due to 'the Parnellites, the Scottish Crofters, the ILP's and the SDF's' who had 'stabbed in the back' the Liberal and Home Rule alliance. Indeed, he credited the nine Parnellites not only with ruining Rosebery's strategy of 'filling up the cup' (that is, by provoking the Lords to stop popular legislation), but also with 'ruthlessly smashing it to pieces when more than half-full of very tolerable democratic liquor'. Useful, necessary measures including 'the factory, Irish Land, Crofters' and Welsh Disestablishment Bills' had come to nothing 'because of an adverse majority of seven on Cordite'. It was an indictment not of the Liberals, but of 'Party Government and methods of parliamentary legislation'. The greatest loser was Ireland, which 'has ... been ... most loyal to the Liberal alliance; more loyal than many Liberal members themselves'. The anti-Parnellites were singled out for special praise: they were 'mostly poor, but nearly all able men'.[74] He concluded with a prophecy about the Liberal party, which

has been sloughing off 'Class' after 'Class' and 'interest' after 'interest', but its grand mission is not yet fulfilled. That mission is not to disestablish Churches and Public Houses, or even to pass Factory Bills, but to give the people One Adult One Vote of Equal Value; Annual or Biennial Parliaments; Second Ballot; Paid

---

[71] See his serialized work signed J. M. D., 'The Book of Erin, Chapter XVI', *RN*, 26 Feb. 1888, 2 and 'Our glorious constitution: how it came about', *RN*, 7 Oct. 1900, 7 (one of a series on this topic).

[72] J. Morrison Davidson, 'The cordite coalition', *WT&E*, 30 June 1895, 6.

[73] Ibid. Suspicion of Gladstone's 'crafty' approach had been recurrent in the popular radical press at least since 1886: see for an example l.a., 'The autumn campaign', *RN*, 9 Oct. 1887, 1.

[74] J. Morrison Davidson, 'The cordite coalition'. However, the 'cordite affair' – the allegedly inadequate supply of explosives, on which Campbell Bannerman resigned – actually elicited some animosity from *Weekly Times* contributors, who claimed to be concerned both about national security in case of a war, and about the welfare of government workers in arsenals and arms factories: see letter by 'Nemesis', 'The late Liberal government and government workers', *WT&E*, 30 June 1895, 6.

membership and Election Expenses; federal Home Rule; the Initiative and Referendum.[75]

The 'initiative and referendum' – the former to empower citizens to start legislation, the latter to enable them to enact it by plebiscite – would shift the balance of power away from Parliament towards the electorate, who would acquire the power to initiate legislation and to vote directly on specific Bills. These radical changes would in turn be the first step towards what the author described as 'the Cooperative Commonwealth'. The latter should be a decentralized democracy with separate provincial assemblies for '"Greater" London, Scotland, Wales, Ulster [and] Erin (that is, the rest of Ireland)'.[76] This proposal was vaguely reminiscent of Chamberlain's 1885 plan, but Morrison Davidson also borrowed liberally from the continental tradition of radical democracy and socialism. In particular, 'the initiative and referendum' had long been debated within socialist circles and endorsed by the Second International at the 1893 Zurich Congress.[77] Much of it – such as the second ballot, manhood suffrage and payment of both MPs and their electoral expenses – had already been adopted by Liberal and Radical clubs around the country.[78]

By the summer of 1894 one of the readers of the *Weekly Times* congratulated the editors on their dropping the Unionist cause in favour of a new line, which sought to foster a 'progressive' alliance between socialism and a regenerated post-Gladstonian Liberal party.[79] The leaders of such an alliance were to be Keir Hardie and Rosebery, imaginatively joined in an improbable but suggestive partnership – a reminder of the extent to which the Scottish peer was regarded as a radical.[80] For Morrison Davidson a Liberal–Labour electoral alliance was essential to avoid

---

[75] Morrison Davidson, 'Cordite coalition'.

[76] J. Brailsford Bright, 'A possible Labour Parliament', *WT&E*, 23 Dec. 1894, 6.

[77] Barrow and Bullock, *Democratic ideas*, 50–6. The referendum was to be widely discussed in both Liberal and Conservative circles in the run up to the constitutional crisis of 1911: L. Atherley-Jones, 'The Liberal party and the House of Lords', *The Nineteenth Century Review*, 62 (1907), 170; J. A. Hobson, *The crisis of Liberalism: new issues of democracy* (1909), 37–8. Cf. G. Guazzaloca, *Fine secolo: gli intellettuali italiani e nglesi e la crisi fra otto e Novecento* (2004), 151–63.

[78] See, for example, the 'Social and political programme' of the Partick Liberal Association (Mitchel Library, Glasgow), 18 Mar. 1891. Partick was at the time an inner-city ship-building district.

[79] 'The articles by J. C. Kenworthy, Keir Hardie, and Morrison Davidson are splendid. At last I am firmly convinced that the position you have taken up in regard to politics and labour is right. Six months ago I had almost given your paper up because of what you were constantly saying about the Liberal Party. But you were always right. From Kenworthy's article on Hardie I could see Hardie was a man to be trusted. He is the only true Democrat in the House of Commons.' (Letter by 'A Primitive Methodist', 'Driving it home at last!', *WT&E*, 15 July 1894, 6.)

[80] L. McKinstry, *Rosebery: statesman in turmoil* (2005), 123–4, 140–2, 301.

splitting the 'progressive' vote against 'aristocratic forces and plutocratic fraud [which for centuries] have robbed you and your forefathers of the two most elementary Rights of Man – the Right to the Suffrage and the Right to the Soil'.

At most General Elections, of late years, there has been little or nothing to choose between the two historical parties – the Liberals and the Tories – who have been about equally your enemies when *in office* . . . But in the present instance the case is different. The late Liberal Government may not have adopted . . . the best methods of affecting imperative reforms, but that it did achieve several of considerable magnitude and seriously attempt others cannot in justice be gainsaid.

In particular, the 1894 budget 'affirmed the great principle that in taxation the heaviest burden should be laid on the most burdensome (the landlords and the capitalists) and not the most burdened members of the community'. Moreover, 'to the villagers [the Liberal government] gave their Magna Charta' in the shape of parish councils and 'to Londoners the Equalization of their Rates'.[81] While '*Collectivism* was the goal', the Liberals could provide the means to reach it. They were a 'reclaimable, and . . . at present a *reclaimed* party'. Morrison Davidson proposed a programme of political, social and economic reforms which combined radical liberalism with socialist and anarchist demands. They comprised universal suffrage (women and 'paupers especially included'), church disestablishment, Home Rule All Round, decentralization on the US, 'or better the Swiss model', and payment of MPs. He went beyond parliamentary democracy with his insistence on 'the Initiative and Referendum' and the reform or abolition of both the House of Lords and the monarchy. He recommended economic and social reforms ranging from old age and widows' pensions, municipal control over the liquor trade and free education (including university), to the Eight-Hour Bill, parish ownership of land and mines, a 'Cooperative Commonwealth' to

---

[81] J. Morrison Davidson, 'To the electors and non-electors of Great Britain and Ireland', *WT&E*, 7 July 1895, 6. For another correspondent (W. Saunders, 'Toryism in Liberal disguise', *WT&E*, 1 July 1894, 6) the alliance was supposed to work along lines which anticipated the 1903–6 Herbert Gladstone–MacDonald pact: 'A mere tactical but loyal alliance, offensive and defensive, is all that is wanted. Let the Labourist candidate be withdrawn in constituencies in which their chance is hopeless, and where they have reasonable prospect of winning let the Liberals do so likewise, and thus make common cause against the unprincipled alliance of King Salisbury and the shameless Brummagem apostate.' Other contributors were less favourably disposed towards the Liberal government: 'The most important proposals of the Newcastle Programme, those upon which the present Cabinet obtained office, have been left without any attempt at fulfilment . . . The leaders of the Liberal Party have for eight years kept an impossible Home Rule Bill across the path of progress; and as an additional obstruction they have now got up an agitation against the House of Lords, which can have no practical effect.'

provide jobs or living wages for the unemployed at the expense of the wealthy classes, land nationalization, and free transport by rail or tram. It also demanded the repudiation of the National Debt – a revolutionary proposal if ever there was one in England. Of these proposals, he regarded full parliamentary democracy as the most important.[82]

These articles marked a final shift in editorial policy, away from any residual Unionism. As early as March 1895 the *Weekly Times* had strongly supported Asquith's Welsh Disestablishment Bill[83] and at the ensuing general election it endorsed both Liberal and ILP/socialist candidates, including Keir Hardie, Ben Tillet, Tom Mann, Pete Curran, James Sexton, J. Ramsay MacDonald, George Lansbury and H. M. Hyndman.[84] Morrison Davidson's influence was also reflected in the fact that the newspaper's *official* stance now included both 'Home Rule All Round' and 'the Democratic Federation of the Colonies'. Its social and economic agenda ranged from 'the nationalization of the railways, mines, factories and the land' to 'a minimum wage of thirty shillings in all State and Municipal employment, and a maximum Eight Hour Day in all businesses'.[85] The 'well-expressed essence' of 'Social-Democracy' was the policy which 'a revitalized and real' Liberal party should champion. This was of course an idea which was also becoming popular in Liberal circles, with important consequences over the next twenty years.[86]

Sectionalism or class struggle?

These developments within the Radical Unionist camp were somehow paralleled in Ireland by the growth of agrarian radicalism – which caused both the left-wing Unionists and the Nationalists to adopt similar demands by the end of the century. In particular, in Ulster T. W. Russell was persuaded that the Irish question mainly concerned class conflict over land ownership: if the latter could be solved, 'the Irish peasant would settle down like an ordinary citizen'.[87] Moreover, he believed that the solution lay in compulsory purchase which, contrary to what many of his contemporary critics argued, he started to demand as

---

[82] J. Morrison Davidson, 'To the electors and non-electors of Great Britain and Ireland', *WT&E*, 7 July 1895, 6.

[83] L.a., 'Welsh disestablishment', *WT&E*, 3 Mar. 1895, 8.

[84] L.a., 'New lamps for old ones', *WT&E*, 30 June 1895, 8.

[85] L.a., 'The dissolution, and after', *WT&E*, 7 July 1895, 8.

[86] P. F. Clarke, 'The progressive movement in England', *Transactions of the Royal Historical Society*, 24 (1974), 159–81 and *Liberals and social democrats* (1978), 9–61; A. F. Havinghurst, *Radical journalist: H. W. Massingham (1860–1924)* (1974), 45–53.

[87] Rep., 'Mr T. W. Russell at Birmingham', *The Northern Whig*, 13 Apr. 1889, 6. For Balfour's view see Shannon, *Balfour*, 48, 72–3.

early as 1887, largely in response to his constituents' views, and in the teeth of strong opposition from other Ulster Unionists.[88] In fact, he later wavered in his resolve,[89] being frequently berated by other Liberal Unionists for his opportunism and 'confiscatory' proclivities. However, they too were rather confused about the issue.

The problem was that the landlords were caught between falling rents and a militant peasantry enjoying dual-ownership status under the remarkably favourable conditions created by the Land Acts. Aware of the value of Gladstone's Act for appeasing the peasants, Balfour had extended its benefits to the leaseholders in 1887. By 1888, as a consequence of both judicial reductions and the Plan of Campaign, net rentals had fallen considerably. Lord Lansdowne – who saw his Irish rents drop from £23,000 to £500 – thought that compulsory purchase 'would be an immense relief' provided 'the terms would stop 'short of confiscation'.[90]

Thus the divide between Russell and the other Liberal Unionists was less pronounced than his fierce rhetoric and their indignant denunciations would suggest. Landowners feared 'compulsion' only in so far as it might involve 'confiscation' or sale at a low price. This was widely expected to be the outcome of such an operation unless it was underwritten by the Treasury. The short shrift given by Parliament to Gladstone's 1886 Bill suggested that there was little chance of any government committing large amounts of tax-payers' money to a policy which would benefit one class, and especially the Irish landowners. Moreover, they feared that compulsion would create a dangerous precedent: for 'the principle once admitted – there is nothing to prevent a radical government applying it to any body of Protestant occupiers that a Popish or Fenian majority wish removed from any part of Ireland to make room for "men of their own"'.[91] For all these reasons the moderate or Whig section of the Ulster Liberal Unionists favoured gradual, *voluntary* sale under some extended version of the Ashbourne Act.[92]

The problem with this strategy was that, as the tenant agitation spread to Protestant districts, time was running out for the landowners. They thought that the National League was deliberately causing a further depreciation of land, in the hope that tenants would be able to buy

[88] T. W. Russell, 'The government land proposals', *The Liberal Unionist*, 6 Apr. 1887, 18–19 and 'The Irish land settlement', ibid., Apr. 1890, 161–2.

[89] See the introduction to *'Compulsory Purchase' in Ireland: five speeches made by Mr T. W. Russell MP* (1901), PRONI, D/1507/A/2/3.

[90] Cited in Geary, *Plan of Campaign*, 49; Shannon, *Balfour*, 48; Solow, *The land question*, 184–5.

[91] J. Porter Porter to H. de F. Montgomery, 27 June 1892, PRONI, D/627/428/205.

[92] J. Britton to E. N. Herdman, 16 Apr. 1889, PRONI, D/627/428/95.

cheaper when the time came for wholesale purchase. Thus, 'the sooner a final settlement can be arranged, *the better for the landlords*, as in the present temper of times, and with the loose views that are being propagated ... as to the rights of all kind of property, delay in finding out some satisfactory solution of the present difficulty is likely to be more detrimental to the interests of the *few*, than of the *many*'.[93] As a leading Liberal Unionist privately observed in 1889, '[i]f in some counties or districts farmers are not agitating or anxious for this issue [compulsory sale], it may be that they are not fully conversant with all the advantages to themselves, or possibly that they are biding their time, waiting for a drop in rents to a lower level'.[94] In a similarly despondent mood another Liberal Unionist reported in 1892:

A candidate will not get in unless he supports Com.[pulsory] Sale. I went over to see my brother yesterday purposely to ask how D'[erry]gonnelly our hottest Orange quarter took [the Radical candidate Mr] Dane & if mention of Com.[pulsory] Sale. Edward replied 'not a man would have listened one minute to him if he had not said he was for it['] ... I personally feel very strongly against Comp.[ulsory] Sale but I'm not a narrow minded woman that can't drink tea out of a different cup & I see country clamour must be given in to & our own views laid aside, & I must support the Unionist candidate, even though he is a *Dane*, & that pretty *heartily* or the country men see thro' you & know you are very luke warm [*sic*].[95]

Indeed, tenant opinion soon forced even the ULUA to endorse compulsion 'upon equitable terms'.[96] By then Russell had made himself indispensable to his party. Both Hartington (by then Devonshire) and Chamberlain feared that 'if he were to leave us in dudgeon the greatest possible injury would be done to the Unionist cause, and therefore it is necessary to bear with him even when his actions are unwise or ill-conceived'.[97]

In this context, Russell's opportunism reflected widely acknowledged electoral constraints, compounded, in his specific case, by his comparatively vulnerable position as a Scottish radical of working-class background trying to retain the support of his Ulster constituents. In 1895 many Unionists were exasperated by his support for Morley's Land Bill, which made stringent provision for the imposition of judicial rents and

[93] R. MacGeagh to H. de F. Montgomery, 21 Apr. 1889, PRONI, D/627/428/98; emphasis in the original.
[94] Ibid.
[95] J. Porter Porter, Jamestown, Ballinamallard, Co Fermanagh, to H. de F. Montgomery, 27 June 1892, D/627/428/205 (emphasis in the original).
[96] In 1894: *Ulster Liberal Unionist Association*, 60–3.
[97] J. Chamberlain to H. de F. Montgomery, 9 Oct. 1894, PRONI, T/1089/261. Cf. the Duke of Devonshire to H. de F. Montgomery, 21 Mar. 1894, PRONI, T/1089/259.

stipulated that the latter should not be assessed on any increased value of the land due to the tenant's own improvements. Both provisos elicited considerable cross-community support from the tenants, with William O'Brien describing it as 'the best Land Bill ever introduced by an English Government',[98] Russell '[aligning] an impressive section of northern farming opinion behind Morley'[99] and the Nationalists enthusiastically supporting the Ulster Protestant land reformers.[100] For some time it seemed as though Radical Unionism would break away from the Unionist alliance: while a few Radical Unionist MPs supported the Liberal Welsh Disestablishment Bill,[101] the party bosses were most alarmed by the Antrim tenants' cry that 'they had no representatives' in the House of Commons to 'make their voices heard'.[102] Such claims suggested that even in Ulster the anti-Home Rule alliance could not be taken for granted and certainly had not overcome old class tensions. Moreover, between Catholic and Protestant tenants there was a basic convergence of *economic* interests, which was occasionally reflected in practical co-operation between them.[103] After all, agrarian radicalism had long been one of the Liberal strategies for attracting cross-community support in Ulster.[104] Although in 1885–92 it had been pushed to the back of the stage by the more pressing patriotic issues of the Union and Home Rule, T. W. Russell was aware that it was still viable.

---

[98] Rep., 'Mr Wm O'Brien, MP, in Cork', *FJ*, 9 Mar. 1895, 5 and l.a., *FJ*, 5 Mar. 1895, 4; T. W. Russell, 'Mr Morley and the Irish Land Bill', *Fortnightly Review*, 339 (1895), 348–51.

[99] Jackson, *Saunderson*, 122. See rep., 'Ulster and the Land Bill: important meeting of Unionist farmers in Derry: unanimous support for Mr Morley's proposals: "The most important parliamentary step since the Act of '81"', *FJ*, 7 Mar. 1895, 6.

[100] '[T]he people of the south and east and west of Ireland were standing shoulder to shoulder with the Presbyterians and Protestants of the north' in their demand for Morley's Land Bill: speech by T. J. Healy, cited in rep., 'Reorganisation in North Wexford', *FJ*, 8 Jan. 1895, 6. T. J. Healy (not to be confused with T. M. Healy) was MP for North Wexford. See also the welcome reserved to J. M. Armour in rep., 'Land meeting in Co. Derry', *FJ*, 11 Jan. 1895, 6, as well as J. R. B. McMinn, *Against the tide: a calendar of the papers of the Reverend J. M. Armour, Irish Presbyterian minister and Home Ruler, 1869–1914* (1985).

[101] Barker, *Gladstone and radicalism*, 97.

[102] J. W. Currie, cited in rep., 'The land question in Ulster: Antrim farmers and the Land Bill', *FJ*, 26 Feb. 1895, 5.

[103] Rep., 'The land agitation in Ulster: meeting of farmers in County Antrim', *FJ*, 9 Jan. 1895, 5; rep., 'Ulster farmers and the Land Bill', *FJ*, 9 Mar. 1895, 5. For the context see Jackson, 'Irish Unionism', 381–3.

[104] For evidence of inter-confessional co-operation against coercion in 1887 see rep., 'Gladstonian demonstration at Ballymoney,' *FJ*, 4 Nov. 1887, 7. On Liberal strategies in the North see Bew and Wright, 'The agrarian opposition in Ulster politics', 213–27; B. M. Walker, 'The land question and elections in Ulster, 1868–86', ibid., 230–69; and Greenlee, 'Land, religion and community'.

Morley's 1895 Bill died with the Liberal government, but from the new Unionist administration Russell demanded a further measure of land reform as the condition for his acceptance of office. They needed him and a Bill was duly introduced. Russell then further demonstrated his bargaining skills by forcing the government to withdraw a number of undesired pro-landowner amendments. This resulted in the 1896 Act.[105] However, by 1900 Russell's relentless support for tenant rights brought his partnership with Chamberlain to an end. Undeterred, he himself orchestrated the final break 'to ensure that he would not only be sacked, but would be sacked for reasons that would rally Ulster farmers in his support'.[106] Meanwhile he had energetically renewed his old policy of compulsory land purchase and presented it in 'revolutionary' terms as a scheme for the general state-sponsored transfer of all agricultural land in Ireland, except for that directly occupied by the landlords. His plan convinced William O'Brien, and the United Irish League (UIL) adopted it as part of their strategy – indeed, used it to expand their appeal from the 'congested' counties of the west to the prosperous tenant farmers in the east.[107] Thus, although as Bew has written, Russell was 'a rather unlikely friend of the UIL',[108] especially in view of his virulent anti-Catholicism, his Parnell-style hostility to the landowners and commitment to compulsory sale eventually brought him closer to O'Brien. In turn, the latter gradually overcame his aversion to what he had frequently described as 'the bigot of South Tyrone'. From December 1901 Russell started to support the UIL in its struggle over the De Freyne estate in Roscommon; then, with Nationalist help, Russellite candidates won by-elections at East Down (February 1902) and North Fermanagh (March 1903), which had previously been held by the Unionists. Once again the spectre of class-based radical politics was weakening Unionism and challenging Nationalist certainties.

Russell had always been a very independent MP, but in June 1901, after his break with Chamberlain, he actually established his own organization, the Ulster Farmers' and Labourers' Union and Compulsory Purchase Association, building on a pre-existing network of tenant groups in the province. Like the UIL, it demanded that the policy of compulsory purchase also be applied to grazing tracts in the west, which

---

[105] T. W. Russell, *Ireland and the empire: a review, 1800–1900* (1901), 126–7; Jackson, 'Irish Unionism and the Russellite threat', 381–9; Loughlin, 'Russell', 55, 58.
[106] Loughlin, 'Russell', 59; Jackson, *The Ulster party*, 226–7.
[107] Campbell, *Land and revolution*, 47–50.
[108] P. Bew, *Conflict and conciliation in Ireland, 1890–1910: Parnellites and radical agrarians* (1987), 87.

should '[be] cut up and made into workable holdings'.[109] Despite this, he believed that such a radical reform would result not in the extinction, but in the regeneration of the landowners as a ruling elite. In ways reminiscent of Parnell and Gladstone's vision in the mid-1880s, he thought that '[t]he Irish landlord, freed from all the friction attached to ownership of land, has a great future before him in the country. By birth, education and position, he is entitled, and oftentimes he is well-qualified, to lead in a country where leadership is the one thing necessary.'[110]

Despite this 'conservative' dream, Russell, again like Gladstone and Parnell before him, played on the growing class polarization in Irish politics, one which had recently been illustrated by the first elections held under the 1898 Local Government Act. The latter established county and district councils, elected triennially on simple household franchise which included women. Although the Ulster Liberal Unionists had always protested their support for the establishment of county councils, Loughlin's claim that they 'strongly pressed' for it should not be taken without qualification. Only the tenant-rights faction of the party was consistently in favour of local democracy. By contrast, the landowners had long been worried by Chamberlain's proposals and regarded radicals like Russell as class enemies.[111] They had reason to fear that democracy would involve '[the] absolute transfer of administrative control over county affairs from the representatives of the landlord class and the larger ratepayers to occupiers at large', resulting in 'the interests of the larger ratepayers [being] completely swamped', with a consequent 'complete divorce between taxation and representation'.[112] In a last-ditch attempt to avoid such an outcome, they pressed, unsuccessfully, for two-member constituencies. Eventually Gerald Balfour, perhaps playing to the British and essentially 'liberal' voters,[113] pushed through a Bill whose electoral consequences were indeed as radical as the ULUA had anticipated. Despite Unionist reforms and the Congested Districts Board, Nationalist feeling ran high, and its representatives

---

[109] Russell, *Ireland and the empire*, 204; and *'Compulsory purchase' in Ireland: five speeches made by Mr T. W. Russell MP* (1901), PRONI, D/1507/A/2/3.

[110] T. W. Russell, 'Ireland and Irish land once more', *Fortnightly Review*, 409 n.s., 1 Jan. 1901, 19.

[111] A. C. Sellar to H. de F. Montgomery, 13 Mar. 1888, PRONI, D/627/428/36; J. Sinclair to H. de F. Montgomery, 1 May 1888, D/627/428/44; W. Kenny to H. de F. Montgomery, 21 Apr. 1889, D/627/428/97; J. M. Stewart, MP to H. de F. Montgomery, 1 July 1892, D/627/428/187.

[112] *Ulster Liberal Unionist Association*, 89.

[113] A. Gailey, 'Unionist rhetoric and Irish local government reform, 1895–9', *Irish Historical Studies*, 24, 93 (1984), 52–68. Cf. C. Shannon, 'The Ulster Liberal Unionists and local government reform, 1885–1898', *Irish Historical Studies*, 18, 71 (1973), 407–23.

gained a convincing victory at the next election: 551 seats against 125 Unionist seats (86 of which were in Ulster).[114] Worse still, the election destroyed not only Unionist power in the South, but also landlord influence in the North-East. The decline of landlordism was then further accelerated by George Wyndham, whose 1903 scheme of land purchase was voluntary – for compulsion would have been met with strong cross-class resistance except in Ulster and the west of Ireland – but effective. Under the Act nearly 200,000 tenants became owner-occupiers eventually.[115]

Russell was still ostensibly a Unionist, but argued that, with the defeat of Home Rule, Protestant tenant farmers could at last afford to vote for their *economic* interests rather than their patriotic allegiances, which meant against the landlords, irrespective of party affiliation. Thus his agrarian radicalism implied the politics of class struggle supplanting the anti-Nationalist alignment, which now appeared irrelevant and obsolete.[116] Not surprisingly, his strategy both alienated orthodox Liberal Unionists and brought about a rapprochement between Russell and the British Liberals: from the beginning of 1904 he was in receipt of financial support from Herbert Gladstone.[117] By 1906, although still claiming to be a Radical Unionist, he openly campaigned against both Conservatives and Liberal Unionists. His priority remained the achievement of compulsory purchase despite the fact that the unexpected cost of 'Mr Chamberlain's war' (in South Africa) limited the government's ability to implement further land reform in either Ireland or Britain.[118]

On the other hand, Irish remedies were not universally applicable, as illustrated by a comparison with the Scottish Highlands, where the situation was supposedly similar to that in the west of Ireland. In 1897 the Unionist government established a Congested District Board for Scotland, hoping that it would replicate the success already achieved by its Irish namesake since 1891. In particular, the Scottish Board was instructed to carry out a policy of land purchase which – the government hoped – would free the landlords from the embarrassment associated with the dual-ownership regime of the 1886 Crofter Act. As Ewen Cameron has shown, the Board pursued this policy with some determination but against the hostility of the crofters, who feared the loss of the protection

---

[114] Shannon, *Balfour*, 103.
[115] M. O'Callaghan, *British high politics and Nationalist Ireland: criminality, land and the law under Forster and Balfour* (1994), 149; Campbell, *Land and revolution*, 79–80; T. Dooley, *The decline of the big house in Ireland* (2001).
[116] Russell, *Ireland and the empire*, 126–7.   [117] Bew, *Conflict and conciliation*, 90–1.
[118] Four-page leaflet of a speech by 'Mr Russell on land reform', 1906, PRONI, D/3036/F/3.

they enjoyed under the 1886 Act and were reluctant to commute their 'fair' rent for the (higher) purchase annuity. Most crofters managed to resist purchase until the Liberal government reversed the Unionist strategy and instructed the Board to act as landlord on the estates already purchased, allowing the crofters to remain as tenants.[119] Worse, those who had purchased 'petitioned the government to resume their crofting status'.[120]

Here then we have a complete reversal of the Irish scenario, and this was not simply a result of the crofters being less politicized and assertive than the Irish tenants. For even in Ulster, where the farmers were not nationalist and their relationship with the gentry was less frayed than in the South, agrarian radicals of all party persuasions campaigned for compulsory purchase. By contrast, in the Highlands the Liberals campaigned for a retention of the dual-ownership system against voluntary land purchase, which the Unionist government wanted to make virtually 'compulsory' at the tenants' expense. Part of the difference was certainly owing to the fact that the Irish, empowered by nationalism, had obtained more generous terms which the government was not prepared to extend to the Highland crofters. But the difference was also that the crofters' real pressing need was to secure more land and larger allotments, rather than ownership of the usually inadequate and unprofitable small crofts they already held. Furthermore, while the Irish tenants were small entrepreneurs who improved their farms and demanded compensation, the latter was not a major concern for the crofters, who depended more on the landlords' investments. In these respects the difference between crofters and Irish farmers was one of class, the crofters being somehow closer to the Irish labourers than to the comparatively more prosperous and ambitious Irish tenants.[121]

The closest parallel to the sectionalism and rural radicalism in North-East Ulster is therefore offered by the developments in the Nationalist camp. There Gladstone's 1894 resignation had been a signal for renewing the struggle for the party's soul. In particular, John Redmond and the Parnellites courted agrarian radicalism and Fenianism.[122] Healy seemed bent on destroying what remained of the party 'machine' through his

---

[119] E. A. Cameron, 'Politics, ideology and the Highland land issue, 1886 to the 1920s', *Scottish Historical Review*, 72, 193 (1993), 68–71 and Cameron, 'The Scottish Highlands as a special policy area, 1886 to 1965', *Rural History*, 8 (1997), 196–201.

[120] Cameron, 'Communication or separation?', 662; see also 657–9.

[121] Although scholars are now beginning to explore the tensions, within the crofting community, between the crofters and the even poorer class of landless Highland cottars: Cameron, 'Communication or separation?', 655, 645 n. 71.

[122] Bew, *Conflict and conciliation*, 23–4; M. Kelly, '"Parnell's Old Brigade": the Redmondite–Fenian nexus in the 1890s', *Irish Historical Studies*, 33, 130 (2002), 209–32.

People's Rights Association, which campaigned for a return to local constituency autonomy in close alliance with the clergy. Even before the 1895 electoral campaign, 'Healyism' had generated strong tensions within both the parliamentary group and the rank and file.[123] As we have seen (chapter 3), such tensions came to a head during the election, when Healy publicly attacked the 'pro-Liberal' leaders – Justin McCarthy, John Dillon, Edward Blake, Thomas Sexton, William O'Brien and Michael Davitt – famously claiming that they had 'sold' parliamentary seats in the North to the Liberals for £200 each.[124]

The virulence of the now multiple split reflected not just differences about internal party matters, but also fundamental divergences about the overall Nationalist strategy. Redmond and Healy reverted to a policy of independence from British parties, dismissing the differences between Liberals and Unionists as irrelevant while being prepared to accept further reforms from whatever quarter they might come. By contrast, Dillon and the Federationists – so named after the main anti-Redmondite organization, the Irish National Federation (INF) – clung resolutely to the Liberal alliance and perceived the Nationalist cause in terms of Home Rule alone.

A majority of the nationalists agreed: 'The Liberal party of England had been their allies, – insisted the Rev. M'Polin of Newry (Co. Down) – and take them all in all, they had been faithful allies; and if the Irish people and the Irish representatives were faithful to themselves and to their country the English Liberals would also do their part, he was sure, honourably and efficiently.'[125] In particular, they denied that the Liberal alliance was weakened by Rosebery's accession to the leadership, despite his unpromising attitude to Home Rule. For Dillon, if the latter was 'taking a back seat' in Liberal politics, it was largely because of sectionalism and 'futile disputes' among the Nationalists themselves.[126] They reaffirmed their confidence in Lord Rosebery and especially in John Morley. The divergences between the two Liberal leaders were known, but were brushed aside, partly because the defeat of Gladstone's 1893 Bill meant that, irrespective of who led party, there would be little chance of achieving

---

[123] Rep., 'Great Nationalist meeting in Galway', *FJ*, 7 Jan.1895, 6.

[124] For an account of the split see Lyons, 'The Irish parliamentary party', 191–5. For the Nationalist response see l.a., *FJ*, 11 July 1895, 4, and 'Mr Healy's charges against his colleagues: letter from the chairman of the Irish party', *FJ*, 15 July 1895, 5.

[125] Revd M. M'Polin, chairman of the meeting, cited in rep., 'The conventions', *FJ*, 10 July 1895, 5; similar views were expresses in l.a., *Cork Examiner*, 25 June 1895, 4.

[126] Cited in rep., 'The National movement: great meeting in Co. Wexford', *Cork Examiner*, 2 Jan. 1895, 6; *Cork Examiner*, 26 May 1895, 4; Lyons, *Irish parliamentary party*, 48.

self-government in the near future,[127] and partly because the new leader would have to accept the case for Home Rule out of 'necessity' – black, unpleasant necessity . . . arising out of . . . the events of 1885 – that alone, but amply, justified H.[ome] R.[ule]'.[128] Alfred Webb saw an opportunity in this challenge: instead of whingeing about the defunct Home Rule Bill, he felt that the time had come for the Irish patriots to help the British Liberals. He argued that '[the Nationalists] hold themselves quite independent, but they held that it did not show independence to refuse to help those who had proved their willingness and anxiety to help them (hear, hear). He believed in helping the English, Scotch and Welsh people who had aided them when they most needed help.'[129]

Thus in the aftermath of the defeat of the second Home Rule Bill, there were Federationists who welcomed the prospect of a campaign against the House of Lords, 'the citadel of the opponents of reform', who had always supported iniquity and injustice: '[s]lavery, religious ascendancy, political corruption had there their last and their belated defenders. It has defeated, delayed, mutilated every reform that was ever submitted to its judgement.' For the *Freeman's Journal* '[t]he time has come to make an end of its absurd privileges, and to clear the path of popular reform of the last and biggest obstruction'.[130] Michael Davitt thought that, '[i]f the movement against the Lords is encouraged by Gladstone & the Cabinet I think the next general election will be carried by the Liberals'.[131] This did not mean that in 1894–5 they were eager to see a dissolution. On the contrary, they hoped that the government would stay on to implement the work promised for the 1895 session. Its resignation in June caused 'surprise and some disappointment'. Nationalists regretted '[t]he abandonment of a programme of most useful legislation, that had been carried to the verge of success', particularly Welsh disestablishment and Morley's Land Bills. 'The passage of those measures, even through the House of Commons, would have been of enormous advantage to the two countries,' but, being 'stabbed in the back', the 'Home Rule ministry' had no choice. 'By resigning at this stage they have saved the cause of religious freedom in Wales and the cause of Irish Land Reform one disaster at least – the disaster of a treacherous defeat in a Liberal House of Commons.'[132]

---

[127] Lyons, 'The machinery of the Irish parliamentary party', 115.
[128] As Campbell-Bannerman wrote to Rosebery on 8 Sep. 1893: Rosebery Papers, NLS, MS 10002, 114–15.
[129] A. Webb, cited in rep., 'The conventions: Longford', *FJ*, 10 July 1895, 5.
[130] L.a.,'Lord Rosebery and his colleagues', *FJ*, 9 May 1895, 4.
[131] M. Davitt to E. Blake, 19 Feb. 1894, NLI, Blake Letters, 4681.
[132] L.a., 'The resignation of the government', *FJ*, 24 June 1895, 4; l.a., *Cork Examiner*, 25 June 1895, 4. For Morley's popularity among the Irish see Heyck, *Dimensions*, 221–6.

They blamed not Rosebery, but the Irish and Welsh 'sectionalists' – namely Redmond, Healy and David Lloyd George – and also, significantly, 'the socialists' and Keir Hardie in particular.

This concern for the socialist challenge in Britain corresponded to a revival of the awareness in Ireland of the political importance of both farm labourers and town workers. The Federationists had traditionally campaigned on the 'Chartist' assumption that the necessary prerequisite for *social* reform was *political* democracy.[133] This could easily become an excuse to neglect social reform. However, when the election came, they felt they needed to make some gesture to appease the farm workers and promised 'a practical scheme to give the labourers good houses and plots of land at fair rents'.[134] Sensitivity for the labourers' vote was compounded by a growing concern about the alienation from the constitutional movement of the younger generation – those who eventually flocked to Sinn Fein[135] – as well as about the general public apathy which produced a drop of about 70 per cent in the combined membership of the main Federationist and Redmondite organizations by 1894.[136]

In the following years, the impotence of the Liberals and the ongoing splits in the Nationalist camp encouraged the formation of associations which eschewed party politics, but focused on specific measures – such as the reform of the franchise for the election of Poor Law boards and the extension to Ireland of the allotment clause of the Parish Councils Act.[137] From as early as 1891 William O'Brien had been working with the Congested District Board, both contributing to several projects and starting some himself. This co-operation continued after 1895, while T. C. Harrington, Redmond and others liaised even with the Grand Master of the Belfast Orangemen and Unionist peers in Horace Plunkett's Recess Committee.[138] Thus, in the Irish context land reform made the Unionists the real 'collectivists' and, at the same time, took the

---

[133] See speeches by A. Webb, MP and P. J. Power, MP, in 'Nationalist convention in Waterford', *FJ*, 20 Apr. 1895, 5; and rep., 'The East Wicklow election: vigorous campaign of the Nationalists', *FJ*, 22 Apr. 1895, 5.

[134] G. J. Engldew (Nationalist candidate), in rep., 'Kildare', *FJ*, 9 July 1895, 6. The Irish farm workers constituted one of the most neglected and economically depressed social groups in the United Kingdom (Horn, 'The National Agricultural Labourers' Union in Ireland', 352).

[135] F. Campbell, 'The social dynamics of Nationalist politics in the west of Ireland, 1898–1918', *Past & Present*, no. 182, (2004), 180–1; Silverman, *An Irish working class*, 227.

[136] O'Brien, *William O'Brien*, 97–8.

[137] Rep., 'Irish Land and Labour Association: meeting of Central Council', *Cork Examiner*, 7 June 1895, 5.

[138] O'Brien, *William O'Brien*, 102–3.

wind out of the Nationalist sails for a while, even if it failed to shake the party's hold on the Irish constituencies.

There were plenty of good reasons to be concerned about economic problems. In 1896–7, for two consecutive years, the potato crop was poor. By the end of 1897, at a time of growing economic distress, O'Brien realized that the time was ripe for a resumption of the land campaign as a means of renewing Nationalist agitation: material distress could be linked, in the minds of voters, with the political and constitutional dimension. In this respect the Federationist 'Chartist' electoral strategy was fundamentally correct. In order to make it work, however, it was necessary to re-establish the link with the grass-roots and revive popular enthusiasm. In 1879–82 the land agitation began among the smallholders of Mayo, although subsequently Davitt and Parnell mobilized the farmers who were better off. This time an opportunity was provided, again, by the grievances of the tenants and labourers of Mayo, Roscommon and Galway. They scraped a bare existence on reclaimed bogs on the margins of vast grasslands let to graziers, and often integrated their meagre earnings with the wages they earned as seasonal migrants.[139] By contrast the graziers formed a new 'middle class' consisting of people of various social backgrounds (including landowners and 'strong' farmers, but also Catholic priests, retired policemen and shopkeepers), often actively involved in Nationalist politics: after all, from the 1880s Nationalism had relied on the rural middle class and the 'small western farmers were doomed to become the victims not the victors of the "Land League revolution"'.[140] Such small farmers were obliged to rent from the grazing ranches land for their cattle. O'Brien demanded a redistribution of the grasslands for their benefit and for the benefit of tillage farmers – a class that by 1898 had come under pressure in terms of either general hardship or 'insecurity revived and exacerbated by the sufferings of a relatively small minority'.[141]

The problem had been known for years, and in fact had already led to outbursts of conflict between graziers and peasants in 1879–80 and after 1885.[142] In 1895 some INF local branches had actually called for reform.

---

[139] Boyle, 'A marginal figure', 320.
[140] Bew, *Conflict and conciliation*, 36; for the social composition of the graziers see also pp. 41, 86 and M. D. Higgins and J. P. Gibbons, 'Shopkeeper-graziers and land agitation in Ireland, 1895–1900', in P. J. Drudy (ed.), *Ireland: land, politics and people* (1982), 93–118; L. Kennedy, 'Farmers, traders, and agricultural politics in pre-independence Ireland', in Clark and Donnelly, *Irish peasants*, 346–7.
[141] P. Bull, 'The formation of the United Irish League, 1898–1900: the dynamics of Irish agrarian agitation', *Irish Historical Studies*, 33, 132 (2003), 411.
[142] Jones, 'The cleavage between graziers and peasants', 381.

In 1896 O'Brien had unsuccessfully asked that powers of compulsory purchase be given to the Congested District Board under that year's Land Bill. When nothing came of it, O'Brien, with the support of M. Davitt and T. C. Harrison, established the UIL (January 1898), as a new tenants' organization with the aim of breaking up the large grass farms. As Bew has written, '[t]he agitation against the graziers explicitly opened the door to the politics of envy in particular and socialism in general'.[143] O'Brien's readiness to adopt a 'class struggle' approach, irrespective of established Nationalist allegiances, proved very successful, and by October the UIL had already established 53 branches (at the time the INF had 221 and the Redmondite INL only 6). After espousing T. W. Russell's plan (see p. 295), the UIL spread from the west of Ireland to the rest of the country by targeting not only the 'grass-grabbers', but also the landowners. Ruthlessly adopting semi-lawful and illegal practices like boycotting and intimidation, the UIL rapidly acquired a higher profile since it was increasingly seen as the response to popular demands for Nationalist unity.

After the 1895 electoral defeat – which was acknowledged to be 'complete and absolute'[144] – the question of reunification had become paramount and for the founders of the UIL was one of the aims from the start.[145] It was the 'ever-widening public recognition of the collapse of morale within the parliamentary party' which shifted the UIL towards a more assertive strategy.[146] There was talk of holding a National Convention 'to remove the present misunderstanding and consolidate the Irish political movement both in and out of Parliament'.[147] From 1898 this demand was effectively voiced not only by UIL branches but also by popularly elected authorities which had started to provide a forum for hitherto marginalized social groups, in a pre-run of a generational and social revolution which was to take shape on a larger and more dramatic scale twenty years later.[148] In this context the UIL continued to grow rapidly, with 279 branches in August 1899, 462 by the spring of 1900 and 758 by November of that year.[149] Each branch was self-governing, and membership was open to Parnellites and anti-Parnellites alike. Both provisos were important, because the UIL started to pre-select candidates

---

[143] Bew, *Conflict and conciliation*, 41–2.   [144] L.a., *Cork Examiner*, 29 July 1895, 4.

[145] Bew, *Conflict and conciliation*, 46; Bull, 'The formation of the United Irish League', 405.

[146] P. Bull, 'The United Irish League', 63.

[147] Last resolution, cited in rep., 'Kildare', *FJ*, 9 July 1895, 6.

[148] O'Brien, *William O'Brien*, 105–7; Bull, 'The formation of the United Irish League', 407–8, 411, 418; Shannon, *Balfour*, 134; Campbell, 'Social dynamics', 203–5.

[149] O'Brien, *William O'Brien*, 108–12; Bull, 'Reunion', 76.

for both local and parliamentary elections bypassing the old cliques and related animosities.[150]

The Claremorris (Co. Mayo) convention of January 1899 confirmed that the UIL's focus had shifted from land redistribution to parliamentary politics. The path towards Nationalist reunification was now open. In order to facilitate this development, more than a hundred graziers claimed to be willing to give up some of their land on certain terms; although this move left agrarian militants sceptical, it was welcomed by the leadership.[151] However, while O'Brien, Dillon and Blake hoped that the UIL would be able to impose unification *from below*, the initiative soon fell into the hands of Redmond and Healy, whose negotiations for a reunification of the parliamentary party forced the others to join in. The momentum created by the centennial celebrations of the rising of 1798 and the pro-Boer sentiment in 1899–1900 contributed towards speeding up the realignment; eventually the party was formally reunited – but not reformed – at a meeting in the House of Commons on 30 January 1900.[152]

'No voice at Hawarden'?

Not only in Ireland, but also in Britain the 1895 election was important in clearing the air.[153] It brought to an end a cycle which had started in 1886. The case of sectionalism in Wales is in this respect interesting. From the beginning of the 1890s Gladstone's unwillingness to act on disestablishment began to test the loyalty of the Welsh Liberals.[154] To the horror of the local branches of the Irish Land League, the cohesion of the Home Rule alliance began to disintegrate into single-issue faddism,[155] as the pressure groups which had supported the campaign, tired of Ireland dominating the Liberal agenda, started to prioritize their own specific concerns and threatened to rebel against the leadership unless they

---

[150] Bull, 'The formation of the United Irish League', 421.

[151] Bew, *Conflict and conciliation*, 56.

[152] S. Paseta, 'Nationalist responses to two royal visits to Ireland, 1900 and 1903', *Irish Historical Studies*, 31, 124 (1999), 489; Bull, 'Reunion', 67–8.

[153] The election and the causes of the Liberal defeat are elegantly discussed in P. Readman, 'The 1895 general election and political change in late Victorian Britain', *Historical Journal*, 42, 2 (1999), 467–93.

[154] Montgomeryshire Liberal Association, copy of resolution adopted at the Annual Meeting of the Council, 2 June 1890, in NLW, Stuart Rendel Papers, 19446E, V4; see also Montgomeryshire Central Liberal Association, 12 June 1890, ibid., 19448B, vii, 3, and L. D. Roberts to T. E. Ellis, 25 Oct. 1890, in NLW, T. E. Ellis MSS, 1806.

[155] Letter by E. Griffin, 'Mr Alfred Thomas, MP, and his constituents', *Pontypridd Chronicle*, 18 Dec. 1891, 8.

obtained satisfaction. But the rank and file were divided between those overwhelmed by resentment and a sense of betrayal for Gladstone's inactivity,[156] and those who continued to insist that 'the GOM's conduct is such as to demand a reverence akin to worship from all true Rad[ical]s'.[157] The MPs considered setting up their own party and adopting Parnellite tactics to remind 'the phlegmatic Saxon' that 'Wales [can also] block the way'.[158] Despite his initial reservations about Irish Home Rule, even Lloyd George accepted that only a 'National Parliament' could solve the Welsh question in all its facets, including disestablishment, land reform, education and that, therefore, 'all our demands for reform ought to be concentrated in one general agitation for National Self-Government',[159] which was 'the way whereby all social evils in Wales would be cured'.[160] However, throughout the period from 1890 '[the] real and only question [was] this. Can Wales venture to say like Italy "Italia fara [sic, sc. farà] da se." Can Wales accomplish alone & unaided & in defiance of her friends as well as her opponents her own deliverance?'[161] On the whole, the answer was in the negative: 'The only reason why Wales had not had her own way in this matter ... was simply because she was a comparatively small nationality.'[162] As a consequence even in 1895 Irish Home Rule and the alliance with the English Liberals remained close to the top of the political agenda of many Welsh radicals, as a matter of both expediency and principle.[163]

Thus Lloyd George's strategy involved the permeation, not the destruction, of the Liberal party. By 1895 he believed that '[the] Liberal organizations [had] been captured already by Welsh Nationalism',[164] although he would have been more accurate to say that 'the voice of Wales is the voice of the Liberal party in all questions except those matters in which ... she is called on to be a pioneer viz. the question of Home Rule & that of religious equality'.[165]

---

[156] See two telegrams of protest from Welsh radicals to T. E. Ellis, dated 17 Feb. 1893, in NLW, Ellis MSS, 2975, and resolution passed by the Carmarthenshire and Cardiganshire Welsh Baptist Association, 3 Aug. 1893, in NLW, T. E. Ellis MSS, 168.
[157] W. R. Davies to T. E. Ellis, 1 Aug. 1893, in Ellis MSS, 2304. For Gladstone's 1891 views see rep., 'Great speech by Mr Gladstone', *The Scottish Highlander*, 8 Oct. 1891, 2.
[158] L. a., 'Mr Gladstone and the Welsh party', *Pontypridd Chronicle*, 24 Feb. 1893, 5, and l. a., 'Welsh members forcing the battle', ibid., 7 July 1893, 5.
[159] D. Lloyd George to T. Gee, 9 Oct. 1895, in NLW, T. Gee MSS, 8310D, 501a.
[160] C. J. Wrigley, *David Lloyd George and the British Labour movement* (1976), 8.
[161] Stuart Rendel to T. Gee, 26 Dec. 1890, in NLW, T. Gee MSS, 8308D, 265a.
[162] J. Herbet Lewis, MP, at the 1893 Liverpool meeting of the NLF, NLFAR, 73.
[163] See J. H. Lewis' election addresses for 1891 and 1895, NLW, Flintshire parliamentary Elections, MS 9494E.
[164] D. Lloyd George to Miss Gee, 29 Jan. 1895, in NLW, T. Gee MSS, 8310D, 500a.
[165] M. F. Roberts to T. E. Ellis, 9 Mar. 1894, in NLW, T. E. Ellis MSS, 1855.

This closing of ranks around the post-Gladstonian Liberal party was a more general phenomenon, although some historians have argued that the reluctance on the part of many Liberal MPs to embrace collectivism was both a weakness and a cause of the 'socialist revival'. The Liberals believed that 'ideas could win votes',[166] and after the election engaged in a considerable amount of soul searching about ideas. Their concern has been mirrored by the historiography, which has created a circular effect (with scholars often reproducing, rather than critically analysing, the post-Gladstonian diagnosis about what was 'wrong' with the Liberal party).[167]

But was the Liberal problem really about ideological arteriosclerosis? Let us take the case of George Howell, a veteran Lib-lab and one of a number of 'typical Gladstonians' whose electoral defeat in 1895 was, as Maccoby argued, a sign of the times.[168] He lost his seat never to return to Parliament. In his last electoral address to his constituents in Bethnal Green, he restated all the radical causes which he had been advocating since 1886 – including Irish self-govenrment – but emphasized a number of domestic issues selected from recent Liberal reform proposals. They ranged from the equalization of the rates and the reduction of government expenditure, to land reform. He further proposed to bring the Poor Laws 'into conformity with the age in which we live, and render them more humane' in their provision of relief for the deserving poor, yet 'mindful at all times that any increase in the rates must fall upon the ratepayers'. For Howell and many other radicals the fiscal touchstone was the taxation of land values, which would relieve industry from the burden which was allegedly the main cause of unemployment.[169] Obviously this was neither a socialist nor a 'New Liberal' programme. Indeed for the rest of his life Howell professed himself a 'Radical of the old school', a 'proud ... disciple of Jeremy Bentham ... John Stuart Mill, Henry Fawcett, [and] P. A. Taylor', as well as an admirer of Charles Bradlaugh.[170] Ostensibly, then, his defeat marked the end of a generation who had outlived the political relevance of their ideas.

---

[166] H. C. G. Matthew, *The Liberal imperialists: the ideas and politics of a post-Gladstonian elite* (1973), viii.
[167] M. Freeden, *The New Liberalism: an ideology of social reform* (1978); Emy, *Liberals, radicals and social politics*; J. Lawrence, 'Popular radicalism and the socialist revival in Britain', *Journal of British Studies*, 31 (1992), 163–86; G. Johnson, '"Making reform the instrument of revolution": British social democracy, 1881–1911', *Historical Journal*, 43, 4 (2000), 977–1002.
[168] S. Maccoby, *English radicalism, 1886–1914* (1953), 199.
[169] G. Howell, 'To the electors and other residents in the North East Division of Bethnal Green', July 1895, in Howell Collection, microfilm edition, I/5. Cf. William Saunders to T. E. Ellis, 23 Mar.1894, in Ellis Papers, 1925.
[170] G. Howell, 'Labour politics, policies and parties: a striking indictment', *RN*, 4 June 1905, 3.

The main problem with this interpretation is that all the *socialist* candidates, including the sitting ILP MPs, were also defeated, together with many Liberals, irrespective of their views on 'collectivism'. Many socialists stood on platforms which included Irish Home Rule 'on the ground that the government of the people should be *by* the people *for* the people'.[171] In other words, there is little evidence that in 1895 social radicals were in greater demand than the Cobdenite variety. Partly because of the rising tide of military expenditure 'old' liberalism was still credible and relevant.[172] Indeed, despite his staunchly 'old' Liberal and anti-socialist ideology Charles Bradlaugh had been by far the most popular radical leader for as long as he lived, and his memory continued to be honoured well after his death in 1891.[173]

In particular, many felt that the credibility of the radicals – whether Gladstonian or socialist – had been undermined by Home Rule. However, as Readman has shown, in 1895 it was canvassing and party organization, not ideas, that determined the result of the election. The defeat of the candidates listed above had little to do with Home Rule or anything else in their programme, and everything to do with inadequate organization. The ILP and the NLF, for all their democratic aspirations and effectiveness as a forum for thrashing out ideas, were no match for the more numerous members of the less demanding and ambitious Primrose League.[174]

Like his colleague Randal Cremer, Howell stood as a Radical rather than a trade-union representative not because his ideology was 'old fashioned', but because of the weakness and disorganization of the labour movement in his London constituency, especially during the slump of 1895, when 'unions were fighting to survive, and had little surplus energy to put into politics'.[175] Interestingly enough, Keir Hardie, the man who more than anybody else personified ILP politics, was in a comparable position in his West Ham constituency, where he relied on the temperance lobby more than on the trade unions, and claimed to stand as the 'United Liberal, Radical and Labour party' candidate.[176] Moreover, although his programme was different from Howell's, it was not

---

[171] Frank Smith, 'Address for the Tradeston Division of Glasgow, general election of 1895', in Glasgow parliamentary literature, Mitchel Library, G.394.2 (emphasis in the original).

[172] Howe, *Free trade and Liberal England*, 223–4.

[173] For Bradlaugh's popularity see Royle, *Radicals, secularists and republicans*, 233–5. For his rejection of socialism see the pamphlets *Debate between H. M. Hyndman and Charles Bradlaugh. Will socialism benefit the English people?* (1884), C. Bradlaugh, *Socialism: its fallacies and dangers* (1887) and Bradlaugh, *The radical programme* (1889).

[174] Readman, 'The 1895 general election', 482–7.

[175] P. Thompson, *Socialists, liberals and labour: the struggle for London, 1885–1914* (1967), 43, 107.

[176] F. Reid, *Keir Hardie: the making of a socialist* (1978), 130.

distinctively 'socialist': its seven points consisted of three traditional Radical demands (free non-sectarian education, taxation of unearned increments and international arbitration), the Eight-Hour Bill, the abolition of overtime for children under fourteen, work for the unemployed, and 'provision for the sick, disabled, aged, widows, and orphans, the necessary funds to be obtained by a tax upon unearned incomes'. He used the rhetoric of both humanity and class struggle. While what he said was sufficiently vague to fit any political complexion on the left, his insistence that the ILP was '[f]or the present, strongly anti-Liberal in feeling'[177] did not help. His dismissal of radical causes – including church disestablishment and Home Rule – ensured that he would at once unnecessarily antagonize both the Nonconformist and the Irish vote.[178] In the end, if the socialists could claim a 'success', it was in splitting the anti-Unionist vote in several parts of the country. This resulted in a series of three-cornered contests in which the Liberals lost constituencies such as Newcastle upon Tyne, Halifax and North-East Manchester. While the wisdom of this course of action was open to debate (as even Hardie came to admit by 1900), David Howell has pointed out that for the ILP '[t]he 1895 election was … the death of easy optimism'.[179]

The election was a turning point also for the Liberals. On the one hand, it showed that there was nothing to gain from pursuing a 'progressive' alliance with the ILP.[180] On the other, it felt like the end of the Gladstonian era – and ostensibly it was. Defeat and repeated leadership changes in 1895–1900 generated confusion, but also helped to reopen the debate about the future. Irish Home Rule was indeed taking 'a back seat', but the NLF and the SLA would not have allowed it to be thrown out altogether. Nor was the old enthusiasm for Ireland completely quenched among the Nonconformists and rank-and-file radicals in general.[181] Let us take London, where the swing against Liberalism was more pronounced than anywhere else in the country. Although a majority of the London Congregational deacons interviewed in an 1894 survey of Metropolitan Dissent indicated that they wished Irish self-government could be forgotten and Liberal party unity re-established, 54 per cent of

[177] For three examples of his rhetoric see 'Mr Keir Hardie at Newcastle', *WT&E*, 21 July 1895, 5 and 'Mr Hardie on his defeat', ibid.; and J. Keir Hardie, 'The Independent Labour Party', *The Nineteenth Century*, 215, Jan. 1895, 9, 12.

[178] Emy, *Liberals*, 53; Thompson, *Socialists*, 27, 131; Morgan, *Keir Hardie*, 80.

[179] D. Howell, *British Workers and the Independent Labour Party, 1888–1906* (1983), 309; Thompson, *Socialists*, 164; Heyck, *Dimensions*, 203.

[180] J. R. Moore, 'Progressive pioneers: Manchester liberalism, the Independent Labour Party, and local politics in the 1890s', *Historical Journal*, 44, 4 (2001), 989–1013.

[181] Searle, *The Liberal party*, 34.

them supported the second Home Rule Bill, 35 per cent opposed it and 11 per cent were undecided.[182] Some of the Gladstonians held very strong views: as one Dissenter publicist wrote in 1895, '[i]t would be better that Liberals should remain out of office for fifty years, than they should ... abandon the policy of Irish Home Rule'.[183]

The complex and ambitious 1891 Newcastle Programme had failed to deliver an effective and sustainable electoral revival, but, as we have seen (pp. 187–8), it did lead to a serious debate within the NLF and the parliamentary party about the role of the mass organization. It also led to a rejection of the notion of 'programme' politics, which many felt had been 'imposed' on the party by the Federation. In particular, the Newcastle Programme now appeared to have been too wide-ranging to be feasible and so ambitious that it had raised expectations only to disappoint them – although arguably in 1891–2 it had done its job by helping to bring about a Liberal recovery, despite the demoralization and loss of support caused by the Parnell split.[184]

This dismissal of 'programme politics' was therefore partly irrational and partly a feature of the parliamentary party's attempt to deprive the NLF of its policy-making powers; but it also revealed exasperation with faddism and the younger Liberals' impatience with the non-social side of the old programme. In turn, such intolerance was evidence of the wide-spread acceptance of the primacy of social reform – a back-handed tribute to Chamberlain's 'materialist approach' to Liberalism. In particular, many Radicals feared that the GOM's snubbing of what they supposed to be the working-class demand for social reform would weaken the party's electoral prospects.[185] In their view the NLF had missed a historic opportunity when it failed to redress the balance at its 1893 (Liverpool) meeting: as Tuckwell noted, 'I had hoped for clear-eyed and exultant handling of the great social problem, whose solution was now once more attainable; I heard only the old, tame, passive, abject reliance on Gladstone.'[186] Instead of the usual enthusiasm, 'misgivings were expressed, in veiled language on the platform, frankly and angrily in the private talk of delegates'. '[A]nd the Independent Labour Party was the consequence',[187] with 'the ominous defection of the Labour vote' posing a threat to the future of the Liberal party, one which the latter could face

---

[182] D. W. Bebbington, 'Nonconformity and electoral sociology, 1867–1918', *Historical Journal*, 27, 3 (1984), 644.
[183] C. J. Shebbear, *The Greek theory of the state and the Nonconformist conscience* (1895), v.
[184] Hamer, *Liberal politics*, 213–14.
[185] Ben Tillett, 'Thirty minutes with Gladstone', *WT&E*, 12 Mar. 1893, 9.
[186] Tuckwell, *Reminiscences*, 207.   [187] ibid., 223.

down only by choosing new leaders and adopting 'the new and living principles which the necessity of the hour demand'.[188]

Quite apart from exaggerating the electoral significance of the ILP, this criticism was not entirely fair on the NLF. Labour questions had been vigorously discussed at Liberal meetings for years. Meanwhile, as Peter Clarke has pointed out, even if the Home Rule campaigns had failed to achieve their principal aim, they '[had] precipitated a move to the left' among Liberal and Radical activists,[189] in particular creating new expectations of state intervention in social reform in mainland Britain. In this sense at least, social engineering in Ireland was also affecting British politics: observers as diverse as George Lansbury and H. W. Massingham contrasted the eagerness with which both parties had offered state assistance to Irish farmers with the still prevalent laissez-faire orthodoxy in domestic affairs. It was to these activists and opinion makers – more than to the ordinary working-class elector steeped in the ways of self-help and dogmas of free trade – that 'the New Liberalism' offered hope.

In 1888–90 Massingham was assistant editor, and then editor, of *The Star* – the halfpenny evening newspaper established in London in 1887 by T. P. O'Connor, the Irish Nationalist and Radical leader. With a circulation which rose from 140,000 to 279,000 (by 1889), *The Star* was a resounding success. It articulated the new 'progressive' concerns – emphasizing working-class housing, land reform and free education – but took a Gladstonian line on imperial affairs and the Liberal–Nationalist alliance (O'Connor's top priority). With social analysts and reformers of the calibre of Sidney Webb and George Bernard Shaw, its staff was arguably one of the most talented ever assembled for a popular newspaper.[190] Soon, however, O'Connor's Irish priorities exasperated Massingham, who, although a keen Home Ruler himself, was becoming increasingly excited about the wider social agenda of what was beginning to be called the 'New Liberalism'.[191] As L. Atherley Jones, the son of the last Chartist leader Ernest Jones, put it in his famous 1889 article, this was to be a Liberalism *for* the working classes – targeting their needs, 'as yet inarticulate' but identified for them by the party's intellectual elite of journalists, academics and civil servants. It was this elite who

---

[188] L.a., 'The Liberal collapse', *WT&E*, 21 July, 1895, 8.
[189] Clarke, *Lancashire and the New Liberalism*, 154.
[190] O'Connor, *Memoirs of an old parliamentarian*, vol. II, 256, 265–6; Thompson, *Socialists*, 97–9; Brady, *T. P. O'Connor*, 103–9.
[191] Brady, *T. P. O'Connor*, 114–17; Havinghurst, *H. W. Massingham*, 18–40.

insisted that the 'New Liberalism' was to be about 'a wider diffusion of physical comfort'.[192]

Meanwhile, it was not quite clear which particular working-class issues the party should prioritize. The 1885 electoral success with the farm workers had proved difficult to repeat – also because the Conservatives did not raise the tariff reform issue again, the latter being the single most important factor in causing the labourers to come out and vote Liberal.[193] The Liberal government had tried to tackle some of the specific concerns of the farm workers, but the 1895 election results suggested that parish councils and allotments were not enough to earn their gratitude: Liberal results in the English counties were only marginally better than in 1886.[194] But what delayed further moves in this direction was neither lack of ideas nor dogmatic laissez-faire within the party, but tactical and ideological divisions inside the trade union movement, in particular between the proponents and opponents of a statutory eight-hour day. Rosebery, on becoming Prime Minister, made an attempt to seize the social reform agenda by personally endorsing the eight-hour day (in March 1894). Significantly, both the War Office and the Admiralty adopted it for their workers. Moreover, Asquith pushed through his Factory Bill, which was approved in 1895.[195]

Ultimately, however, the single most important obstacle to Liberal reform was the House of Lords. In a further instance of that *fin-de-siècle* radical phenomenon which Barrow and Bullock have described as 'the survival of Chartist assumptions',[196] the NLF, like the INF in Ireland, insisted that *political* democracy was the precondition for *social* reform. This growing concern for the social question was accompanied by renewed interest in the question of democracy. The Lords' rejection of most of the Bills endorsed by the Home Rule majority in the Commons prompted the NLF to demand the reform of the national representative system as a whole. Various other proposals emerged from the deliberations of local caucuses and were adopted by the General Committee in

---

[192] L. Atherley Jones, 'The new liberalism', *The Nineteenth Century*, 26 (1889), 192; see also Clarke, *Liberals and social-democrats*, 22–7.

[193] Pelling, *Popular politics*, 6. The Liberals won a majority of the country seats only in 1885 and 1906, and in both cases free trade was at stake. Cf. Lynch, *Liberal party*, 38. For free trade as an electoral issue in 1885 see Biagini, *Liberty*, 133–4, and Howe, *Free trade and Liberal England*, 185.

[194] Hamer, *Liberal politics*, 204; Packer, *Lloyd George*, 25; Lynch, *Liberal party*, 147–9.

[195] D. Powell, 'Liberal ministries and labour, 1892–1895', *History*, 68 (1983), 417, 425–6.

[196] 'The Liberals and the agricultural labourers', Liberal leaflet, No. 1553, in J. Johnson Collection, 'Creed, Parties and Politics', box 18. This was similar to the strategy adopted by the Irish Nationalists (see above, pp. 110–11, 301). Cf. Barrow and Bullock, *Democratic ideas*, 9.

April 1893. They included the removal of the value qualification for lodgers, registration of new electors to take place twice a year and the abolition of disqualification through either change of residence or receipt of temporary Poor Law relief.[197] Once again the NLF was critical of the parliamentary party and the government, whose Registration Bill they regarded as timid and inadequate. This concern for democratic reform continued over the few next years. In 1895 a canvassing of constituency opinion conducted by the Liberal party's Radical Committee indicated that the rank and file regarded the reform of the House of Lords as a matter of utmost urgency. Other concerns were the democratization of the electoral system, including one man one vote, the abolition of plural votes[198] and the reform of the existing system of registration. The last of these was identified as one of the causes of the systematic disfranchisement of working men and potential radical electors. In January 1895 the Registration Committee of the Scottish Liberal Association proposed the abolition of the qualifying period, demanding that the simple registration on the Valuation Roll be sufficient to qualify a man to vote, in order to ensure that 'every person who is a householder or owner would be on the Register of voters somewhere'. As for the lodgers, they also insisted that '[i]t would simply be suicidal to leave the franchise as it is' and proposed the abolition of all property qualification so that all lodgers be given the vote. Furthermore, they recommended the enfranchisement of 'persons occupying a dwelling house jointly', the abolition of disqualification for the non-payment of the rates and the abolition of plural votes.[199]

In contrast to the party's programmatic activism of 1891, in 1893–5 Liberal strategy seemed dominated by their struggle against the House of Lords, now a Unionist-controlled chamber which vetoed or mutilated most government Bills. At first the new approach seemed to work: the anti-Lords campaign filled the NLF with renewed radical zeal. At the

---

[197] 'Registration reform', meeting of the General Committee of the NLF, Westminster Town Hall, 19 Apr. 1893, NLF Reports, 16–17.

[198] Proceedings of the Annual Meeting of the Council of the NLF, Cardiff, 17–18 Jan. 1895, 5, 9. Emy, Liberals, 66. J. Moon (Liverpool) to T. E. Ellis, 24 July 1895, in Ellis Papers, 3605. In the Glasgow constituencies from 1894 to 1897 the lodger voters for the Unionists had increased from 3,830 to 4,238; during the same period, the Liberal lodger vote had only increased from 1,165 to 1,209: figures in the Minutes of the Meeting of the Western Committee of the Scottish Liberal Association, Glasgow, 13 Oct. 1897, 338, NLS, Acc. 11765/6.

[199] Meeting of Registration Committee of the SLA, Glasgow, 14 Jan. 1895, 343–5, NLS, Acc. 11765/5; for the subsequent debate see Meeting of the Executive Committee, 24 Jan. 1895, 304–7, ibid., and Meeting of the Eastern Committee of the SLA, 1 July 1895, 375, ibid.

1894 conference in Portsmouth, 'Mr Acland's speech against the Lords [was] received with mad enthusiasm. At the evening meeting, where Sir W. Harcourt spoke, "God save the Queen" was hissed – a thing I never heard before or since.'[200] Perhaps for the first time since 1886, a Liberal agitation was favourably echoed in the Radical Unionist weekly press,[201] and this suggested that the Liberal rank and file desired party reunion as much as the Nationalists and agrarian radicals did in Ireland. Such an aspiration was confirmed in 1894 by the favourable responses elicited by Rosebery's succession to the party leadership.[202] However, in the end the anti-Lords campaign failed to ignite the imagination of the wider public: as in 1886, rank-and-file zeal did not spread the radical contagion to the mass of the electors.[203] When this became apparent, there followed loss of morale and self-confidence among Liberal associations even in traditionally Gladstonian areas, especially in England and Scotland. In such a context, the ILP denounced what they regarded as the Liberal infatuation with 'merely political' reform. Yet, the Upper House's rejection of the 1893–4 Employers' Liability Bill indicated the extent to which an undemocratic constitution hindered social and economic reform and directly affected the interests of labour.[204] Although Chamberlain pushed through workmen's compensation in 1897, his Bill neglected the crucial issue of workplace safety and the prevention of accidents, for which both the Liberals and the labour movement had long been campaigning.[205]

Despite the anxiety expressed by Tucker and other social Liberals, the chief significance of the early ILP was not its socialism, but its democratic politics, which revived a tradition of independent popular radicalism stretching back to the Chartists and beyond, and for which the Liberal split had again created a political space. By the same token, as Alastair

---

[200] Tuckwell, *Reminiscences*, 208; cf. W. Reid, 'The Leeds Conference' and rep., 'Leeds: June 20th, 1894', in *The Liberal Magazine*, 2, 10, July 1894, 200–3.

[201] L.a., 'Hopeless obstruction', *LW*, 20 Aug. 1893, 8; l.a., 'Welsh disestablishment', *WT&E*, 3 Mar. 1895, 8.

[202] L.a., 'Lord Rosebery's opportunity', *LW*, 4 Mar. 1894, 8; l.a., 'Federal Home Rule', *WT&E*, 23 Apr. 1893, 8, suggesting federalism as the solution to the 'British constitutional problem' as well as a policy which would reunite the Liberal party.

[203] McKinstry, *Rosebery*, 328–31.

[204] W. Abraham ('Mabon' in NLFAR 1895 (Cardiff)), 7, 103–6. The Lords' opposition focused on contracting out, a procedure which the Bill proposed to abolish: see Powell, 'Liberal ministries and labour', 422 and n. 65, Clegg et al., *A history of British trade unions*, 253 n. 1 and E. P. Hennock, *British social reform and German precedents: the case of social insurance, 1880–1914* (1987), 56–7.

[205] V. Markham Lester, 'The employers' liability/workmen's compensation debate of the 1890s revisited', *Historical Journal*, 44, 2 (2001), 471–95.

Reid has stressed, the foundation of the Labour Representation Committee (LRC) did not signal a new start, but rather 'a revival of the spirit of the 1860s and 1870s' and the demand both for a return to the Gladstonian settlement and for working towards stronger trade union representation in Parliament as a means to an end.[206] Apart from the mid-Victorian Labour Representation League there were other precedents for this strategy. In 1887 a National Labour Party had demanded 'Home Rule, County Government and Religious Equality' together with payment of members and their electoral expenses. One of its most radical demands was ' "Adult Suffrage" and the right for women to sit as MPs'.[207] For *Reynolds's Newspaper* the proposed party was to be modelled on Parnell's National party, rather than on the socialist ones already existing in other Western European countries. Ideologically, it wanted the new party to be democratic and liberal, as indicated by its proposed leaders, who included Lib-labs like Fenwick and Burt and radicals such as Bradlaugh.[208] In a similar spirit, a new Labour Representation League was set up in 1891 by the London Trades Council in an attempt to bring together labour candidates 'irrespective of creed or sect'.[209]

Within the Liberal party these developments created a renewed awareness of the need for a 'progressive alliance'.[210] In one shape or another, such a 'progressive alliance' had been Liberal policy since 1868 at least, when Gladstone's party had managed to secure the support of the Reform League and other organizations of artisan radicalism. From 1877 the NLF had tried to 'institutionalize' such an alliance, but with limited success. On the other hand, although the government had been unable to implement most of the proposals included in the 1891 Newcastle Programme (see chapter 4, pp. 187–8), the policy aims which it had articulated continued to dominate the outlook of the radicals. In fact, in this way those debates contributed to the making of the 'New Liberalism' – if not as a philosophy, certainly as a set of practical demands and humanitarian standards. In particular, land reform and the principle of taxing its value

---

[206] A. J. Reid, *United we stand: a history of Britain's trade unions* (2004), 260.

[207] 'The remuneration of female labour, and the conditions under which women too frequently work are simply barbarous, and will never be adequately rectified, until we have a score or two of competent ladies like Miss Helen Taylor, and Miss Amy Mander, the Newnham College Undergraduate [*sic*], who gave such clear and convincing evidence the other day respecting the brutalities of the police at Mitchelstown, have seats in the House of Commons.' (L.a., 'The National Labour Association', *RN*, 25 Sep. 1887, 1.)

[208] L.a., 'The representation of labour', *RN*, 25 Sep. 1887, 4; Gracchus, 'The advance of socialism', *RN*, 2 Oct. 1887, 2.

[209] Thompson, *Socialists*, 103.

[210] Matthew, *The Liberal imperialists*, 22; Clarke, *Lancashire*, 166.

retained considerable appeal not only in the 'Celtic Fringe'[211] and in rural England (where the Liberals more than doubled their seats),[212] but also in urban constituencies. Land reform, 'Progressivism' and the emergence of an interventionist agenda of social reform, helped the party to make considerable, though ephemeral, advances in various boroughs, especially in London, in 1892.[213] Even Home Rule continued to be close to the heart of a minority within working-class radicalism – but one holding strong views.[214] Some hoped that land reform would result in an Irish equivalent of the 'Homestead Act', under which settlers in the USA were granted land, and demanded the nationalization of minerals.[215]

This indicates that the Liberal party's problem lay not in ideas, and not merely in inadequate organization, but ultimately in lack of effective leadership. 'Liberalism, if it is, as we trust, to rise once more ... must seek leaders of a very different stamp,' proclaimed the *Weekly Times* in 1895, '[o]therwise, the ominous defections of the Labour vote will increase rapidly'.[216] But the problem of competent leadership was also shared by the new labour and socialist organizations, as the *Weekly Times* had conceded at least since 1889.[217] In 1893 Keir Hardie launched his bid in an article which, at the time, must have been one of his most widely circulated publications – arguably more so than his contributions to the *Labour Leader*.[218] He claimed that the political differences between the bourgeois parties were 'minor' and that the 'experiment of a Socialistic party ... will ... hasten the time ... when the dividing lines of politics will no longer be the more or less shadowy line which divides Liberalism from Toryism, but that of Collectivism v. Individualism'.[219] Yet his messianic socialism appeared somehow vague and utopian: he deprecated state intervention, exalted collective working-class self-help and invested his best hopes in the ballot box – which was precisely what the despised Liberals also did.[220] Likewise, the joint

---

[211] William Saunders to T. E. Ellis, 24 Mar. 1894, in Ellis Papers, 1925.

[212] Packer, *Liberalism and the land*, 201.

[213] Thompson, *Socialists*, 96; Howell, *British workers*, 258; Moore, *Transformation of urban liberalism*, 124, 214–34.

[214] E. W. Yates, Organiz. Secretary, Somerset, Gloucester and Wilts. Agricultural and General Labourers' Union, to E. Blake, Dec. 1892, in NLI, Blake Letters, [523–4] 4685. E. L. Gales wrote to Blake about the attention he commanded among 'those men who are the *unlettered* & *despised working men*'. 25 Apr. 1894 Blake Letters, [1450] 4686 (emphasis in the original).

[215] 'A Cornish Quaker' to E. Blake, 16 Mar. 1893, Blake Letters, [1823] 4685.

[216] L.a., 'The Liberal collapse', *WT&E*, 21 July 1895, 8.

[217] L.a., 'Socialism in the north', *WT&E*, 2 June 1889, 8.

[218] The paper had a circulation of about 50,000 in 1894: Morgan, *Keir Hardie*, 67.

[219] Keir Hardie, 'Independent Labour Party conference', *WT&E*, 22 Jan. 1893, 9.

[220] Keir Hardie, MP, 'Marching orders for the Labour army', *WT&E*, 15 Jan. 1893, 9: 'I confess to having great sympathy with those who honestly deprecate State interference

manifesto of the 'Socialist bodies' (including Fabians, SDF, the Hammersmith Socialist Society and other such groups) was strongly anti-anarchist but very ambiguous about socialism, which it defined in terms of *individual* freedom more than anything else.[221]

Although such evidence may be read in different ways, in context it suggests that these socialist groups were aware that they operated within a popular culture dominated by values that were essentially liberal and individualistic. In other words, they realized that disgruntled artisans and working-class radicals could perhaps be persuaded to turn away from the Liberal party, but were not likely to reject self-help and related values. By the same token, the main motivation for the *Weekly Times* supporting the ILP and the SDF was not enthusiasm for 'socialism', but 'disgust' with the alternatives facing 'the English Democracy'. It praised and endorsed the ILP for being both 'above' party squabbles and single-mindedly devoted to 'the promotion of the welfare of the workers'.[222]

Then, the real question was to find a leader who could unify such currents of radicalism and forge them into an effective political force again. For the *Weekly Times* the rising stars were H. H. Asquith, R. B. Haldane, H. Fowler and A. H. D. Acland.[223] It prophesied, quite accurately, that Asquith 'has but to wait, and wisely begin to reorganise a new *real* Liberal Party and he may be its chief, and Prime Minister ere the coming century has scored many years'.[224] As for Acland, his strength was that he could reconcile the crusading humanitarianism of the Gladstonian tradition with the social radical vision of 'positive' liberty, which would 'improve, directly or indirectly … the hard lot of, and increase the leisure of many of the workers … develop[ing] … for those who were at a disadvantage in the struggle of life, fuller and wider opportunities to attain better things'.[225]

---

with the conditions of Labour … We say to the workers that they have no right to look to rich sympathisers for aid; they have themselves the power to do all that is necessary if they will but organize their forces and give expression to their wishes at the ballot-box … For it is not an eight-hour day by law enacted, nor a pension to every disabled worker, nor colonies for the unemployed that is the goal. These are but easy stages on the march. There can be no final solution of the Labour problem till Rent and Usury cease, and production is maintained to supply the necessities of the community.'

[221] 'Manifesto of the joint committee of Socialist bodies', *WT&E*, 7 May 1893, 1.

[222] L.a., 'The Independent Labour Party', *WT&E*, 22 Jan. 1893, 8; this reaction against party politics had been going on for years, especially since 1886: see, for example, l.a., 'Humbug all round', *WT&E*, 14 July 1889, 8.

[223] L.a., 'New lamps for old ones' and 'The future of Liberalism', in *WT&E*, 30 June 1895, 8.

[224] 'Powder and shot', *WT&E*, 21 July. 1895, 9.

[225] A. H. D. Acland, 'Liberalism and Labour', NLF Reports, 1893, 40.

Armenian atrocities

Acland failed to rise to these expectations, but crusading humanitarianism continued to be the common feature of various currents of radicalism, including the ILP. Indeed, in October 1896 Rosebery resigned the party leadership, apparently feeling himself to be no match for the octogenarian Gladstone, who continued to mesmerize what Rosebery described as 'the intriguers' among the Liberals.[226] His words reflected not only his failure to unify the party, but also his awareness that he was 'in apparent difference with a considerable mass of the Liberal party on the Eastern Question'.[227] He was alluding to the Armenian atrocities.

The government had found out about them in December 1894 and Rosebery, the then Prime Minister, protested to the Porte in January 1895, but Harcourt and others within the government found his action weak and indecisive. In June Bryce urged the Foreign Secretary, Lord Kimberley, to publish a report on the massacres in order to awaken the public conscience, but he refused.[228] Although the Ottoman authorities tried to prevent foreign journalists from visiting the areas involved in the disturbances, news leaked out through the Russian border. Rumours and early reports were eventually confirmed in February 1895.[229] The women's Liberal associations were among the first to take up the issue.[230] From April spontaneous non-partisan meetings were organized in various parts of the country: Gladstone was invited to speak at Chester, but declined on account of bad health, although in May he did send a letter of support to the organizers of the National Protest Demonstration Committee.[231]

Meanwhile, important gatherings had taken place in various parts of the country. At St James' Hall, in early May, the Duke of Argyll, the Duke of Westminster (both of whom had already been active in the 1876 Bulgarian agitation[232]), the Moderator of the Church of Scotland, the Archbishop of York and various bishops, as well as Nonconformist leaders, spoke at a 'weighty and impressive' demonstration which 'testifie[d] to the passionate feeling aroused in this country by the accounts . . . of the cruel and shameful treatment of some of the subjects of the Sultan, whose rights and liberties

---

[226] Rosebery to C. Geake, 6 Oct. 1896 and 7 Oct. 1896, in National Liberal Club Collection, Bristol Univ. Library, P14560 and P14561.

[227] Cited in NLFAR, Norwich, 18 Mar. 1897, 5.

[228] Stansky, *Ambitions and strategies*, 125–7; McKinstry, *Rosebery*, 389–92.

[229] *The Times*, 4 Feb. 1895, 6; 23 Feb. 1895, 5; 29 Mar. 1895, 9.

[230] See meeting of 15 Feb. 1895 and Maria Richards' circular of the same date in U. Masson (ed.), *'Women's rights and womanly duties': the Aberdare Women's Liberal Association, 1891–1910* (2005), 156–7.

[231] *The Times*, 11 Apr. 1895, 3; 7 May 1895, 12.

[232] Foster, 'The intellectual duke', 155–7; Thompson, *William Morris*, 211.

had been especially placed under the safeguards of the last great European settlement of Eastern affairs'. A letter from Gladstone was read out: the former Liberal leader 'expressed the hope that the Turkish Government would be forced "by moral means, if possible" to give securities against the recurrence of the horrors'.[233] He was eventually persuaded to address a meeting in August, at a time (after the general election) when it would not be open to the criticism that it was held in a partisan spirit – a concern shared by all the Liberal leaders.[234] Although they meant to support the Unionist government, rather than embarrass it, the rank and file and Nonconformists took a different line. In early December John Clifford, speaking at the Council of the Free Churches, sounded a defiant note:

> It is impossible to sit still and read the disclosures made in the Press from day to day. It makes one's blood boil ... Whilst the diplomatists debate the people perish. Little children are butchered like sheep, women are so brutally treated that they dread death less than the arrival of the Turk ... Our own 'treaty obligations' are trampled under foot. Our Governments have withheld from us the 'Consular reports' ...[235]

A few days later Gladstone came out in his support. In a public letter to Clifford, he stated his confidence that Britain '[was] quite able to cope not only with Turkey, but with five or six Turkeys, and she is under peculiar obligations'. He added that he *hoped* that 'the Government has not been in any degree responsible for bringing about the present almost incredible ... situation'.[236] On both counts his words implied criticism of Salisbury's policy and were interpreted as such. Meanwhile the deep link between Nonconformist Christianity and Liberal politics characterizing many parts of the country ensured that the issue remained at the forefront of local associations, with the women in particular becoming passionately involved and invoking the application of 'Gladstone's "bag and baggage" policy with regard to the Sultan'.[237] In March 1896, in a speech at Swansea, Asquith criticized Salisbury for what he regarded as his inept and counterproductive handling of the situation.[238]

---

[233] *The Times*, 8 May 1895, 9.

[234] 'Mr Gladstone on the Armenian question', *The Times*, 7 Aug. 1895, 4; l.a., ibid., 7.

[235] 'Armenia and the Church Council of the Free Churches of London', *The Times*, 7 Dec. 1895, 7.

[236] 'Mr Gladstone and the Armenian question', *The Times*, 18 Dec. 1895, 12 (my emphasis).

[237] See, for example, Masson (ed.), *Aberdare Women's Liberal Association*, meetings of 24 Jan. and 27 Jan. 1896, 175–6. This association continued to support the victims of the Armenian massacres at least until the spring of 1900: see the entries for 23 and 27 Apr. and 4 May 1900 in ibid., 216–17.

[238] *The Times*, 23 Mar. 1896, 7.

While Rosebery and Spencer insisted that the question should not be treated as a party issue, the wave of popular meetings went the other way: at Bradford, Rochdale, Shoreditch, Coventry, Glasgow, Northampton, Bolton, Nottingham and elsewhere well-attended demonstrations addressed by local Liberal and socialist leaders, as well as Nonconformist and Anglican clergymen, demanded immediate action, of an unspecified but presumably military character, to stop the atrocities.[239] H. W. Massingham, then editor of the *Daily Chronicle*, tried to galvanize the Liberal leaders into taking up the Armenian crusade, and, with the help of other humanitarians, including James Bryce, reassured Gladstone about the strength of the popular agitation.[240] Eventually, the GOM overcame his reluctance and on 24 September addressed a popular meeting at Hengler's Circus in Liverpool. It was an important political endorsement of an otherwise largely spontaneous campaign, which had experienced no encouragement from the Liberal party leaders. Gladstone called for a 'humanitarian crusade', taking care to stress that this was no religious campaign of Christians against Muslims, nor of Europeans against Turks: 'The ground on which we stand here it is not British nor [*sic*] European, but it is human.'[241] He demanded the issuing of a 'peremptory note' indicating the suspension of diplomatic relations. Britain should stop short of any action which could precipitate a general European war, but should renounce 'neutrality' in this matter, declaring that 'we will not acknowledge as a nation within the family of nations the ruler who is himself the responsible agent of these monstrous acts', and only resorting to military action if and when it was deemed appropriate.

As *The Times* pointed out, it was not clear what course of action Gladstone was actually recommending,[242] but the spirit of moral outrage pervading his speech was echoed at popular meetings in Carlisle, Newcastle, Leicester, Portsmouth, Guildford, Leith, Sheffield and Reading (the last convened by the Evangelical Alliance).[243] Such popular demonstrations became increasingly belligerent. At West Bromwich a meeting was introduced by a band playing 'Rule Britannia' and the National Anthem, and concluded by a resolution pledging 'loyal support in any resolute steps which they may consider expedient to take in order to put an end to the barbarities'.[244] In October two important meetings took place in Hyde Park, attended by many labour leaders including Henry Broadhurst and John Burns, and at St James' Hall, chaired by the

---

[239] *The Times*, 16 Sep. 1896, 3; 21 Sep. 1896, 3; 22 Sep. 1896, 4; 24 Sep. 1896, 4 (including a resolution of the SDF).
[240] Stansky, *Ambitions and strategies*, 207.
[241] 'Mr Gladstone on the Armenian question', *The Times*, 25 Sep. 1896, 5.
[242] L.a., *The Times*, 29 Sep. 1896, 7.   [243] *The Times*, 26 Sep. 1896, 5; 28 Sep. 1896, 5.
[244] *The Times*, 29 Sep. 1896, 8.

Duke of Westminster, a member of the Anglo-Armenian Association, and supported by many Anglican and Nonconformist clergymen, including Dr Kane of Belfast.[245] Although Bryce and other Liberal leaders tried to restrain rank-and-file criticism of the government, the feelings expressed at these demonstrations were endorsed by the NLF.[246] Many Liberals wanted their leaders to exploit the emotion generated by reports of indiscriminate massacres in the Ottoman Empire in order to create a 'Bulgarian atrocities' effect – similar to when in 1876 the party had been lifted up from the slough of despond by the People's William's enlivening gospel.[247] They included a broad cross-section of supporters and activists – ranging from the 'Liberal Forwards' group to the peace movement and Nonconformist leaders such as Clifford and Hugh Price Hughes.[248]

Perhaps because of its limited electoral consequence, the Armenian agitation has been neglected by historians,[249] but at the time it caused a remarkable display of political emotion and stirred up radical opinion not only in Britain, but also in Ireland, where a vigorous campaign involved both the Parnellites and the anti-Parnellites. While there was hardly any Nationalist contribution to the debate at Westminster,[250] and no official reaction from either the INL or the INF, the press was up in arms about the issue. Irish newspapers had no special correspondents in the Ottoman Empire, and relied on the London press for their supply of news,[251] but the Armenian crisis was regularly covered by detailed reports from as early as December 1894–January 1895.[252] The opening salvo in the Irish agitation coincided with Gladstone's eighty-sixth birthday. On

---

[245] 'The Armenian demonstration', *The Times*, 12 Oct. 1896, 6; Brown, *John Burns*, 75; 'The Armenian question: great meeting in St James' Hall', *The Times*, 20 Oct. 1896, 4.

[246] *The Times*, 24 Nov. 1896, 10; 22 Dec. 1896, 4.

[247] Minutes of the Western Committee (Glasgow) of the Scottish Liberal Association, 7 Oct. 1896, 264, and of the Executive Council of the Scottish Liberal Association, 9 Oct. 1896, 266, NLS, Acc. 11765/36. H. W. Massingham attacked Rosebery for following 'the dogma of "British interests" as against the interests of humanity' (Laity, *British peace movement*, 143).

[248] Laity, *British peace movement*, 138–9. The 'Liberal Forwards' were to play an active role on the pro-Boer side during the political debates surrounding the South African war at the turn of the century: A. Davey, *The British pro-Boers, 1877–1902* (1978), 72–3.

[249] But see P. Marsh, 'Lord Salisbury and the Ottoman massacres', *Journal of British Studies*, 11, 2 (1972), 62–83, R. Douglas, 'Britain and the Armenian question, 1894–7', *Historical Journal*, 19 (1976), 113–33, and the rather partisan J. Salt, *Imperialism, Evangelism and the Ottoman Armenians* (London, 1993).

[250] Questions as to the massacres were asked by J. C. Flynn (Cork North), HPD, 4th series, XLI, 1435, 1435 and XLII, 25 June 1896, 69. Michael Davitt, usually very responsive to issues of human rights, was silent on the Armenian question.

[251] Especially on the *Daily News* and *Daily Telegraph*: l.a., 'Armenia', *FJ*, 16 May 1895, 4; l.a., *Cork Examiner*, 22 Mar. 1895, 4.

[252] Rep., 'The Armenian atrocities: a veritable reign of terror: graphic account of the Sasun massacre: horrible butcheries of women and children', *FJ*, 9 Jan. 1895, 5.

29 December 1894 the GOM received a deputation from the Armenian National Church, delivering – in the *Freeman's* words – an 'address of the greatest possible portent':

'As long as I have a voice I hope that voice upon occasion will be uttered on behalf of humanity and truth.' Mr Gladstone spent his birthday in doing another good deed for the sacred cause of humanity and Christian civilisation. His long silence has been broken, and broken by words which will ring throughout Europe, and instil a healthy fear into the Power that is supposed to control the butchers of Armenia ... Mr Gladstone recalls the story of Bulgaria. It was thought a great extravagance then ... when he declared that the Turk and all his belongings should go out of Bulgaria bag and baggage. But they did go out of Bulgaria, and it is evidently Mr Gladstone's thought, 'if these tales of murder, violation and outrage be true,' they ought to be cleared out of Armenia as well.[253]

The *Cork Examiner* took a very similar line from March 1895,[254] while the *Freeman's* returned to the topic in April. Once again Gladstone, who had received a second Armenian deputation, provided the opportunity. 'Everything connected in any way with Mr Gladstone is of interest to the public,' argued the Dublin daily:

He has attained a position unique amongst living men. The blatant voice of calumny is silenced in his regard and admission universally expressed. The pilgrimage of Armenian refugees to Hawarden on Easter Saturday is an incident of very special interest indeed. They came with a chalice and rare MS for the great man who has fixed the gaze of the civilised world on the atrocities they have endured and kindled universal indignation against their persecutors.[255]

Gladstone's attitude to foreign policy – and his Liberalism in general – were perceived to be primarily about humanitarianism, the political relevance of Christian ethics and the priority of moral imperatives on *Realpolitik*. This was the line for the Irish to follow, as they 'place[d] the cause of humanity above that spirit which is given the name of Jingoism, and with a double dose of which Englishmen seem to have been born'.[256] 'Mr Gladstone is too much of a Christian to believe that great nations can with honour to themselves and without treason to their mission ask "Am I my brother's keeper?" There is a conscience that prescribes a duty of charity here as in the narrower scope of social and individual action.'[257]

---

253 L. a., 'The unteachable Turk', *FJ*, 31 Dec. 1894, 4.
254 L. a., *Cork Examiner*, 1 Mar. 1895, 4.
255 L. a.,'Mr Gladstone at Hawarden', *FJ*, 16 Apr. 1895, 4.
256 L. a., *Cork Examiner*, 22 Mar. 1895, 4.
257 L. a., 'The unteachable Turk', *FJ*, 31 Dec. 1894, 4. See also l.a., 'Mr Gladstone at Hawarden', *FJ*, 16 Apr. 1895, 4: 'the magnitude of Mr Gladstone's services to humanity ... weak as his voice has become, it is strong enough to thrill Christian Europe still with a sense of the duty to the victims of the Turk's oppression'.

What the Ottomans had perpetrated against both the Bulgarians and the Armenians was enough to raise the question of 'whether the Turkish Empire in its present shape can continue to exist'.[258] Already in 1883 the Dublin daily had argued that the one advantage which the friends of liberty could derive from the otherwise deplorable British invasion of Egypt was that it had finally exploded the old doctrine that the Ottoman Empire was to be preserved as 'the Western outpost of the English seizure of India'. After Egypt had been sacrificed for the perceived advantage of the British Empire, it was to be hoped that Ireland and the rest of the United Kingdom would not 'be dragged into another disreputable war to sustain the hideous and corrupt Mahomedan [*sic*] power for the benefit of the commercial class in England'.[259] In the context of the 1895–6 crisis, this change in the geo-political priorities of British imperialism meant that '[i]f Russia takes the case into its hands the sympathy of the world will go with it, whatever the remedy'.[260] Unilateral action by Russia would be better than inertia, though joint intervention by the powers was the best way forward. This of course involved reactivating the 'Concert of Europe' – or the Berlin 'Treaty Powers' – for the carrying out of its classical Gladstonian function of international tribunal and policing. However, the *Freeman's Journal* was firmly opposed to any policy which might reopen the Eastern crisis in the shape of a general European war,[261] and indignantly denounced the Ottomans' claim that their methods in the Armenian provinces were no worse than British coercion in Ireland.

Though the emphasis was usually on the 'non-partisan' nature of the campaign, support for Gladstone during this crisis was explicitly acknowledged to be evidence of the Irish 'devotion to one Liberal doctrine, the support of the Christian races in the East'.[262] Each and every public statement by the GOM on the matter was not only reported, but also extensively commented upon in terms which were as flattering as if Gladstone had been Parnell's one and only true successor, rather than a retired British statesman. He continued to be honoured as the only hope that Ireland, and indeed the cause of international justice, still had.[263]

---

[258] L. a., 'The unteachable Turk', *FJ*, 31 Dec. 1894, 4.   [259] L. a., *FJ*, 13 Jan. 1883, 4.

[260] L. a., *FJ*, 22 Mar. 1895, 4.

[261] L. a., 'Armenia', *FJ*, 9 May 1895, 4. Likewise, in March 1885 the *Freeman's Journal* had praised Gladstone's handling of the 1885 Afghan crisis, since his 'happy audacity' avoided a war with Russia (L. a., *FJ*, 9 Mar. 1885, 4).

[262] L. a., 'Armenia', *FJ*, 9 May 1895, 4.

[263] L. a., 'Mr Gladstone on Armenia', *FJ*, 7 Aug. 1895, 4; 'Mr Gladstone on the Armenian atrocities: he calls for firm and determined action', *FJ*, 8 May 1895, 5; l.a., *Cork Examiner*, 31 May 1895, 4.

Gladstone was indeed the only hero at the time, and the Armenian massacres offered further evidence of the unparalleled standing of the Grand Old Man in the Constitutional Nationalist pantheon (although the Parnellites accused him of giving mere verbal sympathy when he knew that he would never have to act on his rhetoric). In September 1896 the announcement that he would deliver a speech in Liverpool was repeated several times in various articles during the days preceding the event.[264] Eventually, the full report of Gladstone's speech[265] was accompanied by a leader expressing unreserved support for the GOM's 'clear, strong, eloquent pronouncement in favour of a definite, practical, and feasible policy on the Turkish question'. The article further argued

That the opinion of Ireland is absolutely unanimous on this question was shown by the successful meeting held last evening in Dublin. The platform represented every party and every section in the country. His eminence cardinal Logue sent his good wishes and a generous donation to the Armenian Relief Fund. The Protestant Primate proposed the chief resolution, which was seconded by Revd Father Lynch, OSF ... The declaration of Mr Swift McNeill, that 'this devil's work must cease', commended itself to the sentiment of the meeting. No suffering people ever appealed to Ireland in vain for sympathy. The Armenians are being persecuted for their nationality as well as for their religion ... Those who have known suffering themselves are the best messengers of consolation.[266]

The meeting had taken place in Leinster Hall, Dublin, in the evening of 24 September. According to the report, the meeting was both popular and representative: '[t]he Hall was crowded, and amongst the audience there was a very large percentage of ladies'.[267] On the platform, together with Catholic priests, Protestant ministers and Episcopalian bishops, there was the Lord Mayor, Alfred Webb (the former president of the Indian National Congress) and Swift McNeill, a Protestant Nationalist MP.[268] In October a non-partisan Armenian Relief Fund was established as an inter-confessional Christian and humanitarian association, operating with the blessing of Cardinal Logue, the Archbishop of Armagh.[269] The Roman Catholic hierarchy in Ireland was echoed by the British

[264] 'Mr Gladstone to speak on Thursday', *FJ*, 22 Sep. 1896, 3; 'The Liverpool meeting', *FJ*, 23 Sep. 1896, 3.
[265] Rep., 'Mr Gladstone and the Armenian horrors', *FJ*, 25 Sep. 1896, 5.
[266] L. a., 'A policy for Lord Salisbury', *FJ*, 25 Sep. 1896, 4.
[267] Rep., 'Sympathy for the Armenians: enthusiastic meeting in Dublin', *FJ*, 25 Sep. 1895, p. 3.
[268] Ibid. However, when one 'who appeared to be a working man' came forward and climbed the platform for the purpose of moving an amendment, he was forcibly ejected twice. The incident provided a suitable illustration of the subordination of working men in Irish politics, in so far as the 'notables' – whatever their confessional allegiance – retained what in Gramscian terms was their 'hegemony'.
[269] Rep., 'Irish Armenian Relief Fund', *FJ*, 22 Sep. 1896, 3.

branches of that confession, with 'some outspoken utterances' being voiced by bishops in England, and the Vicar apostolic of Wales, who expressed 'heartfelt detestation of the horrible outrages . . . perpetrated by the "Great Assassin" [the Sultan]'.[270]

During the following weeks and months the *Freeman's Journal* continued to conduct an unrelenting campaign to stop the atrocities. Graphic reports of the massacres were published almost daily, while leading articles thundered with Gladstonian zeal. One of the reports, entitled 'An Irish eyewitness describes the butcheries', narrated how

> The Turks started to murder the Armenians the day we arrived . . . It was awful. Thousands and thousands of them were killed. I have not yet heard how they took the news in England, or how it was reported home, but we were expecting to see the English fleet coming up every morning to blow the place to pieces. I would have lent a willing hand, for I never saw such cruelty . . . All through the night I could hear the cries of the people who were being killed close to where the ship was lying. I believe the Armenians are exterminated in some districts of the town . . .[271]

It soon became clear that the Royal Navy would not come, and Britain's inability to intervene was sarcastically described as 'the brilliant result of the policy of the Jingoes in Egypt'.[272] Though Gladstone had arguably contributed more than anyone else to the latter policy, he was again exempted from most of the blame: '[t]he impotence of England is . . . Lord Salisbury's doing. Jingoism has met its nemesis. The spirit of it, expressed in British foreign policy, has provoked that distrust in which the Sultan has found his protection.'[273] The Conservatives were responsible because they had opposed the 1878 treaty of San Stefano (which had tried to force the Ottomans to reform their government of Crete and other Christian regions of their empire) and accepted responsibilities which the United Kingdom found quite impossible to discharge.[274] Moreover, by fostering the suspicion that British foreign policy was inevitably aimed at '[grabbing] the asset upon the smash up of the Turkish Empire', Salisbury '[had] led England into a position of utter isolation and utter powerlessness

---

[270] Cited in *FJ*, 29 Sep. 1896, 4.

[271] 'An Irish eyewitness describes the butcheries', *FJ*, 23 Sep. 1896, 3. This was a letter sent by a merchant marine officer to his brother in Newry. The officer happened to be in Constantinople when the pogrom against the Armenians began. This quotation offers an interesting illustration of how Irishmen overseas could occasionally feel 'English' when confronting hostile cultures – in this case militantly anti-Christian Ottomans. A similar attitude inspired Irish Nationalist *anti*-Boer feeling in 1899–1902: D. P. McCracken, *The Irish pro-Boers, 1877–1902* (1989), 120.

[272] L. a., *FJ*, 'The Armenian question', 6 June 1895, 4.

[273] L. a., 'Lost Armenia', *FJ*, 17 Sep. 1895, 4; for the similarity with contemporary Liberal criticisms of Salisbury cf. l.a., 'Lord Rosebery and his critics', *FJ*, 21 Oct. 1896, 4.

[274] L. a., 'Armenia', *FJ*, 16 May 1895, 4.

for good by reason of mistrust which his policy has engendered. The Armenian nation is lost, and lost through the policy that won its fatal triumph at Berlin.'[275] If Salisbury was responsible for past mistakes and present impotence, Lord Rosebery, the Liberal leader, had grievously sinned by 'combating the bold policy of bold intervention, single-handed if need be, to stop the massacres which are an outrage on humanity'.[276] He was now out of step with public opinion in both Ireland and Britain, and his resignation from the leadership in reaction to Gladstone's Liverpool speech was 'his one honourable escape' from an untenable position.[277]

At that stage the partisan nature of the agitation was explicit also in Britain, where it was encouraged by James Bryce, Newman Hall and Herbert Gladstone, as well as Harcourt, Labouchere and Morley.[278] They presented the issue in terms increasingly critical of the government. Having both publicly described the Sultan as 'the great Assassin' and effectively called for the union of Crete with Greece, W. E. Gladstone adopted a partisan line himself in the letter which he wrote in support of Bonham Carter for the Petersfield (Hampshire) by-election at the end of May, criticizing the government not only for their inactivity in Armenia, but also for their support for the Ottomans in Crete.[279] Although Petersfield remained Tory, there followed a string of Liberal victories at by-elections throughout the country.[280] The partisan nature of the agitation was then further intensified by the Colonial Secretary's intervention. As we have seen in the previous chapter, Chamberlain had always been unable to sympathize with the 'sentimental' politics of humanitarianism – a failure further exacerbated by the Home Rule split. Not surprisingly, in 1897 he reacted to the Liberal adoption of the Armenian and Cretan issues by denouncing the 'forward party'. He minimized the massacres in Crete by comparing them with the violence which had been going on for centuries on the Afghan frontier, and insisted that Britain's interests in the Sudan should be regarded as the country's paramount obligation.[281]

[275] L. a., 'Lost Armenia', *FJ*, 17 Sep. 1895, 4.
[276] L. a., 'Lord Rosebery's apologia', *FJ*, 10 Apr. 1895, 4.
[277] L. a., 'Retirement of Lord Rosebery', *FJ*, 8 Oct. 1895, 4.
[278] See reports in *The Times*: 'Greece and Crete', 20 Feb. 1897, 12, 'Sir W. Harcourt in Stepney', 5 Mar. 1897, 11; 'The Radicals and Greece', 6 Mar. 1897, 12; 'The Cretan question', 13 Mar. 1897, 9; 'The Cretan question: Mr Gladstone's letter', 19 Mar. 1897, 8; 'Mr Morley at Merthyr Tydvil', 8 May 1897, 16.
[279] W. E. Gladstone, *The Eastern crisis. A letter to the Duke of Westminster, KG* (1897), 3, 13–15; *The Times*, 31 May 1897, 13.
[280] See 'Election intelligence', *The Times*, 30 Oct. 1897, 8 and 5 Nov. 1897, 7; 'Mr Asquith at Rochdale', ibid., 11 Nov. 1897, 9.
[281] 'Mr Chamberlain in Birmingham', *The Times*, 1 Feb. 1897, 8; 'Mr Chamberlain in Glasgow', ibid., 5 Nov. 1897, 7.

His remarks came across as even more callous than Disraeli's response to the Bulgarian massacres of 1876. Chamberlain's 'neo-Beaconsfieldism' was soon further compounded by the embarrassing Jameson raid in South Africa and by a new war on the Indian North-Western Frontier. As in 1879, humanitarian pressure groups protested against '[t]he ruthless destruction and burning of villages ... thus causing suffering upon women and children who can have done us nothing wrong', amounting to 'a return to methods of barbarous vengeance, and a discredit of professedly Christian Empire'.[282]

As usual, part of this enthusiasm for humanitarian concerns in imperial affairs was due to a perceived link between the cause of Home Rule and that of any people 'struggling to be free'.[283] That the latter proved to be the guiding consideration in Nationalist responses to imperial and foreign affairs was confirmed by Michael Davitt's plea for the Ashanti,[284] and his denunciation both of 'the killing of helpless wounded foes [the Dervishes] on the battlefield of Omdurman' and of 'the conduct of Soudanese and Egyptian soldiers under the orders of British officers in perpetrating nameless outrages inside the city after the battle was won'.[285] Press reactions to the 1896 Jameson raid were similarly informed by Gladstonian imperatives. Gladstone himself set the example by expressing his support for Kruger and 'surprise and disgust' at the 'outrage committed on the Republic'.[286]

There were alarming parallels between the Boer republics and Ireland. Transvaal and Orange had been granted 'home rule' by the Liberals in 1881: now they were being threatened by a Unionist government whose Colonial Secretary, Chamberlain, was the *bête noire* of both the Gladstonians and the Nationalists, and 'lectured' the Boers on their alleged ineptitude for self-government. 'Very rarely, even from the English Colonial Office, has a document more unconstitutional, insulting and misleading been issued to the world.'[287] In such a context the chief aim of 'Ireland's foreign policy' was 'to prove that the Hottentot system of governing Ireland won't pay the British Empire'.

Thus the Nationalists' pro-Boer stance in 1899–1902 should not be regarded as a mere reflection of their Anglophobia. Nor was it an isolated

[282] 'British armies on the Indian frontier: a protest', Yorkshire Quarterly Meeting of the Society of Friends, held at Sheffield, 27 Oct. 1897, Sheffield Archives, H. J. Wilson Papers, MD 2590–91. See also 'Scottish Liberal Association', *The Times*, 27 Nov. 1897, 12; Davey, *British pro-Boers*, 39–4.

[283] Wells, *John Redmond*, 58.   [284] HPD, 4th series, XLI, 9 June 1896, 1440.

[285] HPD, 4th series, LXXII, 8 June 1899, 667–8, 675–6.

[286] 'Mr Gladstone on the Transvaal', *FJ*, 22 Jan. 1896, 5.

[287] L. a., 'Mr Chamberlain lectures the Boers', *FJ*, 8 Feb. 1896, 4.

instance of Irish sympathy for the victims of jingoism.[288] Moreover, it was not unanimous: though in Ireland there was 'a powerful identification across a wide spectrum of ... opinion with the Boers ... [and] abhorrence at British actions in South Africa',[289] many Home Rulers in Australia, New Zealand, Canada and even in the USA protested strongly against this approach, fearing that it would damage the prospects of Ireland obtaining self-government. As Edward Blake – himself a Canadian – admitted, 'I was always conscious ... of the injury ... to the case of Home Rule which would be done by an Irish National opposition to the war. Nevertheless I personally believe ... that the war was unjust and to the highest degree impolitic.'[290] John Redmond, the leader of the newly unified party, was equally undeterred by the imperialist mood of the Irish diaspora, ready to press on along essentially Gladstonian lines, and concerned to voice the point of view of the Afrikaners against Chamberlain, rather than against the British as a nation.[291]

These episodes generated a wave of emotion which transcended religious, class and party divides and indicated the potential for a popular front, not one of progressivism, despite significant steps in this direction in the north-west and elsewhere,[292] but a Gladstonian popular front of moral outrage. Even Keir Hardie seemed to adopt the cause of radical unity. In October–November 1896, campaigning at Bradford East in a three-cornered contest, he proposed 'a fusion of advanced forces'.[293] Moreover, he reasserted his support for Irish Home Rule, church disestablishment, temperance reform and taxation of land values, claiming to be not only 'the best Liberal candidate available', but also the worst enemy of 'the Sultan of Turkey'. Incredibly, however, he denounced Gladstone's stance on Armenia and praised Gordon of Khartoum as 'the most Christ-like man this country had ever seen'. He was defeated, and finished at the bottom of the poll. In any case, his rediscovery of radical unity seemed short lived and from 1897 he lapsed in his typical

---

[288] McCracken, *The Irish pro-Boers*; K. Jeffery (ed.), *An Irish empire? Aspects of Ireland and the British Empire* (1996).

[289] Bull, *Land*, 113.

[290] Blake to the Hon. M. Grace, Wellington, New Zealand, 27 Sep. 1900, Blake Letters, 2342, NLI, 4688. For a few examples of abusive correspondence by supporters of the war in Canada and the USA see J. Connor to Blake, 10 Feb. 1900, ibid., 2328; TS, 'A national disgrace', *Ontario Free Press*, 10 Feb. 1900 (on Blake's vote for Redmond's pro-Boer amendment), ibid., 2329; and R. E. A. Land (from Florida), to Blake, 11 Feb. 1900, ibid., 2330.

[291] Redmond to W. O'Brien, 24 Apr. 1901, in J. Redmond Letters, NLI, MS 10,496 (4).

[292] Clarke, *Lancashire*, 163ff.; Blaazer, *Popular front*, 60–85; Moore, 'Progressive pioneers', 989–1013.

[293] 'Election intelligence', *Ti*, 17 Oct. 1896, 10.

warfare against the Liberals, despite the fact that the latter showed signs of revival in a series of by-election victories, while ILP candidates were humiliated everywhere. But by the summer of 1898, as further electoral results urged pragmatism, the ILP Parliamentary Committee (which included Hardie, MacDonald and Brocklehurst) started covert negotiations with the Liberal chief whip Ellis for an electoral pact in eight constituencies, in return for ILP support for a future Liberal government.[294]

From the end of 1899 the Boer War provided further fuel for a latter-day Gladstonian revival, which started to attract well-known Liberal Unionists like Albert Bright and Leonard Courtney back to the fold.[295] When Morley delivered an electrifying peroration at the St James' Hall in Manchester in September 1899, it seemed that the agitations of the previous years would now turn into a real movement, but he was unable to sustain the enthusiasm for long and turn it into a national uprising. Nevertheless, as Grigg has written, the war in South Africa gave 'new urgency and relevance' to the anti-jingoist vein in the radical tradition and increased the standing both of the leaders who championed it, including Campbell-Bannerman, and of the more ambiguous, though incredibly resourceful, Lloyd George.[296] Pro-Boer sentiment – although divisive within the parliamentary Liberal party – was consistent with many of the currents of radicalism which had contributed to the Liberal alliance in 1879–86. In particular, it attracted agrarian radicals throughout the United Kingdom and mobilized both ethical socialists and unreconstructed Gladstonians in a 'popular front' of moral outrage. It brought together old friends and created new alliances, ranging from John Dillon, Michael Davitt, John and Willie Redmond to Thomas Burt, John Clifford, F. W. Hirst, Jane Cobden-Unwin and other representatives of different shades of Cobdenism. It also attracted social radicals and New Liberals such as J. Ramsay MacDonald, Lloyd George, C. P. Scott, J. A. Hobson and J. L. Hammond. While Hobson had been a Liberal Unionist in 1887, Hammond symbolized the ideological affinity between pro-Boerism and Home Rule.[297] At last there was co-operation between

[294] Howell, *Independent Labour Party*, 189–93; Morgan, *Keir Hardie*, 90–4, 96.

[295] Clarke, *Lancashire*, 178–9.

[296] J. Grigg, 'Lloyd George and the Boer War', in A. J. A. Morris (ed.), *Edwardian radicalism, 1900–1914* (1974), 16.

[297] McCracken, *The Irish pro-Boers*; Davey, *The British pro-Boers*, 150–1; Laity, *The British peace movement*, 153; Cameron, *Mackintosh*, 211–12; A. Howe, 'Towards the "hungry forties": free trade in Britain, c.1880–1906', in Biagini *Citizenship and community*, 206–10, 214–15; J. W. Auld, 'The Liberal pro-Boers', *Journal of British Studies*, 14 (1975), 78–101; B. Porter, 'The pro-Boers in Britain', in P. Warwick (ed.), *The South*

socialists (including the SDF) and Liberals in many constituencies, particularly in Lancashire.[298] While Davitt thundered for Boer freedom, Hardie, to the astonishment of some of his supporters, adopted distinctly radical arguments, which 'differed very little in kind from Bright's and Cobden's denunciation of the Crimean War almost fifty years earlier'.[299] Even more remarkable was the extent to which his former anti-Liberalism was replaced by eulogies of the leading anti-war radicals. He even went as far as making overtures to John Morley, whom he had long denounced as the arch-individualist apologist of unbridled capitalism.

McCracken has argued that the British and Irish pro-Boers had little in common. There is no question that the Anglophobia which accompanied the Nationalist response to the war had no parallels in Britain. However, Anglophobia was certainly not the main motivation for Michael Davitt, a member of the Humanitarian League, which also included Keir Hardie as well as a number of other socialists, radicals and feminists.[300] As for the rest of the Nationalists, one factor was the sympathy for the small nations 'rightly struggling to be free' – a sentiment which was to prompt tens of thousands of Nationalists (and as many Ulster Unionists) to join the Crown forces in 1914, on behalf of 'gallant little Belgium'. Finally, if we set aside for a moment the negative dimension of Nationalism (the rejection of the British link) and compare the *positive* values with which the Boers were associated in radical circles both in Ireland and Britain, substantial common ground emerges between the two pro-Boer camps. In particular, both shared a commitment to agrarian radicalism at home and admiration for the Spartan democracy and public spirit of the people of the *Veld*, exemplified by their readiness to serve the fatherland in the citizens' army.[301] Their 'neo-roman' virtue was praised by Keir Hardie, and had long been celebrated by Tom Ellis. He may have been 'an ardent admirer of Rhodes and the close colleague of Salisbury', as K. O. Morgan has argued, but his views of the Boers were clear. The latter were

brave, dogged, independent, conservative, religious. The deep religious feeling which still characterizes the Dutch population in South Africa is due largely to the splendid stance made by Holland for the right of conscience, and largely to the immigration into the Cape of the French Huguenots after the Revocation of

---

African war: the Anglo-Boer war, 1899–1902 (1980), 239–57; P. Cain, *Hobson and imperialism* (2002), 83–9; D. Marquand, *Ramsay MacDonald* (1997), 64–5; Weaver, *The Hammonds*, 57–62; Peatling, *British opinion*, 61.

[298] Clarke, *Lancashire*, 312.

[299] Morgan, *Keir Hardie*, 106. For Michael Davitt's views see his *The Boer fight for freedom* (1902).

[300] Gill, 'Calculating compassion in war', 117.

[301] McCracken, *Irish pro-Boers*, 159; cf. Davey, *British pro-Boers*, 60–4, 137, and Newton, *British labour, European socialism*, 133.

the Edict of Nantes in 1685. These Dutchmen or Boers as they are generally called in South Africa, have plenty of manly stuff in them. The Transvaal war showed that they had the courage of freemen. They refuse to let their language be swamped in public schools ... The Dutch farmer likes a lonely life and hates taxes, railways, officials, bustle. His primary principle in politics is to be let severely alone ... They have no privileged class, no Established Church, no State-aided sectarian education. They have not to struggle against militarism and centralization ... their educational system ... seems to me framed in a liberal spirit, and it has lessons for us in Wales.[302]

Ellis died on 5 April 1899 – well before the start of the Boer War. But it is interesting that in the 1900 election Wales did not experience that swing towards the Unionists which characterized other parts of the United Kingdom: in fact, it was the only part of the country which showed a shift towards the Liberals.[303] Of course, the extent to which the Welsh vote was motivated by pro-Boerism, rather than traditional Nonconformist issues, is debatable.[304] On the other hand, the government's failure to capitalize on the 'khaki' issue – which was improving the Unionist vote elsewhere in Britain – is in itself indicative of the weakness of imperialism in Wales, where the Liberal Imperialist 'has little influence and less interest'.[305] In any case, all scholars agree that the electoral behaviour of all social, ethnic and religious groups in the United Kingdom was influenced by a variety of disparate causes, with no simple relationship to the rights and wrongs of the South African war. For example, despite their supposed hostility to the war, some Irish electors in Britain voted Tory in 1900 over the demand for a Catholic university for Ireland, to which the Unionists were more favourably disposed than the Liberals.[306] Moreover, irrespective of politics or religion, any personal connection with soldiers at the front was enough to generate some sort of emotional commitment to the army, if not to the war, among working-class families both in Wales and in Ireland. In fact, in the latter case, where pro-Boerism was general, the many relatives of Irishmen serving in the forces could be passionately proud of British 'invincibility' on the field and yet vote Nationalist.[307]

---

[302] T. E. Ellis, draft article for the *South Wales Daily News*, MS dated 12 Dec. 1890, in NLW, Ellis MSS, 2961 (a) and (b). Cf. Morgan, *Rebirth of a nation*, 31.
[303] Davey, *British pro-Boers*, 128; H. Pelling, 'Wales and the Boer War', *Welsh Historical Review*, 4 (1969), 363–5.
[304] K. O. Morgan, 'Wales and the Boer War – a reply', *Welsh Historical Review*, 4 (1969), 368, 373. Although Wales as a whole went Liberal, there were important regional and local differences, with the Welsh-speaking north and Welsh-language press being strongly pro-Boer, in contrast to the Anglophone areas in the south.
[305] Matthew, *Liberal imperialists*, 56.   [306] Pelling, *Popular politics and society*, 93.
[307] R. Price, *An imperial war and the British working class* (1972), 95; McCracken, *Irish pro-Boers*, 120, 123. Cf. Morgan, *Wales in British politics*, 179.

Specific election results are not always easy to interpret. For example, one of the pro-Boer Liberal candidates in Wales was John Albert Bright, whose stance on the issue was certainly not 'explained by his parentage', contrary to what Morgan has suggested.[308] As we have seen (chapter 5), he had been a Liberal Unionist and friend of Chamberlain for years. He was then gradually attracted back to the Gladstonian fold first by the Armenian agitation, and then by the South African war. That the Birmingham Unionists were tired of him may have contributed to his final decision to stand as a Liberal. In any case, his 1900 defeat does not say much about the feelings about the war in the Montgomery District. Organizational and broadly cultural factors must instead be considered, bearing in mind that Bright was not only a newcomer to the constituency, and therefore at a disadvantage, but also a notoriously ineffective politician and a lazy campaigner.[309]

Lack of leadership was certainly one of the problems for the pro-Boers. Hardie was aware that only a strong and widely accepted leader could effectively harness all these currents of radicalism to the cause of 'humanity'. The new priorities created by the war again made him ready even to contemplate co-operation with Morley. But, as in 1896–7, the latter failed to rise to the challenge. He was clearly keener on writing Gladstone's biography than on following in the GOM's footsteps. Hardie soon had reason to regret that '[there was] no voice at Hawarden'.[310] This was indeed both a problem and a paradox. Already in 1898 an acute observer had remarked: 'the old hero of high political morality is dying by inches at Hawarden Castle and all that goes on in the world a sealed book to him'. Yet, she concluded, 'How difficult it is to do without him.'[311] Then the unexpected happened: a radical newspaper editor emerged proposing himself as the leader of a new popular agitation.

The National Democratic League

The foundation of the Labour Representation Committee (LRC) did not arouse as much interest as the launching of a 'democratic convention'

---

[308] Morgan, 'Wales and the Boer War', 371.
[309] Pelling, 'Wales and the Boer War', 36 3–5.
[310] Hardie to Hodgson Pratt, cited in Price, *Imperial war*, 44–5; cf. G. Stedman Jones, *Languages of class: Studies in English working class history, 1832–1982* (1983), 181. In June 1899 C. P. Scott of the *Manchester Guardian* was also considering Morley as the potential leader of a 'progressive' party; Clarke, *Lancashire*, 174.
[311] Elizabeth Rhys to T. E. Ellis, 4 May 1898, in NLW, T. E. Ellis MSS, 1747.

by *Reynolds's Newspaper* a few months later, in September 1900.[312] The unrelentingly radical London weekly was then partly owned by J. H. Dalziel, a Scottish Home Ruler and Liberal MP for Kirkcaldy Burghs, who was close to Lloyd George.[313] Its chief editor was W. M. Thompson, who had succeeded Edward ('Gracchus') Reynolds in 1894. Although he was a member of the Radical Committee of the Liberal party, his articles were critical of the party leadership and in most respects he wrote and acted as an independent democrat. Fiercely hostile to Chamberlain (whom he routinely abused as 'that vulgar bully'[314]), he managed to oppose the Boer War without alienating the soldiers who traditionally formed a significant part of *Reynolds's* readership. He emphasized their humble and heroic efforts and championed their grievances, but condemned the ruling 'Oligarchy' who had started an unjust war for base self-interest, and were recklessly and unpatriotically 'LOOTING THE BRITISH EMPIRE'.[315] In short, he took a line which was more 'pro-Briton' than pro-Boer, similar to the 'critical' but 'patriotic' line adopted by Labouchere as well as C. P. Scott and J. A. Hobson in the *Manchester Guardian*.[316]

The Convention that Thompson called was not only against the war, but also against the existing parties and in favour of a democratic reform of the state. He proposed 'the formation of a DEMOCRATIC PARTY ... representative of the People, uncontrolled by official wire-pullers ... representative, in no narrow spirit, of all shades of Democratic opinion'.[317] Thompson criticized for their 'apathy' and 'timidity' '[the] men generally recognized as leaders in working-class movements' and was dismissive of the recently established LRC. According to Barrow and Bullock, his was 'a conscious revival of Chartism', but it was also an attempt to harness working-class radicalism to the twin causes of antiwar and social reform.[318] The initiative contained allusions both to the 1866–7 Reform agitation and to various other radical causes. For example, the Convention adopted an official flag: a tricolour of white, red and

---

[312] Morgan, *Keir Hardie*, 109; G. D. H. Cole, *History of socialist thought*, vol. III (1956), 1, chapter 4.

[313] Lee, 'Radical press', 51–2; M. Brodie, 'Dalziel, J. H., Baron Dalziel of Kirkcaldy (1868–1935)', *ODNB*, vol. xv, 21–2.

[314] W.M.T., 'A working man's government', *RN*, 14 Oct. 1900, 1.

[315] W.M.T., 'Labour first', *RN*, 23 Sep. 1900, 1 (emphasis in the original).

[316] Hind, *Henry Labouchere*, 33; M. Hampton, 'The press, patriotism, and public discussion: C. P. Scott, the *Manchester Guardian*, and the Boer War, 1899–1902', *Historical Journal*, 44, 1 (2001), 177–97.

[317] 'A democratic convention', *RN*, 16 Sep. 1900, 1.

[318] Barrow and Bullock, *Democratic ideas*, 141; Davey, *British pro-Boers*, 123; Price, *Imperial war*, 92–4 and App. II.

green, like that of the Reform League and 'also the flag of the Italian Republicans in the days of Mazzini and Garibaldi'. It was meant to symbolize the unity of all currents of radicalism in the British Isles, and their link with the early nineteenth-century revolutionary tradition.

Red, for the Socialists, is the emblem of the sun, green, for Irish Nationalists, is the colour of the earth, and white is the emblem of light, the hue of the friends of peace. It is also the flag of the English Republican conspirators of 1816 – Watson, Thirstlewood, and Preston, and was raised as the flag of insurrection in Spa Fields. It is a noble flag that should gather all around it.[319]

The tone and style was consistently 'Mazzinian' with its typical combination of idealism and sublimely vague, quasi-religious democratic rhetoric.

   In a spectacular display of political identification between a newspaper and its readers – a relationship which historians are more accustomed to associate with the *Northern Star* and the old Chartist press than with Edwardian journalism – Thompson appealed to his readers to mobilize *instantly*. He referred to them as 'the Old Guard of the English Democracy', and relied on their loyalty as confidently as the editor of a continental European socialist party organ – such as *Vorwärts* or *l'Avanti!* – might have done on that of its reader-activists:

In every constituency in Great Britain the readers of *Reynolds's* are invited to assemble outside the local Radical or Working Man's Club, Parish Council Room, or Parish Church, as the case may be, at eight o'clock this (Sunday) evening, or, if that day be inconvenient, on Monday evening, and thence proceed to any place of meeting which shall be convenient. There a Provisional Emergency Committee shall be immediately formed, consisting of all present.[320]

If such mobilization was not unprecedented (arguably the onset of the Bulgarian agitation in August 1876 had seen something similar in the north of England[321]), it was unknown for one newspaper editor to call for anything like it on a *national* scale.

   In the short term at least, this *levée en masse* was quite effective. The proposal was immediately welcomed by both the Metropolitan Radical Federation and a number of prominent Lib-labs and Radical leaders, including Thomas Burt and Wilfrid Lawson. As Richard Price has shown, it was especially successful with the Club and Institute Movement – which by 1903 comprised about 900 clubs and 320,000 members[322] – but was also enthusiastically endorsed by many trade

---

[319] 'The Democratic Colours', *RN*, 21 Oct. 1900, 5.
[320] 'A democratic convention, emergency provisional organization', *RN*, 30 Sep. 1900, 1.
[321] Shannon, *Bulgarian agitation*, 75.   [322] Price, *Imperial war*, 47, 68–9, 93–4.

unions, including the navvies, the General Labourers' Amalgamated Union and several groups of Jewish workers as well as trade councils, anti-war committees and radical clubs from all over the country.[323] Among the larger unions, Will Thorne's Gas Workers and General Labourers and Richard Bell's Railway Servants were prominent. It was indicative of the Convention's pull that J. Ramsay MacDonald himself sent in his adhesion on behalf of the LRC. So also did twenty ILP and twelve SDF branches.[324] Among the early supporters there were champions of both agrarian radicalism and anti-imperialism, such as G. B. Clark of the Scottish crofters and the Irish Nationalist F. H. O'Donnell.[325]

By the time the Convention met to the tune of the *Marseillaise* at the end of September, its 700 delegates claimed to represent one million people of both sexes. Besides 'WMT' (as Thompson was familiarly known to his readers), the main speakers included Tom Mann, George Howell and Pete Curran. The original programme included: '1. Automatic registration, with a three months qualification. 2. One man one vote, so as to abolish the half million bogus votes. 3. The official election expenses placed on State funds. 4. A second ballot. 5. Abolition of the hereditary principle in the Legislature.'[326] The meeting's openness and its organizers' commitment to internal democracy was suggested by the extent to which the views of those speaking from the floor (many did) were taken seriously: it was one of them who proposed amending the programme to include political rights for women through 'adult', instead of 'manhood', suffrage. The Convention then proceeded to appoint a council, which included several women.[327]

This resulted in the formation of the National Democratic League (NDL). Its philosophy was quintessentially Chartist, based on the assumption that class discrimination and the unequal distribution of wealth were the *consequence* of political inequality, rather than its *cause*,

---

[323] 'The Metropolitan Radical Federation', *RN*, 16 Sep. 1900, 1; 'A democratic convention', *RN*, 23 Sep. 1900, 1.

[324] Price, *Imperial war*, 247.

[325] 'A Democratic Convention: new political epoch', *RN*, 23 Sep. 1900, 5; 'National Democratic Convention', *RN*, 21 Oct. 1900, 5. On Clark see Foster, 'The intellectual duke', 156, n. 100; on O'Donnell see D. Fitzpatrick, 'Ireland and the Empire', in Porter, *The nineteenth century*, 505–6; H. V. Brasted, 'The Irish connection: the Irish outlook on Indian nationalism, 1870–1906', in K. Ballhatchet and D. Taylor (eds.), *Changing South Asia: politics and government* (1984), 73.

[326] 'Great National Democratic Convention', 28 Oct. 1900, 8.

[327] The revised programme was published in *RN*, 24 Nov. 1900, 1. Among the women on the council there was Mrs W. M. Thompson, described as a member of the Women's Liberal Federation: 'The Great Convention', *RN*, 4 Nov. 1900, 1.

as the Marxists argued. Its strategy was 'to democratise Parliament' *in order* to secure social and industrial legislation.[328] This understanding was aptly expressed in a cartoon.[329] It showed Parliament, its gate locked and a notice posted saying 'Capitalistic legislation only'. Outside the gate six figures were waiting impatiently. These were 'The Outcasts': Housing of the Poor, Old Age Pensions, Infant Mortality, Poor Law Reform, the Unemployed and Temperance Reform. Only Democracy could unlock the gate and remove the class-exclusive notice from it. The NDL also campaigned for most of the then current radical concerns, including free trade and secular education (against Balfour's Bill),[330] but not explicitly for Irish Home Rule, despite W. M. Thompson's personal convictions.[331]

The NDL has been comparatively neglected by modern scholars. Yet G. D. H. Cole, an informed contemporary as well as a historian, argued that for a few years it enjoyed 'much more of the limelight' than the LRC, a view shared by Price and endorsed by Davey.[332] It certainly attracted substantial backing from Liberals and democrats nationwide and was strongly supported by the radical clubs (in London they accounted for one-third of the NDL branches). In addition it was championed by Club Life and the maverick *avant garde* journal *New Age*.[333] Its activities were carefully reported by *The Democrat*, its official magazine, and even more effectively by *Reynolds's*, which simultaneously acted as its sounding board and chief source of inspiration. Contrary to what Price has suggested,[334] the anti-war dimension was central to the NDL *from the start*, rather than emerging as a fall-back strategy for attracting support which the League's 'Chartist' platform would otherwise have lacked. In fact, the NDL's pro-Boer stance was the reason why the Fabian Society (which supported the war) refused to participate in its founding Convention.

---

328 D. Torr, *Tom Mann and his times*, vol. I: *1856–1890* (1956), 92; *RN*, 2 Dec. 1900, 5. See also T. Mann, *Why I joined the National Democratic League* (1901).
329 *RN*, 2 June 1901, 5.
330 See reports in *Ti*, 12 May 1902, 9, and 18 July 1902, 6; see also *The Democrat*, June–Nov. 1902.
331 His newspaper continued to report sympathetically the meetings of the Irish National Convention and appropriated Nationalist notions and language, calling for the democrats' 'Plan of Campaign' and revelling in examples of government repression – such as when the circulation of *Reynolds's* and *Lloyd's Weekly* was prohibited in martial-law districts in the Cape Colony: *RN*, 16 Dec. 1900, 4 and 13 Jan. 1901, 4; 'The Jingo and Tory government and *Reynolds's Newspaper*: English press censorship: imperialism means tyranny', *RN*, 17 Feb. 1901, 1.
332 Cole, *History of socialist thought, The Second International* (1956), 195–6; Price, *Imperial war*, 93–4; Davey, *British pro-Boers*, 123.
333 Price, *Imperial war*, 92–3; on the political trajectory of the *New Age* see T. Villis, *Reaction and the avant-garde: the revolt against liberal democracy in twentieth-century Britain* (2006).
334 Price, *Imperial war*, 249; cf. Thompson, *Socialists*, 212–13.

The League was chaired by Thompson himself. Its vice-presidents included David Lloyd George, Charles Fenwick and Sam Woods (the secretary of the parliamentary Committee of the TUC). Among its most active supporters were John Burns, Robert Smillie of the Scottish miners, John Ward of the navvies and George Howell, the veteran Lib-lab. Its first secretary was Tom Mann. Although the ILP and SDF refused to join because of the League's links with the Liberal party, some of their local branches did and several individual socialists were prominent in its ranks. From the start individual, as well as corporate, membership was welcomed, and the NDL attracted a number of disgruntled Liberals and feminists who demanded 'a reorganized and reinvigorated party of justice'.[335]

Paul Thompson has argued that the NDL's reliance on the services of SDF members indicated 'the extent to which Social Democracy had replaced radicalism among the politically-minded working class'.[336] However, if we accept that the Boer War was important, Thompson's evidence must be read in a different way. The League claimed to represent 'the electoral army of Labour' with the mission of joining together democrats of all classes and backgrounds and both sexes, children included, against 'Territorialism, Capitalism and Privilege'.[337] That it attracted the support of SDF members is evidence of its success, not of its failure. Such co-operation was facilitated by the porous nature and continuous exchange of ideas and personnel between radical and socialist groups at the turn of the century, a situation involving the fluidity of party boundaries and compatibility between different allegiances on the left.[338] If the NDL attracted socialists of various affiliation, the SDF and the ILP had reason to find the trend alarming, rather than encouraging, because it betrayed the continuing appeal of liberal radicalism, which, as Paul Thompson admits, eventually triumphed in the election of 1906, when the Liberals attracted more than 60 per cent of the London working-class vote. For Cole that triumph was indeed partly the result of the NDL's activities, which had helped to reorient the Liberal party towards

---

[335] See the reports and letters under 'National Democratic Convention', *RN*, 14 Oct. 1900, 1 and 'The Great Convention: list of delegates', *RN*, 21 Oct. 1900, 5.

[336] Thompson, *Socialists*, 108, 194–5.

[337] 'National Democratic League: are we a debating society or an army?', *RN*, 18 Nov. 1900, 1; l.a., 'The People's League: appeal to democrats', *RN*, 13 Jan. 1901, 1.

[338] M. Bevir, 'The British Social Democratic Federation, 1880–1885: from O'Brienism to Marxism', *International Review of Social History*, 37 (1992), 207–29; Lawrence, 'Popular radicalism', 177–8; Johnson, '"Making reform the instrument of revolution"', 987–8. What Johnson writes about the sympathy of some SDF members for the Liberal party contrasts with his later insistence that for SDF members 'it was important that their politics continued to derive its inspiration from Marx' (999).

radicalism and – by the same token – had considerably slowed down the movement towards independent labour party politics.[339]

As we have already seen, despite Dalziel's links with Lloyd George, *Reynolds's* support for the Liberal party was at best conditional. In fact, both W. M. Thompson and the other *Reynolds's* editors missed no opportunity to criticize the NLF for its lack of adequate social policies, describing it as 'a middle-class party' and going so far as to suggest that 'Liberalism [had] exhausted its role.'[340] However, as had been the case so often in the paper's history, at least since 1864, what mattered most in defining *Reynolds's* attitude to parliamentary Liberalism was not what the party actually *did*, but what its *critics* claimed it was doing. In this matter, the editors reacted vigorously against Liberal Imperialist allegations that the Gladstonians had sold out to the Boers for the sake of some abstract principle, in disregard for the national interest. For example, Lord Rosebery's singling out of Charles James Fox as the putative father of pro-Boer liberalism motivated *Reynolds's* to adopt the eighteenth-century Whig leader as one of its heroes: Fox became overnight a model for modern democrats. He was a real patriot for '[he] knew that unjust wars were the destruction of liberty'. By contrast,

[t]hose who defend the present war in South Africa ... have not got beyond Machiavelli, whose central doctrine was that the individual exists for the State and not the State for the individual. Self-interest, backed by material force, was the right principle of State action according to the author of 'The Prince' and our Chamberlains and Roseberys have succeeded in reviving this idea, the idea on which the Roman Empire and old-world Pagan States were built. But the world's greatest martyrs, Socrates and Jesus, gave to mankind a higher conception, a conception of a universal moral law, which States and individuals alike must obey.

Seizing the high moral ground of Christian ethics, *Reynolds's* proclaimed that the allegedly patriotic motto 'my country, right or wrong' embodied 'not a Christian but a Pagan doctrine and, if adopted, will lead us back to barbarism'.[341]

Imperialism was of course the key issue in the general election of 1900 (28 September to 24 October). As Rebecca Gill has shown, in the run-up

---

[339] Cole, *History of socialist thought*, 196; Thompson, *Socialists*, 166–7; cf. C. Wrigley, 'Liberals and the desire for working-class representatives in Battersea, 1886–1922', in K. D. Brown (ed.), *Essays in anti-Labour history: responses to the rise of Labour in Britain* (1974), 126–58.

[340] WMT, 'A manifesto to the democracy', 19 Jan. 1902, 1; see also the editorials 'The Whig rump', 23 June 1901, 1; 'The Whig secession', 30 June 1901, 1; 'Radicals v. Whigs', 7 July 1901, 1; 'The National Democratic League Congress', 27 Oct. 1901, 1; 'A middle class party', 23 Feb. 1902, 1.

[341] L.a., 'The Rosebery manifesto', *RN*, 21 July 1901, 4. For C. J. Fox and the pro-Boers see also Weaver, *The Hammonds*, 62.

to the election humanitarian concerns had been canvassed by the Transvaal Peace Committees, started by the Liberal Forwards in June 1899 with the participation of a number of Liberals who had previously been involved in the Bulgarian and the Armenian agitations – including John Morley, C. P. Scott, H. A. L. Fisher and Goldwin Smith. With the start of the war these committees lost their purpose, but many of their members joined the South African Conciliation Committee. The latter was chaired by Leonard Courtney, and included, among others, Kate Courtney, Emily Hobhouse, George Cadbury, Bernard Bosanquet and his wife, T. Fisher Unwin and his wife Jane Cobden, Frederic Harrison, L. T. Hobhouse, J. A. Hobson, G. Murray, C. P. Scott, Beatrice Webb, Keir Hardie, John Burns and Edward Carpenter (for the Humanitarian League)[342] – an impressive combination of Gladstonians and social radicals.

Although Lord Roberts had already started to burn farms in South Africa, the British army's 'methods of barbarism' to crush Boer resistance had not yet been exposed by the press. In fact, most of the press did not dare to throw 'mud' on the 'gentlemen in khaki' who were fighting for Queen and Empire.[343] It was only on 26 November that Charles Trevelyan first expressed concern publicly in a letter to *The Times*, demanding that the government provide trustworthy information and statistics about the destruction of Boer homes.[344] On 6 December, in a speech in the House of Commons, Campbell-Bannerman took up this issue. He referred to farm burning as something which had 'moved the country', adding that 'many a heart revolt[ed] against them'. However, he refused to criticize such a policy on the ground that Parliament had been denied access to the relevant evidence.[345] This prudent course of action was part of what Jose Harris has described as his 'self-effacing' strategy to disarm and neutralize his competitors for power within the party, the Liberal Imperialists, until he was strong enough to take them on.[346] Other and less cautious Liberals, such as Bryce, displayed no such qualms and openly called for an immediate halt to the policy of farm burning and for generous terms to be offered 'to the representatives of the two Republics and to the burghers who were now in arms'.[347]

---

[342] Gill, 'Calculating compassion', 107–8.
[343] T. Pakenham, *The Boer War* (1979), 493. *Reynolds's* stood out, as usual: see 'Lord Roberts as a barbarian', 2 Sep. 1900, 4.
[344] *Ti*, 26 Nov. 1900, 12.   [345] HPD, 4th Series, LXXXVIII, 6 Dec. 1900, 114–17.
[346] J. Harris and C. Hazlehurst, 'Campbell-Bannerman as prime minister', *History*, 55, 185 (1970), 364, 371.
[347] *Ti*, 13 Dec. 1900, 10: he issued the invitation in a public speech and articulated his views more fully in a speech in the House of Commons.

In the new Parliament the issue was then raised by, among others, Campbell-Bannerman himself, John Ellis and William Redmond. The Nationalist Redmond went so far as to claim that indignation was creating a new solidarity among the people of England, Scotland and Ireland. '[W]hen they read of the burning of the homesteads of people whose only crime was that they fought for their own country' they could not but deplore the 'ruthless and cowardly persecution to which women and children [were] subjected from one end of South Africa to the other'.[348] One of the MPs who spoke most frequently and forcefully on the question was another Nationalist, John Dillon. He denounced the suppression of English newspapers in the Cape Colony,[349] and attacked the 'deportation of women and children' as a 'most disgraceful and most cowardly', 'unheard-of breach of the usages of war'.[350] *Reynolds's* was quick to echo Dillon's denunciation of 'the policy of brigands'[351] and, later, to endorse Campbell-Bannerman's famous attack on the 'methods of barbarism'. The latter turned out to be an important episode in the rapprochement between the NDL and the Liberal party.

Campbell-Bannerman, or 'CB' as he was often referred to, was identified with the 'Liberal centre' rather than the most uncompromising Gladstonian faction, and what he said was likely to be perceived as representative of the views of party as a whole.[352] From the start he had doubts about the Boer War, which he first publicly condemned at the Aberdeen conference of the Scottish Liberal Association (SLA) on 19 December 1899. Because Rosebery and so many of the other Liberal leaders (including of course 'CB' himself) were either Scots or MPs for Scottish constituencies, what the SLA decided would be of considerable strategic importance and could affect the future of the party leadership. When the executive (dominated by Liberal Imperialists) rebuffed Campbell-Bannerman, it attracted the radicals' ire. Speaking from the conference floor, a number of them denounced the executive, suggesting that it was acting on Rosebery's instructions. Then the General Council took the extraordinary course of breaking with the executive, approving both an 'unofficial' resolution and a programme which included 'Home Rule All Round', women's suffrage, the abolition of the House of Lords, church disestablishment and the taxation of land values. The Liberal

---

[348] HPD, 4th Series, XC, 14 Feb. 1901, 123.
[349] HPD, 4th Series, XC, 22 Feb. 1901, 841–2.
[350] HPD, 4th Series, XC, 25 Feb. 1901, 1163; cf. 'Sir H. Campbell-Bannerman at Oxford', *Ti*, 3 Mar. 1901, 15. On the context see Davey, *British pro-Boers*, 56–60, and McCracken, *Irish pro-Boers*, 106–7.
[351] Rep., 'Farm burning in South Africa', 8 Mar. 1901, 4.   [352] Pakenham, *Boer War*, 112.

Imperialists, and Rosebery in particular, were humiliated. He resigned as president of the SLA on 26 January 1900.[353]

At this stage, the Roseberyites were still under the impression that time was on their side, but, despite the jingoist backlash of the following months, there was evidence that public opinion was beginning to change. In March the Edinburgh Trades Council held a special meeting to protest against recent attacks on free speech (pro-Boer meetings had been broken up by jingo mobs). Yet the party continued to be hopelessly divided on everything except dislike for Chamberlain. In particular, Irish Home Rule – despite having taken 'a back seat' from 1895 – remained a powerful symbol for the Gladstonians and a thorn in the flesh for the imperialists. Many young MPs and candidates did not want to know about it, and Campbell-Bannerman and Herbert Gladstone (who had become chief whip upon the death of Tom Ellis) had to reassure them that 'they would not be committed to support a bill in the next parliament'.[354] In the fervidly imperialistic climate of the 'Khaki' election, there was a 2 per cent swing against the Liberals nationwide. However, they did well in Wales, as we have already seen, and gained a slight majority of the popular vote in Scotland. Overall, they improved marginally on their disastrous result of 1895, securing seven more seats. There were now 184 Liberal, 82 Nationalists and 2 Labour MPs contrasting with 402 Conservatives and Unionists. However, in terms of the popular vote, the United Kingdom was more equally divided, with about 1,797,000 votes for the government and 1,721,000 for the opposition (including Labour and the Irish).

From then on Campbell-Bannerman mounted a consistent attack on the Liberal Imperialists, challenging them either to reaffirm their loyalty to the party leader and the 'old Liberal faith', or to leave the party altogether and join the Liberal Unionists. The clash was not merely over imperialism but also – and largely – over the question of whether Irish Home Rule should remain part of the official programme.[355] The Liberal Imperialists had long been wishing to drop Home Rule anyway and had recently become even more disenchanted with the Irish because of the latter's opposition to the Boer War. The fact that the reunited Irish party had just proclaimed their wish to resume Parnell's old policy of independence from all British parties further strengthened their

---

[353] S. J. Brown, ' "Echoes of Midlothian": Scottish Liberalism and the South African war, 1899–1902', *The Scottish Historical Review*, 71, 191/2 (1992), 165–6.

[354] H. W. McCready, 'Home Rule and the Liberal party, 1899–1906', *Irish Historical Studies*, 13, 52 (1963), 319; Pakenham, *Boer War*, 492.

[355] McCready, 'Home Rule and the Liberal party', 326–8.

resolve.[356] However, 'CB', John Morley, Sir William Harcourt and Lords Kimberley and Spencer – who had all held prominent posts in the last Gladstone government – remained committed to Home Rule in principle. They rejected even the 'step-by-step' approach, proposed by Asquith and Sir Edward Grey and supported by some New Liberal imperialists, including Herbert Samuel. It consisted of a vague endorsement of 'as liberal a devolution of local powers and local responsibilities as statesmanship can from time to time devise'.[357] 'CB' and his friends continued to regard Home Rule as the central plank of the Liberal solution to the Irish problem. It was based, as they put it, on both 'principles' (self-government and an appreciation of national sentiment and popular will in Ireland) and 'facts' (the solid Nationalist majorities in election after election from 1885).[358] Meanwhile Lloyd George, the leading Liberal pro-Boer, further infuriated the Roseberyites by vigorously denouncing both the war and some of the British officers who were conducting it. On 27 February 1901 the NLF passed a resolution condemning army brutality in South Africa. In March two Radical MPs (John Ellis and C. P. Scott, of the *Manchester Guardian*) first used the expression 'concentration camps' to describe the places where Boer women and children were kept.[359] According to the government they were places of 'refuge',[360] but Scott and Ellis compared them to the notorious *reconcentrado* camps used by the Spaniards in 1898 in their vain attempt to defeat the Cuban rebels.[361]

It was only on 14 June that Campbell-Bannerman delivered his first 'methods of barbarism' speech, following the publication of Emily Hobhouse's famous indictment, which confirmed the worst allegations about the camps.[362] The report was based on first-hand evidence collected during her five-month visit to South Africa (December 1900 to May 1901). As Rebecca Gill has argued in her brilliant work, '[i]n engaging

---

[356] J. Redmond, E. Blake, J. F. X. O'Brien and T. Harrington, 'Irish party manifesto', *Ti*, 12 Feb. 1900, 8.

[357] Asquith on 30 Sep. 1901. Cited in McCready, 'Home Rule and the Liberal party', 332; B. Wasserstein, *Herbert Samuel: a political life* (1992), 47.

[358] McCready, 'Home Rule and the Liberal party', 332. Campbell-Bannerman reaffirmed these views in the *Liberal Magazine*, Mar. 1902, 98ff.

[359] J. Ellis, HPD, 4th Series, XC, 1 Mar. 1901, 180; and C. P. Scott, ibid., 5, Mar. 1901, 554.

[360] Secretary of State for War (Brodrick), HPD, 4th Series, LXXXIX, 25 Feb. 1901, 1021, and XC, 1 Mar. 1901, 180.

[361] Pakenham, *Boer War*, 535; R. Fry, *Emily Hobhouse: a memoir* (1929).

[362] More than 20,000 women and children died in the camps, with mortality rates of between 117 and 500 per thousand among children: Pakenham, *Boer War*, 536–41; Grigg, 'Lloyd George', 18; K. O. Morgan, 'The Boer War and the media (1899–1902)', *20th Century British History*, 13, 1 (2002), 12.

the language of "atrocity", Emily Hobhouse and her supporters in the Liberal party were able to transform the question of the Government's policy in South Africa from a minority cause into a pressing "humanitarian" issue necessitating immediate redress'.[363]

'CB' then used the expression 'methods of barbarism' again in a speech in the Commons on 17 June. Although a majority of Liberal MPs refused to vote with their leader, it soon emerged that Campbell-Bannerman had Scottish opinion on his side. In early September the Liberals openly split at the North-East Lanark by-election, when 'CB' and the Scottish whip John Sinclair supported Robert Smillie, the Labour candidate (a pro-Boer, Home Ruler and leading NDL figure), against the official Liberal candidate, Cecil Harmsworth, a Liberal Imperialist from the powerful newspaper family. The contest resulted in a Liberal Unionist being elected. In response, the Liberal Imperialist leaders – including Asquith, Haldane and Grey – campaigned in Scotland from the end of the month, demanding the abandonment of Irish Home Rule and the subordination of other radical causes to imperialism and national efficiency. However, they met with limited success and within a month their campaign had petered out. In any case, on 25 October the SLA strongly endorsed Campbell-Bannerman as party leader and denounced the war. This was followed by a large anti-war meeting in Edinburgh (30 October), with Lloyd George as the main speaker. The formation of the Young Scots Society further confirmed the trend. Its members, whose motto was 'For Scotland and Gladstone', organized another large anti-war meeting in the Waverley Market in April 1901. Various Liberal Imperialist attempts to launch their own popular association to counteract the SLA failed, but they eventually rallied around the Liberal League (launched in London on 25 February 1902). The latter concentrated its organizational efforts on Scotland, Rosebery's home, but with limited results. By then Rosebery had clearly failed not only to steer the party towards imperialism, but also to induce it to abandon Irish Home Rule.[364]

Not only was the Scottish Liberal party closing ranks around Campbell-Bannerman, but it was also adopting the anti-imperialist, Gladstonian platform of democracy, peace, retrenchment and reform.[365] For the Liberal Imperialists this meant complete defeat. As S. J. Brown

---

[363] Gill, 'Calculating compassion in war', 130.
[364] McCready, 'Home Rule and the Liberal party', 336.
[365] Minutes of meeting of Executive Council of Scottish Liberal Association, 16 Oct. 1901, NLS ACC. 11765/7. Brown, ' "Echoes of Midlothian" ', 167–81; Matthew, *Liberal Imperialists*, 74–5.

points out, while they 'had called for the subordination of Scottish national identity to the mission of the British imperial state, and the subordination of popular government to the guidance of a wealthy educated elite', the party rebelled, and the rank and file 'rejected the idea of subordination and revived a Scottish radical identity. The benefits of empire no longer seemed worth the sacrifice, and the elite no longer commanded such confidence.'[366]

The war had been central to both the NDL's rise and Campbell-Bannerman's seizure of effective power within the Liberal party. In the spring of 1902, as even the guerrilla phase of the Boer War was drawing to a close, the League's importance declined. By then, however, the prospect of tariff reform was creating a new popular agitation, mobilizing, in particular, powerful pressure groups, including the Co-operative Union, which, with a membership of two million, was comparable to Nonconformity in terms of its electoral muscle.[367] The NDL decided to run eight parliamentary candidates against the government. In this connection it is important to bear in mind that opposition to the war and tariff reform were interlinked. As Howe has pointed out, '[t]he Boer War, acting as the mother of fiscal re-invention, had spawned a series of expedients which posed an obvious and cumulative threat to fiscal orthodoxy'.[368] The 'Chinese slavery' issue strengthened the suspicion that the government was involved in a sinister conspiracy against the rights of labour. The Transvaal had been purchased by British blood and money, allegedly in order to liberate the Uitlanders and offer a brighter future to British immigrants; but now it was handed over to 'foreign Jews', while Chamberlain allowed the mine-owners to import indentured Chinese workers, who made Uitlander labour redundant.[369] Compounding damage by insult, the government gave the impression that it intended to pay for such an unjust and expensive war by taxing the British workman's necessities and industry: the 1901 Budget brought back both a sugar duty (which had been repealed in 1874) and a coal export duty (repealed in

---

[366] Brown, ' "Echoes of Midlothian" ', 182–3.

[367] F. Trentmann, 'The strange death of free trade: the erosion of "liberal consensus" in Great Britain, c.1903–1932', in Biagini, *Citizenship and community*, 231.

[368] Howe, *Free trade*, 227. Cf. P. J. Cain, 'British radicalism, the South African crisis and the orgins of the theory of financial imperialism', in D. Omissi and A. S. Thompson (eds.), *The impact of the South African war* (2002), 186.

[369] Although the latter issue had an obvious humanitarian dimension, the conditions under which Chinese workers were brought to and kept in South Africa did not feature prominently in *Reynolds's*, the *Labour Leader* or the *ILP News*. What mattered to them was the patriotic issue of the 'white' man being robbed of his wages by his 'yellow' competitor, thanks to a conspiracy of Tories and Jews: See Ward, *Red flag and Union Jack*, 67.

1845). The NDL felt that Chamberlain's tariff reform ideas were even more insulting and inequitable, and damned them as 'the widow's loaf tax'. The fact that this fiscal strategy coincided with the Taff Vale reversal of Gladstone's 1871 trade union legislation further contributed towards casting it in a sinister light.

Such were the themes discussed at a League demonstration in Hyde Park on 11 May 1902. Participants included members of trade unions, friendly societies and various democratic organizations, as well as a number of MPs. The previous day a demonstration for the same purpose had taken place in Newcastle upon Tyne, involving the Northumberland and Durham miners.[370] *Reynolds's* hoped that the two meetings would signal 'the awakening' of democracy. Praising the Irish Nationalist MPs for being 'loyal as usual to great principles', it highlighted the similarities between the present situation and the 1879 anti-Beaconsfield agitation, in that both represented a radical reaction against an imperialist government intent on wasting British lives and national revenue on reckless imperial adventures.[371] Although the Hyde Park rally attracted only about 20,000 people – a comparatively small number – participants comprised a cross-section of London progressive politics, with both social radicals and Cobdenite Liberals marching to the tune of the *Marseillaise* and the *Carmagnole*. In *Reynolds's* the page reporting the meeting was writ large with a sizeable portrait of Richard Cobden – the man 'who abolished the tax on bread' and the champion of peace and anti-imperialism. 'WMT' used the opportunity to launch a final appeal for the formation of a new People's party.[372]

When his plea went unheeded, he tendered his resignation as NDL president – only to hold it back when it proved impossible to find an immediate successor.[373] He claimed that it had become increasingly difficult to reconcile his duties to the NDL with his professional commitment to his newspaper. But there is evidence to suggest that he had also become disenchanted with the League. While reports of NDL meetings – which had been so prominent during the previous eighteen months – suddenly disappeared (although they were reintroduced at the end of September), Thompson looked to the TUC and LRC, hoping they would become the kernel of his new 'People's party'. In a curious reversal of

---

[370] See the reports 'The Budget proposals', *Ti*, 12 May 1902, 9 and 'THE FOOD OF THE PEOPLE: widow's loaf taxed: National protest in Hyde Park', *RN*, 11 May 1902, 1.

[371] L.a., 'The awakening', *RN*, 18 May 1902, 4.

[372] Rep., 'The Hyde Park protest', *RN*, 18 May 1902, 5; WMT., 'National Democratic League: special appeal', ibid., 1.

[373] Rep., 'The democratic world: Mr W. M. Thompson resigns NDL presidency', *RN*, 27 July 1902, 1.

1900, the NDL (unsuccessfully) sought affiliation to the LRC. This signalled a change of tactics, but was hardly one of either strategy or ideology. In fact, Thompson continued to campaign for a popular front which would involve not only Labour and the Liberals, but also the Irish National party and even the Ulster Radical Unionists.[374] In February 1903 he was finally able to have his resignation accepted when G. J. Holyoake agreed to become his successor. The octogenarian Holyoake – a veteran, as he boasted, of the 1832 agitation for the Great Reform Bill – was largely a figurehead, who did not play a very active role, although he did produce the occasional stirring appeal.[375] The League had run out of steam and its future was uncertain: lack of funds prevented effective action, and the need for a relaunch was explicitly admitted by many of its delegates: as John O'Connor put it, '[i]f the NDL was to live, it must be composed of different members than those of the past two years'.[376]

However, by then the revival of radical causes was well under way. The reaction to Chamberlain's tariff reform proposal prompted old and new radicals to champion free trade as a vital part of the constitution, one which allegedly provided 'virtual' representation to the interests of groups – such as women – who were excluded by the formal democratic process.[377] Meanwhile Balfour's Education Bill brought out a number of 'Progressive, Labour and other [radical] bodies', prompting *Reynolds's* to launch a new crusade against 'clericalism'.[378] In April 1902 the NDL individual membership, 'not reckoning [that] of affiliated societies', amounted to about 6,000 – more or less the same as for the ILP at the time.[379] Soon, however, there were reports of a 'great increase in the

[374] WMT, 'The Trades Union Congress', *RN*, 7 Sep. 1902, 1; rep., 'Labour demonstration', ibid., 3; rep., 'The Trades Union Congress', ibid., 5; WMT, 'Ireland for the Irish', *RN*, 21 Sep. 1902, 1.

[375] 'A great democrat's last appeal: George Jacob Holyoake to the democracy', *RN*, 14 Jan. 1906, 1. His experience with the NDL was barely mentioned in McCabe's *Life and letters*, and not at all in Holyoake's own *Bygones worth remembering* (1906). He was, however, highly regarded in radical circles and in 1902 was also elected vice-president of the Land Nationalization Society: J. McCabe, *Life and letters of George Jacob Holyoake*, (1908), vol. II, 296.

[376] Rep., 'National Democratic League: annual meeting', *RN*, 1 Feb. 1903, 1.

[377] F. Trentmann, 'Bread, milk and democracy: consumption and citizenship in twentieth-century Britain', in M. Daunton and M. Hilton (eds.), *The politics of consumption* (2001), 134.

[378] Rep., 'The Education Bill', *Ti*, 18 July 1902, 6; 'Demonstration against the Education Bill and the Bread Tax', *RN*, 17 Aug. 1902, 1; l.a., 'Clericalism', *RN*, 7 Sep. 1902, 1; WMT, 'Bishops and education', *RN*, 2 Nov. 1902, 1; rep., 'The clerical conspiracy! . . . Great protest in Hyde Park yesterday: march of the Free Churches', *RN*, 24 May 1903, 1.

[379] 'NDL new resolves: great demonstration in Hyde Park: protest against the bread tax: eight candidates for Parliament', *RN*, 27 Apr. 1902, 1. For the membership of the ILP at the time see Howell, *Independent Labour Party*, 328.

membership' in South Wales, especially in the mid-Rhondda, partly in response to the adoption of a club system. At that stage the League counted fifty-one metropolitan and sixty provincial branches.[380] Then came the Woolwich by-election, where Will Crooks triumphed as the Liberal and NDL candidate.[381] This sparked off a polemic between the League and the LRC over political co-operation with the Liberals. Richard Bell – an LRC member on a collision course with his party leaders over this issue – had unsuccessfully proposed a conference of Liberal and LRC MPs. Keir Hardie's decision to reject it was criticized by the NDL as 'suicidal'.[382] The polemic broadened when F. Maddison pointed out that not only Hardie himself owed his seat to the Liberals, but that both D. J. Shackleton at Clitheroe and Will Crooks at Woolwich had stood as 'progressive' candidates.[383]

The battle lines between the advocates of the 'popular front' and those of independent socialist action were now finally drawn. In July Morrison Davidson started a new series of articles on 'Dear Bread – Imperialism'.[384] In October 1903 *Reynolds's* launched a campaign for a public inquiry into allegations that the ILP had been 'secretly acting in the interest of the Tories'.[385] In June 1905 the newspaper was to attack the SDF for the same reason.[386] While Keir Hardie renewed his campaign against Liberalism, Richard Bell (of the Railway Servants, who had been the first victims of the Taff Vale judgement), Sam Woods and John Ward, general secretary of the Navvies' Union, advocated the NDL line of close co-operation with the Liberals.

Thompson had now reached the conclusion that the Liberal party, rather than the LRC, was to be the kernel of the popular front, while the ILP was a mere faction and an obstacle.[387] Between May and September 1903 *Reynolds's* hosted a series of seventeen articles by Lib-lab and Radical leaders advocating the Liberal alliance. Holyoake wrote an address as NDL president condemning the politics of ILP exclusivism, which he compared to the strategy adopted by the Chartists in 1837–46: then, as now, competition between Liberals and socialists would benefit

[380] Rep., 'National Democratic League: annual meeting', *RN*, 1 Feb. 1903, 1.
[381] See the reports in *RN*, 8 Mar. 1903, 1 and 15 Mar. 1903, 1.
[382] Rep., 'Labour in politics', *RN*, 5 Apr. 1903, 1.
[383] Rep., 'Labour and Liberalism', *RN*, 3 May 1903, 5.   [384] *RN*, 5 July 1903, 3.
[385] 'The Independent Labour Party: serious accusations: an inquiry necessary', *RN*, 4 Oct. 1903, 1; see also the exchange of letters the following week, 11 Oct. 1903, 4.
[386] L.a., 'SDF and Tory funds', *RN*, 11 June 1905, 8.
[387] TAC, ' "WMT" at Portsmouth', *RN*, 12 Apr. 1903, 3; 'Labour and liberalism', *RN*, 3 May 1903, 5; Morgan, *Keir Hardie*, 127–9.

only the Tories.[388] This remained the line which *Reynolds's* canvassed in its columns, often through the pen of George Howell. He deployed the Gladstonian rhetoric of the 'masses versus the classes', according to which 'class' politics was vicious and incompatible with the public interest (the 'masses'). In the tradition of John Bright, he proclaimed 'we do not claim class representation; we want to break it down'.[389] As Blaazer has pointed out, it was this divergent attitude to 'class' representation which, more than the clash between 'socialism' and 'individualism', represented 'the real barrier' between the NDL and the ILP.[390]

The 'Chinese labour' question allowed *Reynolds's* to exploit the English working man's xenophobic instincts by denouncing the 'the pro-pigtail' government and their Chinese 'serfs'.[391] If its attitude to the Chinese smacked of racism, the London weekly vindicated its liberal credentials by advocating the cause of the Jewish immigrants. In Britain (and to a lesser extent Ireland) the Russian pogroms and the Dreyfus affair had begun to create a new rallying point for radicals and democrats in the late 1890s.[392] In London, the three newspapers of Chartist tradition – *Reynolds's*, *Lloyds* and the *Weekly Times* – rediscovered a common ground in their response to anti-Semitism when they all joined the radical and Nonconformist campaign in support of Alfred Dreyfus.[393]

Reynolds's fearlessly championed the cause of the Jewish refugees and workers, who in politics were solidly radical (their concentration in Whitechapel guaranteed this being a safe Liberal seat).[394] In the process it managed to appropriate the anti-capitalist side of anti-Semitism without renouncing its traditional defence of the underdogs of 'every creed and nation'. This is best illustrated by its stance in the Mile End by-election, which saw an unprecedented display of anti-Semitic

---

[388] The first article was by George Howell, 'Liberalism and Labour', *RN*, 17 May 1903, 1; the last was by Sir Charles Dilke, *RN*, 6 Sep., 1903, 5; for Holyoake see 'National Democratic League: address by the president', ibid.

[389] G. Howell, 'Labour politics, policies and parties: a striking indictment', *RN*, 4 June 1905, 3.

[390] Blaazer, *Popular front*, 54.

[391] WMT, 'The pro pig-tail party', *RN*, 22 Jan. 1905, 1 and the cartoon 'The Tory–Jingo policy', *RN*, 21 May 1905, 5.

[392] B. Porter, *The refugee question in mid-Victorian politics* (1979); S. Howe, *Ireland and the empire economical legacies in Irish history and culture* (2000), 46.

[393] See 'The Dreyfus trial: his innocence clearer every day', *LW*, 3 Sep. 1899, 5 and l.a., 'Dreyfus again condemned', *LW*, 10 Sep. 1899, 1. For the Nonconformist dimension see W. D. Rubinstein, 'The anti-Jewish riots of 1911 in South Wales: a re-examination', *Welsh History Review*, 18 (1996–7), 673–4. For reactions elsewhere in Europe see B. Croce, *Storia d'Italia dal 1871 al 1915* (1991), 272; Guazzaloca, *Fine secolo*, 100; R. Bellamy, *Liberalism and modern society* (1992), 88–9; Newton, *British Labour, European socialism*, 129.

[394] Thompson, *Socialists*, 20.

propaganda for the benefit of the Tory candidate, although the latter was himself a Jew who had adopted the English name of Lawson. The Liberal candidate was also a Jew, but one who had retained his family name of Straus. '[W]hat a sight,' commented *Reynolds's*. 'A naturalized Jew barking at Jews not yet naturalized! A Jew defending the importation of Chinese in South Africa by the Jewish mine owners and denouncing the importation of Jewish tailors by Jewish employers of labour in East London!' Perceptively, it concluded that the real issue was not Jewishness, but class exploitation and access to the empire's labour market, inviting its readers to 'VOTE FOR STRAUS, CHEAP FOOD, AND NO ALIEN LABOUR IN SOUTH AFRICA!'[395]

The episode reinforced *Reynolds's* alliance with the Liberal left, which was pursuing a similar rhetorical strategy, based both on the primacy of class over race and on distinction between wealthy and poor Jews. Such collaboration was further strengthened by the struggle against the 1905 Aliens Bill. Vigorously opposed by the Liberals, including Winston Churchill,[396] the Bill was first withdrawn, then reintroduced in a revised form. Although at this stage most Liberals adopted a less confrontational strategy, because they realized the popularity of the government measure, the latter continued to be staunchly opposed by a group of Radicals, including C. P. Trevelyan and Sir Charles Dilke (who was close to the NDL),[397] as well as by *Reynolds's*.[398] Denouncing '[t]he aliens question' as 'an impudent bogey and a political red herring', it appropriated the high moral ground of patriotism and the defence of English liberty by advocating the maintenance of 'the noble traditions of this nation as the hosts of public-spirited men who have had to flee from their own countries for lifting up their voice against the tyrannies practised on the poor by foreign rulers and Governments'.[399] Having established its patriotic credentials, the editors felt free to champion other and more controversial forms of imperial devolution: in a throwback to its bold stance during the Indian Mutiny of 1857–8, *Reynolds's* praised Indian nationalism and called for the formation of 'the United States of India'.[400]

On both the Chinese and Jewish issues the Liberals and some Nationalists (Michael Davitt in particular) had been in the forefront of the anti-government campaign, while the LRC had kept a low profile.

---

[395] L.a., 'The Jews in England', *RN*, 1 Jan. 1905, 2; eventually 'Levi' Lawson won. For the context of these inter-Jewish, class-based clashes between the existing community and the new East End immigrants see G. Alderman, *Modern British Jewry* (1998), 117–33.
[396] R. Jenkins, *Churchill* (2002), 108.
[397] Clarke, *Lancashire*, 259; Alderman, *British Jewry*, 137.   [398] L.a., 2 July 1905, 4.
[399] 'The Mile End fight', *RN*, 8 Jan. 1905, 7.
[400] Editorial by A. E. F.[letcher], *RN*, 1 Jan. 1905, 4.

This further contributed to *Reynolds's* scepticism about the claims of the proponents of independent Labour politics, whose party appeared pusillanimous on issues of civil liberty, sectarian in terms of electoral strategy, and directionless in terms of programmes. The expulsion of Richard Bell from the LRC for his refusal to sign the party's constitution in 1904–5 and the reprimanding of both Shackleton and Arthur Henderson[401] signalled the beginning of a new phase in this campaign. *Reynolds's* now targeted the LRC as an unrepresentative 'caucus' which took into account the views of '[o]nly a mere fraction of the workers', that is, 'Trade Unionists, who personally choose to subscribe to the funds, and a few Socialists'. Like the caucus, the LRC was undemocratic, because of the 'sinister secret influence' disproportionately wielded by small socialist societies of 'middle-class people' on the party's committee.[402] Unlike the NDL, the LRC had no programme and demanded a 'blank cheque' from its supporters – surely a course of action incompatible with the democratic expectation that citizens would vote for measures, not men. Later the editors expressed their dismay at the election of Keir Hardie as chairman of the group because of his 'bitter antagonism to Liberalism'. His policy amounted to mere sectarianism in view of the fact that it was difficult to detect any distinctiveness in either the aims of the LRC or those 'which the Radical-Democrats have been advocating for years before the formation of the new party'. A contemporary cartoon showed Campbell-Bannerman as the foreman on a building site and 'Honest John' as his worker: the former notes 'we shall want a lot of Labour on this job', to which the worker replies 'I think we can manage it between us.'[403]

At the same time *Reynolds's* stressed its own independence from the Liberals and its commitment to 'Radical Democracy'. It argued that the latter should 'use' the Liberal party as its vehicle for as long as it worked, but should always be on the outlook for the 'tricks of Whiggery' which the landowning faction within the party was likely to employ.[404] The League's most popular politicians were John Burns and John Ward, who, by the end of 1905, was the new NDL chairman. Ward was enthusiastically described as 'a people's candidate; a Democratic candidate; a Reynolds's candidate'.[405]

---

[401] C. Wrigley, *Arthur Henderson* (1990), 37–8; Pelling, *Origins of the Labour party*, 225.
[402] L.a., 'Labour representation', *RN*, 15 Jan. 1905, 1.
[403] L.a., 'The Socialist-Labour group', 18 Feb. 1906, 4; the cartoon 'Tackling the wreckage', ibid., 9.
[404] See the leaders 'The decline and fall of Socialism', 24 Sep. 1905, 1 and 'Radical democracy and Liberalism', 1 Oct. 1905, 1.
[405] L.a., 31 Dec. 1905, 1.

Largely thanks to Chamberlain, the NDL's strategy of a popular front was now succeeding. The election turned into a crusade: 'If we are beaten ... the clock will be set back fifty years.' A Unionist victory would be '[t]he triumph everywhere of insolent privilege, rapacious Capitalism, insidious priestism, truculent militarism, and profligate extravagance'.[406] As in 1880, the Liberal government should be given a popular mandate to reverse 'folly and wickedness'. It was a holy war against 'Dear Food, Heavy Taxation, More Wars, Bad Times at Home, and the Merciless Exploitation of Labour for the benefit of Capital'. Although the *Weekly Times* by then had shed much of its old militancy, in 1906, like *Reynolds's*, it appealed to its readers as if they represented a distinct and self-contained component of 'the Democracy' on the march. In particular, it named a long list of Liberal and Labour candidates for constituencies throughout Britain, recommending them to its readers and issuing the general instruction that '[w]here no names are given, readers will, of course, vote for the Liberal candidate, *except in a very few instances, where private information is given to abstain*'.[407] However, bearing in mind the newspaper's long-standing Unionism, the most extraordinary recommendation was directed to the Irish: 'In Ireland we have comparatively little influence, few agents, and not much local information. It goes without saying that if we were Irish we would vote solidly Nationalist always.' Furthermore, the editor continued, '[i]f we were living in Ireland, and entitled to a vote, [as Englishmen] we should do the same, believing that the Irish people know their interest best'.[408]

W. M. Thompson's emphasis on a comprehensive and united democratic party chimed in with Herbert Gladstone's strategy, and the two men also agreed in their distaste for those partisan sectionalists who '[looked] too much to adjectives and names'.[409] In the aftermath of the election Thompson claimed that the NDL had secured the return of twenty of its members to Parliament.[410] Its success enabled him confidently to assert that '[t]he new Liberal party is a Radical and Labour party, or it is nothing. The word "Liberal" is a convenient nickname to describe the various shades of Radicalism and Labour.'[411]

---

[406] L.a., 'Why we must win', *WT&E*, 7 Jan. 1906, 8.
[407] 'General election 1906: Special recommended candidates', *WT&E*, 7 Jan. 1906, 12 (emphasis in the original).
[408] Ibid.
[409] Gladstone in May 1903, cited in Clarke, *Lancashire*, 314.
[410] 'National Democratic League', *Ti*, 26 Feb. 1906, 3.
[411] L.a., 'The Radical-Labour Programme', *RN*, 28 Jan. 1906, 1. Paul Thompson has used this quotation as if it lends itself to illustrating the extent to which radicalism 'was

Although there were no direct references to Home Rule, *Reynolds's* had never disclaimed its support for Irish self-government, but now hoped that, in the spirit of the newly established popular front, the 'Orangemen' – as 'good Democrats' – would at last see the light and convert to Gladstonianism.[412] The newspaper demanded the liberation of 'political' prisoners and the repeal of coercion. Moreover, in its campaign against the 'sectionalism' of the left, it missed no opportunity to insinuate that 'the Labour Socialist members' were both anti-Home Rule and 'anti-Catholic' and argued that that they would be completely isolated in a future 'Radical Parliament', also because the Irish Nationalists were hostile to the whole ideology of socialism.[413] In the end, ethical and Gladstonian issues such as that of Chinese labour and free trade played a crucial role in the Liberal victory of 1906.[414] Moreover, they 'had the effect of reconciling Gladstonians, collectivists and organised labour',[415] creating a coalition which was as much backward- as forward-looking, but which provided an effective vehicle for the New Liberalism. Would it be the harbinger of the democratic utopia? The veteran Christian socialist Morrison Davidson thought so: 'the Masses may safely repose a hitherto inexperienced and unknown measure of confidence that their just interests will not be over-looked in the future as in the past . . . [I] am naturally disposed, Anarchism apart, to look to the new Government for a reasonable installment of the millennium before long.'[416]

The NDL remained active until the end of the decade: perhaps its last success came in December 1909, when it organized a demonstration in Trafalgar Square to support Lloyd George's 'People's Budget' against the Lords' veto. *The Times* – hardly a sympathetic observer – reported that the square 'was filled with an immense crowd of people. A large number of speakers addressed the gathering from six platforms.'[417] By then the

---

increasingly an outdated concept' in 1906 (*Socialists*, 179) – an appraisal which later generations of scholars may perceive as reflecting the ideological concerns of the late 1960s more than the political reality of the 1900s.

[412] WMT, 'Home Rule inevitable', *RN*, 26 May 1905, 1.

[413] L.a., 'Victory!', *RN*, 26 May 1905, 1; l.a, 'Ireland in the new Parliament', *RN*, 11 Feb. 1906, 4.

[414] E.g. *The Clarion*, 29 Apr. 1904, 14; J. Ramsay MacDonald, 'The Labour party and its policy', *The Independent Review*, 6, 23 (1905), 268; *Ti*, 17 Jan. 1906, 9; H. Samuel, *Memoirs* (1945), 45; L. Masterman, *C. F. G. Masterman: a biography* (1968), 61–4. For two scholarly analyses see A. K. Russell, *Liberal landslide: the general election of 1906* (1973), 196–200 and M. M. Kim's unpublished work, 'The Chinese labour question and the British labour movement, 1903–1906', M.Phil. dissertation, University of Cambridge, 1997.

[415] Clarke, *Lancashire*, 151.

[416] J. Morrison Davidson, 'The Liberal Pentecost', *RN*, 21 Jan. 1906, 1.

[417] Rep., 'Demonstration against the House of Lords', *Ti*, 6 Dec. 1909, 11; see rep., 'London's great meeting of protest', *RN*, 5 Dec. 1909, 1.

League was led by C. F. G. Masterman, but had lost none of the original *Reynolds's* idealism – standing as it did for 'adult suffrage', free trade and Indian self-government among other causes.[418] The paper campaigned on unemployment legislation and strongly supported Asquith and Lloyd George in their confrontation with the Lords. Lloyd George in particular '[had] established a claim to rank in the apostolic succession of great Liberal finance statesmen', together with Gladstone.[419] But in the new context, it also found a way to praise the new Labour as a stalwart of 'humanitarianism'. The latter was, in the last analysis, what *Reynolds's* had effectively always advocated, and would continue to champion, irrespective of party politics, until the newspaper ceased publication in 1924.[420]

[418] Rep., 'Political engagements', *Ti*, 19 Mar. 1909, 13.
[419] See the editorials 'The tragedy of unemployment', *RN*, 3 Jan. 1909, 2 and 'A democratic Budget', *RN*, 2 May 1909, 1.
[420] L.a., 'Labour in conference', *RN*, 18 Apr. 1909, 1. The Reynolds tradition of left-wing Sunday papers continued through the *Reynolds's Illustrated News* (1924–36), *Reynolds News* (1936–44) and *Reynolds News and Sunday Citizen* (1944–62).

7   Democracy and the politics of humanitarianism

[Tories and Whigs] are full of class prejudice, blind and selfish, and do not appear to understand what Christ came into the World for. It was to destroy selfishness and unite the whole human race in one holy brotherhood. Priests, Pashas, Sultans, Emperors and the privileged classes generally in all lands do not yet appear to comprehend this, but the people do or will very shortly.[1]

[T]he Irish controversy ... affects much more even than the relations between England and Ireland; it touches those great difficulties for which Socialism is endeavouring to suggest a remedy; it is but one of the many phases of the conflict between privileged classes and the people.[2]

Home Rule and the politics of humanitarianism

In 1876–80 Gladstone shifted popular liberalism towards emotional crusades for humanitarian causes 'above' party politics. The Palmerstonians within both the parliamentary party and the rank and file were distressed by the GOM's apparent disregard of national interest. As an 'Independent Liberal working man and one who loves his country better than Mr Gladstone & party' wrote to the People's William, 'your speeches have converted me and many of my Liberal friends to the Conservative party, as we cannot but think that your foreign Policy is unsafe'.[3]

However, whether or not foreign policy was 'unsafe' in Gladstone's hands, these people were mistaken if they feared that he was prepared to pursue the politics of humanitarianism to the detriment of what *he* regarded as the national interest. For, in the first place, as Shannon has argued, Gladstone's charismatic campaigning was merely 'limited-application demagogy', in the sense that, once he had achieved the

---

[1] 'A Scotchman' to Gladstone, 5 Jan. 1878, Glynne–Gladstone Papers, 702.
[2] 'The Liberal party and its leaders', *The Congregationalist*, Apr. 1886, 305.
[3] Letter dated 23 Mar. 1880, in Glynne–Gladstone Papers, 703.

central object of a great crusade, the GOM expected to be able to revert to his 'Peelite persona'.[4] Second, as Matthew has written, 'Gladstone was, outside free trade, no Cobdenite.' While Cobden himself always opposed intervention, Gladstone 'saw [it] as a natural part of the maintenance of the civilized order of the world . . . Every Cabinet he had sat in since 1843 had dispatched a military expedition.'[5] In fact as early as 1862 John Bright had noted that 'Gladstone with his professions of piety, [always found] some way of reconciling his conscience to a retention of office and the justification of crimes that [seemed] to carry us back to an age of barbarism.'[6] In any case, the GOM's philosophy of international relations implied almost universal intervention – provided not only that it was sanctioned by either the Concert of Europe or some overriding Christian imperative, but also (and crucially) that it was consistent with British interest, as perceived from the Treasury's point of view.

Such a philosophy was based on a version of *inter*-nationalism that ascribed to nation-states a leading role in human progress. In pursuit of this vision, far from being idealistic, Gladstone was essentially a pragmatist, as illustrated by his ruthless 1882 invasion of Egypt – where British economic and strategic interests were at stake. By contrast, he opposed imperialism in Sudan and Uganda – where Britain only had vague and intangible reasons for intervention, albeit linked to lofty aims such as the suppression of the slave trade and the protection of a Christian minority against a possible Islamic backlash.[7] He even refused to discontinue the opium trade from India to China in 1892, when lobbied by the Quakers – who objected to the trade on moral and health grounds – because he was aware of its importance for the revenue of the Raj (and the profits of the Indian mercantile bourgeoisie).[8] Thus, while Bright had consistently been a genuine critic of empire, and some of the Methodist leaders became fervent advocates of high-minded imperialism,[9] Gladstone himself was always an unreconstructed wielder of imperial power for 'conservative' aims. And, although he was attacked as an 'anti-imperialist' in the jingoistic climate of 1876–8, even his speeches to stop the Bulgarian

---

[4] Shannon, *Bulgarian agitation*, 11.

[5] Matthew, *Gladstone 1875–1898*, 123; cf. W. Hinde, *Richard Cobden* (1987), 202–3, 207–8, 270–1.

[6] John Bright to James White, Rochdale, 14 Nov. 1863, Bristol Univ. Library, National Liberal Club Collection, P14814.

[7] R. T. Harrison, *Gladstone's imperialism in Egypt* (1995); A. Low, 'Public opinion and the Uganda question, October–December 1892', *Uganda Journal*, 18, 2 (1954), 81–100.

[8] J. Y. Wong, *Deadly dreams: opium and the Arrow War (1856–1860) with China* (1998), 433.

[9] J. L. Sturgis, *John Bright and the empire* (1969); G. Cuthbertson, 'Preaching imperialism: Wesleyan methodism and the war', in Omissi and Thompson, *The impact of the South African war*, 157–72.

atrocities contained the 'implicit reaffirmation of Britain's right to dictate events in the eastern Mediterranean'. If such a claim was 'delivered with the charisma of an Old Testament prophet', it was also 'calculated to appeal to Britons, whatever their background'.[10]

The years 1876–9 saw 'the emotional apex of Victorian politics',[11] not only because of the size of the crowds mobilized by Gladstone's political sermons, but also because of the nearly as large and certainly equally emotional masses involved in the Jingo counterdemonstrations.[12] The politics of humanitarianism were not only influential, but also divisive. Yet, as the Liberal triumph in the 1880 election suggested, Gladstone could be justified in his belief that humanitarianism would be at least as electorally viable as the politics of jingoism. In 1886 the new 'Democracy' was an unknown quantity. He tested its fibre with his spectacular proposal to 'pacify' Ireland by means of parliamentary self-government and land purchase. Although his decision was not shaped by electoral calculation, he had reason to hope that the plan would attract substantial support. After all, in 1881–5 many among his followers – including the Lib-lab MPs – had made no secret of the fact that they perceived Ireland as a legitimate target for the application of humanitarian imperatives, drawing analogies between the latter and Bulgaria, Poland and other countries 'rightly struggling to be free'. The unpopularity of coercion among the British public and reports of the wanton cruelty and suffering associated with the evictions of tenant farmers in Ireland contributed towards establishing a close link between Home Rule and the politics of humanitarianism.

These factors were certainly crucial in generating emotional and political support for the cause in Britain – especially among Dissenters, working-class radicals, Liberal women, and Scottish and Welsh revivalists. Each of these groups 'appropriated' Home Rule and turned its advocacy into an opportunity for fostering its own specific agenda, including land reform and devolution for both Scotland and Wales. The WLF exploited the affinity between humanitarianism and emotionalism – a supposedly central feature of the feminine character – to claim that women had a special moral mission in the public sphere, namely to purge democracy of selfishness and callous self-interest. However, the 'feminization' of Gladstonian politics reflected not so much – and certainly not only – WLF activism, but especially the broader, non-gendered humanitarian

---

[10] Pottinger Saab, *Reluctant icon*, 94.
[11] G. L. Goodman, 'The Liberal Unionist party, 1886–1895', D.Phil. thesis, University of Chicago, 1956, 7.
[12] Pottinger Saab, *Reluctant icon*, 167–73.

campaigns which periodically mobilized all currents of radicalism in the British Isles from 1876 to 1906.

Moreover, humanitarian rhetoric helped to disarm Gladstone's left-wing critics, like Keir Hardie, for whom 'internationalism ... was a central theme'.[13] Among the Lib-labs, it is remarkable that Home Rule was prominent in the programmes not only of Benthamites like George Howell, but also of more socially oriented radicals, such as the Mazzinian Fred Maddison and Benjamin Pickard, the advocate of coal mine nationalization.[14] On the whole in Britain, the left remained loyal to Gladstone despite his old-fashioned views on social policy, and even those who had supported Radical Unionism in 1886 gradually returned to the Gladstonian fold over the next ten years. At the elections of 1892 the working men's candidates – both Liberal and Independent – all stood on platforms which invariably included Home Rule. Those who did not (there were a few Tory–labour candidates), failed to be elected. Independent socialists were returned only if endorsed by the Liberals and their ecclesiastical allies. Throughout the period 1894–1905 there are examples of frustrated ILPers complaining of how 'Church ... Nonconformist conscience [and] ... party caucuses ... are arrayed against us.'[15] If they fought the caucus and tried to split the anti-Unionist vote, they would attract the wrath of the Irish, as Keir Hardie discovered to his cost in South-West Ham in 1894–5.[16]

By then Gladstone had retired and Home Rule was no longer an immediate prospect. There was a general demand for the Liberals to move on with their programme, and even the Irish Nationalists were prepared to support the government in this. On the other hand, social radicalism, supposedly the new touchstone, was a vague and divisive concern. Rosebery, Gladstone's immediate successor, had a chance of squaring the circle by appeasing the left while simultaneously holding on to the vote of the right through his social imperialist policies. Despite his anti-Gladstonian rhetoric, his technique was essentially Gladstonian, as Hamer has pointed out.[17] When he failed, he blamed others, decrying 'programmatic' politics, 'faddism' and disloyal colleagues, although, as Readman has shown, at the 1895 election the Liberals' main weakness was not lack of ideas, but inadequate party organization. After Rosebery's resignation, substantial numbers of Liberal MPs remained loyal to him.[18] They

[13] Morgan, *Keir Hardie*, 41.
[14] Election addresses 1892, vol. I, in National Liberal Club Collection, f. 4a (Howell), f. 54b (Maddison) and f. 51 (Pickard).
[15] Ben Tillett, 'The lesson of Attercliffe', *WT&E*, 15 July 1894, 6.
[16] Morgan, *Keir Hardie*, 79–80.   [17] Hamer, *Liberal politics*, 248–9.
[18] Matthew, *Liberal Imperialists*, 20–1; Stansky, *Ambitions and strategies*, chapter 2.

included most of the young generation and rising stars such as Asquith, Haldane and Grey. Tired of Home Rule, they disapproved of Gladstone's endless revivalism and 'sop-throwing' to NLF 'faddism', and were attracted by Rosebery's unconventional patriotism. They stood for a new approach to Liberalism, based on pragmatism and 'national efficiency'.

The problem was that Rosebery's ideas and tactics further divided the faithful within the SLA and the NLF and had limited mileage within the country as a whole. On the one hand, as Davitt wrote to Blake, the Liberal leaders 'were discovering that Home Rule had a far stronger hold upon the abiding convictions of the Liberal rank and file than they had hitherto believed'.[19] On the other hand, Rosebery could not really compete with the Unionists in terms of imperialism and, anyway, it is not clear to what extent people really cared about it, except as a sideshow and for as long as it did not affect the income tax rate or interfere with the workman's 'free breakfast table', that is the traditionally low duties on the necessities of life.[20] Moreover, his aspirations in terms of social reform were, so to speak, ahead of working-class expectations, which focused on trade union rights, self-help and free trade rather than on 'welfare'. Thus, in electoral terms, social radicalism proved little more than a fashionable diversion. It affected only the elite in each of the parties – including the ILP.

By contrast, there was evidence that the politics of humanitarianism was still viable after 1895. While the Liberal Imperialists were annoyed by 'the excessive degree to which the party had become a party of protest',[21] a growing number of people and pressure groups in the country believed that there was in fact much to protest about. In a two-party system political success depends largely on the other side's mistakes, and in the period 1896–1903 the Unionist government provided ample scope and opportunity for the revival of the opposition. Questions of foreign and imperial policy and issues of broad humanitarian concern could be used both to appeal to disaffected Liberal voters with little sympathy for the cause of Home Rule, and to encourage the recovery of a degree of solidarity among the fractious Irish Nationalists. This was first indicated by the protest surrounding the events of 1895–7: the Armenian and Cretan massacres and the Jameson raid. In the aftermath of a largely spontaneous agitation, by-elections showed a 5 per cent swing in favour of the Liberals. Bearing in mind that in 1895 about sixty former Liberal seats were won by the Unionists with a majority of 5 per cent or less,[22] the potential and significance of the protest are clear.

[19] M. Davitt to E. Blake, 21 Oct. 1897, NLI, Blake Letters, 4681.
[20] Porter, *The absent-minded imperialists*.   [21] Matthew, *Liberal Imperialists*, 133.
[22] Readman, '1895 general election', 486.

However, neither Rosebery nor Harcourt, nor, for that matter, Campbell-Bannerman, was able to unify the anti-imperialist vote around this or any other rallying cry. Astonishingly, as Taylor has pointed out, the Radicals and Irish Nationalists, including Labouchere and Blake, failed to exploit the Jameson fiasco to ruin and drive Chamberlain out of politics.[23] On the contrary, in September 1898 the Fashoda incident indicated the extent to which the parliamentary party was divided over foreign policy. Eventually, a concerted Liberal Imperialist attack on the 'Little Englander' Harcourt and Morley brought about the former's resignation as party leader.[24] The opportunity to challenge jingoism came again within months, when the government blundered into the Second Boer War. As John Grigg has written, in the election of 1900 'the Liberals lost because they were divided on the war, rather than because some of them were opposed to it'.[25] The impression that the Liberal Imperialists dominated the parliamentary party and could cause a new and catastrophic split like the one of 1886 forced Campbell-Bannerman to adopt a prudent and tolerant tactic. Soon, however, the cost and consequences of the war exposed the Liberal Imperialists as an isolated sect, rather than the party orthodoxy.

As in 1876, opposition to the war started not with the parliamentary party, but with the radical press and peace movement – such as the International Arbitration League, dominated by artisans of the Lib-lab type such as Tom Burt and Randal Cremer.[26] However, soon the agitation involved also most other radical working-class groups, including the ILP and SDF. Although the Fabian Society supported the war, J. Ramsay MacDonald opposed it.[27] Keir Hardie denounced it as the 'murder' of 'two freedom-cherishing Republics' and described the Boer fighters as 'serving humanity in the struggle against capitalist imperialism'.[28] Hobson thought that the time was ripe for 'an effective Labour party' to take off.[29] It is highly significant that such an eminent social radical considered that a party realignment in favour of independent Labour could be brought about not by some collectivist crusade on underconsumption or other such social reform issues, but by opposition to imperialism. Indeed, as Gill has shown, the two were intimately interconnected as part of what she brilliantly describes as 'the rise of

---

[23] Taylor, *Trouble makers*, 108; J. Butler, *The Liberal party and the Jameson raid* (1968).
[24] Matthew, *Liberal Imperialists*, 29–30.   [25] Grigg, 'Lloyd George', 16.
[26] P. Laity, 'The British peace movement', in Omissi and Thompson, *The impact of the South African war*, 143.
[27] Davey, *British pro-Boers*, 126.   [28] Ibid., 124–5.
[29] Cited in J. Townshend, 'Introduction' to J. A. Hobson, *Imperialism: a study* (1988), 18.

scientific humanitarianism' – an organic combination of Gladstonian voluntaryism and technocratic altruism.[30]

Indeed the war did bring about a realignment, but the beneficiaries were the Liberals. By 1901 Campbell-Bannerman felt confident enough as party leader to challenge the Liberal Imperialists. He helped to co-ordinate and focus the efforts of the various groups involved in this groundswell of protest and built a popular front of moral outrage – one which also included the Irish Nationalists, but avoided divisive issues by keeping Home Rule on the backburner. Asquith and the other younger party leaders were shrewd enough to understand that this was the time to support him.

From then on the Liberals retained the initiative within the left. They were in the forefront of the moral opposition to Chinese labour, a practice which in 1903 they denounced as an abomination to humanity. At that time only Keir Hardie, among the Labour leaders, shared any interest in the question. By contrast, as Kim has demonstrated, the TUC, LRC, ILP and even Ramsay MacDonald paid scant attention to the issue until February 1904.[31] But then the agitation gathered momentum, with resolutions by the SDF, ILP, Baptist Union, London Radical clubs, National Liberal Club and NLF, sponsored by *Reynolds's* and the *Manchester Guardian*. Once again the leadership devolved on the Liberals, including Morley and Asquith, while the Labour engagement was, as Kim has pointed out, 'essentially reactive' in nature.[32]

As already noted above (pp. 36–7), Pottinger Saab has explained the large-scale popular support for the 1876 Bulgarian agitation in terms of working-class alienation from the political process. It is questionable whether there was any such estrangement in 1876, but by 1905 there was plenty of alarm among both the trade unions and the working classes in general. By then they had been exposed to a series of episodes which challenged late Victorian expectations about the proper, 'British' relationship between the state and society. First, with Taff Vale, judge-made 'law' undermined the immunity which trade unions had enjoyed since 1871. Then 'methods of barbarism' – which eventually received considerable media coverage – exposed a very 'un-English' way of fighting wars by starving Boer women and children in concentration camps. Peace had hardly been re-established when 'Chinese labour' suggested that the British immigrant could, after all, be cheated out of his job in the newly acquired empire. Apart from the humanitarian issues discussed above, this created

---

[30] Gill, 'Calculating compassion', 111.   [31] Kim, 'Chinese labour', 38–9.
[32] Ibid., 48. On the political role of the National Liberal Club see R. Steven, *The National Liberal Club: politics and persons* (London, 1925).

a powerful solidarity 'between the self-interest of the worker' and 'the self-righteousness of the Nonconformists'.[33] The 1902 Education Act abolished the School Boards established in 1870 which had provided an effective system of representation for religious minorities and a framework to monitor religious freedom in local authority schools. The Act further alienated the Nonconformists at the very time their numbers and political self-confidence were being boosted by revival.[34] Not surprisingly, the election mobilized their ministers and in some constituencies they came out *en masse* against the Unionist candidates. As Victor Cavendish wrote to Devonshire, '[l]eading members of the different Nonconformist bodies [stood] outside the polling booths [at Bakewell] and every elector had to run the gauntlet of this cross-fire of ecclesiastical influence'.[35]

Simultaneously, the Tariff Reform campaign was widely denounced as a further conspiracy intended to make the impoverished working man pay for a war which had only benefited the 'Jewish' capitalist. Consumers were generally alarmed, especially women. Although the *Daily Telegraph* contemptuously dismissed 'the ignorant female mind, unable to look beyond the limitations of the ... weekly wage', *Women's Weekly* emphatically declared that 1906 was a 'women's election'.[36] As A. K. Russell has noted, 'influenced by a combination of cheap food and suffrage issues', women played an important role, canvassing and 'prevailing' upon undecided electors.[37] In particular, the WLF was able to extend its registration and propaganda network, 'quite outstripping the Primrose League'[38] – not in numerical terms, but in terms of its effectiveness as an electoral machine.

These events had further repercussions. The Boer War and the Education Act helped Lloyd George 'break away from his roots as a purely Welsh politician to become a significant figure in the Liberal leadership'.[39] On the basis of other, similarly Old Liberal issues, a number of prominent 'New Liberal' careers were launched, including that of Churchill, who broke with the Tories on 31 May 1904, protesting against their 'Imperialism on the Russian model', 'insular prejudice against foreigners ... racial prejudice against Jews, and ... labour prejudice against

---

[33] Russell, *Liberal landslide*, 205.
[34] S. E. Koss, '1906: revival and revivalism', in A. J. A. Morris (ed.), *Edwardian radicalism, 1900–1914* (1974), 75–96; C. R. Williams, 'The Welsh religious revival, 1904–1905', 77, Journal3 (1952), 242–59.
[35] Russell, *Liberal landslide*, 184–5.   [36] Ibid., 177.   [37] Ibid., 176.
[38] A. K. Russell, 'Laying the charges for the landslide: the revival of Liberal party organization, 1902–1905', in Morris, *Edwardian radicalism*, 69.
[39] Grigg, 'Lloyd George', 19; Packer, *Lloyd George*, 16.

competition'.[40] The close links between Old and New Liberalism we further illustrated by J. A. Hobson, whose 'underconsumptionist' ideas were refined in the context of his critique of British imperialism and the Boer War.[41]

The significance of the 'New Liberalism'

In an influential piece of historical revisionism, Duncan Tanner has presented Liberalism and Labour in 1900–18 as two anti-Unionist parties competing for the same social constituency.[42] In this contest, at least until 1910, the Liberals enjoyed an important advantage. For those who proposed left-wing alternatives to Liberalism discovered, to their cost, that they were locking horns with the combined forces of Christian radicalism and Celtic nationalism, the latter being strongly Catholic in Ireland and staunchly Nonconformist in Wales. Many thought that 'religion and radical politics [were] inseparably connected'[43] and behaved accordingly.

In particular, the supposed link between liberty and Home Rule developed into something of a dogma and semi-religious faith. In the process popular liberalism as a whole became similar to religious revivalism, being driven by lofty ideals rather than practical policy aims. For these reasons it was often ineffective and would have suffered from competition from the new socialist organizations, had it not been for the fact that they, too, were similar to Dissenting religious sects. However, unlike the Liberals and the Protestant Dissenters, the socialist groups, for all their prophetic zeal, experienced little in the way of revivals between 1895 and 1913.[44] Far from challenging the Gladstonians' hold on the working-class vote, at the turn of the century they came under pressure from the neo-Chartist NDL.

Patricia Jalland has argued that Home Rule delayed the rise of a new Liberal leader who could appeal to labour and that it 'paralys[ed] the party's development in other areas by lack of direction'.[45] But Gladstone's political longevity did not hinder the debate on collectivism and 'progressivism' within the NLF and Liberal intellectual circles, or, for that matter, the government itself. In fact, collectivist legislation

---

[40] Cited in M. Gilbert: *Churchill: a life* (1991), 165.
[41] J. A. Hobson, *The problem of the unemployed* (1896); P. J. Cain, 'British radicalism, the South African crisis, and the origins of the theory of financial imperialism', in Omissi and Thompson, *South African war*, 176–81.
[42] Tanner, *Political change*.   [43] 'The plebiscite', *The Congregationalist*, August 1886, 603.
[44] Thompson, *Socialists, liberals and labour*, 195, 226.
[45] P. Jalland, *The Liberals and Ireland: the Ulster question in British politics to 1914* (1980; 1993), 21–2.

started very early – from 1881 in Ireland and 1886 (Crofters Act) in Scotland. Moreover, as we have seen, the 1887 agitation against coercion in Ireland was a formative experience for a whole generation of radicals and future Labour leaders, including George Lansbury, W. H. Massingham and Sidney Webb, who derived from the Irish crisis wide-ranging conclusions about social injustice and the importance of remedial political action – principles which contributed to the rise of the 'Progressive' or New Liberal agenda both in municipal and in national politics.[46] Thus in terms of formulating new social policies the Liberal party was far from 'paralysed' in 1891–1905.

In any case, given the rise of Parnellism as a mass movement in the early 1880s and the unpopularity of coercion, which was necessary to hold it back, the British 'Democracy' could not have ignored the question of Irish self-government. It is hardly surprising that it arose when it did and that it split the Liberals. Without a Gladstone, it would have severed the Liberals from labour, with a Joseph Cowen or Charles Bradlaugh playing the role subsequently, and rather ineffectively, adopted by Keir Hardie in setting up an independent democratic party.

Moreover, it is not clear whether more aggressive 'statist' social reform was an electoral asset at any stage before 1914. In fact, it is likely that Chamberlain-style proposals would have been electorally counterproductive had they been tried in the 1880s: they could easily have provided the Tories with a rallying cry in defence of the Englishman's liberty against the 'Prussian police state' associated with state intervention. Even in 1891 national insurance was opposed by the friendly societies. The latter feared that, if the government provided insurance, the state 'would be competing in the same limited market for working-class savings as the friendly societies themselves'.[47] From 1910 Lloyd George was more successful not only because the general ethos was then different, but also because, although his basic premises were similar to those of Chamberlain, he was more skilful than the Unionist leader and better at playing the politics of emotionalism.[48] Even so, national insurance did not make the government more popular in 1911.

Like Lloyd George, Chamberlain was one of those radicals who liked to 'get things done'. This required power at the centre and the preservation of the Union, which Gladstone regarded as a constitutional quagmire. The GOM's rhetoric suggested the impression that, largely for moral

---

[46] Barker, *Gladstone and radicalism*, 90; Maccoby, *English radicalism, 1886–1914*, 59–63; Moore, *Transformation of urban liberalism*, 278–9.
[47] G. Stedman Jones, *An end to poverty? A historical debate* (2004), 215.
[48] Grigg, 'Lloyd George', 13.

reasons, he considered the political 'process' more important than its 'results'. Although this was not necessarily what he actually thought – most of the time he was more interested in achieving practical solutions than in crusading for ethical imperatives – it was enough to exasperate Liberals of the younger generation, like Acland and Samuel. By contrast, popular radicals and the labour movement tended to agree with Gladstone, not because they shared his moral concerns, but because they feared that, without democratic control over the process, they could not trust the government to deliver desirable policies. This was the rationale behind the turn-of-the-century resurgence of the old Chartist demand for full democracy as a precondition of real social reform.

After the intense debates about collectivism and socialism in the 1890s, and the parallel emphasis on 'constructive unionism' in Ireland, the 'neo-Chartism' of the beginning of the twentieth century could be perceived as something of an anti-climax. But in fact it revealed a new awareness of the limitations of 'democracy' in its 'household franchise' dispensation, and, as Barrow and Bullock have pointed out, highlighted a plan for a 'radical political democracy' in which Parliament and local assemblies would be more directly accountable and citizens would be empowered by the referendum and the 'initiative'.[49] However, in contrast to what they have argued,[50] there is little evidence that 'greater democracy and full-blooded socialism' were regarded as 'but two sides of the same coin', except by a small minority. While 'socialism' was a vague notion, a new jargon for most British and Irish people, in 1905 many believed that the real issue was neither 'collectivism' or 'statism', but democracy. In hindsight we can only say that they were right. Democracy – or lack thereof – was the problem then and would continue to be so for a long time afterwards. This is related to another apparent 'anachronism', namely the fact that land reform was a major issue in English, as much as in Irish, Scottish and Welsh, politics. This reflected not only the complexity and importance of the issue (which affected urban, as well as rural, land values and the ownership of the mines), but also an old radical dream, a form of *economic* democracy (instead of *social* democracy), based on the independence and self-reliance that a plot of land was supposed to confer on its peasant owner.[51]

---

[49] Barrow and Bullock, *Democratic ideas*, 14.   [50] Ibid., 57.

[51] M. Tichelar, 'Socialists, labour and the land: the response of the Labour party to the land campaign of Lloyd George before the First World War', *Twentieth Century British History*, 8, 2 (1997), 127–44; G. Stedman Jones, 'Rethinking Chartism', in Jones, *Languages of class: studies in English working class history, 1832–1982* (Cambridge, 1983), 90–178.

Thus, in contrast to Collini, I am not sure that we can indicate a precise point in time when collectivism fully replaced the old creed of 'peace, retrenchment and reform' as a credible political strategy.[52] But arguably 1906 was the last election of the late Victorian cycle which had started in 1880. Then 'Gladstone's speeches [had given] a moral dignity to a struggle against a policy which claimed to be based on a sensible, realistic approach',[53] by showing that Beaconsfield's imperialism and 'profligate' mismanagement of the Treasury were both immoral and impolitic. In 1906 there was no equivalent of the GOM, though something like a build-up of collective Gladstonianism had taken place over the previous three years. As in 1880, so also in 1906 Home Rule played no direct role, but in both cases there was a reasonable expectation on the part of the Irish Nationalists that a Liberal victory would indirectly benefit the cause of Irish self-government. In particular, there was widespread awareness that Home Rule was not an isolated issue, but one of the broader aspects of imperialism and democracy.

It is certainly true, as Laybourn writes, that, despite the fact that political allegiances are hard to break, once the Labour party came into existence it offered an alternative focus of activity.[54] Indeed, this is one of the points made in chapter 6. Political identities and loyalties were in a state of flux after Gladstone's retirement. Radical activists of various hues could vote for and support a range of diverse and ultimately conflicting organizations without feeling that this involved a betrayal of any partic-ular cause, because many thought that Liberals, radicals, the socialist societies, the NDL and the LRC were all – though in different ways – championing the overriding and all-encompassing causes of democracy and 'humanity'.

If 1906 was a victory for Gladstonianism and 'the old Liberal faith', the economic crisis of 1908 and the electoral victories of 1910 helped the new social radicals to promote their creed of reform.[55] Although there was often a generational clash between 'Old' and 'New' Liberals, they both included a strong Nonconformist component.[56] Moreover, there was no necessary contradiction between the policies advocated by each group. The continuity between the two was best personified by Lloyd George, whose 1909 land campaign 'retained the form of a traditional crusade against "privilege" ... [but] its content became major social reform',

---

[52] S. Collini, *Liberalism and sociology: L. T. Hobhouse and political argument in England, 1880–1914* (1979), 42.

[53] T. Lloyd, *The general election of 1880* (1968), 160.

[54] K. Laybourn, 'The rise of Labour and the decline of Liberalism: the state of the debate', *History*, 80, 259 (1995), 225.

[55] S. J. Brown, '"Echoes of Midlothian"', 71, 182–3.   [56] Searle, *The Liberal party*, 64.

focusing on urban land values, minimum wages and housing developments.[57] With the notable exception of old age pensions, the measures
introduced by the new government in 1906–9 tested and vindicated the
enduring relevance of Old Liberalism. This was obviously the case with
free trade and the 1906 Trades Disputes Act.[58] 'Home Rule' for South
Africa in 1909 was not in the same league, but was important for the
Liberals: it vindicated the pluralistic view of the empire and United
Kingdom celebrated by Gladstone from 1886.[59] It was also consistent
with the New Liberal 'inclusive' patriotism which sought to transcend
conventional class struggle. As Readman has shown, despite the Radicals'
display of social hatred for 'landlordism', even their advocacy of land
reform 'largely stemmed from a conviction that it would do much to
bolster the national character of the people'.[60] The 'feudal' nobility and
the House of Lords were attacked in the name of the 'public good', rather
than of class struggle. It was a refined version of Gladstone's 'masses
versus classes', not the watered-down variety of Marx's proletarian gospel, which inspired Lloyd George's rhetoric and helped to contain the
Labour party in 1910.[61]

This is not to deny that, already before 1914, the shift from cultural to
class politics was eroding the viability of Old Liberalism.[62] But it is to
remind us of the extent to which the period under consideration was one
of transition. In this respect, Clarke's theory about the importance of the
Liberals being ready for the politics of class is still persuasive. For
Asquith's party was, so to speak, ahead of the game, and well provided
with a supply of men, ideas and experience which would shape the
collectivist consensus throughout the period 1918–1945. The real question is why, *after* 1918, so many of these men and ideas 'migrated'
into Conservatism, National Liberalism and especially the Labour
party, whose first two governments included a number of former
Liberal ministers and MPs such as Haldane, Trevelyan, Ponsonby and
Wedgwood. In other words, Clarke helps us to identify the problem
behind Liberalism's decline. The latter had little to do with the alleged
inadequacy of the party's ideas and policies. Instead it was about the

---

[57] Packer, *Lloyd George*, 194.
[58] J. Thompson, 'The genesis of the 1906 Trades Disputes Act: liberalism, trade unions and the law', *Twentieth Century British History*, 9, 2 (1998), 175–200.
[59] Ellis, 'Reconciling the Celt', 391–418.
[60] P. Readman, 'The Liberal party and patriotism in early twentieth century Britain', *Twentieth Century British History*, 12, 3 (2001), 295.
[61] N. Blewett, *The peers, the parties and the people* (1972).
[62] P. F. Clarke, 'Liberals, Labour and the franchise', *English Historical Review*, 92 (1977); Bebbington, 'Nonconformity', 655.

post-war generation believing that traditional liberal values were best promoted through other party organizations.[63] The Irish equivalent of this problem is, in a sense, easier to solve. The decline and fall of parliamentary Nationalism is closely linked to generational clashes, cultural shifts and the disruption caused by war and terrorism in 1916–18.[64]

There is no equivalent of the electoral collapse of Redmond's party in post-war British politics. The oft-quoted rebuttal of Clarke's *Lancashire* thesis – namely that the New Liberalism was much less prominent in other parts of the country, where the party stuck to its Old agenda – is not completely convincing.[65] Of course, 'constituency parties could emphasise particular aspects of the "national" image'.[66] But, while local electoral outcomes essentially depended on party organization (rather than ideas), in order to be effective New Liberalism needed to be established not so much in the constituencies as at the centre, where it was indeed well entrenched before the First World War. Moreover, among many of their supporters in the country, 'peace, retrenchment and reform' continued to provide an adequate battle cry for the local Liberal parties well into the twentieth century.[67] In fact the combination of a New Liberal ministry and Old Liberal caucuses and MPs in parts of the country may have been highly suited to a time of change – when ideas of state intervention were still controversial and less than welcome to many of the working class, its intended beneficiaries.[68] In so far as the latter preferred 'independence', trade union rights and fair wages sufficient for them to save for hard times, they too, and even the early Labour party, were closer to Old Liberalism than to any variety of socialism or New Liberalism which might lie ahead in the future.[69]

---

[63] B. M. Doyle, 'Urban liberalism and the "lost generation": politics and middle class culture in Norwich, 1900–1935', *Historical Journal*, 38, 3 (1985), 617–34.

[64] Bew, 'Moderate nationalism'; Garvin, *1922: the birth of Irish democracy*, 123–55; Laffan, *Resurrection of Ireland*, Campbell, *Land and revolution*, 166–225; M. Wheatley, *Nationalism and the Irish party: provincial Ireland, 1910–1916* (2005).

[65] K. O. Morgan, 'The new Liberalism and the challenge of Labour: the Welsh experience, 1885–1929', in K. D. Brown (ed.), *Essays in anti-Labour history* (1974), 164, 170; Laybourn, 'The rise of Labour', 215.

[66] Tanner, *Political change*, 15.

[67] M. Dawson, 'Liberalism in Devon and Cornwall, 1910–1931: 'The old time religion''', *Historical Journal*, 38, 2 (1995), 425–37; C. P. Cook, 'Wales and the general election of 1923', *Welsh History Review*, 4 (1968–9), 387–95; M. D. Pugh, 'Yorkshire and the New Liberalism?', *Journal of Modern History*, 50, 3, (1978), D1139–55.

[68] H. Pelling, 'The working class and the origins of the welfare state', in Pelling, *Popular politics and society in late Victorian Britain* (1979), 1–18.

[69] P. Thane, 'The working class and state "welfare" in Britain, 1880–1914', *Historical Journal*, 27, 4 (1984), 877–900; Thane, 'The Labour party and state welfare', in K. D. Brown (ed.), *The first Labour party, 1906–1914* (1985), 183–216.

Laybourn's claim that '[t]he primary cause of the Liberal decline and Labour growth was obvious' – namely, that 'the voters had abandoned the Liberal party in favour of its Labour or Conservative rivals'[70] – appears so self-evident and yet is wide of the mark. For, in absolute terms, the Liberal vote continued to grow after 1918, reaching its peak in 1929, when the party had twice as many votes as in 1906. But by then they amounted to only 23 per cent of the votes cast under the recently introduced universal suffrage. Thus the Liberals' problem is not that they were 'abandoned' by their old supporters, but rather that in the 1920s they attracted a smaller share of the *new* voters than their competitors. Moreover, in terms of their ability to offer new policies, although they had been leading 'progressive' opinion until 1914, they seemed to have lost the initiative during the war, when free trade and humanitarianism were discredited and New Liberal strategies were also adopted by the other two parties. They managed to regain their dynamism only in 1929. But by then Lloyd George had wasted much of his credibility as a national leader and the party was unable to match its rivals in terms of organization and funding.

Meanwhile Nonconformity (or the Free Churches, as they began to be called) remained a potentially powerful force in politics. Lloyd George unsuccessfully sought to mobilize this constituency in the inter-war period. He claimed, not without some justification, that 'when the Evangelical Free Churches have failed to play any notable and active part in the struggle for social reform and for international justice and freedom, they have been weak and negligible'. By contrast, 'they [have become] strongest when they are fired with enthusiasm for some living cause which vitally affects the practice of Christianity in human life'.[71] However, for the Liberals the problem was that, although the Dissenters never did become committed supporters of the Labour party, in the 1920s and 1930s their allegiances were divided, as Labour MPs became the main advocates of the 'Nonconformist conscience' in matters such as drink control and gambling.[72]

In any case, what is most remarkable in the post-war era of universal suffrage is not the rise of Labour, which was very slow and painful, but the continued electoral dominance of a rejuvenated Conservative party, which was able to recast Unionism in terms of national unity above social strife, instead of territorial integrity against the claims of separatist

---

[70] Laybourn, 'The rise of Labour', 207.

[71] Lloyd George's memorandum, 18 May 1938, cited in S. Koss, 'Lloyd George and Nonconformity: the last rally', *English Historical Review*, 89, 350 (1974), 108.

[72] P. Catterall, 'Morality and politics: the Free Churches and the Labour party between the wars', *Historical Journal*, 36, 3 (1993), 667–85.

nationalisms.[73] This involved stealing the New Liberals' mantle, which, as Daunton has shown, they did with some success in 1925–9, with the help of Churchill as Chancellor of the Exchequer.[74] It is also significant that, at least as late as 1920–3, the Conservatives felt that they ought to make a real effort to 'deactivate' Old Liberal time-bombs – such as Welsh disestablishment, the relationship between church and state in Scotland, and the 'Irish question' – which Lloyd George might have been able to use in order to mobilize an anti-Unionist popular front. Baldwin contributed promptly to the settlement of all these questions, including Home Rule (in the shape of the Irish Free State and devolution in Northern Ireland) and prevented the Lords from precipitating a new 1910-style constitutional crisis.[75] However, he could not avoid defeat on another 'Old Liberal' sacred cow – free trade – around which the anti-Conservative vote rallied both in 1923 and 1929.[76]

The role of the mass party

Despite the NLF's reputation as the cutting edge in 'caucus' and 'machine' politics, it remained anchored to the idea of the supremacy of its representative council even when this formula proved inadequate. The same Liberal veneration for local democracy which inspired popular support for Home Rule militated against the creation of a more effective electoral machine. Continual changes in the constitution illustrated the difficulty of finding, to the question of 'what the party was', a liberal answer which would also be an effective solution to the problem of 'how the party should work', that is, how it could win elections. It may be significant that, when the supremacy of the representative councils and the practical need to win elections became incompatible, it was to the preservation of the former that priority was given.

Furthermore, the NLF was unable to reconcile two notions of representation then current among popular radicals. The one prevalent within the NLF, and embodied in its constitution – in all of its many drafts – was that representation meant representation of individual members: the

---

[73] S. Evans, 'The Conservatives and the redefinition of Unionism, 1912–21', *Twentieth Century British History*, 9, 1 (1998), 1–27.

[74] M. Daunton, *Just taxes: the politics of taxation in Britain, 1914–1971* (2002), 124–35.

[75] G. I. T. Machin, *Politics and the churches in Great Britain, 1869 to 1921* (1987), 313–6, 226; K. Matthews, 'Stanley Baldwin's "Irish question"', *Historical Journal*, 43, 4 (2000), 1027–49.

[76] Howe, *Free trade*, 274–308; Trentmann, 'Bread, milk and democracy'.

NLF's motto was the old radical watchword of 'one man one vote'[77] (later women were also included[78]). However, there was another, community-based, specifically working-class notion of representation, which entailed that of communities rather than individuals. This was best exemplified by the 'block vote' exercised by the north-eastern miners' unions in the selection of parliamentary candidates: in practical terms, it was achieved either internally, by infiltrating the Liberal caucuses, or from the outside, by imposing on the Liberals conditions for the trade unions' electoral co-operation.

A possible way of reconciling such conflicting notions of representation could have taken the shape of something like the secret 1906 agreement between the German trade unions and the social democratic (SPD) leadership: the latter 'undertook to avoid and play down policies offensive to the trade unions. In return, the trade union leaders renounced any attempt at establishing a separate political line for themselves.'[79] Thus the unions became the main prop of the party leadership against the militant left, demonstrating the truth of Toqueville's maxim that 'democracy is not the enemy of oligarchy but perhaps its most fertile soil'.[80] The SPD developed into a model of Weber's 'bureaucratic mass party', that is one which was held together by oligarchic organization (in which the trade union bosses played a major role).[81] Moreover, such a solution, had the Liberal party been able to adopt it, would have provided the leadership with the power to control the rank-and-file organization. However, this would have required a degree of centralization that neither the NLF nor the Liberal party as a whole possessed at the time.

A more feasible alternative would have been to accommodate, within the NLF constitution, both individual and corporate membership for trade unions and other associations and leagues, such as the Liberation Society, which could then be allotted some form of 'block vote'. That this was not attempted was one of the reasons why the NLF was unable to absorb other radical pressure groups, a failure which remained its major long-term weakness,[82] especially in contrast to its Irish counterparts. On

---

[77] Report of the Conference, 31 May 1877, 15, in NLFAR. As J. Chamberlain emphasized, 'The vote of the poorest member is equal to that of the richest. It is an association based upon universal suffrage' (ibid.).

[78] In fact, from as early as 1877 Chamberlain felt he had to allude to prospective women's membership: 'I don't say anything about women, although it may appear ungallant not to allude to them, and although I am aware that there are many good Liberals who think that they, too, might be consulted as to the legislation by which they are considerably affected.' (Report of the Conference, 31 May 1877, 23, in NLFAR.)

[79] Nettl, 'German Social Democratic party', 78.   [80] Cited in ibid., 79.

[81] W. J. Mommsen, *The political and social theory of Max Weber* (1989), 74, 80.

[82] Marsh, *Chamberlain*, 119.

the other hand, though pragmatically justifiable and not irreconcilable with British Liberal party traditions, the corporatist notion of representation which collective affiliation would have entailed was different from the mainstream Liberal and democratic emphasis on individual rights. The latter was the backbone of traditional English libertarian radicalism, and still widely accepted by many artisans and skilled workers outside the mining regions.[83] Even in the north-east, the workers articulated their communitarian ideology in liberal-individualist terms, which compounded the problem by creating misunderstandings and additional tension between local leaders and their followers, and between trade unions and their members.

While these were real problems from an electoral point of view, throughout the 1890s the NLF rank and file continued to worry about both the accountability of the parliamentary party to the council and a reduction of bureaucratic centralization within the NLF. Such demands showed the extent to which many members wanted the NLF to remain 'a Parliament outside Parliament', rather than become a modern party machine. To their demands Gladstone had offered a charismatic, rather than an institutional, answer. He managed to reconcile their democratic aspiration with the needs of electioneering and party discipline through his own personal prestige. In the short run, it worked: Liberal associations and working-class pressure groups trusted him even when they did not really approve of what he did. As we have seen, Irish Nationalists regarded Parnell – and eventually Gladstone himself – with similar feelings and attitudes. However, the GOM's retirement, like Parnell's fall and subsequent death, opened up a Pandora's box of constitutional troubles. Eventually, Herbert Samuel told the 1897 council that there were three ways forward for the NLF if they wanted 'to make that assembly the real Parliament of the Liberal party':

One was that there should be subordinate federations, which would discuss in provincial assemblies the various resolutions, and, after sifting them, send them up to the General Council. A second proposal was that they should do as the Trade Union Congress did, and sit a week for the discussion of the various questions in which they were interested; and the third proposal was that [the] assembly should, by some means, be split up into committees for the discussion of the various groups of questions that went to the formation of the programme of the party.[84]

---

[83] Especially in large cities, with a differentiated economic and labour structure, attempts to pledge trade union support for specific causes or candidates had often been resisted by members, and the right of the leaders to do so publicly challenged: for an example see the letter by 'A [trade] Unionist', *Leeds Mercury*, 2 Feb. 1874, 3.

[84] Samuel, NLFAR, 1897, 78–9.

The second alternative would have been consistent with the tradition of charismatic democracy; the third the most innovative and democratic, as well as closest to a more modern model of a political party. However, it is significant that it was the first one – the effective dismemberment of the council in regional federations – which eventually triumphed, with the Herbert Gladstone reforms at the turn of the century. Such a solution favoured concerns of 'representation' and direct participation over those of national debate and rank-and-file control of the party. Members would be better able to 'voice' their views; however, the NLF became less able to influence the parliamentary party and its programme. Effectively, it was deprived of a national voice, and made more similar to the mass organizations of the Irish National party before 1895, but without the electoral advantage which the latter had enjoyed – namely, centralization under decisive parliamentary leadership.

In 1885–1910 there was little working-class demand for a 'socialist', or even 'independent labour', party. However, there was need for an effective *democratic* party, willing and able to represent and defend the interests of the Nonconformist middle classes and organized labour. Such a party would voice, propose and elaborate relevant policies, and provide the electoral organization for carrying them into the realm of practical politics. The NLF was a debating arena, but its relationship with the parliamentary party was ambiguous and unclear. It incorporated two 'souls' at war with each other: the autocratic electoral 'machine', and the democratic assembly. Neither was ever able to triumph over the other, though for as long as Gladstone was active, his charisma maintained an equilibrium. After him, the party went through a number of constitutional changes and adaptations, but, in the end, still required charismatic leadership to operate effectively. In the new century, the Liberals were fortunate enough to find Asquith, Churchill and Lloyd George, who became viable popular leaders. However, the NLF as such could not really become the 'machine' it was required to be and which the party's labour constituency needed in order to assert its influence. This failure must be regarded as one of the reasons for the 'rise of Labour'.

In Ireland, the INL and its successors dealt with similar problems in different ways, with interesting outcomes. Partly because of the need to assert Irish unity against both Unionists and Liberals, partly because of the clerical 'block vote', but largely because of Parnell's unique historical role, the INL prioritized the electoral machine at the expense of the representative assembly. Yet, finding a satisfactory balance between parliamentary party and mass organization was a difficult and delicate operation, which frequently had to be renegotiated, especially after Parnell's fall. Despite various attempts and the rise of the INF, no effective solution was reached until 1900, with the emergence of the UIL and the reunification of the parliamentary party. Even then, many complained that the parliamentary masters of the 'machine' were suffocating the political energy of the new generation. From 1906, Sinn Fein began to offer an alternative source of political identity. As a party, it evolved a structure which – with its emphasis on participatory citizenship, representative bodies and large, unwieldy sovereign general assembly[85] – was reminiscent of what the NLF and its modern *ekklesia* had tried to be between 1891 and 1895. But the political and social context was different and, whether or not Sinn Fein was as 'clericalist' as John Dillon thought (see chapter 1, p. 32), the Catholic clergy on whose help they relied were increasingly anti-modernist and anti-liberal in outlook.[86]

Conclusion

By August 1918 Dillon was aware that his party would face 'destruction' at the next general election, accurately expecting it to secure no more than seven to ten seats.[87] With the obliteration of the National party, both liberalism and internationalism were temporarily eclipsed in Ireland. Internationalism re-emerged, in various ways, especially from the 1950s, when the republic began to play an active role in the politics of the United Nations and Amnesty International.[88] Likewise, 'liberal' nationalism did not die out in 1918 since its basic values and principles were reasserted from 1922, when the country emerged from civil war to become one of the most stable parliamentary democracies in the world.

Throughout the period from 1865 at least, the affinities between Irish Home Rulers and British radicals were based on their shared assumption that 'liberty' primarily meant self-government. This was what political theorists often refer to as 'positive' or 'neo-roman' liberty. Of course, it

---

[85]   Laffan, *Resurrection*, 171–3.

[86]   T. Garvin, 'Priests and patriots: Irish separatism and fear of the modern, 1890–1914', *Irish Historical Studies*, 25, 97 (1986), 67–81; S. Pašeta, 'Ireland's last Home Rule generation: the decline of constitutional nationalism in Ireland, 1916–30', in M. Cronin and J.M. Regan (eds.), *Ireland: the politics of independence, 1922–49* (Basingstone, 2000), 13–31.

[87]   C.P. Scott's diary entry for 7–8 Aug. 1918, in T. Wilson (ed.), *The political diaries of C.P. Scott, 1911–1928* (1970), 352.

[88]   E. Keane, *An Irish statesman and revolutionary* (2006); M. Kennedy and J. Morrison Skelly (eds.), *Irish foreign policy 1919–1969: from independence to internationalism* (Dublin, 2000); M. Kennedy and E. O'Halpin (eds.), *Ireland and the Council of Europe: from isolation towards integration* (2000); O. O'Leary and H. Burke, *Mary Robinson* (1998). For the internationalist dimension see M. Kennedy, *Ireland and the League of Nations, 1919–1946* (1996); R.A. Stradling, *The Irish and the Spanish Civil War, 1936–1939* (1999), 145–85; and English, *Ernie O'Malley*, 130–73.

was merely one among many competing – and sometimes conflicting – understandings of liberty discussed at the time in the British Isles. In particular, an alternative definition assumed importance during the Home Rule split and subsequent debate: namely, one rooted in both a concern for the preservation of religious freedom and a fear of the political intolerance and 'economic bigotry' of the Catholic peasantry in a Home Rule Ireland. This understanding of liberty – close to what Isaiah Berlin has described as 'negative' liberty – inspired many Radicals to reaffirm their support for the 1800 Act of Union. Their belief that the centralized Westminster model would be the best parliamentary framework for reconciling order with progress, minority rights and individual originality was based on a long-established constitutional tradition. Therefore it is not surprising that so many 'advanced' Liberals continued to support it after 1886. Instead, what *is* surprising is that not more of them did, and that the schism was not even more devastating for the Liberal party, which soon recovered from the split and evolved into a radicalized political force, able to compete successfully with the new socialist and independent labour left.

The latter was the main casualty of the prolonged Home Rule crisis. In Ireland it was permanently marginalized by Unionism in the North and constitutional Nationalism in the South.[89] In Britain, the ILP, SDF and early Labour party were long constrained by the Liberal straitjacket – the most they could do was to insist that they were 'better' or more 'real' liberals than those belonging to the party of Gladstone, Asquith and Lloyd George. Until 1918 such claims were hardly credible.

Thus another conclusion that can be drawn from the present work is that throughout the British Isles the Home Rule crisis was essential to securing the viability of what Kissane describes as 'democratic elitism' – 'whereby a dominant political elite proves able to absorb a variety of influences while at the same time maintaining their pivotal position within the system'.[90] In Ireland this reflected the Nationalist party's 'sole rights' over the goal of parliamentary self-government, '[a] most richly ambiguous and winningly incoherent political concept', as Jackson puts it.[91] In Ulster, Unionist hegemony developed along parallel lines, and relied on political concepts which were similarly 'ambiguous' and 'incoherent', and equally 'winning' in terms of popular support. In

---

[89] G. Walker, *The politics of frustration: Harry Midgley and the failure of Labour in Northern Ireland* (1985); C. Fitzpatrick, 'Nationalising the ideal: Labour and nationalism in Ireland, 1909–1923', in Biagini (ed.), *Citizenship and community*, 276–304; R. English, *Radicals and the republic: socialist republicanism in the Irish Free State, 1925–1937* (1994).
[90] Kissane, *Explaining Irish democracy*, 228.   [91] Jackson, *Home Rule*, 106.

Britain, the Home Rule agitation played a key role in bringing about what Peter Clarke has described as 'the greatest achievement of Gladstonian populism', namely '[running] a democratic party by keeping class out of politics'.[92] Irish working-class support for Gladstone and the rise of Liberal nationalism in Wales deprived budding socialist groups of potential constituencies. The dawn of a new era of 'class politics' – which contemporaries had long been predicting and modern historians are eager to identify – was postponed for two generations. While between 1896 and 1906 social radicalism failed to sideline religion as the normal source of political alignment, the rise of the Labour party was largely a phenomenon of the 1920s. Indeed, even by 1929 the Labour leader Ramsay MacDonald was more comfortable championing traditional Gladstonian policies – such as humanitarianism, free trade and a principled foreign policy – than the socialist New Jerusalem.[93]

Between 1906 and 1914 Liberal governments initiated groundbreaking social legislation and managed to overcome all sorts of constitutional challenges, but were unable to solve the Irish Home Rule crisis. This failure was closely related to the outbreak of the First World War, in itself but the culmination of a series of international crises for whose 'mismanagement' Sir Edward Grey, the Foreign Secretary, was widely criticized by both Radicals and Irish Nationalists, often in terms reminiscent of the Gladstonian tradition.[94] The latter also surfaced in John Redmond's 1916 denunciation of the government's repression of the Easter Rising.[95] It was a speech which the GOM would have been better able to appreciate than either Lloyd George or the leaders of Sinn Fein. But it was to them that the future belonged. In both countries, such a future was to be dominated by parliamentary centralism, 'national' values and the power of the executive, in contrast to the old Gladstonian advocacy of local initiative and self-government. In a way, it was Chamberlain's posthumous revenge.

Yet, the Liberal party had no shortage of post-Gladstonian idealists or humanitarian crusaders, including intellectuals, politicians and publicists such as C. P. Trevelyan, Norman Angell, Arthur Ponsonby, J. A. Hobson, E. D. Morel and H. N. Brailsford. The last of these embodied many of the trends surveyed in the present book: a strong critic of British rule in Ireland, he started his career in 1898 as a *Manchester Guardian* special correspondent in Crete, in the aftermath of the massacres, and

---

[92] Clarke, *Liberals and social democrats*, 7.
[93] Marquand, *Ramsay MacDonald*, 328–9; D. Howell, *MacDonald's party: Labour identities and the crisis, 1922–1931* (2002), 227–31.
[94] Lyons, *Dillon*, 322, 355–6.   [95] Ibid., 405.

was an active pro-Boer from 1899. With Bryce and the Buxton brothers he was a founding member of the Balkan Committee in 1902 and from 1907 became the censor of the government's foreign policy (he joined the ILP in protest against Liberal imperialism in Egypt). From 1914 he was a leading light in the Union of Democratic Control (UDC), and after the war went on to champion the League of Nations and a revision of the Versailles Treaty for the purpose of redressing the vindictive peace terms imposed upon Germany.[96] Like other radicals of his generation, he was enthusiastic about the Bolshevik revolution, a cause which at first attracted considerable sympathy in Britain, largely on account of the combined influence of internationalism, democracy and pacifism.[97]

Meanwhile, in 1919–21 H. W. Massingham fulminated against the repressive policies introduced by the Lloyd George government for the purpose of crushing the republican revolution in Ireland. It was like a re-enactment of the Gladstonian anti-coercion campaigns, but with a difference: now British Radicals advocated full independence for Dublin and, despairing of the Liberal party's inability to stand up for liberty, many of them defected to Labour.[98] Moreover, James Bryce, one of the supporters of the Armenians in 1895–6, became the chairman of a group of Radical and UDC politicians and journalists which drafted the 1915 'Proposals for the prevention of future wars', which became one of the most important preliminary schemes for the League of Nations.[99]

The Liberals emerged from the war hopelessly divided, while the UDC facilitated the exodus of a significant number of both Cobdenite and social radicals to Labour by championing the old Gladstonian faith in rationalism and humanitarianism in foreign politics. Again, the decisive factor was not social radicalism, but the assertion of the traditional principles of 'peace, retrenchment and reform' together with democratic control over foreign policy (the cause for which Gladstone had made his famous stand in appealing to 'the masses' in 1879).[100] Yet, even for most

[96] Taylor, *Trouble makers*, 132–66; Havinghurst, *Massingham*, 226–68; Cain, *Hobson*, 165–99; C. A. Cline, 'E. D. Morel: from the Congo to the Rhine', in Morris, *Edwardian radicalism*, 234–45; H. N. Brailsford, *A League of Nations* (1917) and *After the peace* (1920). See F. M. Leventahl, 'H. N. Brailsford and the search for a new international order', in Morris, *Edwardian radicalism*, 204–5; M. Swartz, *The Union of Democratic Control in British politics during the First World War* (1971).

[97] S. Grabard, *British Labour and the Russian Revolution, 1917–1924* (1956); R. Page Arnot, *The impact of the Russian Revolution in Britain* (1967); K. Robbins, *The abolition of war: the 'peace movement' in Britain, 1914–1919* (1976).

[98] Havinghurst, *Massingham*, 283–6, 307–10.

[99] G. W. Egerton, *Great Britain and the creation of the League of Nations* (N.C., 1978), 3–23. The group included the Churchman and Liberal MP W. H. Dickinson, along with Graham Wallas, J. A. Hobson, Ponsonby and others.

[100] Swartz, *The Union of Democratic Control*, 1–2, 6–7.

of those who remained within the party the internationalism of the League of Nations was now the orthodoxy, backed by intellectuals like Gilbert Murray and idealists like Lord Lothian and further strengthened by the influence of US President Woodrow Wilson.[101] By contrast, Liberal Imperialism was now totally discredited: although it continued, in a mitigated form, under the name of 'trusteeship', even Ramsey Muir, a supporter of that idea, accepted that there was 'a natural antithesis or antipathy between the words "Liberalism" and "Empire"'.[102] Instead, international co-operation was powerfully canvassed by J. M. Keynes in his best-selling *The economic consequences of the peace* (1919). The latter was certainly no Gladstonian tract, but its message was consistent with the GOM's vision of economic interdependence and free trade. Applauded by the radical press and statesmen such as H. H. Asquith and Austen Chamberlain, who embodied the Liberal Unionist tradition,[103] *The economic consequences of the peace* symbolized a strange post-war paradox: despite the Liberal party being in disarray and slow decline, its intellectuals were as influential as they had been in the days of John Stuart Mill.

The enduring power of the Gladstonian tradition and the appeal of the politics of humanitarianism were also evident in the Labour party. In November 1918 its programme advocated free trade, 'freedom' for both Ireland and India, the right of self-determination for all peoples within a 'British Commonwealth of Free Nations' and a 'Peace of International Co-operation' in Europe.[104] In fact, as A. J. P. Taylor has written, after the war '[t]he Union of Democratic Control and the Labour movement were one so far as foreign policy was concerned'.[105] Of course, this did not prevent Ramsay MacDonald – like the GOM, a pious preacher of sentimental radicalism – from acting as ambiguously as Gladstone had done whenever 'the dictates of morality' landed him 'in difficulties'.[106]

The argument put forward in the present book is that between 1876 and 1906 the crisis of public conscience caused by the debate over Home Rule acted as the main catalyst in the remaking of popular radicalism in both Britain and Ireland. It did so not only because of Ireland's intrinsic importance as a constituent part of the United Kingdom, at the heart of

---

[101] L. W. Martin, *Peace without victory: Woodrow Wilson and the British Liberals* (1973); R. S. Grayson, *Liberals, international relations and appeasement* (2001), 36–40, 50–3.

[102] R. Muir, 'Liberalism and the empire', in H. L. Nathan (ed.), *Liberal points of view* (1927), 253; on Muir's views see Grayson, *Liberals*, 42–3.

[103] R. S. Grayson, *Austen Chamberlain and the commitment to Europe: British foreign policy, 1924–29* (1997).

[104] 'Labour manifesto – "A challenge to reaction"', *Ti*, 28 Nov. 1918, 8.

[105] Taylor, *Trouble makers*, 165.   [106] Ibid., 94.

the empire, but also because the 'Irish cause' came to be identified with democracy, constitutional freedoms and 'the claims of humanity'. The related politics of emotionalism were no help in finding a solution to either the Home Rule or the Ulster problem and created the conditions for the renewal of 'democratic elitism' throughout the British Isles. However, they also contributed towards establishing a popular culture of human rights based on the conviction that, ultimately, politics should be guided by non-negotiable moral imperatives. Often, especially in Ireland, this had the consequence of deepening existing political and community divides. But it also gave new urgency to economic and social reform and enabled people belonging to various currents of radicalism to become more aware of the implications which the Irish question had for the wider world, bearing in mind, as Gladstone once famously said, that 'mutual love is not limited by the shores of this island'.

Bibliography

1 MANUSCRIPT SOURCES

Birmingham Liberal Unionist Association Papers, Birmingham Central Library
Bishopsgate Institute, London
Edward Blake Letters, microfilm edition, National Library of Ireland, Dublin
    (original manuscripts in the Public Archives of Canada, Ottawa)
James Bryce Papers, Bodleian Library, Oxford
Joseph Chamberlain Papers, Birmingham University Library
County Union, Reports and Balance Sheets, National Library of Scotland,
    Edinburgh
Joseph Cowen Papers, Tyne and Wear Archives, Newcastle upon Tyne
C. Dilke Papers, Churchill Archives, Cambridge
Dunbartonshire Liberal Association Papers, National Library of Scotland
Durham Miners' Association Papers, Durham County Record Office
T. E. Ellis Papers, National Library of Wales, Aberystwyth
Bulgarian Agitation Petitions, FO 78/2551, 78/2556 and 78/2931, National
    Archives, London
Papers re. the *Lloyd's Weekly Newspaper*, BT31, No. Company 96714, National
    Archives, London
T. Gee Papers, National Library of Wales
Gladstone Papers, British Library, London
Glasgow Parliamentary Literature, Mitchel Library, Glasgow
Glynne–Gladstone Papers, Flintshire Record Office, Hawarden
William Haley Papers, National Library of Ireland, Dublin
T. C. Harrington Papers, National Library of Ireland
Heffernan Papers, National Library of Ireland
J. Keir Hardie Papers, microfilm edition, original in National Library of Scotland
G. Howell Papers, Bishopsgate Institute, London
John Johnson Collection, Bodleian Library, Oxford
Labour Representation League Papers, British Library of Political and Economic
    Science, London
J. F. Lalor Papers, National Library of Ireland
Leader Papers, Sheffield University Library
Liberal Unionist Association, Library of Queen's University Belfast
Archivio Linton, Biblioteca Feltrinelli, Milan
George C. Mahon Papers, National Library of Ireland

J. Mc Carthy to R. M. Praed, letters, National Library of Ireland
H. de Fellenberg Montgomery Papers, Public Record Office of Northern Ireland
A. J. Mundella Papers, Sheffield University Library
Newcastle upon Tyne Liberal Club Papers, Tyne and Wear Archives, Newcastle upon Tyne
Parnell Letters, National Library of Ireland
Parry MSS, National Library of Wales
Partick Liberal Association, Mitchel Library, Glasgow
J. Redmond Papers, National Library of Ireland
Stuart Rendel Papers, National Library of Wales
Rosebery Papers, National Library of Scotland
Scottish Home Rule Association Papers, National Library of Scotland
Scottish Liberal Association Papers, National Library of Scotland
Scottish Women's Liberal Federation Papers, National Library of Scotland
W. T. Stead Papers, Churchill Archives, Cambridge
H. J. Wilson Papers, Sheffield University Library

2 PRINTED PRIMARY SOURCES

PARLIAMENTARY DEBATES AND PARLIAMENTARY PAPERS

Hansard Parliamentary Debates (HPD), 3rd *series*, 1882–87
Hansard Parliamentary Debates, 4th *series*, 1892–1901
National Liberal Club Collection, Bristol University Library
National Liberal Federation Annual Reports, Microfilm edition (Harvester Press) in Cambridge University Library
Newcastle upon Tyne Central Library, pamphlets
Nuffield Collection of Electoral Posters, Nuffield College, Oxford
Report of Her Majesty's Commissioners of Inquiry into the Working of the Landlord and Tenant Act, PP, xviii (London, 1881)

PERIODICALS

The Baptist Magazine, 1886
The Bee Hive, 1868–72
Birmingham Daily Post, 1885–9
Birmingham Gazette, 1889
Birmingham Times, 1889
Cardiff Times & South Wales Weekly News, 1885–6
The Congregational Review, 1887–9
The Congregationalist, 1883–6
Co-operative News, 1880
Cork Examiner, 1876–95
The Cotton Factory Times, 1886–1900
Daily Telegraph, 1895
Daily News, 1895
The Debater. A Weekly Record of the Newcastle Parliamentary Debating Society, 1882
The Dublin Evening Mail, 1869

The Durham Chronicle, 1886
Financial Times, 2006
Folkestone Express, 1894
Fortnightly Review, 1878–1901
Freeman's Journal, 1876–97
Glamorgan Free Press, 1891–5
The Humane Review
The Humanitarian
The Irish People, 1900
The Irish Times, 1869–91
Journal of the Home Rule Union, 1888
Labour Tribune, 1886
The Leeds Mercury, 1874–85
The Liberal, 1895
The Liberal Magazine, 1894
The Liberal Unionist, 1887–92
Lloyd's Weekly, 1874–95
Macmillan's Magazine, 1876–7
The National Reformer, 1880
National Review, 1892–5
Newcastle Daily Chronicle, 1868–85
Newcastle Weekly Chronicle, 1873–86
Newspaper Press Directory, 1886–94
The Nineteenth Century, 1882–95
North American Review, 1891
The North-Eastern Daily Gazette, 1886
The Northern Echo, 1886
Northern Whig, 1885–9
Ontario Free Press, 1900
Pontypridd Chronicle, 1885–93
Potteries Examiner, 1873
Primitive Methodist Quarterly Review, 1886–95
The Primitive Methodist Quarterly Review and Christian Ambassador, 1881–91
The Quarterly Magazine, 1878
Reynold's Newspaper, 1867–1909
The Scottish Highlander, 1891
The Scotsman, 1886
South Wales Daily News, 1890
The Times, 1878–1909
United Ireland, 1886
Weekly Times, 1886–8
Weekly Times & Echo, 1888–95

AUTOBIOGRAPHIES, DIARIES AND CONTEMPORARY BIOGRAPHIES

Aberdeen, Lady, *'We Twa'. Reminiscences of Lord and Lady Aberdeen*, vol. I (London, 1925).
Arch, J., *The autobiography of Joseph Arch*, ed. by J. G. O'Leary (London, 1966).

Ashby, M. K., *Joseph Ashby of Tysoe, 1859–1919* (London, 1974).

Asquith, M. (Lady Oxford), *More Memoirs* (London, 1933).

Auld, A., *Life of John Kennedy, DD* (1887; Lewes, 1997).

Brooks, G., *Gladstonian liberalism: in idea and in fact. Being an account, historical and critical, of the second administration of the Right Hon. W. E. Gladstone, MP, from April 29th, 1880 to June 25th, 1885* (London, 1885).

Cashman, D. B., *Life of Michael Davitt, with a History of the Rise and Development of the Irish National League* (Dublin, 1881).

Chamberlain, J., *A political memoir, 1880–92*, ed. by C. H. D. Howard (London, 1953).

Friederichs, H., *The life of Sir George Newnes* (London, 1911).

The Gladstone diaries, ed. by M. R. D. Foot and H. C. G. Matthew, 14 vols. (Oxford, 1968–94).

Gwynn, S. and G. M. Tuckerwell, *The life of the Rt Hon. Sir Charles Dilke, MP* (London, 1917).

Haldane, R. B., *An autobiography* (London, 1929).

Healy, T. M., *Letters and leaders of my day*, 2 vols. (London, n.d. [1928]).

Holyoake, G. J., *Bygones worth remembering* (London, 1906).

McCabe, J., *Life and letters of George Jacob Holyoake*, 2 vols. (London, 1908).

MacKnight, T., *Ulster as it is or twenty-eight years experience as an Irish editor*, 2 vols. (London, 1896).

Narikoff, O., *The MP for Russia: reminiscences and correspondence of Madame O. Narikoff*, vol. I, ed. by W. T. Stead (London, 1909).

O'Connor, T. P., *Memoirs of an old parliamentarian*, 2 vols. (London, 1929).

O'Toole, E., *Whist for your life, that's treason. Recollections of a long life* (Dublin, 2003).

Potter, G., *Life of W. E. Gladstone*, reprinted in his 'Gladstone, the friend of the people', 'Leaflets for the new electors' (London, 1885) Bishopsgate Institute.

Samuel, H., *Memoirs* (London, 1945).

Gordon, P. (ed.), *The Red Earl: the papers of the Fifth Earl Spencer, 1835–1910*, 2 vols. (Northampton, 1981, 1986).

Tuckwell, Revd W., *Reminiscences of a radical parson* (London, 1905).

Walling, R. A. J. (ed.), *The diaries of John Bright* (London, 1930).

Webb, B., *My apprenticeship* (Harmondsworth, 1950).

Wells, W. B., *John Redmond. A biography* (London, 1919).

Wemyss Reid, T., *The life of the Rt Hon. W. E. Forster*, 2 vols. (Bath, 1888; New York, 1970).

OTHER PRINTED PRIMARY SOURCES

[Anon.], *Chartism and Repeal. An address to the Repealers of Ireland, by a Member of the Irish Universal Suffrage Association* (Dublin, 1842).

[Anon.], *Scotland's welcome to Mr Parnell: A souvenir of his first political visit to Scotland* (Edinburgh, 1889).

[Anon], *The Ulster Liberal Unionist Association. A sketch of its history 1885–1914. How it has opposed Home Rule, and what it has done for remedial legislation for Ireland*, introduction by Mr J. R. Fisher, published by the authority of the Executive Committee of the Ulster Liberal Association, Ulster Reform Club (Belfast, 1913).

Atherley-Jones, L., 'The Liberal party and the House of Lords', *The Nineteenth Century Review*, LXII (1907), 167–76.

'The New Liberalism', *The Nineteenth Century Review*, XXVI, (1889), 186–93.

Beesly, E. S., *Socialists against the grain: or, the price of holding Ireland* (London, 1887).

Besant, A., *Egypt* (London, 1882).

Binney, F. A., *Why working men should be Liberals* (London and Manchester, n.d. [1885]).

Blackie, J. S., *Home Rule and political parties in Scotland. A review* (Edinburgh, 1889).

Bradlaugh, C., *Debate between H. M. Hyndman and Charles Bradlaugh. Will socialism benefit the English people?* (London, 1884).

The radical programme (London, 1889).

Socialism: its fallacies and dangers (London, 1887).

Brailsford, H. N., *After the peace* (London, 1920).

A League of Nations (London, 1917).

Bridges, J. H., *Irish disaffection: four letters addressed to the editor of the 'Bradford Review'* (Bradford, 1868).

Butler, J. E., *Our Christianity tested by the Irish question* (London, n.d. [1886]).

Cameron, J., *The old and the new Highlands and Hebrides* (Kirkcaldy, 1912).

Chamberlain, J., *Home Rule and the Irish question: A collection of speeches delivered between 1881 and 1887* (London, 1887).

Chamberlain, J. et al., *The radical programme* (London, 1885; ed. by D. A. Hamer, 1971).

Collings, J., *The colonization of rural Britain* (London, 1914).

Land reform: Occupying ownership, peasant proprietary and rural education (London, 1906).

Collings, J. and J. L. Green, *Life of the Right Hon. Jesse Collings* (London, 1920).

Cowen, J., *Joseph Cowen's speeches on the near Eastern question* (London, 1909).

Craig, J. D., *Are Irish Protestants afraid of Home Rule? Two speeches delivered by Rev. J. D. Craig Houston and Professor Dougherty at the General Assembly of the Presbyterian Church, held in Belfast, on June 9th, 1893*, The Liberal Publications Department (London, 1893).

Crookshank, C. H., *Memorable women of Irish Methodism in the last century* (London, 1882).

Davitt, M., *The Boer fight for freedom* (New York and London, 1902).

The fall of feudalism in Ireland (London, 1904; 1970).

Leaves from a prison diary (1885; Shannon, 1972).

The settlement of the Irish Question. A speech by Mr Michael Davitt, MP, on Apr. 11th, 1893 in the House of Commons, 'Authorised edition' as a penny pamphlet, Liberal Publications Department (London, 1893).

Denvir, J., *The Irish in Britain from the earliest times to the fall and death of Parnell* (London, 1892).

Dickson, T. A., *An Irish policy for a Liberal government* (London, 1885).

Gladstone's speeches, ed. by A. Tinley Basset, (London, 1916).

Gladstone, W. E., *The Bulgarian horrors and the question of the East* (London, 1876).

Gladstone, W. E., *Coercion in Ireland. Speech delivered by the Right Hon. W. E. Gladstone, MP, in the House of Commons, on Friday, Feb. 17th, 1888*, Liberal Publications Department (London, 1888).

The Eastern crisis. A letter to the Duke of Westminster, KG (London, 1897).

Egypt and the Soudan, a speech republished delivered to the House of Commons, Liberal Central Association (London, 1884).

'The future policy of the Liberal party, Newcastle, October 2, 1891', in A. W. Hutton and H. J. Cohen (eds.), *The speeches of the Right Hon. W. E. Gladstone* (London, 1902), 383–5.

Midlothian Speeches, 1879 (Leicester, 1971).

The Gladstone diaries, ed. by M. R. D. Foot and H. C. G. Matthew, 14 vols. (Oxford, 1968–94).

The Government of Ireland Bill (London, 1886).

The Irish Land Bill (London, 1881).

The Irish question (London, 1886).

The Treatment of the Irish Members and the Irish Political Prisoners, a speech by the Right Hon. W. E. Gladstone, MP, to the Staffordshire Liberals, Liberal Publications Department (London, 1888).

Gordon, P. (ed.), *The Red Earl: the papers of the Fifth Earl Spencer, 1835–1910*, 2 vols (Northampton, 1981, 1986).

Gray, E. Dwyer, correspondence in T. W. Moody, 'Select documents: Parnell and the Galway election of 1886', *Irish Historical Studies*, 8, 33 (1954), 319–38.

Griffith, A., *The resurrection of Hungary: a parallel for Ireland* (Dublin, 1904).

Harrison, F., *The crisis in Egypt*, Anti-Aggression League Pamphlet No. 2 (Dublin, 1882).

Healy, T. M., 'The Irish parliamentary party', *Fortnightly Review*, 32, n.s. (1882), 625–33.

Hobson J. A., *The crisis of Liberalism: new issues of democracy* (London, 1909).

Imperialism: a study (London, 1902; 1988).

The problem of the unemployed (London, 1896).

The psychology of Jingoism (London, 1901).

Hogan, J. F., *The Irish in Australia* (London, 1887).

Kemp, D. W., *The Sutherland democracy* (Edinburgh, 1890).

Lubbock, J. and H. O. Arnold-Forster, *Proportional representation: a dialogue* (London, 1884).

Mabellan, D., *Home Rule and imperial unity, an argument for the Gladstone–Morley scheme* (London, 1886).

MacCarthy, J. G., *The principles of Home Rule as explained by Isaac Butt, Esq., MP. Is it reasonable & what practical advantages are expected from it?* (Sheffield, 1873).

MacDonald, J., 'Is the caucus a necessity'? *Fortnightly Review*, 44 (1885), 780–90.

MacDonald, J. R., 'The Labour party and its policy', *The Independent Review*, 6, 23 (Aug. 1905).

McMinn, J. R. B., *Against the tide: a calendar of the papers of the Reverend J. M. Armour, Irish Presbyterian minister and Home Ruler, 1869–1914* (Belfast, 1985).

Maine, H., *Village communities in the East and the West* (London, 1876).

Mann, T., *Why I joined the National Democratic League* (London, 1901).

Mill, J. S., *Collected works*, vol. 19, *Essays on politics and society*, ed. by J. M. Robson, (Toronto and London, 1977).

Milner, Lord, J. A. Spender, Sir Henry Lucy, J. Ramsay Macdonald, H. Cox and L. S. Amery, *Life of Joseph Chamberlain* (London, 1914).

Nicholas, Revd W., *Why are the Methodists of Ireland opposed to Home Rule* (1893).
Nulty, T., *To the clergy and laity of the Diocese of Meath* (Mulligar, 1888).
Ostrogorski, M., *Democracy and the organization of political parties* (1902; New York, 1964).
Reynolds, S., Bob and Tom Woolley, *Seems so! A working-class view of politics* (London, 1911).
Russell, T. W., *Disturbed Ireland. The plan of campaign estates* (London, 1889).
   Ireland. No. XXIX. The case for Irish Loyalists, published by the Irish Loyal and Patriotic Union (Dublin, 1886).
   Ireland and the empire. A review, 1800–1900 (London, 1901).
   'The Irish question from the standpoint of a Liberal', *Dublin University Review*, 2 (Feb. 1886), 105–14.
   The Plan of Campaign illustrated (London, 1889).
Seeley, J., *The expansion of England* (London, 1882).
Shaw Lefevre, G., *Incidents of coercion: a journal of visits to Ireland in 1882 and 1888* (London, 1889).
   Mr John Morley, MP, in Tipperary. Why he went and what he saw (London, 1890).
Shebbear, C. J., *The Greek theory of the state and the Nonconformist conscience* (London, 1895).
Stead, W. T., *Truth about Russia* (London, 1888).
Watson, R. Sperce, *The National Liberal Federation: from its commencement to the general election of 1906* (London, 1907).
Webb, A., *An address to the electors of Waterford* (Dublin, 1888).
Wilson, T. (ed.), *The political diaries of C. P. Scott, 1911–1928* (New York, 1970).

3 SECONDARY SOURCES

Alberti, J. *Eleanor Rathbone* (London, 1996).
Alderman, G., *Modern British Jewry* (Oxford, 1998).
Al-Sayyid-Marsot, A. L., 'The British occupation of Egypt from 1882', in A. Porter (ed.), *The Oxford history of the British Empire, vol. III: The nineteenth century* (Oxford, 1999), 651–64.
Anderson, J., 'Ideological variations in Ulster during Ireland's first Home Rule crisis: an analysis of local newspapers', in C. H. Williams and E. Kofman (eds.), *Community conflict, partition and nationalism* (London, 1989).
Anderson, M., *Henry Joseph Wilson: fighter for freedom* (London, 1953).
Andreucci, F. 'La questione coloniale e l' imperialismo', in E. J. Hobsbawm et al. (eds), *Storia del marxismo, Vol. 2, Il marxismo nell' età della seconda internazionale* (Turin, 1979), 868–96.
   Socialdemocrazia e imperialismo (Rome, 1988).
Armour, N., 'Isabella Tod and Liberal Unionism in Ulster, 1886–1896', in A. Hayes and D. Urquhart (eds.), *New perspective on Irish women* (Dublin, 2004), 72–87.
Armytage, W. H. G. and A. J. Mundella, 1825–1897: *The Liberal background to the labour movement* (London, 1951).
Arnstein, W. J., 'Parnell and the Bradlaugh case', *Irish Historical Studies*, 13, 51 (1963), 212–35.
Arnot, R. Page, *The impact of the Russian Revolution in Britain* (London, 1967).

Ashby, M. K., *Joseph Ashby of Tysoe* (London, 1974).

Auld, J. W., 'The Liberal pro-Boers', *Journal of British Studies*, 14 (1975), 78–101.

Bakshi, S. R., *Home Rule movement* (New Delhi, 1984).

Banks, M. B., *Edward Blake, Irish Nationalist: a Canadian statesman in Irish politics, 1892–1907* (Toronto, 1957).

Barker, M., *Gladstone and radicalism: the reconstruction of Liberal policy in Britain, 1885–1894* (Hassocks, 1975).

Barrow, L. and I. Bullock, *Democratic ideas and the British labour movement, 1880–1914* (Cambridge, 1996).

Barry O'Brien, R., *John Bright* (London, 1910).

Bassett, T. M., *The Welsh Baptists* (Swansea, 1977).

Bayly, C. A., 'Ireland, India and the empire, 1780–1914', *Transactions of the Royal Historical Society*, 6th series, 10 (2000).

Beales, D. E. D., 'Parliamentary parties and the "independent" member, 1810–1860', in R. Robson (ed.), *Ideas and institutions of Victorian Britain* (London, 1967), 1–19.

Bebbington, D. W., 'Gladstone's Christian liberalism', *Chf Bulletin*, (Summer 2005), 11–17.

The mind of Gladstone (Oxford, 2004).

The Nonconformist conscience: chapel and politics, 1870–1914 (London, 1982).

'Religion and national feeling in nineteenth-century Wales and Scotland', in S. Mews (ed.), *Religion and national identity* (Oxford, 1982), 489–503.

'Nonconformity and electoral sociology, 1867–1918', *Historical Journal*, 27, 3 (1984), 633–56.

Belchem, J., 'Nationalism, republicanism and exile: Irish emigrants and the revolutions of 1848', *Past and Present*, no.146 (1995), 103–35.

Bellamy, E., *Liberalism and modern society* (Cambridge, 1992).

Bellamy, J. M. and J. Saville (eds.), *Dictionary of Labour Biography* (London, 1972–).

Berridge, V., 'Popular journalism and working-class attitudes', Ph.D. thesis, University of London, 1976.

Bevir, M., 'The British Social Democratic Federation, 1880–1885: from O'Brienism to Marxism', *International Review of Social History*, 37 (1992), 207–29.

Bew P., *Charles Stewart Parnell* (Dublin, 1991).

Conflict and conciliation in Ireland, 1890–1910: Parnellites and radical agrarians (Oxford, 1987).

Ideology and the Irish question: Ulster Unionism and Irish nationalism, 1912–1916 (Oxford, 1994).

Land and the national question in Ireland, 1858–82 (Dublin, 1978).

'Liberalism, nationalism and religion in Britain and Ireland in the nineteenth century', in S. Groeveld and M. Wintle (eds.), *Britain and the Netherlands, vol. XII: Under the sign of liberalism* (Zutphen, 1997), 93–101.

'Moderate nationalism and the Irish revolution, 1916–1923', *Historical Journal*, 42, 3 (1999), 729–49.

Bew, P. and F. Wright, 'The agrarian opposition in Ulster politics, 1848–87', in S. Clark and J. D. Donnelly (eds.), *Irish peasants, violence and political unrest, 1780–1914* (Dublin, 1986), 192–229.

Bew P., K. Darwin and G. Gillespie (eds.), *Passion and prejudice: Nationalist–Unionist conflict in Ulster in the 1930s and the founding of the Irish Association* (Belfast, 1993).

Biagini, E. F., 'The Anglican ethic and the spirit of citizenship: the political and social context', in T. Raffaelli, E. Biagini and R. McWilliams Tullberg (eds.), *Alfred Marshall's lectures to women* (Aldershot, 1995), 24–46.

'British trade unions and popular political economy, 1860–1880', *Historical Journal*, 30, 4 (1987), 811–40.

'Exporting "Western and beneficent institutions": Gladstone and empire, 1880–1885', in D. Bebbington and R. Swift (eds.), *Gladstone centenary essays* (Liverpool, 2000), 202–24.

'Liberalism and direct democracy: John Stuart Mill and the model of ancient Athens', in Biagini (ed.), *Citizenship and community: liberals, radicals and collective identities in the British Isles, 1865–1931* (Cambridge, 1996), 21–44.

Liberty, retrenchment and reform: popular liberalism in the age of Gladstone, 1860–1880 (Cambridge, 1992).

'Neo-Roman liberalism: "republican" values and British liberalism, ca. 1860–1875', *History of European Ideas*, 29 (2003), 55–72.

'Per uno studio del liberalismo popolare nell'età. di Gladstone', *Movimento operaio e socialista*, 5, 2 (1982), pp. 209–38.

'Popular liberals, Gladstonian finance and the debate on taxation, 1860–1874', in E. F. Biagini and A. J. Reid (eds.), *Currents of Radicalism* (Cambridge, 1991), 134–62.

Blaazer, D., *The Popular Front and the progressive tradition: socialists, liberals and the quest for unity, 1884–1939* (Cambridge, 1992).

Blewett, N., *The peers, the parties and the people* (London, 1972).

Bowman, T., *People's champion: the life of Alexander Bowman, pioneer of labour politics in Ireland* (Belfast, 1997).

Boyce, D. G., 'Federalism and the Irish question', in A. Bosco (ed.), *The federal idea, vol. I: The history of federalism from the Enlightenment to 1945* (London, 1991).

The Irish question and British politics, 1886–1996 (Basingstoke, 1996), 34.

Nationalism in Ireland (London, 1991).

'Parnell and Bagehot', in D. G. Boyce and A. O'Day (eds.), *Parnell in perspective* (London, 1991).

Boyce, D. G. and A. O'Day (eds.), *The making of modern Irish history: revisionism and the revisionist controversy* (London, 1996).

Boyle, J. W., 'A marginal figure: the Irish rural labourer', in S. Clark and J. D. Donnelly (eds.), *Irish peasants, violence and political unrest, 1780–1914* (Dublin, 1986), 311–38.

Bradley, I., *The optimists: themes and personalities in Victorian liberalism* (London, 1980).

Bradshaw, B., 'Nationalism and historical scholarship in modern Ireland', *Irish Historical Studies*, 26, 104 (1989), 329–51.

Brady, L. W., *T. P. O'Connor and the Liverpool Irish* (London, 1983).

Brasted, H. V., 'The Irish connection: the Irish outlook on Indian nationalism, 1870–1906', in K. Ballhatchet and D. Taylor (eds.), *Changing South Asia: politics and government* (Hong Kong, 1984).

Briggs, A., *Victorian people* (London, 1954).

Brown, H., 'An alternative imperialism: Isabella Tod, internationalist and "Good Liberal Unionist"', *Gender and History*, 10, 4 (1998), 358–80.

Brown, K. D., *John Burns* (London, 1977).

Brown, S. J., ' "Echoes of Midlothian": Scottish liberalism and the South African war, 1899–1902', *The Scottish Historical Review*, 71, 191/2 (1992), 156–83.

Brownlee, R. S., *Gray ghosts of the Confederacy: guerrilla warfare in the West, 1861–1865* (1986).

Buckland, P. (ed.), *Irish Unionism, 1885–1923* (Belfast, 1973).

Bull, P., 'The formation of the United Irish League, 1898–1900: the dynamics of Irish agrarian agitation', *Irish Historical Studies*, 33, 132 (2003), pp. 404–23.

Land, politics and nationalism (Dublin, 1996).

'The United Irish League and the reunion of the Irish parliamentary party, 1898–1900', *Irish Historical Studies*, 26, 101 (1988), 51–78.

Burness, C., *Strange associations: the Irish question and the making of Scottish Unionism, 1886–1918* (Edinburgh, 2003).

Burrow, J. M., 'Henry Maine and the mid-Victorian idea of progress', in A. Diamond (ed.), *The Victorian achievement of Sir Henry Maine* (Cambridge, 1991), 55–69.

Butler, J., *The Liberal party and the Jameson raid* (Oxford, 1968).

Cain, P., *Hobson and imperialism* (Oxford, 2002).

Cain, P. J., 'British radicalism, the South African crisis, and the origins of the theory of financial imperialism', in D. Omissi and A. S. Thompson (eds.), *The impact of the South African War* (Basingstoke, 2002), 173–93.

Caine, B., *Victorian feminists* (Oxford, 1993).

Callanan, F., *T. M. Healy* (Cork, 1996).

Cameron, E. A., ' "Alas, Skyemen are initiating the Irish": a note on Alexander Nicolson's "Little Leaflet" concerning the crofters' agitation', *The Innes Review*, 55, 1 (2004), 83–92.

'Communication or separation? Reactions to Irish land agitation and legislation in the Highlands of Scotland, c.1870–1910', *English Historical Review*, 120, 487 (2005), 633–66.

' "A far cry to London": Joseph Chamberlain in Inverness, September 1885', *The Innes Review*, 57, 1 (2006), 36–53.

The life and times of Fraser Mackintosh Crofter MP (Aberdeen, 2000).

'Politics, ideology and the Highland land issue, 1886 to the 1920s', *Scottish Historical Review*, 72, 193 (1993), 68–71.

'The Scottish Highlands as a special policy area, 1886 to 1965', *Rural History*, 8 (1997), 196–201.

Cammarano, F., '*To save England from decline': the national party of common sense: British Conservatism and the challenge of democracy (1885–1892)* (Lanham, 2001).

Campbell, F., *The dissenting voice: Protestant democracy in Ulster from Plantation to Partition* (Belfast, 1991).

Land and revolution: Nationalist politics in the west of Ireland, 1891–1921 (Oxford, 2005).

'The social dynamics of Nationalist politics in the west of Ireland, 1898–1918', *Past & Present*, no. 182 (2004).

Catterall, P., 'Morality and politics: the Free Churches and the Labour party between the wars', *Historical Journal*, 36, 3 (1993), 667–85.

Chevalier, L., *Classes laborieuses et classes dangereuses à Paris pendant la première moitié du XIXe siècle* (Paris, 1958).

Clark, S. and J. S. Donnelly, Jr. (eds.), *Irish peasants: violence and political unrest, 1780–1914* (Dublin, 1986).

Clarke, P. F., 'Electoral sociology of modern Britain', *History*, 57, 189 (1972), 31–55.

Lancashire and the New Liberalism (Cambridge, 1971).

'The progressive movement in England', *Transactions of the Royal Historical Society*, 24 (1974), 159–81.

'Liberals, Labour and the franchise', *English Historical Review*, 92 (1977), 582–90.

Liberals and social democrats (Cambridge, 1978).

Clarke, P., *A question of leadership* (London, 1991).

Clarke, S., 'The social composition of the Land League', *Irish Historical Studies*, 17, 68 (1971), 447–69.

Claydon, T., 'The political thought of Charles Stewart Parnell', in D. G. Boyce and A. O'Day (eds.), *Parnell in perspective* (London, 1991), 151–70.

Clegg, H. A., A. Fox and A. F. Thompson, *A history of British trade unions since 1889, vol. I: 1889–1910* (Oxford, 1977).

Cline, C. A., 'E. D. Morel: from the Congo to the Rhine', in A. J. A. Morris (ed.), *Edwardian radicalism, 1900–1914* (London, 1974), 234–45.

Coffey, J., 'Democracy and popular religion: Moody and Sankey's mission to Britain, 1873–1875 campaign', in Biagini, *Citizenship and community*, 93–119.

Cole, G. D. H., *British working class politics* (London, 1941).

A history of socialist thought, The Second International, 1889–1914 (London, 1956).

Collini, S., 'The idea of "character" in Victorian thought', *Transactions of the Royal Historical Society*, 5th series, 35 (1985), 29–50.

Liberalism and sociology: L. T. Hobhouse and political argument in England, 1880–1914 (Cambridge, 1979).

Public moralists: political thought and intellectual life in Britain, 1850–1890 (Oxford, 1991).

Comerford, R. V., *The Fenians in context: Irish politics and society, 1848–82* (Dublin, 1985).

Ireland (London, 2003).

'The land war and the politics of distress, 1877–82', in W. E. Vaughan (ed.), *A new history of Ireland*, vol. VI (Oxford, 1996), 26–52.

'The Parnell era, 1883–91', in W. E. Vaughan (ed.), *A new history of Ireland*, vol. VI (1996), 53–80.

Cook, C., *A short history of the Liberal party, 1900–2001* (Basingstoke, 2002).

Cook, C. P., 'Wales and the general election of 1923', *Welsh History Review*, 4 (1968–9), 387–95.

Cook, S. B. 'The Irish Raj: social origins and careers of Irishmen in the Indian Civil Service, 1855–1914', Journal of Social History, 20, 3 (1987), 507–29.

Cooke, A. B. and J. R. Vincent, *The governing passion* (Brighton, 1974).

'Herbert Gladstone, Forster and Ireland (I)', *Irish Historical Studies*, 17, 68 (1971), 521–48.

Corfe, T., *The Phoenix Park murders* (London, 1968).

Corish, P. J., 'Cardinal Cullen and the National Association of Ireland', in *Reactions to Irish Nationalism* (London, 1987), 117–66.

Croce, B., *Storia d'Italia dal 1871 al 1915* (Bari, 1991).

Crosbie, B., 'Collaboration and convergence: the Irish expatriate community in British India, *c*.1798–*c*.1898', Ph.D. thesis, University of Cambridge, 2005.

Crossman, V., *Politics, law and order in nineteenth-century Ireland* (Dublin, 1996).

Cruise O'Brien, C., *Parnell and his party, 1880–90* (Oxford, 1957).

Cunningham, H., 'Jingoism in 1877–78', *Victorian Studies*, 14, 4 (1971), 419–53.

Curtis, L. P., *Anglo-Saxons and Celts: a study of anti-Irish prejudice in Victorian England* (New York, 1968).

   Apes and angels: the Irishman in Victorian caricature (Newton Abbot, 1971).

   Coercion and conciliation in Ireland, 1880–1892 (Princeton, 1963).

   'Government policy and the Irish party crisis, 1890–92', *Irish Historical Studies*, 13, 52 (1963), 295–315.

Curtis, L. P., J. Belchem, D. A. Wilson and G. K. Peatling, 'Roundtable', *Journal of British Studies* 44, 1 (2005), 134–66.

Cyr, A., *Liberal party politics in Britain* (London, 1977).

Daunton, M. J., *Just taxes: the politics of taxation in Britain, 1914–1971* (Cambridge, 2002).

   Trusting Leviathan: the politics of taxation in Britain, 1799–1914 (Cambridge, 2001).

Davey, A., *The British pro-Boers 1877–1902* (Cape Town, 1978).

Davies, J., *A history of Wales* (London, 1994).

Davis, J., 'Radical clubs and London politics, 1870–1900', in D. Feldman and G. Stedman Jones (eds.), *Metropolis – London: histories and representations of London since 1800* (1989).

Davis, R. P., *Irish issues in New Zealand politics, 1868–1922* (Dunedin, 1974).

Dawson, M., 'Liberalism in Devon and Cornwall, 1910–1931: "The old time religion"', *Historical Journal*, 38, 2 (1995), 425–37.

de Nie, M., *The eternal Paddy: Irish identity and the British press, 1798–1882* (Madison, Wis., 2004).

Devine, T. M., *Clanship to crofters' war* (Manchester, 1994).

Dooley, T., *The decline of the big house in Ireland* (Dublin, 2001).

Douglas, R., 'Britain and the Armenian question, 1894–7', *Historical Journal*, 19 (1976), 113–33.

Doyle, B. M., 'Urban liberalism and the "lost generation": politics and middle class culture in Norwich, 1900–1935', *Historical Journal*, 38, 3 (1985), 617–34.

Dunne, T., '*La trahison des clercs*: British intellectuals and the first home-rule crisis', *Irish Historical Studies*, 23, 9 (1982), 134–73.

Edwards, J. H., *David Lloyd George*, 2 vols. (New York, 1929).

Egerton, G. W., *Great Britain and the creation of the League of Nations* (Chapel Hill, N.C., 1978).

Ellis, J. S., 'Reconciling the Celt: British national identity, empire and the 1911 investiture of the Prince of Wales', *Journal of British Studies*, 37, 4 (1998), 391–418.

Emy, H. V., *Liberals, radicals and social politics, 1892–1914* (Cambridge, 1973).

English, R., *Ernie O'Malley: IRA intellectual* (Oxford, 1998).

   Radicals and the republic: socialist republicanism in the Irish Free State, 1925–1937 (Oxford, 1994).

Ensor, R. C. K., 'Some political and economic interactions in later Victorian England', in L. Schuyler and H. Ausbel (eds.), *The making of English history* (New York, 1952), pp. 534–42.

Epstein, J., *In practice: studies in the language and culture of popular politics in modern Britain* (Stanford, 2003).

Evans, S., 'The Conservatives and the redefinition of Unionism, 1912–21', *Twentieth Century British History*, 9, 1 (1998), 1–27.

Fest, W., 'Jingoism and xenophobia in the electioneering strategies of British ruling elites before 1914', in P. Kennedy and A. Nicholls (eds.), *Nationalist and racialist movements in Britain and Germany before 1914* (London, 1981), 171–89.

Fetscher, I., 'Bernstein e la sfida all'ortodossia', in E. J. Hobsbawm, *Storia del marxismo*, vol. II (Turin, 1979), 237–78.

Fielding, S., 'Irish politics in Manchester, 1890–1914', *International Review of Social History*, 23 (1988), 261–84.

Finn, M., *After Chartism: class and nation in English radical politics, 1848–1874* (Cambridge, 1993).

Fitzpatrick, C., 'Nationalising the ideal: Labour and nationalism in Ireland, 1909–1923', in E. F. Biagini (ed.), *Citizenship and community: liberals, radicals and collective identities in the British Isles, 1865–1931* (Cambridge, 1996), 276–304.

Fitzpatrick, D., 'Ireland and the empire', in A. Porter (ed.), *The Oxford history of the British Empire: the nineteenth century* (Oxford, 1999), 495–521.

Foner, E., *Free men, free soil and free land: the ideology of the Republican party on the eve of the Civil War* (New York, 1970).

Foster, K. M., 'The intellectual duke: George Douglas Campbell, 8th Duke of Argyll, 1823–1900', Ph.D. thesis, University of Edinburgh, 2005.

Foster, R. F., *Charles Stewart Parnell: the man and his family* (Hassocks, 1979).
    Paddy and Mr Punch: connections in Irish and English history (London, 1993).

Fowler, W. S., *A study in Radicalism and Dissent: the life and times of Henry Joseph Wilson, 1833–1914* (London, 1961).

Fraser, P. S., *Joseph Chamberlain: radicalism and empire, 1868–1914* (London, 1966).

Freeden, M., *The New Liberalism: an ideology of social reform* (Oxford, 1978).

Fry, R., *Emily Hobhouse: a memoir* (London, 1929).

Gailey, A., *Ireland and the death of Unionism: the experience of constructive Unionism, 1890–1905* (Cork, 1987).
    'Unionist rhetoric and Irish local government reform, 1895–9', *Irish Historical Studies*, 24, 93 (1984), 52–67.

Gallissot, R., 'Nazione e nazionalità nei dibattiti del movimento operatio', in E. J. Hobsbawm, *Storia del marxismo, vol II: Il marxismo nell' età della Seconda Internazionale* (Turin, 1979), 787–867.

Gardiner, A. G., *The life of Sir William Harcourt*, 2 vols. (New York, n.d.).

Garvin, J. L., *The life of Joseph Chamberlain*, 3 vols. (London, 1938–69).

Garvin, T., *1922: the birth of Irish democracy* (Dublin, 1996).
    The evolution of Irish nationalist politics (Dublin, 1981, 2nd edn 2005).
    Nationalist revolutionaries in Ireland, 1858–1928 (Oxford, 1987).

'Priests and patriots: Irish separatism and fear of the modern, 1890–1914', *Irish Historical Studies*, 25, 97 (1986), 67–81.

Geary, L. M., 'John Mandeville and the Irish Crimes Act of 1887', *Irish Historical Studies*, 25, 100 (1987), 358–75.

The Plan of Campaign, 1886–1891 (Cork, 1986).

Georghallides, G. S., *A political and administrative history of Cyprus, 1918–1926, with a survey of the foundations of British rule* (Nicosia, 1979).

Gibbon, P., *The origins of Unionism* (Manchester, 1975).

Gilbert, B., 'David Lloyd George and the great Marconi scandal', *Historical Research*, 62 (1989), 295–317.

Gilbert, M., *Churchill: a life* (London, 1991).

Gill, R., 'Calculating compassion in war: the "New Humanitarian" ethos in Britain, 1870–1918', Ph.D. thesis, University of Manchester, 2005.

Gilley, S., 'English attitudes to the Irish in England, 1780–1900', in C. Holmes (ed.), *Immigrants and minorities in British society* (London, 1978).

Glaser, J. F., 'Parnell's fall and the Nonconformist conscience', *Irish Historical Studies*, 12, 46 (1960), 119–38.

Goodlad, G., 'Gladstone and his rivals: popular Liberal perceptions of the party leadership in the political crisis of 1885–1886', in E. F. Biagini and A. J. Reid (eds.), *Currents of radicalism: popular radicalism, organised labour and party politics in Britain, 1850–1914* (Cambridge, 1996), 163–83.

Goodlad, G. D., 'The Liberal party and Gladstone's Land Purchase Bill of 1886', *Historical Journal*, 32, 3 (1989), 627–41.

Goodman, G. L., 'The Liberal Unionist party, 1886–1895', D.Phil. thesis, University of Chicago, 1956.

Graham Jones, J., 'Michael Davitt, David Lloyd George and T. E. Ellis: the Welsh experience, 1886', *Welsh History Review*, 18 (1996–7), 450–82.

Grabard, S., *British labour and the Russian Revolution, 1917–1924* (Cambridge, 1956).

Grant, K., *A civilised savagery: Britain and the new slaveries in Africa, 1884–1926* (London, 2005).

Grayson, R. S., *Austen Chamberlain and the commitment to Europe: British foreign policy, 1924–29* (London, 1997).

Liberals, international relations and appeasement (London, 2001).

Greenlee, G., 'Land, religion and community: the Liberal party in Ulster, 1868–1885', in E. F. Biagini (ed.), *Citizenship and community: liberals, radicals and collective identities in the British Isles, 1865–1931* (Cambridge, 1996), 253–75.

Gregory, A. and S. Pašeta (eds.), *Ireland and the Great War* (Manchester, 2002).

Grigg, J., 'Lloyd George and the Boer War', in A. J. A. Morris (ed.), *Edwardian radicalism, 1900–1914* (London, 1974), 13–25.

Groh, D., *Negative Integration und revolutionarer Attentismus. Die deutsche Sozialdemokratie am Vorabend des Ersten Weltkrieges*, (Frankfurt am Main, Berlin and Vienna, 1973).

Guazzaloca, G., *Fine secolo: gli intellettuali italiani e inglesi e la crisi fra Otto e Novecento* (Bologna, 2004).

Gullie, E. E., *Joseph Chamberlain and English social politics* (New York, 1926).

Haire, D., 'In aid of the civil power, 1868–1890', in F. S. L. Lyons and R. A. J. Hawkins (eds.), *Ireland under the Union: varieties of tension* (Oxford, 1980), 115–48.

Hall, C., *Civilising subjects: metropole and colony in the English imagination, 1830–1867* (Cambridge, 2002).

Hamer, D. A., 'The Irish question and Liberal politics, 1886–1894', in *Reactions to Irish Nationalism*, introd. by A. O'Day (London, 1987), 237–58.

John Morley: Liberal intellectual in politics (Oxford, 1969).

Liberal politics in the age of Gladstone and Rosebery (Oxford, 1972).

The politics of electoral pressure: a study in the history of Victorian reform agitations (Hassocks, 1977).

Hames, T., review of R. Douglas, *Liberals*, in *Times Literary Supplement*, 8 Apr. 2005, p. 4.

Hammond, J. L., *Gladstone and the Irish nation* (London, 1938).

Hampton, M., 'The press, patriotism, and public discussion: C. P. Scott, the *Manchester Guardian*, and the Boer War, 1899–1902', *Historical Journal*, 44, 1 (2001), 177–97.

Hanham, H. J., *Elections and party management: politics in the age of Disraeli and Gladstone* (Hassocks, 1978).

'Tra l'individuo e lo stato,' in P. Pombeni (ed.), *La trasformazione politica nell'Europa liberale 1870–1890* (Bologna, 1986), 93–102.

Hansen, M. H., *The Athenian ecclesia* (Copenhagen, 1983).

Harris, J., *Private lives, public spirit: Britain, 1870–1914* (London, 1994).

Harris, J. and C. Hazlehurst, 'Campbell-Bannerman as prime minister', *History*, 55, 185 (1970), 360–83.

Harrison, R., *The English defence of the Commune (1871)* (London, 1971).

Harrison, R. T., *Gladstone's imperialism in Egypt* (Westport, Conn., 1995).

Hart, J., *Proportional representation: critics of the British electoral system, 1820–1945* (Oxford, 1992).

Hart, P., *The IRA at war, 1916–1923* (Oxford, 2003).

Harvie, C., 'Ideology and Home Rule: James Bryce, A. V. Dicey and Ireland, 1880–1887', *English Historical Review*, 91, 359 (1976), 298–314.

The lights of liberalism: university liberals and the challenge of democracy, 1860–86 (London, 1976).

Havinghurst, A. F., *Radical journalist: H. W. Massingham (1860–1924)* (London and New York, 1974).

Hennock, E. P., *British social reform and German precedents: the case of social insurance, 1880–1914* (Oxford, 1987).

Herrick, F. H., 'The origins of the National Liberal Federation', *Journal of Modern History*, 17 (1945), 116–29.

Hesse, C., 'The new empiricism', *Cultural and Social History*, 1 (2004), 201–7.

Heyck, T. W., *The dimensions of British radicalism: the case of Ireland, 1874–1895* (Urbana, Ill., 1974).

'Home Rule, radicalism and the Liberal party, 1886–1895', in *Reactions to Irish Nationalism*, introd. A. O'Day (London, 1987), 259–84.

Higgins, M. D. and J. P. Gibbons, 'Shopkeeper-graziers and land agitation in Ireland, 1895–1900', in P. J. Drudy (ed.), *Ireland: land, politics and people* (Cambridge, 1982), 93–118.

Hill, C., 'The Norman yoke', in J. Saville (ed.), *Democracy and the labour movement* (London, 1954), 15–46.

Hind, R. J., *Henry Labouchere and the empire, 1880–1905* (London, 1972).

Hinde, W., *Richard Cobden* (London, 1987).

Hirst, C., *Religion, politics and violence in nineteenth-century Belfast: the Pound and Sandy Row* (Dublin, 2002).

Hollis, P., *Ladies elect: women in English local government, 1865–1914* (Oxford, 1987).

Hoppen, K. T., *Elections, politics and society in Ireland, 1832–1885* (Oxford, 1984).
  'Riding a tiger: Daniel O'Connell, reform and popular politics in Ireland, 1800–1847', *Proceedings of the British Academy*, 100 (1999), 121–43.

Horn, P., *Joseph Arch (1826–1919): the farm workers' leader* (Kineton, 1971).
  'The National Agricultural Labourers' Union in Ireland, 1873–9', *Irish Historical Studies*, 17, 67 (1971), 340–52.

Horton, J. M. Jr.,'The case of the American Civil War in the debate over Irish Home Rule', *American Historical Review*, 69 (1964), 1022–36.

Howard, C. H. D., 'Joseph Chamberlain, Parnell and the Irish "central board" scheme, 1884–5', *Irish Historical Studies*, 8 (1953), 324–63.

Howe, A., *Free trade and Liberal England, 1846–1946* (Oxford, 1997).
  'Towards the "hungry forties": free trade in Britain, *c.*1880–1906', in E. F. Biagini (ed.), *Citizenship and community: liberals, radicals and collective identities in the British Isles, 1865–1931* (Cambridge, 1996), 193–218.

Howe, S., *Anticolonialism in British politics: the left and the end of empire, 1918–1964* (Oxford, 1993).
  Ireland and the empire: colonial legacies in Irish history and culture (Oxford, 2000).

Howell, D., *British workers and the Independent Labour Party, 1888–1906* (Manchester, 1983).
  MacDonald's party: Labour identities and the crisis, 1922–1931 (Oxford, 2002).

Huard, R., 'La genesi dei partiti democratici moderni in Francia', in M. Brigaglia (ed.), *L'origine dei partiti nell' Europa contemporanea, 1870–1914* (Bologna, 1985), 127–46.

Hurst, M. C., 'Joseph Chamberlain, the Conservatives and the succession to John Bright, 1886–89', *Historical Journal*, 7, 1 (1964), 64–93.
  Joseph Chamberlain and Liberal reunion: the Round Table Conference of 1887 (Toronto, 1967).
  'Parnell in the spectrum of nationalisms', in D. George Boyce and A. O'Day (eds.), *Parnell in perspective* (London, 1991), 77–106.

Hussain, A. and K. Tribe, *Marxism and the agrarian question*, vol. I (London, 1981).

Hutchison, I. G. C., 'Glasgow working-class politics', in R. A. Cage (ed.), *The working class in Glasgow, 1750–1914* (London, 1987), 98–141.
  A political history of Scotland, 1832–1924 (Edinburgh, 1986).

Jackson, A., *Coronel Edward Sounderban: Land and loyalty in Victorian Ireland* (Oxford, 1995).

Home Rule: an Irish history, 1800–2000 (London, 2003).

'Irish Unionism, 1870–1922', in D. George Boyce and A. O'Day (eds.), *Defenders of the Union* (London, 2001), 115–37.

'Irish Unionism and the Russellite threat', *Irish Historical Studies*, 25, 100 (1987), 376–404.

The Ulster party: Irish Unionists in the House of Commons, 1884–1911 (Oxford, 1989).

Jalland, P., *The Liberals and Ireland: the Ulster question in British politics to 1914* (1980; Aldershot, 1993).

Jeffery, K. (ed.), *An Irish empire? Aspects of Ireland and the British Empire* (Manchester, 1996).

Jenkins R., *Churchill* (London, 2002).

Dilke: a Victorian tragedy (London, 1996).

Jenkins, T. A., 'Hartington, Chamberlain and the Unionist alliance, 1886–1895', *Parliamentary History*, 2, 1 (1992), 108–38.

The Liberal ascendancy, 1830–1886 (London, 1994).

Johnson, G., '"Making reform the instrument of revolution": British Social Democracy, 1881–1911', *Historical Journal*, 43, 4 (2000), 977–1002.

Jones, D. S., 'The cleavage between graziers and peasants in the land struggle, 1890–1910', in S. Clark and J. D. Donnelly (eds.), *Irish peasants, violence and political unrest, 1780–1914* (Dublin, 1986), 374–413.

Jones, G., 'Scientists against Home Rule', in D. G. Boyce and A. O'Day (eds.), *Defenders of the Union: a survey of British and Irish Unionism since 1801* (London, 2001), 188–208.

Jordan, D., 'The Irish National League and the "unwritten law": rural protest and nation building in Ireland, 1882–1890', *Past & Present*, no. 158 (1998), 146–71.

'John O'Connor Power, Charles Stewart Parnell and the centralization of popular politics in Ireland', *Irish Historical Studies*, 25, 97 (1986), 46–66.

Land and popular politics in Ireland: County Mayo from the Plantation to the Land War (Cambridge, 1994).

Jordan, J., *Josephine Butler* (London, 2001).

Joyce, P., *Democratic subjects: the self and the social in nineteenth-century England* (Cambridge, 1994).

Visions of the people: industrial England and the question of class, 1840–1914 (Cambridge, 1991).

Judd, D., *Radical Joe* (London, 1977).

Kadebo, T., *Ireland and Hungary: a study in parallels with an Arthur Griffith bibliography* (Dublin, 2001).

Kavanagh, D., 'Organization and power in the Liberal party', in V. Bogdanor (ed.), *Liberal party politics* (Oxford, 1988), 123–42.

Keane, E., *An Irish statesman and revolutionary: the nationalist and internationalist politics of Sean MacBride* (London, 2006).

Keith-Lucas, B., 'The Liberal party, local government and community politics', in V. Bogdanor (ed.), *Liberal party politics* (Oxford, 1983).

Kelly, M., '"Parnell's Old Brigade": the Redmondite–Fenian nexus in the 1890s', *Irish Historical Studies*, 33, 130 (2002), 209–32.

Kendle, J., *Ireland and the federal solution: the debate over the United Kingdom constitution, 1870–1921* (Kingston and Montreal, 1989).

Kennedy, L., 'The economic thought of the nation's lost leader: Charles Stewart Parnell', in D. G. Boyce and A. O'Day (eds.), *Parnell in Perspective* (London, 1991).

'Farmers, traders, and agricultural politics in pre-independence Ireland', in S. Clark and J. S. Donnelly, *Irish peasants: violence and political unrest, 1780–1914* (Dublin, 1983), 339–73.

Kennedy, M., *Ireland and the League of Nations, 1919–1946* (Dublin, 1996).

Kennedy, M. and J. Morrison Skelly (eds.), *Irish foreign policy 1919–1969: from independence to internationalism* (Dublin, 2000).

Kennedy, M. and E. O'Halpin (eds.), *Ireland and the Council of Europe: from isolation towards integration* (Strasbourg, 2000).

Kim, M. M., 'The Chinese labour question and the British labour movement, 1903–1906', M.Phil. dissertation, University of Cambridge, 1997.

Kinzer, B. L., A. Robson and J. M. Robson, *A moralist in and out of Parliament: John Stuart Mill at Westminster, 1865–1868* (Toronto and London, 1992).

Kirshner, A. S., 'Character and the administration of empires in the political thought of Henry Maine', unpublished M.Phil. dissertation, University of Cambridge, 2002.

Kissane, B., *Explaining Irish democracy* (Dublin, 2002).

Knight, A., *The Mexican Revolution, vol. I: Porfirians, liberals and peasants* (Cambridge, 1986).

Koss, S. E., '1906: revival and revivalism', in A. J. A. Morris (ed.), *Edwardian radicalism, 1900–1914* (London, 1974), 75–96.

'Lloyd George and Nonconformity: the last rally', *English Historical Review*, 89, 350 (1974), 77–108.

Laffan, M., *The resurrection of Ireland: the Sinn Féin party, 1916–1923* (Cambridge, 1999).

Laity, P., 'The British peace movement', in D. Omissi and A. S. Thompson (eds.), *The impact of the South African war* (Basingstoke, 2002).

The British peace movement, 1870–1914 (Oxford, 2001).

Lane, F. and D. Ó Drisceoil (eds.), *Politics and the Irish working class, 1830–1945* (London, 2005).

Larkin, E., *The consolidation of the Roman Catholic Church in Ireland, 1860–1870* (Chapel Hill, N.C. and London, 1987).

The Roman Catholic Church and the emergence of the modern Irish political system, 1874–1878 (Dublin, 1996).

The Roman Catholic Church and the Home Rule movement, 1870–1875 (Chapel Hill, N.C., 1990).

The Roman Catholic Church and the Plan of Campaign in Ireland, 1886–1888 (Cork, 1978).

Larsen, T., *Friends of religious equality: Nonconformist politics in mid-Victorian England* (Woodbridge, Suffolk, 1999).

Lawrence, J., 'Popular politics and the limitations of party: Wolverhampton, 1867–1900', in E. F. Biagini and A. J. Reid (eds.), *Currents of radicalism: popular radicalism, organised labour and party politics in Britain, 1850–1914* (Cambridge, 1991), 65–85.

'Popular radicalism and the socialist revival in Britain', *Journal of British Studies*, 31 (1992), 163–86.

Speaking for the people: party, language and popular politics in England, 1867–1914 (Cambridge, 1998).

Laybourn, K., 'The rise of Labour and the decline of Liberalism: the state of the debate', *History*, 80, 259 (1995), 207–226.

Lee, A. J., The radical press', in A. J. A. Morris (ed.), *Edwardian radicalism, 1900–1914* (1974).

Leventahl, F. M., 'H. N. Brailsford and the search for a new international order', in A. J. A. Morris (ed.), *Edwardian radicalism, 1900–1914* (London, 1974), 202–17.

Lewis Solow, B., *The land question and the Irish economy, 1870–1903* (Cambridge, Mass., 1971).

Li Chien-Hui, 'Mobilizing traditions in the animal defence movement in Britain, 1820–1920', Ph.D thesis, University of Cambridge, 2002.

Lloyd, T., *The general election of 1880* (Oxford, 1968).

Loughlin, J., *Gladstone, Home Rule and the Ulster question, 1882–93* (Dublin, 1986).

'Imagining "Ulster": the North of Ireland and British national identity, 1880–1921', in S. J. Connolly (ed.), *Kingdoms united? Great Britain and Ireland since 1500* (Dublin, 1999), 109–23.

'The Irish Protestant Home Rule Association and nationalist politics, 1886–93', *Irish Historical Studies*, 24, 95 (1985), 340–60.

'Joseph Chamberlain, English nationalism and the Ulster question', *History*, 77 (1992), 202–19.

'T. W. Russell, the tenant-farmer interest, and progressive Unionism in Ulster, 1886–1900', *Éire–Ireland*, 25, 1 (1990), 44–63.

Low, A., 'Public opinion and the Uganda question, October–December 1892', *Uganda Journal*, 18 Sep. 1954, 81–100.

Lubenow, W. C., 'Irish Home Rule and the social basis of the great separation in the Liberal party in 1886', *Historical Journal*, 28, 1 (1885), 125–42.

Parliamentary politics and the Home Rule crisis: the British House of Commons in 1886 (Oxford, 1988).

Luddy, M., 'Isabella M. S. Tod, 1836–1896', in M. Cullen and M. Luddy (eds.), *Women, power and consciousness in nineteenth-century Ireland* (Dublin, 1995), 13–18.

Lynch, P., *The Liberal party in rural England, 1885–1910* (Oxford, 2003).

Lyons, F. S. L., *The Irish parliamentary party, 1890–1910* (London, n.d. [c.1951].

'The Irish parliamentary party and the Liberals in mid-Ulster, 1894', *Irish Historical Studies*, 8, 27 (1951), 191–5.

John Dillon: a biography (London, 1968).

'The machinery of the Irish parliamentary party in the general election of 1895', *Irish Historical Studies*, 8 (1952–3), 115–39.

'The political ideas of Parnell', *Historical Journal*, 16, 4 (1973), 749–75.

McBride, T., 'John Ferguson, Michael Davitt and Henry George: land for the people', *Irish Studies Review*, 14, 4 (2006), 421–30.

Macaulay, A., *The Holy See, British policy and the Plan of Campaign in Ireland, 1885–93* (Dublin, 2002).

McCafrey, L. J., 'Home Rule and the general election of 1874 in Ireland', *Irish Historical Studies*, 9, 33 (1954), 190–212.

McCartney, D., *W. E. H. Lecky: historian and politician, 1838–1903* (Dublin, 1994).

Maccoby, S., *English radicalism, 1886–1914*, 6 vols. (London, 1935–61).

MacColl, A. W., 'The churches and the land question in the Highlands of Scotland, 1843–1888', Ph.D. thesis, University of Cambridge, 2002.
   Land, faith and the crofting community: Christianity and social criticism in the Highlands of Scotland, 1843–1893 (Edinburgh, 2006).

MacCracken, D. P., *The Irish pro-Boers, 1877–1902* (Johannesburg, 1989).

McCready, H. W., 'Home Rule and the Liberal party, 1899–1906', *Irish Historical Studies*, 13, 52 (1963), 316–48.
   'Irish Catholicism and nationalism in Scotland: the Dundee experience, 1865–1922', *Irish Studies Review*, 6, 3 (1998), 245–52.

MacDonagh, O., *O'Connell: the life of Daniel O'Connell, 1775–1847* (London, 1991).
   States of mind: a study of Anglo-Irish conflict, 1780–1930 (London, 1983).

MacDonald, C. (ed.), *Unionist Scotland, 1800–1997* (Edinburgh, 1998).

MacDonald, C. M. M., 'Locality, tradition and language in the evolution of Scottish Unionism: a case study, Paisley 1886–1910', in C. M. M. Macdonald (ed.), *Unionist Scotland, 1800–1997* (Edinburgh, 1998), 52–72.

McDougall, H. A., *Racial myth in English history* (Montreal, 1982).

Machin, G. I. T., *Politics and the churches in Great Britain, 1869 to 1921* (Oxford, 1987).

McHugh, P., *Prostitution and Victorian social reform* (London, 1980).

McGill, B., 'Schnadhorst and Liberal party organization', *Journal of Modern History* (1962), 19–39.

McKinstry, L., *Rosebery: statesman in turmoil* (London, 2005).

McMinn, J. R. B., 'Liberalism in North-Antrim, 1900–1914', *Irish Historical Studies*, 13, 89 (1982), 17–29.

Mcminn, R., 'The myth of "Route" liberalism in County Antrim, 1869–1900', *Éire–Ireland*, 17 (1982), 137–49.

MacRaild, D. M., *Irish migrants in modern Britain, 1750–1922* (Basingstoke, 1996).

Mandler, P., 'The problem with cultural history', *Cultural and Social History*, 1 (2004), 94–117.
   'Problems in cultural history: a reply', *Cultural and Social History*, 1 (2004), 326–32.

Mansergh, N., 'John Redmond', in D. Mansergh (ed.), *Nationalism and independence* (Cork, 1997), 23–32.

Markham Lester, V., 'The employers' liability/workmen's compensation debate of the 1890s revisited', *Historical Journal*, 44, 2 (2001), 471–95.

Marquand, D., *Ramsay MacDonald* (London, 1997).

Marsh, P., *Joseph Chamberlain: entrepreneur in politics* (New Haven and London, 1994).
   'Lord Salisbury and the Ottoman massacres', *Journal of British Studies*, 11, 2 (1972), 62–83.

Martin, L. W., *Peace without victory: Woodrow Wilson and the British Liberals* (Port Washington, N.Y., 1973).

Masson, U. (ed.), *'Women's rights and womanly duties': the Aberdare Women's Liberal Association, 1891–1910* (Cardiff, 2005).

Masterman, L., *C. F. G. Masterman: a biography* (1968).

Matikkala, M., 'Anti-imperialism, Englishness and empire in late-Victorian Britain', Ph.D. thesis, University of Cambridge, 2006.

Matthew, H. C. G., *Gladstone, 1875–1898* (Oxford, 1995).

'Gladstone, rhetoric and politics', in P. J. Jagger (ed.), *Gladstone* (London, 1998), 213–34.

The Liberal Imperialists: the ideas and politics of a post-Gladstonian elite (Oxford, 1973).

'Moisei Ostrogorski e la tradizione inglese di studi politici', in G. Orsina (a cura di), *Contro i partiti. Saggi sul pensiero di Moisei Ostrogroski* (Rome, 1993), 47–54.

Matthew, H. C. G. and B. Harrison (eds.), *Oxford dictionary of national biography* (Oxford, 1994).

Matthews, K., 'Stanley Baldwin's "Irish Question"', *Historical Journal*, 43, 4 (2000), 1027–49.

Maume, P., 'From deference to citizenship', in 'Republicanism in theory and practice', *The Republic*, no. 2 (2001), 81–91.

The long gestation: Irish Nationalist life, 1891–1918 (Dublin, 1999).

McL. Côté, J., *Fanny and Anna Parnell: Ireland's patriot sisters* (Basingstoke, 1991).

Meier C. S., 'Democracy since the French Revolution', in J. Dunn (ed.), *Democracy: the unfinished journey, 508 BC to AD 1993* (Oxford, 1992), 125–54.

Michels, R., *Political parties: a sociological study of the oligarchical tendencies of modern democracy* (London, 1915).

Midgley, C., *Women against slavery: the British campaigns, 1780–1870* (London, 1992).

Miller, D. W., *Queen's rebels: Ulster loyalism in perspective* (Dublin, 1978).

Mommsen, W. J., *The age of bureaucracy: perspectives on the political sociology of Max Weber* (Oxford, 1974).

The political and social theory of Max Weber (Cambridge, 1989).

Moody, T. W., *Davitt and the Irish revolution, 1846–82* (Oxford, 1981).

Moore, J. R., 'Progressive pioneers: Manchester liberalism, the Independent Labour Party, and local politics in the 1890s', *Historical Journal*, 44, 4 (2001), 989–1013.

The transformation of urban liberalism: party politics and urban governance in late nineteenth-century England (Aldershot, 2006).

Moran, G., 'James Daly and the rise and fall of the Land League in the west of Ireland, 1879–82', *Irish Historical Studies*, 29, 114 (1994), 189–207.

Morgan, K. O., 'The Boer War and the media (1899–1902)', *20th Century British History*, 13, 1 (2002), 1–16.

'The high and low politics of Labour: Keir Hardie to Michael Foot', in M. Bentley and J. Stevenson (eds.), *High and low politics in modern Britain* (Oxford, 1983), 1285–312.

'The new Liberalism and the challenge of Labour: the Welsh experience, 1885–1929', in K. D. Brown (ed.), *Essays in anti-Labour history* (London, 1974), 164, 170.

Keir Hardie, radical and socialist (London, 1984).

Rebirth of a nation: Wales, 1880–1980 (Oxford, 1982).

'Wales and the Boer War – a reply', *Welsh Historical Review*, 4 (1969), 367–80.

Wales in British politics, 1868–1922 (Cardiff, 1980).

Muir, R., 'Liberalism and the empire', in H. L. Nathan (ed.), *Liberal points of view* (London, 1927), 253–84.

Murphy, C., 'The religious context of the women's suffrage campaign in Ireland', *Women's History Review*, 6, 4 (1997), 549–62.

Murray, B., *The people's budget, 1909–10: Lloyd George and Liberal politics* (Oxford, 1980).

Nettl, J. P., 'The German Social Democratic party 1890–1914 as a political model', *Past & Present*, no. 30 (1965), 65–95.

Newby, A. G., '"Shoulder to shoulder"? Scottish and Irish land reformers in the Highlands of Scotland, 1878–1894', Ph.D. thesis, University of Edinburgh, 2001.

Newton, D. J., *British labour, European socialism and the struggle for peace, 1889–1914* (Oxford, 1989).

O'Brien, J. V., *William O'Brien and the cause of Irish politics, 1881–1918* (Berkeley, Calif., 1976).

O'Callaghan, M., *British high politics and Nationalist Ireland: criminality, land and the law under Forster and Balfour* (Cork, 1994).

O'Day, A., *Parnell and the first Home Rule episode, 1884–87* (Dublin, 1986).

O'Farrell, P. J., *England and Ireland since 1800* (New York, 1975).

Ireland's English question: Anglo-Irish relations, 1534–1970 (London, 1971).

The Irish in Australia: 1788 to the present (Cork, 2001).

O'Leary, O. and H. Burke, *Mary Robinson* (London, 1998).

Omissi, D. and A. S. Thompson (eds.), *The impact of the South African war* (Basingstoke, 2002).

Owen, J., 'The "caucus" and party organization in England in the 1880s', Ph.D. thesis, University of Cambridge, 2006.

Packer, I., *Lloyd George* (Basingstoke, 1998).

Lloyd George, liberalism and the land: the land issue and party politics in England, 1906–1914 (London, 2001).

Pakenham, T., *The Boer War* (New York, 1979).

Parry, J. P., *Democracy and religion: Gladstone and the Liberal party, 1867–1875* (Cambridge, 1986).

'Liberalism and liberty', in P. Mandler (ed.), *Liberty and authority in Victorian Britain* (Cambridge, 2006), 71–100.

The rise and fall of Liberal government in Victorian Britain (New Haven, 1993).

Parsinnen, T. M., 'Association, convention and anti-Parliament in British radical politics, 1771–1848', *English Historical Review*, 88 (1973), 504–33.

Pašeta, S., *Before the revolution: nationalism, social change and Ireland's Catholic elite, 1879–1922* (Cork, 1999).

'Ireland's last Home Rule generation: the decline of constitutional nationalism in Ireland, 1916–30', in M. Cronin and J. M. Regan (eds.), *Ireland: the politics of independence, 1922–49* (Basingstoke, 2000), 13–31.

'Nationalist responses to two royal visits to Ireland, 1900 and 1903', *Irish Historical Studies*, 31, 124 (1999), 488–504.

Peatling, G. K., *British opinion and Irish self-government, 1865–1925* (Dublin, 2001).

Pedersen, S. 'National bodies, unspeakable acts: the sexual politics of colonial policy-making', *Journal of Modern History*, 63 (1991), 647–80.

Pelling, H., *Origins of the Labour party, 1880–1900* (London, 1983).

Popular politics and society in late Victorian Britain (London, 1979).

'Wales and the Boer War', *Welsh Historical Review*, 4 (1969), 363–5.

'The working class and the origins of the welfare state', in Pelling, *Popular politics and society in late Victorian Britain* (London, 1979), 1–18.

Pick, D., *Faces of degeneration: a European disorder, c.1848–c.1918* (Cambridge, 1989).

Polivka, P., 'L'elezione senatoriale di Fallières nel 1906. Militanti e notabili radicali al tempo del "Blocco della sinistre"', in M. Brigaglia (ed.), *L'Origine dei partiti nell' Europa Contemporanea, 1870–1914* (Bologna, 1985), 165–80.

Pombeni, P., *Introduzione alla storia dei partiti politici* (Bologna, 1990).

Partiti e sistemi politici nella storia contemporanea (Bologna, 1994).

'Ritorno a Birmingham. La "nuova organizzazione politica" di Joseph Chamberlain e l'origine della forma partito contemporanea (1874–1880)', *Ricerche di storia politica*, 3 (1988), 37–63.

'Starting in reason, ending in passion: Bryce, Lowell, Ostrogorski and the problem of democracy', *Historical Journal*, 37, 2 (1994), 319–41.

'Trasformismo e questione del partito', in P. Pombeni (ed.), *La trasformazione politica nell'Europa liberale, 1870–1890* (Bologna, 1986), 215–54.

Porter, A., *Religion versus empire? British Protestant missionaries and overseas expansion, 1700–1914* (Manchester, 2004).

Porter, B., *The absent-minded imperialists: empire, society and culture in Britain* (Oxford, 2004).

Critics of empire: British attitudes to colonialism in Africa, 1895–1914 (London, 1968).

'The pro-Boers in Britain', in P. Warwick (ed.), *The South African war: the Anglo-Boer War, 1899–1902* (Harlow, 1980), 239–57.

The refugee question in mid-Victorian politics (Cambridge, 1979).

Pottinger Saab, A., *Reluctant icon: Gladstone, Bulgaria and the working classes, 1856–1878* (Cambridge, 1991).

Powell, D., 'Liberal ministries and labour, 1892–1895', *History*, 68 (1983), 408–26.

Price, R., *An imperial war and the British working class* (London, 1972).

'Lloyd George and Merioneth politics, 1885, 1886 – a failure to effect a breakthrough', *Journal of Merioneth History and Record Society*, 8 (1975).

Pugh, M., *The march of the women: a revisionist analysis of the campaign for women's suffrage, 1866–1914* (Oxford, 2000).

The Pankhursts (London, 2001).

The Tories and the people, 1880–1935 (Oxford, 1985).

'Yorkshire and the New Liberalism?', *Journal of Modern History*, 50, 3 (1978), D1139–55.

Quinault, R., 'Joseph Chamberlain: a reassessment', in T. R. Gourvish and A. O'Day (eds.), *Later Victorian Britain, 1867–1900* (Basingstoke, 1988), 69–92.

Readman, P., 'The 1895 general election and political change in late Victorian Britain', *Historical Journal*, 42, 2 (1999), 467–93.

'The Liberal party and patriotism in early twentieth century Britain', *Twentieth Century British History*, 12, 3 (2001), 269–303.

Regan, J. M., *The Irish counter-revolution 1921–1936: ireatyite politics and the settlement of independent Ireland* (Dublin, 2001).

Reid A. J., 'Old Unionism reconsidered: the radicalism of Robert Knight, 1870–1900', in E. F. Biagini and A. J. Reid (eds.), *Currents of Radicalism: liberals, radicals and collective identities in the British Isles, 1865–1931* (Cambridge, 1996), 214–43.

United we stand: a history of Britain's trade unions (London, 2004).

Reid, F., *Keir Hardie: the making of a socialist* (London, 1978).

Ridden, J., *Making good citizens: Irish elite approaches to empire, national identity and citizenship, 1800–1850* (Cambridge, 2006).

Rix, K., 'The party agent and English electoral culture, 1880–1906', Ph.D. thesis, University of Cambridge, 2001.

Robbins, K., *The abolition of war: the 'peace movement' in Britain, 1914–1919* (Cardiff, 1976).

John Bright (London, 1979).

Roberts, C., *The radical countess: the history of the life of Rosalind Countess of Carlisle* (Carlisle, 1962).

Roberts, M. J. D., *Making English morals: voluntary association and moral reform in England, 1787–1886* (Cambridge, 2004).

Romani, R., 'British views on the Irish national character, 1800–1846: an intellectual history', *History of European Ideas*, 23, 5–6 (1997), 193–219.

Rosen, F., *Bentham, Byron and Greece: constitutionalism, nationalism and early liberal political thought* (Oxford, 1992).

Rossi, J. P., 'Home Rule and the Liverpool by-election of 1880', *Irish Historical Studies*, 19, 74 (1974), 156–68.

Royle, E., *Radicals, secularists and republicans* (Manchester, 1980).

Rubinstein, W. D., 'The anti-Jewish riots of 1911 in South Wales: a re-examination', *Welsh History Review*, 18 (1996–7), 667–99.

Russell, A. K., 'Laying the charges for the landslide: the revival of Liberal party organization, 1902–1905', in A. J. A. Morris (ed.), *Edwardian radicalism, 1900–1914* (London, 1974), 62–75.

Liberal landslide: the general election of 1906 (Newton Abbot, 1973).

Sager, E. W., 'The working-class peace movement in Victorian England', *Histoire Sociale–Social History*, 12, 23 (1979), 122–44.

Salt, J., *Imperialism, evangelism and the Ottoman Armenians, 1878–1896* (London, 1993).

Sarti, R., *Long live the strong: a history of rural society in the Apennine Mountains* (Amherst, 1985).

Savage, D. C., 'The origins of the Ulster Unionist party, 1885–6', *Irish Historical Studies*, 12, 47 (1961), 185–208.

Schlesinger, A. M. Jr., *The age of Jackson* (Boston, 1953).

Schreuder, D. M., *Gladstone and Kruger: Liberal government and colonial 'Home Rule', 1880–85* (London, 1969).

Scirocco, A. (intro.), *Brigantaggio lealismo repression nel Mezzogiorno, 1860–1870* (Ercolano, 1984).

Scott Rasmussen, J., *The Liberal party: a study of retrenchment and revival* (London, 1965).

Searle, G. R., *Corruption in British politics, 1895–1930* (Oxford, 1987).
  The Liberal party: triumph and disintegration, 1886–1929 (London, 1992).
Shannon, C., 'The Ulster Liberal Unionists and local government reform, 1885–1898', *Irish Historical Studies*, 18, 71 (1973), 407–23.
Shannon, C. B., *Arthur J. Balfour and Ireland, 1874–1922* (Washington, DC, 1988).
Shannon, R. T., *Gladstone and the Bulgarian agitation, 1876* (London, 1963).
Shannon, R., *Gladstone: heroic minister, 1865–1898* (London, 1999).
Sheehan, J., *German liberalism in the nineteenth century* (London, 1982).
Shepherd, J., 'Labour and Parliament: the Lib-labs as the first working-class MPs, 1885–1906', in E. F. Biagini and A. J. Reid (eds.), *Currents of radicalism: popular radicalism, organised labour and party politics in Britain, 1850–1914* (Cambridge, 1991), 187–213.
Silver, A. I., *The French-Canadian idea of confederation, 1864–1900* (Toronto and Buffalo, 1982).
Silverman, M., *An Irish working class: explorations in political economy and hegemony, 1800–1950* (Toronto, 2001).
Skinner, Q., *Liberty before liberalism* (Cambridge, 1998).
Smith F. B., *Radical artisan: William James Linton, 1812–97* (Manchester, 1973).
Smith, H. W., *German nationalism and religious conflict: culture, ideology, politics, 1870–1914* (Princeton, 1995).
Smout, T. C., *A century of the Scottish people, 1830–1950* (London, 1986).
Soboul, A., *Les sansculottes parisiens en l'An II* (Paris, 1962).
Solow, B., *The land question and the Irish economy, 1870–1903* (Cambridge, Mass.).
Stansky, P., *Ambitions and strategies: the struggle for the leadership of the Liberal party in the 1890s* (Oxford, 1964).
Stedman Jones, G., *An end to poverty? A historical debate* (London, 2004).
  Languages of class: studies in English working class history, 1832–1982 (Cambridge, 1983).
Steele, E. D., 'Gladstone and Ireland', *Irish Historical Studies*, 17, 65 (1970), 58–88.
von den Steinen, K., 'The harmless papers: Granville, Gladstone, and the censorship of the Madagascar Blue Books of 1884', *Victorian Studies*, 14, 2 (1970), 165–76.
Steven, R., *The National Liberal Club: politics and persons* (London, 1925).
Stokes, E., 'Milnerism', *Historical Journal*, 5, 1 (1962), 47–60.
Stradling, R. A., *The Irish and the Spanish Civil War, 1936–1939* (Manchester, 1999).
Strauss, E., *Irish nationalism and British democracy* (London, 1951).
Sturgis, J. L., *John Bright and the empire* (London, 1969).
Sutherland, G., *Faith, duty and the power of mind: the Cloughs and their circle, 1820–1960* (Cambridge, 2006).
Swartz, M., *The Union of Democratic Control in British politics during the First World War* (Oxford, 1971).
Taithe, B., *Defeated flesh: welfare, warfare and the makings of modern France* (1999).
Tanner, D., 'Ideological debates in Edwardian Labour politics: radicalism, revisionism and socialism', in E. F. Biagini and A. J. Reid (eds.), *Currents of radicalism: popular radicalism, organised labour and party politics in Britain, 1850–1914* (Cambridge 1991), 271–93.

Political change and the Labour party, 1900–1918 (Cambridge, 1990).

Taylor, A. J. P., *The trouble makers: dissent over foreign policy, 1792–1939* (1957; London, 1985).

Taylor, M., *Ernest Jones, Chartism and the romance of politics, 1819–1869* (Oxford, 2003).

Thane, P., 'The Labour party and state welfare', in K. D. Brown (ed.), *The first Labour party, 1906–1914* (London, 1985), 183–216.

'The working class and state "welfare" in Britain, 1880–1914', *Historical Journal*, 27, 4 (1984), 877–900.

Tholfsen, T., *Working class radicalism in mid-Victorian England* (London, 1976).

Thompson, D., *The Chartists* (London, 1984).

'Ireland and the Irish in English radicalism before 1850', in D. Thompson and J. Epstein (eds.), *The Chartist experience: studies in working-class radicalism and culture, 1830–60* (London, 1982), 120–51.

Thompson, E. P., *William Morris, romantic to revolutionary* (London, 1988).

Thompson, F., *The end of liberal Ulster: land agitation and land reform* (Belfast, 2001).

Thompson, J., 'The genesis of the 1906 Trades Disputes Act: liberalism, trade unions and the law', *Twentieth Century British History*, 9, 2 (1998), 175–200.

Thompson, P., *Socialists, liberals and labour: the struggle for London, 1885–1914* (London, 1967).

Thorne, S., *Congregational missions and the making of an imperial culture in 19th-century England* (Stanford, 1999).

Thornley, D., 'The Irish Home Rule party and parliamentary obstruction, 1874–1887', *Irish Historical Studies*, 12, 45 (1960), 38–57.

Isaac Butt and Home Rule (London, 1964).

Tichelar, M., 'Socialists, Labour and the land: the response of the Labour party to the land campaign of Lloyd George before the First World War', *Twentieth Century British History*, 8, 2 (1997), 127–44.

Tinker, H., *The foundations of local self-government in India, Pakistan and Burma* (New York, 1965).

Todd, N., *The militant democracy: Joseph Cowen and Victorian radicalism* (Whitley Bay, 1991).

Torr, D., *Tom Mann and his times, vol. I: 1856–1890* (London, 1956).

Townshend, C., 'The meaning of Irish freedom: constitutionalism in the Free State', *Transactions of the Royal Historical Society*, 6th series, 8 (1998), 45–70.

Trentmann, F., 'Bread, milk and democracy: consumption and citizenship in twentieth-century Britain', in M. Daunton and M. Hilton (eds.), *The politics of consumption* (Oxford, 2001), 129–64.

'The strange death of free trade: the erosion of "liberal consensus" in Great Britain, *c.*1903–1932', in E. F. Biagini (ed.), *Citizenship and community: liberals, radicals and collective identities in the British Isles, 1865–1931* (Cambridge, 1996), 219–50.

Trevelyan, G. M., *The life of John Bright* (London, 1925).

Varouxakis G., '"Patriotism", "cosmopolitanism" and "humanity" in Victorian political thought', *European Journal of Political Theory*, 5, 1 (2006), 100–18.

Vernon, J., *Politics and the people* (Cambridge, 1993).

Villis, T., *Reaction and the avant-garde: the revolt against liberal democracy in twentieth-century Britain* (London, 2006).

Vincent, J., *Formation of the British Liberal party* (Harmondsworth, 1972).

'Gladstone and Ireland', *Proceedings of the British Academy*, 62 (1977), 193–238.

Viotti, A., *Garibaldi: the revolutionary and his men* (Poole, 1979).

Wahlin, V., 'The growth of bourgeois and popular movements in Denmark ca. 1830–1870', *Scandinavian Journal of History*, 5 (1980), 151–83.

Walker, B. M., 'The land question and elections in Ulster, 1868–86', in S. Clarke and J. D. Donnelly (eds.), *Irish Peasants, Violence and Political unrest, 1780–1914* (Dublin, 1986), 230–69.

Ulster politics: The formative years, 1868–86 (Belfast, 1989).

Walker, G., 'Empire, religion and nationality in Scotland and Ulster before the First World War', in I. S. Wood (ed.), *Scotland and Ulster* (Edinburgh, 1994), 97–115.

A history of the Ulster Unionist party (Manchester and New York, 2004).

The politics of frustration: Harry Midgley and the failure of Labour in Northern Ireland (Manchester, 1985).

Walker, L., 'Party political women: a comparative study of Liberal women and the Primrose League', in J. Rendall (ed.), *Equal or different: women's politics, 1800–1914* (Oxford, 1987), 159–91.

Walker, W. M., 'Irish immigrants in Scotland: their priests, politics and parochial life', *Historical Journal*, 15, 4 (1972), 649–67.

Walkowitz, J., *Prostitution and Victorian society* (Cambridge and New York, 1990).

Walling, R. A. J. (ed.), *The diaries of John Bright* (London and Toronto, 1930).

Ward, P., *Red flag and Union Jack: Englishness, patriotism and the British left, 1881–1924* (Woodbridge, 1998).

Warren, A., 'Gladstone, land and social reconstruction in Ireland, 1881–1887, *Parliamentary History*, 2 (1983), 153–73.

Wasserstein, B., *Herbert Samuel: a political life* (Oxford, 1992).

Watson, G., *The English ideology: studies in the language of Victorian politics* (London, 1973).

Weaver, S. A., *The Hammonds: a marriage in history* (Stanford, 1998).

Weber, M., 'Politics as a vocation', in H. H. Gerth and C. Wright Mills, *From Max Weber: Essays in Sociology* (London, 1948), 77–128.

Wedderburn, W., *Allan Octavian Hume*, ed. by E. C. Moulton (New Delhi and Oxford, 2002).

Wheatley, M., *Nationalism and the Irish party: provincial Ireland, 1910–1916* (Oxford, 2005).

White, T. J., 'Nationalism vs. Liberalism in the Irish context: from a post-colonial past to a post-modern future', *Éire–Ireland*, 37, 3–4 (2002), 25–38.

Williams, C. R., 'The Welsh religious revival, 1904–1905', 77, Journal3 (1952), 242–59.

Wong, J. Y., *Deadly dreams: opium and the Arrow war (1856–1860) with China* (Cambridge, 1998).

Wormell, D., *Sir John Seeley and the uses of history* (Cambridge, 1980).

Wrigley, C., *Arthur Henderson* (Cardiff, 1990).

David Lloyd George and the British Labour movement (London, 1976).

'Liberals and the desire for working-class representatives in Battersea, 1886–1922', in K. D. Brown (ed.), *Essays in anti-Labour history: responses to the rise of Labour in Britain* (London, 1974), 126–58.

Zebel, S. H., 'Joseph Chamberlain and the genesis of Tariff Reform', *Journal of British Studies*, 7, 1 (1967), 131–57.

Index